*fifth*
*edition*

# Writing in the Disciplines

## A Reader for Writers

WITHDRAWN

**Mary Lynch Kennedy**
*SUNY Cortland*

**William J. Kennedy**
*Cornell University*

**Hadley M. Smith**
*Ithaca College*

PEARSON
Prentice
Hall

Upper Saddle River, NJ 07458

Library of Congress Cataloging-in-Publication Data

Kennedy, Mary Lynch
  Writing in the disciplines : a reader for writers / Mary Lynch Kennedy, William J. Kennedy,
Hadley M. Smith.—5th ed.
    p. cm.
Includes bibliographical references and index.
  ISBN 0-13-182382-5
  1. College readers.   2. Interdisciplinary approach in education—Problems, exercises, etc.
3. English language—Rhetoric—Problems, exercises, etc.   4. Academic writing—Problems,
exercises, etc.   I. Kennedy, William J. (William John)   II. Smith, Hadley M.   III. Title.
  PE1417 .K45 2003
  808'.0427—dc21

                                                                    2003004018

**Acquisitions Editor:** Corey Good
**Assistant Editor:** Karen Schultz
**Editor-in-Chief:** Leah Jewell
**Senior Managing Editor:** Ann Marie
  McCarthy
**Editorial Assistant:** Steve Kyritz
**Senior Marketing Manager:** Brandy
  Dawson
**Production Liaison:** Fran Russello
**Project Manager:** Karen Berry/Pine
  Tree Composition, Inc.
**Permission Specialist:** Katie Huha
**Manufacturing Buyer:** Mary Ann
  Gloriande

**Art Director:** Jayne Conte
**Cover Designer:** Bruce Kenselaar
**Cover Illustration/Photo:** Piet Mon-
  drian, Dutch (1872–1944), "Composition No. 7 (Facade)" 1914, Oil on can-
  vas, 47½ × 39⅞ in. (120.6 × 101.3). Kim-
  bell Art Museum, Fort Worth, Texas.
  Photographer Michael Bodycomb '99.
  © 2004 Mondrian/Holtzman Trust,
  c/o Beeldrecht/Artists Rights Society
  (ARS), New York. Pixel Height
**Printer/Binder:** Courier Stoughton

Credits and acknowledgments borrowed from other sources and reproduced, with permission, in this textbook appear on appropriate page within text.

Pearson Education LTD., London
Pearson Education Singapore, Pte. Ltd
Pearson Education, Canada, Ltd
Pearson Education–Japan
Pearson Education Australia PTY,
  Limited

Pearson Education North Asia Ltd
Pearson Educación de Mexico,
  S.A. de C.V.
Pearson Education Malaysia, Pte. Ltd
Pearson Education, Upper Saddle River,
  New Jersey

PEARSON
Prentice
Hall

10  9  8  7  6  5  4  3  2  1
ISBN: 0-13-182382-5

# B R I E F
## *contents*

## P A R T   O N E

### Reading and Writing in the Academic Disciplines   1

**1**   Preparing to Write: Active Reading   3

**2**   Writing an Essay in Response to a Source: An Illustration of the Writing Process   37

**3**   Composing Essays Drawing from Two or More Sources: Comparison and Contrast and Synthesis   78

**4**   Essays of Argument, Analysis, and Evaluation   103

**5**   Writing Research Papers   142

## P A R T   T W O

### An Anthology of Readings   191

### *Natural Sciences and Technology*   193

**6**   Cloning   197

**7**   Human/Machine Interaction   239

**8**   Crime-Fighting Technology: Balancing Public Safety and Privacy   285

### *Social Sciences*   331

**9**   The Changing American Family   336

**10**   Social Class and Inequality   398

**11**   Rethinking School   471

## *Humanities*    529

**12**    Religion and Identity    535

**13**    Literatures of Diaspora: Fiction and Nonfiction    586

Appendix: Documenting Sources    639

Rhetorical Index    663

Index    665

# *contents*

Preface   xv

## PART ONE

### Reading and Writing in the Academic Disciplines   1

## 1 Preparing to Write: Active Reading   3

Academic Writing: An Introduction   3

Active Reading Strategies   5

Prereading   6

   Preview the Source and Derive Questions That Will Help You Set Goals
for Close Reading   6

   Freewrite or Brainstorm to Recall Your Prior Knowledge or Feelings
About the Reading Topic   7

Close Reading   8

   Annotate and Elaborate on the Source   9

   Take Content Notes   10

   Pose and Answer Questions About the Source   11

Postreading   15

   Review the Source and Your Notes   15

   Compose Paraphrases and Summaries and Record Quotations
That May Be Useful at a Later Date   16

## 2 Writing an Essay in Response to a Source: An Illustration of the Writing Process   37

The Reading-Writing Process   37

Personal Response in Academic Writing   40

Active Reading Strategies for Response Essays    41
    Analyze the Assignment    41
    Elaborate on Reading Sources    43
Planning    45
    Formulating a Thesis    46
    Organizing    46
Drafting    50
    Planning Individual Paragraphs    52
    Using Quotations, Paraphrases, and Summaries    54
    Writing Introductory Paragraphs    54
    Writing Conclusions    57
    Preparing Lists of References or Works Cited    57
    Titling the Essay    58
Revising the Preliminary Draft    59
    Revising Ideas    62
    Revising Organization    63
    Revising Style    63
Editing    70
    Manuscript Format    72
    Sample Response Essay    73

## 3  Composing Essays Drawing from Two or More Sources: Comparison and Contrast and Synthesis    78

Comparison and Contrast Essay    78
    Identifying Comparisons and Contrasts    79
    Planning Comparison and Contrast Essays    82
    Organizing the Comparison and Contrast Essay    84
    Drafting Comparison and Contrast Essays    86
    Sample Comparison and Contrast Essay    87
    Revising the Preliminary Draft    91
    Editing the Preliminary Draft    93
Synthesizing Sources    94
    Sample Synthesis Essay    97

# *4* Essays of Argument, Analysis, and Evaluation   103

Argument: An Introduction   103
  Developing Support for Arguments   105
  Using Sources in Argument Essays   105
  Organizing Argumentative Essays   112
  Sample Argument Essay   115
  Revising the Preliminary Draft   120
  Editing the Preliminary Draft   122
Analysis and Evaluation: An Introduction   122
Writing an Analytical Essay   124
  Reading the Source and Planning Your Essay   124
  Clarify the Assignment, Set Your Rhetorical Goal, and Consider
  Your Audience   124
  Do a First Reading to Get a General Impression of the Text   125
  Reread and Ask Questions About Analyzing and Evaluating the Text   125
  Review Your Answers to the Questions for Analysis   131
  Deciding on an Organizational Plan   131
  Drafting   134
  Sample Essay of Literary Analysis   135
  Revising the Preliminary Draft   138
  Editing the Preliminary Draft   140

# *5* Writing Research Papers   142

The Research Paper: An Introduction   142
Identifying a Research Topic   143
Developing a Research Strategy   145
  Allocate Sufficient Time for Research   145
  Identify Research Questions   145
  Brainstorm a List of Terms or a Search Vocabulary   146
Virtual Libraries   147
Using Electronic Retrieval Systems   148
  How Computerized Information Retrieval Systems Function   148

    Recall versus Relevancy    150

    Keyword Searching    150

    Truncation    151

    Boolean Searching    151

The Library or the World Wide Web? Choosing a Research Site    153

Locating Information in an Academic Library    156

    The Library Catalog    157

    Periodical Indexes    160

Conducting Research Using the World Wide Web    164

Collecting Information on Your Own: Surveys and Interviews    166

Modifying Your Search Strategy    167

Evaluating Information Sources    168

Excerpting Information from Sources    169

Writing a Preliminary Thesis    170

Planning the Research Paper    172

Writing from Your Outline    174

Revising    174

Editing    175

    Sample Research Paper    176

# P A R T   T W O

## An Anthology of Readings    191

## Natural Sciences and Technology    193

# 6 Cloning    197

JENNIFER AND RACHEL • Lee M. Silver    198

*Defends human cloning as a legitimate reproductive choice.*

ME, MY CLONE, AND I (OR IN DEFENSE OF HUMAN CLONING) •
Jonathan Colvin    208

*Defends cloning as a means for allowing disabled individuals to realize their genetic potential.*

NARCISSUS CLONED • John J. Conley    211

*Maintains that cloning human embryos violates the sanctity of human life and human relationships.*

CROSSING LINES: A SECULAR ARGUMENT AGAINST RESEARCH CLONING • Charles Krauthammer    217

*Argues that therapeutic cloning should not be pursued.*

SPECIES ON ICE • Karen Wright    228

*Discusses how cloning and embryo transplantation technology might be used to save endangered or extinct species.*

BESSIE AND THE GAUR • Malcolm Tait    232

*Argues against relying on cloning as a means of regenerating extinct animal populations.*

# 7  Human/Machine Interaction    239

WE ARE NOT SPECIAL • Rodney A. Brooks    240

*Claims that humans are biological "machines" that are no different, in essence, from machines constructed of plastic and metal.*

CYBORG SEEKS COMMUNITY • Steve Mann    245

*Describes the experiences of a man who has been using wearable computer systems for years.*

LOVING TECHNOLOGY • Sherry Turkle    252

*Describes robot/human relationships and focuses on children's interaction with electronic "pets."*

LIVE FOREVER • Raymond Kurzweil    260

*Predicts the consequences of being able to transfer the contents of a human mind into a computer.*

ISOLATED BY THE INTERNET • Clifford Stoll    269

*Argues that technology cuts us off from contact with other humans.*

THE GIST GENERATION • Jeff Barbian    278

*Claims that using computerized systems have made humans intellectually lazy.*

TIME TO DO EVERYTHING BUT THINK • David Brooks    281

*Maintains that "wireless life" cuts humans off from fully experiencing the "real world."*

## 8  Crime-Fighting Technology: Balancing Public Safety and Privacy    285

COMPUTER PROJECT SEEKS TO AVERT YOUTH VIOLENCE •
Francis X. Clines    286
*Describes Mosaic-2000, a computer program designed to identify students who might be prone to commit violent acts.*

ROOTING OUT THE BAD SEEDS? • Kelly Patricia O'Meara    291
*Highlights the dangers to civil liberties posed by Mosaic-2000, a computer program designed to identify students who might be prone to commit violent acts.*

KYLLO V. UNITED STATES: TECHNOLOGY V. INDIVIDUAL PRIVACY •
Thomas D. Colbridge    298
*Discusses the implications of a recent Supreme Court decision regarding the use of thermal imaging technology to detect indoor marijuana growing operations.*

DC'S VIRTUAL PANOPTICON • Christian Parenti    311
*Describes the expansion of video surveillance in DC in the wake of September 11 events, and highlights the dangers of this technology.*

TRADING LIBERTY FOR ILLUSIONS • Wendy Kaminer    318
*Argues that in the wake of September 11 Americans should not surrender civil liberties in exchange for a false sense of security.*

INVASION OF PRIVACY • Joshua Quittner    321
*Argues that the benefits of modern technological advances are worth the reduction of individual privacy that comes with them.*

## Social Sciences    331

## 9  The Changing American Family    336

BRAVE NEW FAMILY • Kimberly Mistysyn    337
*Describes an alternative family arrangement in which a child has two moms and two dads.*

CHILDREN OF GAY FATHERS • Robert L. Barret and Bryan E. Robinson    340

*Investigates homosexual fatherhood and discusses the ramifications of gay parents for children's development.*

WHAT IS A FAMILY? • Pauline Irit Erera    350

*Traces the rise and fall of the traditional family, and argues that we should embrace and celebrate the unique strengths of diverse, nontraditional families.*

SEVEN TENETS FOR ESTABLISHING NEW MARITAL NORMS • David Popenoe    368

*Recommends a new set of social norms that will allow us to maintain certain elements of the nuclear family.*

COHABITATION INSTEAD OF MARRIAGE • James Q. Wilson    373

*Argues against cohabitation, claiming that its advantages are illusory compared to the advantages of being married.*

PROMOTING MARRIAGE AS A MEANS FOR PROMOTING FATHERHOOD • Wade F. Horn    378

*Argues for a revitalization of marriage as the chief means of strengthening father–child relationships.*

TOWARD REVELS OR A REQUIEM FOR FAMILY DIVERSITY? • Judith Stacey    389

*Argues that in the future we can expect to see even more disruption of the traditional family. Families will become more rather than less diverse.*

## *10* Social Class and Inequality    398

WHAT ARE "CLASS" AND "INEQUALITY"? • Jeremy Seabrook    399

*Situates class in a historical context and explains how it has been redefined as inequality.*

GRANDMA WENT TO SMITH, ALL RIGHT, BUT SHE WENT FROM NINE TO FIVE: A MEMOIR • Patricia Clark Smith    412

*Illustrates through personal experience how individuals can be made to feel out of place because of their social and economic background.*

THE REVOLT OF THE BLACK BOURGEOISIE • Leonce Gaiter    427
*Argues that middle- and upper-class blacks suffer discrimination when they are lumped with economically and socially deprived blacks instead of being treated as individuals.*

THE WAR AGAINST THE POOR INSTEAD OF PROGRAMS TO END POVERTY • Herbert J. Gans    432
*Debunks the concept of "underclass" and similar stereotypes, and offers an intellectual and cultural defense of poor people.*

WHEN SHELTER FEELS LIKE A PRISON • Charmion Browne    442
*Gives a personal account of life in homeless shelters.*

WHITE STANDARD FOR POVERTY • Dirk Johnson    445
*Gives a glimpse of two faces of poverty in the Native American population, and warns against imposing white standards of poverty on Indians.*

SERVING IN FLORIDA • Barbara Ehrenreich    449
*Describes Ehrenreich's experiences as a low-wage worker trying to survive on six to seven dollars an hour in Key West, Florida.*

## *11* Rethinking School    471

HIGH SCHOOL, AN INSTITUTION WHOSE TIME HAS PASSED • Leon Botstein    472
*Argues that we must rethink secondary education and allow students to graduate at sixteen.*

A DAY IN THE LIFE OF RAFAEL JACKSON • Patrick James McQuillan    475
*Provides a vignette of a day in the life of a high-school senior and raises questions about the value of his education.*

EDUCATING BLACK STUDENTS • Shelby Steele    490
*Argues that lack of will to succeed affects black children's performance in school even more than does poverty and racism.*

CHALLENGING OUR ASSUMPTIONS • Janine Bempechat    500
*Takes issue with middle-class parents who claim that their children have too much homework and too little self-esteem, and argues that academic achievement should be at the top of every family's priorities.*

HOMEWORK • Martin L. Gross   510

*Argues that lax homework policies are harmful to American students.*

MYTH 5: SELF-ESTEEM MUST COME FIRST—THEN LEARNING •
Larry E. Frase and William Streshly   514

*Debunks the myth that says students must have high self-esteem in order to learn.*

MANUFACTURING A CRISIS IN EDUCATION • David C. Berliner
and Bruce J. Biddle   522

*Challenges those who claim that American schools are failing our youth.*

## Humanities   529

## *12* Religion and Identity   535

EXCELLENT THINGS IN WOMEN • Sara Suleri   537

*Recounts experiences in the author's Islamic household during her youth in Pakistan.*

POLITICS AND THE MUSLIM WOMAN • Benazir Bhutto   544

*Argues that Islamic law does not regard women as inferior to men or incapable of leadership.*

I STILL HEAR THE CRY • Alina Bacall-Zwirn and Jared Stark   551

*Recounts how the birth of her baby in the concentration camp at Auschwitz challenged the author's identity as a Jew and as a mother.*

THREADS • Elly Bulkin   558

*Affirms the author's Jewish identity but also links it to her other identities as an antiracist lesbian feminist.*

SIN BIG • Mary Daly   565

*Describes a feminist theologian's academic training in Roman Catholic theology.*

THE POPE'S LOYAL OPPOSITION • Garry Wills   569

*Argues that the author considers himself loyal to Catholicism despite his criticism of the Roman papacy.*

AMERICA, A CHRISTIAN NATION • Pat Robertson   574

*Claims that America is a Christian nation and that its Christianity explains its greatness.*

Is America a Christian Nation?  •  Isaac Kramnick and R. Laurence Moore  578
*Argues that the American Constitution separates religion from political institutions and topical political controversy.*


## *13*  Literatures of Diaspora: Fiction and Nonfiction  586

The Proper Respect  •  Isabel Allende  588
*Narrates the dubious rise to prosperity and prestige of an oddly matched husband and wife amid varied immigrant and indigenous groups in Latin America.*

The Journey  •  Primo Levi  595
*Narrates the author's deportation from his native Italy to the German death camp at Auschwitz.*

A Different Mirror  •  Ronald Takaki  604
*Describes various patterns of Japanese immigration to America in the nineteenth century.*

Jasmine  •  Bharati Mukherjee  618
*Narrates the jagged assimilation of an illegal immigrant from the West Indies into the academic community of Ann Arbor, Michigan.*

Everyday Use  •  Alice Walker  628
*Depicts the bonds that relate three generations of African-American women to their ancestors despite the scattering of their origins and dispersal of their roots.*

Appendix: Documenting Sources  639
Rhetorical Index  663
Index  665

# preface

## TO OUR READERS IN APPRECIATION

In preparing the fifth edition of *Writing in the Disciplines: A Reader for Writers*, we listened closely to the suggestions of students and instructors who had used the fourth edition. Since everyone was satisfied with the first part of the book, for the most part we left Part One, "Reading and Writing in the Academic Disciplines," unchanged. As requested, we reworked the second half of the book. A number of the readings are new, and in Chapters 11 and 12, we have introduced new topics. To the readers who suggested these changes, we say "thank you" for helping us strengthen this book.

## ORGANIZATION AND APPROACH

*Writing in the Disciplines: A Reader for Writers* serves two functions. It explains how to use reading sources as idea banks for college papers, and it teaches fundamental academic writing strategies: reading, paraphrasing, summarizing, quoting, organizing, drafting, revising, editing, synthesizing, analyzing, researching, and developing arguments. It also provides an anthology of readings in the humanities, the natural sciences and technology, and the social sciences, with articles representing various rhetorical approaches across academic disciplines. These articles, along with the accompanying instructional apparatus, help develop students' abilities to think critically and reason cogently as they read, compose, and revise. The activities and questions that accompany each reading encourage students to approach academic writing as a process: to preview the source, set reading goals, and ponder the general topic before reading; to annotate the text and think critically while reading; and to reflect on the source and identify information content, form, organization, expository and stylistic features, and rhetorical elements after reading. Students are also shown how to draw on annotations, notes, and preliminary writing to produce first drafts of academic essays and how to revise essays at the drafting stage as well as later in the writing process. Additional activities help students to use ideas from different sources to produce synthesis essays and research papers.

Chapter 1 presents active reading strategies that help students engage the ideas in academic texts and incorporate them in their own writing by paraphrasing, summarizing, and quoting. Chapter 2 presents the writing process, including analyzing the assignment, planning, organizing, drafting, revising, and editing. In addition, Chapter 2 examines essay structures, from the introduction and thesis statement through the body of the essay to its conclusion, and teaches students to write essays of response to a source. Chapter 3 focuses on essays that draw on two or more sources, including compare-and-contrast essays and synthesis. Chapter 4 covers essays of argumentation, analysis, and evaluation, with special attention to literary analysis; and Chapter 5 focuses on library research strategies and writing research papers. In the eight succeeding chapters, we provide fifty-three reading selections. We have organized the anthology in Chapters 6 through 13 by dividing the academic curriculum into three major fields: the natural sciences and technology, the social sciences, and the humanities. Each chapter in *Writing in the Disciplines* deals with a topic that is widely studied in the field. For example, the social sciences section has chapters on redefining the American family and on social class and inequality. The reading selections help students view each topic from a range of perspectives, and they provide diverse views from experts within the discipline and from journalists and specialists in other academic fields. Most of the articles are written for nonspecialized readers, not for majors in particular fields. We believe these articles, derived from popular as well as scholarly sources, represent the types of readings many professors assign in introductory and lower-level courses. Psychology professors, for instance, know that first-year students cannot interpret most psychological research reports until they acquire a basic knowledge of the discipline and learn its principles of experimental methodology and statistical analysis. However, first-year students can read summaries and analyses of psychological research written for nonspecialists. For *Writing in the Disciplines*, we chose readings that might appear on a reserve list as supplements to an introductory-level textbook. We make no assumptions about students' prior knowledge. Our intent is to model first-year-level reading assignments, not to exemplify professional standards within the disciplines.

In the introduction to each section, we characterize the field of study with a discussion of its subdisciplines, methodology, logic, and vocabulary. We then describe writing within the field by examining authors' perspectives, goals, organizational patterns, literary devices, and rhetorical styles. We recognize that there is no absolute standard for categorizing intellectual activities. For example, although we have classified religion as a discipline within the humanities, we could as well have placed it within the social sciences, depending on the methodology the researchers use. Throughout the book, we point out overlaps among disciplines and also capitalize on them in synthesis assignments at the end of each chapter. Despite the imprecision of these categories, we believe that important differences in approaches to scholarship and writing do exist among the three main academic areas. Students who understand these differences will read more critically and write more persuasively.

## Improvements in the Fifth Edition

In the fifth edition of *Writing in the Disciplines*, we have made minor revisions to the initial section on academic writing. The anthology section has changed dramatically. On the advice of our readers, we have removed the fiction excerpts from Chapters 6 through 12 but retained them in Chapter 13. The three anthology chapters on natural sciences and technology include eighteen new readings that focus on recent developments in those fields. The readings in Chapter 6, including five new articles, concern cloning technology and extend beyond the fourth edition's focus on human cloning to cover attempts to save endangered animal species through cloning. The seven readings in Chapter 7, all of which are new, discuss human/machine interaction with special emphasis on the impact that recent and future developments in wireless technology may have on our lives. The six new readings that make up Chapter 8 concern modern crime-fighting technology and its effect on the balance between public safety and privacy, with attention to efforts to combat terrorism since the events of September 11, 2001. We have six new selections on variant forms of family life in Chapter 9 and three new articles about economic disparities and social distinction in Chapter 10.

Chapters 11 and 12 feature new topics: "Rethinking School" and "Religion and Identity" respectively.

We continue to accompany each article with activities and questions that promote critical thinking. Each reading is preceded by a pre-reading activity and followed by groups of questions that encourage students to grasp information and decide what form, organization, and expository features the author uses. Additional questions ask students to analyze rhetorical concerns, such as the context and the author's purpose (see Haas and Flower). As in previous editions, several writing assignments accompany each reading and each topically related chapter.

Finally, we have refined and expanded the guide to documentation and the comparison of the MLA (Modern Language Association) and APA styles in the appendix.


## COLLABORATIVE LEARNING ACTIVITIES

*Writing in the Disciplines* provides a series of collaborative learning activities that require students to work together in groups to clarify and extend their understanding of material presented in Chapters 1 through 5. We have constructed pairs of individual and collaborative exercises for each chapter subsection, so for any particular concept, instructors may assign out-of-class work and follow with in-class collaborative activities. Some instructors may use the collaborative exercises to emphasize points they or their students deem particularly important or problematic.

It is important to prepare students for group work by teaching them the collaborative skills they need in order to work together—requisite social skills, group dynamics, methods of interaction, and strategies for learning from each other as well as from the teacher. Some instructors pair off students at first. Then, when they move the students into groups, they give them time to become acquainted. Another technique is to redefine the groups frequently until everyone in the class has gotten to know each other.

Each collaborative exercise in this textbook requires students to divide into work groups. Experiment with different ways of grouping students together. You might allow them to choose their groups, or you might assign them to groups on the basis of working style, personality types, or role. We have found Kenneth Bruffee's methods for conducting collaborative learning groups particularly useful (28–51). The following procedure, which draws heavily on Bruffee's *Collaborative Learning: Higher Education, Interdependence, and the Authority of Knowledge*, is applicable to all the collaborative exercises in this textbook.

## WORKING IN COLLABORATIVE LEARNING GROUPS

1. Students form groups of five or six by counting off. (Bruffee maintains that groups of five are particularly effective for collaborative activities.)

2. Each group selects a recorder who will write down the results of the group's deliberation and will eventually report to the entire class.

3. Each group selects a reader who then reads the collaborative task from the textbook.

4. Group members attempt to achieve a consensus on the question or issue posed by the collaborrative task. All viewpoints should be heard and considered. (Bruffee recommends that instructors refrain from taking part in or monitoring collaborative learning groups. He believes that teacher interference in groups "inevitably destroys peer relations among students and encourages the tendency of well-schooled students to focus on the teacher's authority and interests" [29].)

5. When a consensus is reached, the recorder reads her or his notes back to the group, and they are revised to make sure they reflect the group's decision. Differences of opinion are also included in the notes.

6. When all groups have completed the assignment, recorders read their notes to the entire class. The instructor may choose to summarize each group's report on the chalkboard. A discussion involving the entire class may follow.

Other methods of forming and conducting collaborative learning groups will also work with the exercises in Chapters 1 through 5. Although we have had success with Bruffee's technique, we encourage instructors to pick the methods that work best for them and their students. The following resources will be helpful:

Angelo, T. A., and K. P. Cross. *Classroom Assessment Techniques: A Handbook for College Teachers*. San Francisco: Jossey-Bass, 1993.

Goodsell, Anne, Michelle Maher, and Vincent Tinto. *Collaborative Learning: A Sourcebook for Higher Education*. University Park, PA: NCTLA, 1992.

Johnson, David W., Roger T. Johnson, Karl A. Smith, and E. Holubec. *Circles of Learning: Cooperation in the Classroom*. Edina, MN: Interaction, 1993.

## ACKNOWLEDGMENTS

Once again, in the fifth edition we have relied on the work of many researchers and scholars in composition and reading. We are particularly grateful to Ann Brown, Kenneth Bruffee, Linda Flower, Christina Haas, John Hayes, and Bonnie Meyer. We used pilot versions of *Writing in the Disciplines* in first-year-level writing courses at Cornell University, Ithaca College, and SUNY at Cortland, and we are indebted to our students for their comments and suggestions. Liam and Maura Kennedy deserve special thanks for their important contributions to Chapters 1, 2, 3, and 4. Hadley Smith would like to acknowledge David Flanagan's and Marlene Kobre's suggestions for articles for Chapters 6, 7, and 8 as well as their collegiality over the years.

We appreciate the assistance we received from Senior Acquisitions Editor Corey Good and Assistant Editor Karen Schultz at Prentice Hall who supervised our project with skill and professionalism. We also appreciate the assistance we received from Editor-in-Chief Leah Jewell, and Editorial Assistant John Ragozzine. Special thanks to our meticulous copyeditor, Carol Lallier. We are also indented to our reviewers for their helpful ideas and suggestions: Deborah E. Stine, California State University, San Bernardino; Marilyn M. Senter, Johnson County Community College; Susan Quarrell, Lehman College; Kami Day, Johnson County Community College; M. Katherine Grimes, Ferrum College; Michael Kuelker, St. Charles Community College; Laima Sruoginis, University of Southern Maine; James M. Baskin, Joliet Junior College; and James A. Voketaitis.

Finally, we are grateful to Liam and Maura Kennedy, Nancy Siegele, and Annie, Colin, and Timm Smith for their patience, support, and understanding.

### WORKS CITED

Bruffee, Kenneth. *Collaborative Learning: Higher Education, Interdependence, and the Authority of Knowledge*. Baltimore: Johns Hopkins UP, 1993.

Haas, Christina, and Linda Flower. "Rhetorical Reading and the Construction of Meaning." *College Composition and Communication* 39 (1988): 167–83.

Mary Lynch Kennedy

William J. Kennedy

Hadley M. Smith

# Reading
and Writing
in the Academic
Disciplines

C H A P T E R

## *one*

---

# Preparing to Write:
# Active Reading

## ACADEMIC WRITING: AN INTRODUCTION

In college, you sometimes find the language used is quite different from what you have encountered in the past. This textbook will prepare you to present your ideas to professors and fellow students by using the conventions of *academic* writing. Academic reading and writing follow a distinct process that we have briefly outlined in the box that follows.

---

### OVERVIEW OF THE ACADEMIC READING-WRITING PROCESS

#### Active Reading

*Prereading.*   Preview the reading sources, freewrite about your topic, and set your goals.

*Close reading.*   Mark, annotate, elaborate on, and pose questions about the reading. Questions address three areas: (1) information; (2) textual form, organization, and expository features; and (3) rhetorical concerns.

*Postreading.*   Record comments, reactions, quotations, paraphrases, and summaries about the readings.

(continued on the next page)

---

### Planning

*Formulating a thesis.*   Arrive at a preliminary understanding of the point you want to make in your paper.

*Organizing.*   Decide how you will use sources in the paper and how you will develop your argument.

### Drafting

*Drafting.*   Weave source material (usually in the form of quotations, paraphrases, and summaries) with your own ideas to create paragraphs and, ultimately, a complete paper, typically with an introduction, a body, and a conclusion.

### Reworking

*Revising.*   Lengthen, shorten, or reorder your paper; change your prose to make it more understandable to your reader; make sentence-level, phrase-level, and word-level stylistic changes; or, in some cases, make major conceptual or organizational alterations to incorporate what you learned during the process of drafting.

*Editing.*   Proofread your paper for errors in sentence structure, usage, punctuation, spelling, and mechanics, and check for proper manuscript form.

Writers do not proceed through the stages of this process in lock-step fashion, beginning with prereading and ending with editing. The movement is recursive, and the processes may be intermixed. You may find yourself revising *while* you draft as well as after you have finished the piece. Even though you will read the sources before you write, you will probably reread portions of them during and after the drafting phase. And writing can occur at any point in the process. You can do freewriting on the assigned topic before you read sources, annotate as you read, or rewrite parts of the paper after you have produced a draft of it.

The first two chapters of this textbook are devoted to describing and illustrating the various stages in the academic reading-writing process. Although we do not apply the actual process sequentially, we will, for convenience, begin with reading and proceed through the phases in the order outlined in the preceding box.

## ACTIVE READING STRATEGIES

Effective reading is essential because academic writing is frequently based on "outside sources." College writers rarely have the luxury of choosing a topic that interests them or of composing an essay based entirely on their own ideas and personal experiences. Typically, professors specify topics and expect students to formulate a thesis or a position and support it by drawing on published sources—textbooks, reserve readings, scholarly books, journals, newspapers, and magazines—along with lecture notes, interviews, and other forms of information. To use outside sources in your papers, you need to practice effective methods of paraphrasing, summarizing, and quoting. In other words, you have to become a skilled reader as well as an accomplished writer.

Skilled readers are *active readers*. They connect what they are reading to texts they have read before and to prior knowledge and personal experiences. Usually when readers have difficulty understanding texts, it is because they lack the appropriate background and cannot make those connections.

To become a more active reader, try some of the strategies listed in the box that follows.

---

### ACTIVE READING STRATEGIES

**Prereading**

1. Preview the source and derive questions that will help you set goals for close reading.
2. Freewrite or brainstorm to recall your prior knowledge or feelings about the reading topic.

**Close Reading**

1. Annotate and elaborate on the source.
2. Take content notes.
3. Pose and answer questions about three aspects of the source: information; textual form, organization, and expository features; and rhetorical concerns.

**Postreading**

1. Review the source and your notes.
2. Compose paraphrases and summaries, and record quotations that may be useful at a later date.

---

## PREREADING

Prereading lays the groundwork for comprehension and understanding. Just as you wouldn't plunge into an athletic activity "cold," you wouldn't set out to read a difficult text without preparation. The more challenging the reading, the more important the prereading activities become. The prereading strategies you select depend on the reading source's character and level of difficulty. Two useful techniques are (1) previewing the source and deriving questions that will help you set goals for close reading, and (2) freewriting or brainstorming to recall your prior knowledge or feelings about the reading topic.

### Preview the Source and Derive Questions That Will Help You Set Goals for Close Reading

Before you do a close reading of the source, thumb through it for a quick inspection. This overview will give you a general idea of the content and organization, and will enable you to understand it better. As you preview the reading, ask yourself the following questions:

1. What does the title indicate the piece will be about?
2. Is there any biographical information about the author? What does this information tell me about the piece?
3. How do the subtitles and headings function? Do they reveal the author's organizational format (for example, introduction, body, conclusion)?
4. Do any topic sentences of paragraphs seem especially important?
5. Does the author provide any other organizational signals, such as enumeration, italics, indention, diagrams, or footnotes?
6. Does the reading end with a summary? What does it reveal about the content of the piece?

Another useful previewing technique is to turn the title and the subheadings into questions that you can try to answer before reading the piece. Consider how one of our students used this technique to preview Jeremy Seabrook's "What Are 'Class' and 'Inequality'?" (Chapter 10). The first subheading is "Global Inequality."

*STUDENT'S CONVERSION OF SUBHEADING INTO QUESTIONS*

What does Seabrook mean by "global inequality"? Is he talking about the differences between wealthy and poor nations?

## STUDENT'S ANSWER (BASED ON SUBSEQUENT CLOSE READING)

There are tremendous disparities and economic injustices in the world. Among the nations, the richest 20% receive 86% of the world's GNP, whereas the poorest 20% get only 1%. In the British population, 26% live in poverty, whereas 74,000 are millionaires. Of the 7 million millionaires in the world, half are in the U.S.

Continue where our student left off. Turn to pages 399–412 and convert the subheadings into questions. Answer them as best you can.

## Freewrite or Brainstorm to Recall Your Prior Knowledge or Feelings About the Reading Topic

The knowledge and experiences you bring to bear on a text affect your understanding of it. While you read, you are constructing new knowledge by relating what you already know to the new material. Prior knowledge paves the way for understanding. For example, if you are reading about alternatives to the traditional nuclear family, as in Pauline Irit Erera's "What Is A Family?" (pp. 350–67), it may help you to process the argument if you first think about kinds of families that you are familiar with: two-parent families, single-parent families, families that include stepparents, families with stepsiblings, and so forth. Or, if you are reading about lax homework policies in Martin L. Gross's "Homework" (see pp. 510–13), it may help you to recall the homework assignments you received in high school.

Two ways to trigger prior knowledge and experiences are freewriting and brainstorming. To freewrite, jot down anything that comes to mind about a topic. Write nonstop for five or ten minutes without worrying about usage or spelling. Put down whatever you want. Brainstorming uses a process of free association. Start the process by skimming the reading source and listing key words or phrases. Then run down the list and record associations that come to mind when you think about these target concepts. Don't bother to write complete sentences; just write down words and phrases. Give your imagination free rein.

For an example, look at the freewriting and brainstorming of our student as she proceeded.

### EXCERPT FROM FREEWRITING

I don't really think about class. My family and all my friends are middle class. Everyone in my neighborhood is middle class. When I got to high school, I met kids from trailer parks and public housing. In some classes they sat next to kids who lived in wealthy suburbs and belonged to the country club. But I think everyone thought they were middle class. I think more in terms of rich and poor than upper and lower class.

### EXCERPT FROM BRAINSTORMING LIST

1. Class vs. caste: India has a caste system. Aren't the people at the bottom called "Untouchables"?

2. Global rich must refer to owners of multinational companies and people in entertainment.

3. I knew Bill Gates is the richest person in the world, but I'm surprised to see the whole Wal-Mart family on the list.

4. Middle class vs. working class: I define working class as blue collar, lower-middle-class people. Everyone works, so who exactly is the working class?

5. Karl Marx's name keeps popping up. Didn't he write about the working class?

6. I remember we talked about Feudalism, lords and nobles and serfs, when we did the Middle Ages in history class.

Once you use freewriting or brainstorming to tap into what you already know about a topic, you will better understand the material and read more objectively. You will also be more conscious of your opinions and biases and less likely to confuse them inadvertently with those of the author. You may also find that freewriting helps break ground for the paper that you will eventually write. The ideas that you summon in freewriting can generate ideas for comparison, contrast, reinforcement, or contestation in your paper. As an argumentative "other" voice that helps to test the claims of your reading, a piece of freewriting can show the direction that your further reading and rewriting might take.

## CLOSE READING

When you read, you are actively constructing meaning. You are not a passive decoder who transfers graphic symbols from the written page to your mind. You are taking part in two-way communication. Visualize and "talk" directly to the author. Let the author know what you are thinking, and ask questions when you need more information or have difficulty understanding.

To keep the interaction between you and the author dynamic, read with pencil in hand, annotating and elaborating on particular ideas, taking separate notes, and posing and answering questions. To illustrate, we apply these strategies to Jeremy Seabrook's article in the examples that follow.

## Annotate and Elaborate on the Source

Annotate by making marginal notes, underlining or highlighting important concepts, and recording your own responses to them. Elaborate on the sources by drawing on your knowledge and experiences to extend, illustrate, or evaluate the particular ideas. You can apply ideas in the text to situations the writer does not envision, or you can provide analogies, examples, or counterexamples of ideas. Note how one of our students annotated and elaborated on a passage from Jeremy Seabrook's "What Are 'Class' and 'Inequality'?"

| *Passage from Seabrook* | *Student Annotations* |
|---|---|
| In pre-industrial society, it was acknowledged that "birth" and "breeding" distinguished those at the top of the social pyramid. The upper classes were separated from the "lower orders" by the "middling rank" of society. In status-conscious society, objects of conspicuous consumption are identified with forms of honor, which formerly clustered around other characteristics—inherited position, property, military prowess. The contemporary iconography of high status is more open—anyone who can afford it can go through the obligatory shopping list of ornate villas with tight security, champagne and caviar, diamonds, yachts, Rolls Royce cars, Armani suits, and accessories bearing the "correct" brand name. | As in the Middle Ages<br><br><br>Draws a comparison<br><br><br>Iconography?<br><br><br>Money buys status.<br><br>Examples |

*ELABORATION OF THE SEABROOK PASSAGE*

Don't birth and breeding still differentiate upper from lower classes in England, India, and some other nations? I thought if you were born into the lower class, you'd have a hard time moving up the ladder. I agree with Seabrook. Money buys mobility. Win the lottery and you can be transformed from poor to rich overnight.

You might want to record your elaborations in a notebook or reading journal. This record will be particularly useful if you intend to write a paper that gives your view on the ideas in the source. It will certainly help your critical analysis of the reading material by pointing to passages that raised questions, offered insights, and provoked your responses the first time you read them.

When you annotate, do not overuse highlighting markers. It is hard to decide what is important as you read through a text for the first time. Every concept may seem significant. But if you highlight a large percentage of the text, you will have a lot to reread when you study for an exam or look for ideas to put in a paper. Another problem with highlighting is that it is a mechanical process that does not actively engage you with the text. It merely gives the illusion that you are reading effectively. Write out summary statements and reactions instead of just highlighting important ideas. Writing makes you process the information, restate it in your own words, and react to it. The ultimate goals of any annotating process are to involve you intellectually with the text and to give you access to it without rereading. Writing out marginal or separate notes is the best way to accomplish this.

## Take Content Notes

When you encounter difficult sources, you may want to take separate notes that will supplement your annotations and elaborations. These notes can be in the form of outlines, summaries, or paraphrases of key passages, lists of particularly significant pages or paragraphs, or any combination of these elements.

When you are taking notes, pay special attention to thesis statements and topic sentences. The thesis is the focal point of the entire piece: the major point, position, or objective the author demonstrates or proves. The main idea of a paragraph or another subdivision of the text is often expressed in a topic sentence. Both the thesis and the topic statement may require more than one sentence, so do not assume that you should always search for a single sentence. Nor should you make assumptions about their location. The thesis statement is typically in the introductory paragraph, but it can also appear elsewhere in the piece. Topic sentences are not always at the beginnings of paragraphs; they can appear in the middle or at the end as well. Some paragraphs do not contain explicit topic sentences; the main idea is implied through an accumulation of details, facts, or examples.

If sources are easy to read and have straightforward content, you can streamline note-taking and annotating procedures to capture only the most basic ideas. But remember that it is natural to forget much of what you have read; even relatively simple ideas can slip from your memory unless you record them in notes or annotations. And of course, when you are working with library sources, note-taking is indispensable.

## Pose and Answer Questions About the Source

A useful method for note-taking is to pose questions about the text and attempt to answer them as you read. Questions provide you with goals for obtaining information from the reading source. If you are reading a textbook chapter, first look at the reader aids: the preview outline at the beginning, the introductory or concluding sections, and the review questions at the end. Also check out chapter or section headings for the concepts or issues that the chapter covers. Using these reader aids, generate some questions about what the chapter will be about, and answer them as you read. This strategy works best if you record your answers as you locate the relevant material. Write your answers in a reading journal so that you can return to them later and find the important ideas you took away from the reading. Too often, students spend hours reading only to find several days later that they remember virtually nothing and must reread all the material. Although it takes extra time to pose and answer questions, it can reduce time spent rereading texts.

A powerful strategy that will increase your chances of understanding even difficult reading sources is to ask questions about three specific aspects of the source: (1) information, (2) form, organization, and expository features, and (3) rhetorical concerns. When you ask these questions, you will be reading in three different but not necessarily separate ways. Skilled readers use all three strategies simultaneously and harmoniously.

## Reading for Information

To read for information, ask the following questions:

> What has the author written?
>
> What is the main idea?
>
> What other content is important?

Asking pointed questions about information or content enables you to set specific goals, to read with an active purpose rather than merely trying to get through all the words on the page. An example of assertive reading is the strategy that our student Sarah Allyn used when she wrote a paper on "Communitarianism Contested" (see pp. 108–20). Instead of accepting the positions of Amitai Etzioni, Christopher Little, and Michael Walzer, the authors of the sources Sarah read for her essay (see Sarah Allyn's works cited, p. 119–20), she developed the opposite position that "communitarians are working to realize a society bereft of many of the hard-fought liberties achieved in our national Constitution." She began to formulate her ideas at the stage of close reading when, as her notes reveal, she started to question Etzioni's remarks. Her questioning led to a series of rebuttals that finally enabled her to produce a statement of her own position.

## Reading for Form, Organization, and Expository Features

To identify form, organization, and expository features, ask questions about how the text functions and what the author is doing as well as saying; for example,

> How has the author written the piece?
>
> Is the author using an identifiable form or genre?
>
> How do the different parts function?
>
> How is the text organized?
>
> What are the text's distinctive characteristics?
>
> Does the author use any special conventions?

Often it is easy to categorize or classify a piece of writing because it has certain regularities. We all recognize the distinguishing characteristics of literary genres, such as short stories, novels, and poems, and the conventions of nonliterary forms, such as thank-you notes, do-it-yourself manuals, and gossip columns. Academic writing also takes identifiable forms. Some, such as the psychological research article, the scientific lab report, and the philosophical essay of reflection, are quite specialized. Others, such as the forms listed here, are more generic:

| | |
|---|---|
| Response | Essay using comparison and contrast |
| Synthesis | Analysis |
| Argument | Evaluation |
| Research paper | Literature review |

We describe each of these forms in detail in Chapters 2 through 5.

Just as you already know something about the different forms that texts take, you are probably aware that many texts regularly have recognizable parts, such as introductions, conclusions, theses or main-idea statements, topic sentences, and paragraphs. Texts are also arranged in identifiable patterns. Most likely, you have organized your own essays using some of the common patterns listed here:

| | |
|---|---|
| Time order, narration, process | Example |
| Antecedent-consequent, cause-effect | Analysis/classification |
| | Definition |
| Description | Analogy |
| Statement-response | Argument/evaluation |
| Comparison/contrast | Problem-solution |

As you read, be mindful of the text's form, parts, and organizational pattern. Continually ask yourself such questions as "Where does this introduction end?" "What point is the author making in this paragraph?" "Will the author explain the causes after having described the effects?"

In addition to identifying form and organizational patterns, proficient readers pay attention to the distinctive expository features, stylistic qualities, and particular characteristics of texts. They observe, for example, that scholarly writers often draw extensively on evidence from published sources or original research that they carefully document. Such readers expect academic writers to adopt rather formal voices and to use sentences with a number of coordinated and parallel elements. They notice when academic writers use conversational, less formal styles or deviate from accepted conventions.

As you become more familiar with academic writing, you will expect particular texts to be organized in certain ways, and you will look for special textual features. For example, once you are acquainted with writing on technological innovation, the subject of the first three chapters in our anthology, you will automatically look for discussions of the costs and benefits of new technologies whenever you read articles on this topic. You will know from your past experiences as a reader that articles on new technology often include, or are entirely structured as, a costs/benefits analysis. You will also take note of any special terminology associated with the technology because you will know that technical vocabulary changes constantly and that mastering the current "buzzwords" is crucial. You will also try to find experimental verification of any new, startling conclusions or look for references to other work in the field. These are just a few of the strategies that skilled readers of technical literature might use.

## Reading for Rhetorical Concerns

Skilled readers are interested in rhetorical concerns as well as in information and textual features (Haas and Flower 167–83). When we speak of rhetoric in this book, we mean an author's attempt to use language to achieve an intended effect. An important word here is *intended*. Both writing and reading are intentional. They are deliberate actions, and each is guided by a purpose or goal. As you read to discover the rhetorical context, ask yourself five questions:

> What prompted the author to write?
>
> What community of readers is the piece intended for?
>
> What impact does the author want to have on the reader?
>
> What role does the author assume with regard to the audience, the subject matter, and his or her own voice?
>
> How does the author view what others have said on the topic?

Answers to these questions help define the rhetorical purpose and the context of the piece. The writer's purpose may not be obvious, but if you ask the right questions, you will discover the imperative—the feeling, view, incident, or phenomenon—that inspired the author to write. For example, consider Wade F. Horn's "Promoting Marriage as a Means for Promoting Fatherhood." Horn's biography suggests that he has a professional commitment to preserving families and fatherhood. He is Assistant Secretary for Children and Families for the U.S. Department of Health and Human Services, and he has served as president of the National Fatherhood Initiative and as Commissioner for Children, Youth, and Families. It seems reasonable to infer that at least part of his goal as a writer is to promote the preservation of traditional mother–father families. This does not mean that Horn is distorting the truth in any way. But if we were to contrast Horn's article with one that is less enthusiastic about maintaining nuclear families, it might be useful to take into consideration each writer's rhetorical goals.

## INDIVIDUAL EXERCISE ON ACTIVE READING

Read Rodney A. Brooks's "We Are Not Special" on pages 240–45 (or another article of your choice from Chapter 7 or 8) using the active reading strategies described on pages 5–15. Write out answers to the questions on information (p. 244); form, organization, and expository features (p. 244); and rhetorical concerns (p. 244).

## COLLABORATIVE EXERCISE ON RHETORICAL READING

1. In preparation for class, each student should read Joshua Quittner's "Invasion of Privacy" on pages 321–29 (or another article from Chapter 7 or 8).
2. Form collaborative learning groups of five students each, as described in the preface, or fashion groups according to your own method.
3. Work collaboratively to answer the following questions about the author's rhetorical purpose. The group recorder should write out your answers.
   a. What prompted the author to write?
   b. What community of readers is the piece intended for?
   c. What impact does the author want to have on the reader?
   d. What role does the author assume with regard to the audience, the subject matter, and his or her own voice? How does the author view what others have said on the topic?
4. Reconvene the entire class. Have each group recorder read the group's answers to the four rhetorical reading questions. After all have been heard from, the entire class can discuss any points on which various groups disagree.

## POSTREADING

### Review the Source and Your Notes

Once you have finished the last page of reading, resist the temptation to lay the book aside and move on to another activity. Take a few minutes to reinforce your understanding by briefly reviewing the source, scanning through your annotations, and looking through your elaborations and notes. Don't hesitate to revise or add to your annotations, elaborations, and notes as you review them. Remember that you can best perform this review activity immediately after reading the text.

## Compose Paraphrases and Summaries and Record Quotations That May Be Useful at a Later Date

Whenever you intend to draw on reading sources in your future writing, take some time immediately after reading to paraphrase, summarize, or quote passages that may be particularly useful. You will continue to paraphrase, summarize, and quote as you compose and revise your essay, but you are best prepared to do this while the reading is still fresh in your mind. Remember that one of the chief goals of active reading is to eliminate the need for rereading the source when you sit down to draft your essay.

### Paraphrasing

When you *paraphrase* a sentence, a paragraph, or some other segment from a reading, you translate the entire piece into your own words. Paraphrasing is a powerful operation for academic writing, but often students do not use it enough. Too many beginning academic writers use direct quotations whenever they refer to information from a reading source. Direct quotations are necessary only when you need the precise wording of the original. We discuss some of the reasons for quoting later in this chapter. Because paraphrasing is an active process that forces you to grapple with the author's ideas, it promotes comprehension. It is no wonder that many professors ask students to paraphrase rather than quote. They know that if you can paraphrase the material in a reading source, then you must be able to understand it.

A paraphrase differs from a summary in that a paraphrase includes *all* the information in the original, whereas a summary contains only the *most important* information. Paraphrase when you want to record the total, precise meaning of a passage. If you are interested in only the gist, summarize it. In general, relatively small sections of the original, often a sentence or two, are paraphrased, and larger chunks of information are summarized.

Paraphrasing requires you to make substantial changes to the vocabulary and sentence structure of the original. It is not enough to substitute a few synonyms and keep the same sentence structure and order of ideas. The following examples, based on an excerpt from Michael

Heim's "From Interface to Cyberspace" (see works cited, p. 35) show adequate and inadequate paraphrases.

> *Original Sentence:* Virtual-reality systems can use cyberspace to repre-sent physical space, even to the point that we feel telepresent in a transmitted scene, whether Mars or the deep ocean.
>
> *Inadequate Paraphrase:* Virtual-reality systems can represent physical space by using cyberspace, even to the extent that people feel tele-present in a scene that is transmitted, perhaps Mars or the deep ocean (Heim 80).
>
> *Adequate Paraphrase:* We can achieve the illusion of being present in remote locations, for example the planet Mars or deep parts of the ocean, by using virtual-reality equipment that creates a cyberspace representation of real-world space (Heim 80).

The writer of the inadequate paraphrase reshuffled the words in the original sentence but retained the vocabulary, sentence structure, and order of ideas. If you do not intend to make major changes to the passage, then quote it word for word. There is no acceptable middle ground between a paraphrase and a direct quotation. An inadequate paraphrase is considered a form of *plagiarism*, since it is interpreted as an attempt to pass off another writer's sentence structure and words as one's own.

You can sometimes paraphrase simply by rewriting the original passage for a new audience. To illustrate, look at an excerpt from "Being and Believing: Ethics of Virtual Reality," a medical journal edi-torial. The sentence describes a computer-based system (virtual reality) designed to simulate a real-world situation.

> The overall effect was that the observer experienced a computer-generated artificial or virtual reality (VR) whose credibility depended largely on the agreement between the simulated imagery and the famil-iar sensible world. (283)

Suppose that your objective is to paraphrase the sentence for an audience of high-school students. Because you do not want to talk over the students' heads, you put the sentence into simpler language.

> The effectiveness of a virtual reality system depends upon the extent to which it can create an environment of computer images that appear life-like ("Being and Believing" 283).

You should notice that in this example the parenthetical documentation gives an abbreviated article title rather than an author's name. That is because the article was written by the medical journal's editorial staff and was not attributed to a specific author. To learn more about documentation conventions, see the appendix.

As the example demonstrates, paraphrasing often requires you to express abstract ideas in a more concrete form. When a passage includes difficult concepts or complex language, it may be hard to reword it and still preserve the original meaning. You will need a more systematic paraphrasing procedure, such as the one in the following box.

---

### PARAPHRASING STRATEGIES

1. Locate the individual statements or major idea units in the original.
2. Change the order of major ideas, maintaining the logical connections among them.
3. Substitute synonyms for words in the original, making sure the language in your paraphrase is appropriate for your audience.
4. Combine or divide sentences as necessary.
5. Compare the paraphrase with the original to assure that the rewording is sufficient and the meaning has been preserved.
6. Weave the paraphrase into your essay in accordance with your rhetorical purpose.
7. Document the paraphrase.

---

Keep in mind that paraphrasing is not a lockstep process that always follows the same sequence. You may use fewer than all seven strategies, and you can vary the order in which you apply them. For illustration, however, we paraphrase a sentence from Carl Sagan's article "In Defense of Robots" (see works cited, p. 36), using all the strategies in approximately the order given in the box. Let's assume that we are writing for an audience of first-year college students.

> There is nothing inhuman about an intelligent machine; it is indeed an expression of those superb intellectual capabilities that only human beings, of all the creatures on our planet, now possess. (Sagan 292)

## Locate the individual statements or major idea units

First, we determine how many major ideas are presented in the passage. We find two central units of information: (1) an assertion about intelligent machines (they are not "inhuman") and (2) an argument to back up the assertion (that these machines demonstrate humans' unique intelligence).

1. There is nothing inhuman about an intelligent machine;
2. It is indeed an expression of those superb intellectual capabilities that only human beings, of all the creatures on our planet, now possess.

## Change the order of major ideas, maintaining the logical connections among them

Now we change the order of the two units of information, placing the second before the first. To accommodate this switch, we substitute the noun phrase *an intelligent machine* for *it* so the subject is clear at the outset of the sentence. Then we add *which demonstrates that* to indicate the logical relationship between the two units.

1. An intelligent machine is indeed an expression of those superb intellectual capabilities that only human beings, of all the creatures on our planet, now possess;
2. which demonstrates that there is nothing inhuman about an intelligent machine.

## Substitute synonyms for words in the original

Think about your audience at this stage. Sagan's original language is relatively easy to understand, but when the words in the original source are too formal or sophisticated, you may want to choose vocabulary more accessible to your readers.

Begin your search for synonyms *without* consulting a dictionary or a thesaurus. Many students rush to such reference books and copy synonyms without considering how they fit into the general sense of the sentence. Paraphrases filled with synonyms taken indiscriminately from a dictionary or a thesaurus can be awkward and confusing.

As a rule of thumb, do not repeat more than three consecutive words from the original. You may occasionally need to repeat a word or a phrase, but whenever possible, substitute synonyms for the original words. It is not necessary to locate a substitute for every word in the sentence you are paraphrasing. Repeat words that are central to the meaning or have no appropriate synonyms, such as the term "inhuman" in our example.

As we return to our example, by substituting synonyms, doing a little more rearranging, and providing context where necessary, we arrive at the following paraphrase:

> Since artificial intelligence results from humans beings' unique intellectual talents, the technology should not be regarded as inhuman (Sagan 292).

### Combine or divide sentences as necessary

Although there is no particular need to divide our paraphrase, for illustration we split it into two short sentences:

> Artificial intelligence results from humans beings' unique intellectual talents. Thus, the technology should not be regarded as inhuman (Sagan 292).

### Compare the paraphrase with the original

Compare the paraphrase with the original sentence to see if you have reworded sufficiently yet have retained the meaning of the original.

> *Original:* There is nothing inhuman about an intelligent machine; it is indeed an expression of those superb intellectual capabilities that only human beings, of all the creatures on our planet, now possess.
>
> *Paraphrase:* Since artificial intelligence results from humans beings' unique intellectual talents, the technology should not be regarded as inhuman (Sagan 292).

In this case, the paraphrase seems adequate. In other cases, you might need to revise the paraphrase, possibly by reapplying one of the strategies we have already discussed.

### Weave the paraphrase into your essay

Weave the paraphrase into your essay in a way that helps further your rhetorical purpose. Consider the following example:

*EXCERPT FROM ESSAY*

Even though we live in a technologically advanced society, many Americans still feel uncomfortable with the idea of machine intelligence. Science fiction abounds with stories of computers whose "inhuman" logic poses a threat to human values. But as Sagan points out, since artificial intelligence results from humans beings' unique intellectual talents, the technology should not be regarded as inhuman (292). These thinking machines are an extension of our own abilities rather than a challenge to our humanity.

Notice that we did not plop the paraphrase into the paragraph. Since Sagan's view contrasts with the preceding sentence, we began with the word "But." Then, we attributed the material to Sagan by writing "as Sagan points out." At the end of the sentence, we provided the page number in parentheses. We cannot be sure that a paraphrase is successful unless we see that it fits smoothly into the essay for which it was intended.

## Document your paraphrase

Failing to document a paraphrase is considered plagiarism, an offense that can lead to failure and permanent expulsion. Always cite the author of the source, enclose in parentheses the page numbers of the information you paraphrased, and provide an entry on the works cited page. Notice how we documented the paraphrase in the preceding example.

### INDIVIDUAL EXERCISE ON PARAPHRASING

1. Apply the steps in the Paraphrasing Strategies box (p. 18) to the following passage taken from Jeremy Seabrook's "What Are 'Class' and 'Inequality'?" (Chapter 10). Work through the steps in the process one by one and record the results of each step, just as we did on pages 18–21 with the sentence from Carl Sagan's article. Write your paraphrase for an audience of first-year college students who have not read the article.

   Inequality is an abstraction. Its great advantage to the rich is that it replaces earlier concepts of class. These were embodied in real living figures of flesh and blood and their relationship to each other. Inequality is a statistical term in which the participants appear only as victims or beneficiaries (paragraph 8).

2. Revise your paraphrase.
3. Submit not only the final paraphrase but also all the preliminary work produced at each stage of the paraphrasing process.

### COLLABORATIVE EXERCISE ON PARAPHRASING

1. Form collaborative learning groups of three students each, as described in the preface, or fashion groups according to your own method.
2. Have each group member take responsibility for one of the following sentences from Jeremy Seabrook's "What Are 'Class' and 'Inequality'?" (Chapter 10). Do not read any sentences other than the one you are responsible for.
   a. Privilege has many methods of self-preservation, not least physical force, but sometimes through a mystical appeal to the special intellectual or spiritual powers the privileged claim to possess (paragraph 1).
   b. For social classes have not been eliminated by the treacherous continuum of inequality, but have been remade, often in ways which make them obscure to the participants (paragraph 12).
   c. In the end, the interests of the nobility merged with those of the new moneyed middle class; a compromise born of expediency, especially when confronted by a rising working class. The heritage of the old rich was maintained by the wealth of the new, a marriage of convenience (paragraph 35).
3. Use the steps listed in the Paraphrasing Strategies box to come up with a paraphrase of your sentence. Write your paraphrase for an audience of first-year college students who have not read the article.
4. When all group members have finished their paraphrases, pass the sheet with your paraphrase to the person on your left and receive the paraphrase of the person on your right. On a new sheet of paper, paraphrase the sentence you received from the person on your right. Do not refer to the original sentence in the book.
5. When all group members have finished their paraphrases, pass sheets once more to the left and once again paraphrase the sentence you receive.
6. Your group should now have serial paraphrases that have gone through three versions for each of the sentences from Seabrook. Working together, compare the original of each sentence with the final version of the paraphrase. Does the paraphrase preserve the

meaning of the original? If not, where did the meaning get lost? Which steps in the paraphrasing process worked well, and which were problematic? Make sure your group recorder notes the conclusions the group comes to.

7. When the class reconvenes, have the recorders explain the conclusions groups reached about the paraphrasing process.

## Summarizing

Whether you are writing a synopsis of a piece of literature, an abstract of a journal article, a précis of an argument, or some other type of summary, the fundamental task is to shorten the original without changing its meaning. Whether summaries are brief or comprehensive, they are attempts to capture the overall gist of the source.

---

### SUMMARIZING STRATEGIES

1. Preview the source and recall your prior knowledge of the topic.
2. Read the source using active reading strategies (annotating, elaborating, taking content notes, and posing and answering questions).
3. Identify and emphasize the most important ideas and the significant connections among those ideas.
4. Construct a graphic overview.
5. Delete unimportant detail, irrelevant examples, and redundancy.
6. Combine ideas in sentences and paragraphs.
7. Identify and imitate the organizational pattern of the source.
8. Identify and incorporate the rhetorical context and the author's rhetorical purpose.
9. Document your summary.

---

You need not apply these strategies in any particular order. Nor do you have to use all nine of them for each summary you write. Simply choose ones that are appropriate for the source you are working with. You can write a short summary simply by explaining the context and the author's rhetorical purpose. Lengthy or complex summaries may require the full range of strategies.

*Preview the source, recall your prior knowledge of the topic, and read the source using active reading strategies*

The first two summarizing strategies recap the active reading techniques that we covered earlier in this chapter. Assertive reading is imperative for summarizing. Annotating the text to draw your attention to main ideas, taking content notes, and identifying the author's organization plan and rhetorical goal are particularly helpful preparation.

*Identify and emphasize the most important ideas and the significant connections among those ideas*

Your annotations and notes should direct you to the most important ideas in the text. Write out the main ideas and explain how they are related to each other. A summary is more than a retelling of main ideas; it should indicate relationships among the ideas and tie them together in coherent paragraphs.

*Construct a graphic overview*

Another way of identifying the principal ideas and of determining how they tie together is to construct a graphic overview. A graphic overview is a diagram that represents the central ideas in a reading source, shows how they are related, and indicates the author's overall purpose. You might think of it as a blueprint charting the source's main ideas.

Let's walk through the process of creating a graphic overview. First, review your reading notes and annotations, and select key words and concepts. Then, try to depict the relationships among those ideas by drawing circles and boxes connected by lines and arrows. Use labels to show how the various points are interrelated. Be creative!

The graphic overview shown in Figure 1-1 was drawn by one of our students to represent the principal content of Isaac Kramnick and R. Laurence Moore's "Is America a Christian Nation?" which appears in Chapter 12. You may want to read the article to get the most out of this example. As you study the example, keep in mind that creating a graphic overview is a highly individual process. A single, definitive graphic overview does not exist for each text. Countless variations are possible.

The graphic overview forces you to think about the big picture. You have to manipulate chunks of information like pieces in a puzzle and determine how they best fit together. The graphic overview allows you to visualize relationships among main ideas and perceive the web of

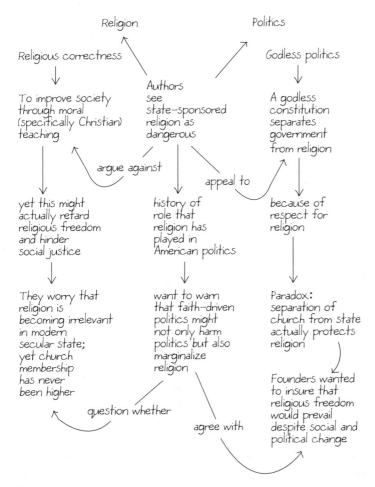

Figure 1-1

meaning in a form other than sentences and paragraphs. Notice that the overview of Kramnick and Moore's article clarifies its focus on a potential conflict between religion and politics. The conflict is represented at the top of the diagram. Lower down in the diagram are specific claims that sharpen the conflict, along with the authors' view that a separation of church and state actually ensures religious freedom. You should find it easy to summarize this source after you have seen all its main ideas diagrammed on a single page. A special advantage of the graphic overview is that it distances you from the author's exact words and thus helps you to avoid plagiarizing. You won't fall back on the author's language as you write out your summary.

## Delete unimportant detail, irrelevant examples, and redundancy

Cross out or label as nonessential any material that is repetitive, excessively detailed, or unrelated to the main idea. Academic sources are often highly redundant because authors repeat or illustrate complex concepts in order to give the reader more than one chance to understand them.

## Combine ideas in sentences and paragraphs

After you delete nonessential material and categorize bits of information, you are often left with disjointed pieces of text. If you want your summary to flow clearly, you have to rearrange these key ideas, make elements parallel, or add logical connectors. You may also want to compress several words or phrases into fewer words and to reduce items in the same class to a single category.

## Identify and imitate the organizational pattern of the source

On page 13, we identified eleven organizational plans for academic writing: (1) time order, narration, process; (2) antecedent-consequent, cause-effect; (3) description; (4) statement-response; (5) comparison/contrast; (6) example; (7) analysis/classification; (8) definition; (9) analogy; (10) argument/evaluation; (11) problem-solution. Rarely do authors restrict themselves to a single plan; they usually use these plans in combination.

Once you identify how the author arranges and orders the piece, you can use a comparable pattern as the skeleton for your summary. Organization conveys meaning, so you will be helping your reader to follow the train of thought.

## Identify and incorporate the rhetorical context and the author's rhetorical purpose

You may want to include in your summary information about the rhetorical context of the source and the author's rhetorical purpose. This is particularly appropriate when you are writing a summary that will stand alone rather than become part of a longer essay. To determine the rhetorical context, ask yourself the questions in the box that follows.

*Rhetorical purpose* or *intention* refers to how the author tries to affect or influence the audience. Sometimes the purpose is easily identified because it emerges as a controlling feature of the piece, such as in an argumentative text or a highly opinionated editorial. At other times the author's purpose may not be self-evident.

---

**QUESTIONS FOR DETERMINING RHETORICAL CONTEXT**

1. What is the author's background? Is he or she an acceptable, credible authority?
2. What feeling, view, incident, or phenomenon brought about the need or motivated the author to write?
3. What role does the author assume in relation to the audience?
4. In what type of publication does the piece appear? If the publication is a journal, magazine, or newspaper, what is the readership?
5. When was the piece published? Is it current or dated?

---

*Document your summary*

Even when you have summarized a text in your own words, you must acknowledge the title and the author. As with paraphrasing, summarizing a source without proper documentation is considered plagiarism. Always cite the source at the point where you use it in your writing and include a complete reference in the works cited list at the end of your paper. We explain how to set up a works cited list on page 57.

We draw on several of the strategies described above to illustrate the process of writing a brief summary. Let's assume that as you are preparing to write an essay on recent controversies over the separation of church and state, you locate Isaac Kramnick and R. Laurence Moore's essay, "Is America a Christian Nation?" (Chapter 12). First, you read the article using the active strategies we described in this chapter—carefully previewing, annotating, taking content notes, and posing and answering questions as you read. Before summarizing relevant parts of the article, you want to be sure to have a good sense of its global structure, so you decide to construct a graphic overview. Let's assume you produced the overview shown in Figure 1-1. The graphic overview makes plain Kramnick and Moore's position that the separation of church and state actually strengthens religion, and it shows how the authors support this position by appealing to the founders of the Constitution. You begin your summary by writing the following account of Kramnick and Moore's central argument:

Kramnick and Moore claim that the separation of church and state actually strengthens religion by protecting it from the hazards of political change.

Consider next which examples are important enough to include in your summary. At this point, as the summarizing strategy suggests, you are identifying and emphasizing the most important ideas. This process also involves another summarizing strategy: deleting peripheral detail, parallel examples, and redundancy.

Next, you must decide on an organizational plan for ordering the material you have selected from the graphic overview. Recalling the summarizing strategy of identifying and imitating the organizational pattern of the source, you return to your annotations and notes to figure out Kramnick and Moore's organizational plan. A strong candidate is the comparison-contrast plan, since Kramnick and Moore describe how views of the modern religious right (comparison) differ from those of the founders of the Constitution (contrast). You could present relevant examples by weighing them against claims that both sides of the argument might make: The religious right might agree with some arguments, while the founders of the Constitution might agree with others.

Finally, you locate in your question-answer notes a statement about Kramnick and Moore's rhetorical purpose, which is to warn readers that faith-driven politics may harm not only politics but religion as well. Here you are applying the summarizing strategy that identifies and incorporates the rhetorical context and the authors' rhetorical purpose.

After adding selected examples to your paraphrase of Kramnick and Moore's central idea, indicating the logical relationships among them, and ending with a statement about the authors' purpose, you come up with the following rough summary:

Kramnick and Moore claim that the separation of church and state actually strengthens religion by protecting it from the hazards of political change. While they discuss the hopes of the religious right to improve society through the moral teaching of the Christian religion, the thrust of this article is on the wisdom of the separation of church and state. Some of the examples they mention show the Constitution's concern for ensuring freedom of conscience, religious toleration, and a belief in moral citizenship. The authors argue that social and political policies tied to specific religious teachings violate this principle. Their goal is to warn that faith-driven politics may harm not only politics but religion as well (578–583).

Note that we have documented the summary by using Kramnick and Moore's names in the text and ending with the inclusive page numbers in parentheses.

## INDIVIDUAL EXERCISE ON SUMMARIZING

1. Read a selection of your choice (other than Kramnick and Moore's essay) from Chapter 12 using the active reading strategies described in this chapter.
2. Decide which summarizing strategies will work best for the article.
3. Locate in this chapter the steps for the summarizing strategy you chose.
4. Work through the process to produce a 250-word summary of the article. Write for an audience of first-year college students who have not read the article.
5. Submit not only the final summary but also all the preliminary work produced at each stage of the summarizing process.

## COLLABORATIVE EXERCISE ON SUMMARIZING

### First-Day Activities:

1. Form collaborative learning groups of five students each, as described in the preface, or fashion groups according to your own method.
2. Assign to each group one of the reading selections from Chapter 12 (other than Kramnick and Moore's essay). Each group should work with a different article. Group members should read their articles outside class.

### Second-Day Activities:

1. Divide into collaborative groups.
2. Identify a summarizing strategy that your group agrees will work best for your article.
3. Apply the summarizing strategy, working as a group and following the steps outlined in this chapter, to produce a 250-word summary of your article. You may want to work through each step in the process together, with the recorder noting the results of your discussion, or you may prefer to subdivide the task among group members and then pool your work. Write for an audience of first-year college students who have not read the article.
4. Reconvene the entire class. Each group recorder should explain what summarizing strategy the group chose and why that choice made

sense, and the recorder should describe any problems that the group encountered using the strategy.

## Quoting

When you compose essays based on sources, try summarizing or paraphrasing rather than stringing together endless quotations. Pack your postreading notes with paraphrases and summaries, not quotations. As a general rule, repeat passages word for word only if they are exceptionally well expressed or contain special forms of writing, such as definitions, key concepts, clever sayings, testimonials, or poetic language. When you take notes on facts and data, paraphrase the original instead of quoting it, unless its wording is particularly striking.

For convenience, we discuss in this section how to incorporate quotations in drafts of your essay as well as how to select quotations for inclusion in your postreading notes.

### Selecting quotations

A typical reason for quoting is to retain the meaning or authenticity of the original source. Assume you are writing about Gene Stephens's "High-Tech Crime Fighting: The Threat to Civil Liberties," an article that discusses individuals' constitutional rights. In your essay, you decide to quote directly from relevant parts of the United States Constitution. It would not be wise to paraphrase the Constitution, since the exact wording is crucial to its interpretation. When precise wording affects your argument, you need to quote.

Another purpose for quoting is to lend support to a literary analysis. When you analyze literature, you need to identify the specific passages that support your interpretation. To illustrate, look at how one of our students used a direct quotation to support his analysis of Mary Ann Rishel's short story "Steel Fires" (see works cited, p. 36).

> The distinction is blurred between workmen and the steel they are producing. When Mike and Rebb, after working hard, begin to tire and lose their momentum, their fatigue is described in terms of the steel production process: "Working metal doesn't always mean it comes out strong" (11).

If the student had paraphrased Rishel's words instead of quoting them directly, the point would not come across as well.

A third purpose for quoting is to capture exactly language that supports your point. In his article on implanting electronic devices in humans, Gareth Branwyn quotes John Anderson, a man who had been totally deaf, about the importance of the electronic hearing implant he received.

> "The silence of those three years when I was totally deaf is still deafening to me these many years later. My life was in the hearing world and it was critical for me to be able to hear like 'everyone else.' " (Branwyn 64)

This quotation lends a sense of reality to Branwyn's discussion. Anderson's exact language tells the reader much more about his attitudes than a paraphrase would reveal.

Another reason to use a direct quotation is *to employ it as a stylistic device*—for example, to open or close a paper. Michael Heim ends his article on human-machine interfaces with a quotation that makes the audience contemplate the future impact of this technology.

> In the 1960s, Jim Morrison saw the danger to sensibility in *The Lords and the New Creatures*, in which he warned: "There may be a time when we'll attend Weather Theatre to recall the sensation of rain." Back then, Morrison could not know that the Weather Theatre will soon be everywhere and that we will need lessons in recalling why we love the sensation of the rain.

A final reason for quoting is *to capture language that you find especially effective or memorable*. Notice how our student Karla Allen employs Charles Dickens's memorable lines:

> In Charles Dickens's words, "It was the best of times, it was the worst of times" (3). While big corporations were reaping larger profits than ever before, many smaller companies and individuals found themselves out of work.

### Altering quotations

It is permissible to alter direct quotations, either by deleting some of the author's words or by inserting your own words, as long as you follow conventions that alert your audience to what you are doing. The sentence below, taken from an editorial in *The Lancet* entitled "Being and Believing: Ethics of Virtual Reality" (see works cited, p. 35), was quoted in a student paper. The student used an *ellipsis*, a set of three spaced periods, to show where words were left out.

> *Editorial:* Although the motives behind clinical VR experimentation may be praiseworthy—e.g., it may replace the prescription of harmful psychotropics—the fact that experimentation may be well intended does not preclude early examination of ethical issues.

> *Student:* Using virtual reality to help disabled people extend their physical capabilities seems attractive, but it is not without pitfalls. As the editors of the medical journal *The Lancet* state, "Although the motives behind clinical VR experimentation may be praiseworthy . . . the fact that experimentation may be well intended does not preclude early examination of ethical issues" (283).

To show omission at the end of quoted material, a normal period is followed by the three spaced periods.

When you insert your own words into a quotation, signal your insertion by placing the words within brackets. Notice how our student uses this convention when she quotes from Rishel's story "Steel Fires":

> *Rishel:* They had a hand in it. Helped make the steel. Forged. Pressed. Rolled. Cast. Hammered steel. But they didn't invent steel. They didn't design a bridge. They didn't think up new uses for steel. They weren't idea men.

> *Student:* But in the end, Mike does not value his own contribution to the industry. "They [laborers] had a hand in it. . . . But they didn't invent steel. . . . They weren't idea men" (13).

By inserting the bracketed word *laborers*, the student clarifies the meaning of the pronoun *they*.

## Documenting quotations

If the quotation occupies no more than four typed lines on a page, enclose it in double quotation marks. If it is longer, set the entire quotation apart from your text by indenting it ten spaces (see Fig. 1-2).

Notice that in the long, set-off quotation in Figure 1-2, the parenthetical citation goes outside the final punctuation. For short quotations, place the parenthetical citation between the final quotation marks and the closing punctuation. The following example draws on Warren Robinett's article "Electronic Expansion of Human Perception," published in *Whole Earth Review* (see works cited, p. 36).

> Robinett states, "Though it [virtual reality] sounds like science fiction today, tomorrow it will seem as common as talking on the telephone" (21).

```
                                                    Nelson 3

At the end of his article Stephens reminds us of both the
promise and threat of high-tech crime fighting.
                Once privacy is gone it will be difficult to
                restore. Once mind control is accomplished it
                will be difficult to reestablish free thought.
                But with proper safeguards the superior
                investigative techniques and more effective
                treatment of offenders that new technology offers
                promise a safer saner society for us all. (25)
        Unfortunately, Stephens overlooks important
advantages of crime fighting technology and the
```

**Figure 1-2**

The phrase "Robinett states" leads into the quotation and acknowledges the author. Other words to use to introduce quotations are listed in the following box.

---

### VERBS FOR ACKNOWLEDGING SOURCES

acknowledges, admits, adds, ascertains, asks, analyzes, assesses, argues, agrees (disagrees), addresses, answers, believes, categorizes, compares (contrasts), critiques, considers, concurs, concludes, cites, defines, delineates, describes, determines, demonstrates, discovers, evaluates, explores, examines, expounds on, emphasizes, envisions, finds, furnishes, investigates, inquires, identifies, lists, makes the case, measures, notes, observes, points out, postulates, presents, proposes, proves, questions, rationalizes, remarks, replies, refers to, reviews, reports, says, shows, states, stipulates, stresses, suggests, summarizes, surveys, synthesizes, traces, views, warns, writes

---

Of course, you can use such introductory phrases and words as lead-ins to summaries and paraphrases as well as to quotations.

*Weaving quotations into your essay*

You can weave a quotation into your writing in several ways. You can refer to the author in the text itself, or you can place the last name within parentheses. When you refer directly to the author, you can cite the name before the quotation, within the quotation, or after it. Consider these examples from a student paper; the page numbers refer to the journal in which the article originally appeared.

---

### WEAVING QUOTATIONS INTO YOUR ESSAY

Here are five options:

> *Option a*—Quotation followed by author's name:
>    "Virtual reality, as its name suggests, is an unreal, alternate reality in which anything could happen" (Robinett 17).
>
> *Option b*—Acknowledgment of author before the quotation:
>    Robinett writes, "Virtual reality, as its name suggests, is an unreal, alternate reality in which anything could happen" (17).
>
> *Option c*—Acknowledgment of author within a quotation:
>    "Virtual reality, as its name suggests," states Robinett, "is an unreal, alternate reality in which anything could happen" (17).
>
> *Option d*—Acknowledgment of author after a quotation:
>    "Virtual reality, as its name suggests, is an unreal, alternate reality in which anything could happen," observes Robinett (17).
>
> *Option e*—Acknowledgment of author in complete sentence followed by a colon:
>    Robinett provides us with a concise definition of this new technology: "Virtual reality, as its name suggests, is an unreal, alternate reality in which anything could happen" (17).

---

Note that all five options require you to cite the page numbers in parentheses. If you are using Modern Language Association (MLA) style, the foregoing method of documentation will suffice. The style of the American Psychological Association (APA) is slightly different in that the publication date follows the author's name, and the abbreviation for page is always included. For example, for option a you would write (Robinett, 1991, p. 17), and for options b, c, d, and e, you would write (1991, p. 17).

When you use option a, don't forget to provide transitions between your own ideas and those of the source author. Inexperienced writers sprinkle their papers with direct quotations that have little connection with the rest of the text. You can avoid this problem by leading into quotations with the verbs listed on page 33.

### INDIVIDUAL EXERCISE ON QUOTING

Scan Pauline Irit Erera's "What Is A Family?" (Chapter 9) for places where the author has quoted directly. Can you make any generalizations about how Erera uses direct quotations to build her argument?

### COLLABORATIVE EXERCISE ON QUOTING

1. Form collaborative learning groups of five students each, as described in the preface, or fashion groups according to your own method.
2. Assume that your group is preparing to write a collaborative essay about school reform. (You will not, in fact, write the essay.)
3. Choose one group member to read aloud the first five paragraphs of Janine Bempechat's "Challenging Our Assumptions" (Chapter 11).
4. After each paragraph, decide which sentences, if any, contain information that you might use in your essay. Which of these sentences would you paraphrase, and which would you quote? Explain your decisions.
5. At the end of the small-group session, the recorder should have a list of sentences and, for each sentence, an indication of whether it would be quoted or paraphrased and why.
6. Reconvene the entire class. Have each group recorder read the list of sentences and explanations. Discuss points of agreement and difference.

### WORKS CITED

"Being and Believing: Ethics of Virtual Reality." Editorial. *The Lancet* 338 (1991): 283–84.

Branwyn, Gareth. "Desire to Be Wired." *Wired* Sept./Oct. 1993: 621.

Dickens, Charles. *A Tale of Two Cities.* New York: Pocket Library, 1957.

Haas, Christina, and Linda Flower. "Rhetorical Reading and the Construction of Meaning." *College Composition and Communication* 39 (1988): 167–83.

Heim, Michael. "From Interface to Cyberspace." *The Metaphysics of Virtual Reality.* New York: Oxford UP, 1993. 72–81.

Rishel, Mary Ann. "Steel Fires." Unpublished short story, 1985.

Robinett, Warren. "Electronic Expansion of Human Perception." *Whole Earth Review* Fall 1991: 17–21.

Sagan, Carl. "In Defense of Robots." *Broca's Brain*. New York: Ballantine, 1980.

Stephens, Gene. "High-Tech Crime Fighting: The Threat to Civil Liberties." *The Futurist* July–Aug. 1990: 20–25.

*t w o*

# Writing an Essay in Response to a Source: An Illustration of the Writing Process

## THE READING-WRITING PROCESS

In Chapter 1, we brought you through the first part of the academic reading-writing process by describing strategies for active reading: prereading, close reading, and postreading. In this chapter, we guide you through the remainder of the process by showing you how to plan, draft, and rework essays.

---

### OVERVIEW OF THE ACADEMIC READING-WRITING PROCESS

**Active Reading**

*Prereading.* Preview the reading sources, freewrite about your topic, and set your goals.

*Close reading.* Mark, annotate, elaborate on, and pose questions about the reading. Questions address three areas: (1) information, (2) textual form, organization, and expository features, and (3) rhetorical concerns.

*Postreading.* Record comments, reactions, quotations, paraphrases, and summaries about the readings.

(continued on the next page)

---

### Planning

*Formulating a thesis.*   Arrive at a preliminary understanding of the point you want to make in your paper.

*Organizing.*   Decide how you will use sources in the paper and how you will develop your argument.

### Drafting

*Drafting.*   Weave source material (usually in the form of quotations, paraphrases, and summaries) with your own ideas to create paragraphs and, ultimately, a complete paper, typically with an introduction, a body, and a conclusion.

### Reworking

*Revising.*   Lengthen, shorten, or reorder your paper; change your prose to make it more understandable to your reader; make sentence-level, phrase-level, and word-level stylistic changes; or, in some cases, make major conceptual or organizational alterations to incorporate what you learned during the process of drafting.

*Editing.*   Proofread your paper for errors in sentence structure, usage, punctuation, spelling, and mechanics, and check for proper manuscript form.

As we mentioned in Chapter 1, rarely do writers methodically work their way through the reading and writing process, beginning with prereading and ending with editing. Sometimes they vary the sequence, or they may return repeatedly to work out particular phases. On page 8, for example, we suggested that some of your freewriting before close reading may provide a basis for your later writing about what you've read. On pages 20–21, we saw that the decision to incorporate a paraphrase rather than a direct quotation may come after you have already drafted your argument and included several quotations, or that you may later rework your paraphrase so that it sounds less like the original to which it refers. On page 28, we saw that you might add illustrative examples to your writing after you have completed substantial parts of your paper. Allow yourself flexibility, but keep in mind that some approaches to the writing process can be more productive than others.

While you are drafting your essay, it would be unwise to stop every few minutes to check spelling, punctuation, or the correct usage. The result could be disjointed, disconnected prose. While drafting, you should concentrate on generating ideas. Save editing for later.

You should also be aware that writers may use different composing styles depending on their purposes. A writer completing a complex history assignment may spend much more time on prewriting activities—reading, underlining, and annotating the materials and taking notes—than would a writer who is composing an essay that recalls prior knowledge or personal experience.

### INDIVIDUAL EXERCISE ON THE WRITING PROCESS

1. Write a one-paragraph description of how you have composed essays in the past. You might consider the following questions: How did you come up with ideas for your writing? What organizational plans did you use? Did you create outlines? Did you write first drafts with or without summaries, paraphrases, or quotations, with or without notes? Did you ask friends, family members, or teachers to read your rough drafts? If so, what types of feedback did you receive, and how did you respond? When you proofread, what specific issues of usage, spelling, punctuation, and mechanics did you focus on?

2. Now consider the overall writing process you used in the past. Over how many days did the process extend? What were the strengths of your approach to writing assignments? What were its weaknesses? What parts of the process were the easiest for you, and what parts were the hardest? Write another paragraph in response to these questions.

### COLLABORATIVE EXERCISE ON THE WRITING PROCESS

1. Form collaborative learning groups of five students each, as described in the preface, or fashion groups according to your own method.

2. Allow ten minutes for each group member to freewrite in response to the first set of questions provided for the Individual Exercise on the Writing Process.

3. Convene your group and have each member read his or her freewriting piece. After each reading, the group should identify strengths and weaknesses in the writer's approach to the composing process. The group recorder should compile lists of strengths and weaknesses.

4. Reconvene the class. Have each group recorder read the lists of individual strengths and weaknesses. Discuss any variations in the lists.

## PERSONAL RESPONSE IN ACADEMIC WRITING

Though the types of writing you usually associate with undergraduate assignments—summaries, research reports, arguments, syntheses of readings, and the like—will determine most of your activities, occasionally you will be assigned papers that are less factual and impersonal. One such typical assignment calls for a personal reaction to designated readings. Consider the following example:

> Write a brief essay in response to one of the reserve readings on the topic of immigration.

Notice that this assignment is not asking you to draw on personal experiences. Nor does it require you to refer only to the source and make minimal use of your own ideas. It asks you to relate two materials—your own views and the views of the author of the text—and in so doing to present an *informed* outlook.

The writing tasks that we focus on in this chapter require a balance between personal expression and textual content. You could fulfill these assignments in an elementary fashion by summarizing the source and tacking on a few sentences of commentary or reaction. But there are much more interesting approaches.

To react and respond to a text, you have to explore the topic and bring your personal experience and knowledge to bear on it in a pertinent way. *Personal response* essays are sometimes called *exploratory* essays because they allow you to probe a topic and examine it by turning it around in the laboratory of your mind. You can use the topic as a catalyst for unraveling personal meaning, uncovering personal relationships, and recalling relevant memories.

You need to frame the author's message in your own context, to carry on a dialogue with the author, and to expand meaningfully on the author's ideas. Your reactions can take a number of forms. You can agree or disagree with the author's ideas, call them into question, express satisfaction or dissatisfaction with them, approve or disapprove of them, elaborate on their consequences, or speculate about them. But you must always take care to treat authors fairly and represent their ideas accurately. The assignment requires you to react in order to learn more about the issues raised in the sources, not just to get your licks in. In academic papers, personal responses should clarify issues rather than cloud the truth or manipulate readers.

## ACTIVE READING STRATEGIES FOR RESPONSE ESSAYS

The active reading strategies we described in Chapter 1 work for all academic essays, including essays of response. We do not repeat those strategies here, but we discuss a task that precedes them. It is the task of analyzing the assignment, an activity that initiates the reading and writing process but that we postponed explaining until we were ready to work with an actual writing task. We also discuss additional elaborating techniques that are particularly useful for response essays. They include strategies for exploring the topic, expressing agreement or disagreement, comparison and contrast, criticism or interpretation, and the like.

### Analyze the Assignment

Throughout your college career, you will receive a variety of writing assignments. Some will include detailed directions and explicit criteria; others will be more loosely structured and open-ended. After you read the assignment two or three times, underline key words that are crucial to your aim and purpose and ask yourself these questions:

1. What is the topic of the paper? Has the professor specified the topic and supplied all the readings? Do I have to select the readings and define and limit the topic myself?
2. What task do I have to perform? What words serve as clues to the nature of this task? The box that follows lists typical directives for assignments. As you read each directive, speculate about what you would have to do.

---

#### DIRECTIVES FOR ACADEMIC ASSIGNMENTS

abstract, agree (or disagree), analyze, appraise, argue, assess, classify, compare/contrast, convince, criticize, critique, defend, define, describe, delineate, demonstrate, differentiate, discuss, distinguish, establish cause-effect, estimate, evaluate, exemplify, explain, explore, expound on, furnish evidence, give examples, identify, illustrate, judge, list, make a case for or against, paraphrase, picture, predict, present, prove, recount, refute, relate, report, respond to, restate, review, show, solve, state, suggest, summarize, support, survey, trace

---

3. What type of paper do I have to write? Does the assignment call for a specialized form of academic writing, such as a research essay, book review, case study, or laboratory report?

4. For whom am I writing—for the professor, classmates, or some other audience? What are the audience's expectations? How much knowledge does my audience have about the topic? Is the audience familiar with the reading source? Will I have to supply background information?

5. What reading sources will I use? Will the professor allow me to include personal reactions, experiences, and subjective interpretations? Does the professor expect me to demonstrate knowledge I have acquired from lectures, discussions, or experiments as well as from readings? Am I limited in the number and kind of reference materials I can use?

6. How shall I document and list my sources? Which style sheet shall I use?

7. What is the approximate length of the paper?

8. Does the professor expect me to submit preliminary drafts as well as the final copy?

These questions will help you develop a mind-set for the assignment and define a rhetorical purpose that will direct your work. If you are unable to answer them, ask your professor for additional information.

Recall the assignment we examined earlier.

> Write a brief essay in response to one of the reserve readings on the topic of immigration.

Maura Grady, one of our students who was working on this assignment, chose to respond to Ronald Takaki's "A Different Mirror" (Chapter 13). As Maura looked over the source and reread the assignment, she was able to answer most of the questions listed above, but she was unsure about how to balance the summary of the source against the personal reaction. When she discussed this issue with her professor, he cautioned her against letting the summary dominate her essay and told her to highlight her own thinking.

After analyzing the assignment once more, Maura turned her attention to her purpose for reading: to explore the topic and generate reactions to the author's ideas. She previewed Takaki's text by asking the set of questions we presented on page 6, and then she spent fifteen minutes freewriting about the issues surrounding American diversity and immigration. Next, she did a close reading of the article by underlining, annotating, and taking down notes in which she elaborated on some of Takaki's points. These prereading, close reading, and postreading strategies are discussed in Chapter 1. Finally, she moved on to the task of elaborating on her reactions to the text so that she could draft an essay in response to the author's ideas.

## Elaborate on Reading Sources

As we explained earlier, elaborating involves probing your memory and making associations between prior knowledge and the propositions in the text. Elaborations can be written as annotations in the margins of the text or as separate notes. Response essays call for a wider repertoire of elaboration strategies than we provided in Chapter 1. A complete set is presented in the box that follows.

---

### STRATEGIES FOR ELABORATING ON READING SOURCES

1. Agree or disagree with a statement in the text, giving reasons for your agreement or disagreement.
2. Compare or contrast your reactions to the topic (for example, "At first I thought . . . , but now I think . . .").
3. Extend one of the author's points.
4. Draw attention to what the author has neglected to say about the topic.
5. Discover an idea implied by the text but not stated by the author.
6. Provide additional details by fleshing out a point made by the author.
7. Illustrate the text with an example, an incident, a scenario, or an anecdote.
8. Embellish the author's point with a vivid image, a metaphor, or an example.
9. Test one of the author's claims.
10. Compare one of the author's points with your own prior knowledge of the topic or with your own or others' experiences.
11. Interpret the text in the light of your own knowledge or experiences.
12. Personalize one of the author's statements.
13. Question one of the author's points.
14. Speculate about one of the author's points by
    a. Asking questions about the direct consequences of an idea
    b. Predicting consequences
    c. Drawing implications from an idea

(continued on the next page)

---

d. Applying the idea to a hypothetical situation

e. Giving a concrete instance of a point made in the text

15. Draw comparisons between the text and books, articles, films, or other media.
16. Classify items in the text under a superordinate category.
17. Discover in the text relations unstated by the author.
18. Validate one of the author's points with an example.
19. Criticize a point in the text.
20. Outline hierarchies of importance among ideas in the text.
21. Make a judgment about the relevance of a statement that the author has made.
22. Impose a condition on a statement in the text. (For example, "If . . . , then. . . .")
23. Qualify an idea in the text.
24. Extend an idea with a personal recollection or reflection.
25. Assess the usefulness and applicability of an idea.

In the following example, notice how Maura embellishes Takaki's points with examples. She draws connections between this selection and the literature she has read in English class and a novel she read the previous summer.

### Takaki's Article

Questions like the one my taxi driver asked me are always jarring, but I can understand why he could not see me as American. He had a narrow but widely shared sense of the past—a history that has viewed American as European in ancestry. "Race," Toni Morrison explained, has functioned as a "metaphor" necessary to the "construction of Americanness": in the creation of our national identity. "America" has been defined as "white."

### Maura's Elaborations

Takaki's experience is summed up in an incisive little poem I just read in English class:

> It must be odd
> to be a minority
> he was saying.
> I looked around
> and didn't see any.
> So I said
> Yeah.

Like Takaki, the poet, Mitsuye Yamada, is Japanese. I'm also reminded of _Snow Falling on Cedars_, the novel about Japanese Americans who were interned in concentration camps during the war.

When you are preparing to write a response essay, it is best to elaborate as fully as you can by annotating the text or taking separate notes. Even if you don't use all these elaborations in your later writing, you will have a rich pool of resources at your disposal.

## INDIVIDUAL EXERCISE ON ELABORATING ON READINGS

Assume that you are working on the following essay assignment:

> In his article, "High School, an Institution Whose Time Has Passed," Leon Botstein maintains that high schools, as they are currently structured, are irrelevant. In a three-page essay, summarize and respond to Botstein's argument.

Turn to "High School, an Institution Whose Time Has Passed" (Chapter 11). As you read the article, elaborate on your reactions in some of the ways we described on pages 43–44. Jot down your elaborations on a separate sheet of paper and submit them to your instructor.

## COLLABORATIVE EXERCISE ON ELABORATING ON READINGS

1. Form collaborative learning groups of five students each, as described in the preface, or fashion groups according to your own method.
2. Select a group member to read aloud, one paragraph at a time, Jeff Barbian's "The Gist Generation" (Chapter 7).
3. After each paragraph is read, group members should suggest elaborations, drawing on the suggestion in the Strategies for Elaborating on Reading Sources box that appears on pages 43–44. The group recorder should compile a list of these elaborations.
4. Reconvene the entire class. Each group recorder should read the group's list of elaborations. Discuss similarities and differences among the lists.

## PLANNING

Active reading strategies such as freewriting, brainstorming, taking content notes, annotating, and elaborating on the text will provide you with raw materials for an essay. Your next challenge is to give form to those raw materials by finding common threads among them, organizing them, deleting extraneous or inappropriate items, and, if necessary, returning to the sources to extract more information. This is the work of planning, the stage when you impose your own rhetorical goal and begin to exercise control over the material you have collected and generated.

## Formulating a Thesis

Your first move should be to establish your *preliminary* or *working thesis*, the central idea you intend to develop in your paper. Have it reflect your rhetorical purpose, the effect you want to have on the audience, and perhaps your organizational plan. In a response essay, the thesis expresses the writer's general reaction to the source, his or her agreement and disagreement, criticism and speculation, qualifications and extensions, and the like. We call the thesis "preliminary" at the prewriting stage because writers often revise their thesis statements later in the writing process.

To form a preliminary thesis, review your reading and elaboration notes as follows:

1. *See if any one type of elaboration predominates.* Are a good portion of your elaborations drawn from your personal experiences? If so, your essay could show how your experiences either validate or contradict the author's claims.
2. *See if several elaborations were triggered by one or two particular ideas in the reading.* Did you elaborate at length on a specific point in the source? If you wish, you can focus your paper on that single aspect of the topic.
3. *Classify your elaborations.* Can you sort your elaborations into workable categories and discard the rest? For example, you could star all the elaborations in which you agree or disagree with the author of the source and then work only with those as you draft your essay.

As our student Maura Grady sorts through her elaborations, she finds a predominance of instances in which she interprets Takaki's text in the light of her own experiences. She jots down the following preliminary thesis:

> Well, I agree that our history books should tell us more about the lives and accomplishments of the diverse groups that settled in the United States. But I also hope the revisionist historians give a strong voice to women, even if evidence about women's lives complicates the account of immigration.

## Organizing

After you come up with a preliminary thesis, your next step is to decide what organizational format you will use. Systematically examine your freewriting, brainstorming, content notes, annotations, and elaborations. Try to derive one or more possible plans by categorizing this information and grouping related information together to see what patterns appear. Try several different grouping schemes to find what works best. Many of the organizational plans that we presented in Chapter 1 are appropriate for response essays.

| | |
|---|---|
| Time order, narration, process | Example |
| Antecedent-consequent, cause-effect | Analysis/classification |
| | Definition |
| Description | Analogy |
| Statement-response | Argument/evaluation |
| Comparison/contrast | Problem-solution |

For example, if your purpose is to show the negative consequences of what an author has proposed, you might develop your essay in a cause-and-effect format. If you want to discuss the similarities and differences between the author's points and your own knowledge or experiences, you could use a plan for comparison/contrast.

Especially useful for a response essay are two variations of the statement-response plan: (1) the summary-response and (2) the point-by-point response. The procedure for each is outlined in the following boxes.

---

### SUMMARY-RESPONSE PATTERN

**Introduction**

1. Identify briefly the issue(s) in the reading source that you intend to focus on.
2. Explain briefly your own view on the issue(s).

**Body Paragraphs**

1. Summarize the source, making sure to explain the issue(s).
2. Give reasons to support your position on the issue(s).

**Conclusion**

See the technique on page 57.

---

---

### POINT-BY-POINT ALTERNATING PATTERN

**Introduction**

1. Identify briefly the issue(s) in the source that you intend to focus on.
2. Explain briefly your own view on the issue(s).

**Body Paragraphs**

1. Mention one issue, one subsection, or one main point from the source.
2. Respond to the material that was just summarized.
3. Repeat steps 1 and 2 for as many aspects of the source as you intend to treat.

**Conclusion**

See the technique on page 57.

---

As Maura studies her elaborations and other reading notes, she realizes that she wants to respond to specific points that Takaki makes with regard to women. She decides that the point-by-point alternating plan best suits her purpose, so she looks back over the annotated article and sketches out the following loose plan:

Bring personal experience to bear on the main point I want to cover: that revisionist historians should give a strong voice to women.

1. Point from Takaki: In the 1800s, Chinese immigrants were predominantly male.

2. My response: This was because they were not allowed to bring wives to the U.S. Nor were they allowed to marry. What was life like for the women they left behind?

1. Point from Takaki: The Japanese men imported women as picture brides.

2. My response: Women are still imported to the United States, as brides and as childcare workers. These women's stories are worth telling.

1. Point Takaki has neglected to mention: Many immigrant women are still marginalized today.

2. My response: Let's hear their stories.

This loose plan suggests that the body of Maura's essay will contain a brief summary of Takaki's main points followed by three point-response units, the first and second beginning with a point made by Takaki and the third beginning with a point that, in Maura's view, Takaki has left out.

You might prefer to organize your notes with the *graphic overview* technique we described in Chapter 1 or with a formal outline. The graphic overview will diagram major ideas and show how they are related. It functions as an idea map for your essay. In Figure 2-1 we have produced a graphic overview of Maura's work.

Some students are more comfortable with a *formal outline* than with graphic overviews or loose plans. Traditional outlines are based on the following structure:

I.
   A.
      1.
         a.
            i.
            ii.
         b.
      2.
   B.
II.

The formal outline provides a clear hierarchical structure useful for imposing order on a topic that is complicated and has a number of discrete subtopics. The following is a segment of a formal outline for Maura's paper on immigration and women.

   B.  Women are imported to the United States.
      1.  Japanese picture brides
      2.  Russian picture brides
      3.  Au pairs and nannies
   C.  Poor immigrant women are still marginalized.
      1.  Women of color
      2.  Female heads of households

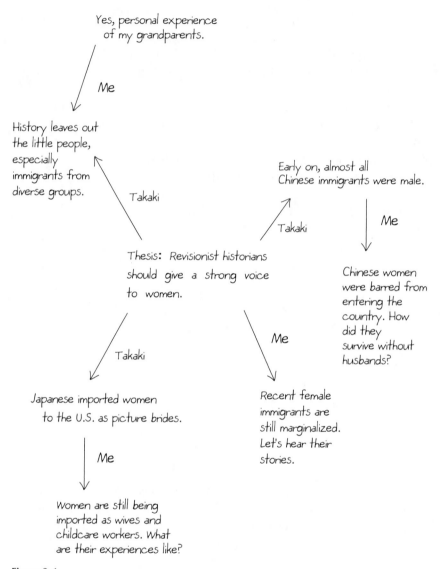

Yes, personal experience
of my grandparents.

Me

History leaves out
the little people,
especially
immigrants from
diverse groups.

Takaki

Early on, almost all
Chinese immigrants were male.

Takaki                                    Me

Thesis:  Revisionist historians
should  give  a  strong  voice
to  women.

Chinese women
were barred from
entering the
country. How
did they
survive without
husbands?

Takaki

Me

Japanese imported women
to the U.S. as picture brides.

Recent female
immigrants are
still marginalized.
Let's hear their
stories.

Me

Women are still being
imported as wives and
childcare workers. What
are their experiences like?

Figure 2-1

## DRAFTING

When you sit down to write your essay, you will find that you have already generated a fair amount of material: the freewriting you produced before reading; the annotations and elaborations you wrote in response to the source; the content notes, including summaries, paraphrases, and quotations, that you extracted from the source; and the outline or the graphic overview that you drew up when you planned your paper. Now comes the challenge. As you weave together bits of information from the reading source and your own thoughts on the topic, you may find it necessary to change, rearrange, or eliminate some of the material you have assembled. This process will be less daunting if you observe the guidelines listed in the following box.

---

### ROUGH-DRAFT GUIDELINES

1. You need not include all your notes in your draft.
2. You don't have to follow your outline religiously or incorporate it completely.
3. You don't have to—and probably shouldn't—begin at the beginning. Many writers start with the body paragraphs and then work on the introduction and the conclusion. After all, you can't introduce a person until he or she is present, so you shouldn't expect to introduce a paper until you've written it.
4. As you revise, you should focus on higher-order concerns, such as ideas and organization, and not get bogged down with spelling, punctuation, and word choice. You can return to these lower-level concerns when you have completed the draft.

---

Keep these guidelines foremost in mind as you consider the six strategies for drafting, shown in the following box. Apply these strategies liberally and flexibly; drafting does not necessarily follow a set procedure or a fixed sequence.

---

### DRAFTING STRATEGIES

1. Select and use organizational plans for individual paragraphs.
2. Weave direct quotations, paraphrases, and summaries in with your own ideas, and supply proper documentation.
3. Decide on an introductory paragraph.
4. Construct a conclusion.
5. Develop a list of references or works cited.
6. Title your essay.

---

For convenience, we describe the strategies in the order in which they appear in the boxed outline. We reemphasize that you need not apply them in that order. For instance, you may find it easier to begin with the introduction and then compose the body of the essay. Whatever you do, don't get stymied by a particular sequence. Try another approach if you find yourself staring at the blank page or waiting for sentences to come to you. Move on to sections you can write readily. Later you can return to the parts that caused difficulty.

## Planning Individual Paragraphs

As you draft the body of your response essay, follow the organizational plan you chose at the prewriting stage: summary-response, point-by-point, or some other format. Develop each paragraph in accordance with this top-level structure. Needless to say, as you compose individual paragraphs, other organizational patterns will come into play. Most writers use multiple patterns to organize their prose. Again, we should point out that if your prewriting plan proves unworkable, or if you discover a new direction for the paper in the process of drafting, don't hesitate to rethink your organizational strategy.

Your paragraphs should be *unified* and *coherent*. Each should develop a central idea, and all the sentences should contribute to that idea in some way. Often, one or more *topic sentences* in each paragraph express the paragraph's dominant ideas. You can achieve coherence by repeating words and ideas, rewording ideas, and using transitional expressions ("also," "for example," "thus," "similarly," "consequently," and so on). All these devices show readers the logical links among sentences.

Notice how Maura Grady unifies the body paragraphs in her final draft with strong topic sentences that add coherence to the essay. Maura intentionally uses repetition to reinforce her thesis: The same topic sentence ends each paragraph. This stylistic device is called anaphora. You may recall Martin Luther King's use of anaphora in his famous refrain, "I have a dream."

```
        Takaki tells us that more women emigrated from Japan
    than China because Japan had a strong government which was
    able to promote female emigration. Though this may be the
    case, when I read Takaki's account of the "predominantly male
    Chinese community in the United States" (248), I am reminded
```

that these young Chinese men were segregated in all-male
ghettos because exclusion laws prohibited them from bringing
wives to the United States and forbade them from marrying
Caucasians. Is it any wonder they turned to "prostitution,
gambling, and drunkeness" (248)? How lonely it must have been
for these men and how devastating for the wives they left
behind in China. Few of these women ever saw their loved ones
again. What hardships these impoverished women must have
endured as they struggled to raise their children. I would
like to hear these women's stories.

It seems the Japanese resolved the problem of male
isolation by negotiating the Gentlemen's Agreement and thus
paving the way for over 60,000 women to enter the United
States, "many as 'picture brides'" for men they had never
met (248). Though arranged marriages were consistent with
Japanese custom, the prospect of crossing the Pacific to wed
an older man, whom she had seen only in a picture, must have
been daunting and traumatic to a young Japanese woman. Such
arrangements still exist. An acquaintance of my father
recently "sent for" and married a Russian woman he had
selected from a catalog of picture brides. A more common
practice is for professional couples to recruit au pair girls
and nannies from other countries. Employment agencies have
placed thousands in American families, sometimes as illegal
aliens in inadequate conditions earning inadequate pay. I
would like to hear these women's stories.

Despite great strides in many areas, poor women, especially immigrants, are marginalized today. Women of color are
still in the lowest paid jobs in the nation, and female heads
of families and their children constitute the poorest of the
poor. New welfare legislation will require millions of these
women to join the workforce, yet childcare facilities are
dreadfully scarce. I would also like to hear these women's
stories.

If you are using the point-by-point pattern to structure your essay,
you might not need to include a summary of the source. Instead, simply
mention the main points to which you are reacting. If you include a
summary, the length depends on your purpose. You may want to provide your readers with a comprehensive summary that covers all the

major aspects of the source, or you may want just to focus in on the aspects that concern you most. Refer to the summarizing strategies in Chapter 1. You will find them very helpful.

Remember that your objective is to integrate the summary of the source with your own ideas on the topic. Once you order and classify your ideas and establish your direction, adapt the summary to your purpose. You need not summarize the entire article, only the sections that relate to your purpose. The summary should highlight the passages that prompted your reaction and refer only incidentally to other portions of the text.

## Using Quotations, Paraphrases, and Summaries

Quotations, paraphrases, and summaries are the principal ways to integrate material from sources into an essay. In Chapter 1, we covered in detail how to compose paraphrases and summaries and how to extract quotations as you take content notes. If you need to supplement your content notes with additional paraphrases, summaries, and quotations, return to those procedures. Remember that the reading-writing process is recursive. It is not uncommon for writers to read the source texts at the drafting stage.

When you employ quotations, paraphrases, or summaries at the drafting stage, be sure to differentiate them from your own words and to cite the sources, as we described in Chapter 1. Always provide your readers with some identification of the source, usually the author and the page number and, if necessary, the title. The reason for including this information is to allow interested readers to locate the complete reference in the list of sources at the end of the paper. Be sure you are aware of the documentation style that your professor requires.

## Writing Introductory Paragraphs

A strong introduction ought to interest readers, announce the topic, disclose a thesis or an attitude toward the topic, and establish the writer's voice. It may also, when appropriate, present background information essential to understanding the topic and indicate the writer's plan.

The opening sentences of an essay are crucial. They should engage the readers and encourage them to read on. These initial sentences also establish the writer's voice as formal or informal, academic or conversational. Some forms of academic writing require you to write in a very professional voice and open your paper in a designated way. For instance, research studies often begin with a one-paragraph abstract or summary of the study's principal findings, which is written in formal, objective language. Response essays give you much more freedom. If you wish, you can use an informal opening that speaks directly to the reader.

There are several openers you could use. For example, if you were writing an essay on cloning human beings, you could open it with a quotation from the reading source.

> "Human embryos are life-forms, and there is nothing to stop anyone from marketing them now, on the same shelves with Cabbage Patch dolls" (Ehrenreich 86). Perhaps we are headed for a future where, as Ehrenreich suggests, we will purchase rather than bear our children?

Or you could start out with an anecdote, a brief story, or a scenario.

> Imagine that you are a clone, an exact copy, of either your mother or your father rather than a combination of genetic material from both of them.

Alternatively, you might begin by providing background information.

> Cloning, a genetic process that makes it possible to produce an exact, living replica of an organism, has been applied to simple organisms for years. Now it is possible to clone complex animals, even human beings.

Other opening strategies might begin with a question, a fact or a statistic, a generalization, a contradiction, or a thesis statement. Avoid opening with clichés or platitudes ("As we contemplate cloning, we should remember that fools rush in where angels fear to tread"), dictionary definitions ("According to *Webster's International Dictionary*, 'cloning' is . . ."), or obvious statements ("Cloning is a very controversial topic").

As you work on the introduction, leave open the possibility of revising the preliminary thesis that you derived at the planning stage (p. 46). Make sure that it still expresses your main idea. You don't have to situate the thesis in any particular place. Although the thesis statement often occurs toward the end of the introduction, after the opening explanation of the general topic and identification of the source, it can occur elsewhere, even at the beginning of the introductory paragraph. Wherever you place it, be sure that you express it adequately and provide your reader with enough context to understand it fully. In academic writing, a thesis statement may occupy several sentences. The complex issues that academic essays deal with cannot always be formulated adequately in a single sentence.

Just as the thesis statement can consist of more than one sentence, the introduction can comprise more than one paragraph. Notice how Maura Grady opens the final draft of her essay with two introductory paragraphs. The first stresses the significance of her personal experience; the second identifies the key topic the paper will address and presents Maura's thesis statement.

> I am a second-generation American. My grandparents emigrated to the United States from the west of Ireland in the 1920s to pursue the American Dream and make a better life for their children. Like most immigrants, they came to this country to labor in low-paying jobs, the Kellys as cab driver and domestic worker, the Gradys as longshoreman and laundress. I never read about "little people" like them in my history textbooks. Textbook writers must think along the same lines as the Irish maid in Ronald Takaki's <u>A Different Mirror</u>: "'I don't know why anybody wants to hear my history. . . . Nothing ever happened to me worth tellin'" (15).
>
> Historically, women fortunate enough to gain entry into the United States, women like my grandmothers--Irish maids, Chicana cleaners, and Japanese "wives who [did] much of the work in the fields"(251)--have been even more silenced than their male counterparts. The women whom male immigrants left behind--wives and lovers barred from entering the country-- have never had the opportunity to tell their tales. As revisionist historians, Takaki and others relate the stories of the "little people," I hope they remember to give women a strong voice. I want my daughters to be able to look into the "'mirror' of history" and through the lens of the present to see "who [women] have been and hence are" (16) and what they have the potential to become.

Lengthy articles in scholarly journals often have a multiparagraph subsection labeled "Introduction" that includes information needed to understand the thesis statement. Sometimes a complex paper opener requires a separate paragraph. For instance, an essay that evaluates the social consequences of cloning human beings might begin with a dramatized scenario, perhaps a description of a family in which the children were clones of their parents, to provide a test case for the author's argument. The details of this scenario might require one or more paragraphs. These opening paragraphs would be followed by a paragraph that zeroes in on the topic and presents the thesis.

## Writing Conclusions

The concluding paragraph should do more than recapitulate the high points of the discussion that precedes it. A summary of the main points is justified, but you should also use techniques such as (1) stressing the significance of your thesis rather than simply repeating it; (2) predicting the consequences of your ideas; (3) calling your readers to action; and (4) ending with a question, an anecdote, or a quotation.

Notice how Maura closes her final draft with a quotation from Takaki and a prediction about the consequences of her proposal.

> Takaki quotes Leslie Marmon Silko's precaution:
>> I will tell you something about stories . . .
>> They aren't just entertainment.
>>> Don't be fooled (15).
> As readers, it may be difficult for some of us to step outside the familiar histories we learned in school to enter the stories of women whose lives are "worth tellin'." To identify with the storyteller, we will have to cross barriers of race, gender, and class. Our reward will be a better understanding of history and ourselves.

## Preparing Lists of References or Works Cited

At the end of your paper, construct a list of sources that includes complete information on anything you quote, paraphrase, summarize, or allude to in the text of your essay. The list should contain an entry for every source you use, and it should be alphabetized according to the authors' last names. The appendix includes detailed information for setting up source lists. Maura's work cited list, constructed according to MLA guidelines, contains only one source, since she draws only on Takaki's article.

Work Cited

Takaki, Ronald. <u>A Different Mirror: A History of</u>
<u>Multicultural America</u>. Boston: Little, Brown, 1993.

## Titling the Essay

Your title should indicate your perspective and, if possible, capture the spirit of the issue you are addressing. The title "A Response to Barbara Ehrenreich's 'The Economics of Cloning'" identifies the subject, nothing more, as it refers to an article in works cited on p. 77. If you prefer a title that is less straightforward, you can choose from a number of options for deriving titles. One alternative is to let the title reflect your organizational plan. An essay that develops according to the comparison/contrast pattern might be titled thus:

The Anti-Cloning Lobby: Humanists or Hypocrites?

You could also title your paper with an apt phrase from the reading source or from your essay itself. Ehrenreich's phrase "genetic immortality" could be used to title an essay that focuses on the implications of cloning for the future of humanity. A catchy saying or a relevant quotation from some other source could also be used:

Cheaper by the Dozen: Cloning and Human Reproduction

The possibilities for titles are limited only by your creativity.

At this point, you will have finished a complete draft of your paper. Congratulations! You are now entitled to take a break from your assignment. But remember that a paper presented only in first-draft form is unlikely to earn you a high grade. A conscientiously revised paper, however, will display your writing to its best advantage. So, you must now turn to a full-scale revision of your paper before you hand it in. This last phase includes both reworking your ideas and your presentation of them and copyediting your paper for errors in standard form or usage. It can be the most rewarding phase because you will see your ideas take stronger, clearer shape and hear your voice emerge with confidence and authority. You will also find that cleaning up your grammar, spelling, punctuation, and other mechanics will reassure you about having written a good paper. First, however, it is wise to set your first draft aside for some time before you revise it. Experience shows that you will come back to it with freshness and alertness, keen to spot weak arguments, poor evidence, awkward transitions, and stylistic mistakes that you did not realize you had made.

## REVISING THE PRELIMINARY DRAFT

To varying degrees, writers revise *while* they are drafting as well as after they have produced full-blown papers. Those who do a great deal of revision as they are composing their drafts may come up with polished products that require minimal changes. Those who prefer to scratch out rough first drafts may make substantial changes as they rewrite in multiple versions. Whether you are an in-process reviser or a post-process reviser, you should keep in mind certain effective principles of revision.

Do not allow your in-process revision to interfere with your draft. Restrict in-process revising to important elements, such as ideas and organization. Check that you have a clear thesis and convincing support, and as you move from one part of the paper to another, be sure you are progressing logically, maintaining your focus, and supplying appropriate transitions. Be sensitive to your readers' needs. But leave concerns like word choice, sentence structure, punctuation, spelling, and manuscript format until after you have finished a full draft of the paper.

The best revisions do more than correct errors in usage, punctuation, and spelling. Notice how Maura revises the first version of her paper.

### EXCERPT FROM MAURA'S FIRST DRAFT

```
Historically, women like my grandmothers, Irish maids, Chi-
cana cleaners, and Japanese "wives who [did] much of the work
in the fields" (251), have been even more silenced than their
male counterparts. As revisionist historians, Takaki and oth-
ers relate the stories of the "little people," I hope they
give these women a strong voice. I want my daughters to be
able to look into the "'mirror' of history" and through the
lens of the present to see "who [women] have been and hence
are" (16) and who we have the potential to become. When I
```

read Takaki's account of the "predominantly male Chinese community in the United States" (248), I am reminded that these
young Chinese men were segregated in all male ghettos because
exclusion laws prohibited them from bringing wives to the
United States and forbade them from marrying Caucasians.
How lonely it must have been for these men and how
devastating for the women they left behind in China. Few of
these women ever saw their loved ones again. I would like to
hear these women's stories. It seems the Japanese resolved
the problem of male isolation by arranging marriages via
photographs. Though arranged marriages were consistent with
Japanese custom, the prospect of crossing the Pacific to wed
an older man whom one had seen only in a picture must have
been daunting and traumatic to a young Japanese woman. Such
arrangements still exist. An acquaintance of my father
recently "sent for" and married a Russian woman he had
selected from a catalog of picture brides. A more common
practice is for professional couples to recruit au pair girls
and nannies from other countries. Employment agencies have
placed thousands of them in American families, sometimes in
inadequate conditions earning inadequate pay. I would like to
hear these women's stories.

> women fortunate enough to gain
> entry into the United States,

> The women male immigrants left
> behind — wives and lovers barred
> from entering the country — have
> never had an
> opportunity
> to tell their tales.

Historically, women like my grandmothers—
Irish maids, Chicana cleaners, and Japanese "wives who
[did] much of the work in the fields" (251), —have
been even more silenced than their male counterparts.
As revisionist historians, Takaki and others, relate
the stories of the "little people," I hope they remember to
give these women a strong voice. I want my daughters
to be able to look into the "'mirror' of history"

and through the lens of the present to see "who
[women] have been and hence are" (16) and who ~~we~~ *they*
have the potential to become.

> Takaki tells us that more women emigrated from Japan than China because Japan had a strong government which was able to promote female emigration. Though this may be the case,

*w*
When I read Takaki's account of the "predominantly
male Chinese community in the United States" (248),
I am reminded that these young Chinese men were
segregated in all-male ghettos because exclusion
laws prohibited them from bringing wives to the
United States and forbade them from marrying
Caucasians. How lonely it must have been for these

> Is it any wonder they turned to "prostitution, gambling, and drunkeness" (248)?

men and how devastating for the ~~women~~ *wives* they left
behind ~~in China~~. Few of these women ever saw their
loved ones again. I would like to hear these
women's stories.

> What hardships these impoverished women must have endured as they struggled to raise their children ⊙

Maura revises the first paragraph by adding two qualifications that allow her to draw a distinction between women "fortunate enough to gain entry into the United States" and women "barred from entering the country." Realizing that the second paragraph begins with a vague reference to male immigration from China, she summarizes Takaki's contrasting point about female immigration policies from Japan. Then she rewords the second sentence to provide a smoother transition to the preceding sentence about immigrant women. In order to flesh out the paragraph's focus on women, she adds two additional sentences, one which draws upon the source and another which expresses her reaction. In both paragraphs, Maura also revises awkward or imprecise word choice and combines related sentences to improve unity and coherence.

## Revising Ideas

When you revise your paper, your first priority should be to make changes in meaning by reworking your ideas. You might add information, introduce a new line of reasoning, delete extraneous information or details, or rearrange the order of your argument. Revision should always serve to sharpen or clarify meaning for your readers. Consider the strategies shown in the following box.

---

### REVISING IDEAS

1. Is your paper an adequate response to the assignment?
2. Is your rhetorical purpose clear? How are you attempting to influence or affect your readers?
3. Does everything in the draft lead to or follow from one central thesis? If not, which ideas appear to be out of place? Should you remove any material?
4. Do individual passages of your paper probe the issues and problems implied by the thesis in sufficient detail? What do you need to add?
5. Will the reader understand your central point?

---

The process of drafting stimulates your thinking and often brings you to new perspectives. You may see links among pieces of information and come to conclusions that had not occurred to you at the planning stage. As a result, first drafts are often inconsistent; they may start with one central idea but then depart from it and head in new directions.

Do allow yourself to be creative at the drafting stage, but when you revise, make sure that your paper expresses a consistent idea throughout the entire piece. Check to see if you have drifted away from your thesis in the subsequent paragraphs or changed your mind and ended up with another position. If you have drifted away from your original goal, examine each sentence to determine how the shift took place. You may need to eliminate whole chunks of irrelevant material, add more content, or reorder some of the parts. After you make these changes, read over your work to be sure that the new version makes sense, conforms to your organizational plan, and shows improvement.

## Revising Organization

When you are satisfied that your draft expresses the meaning you want to get across to your reader, check that your ideas connect smoothly with each other. Your readers should be able to follow your train of thought by referring back to preceding sentences, looking ahead to subsequent sentences, and paying attention to transitions and other connective devices. Keep in mind the organizational concerns shown in the following box.

---

### REVISING ORGANIZATION

1. Is your organizational plan or form appropriate for the kind of paper you've been assigned? If not, can you derive another format?
2. Do you provide transitions and connecting ideas? If not, where are they needed?
3. Do you differentiate your own ideas from those of the author?
4. What should you add so that your audience can better follow your train of thought?
5. What can you eliminate that does not contribute to your central focus?
6. What should you move that is out of place or needs to be grouped with material elsewhere in the paper?
7. Do you use a paper opener that catches the reader's attention?
8. Does each paragraph include a topic sentence(s) and does all the material in this paragraph support it?
9. Does your conclusion simply restate the main idea or does it offer new insights?
10. Does your essay have an appropriate title?

---

## Revising Style

With reference to writing, you may associate the term *style* with works of high literary art—the style, say, of a poem by John Keats or a novel by Emily Brontë. In actuality, however, every piece of writing displays a style of its own, whether it be a business report by a professional analyst or a note of reminders by a roommate or a family member. A style, a tone, a sense of voice and attitude, and above all a sense of liveliness and energy (or their absence) emerge from the writer's choice and use of words, the length and complexity of the writer's sentences, and the writer's focus on sharp, meaningful, reader-based expression.

When you revise for style, you consider the effect your language choices have on your audience. Here are five ways to improve your writing style:

1. Move from writer-based prose to reader-based prose.
2. Add your own voice.
3. Stress verbs rather than nouns.
4. Eliminate ineffective expressions.
5. Eliminate sexist language.

## Moving from Writer-Based Prose to Reader-Based Prose

Throughout this book, we continually stress the importance of audience. It is imperative to keep your readers in mind throughout the entire reading-writing process, especially at the revising stage. Making a distinction between writer-based prose and reader-based prose will help you attend to audience needs as you revise (Flower 19–37). Writer-based prose is egocentric because the writer records ideas that make sense to him or her but makes minimal if any effort to communicate those ideas to someone else. You can compare writer-based prose to a set of personal notes in which the writer puts down information that is meaningful personally but may not make sense to a larger audience. In contrast, reader-based prose clearly conveys ideas to other people. The writer does not assume that the reader will understand automatically but, rather, provides information that will facilitate the reader's comprehension. It is easy to forget about the audience amid all the complications in producing the first draft of an academic essay. That's why first drafts are quite often writer-based. An important function of revising is to convert this writer-based prose to something the reader can readily understand.

To illustrate writer-based prose, we have reproduced a student's reaction to two articles on computer intelligence. As you read the student essay, place checks next to the sentences that are writer-based.

Both of these articles deal with the future and the present status of the computer. Carl Sagan, the author of the article "In Defense of Robots," tends to agree with Ulrich Neisser who is the author of the article "The Imitation of Man by Machine." However, one way they disagree is that Sagan thinks the present state of computers will only remain for a short time. On the other hand, Neisser believes that the status of the computer will remain the same for quite some time.

Both of these articles deal with the issue that computer intelligence is different from human intelligence. To prove that human intelligence is different, Sagan uses the example with a U.S. Senator. Neisser also agrees with Sagan by stating that a computer has no emotions, no motivation, and does not grow. Because of this, Neisser feels that this is where humans have the advantage over computers. As stated in the introductory paragraph, the authors have one contrasting belief. Sagan thinks that the computer's ability will change soon, while Neisser thinks that it will be some time before that happens.

The other issue that is discussed in the articles is about the making of important social decisions. Both the writers feel that the computer being in the stage it is in should not be allowed to make social decisions. Sagan also proves this by his past example. He believes a computer shouldn't make social decisions if it can't even pass the test in the example. Neisser also goes back to his example. He also states that the computer only deals with the problems that it is given, and that it has no room for thought, since it is confined just to finding the answer. Once again, the only place they seem to contrast is about the length of time it will take for the computer to be able to make social decisions.

My reaction to the articles is a positive one. I tend to agree more with Sagan than with Neisser. I feel that the rapid growth of computers will continue. And therefore it is more likely for both these issues to change.

Notice that our writer assumes the audience is familiar with both the assignment and the articles on which it is based. For example, the introduction begins "Both of these articles . . ." as if the reader knows in advance which articles will be discussed (see works cited, p. 77). The first sentence tells us only that the articles discuss the computer's "status," a term that conveys little to anyone who has not read the articles. The second sentence states that Neisser and Sagan agree on something, but it does not indicate what ideas they supposedly share. The writer has simply failed to take into account that the reader may or may not be able to follow the train of thought. Similar failures to consider the audience occur throughout the essay. Below, we have transformed its introduction from writer-based prose to reader-based prose.

```
        The articles "In Defense of Robots" by Carl Sagan and
    "The Imitation of Man by Machine" by Ulrich Neisser both
    deal with the computer's potential to match the intellectual
    accomplishments of humans. Sagan and Neisser agree that
    there is currently a wide gap between machine and human
    intelligence. However, Sagan argues that the gap will quickly
    narrow, whereas Neisser maintains that computer and human
    intelligence will always be significantly different.
```

As you revise your first drafts, make sure that you have provided the necessary context or background for any material that you include from sources. Unless the assignment indicates that the audience has read the sources, do not assume that your readers will share your prior knowledge and experience.

## Adding Your Own Voice

After you've written your paper, read it aloud. Better still, ask a friend to read it aloud to you. Does your writing sound like it's really yours? Or does it sound stiff, wooden, impersonal, colorless? Would your paper be better if it resonated with some of your spoken personality? Richard Lanham devoted his book *Revising Prose* to helping writers project their own voices and breathe life into their writing. Among his suggestions are the following:

1. If too many of the sentences wind endlessly around themselves without stopping for air, try dividing them into units of varying length.

2. Give a rhythm to your prose by alternating short sentences with longer ones, simple sentences with complex ones, statements or assertions with questions or exclamations.

3. Bring your readers into the essay by addressing them with questions and commands, expressions of paradox and wonderment, challenge and suspense.

Try these strategies. They can bring the sound of your own voice into otherwise silent writing and liven it considerably. Be careful, though. Some college instructors prefer a relentlessly neutral style devoid of any subjective personality. Proceed cautiously.

## Stressing Verbs Rather Than Nouns

Pack the meaning in your sentences into strong verbs rather than nouns or weak verbs. See how the following example uses verbs and nouns. We have underlined the nouns and italicized the verbs.

> *Original:* The creation of multiple copies of an individual through the process of cloning *is* now an actual feasibility.
>
> *Revision:* Scientists *can* now *clone* multiple copies of a human.

The first version uses nouns to get the message across, but the revised version uses verbs. Notice that the first version contains only a single verb, *is*. *Is* and other forms of the verb *be* (*are, was, were, be, being, been*) are weak and lifeless because they draw their meaning from the nouns preceding and following them. Sentences that are structured around *be* verbs depend heavily on nouns to convey their central ideas. These "noun-style" sentences are characterized by forms of the verb *be* (*is, are,* and so on) and by nominalization. Nominalization is the practice of making nouns from verbs or adjectives by adding suffixes (*-ance, -ence, -tion, -ment, -sion, -ity, -ing*). The nouns in such sentences often appear in prepositional phrases. An additional sign of nominalization is frequent use of prepositions. In the following example, we have underlined the *be* forms, the instances of nominalization, and the prepositions in the sentence we considered earlier. Notice that the revision does not rely on *be* verbs or nominalization.

> *Original:* The creation of multiple copies of an individual through the process of cloning is now an actual feasibility.
>
> *Revision:* Scientists can now clone multiple copies of a human.

Of course, there are occasions when it is appropriate to use *be* verbs or nominalization. Problems arise only when these forms are overused. Although there is no absolute rule, you should look closely when you find more than one *be* verb or one nominalization per sentence. You need not analyze the nouns and verbs in every paper you write, but it is a good idea to check periodically the direction in which your style is developing. Over time, you will find that less analysis is necessary since you will tend to use more active verbs and fewer prepositions and nominalizations.

## Eliminating Ineffective Expressions

Avoid ineffective expressions and words that do not contribute directly to the meaning of your paper. Notice how the underlined words and phrases in the following passage do not advance the writer's goals.

> Basically, those in support of surrogate motherhood claim that this particular method of reproduction has brought happiness to countless infertile couples. It allows a couple to have a child of their own despite the fact that the woman cannot bear children. In addition, it is definitely preferable to waiting for months and sometimes years on really long adoption lists. In my opinion, however, surrogate motherhood exploits the woman and can be especially damaging to the child. Obviously, poor women are affected most. In the event that a poor couple cannot have a child, it is rather unlikely that they will be able to afford the services of a surrogate mother. Actually, it is fertile, poor women who will become "breeders" for the infertile rich. In any case, the child is especially vulnerable. The given baby may become involved in a custody battle between the surrogate mother and the adopting mother. If the individual child is born handicapped, he or she may be utterly rejected by both mothers. Surely, the child's welfare should be first and foremost in everyone's mind.

The underlined elements are either overused, hackneyed words and phrases or unnecessary qualifiers, intensifiers, or modifiers. None of these words further the writer's intentions. They are inherently vague. Check to see if ineffective expressions occur frequently in your writing.

## Eliminating Sexist Language

Always reread your drafts to check that you have avoided sexist language. Use the masculine pronouns "he" and "his" and nouns with *-man* and *-men* (mail*man*, police*men*, and so on) only when they refer to a male or a group composed entirely of males. Don't use these forms to refer to women. Instead, use the techniques listed in the following box.

## TECHNIQUES FOR AVOIDING SEXIST LANGUAGE

1. Use pronouns that recognize both sexes ("his or her" or "her or his").
2. Use the plural rather than the singular. Plural pronouns by their very nature do not specify gender ("they" and "their").
3. Use nouns that are not gender-specific ("mail carrier" and "police officer").

Observe how we used these techniques in the following example.

### ORIGINAL DRAFT WITH SEXIST LANGUAGE

A physician must consider the broader social consequences of supplying new reproductive technologies to <u>his</u> patients. Likewise, each scientist working on genetic engineering must be aware of the potential social impact of <u>his</u> research.

### REVISION OF SEXIST LANGUAGE

Physicians must consider the broader social consequences of supplying new reproductive technologies to their patients. Likewise, scientists working on genetic engineering must be aware of the potential social impact of their research.

### INDIVIDUAL EXERCISE ON REVISION

1. Obtain a copy (photocopy or extra computer-generated copy) of at least two pages of a paper you have written. Select a paper written for any course, either a final draft or a rough draft. (Your instructor may elect to distribute a single essay to the entire class.)
2. Apply the questions listed in the Revising Ideas and Revising Organization boxes to the piece of writing. Ask yourself each question and handwrite on the essay any revisions that seem necessary.
3. Submit the original essay along with your revised version.

### COLLABORATIVE EXERCISE ON REVISION

1. In preparation for this exercise, the instructor needs to copy a short student essay (not more than two pages) for each class member. A preliminary draft will work best.

2. Form collaborative learning groups of five students each, as described in the Preface, or fashion groups according to your own method.

3. Select one student to read the essay aloud. Other group members should follow along on their own copies.

4. Select another student to read aloud the questions from the Revising Ideas and Revising Organization boxes. After each question is read, discuss whether it suggests any revisions that might improve the essay, and have the recorder write out the changes that the group agrees on.

5. Reconvene the entire class. Each group recorder should report the revisions the group made and explain why they are necessary. Try to account for differences in revisions.

## EDITING

When you have finished your revision, read your paper aloud once again to catch any glaring errors. Then reread the essay line by line and sentence by sentence. Check for correct usage, punctuation, spelling, mechanics, manuscript form, and typos. If you are using a word processing program, apply the spell checker. If you are especially weak in editing skills, and if it is all right with your instructor, go to your campus writing center or get a friend to read over your work.

This stage of revision encompasses all the rules for usage, punctuation, spelling, and mechanics. We cannot begin to review all that material in this textbook. You should think seriously about purchasing a few solid reference books, such as a good dictionary; a guide to correct usage, punctuation, and mechanics; and a documentation manual like the *MLA Handbook for Writers of Research Papers* or the *Publication Manual of the American Psychological Association*. Your campus bookstore and your college library may have a variety of self-help books for improving spelling, vocabulary, and usage. Browse through them and select the ones that best serve your needs.

Here is a list of some features to note as you edit your paper, but remember that you need to keep in mind all the rules of standard written English.

1. Are all your sentences complete?
   *Original:* Certain feminists claim that the new reproductive technologies exploit women. While other feminists argue that these same technologies help liberate women from traditional, oppressive roles.

*Revision:* Certain feminists claim that the new reproductive technologies exploit women, while other feminists argue that these same technologies help liberate women from traditional, oppressive roles.

2. Have you avoided run-on sentences, both fused sentences and comma splices?

   *Original:* Science fiction writers have long been fascinated with the prospect of cloning, their novels and short stories have sparked the public's interest in this technology.

   *Revision:* Science fiction writers have long been fascinated with the prospect of cloning, and their novels and short stories have sparked the public's interest in this technology.

3. Do pronouns have clear referents, and do they agree in number, gender, and case with the words for which they stand?

   *Original:* A scientist who works on new reproductive technologies should always consider the social consequences of their work.

   *Revision:* A scientist who works on new reproductive technologies should always consider the social consequences of his or her work.

4. Do all subjects and verbs agree in person and number?

   *Original:* Not one of the new reproductive technologies designed to increase couples' fertility have failed to incite controversy.

   *Revision:* Not one of the new reproductive technologies designed to increase couples' fertility has failed to incite controversy.

5. Is the verb tense consistent and correct?

   *Original:* Some futurists claim that only eugenics can provide the answers needed to ensure the survival of the human race. They predicted that by the year 2050, human reproduction will be controlled by law.

   *Revision:* Some futurists claim that only eugenics can provide the answers needed to ensure the survival of the human race. They predict that by the year 2050, human reproduction will be controlled by law.

6. Have you used modifiers (words, phrases, subordinate clauses) correctly and placed them where they belong?

   *Original:* Currently, scientists across the nation work to clone various species with enthusiasm.

   *Revision:* Currently, scientists across the nation work enthusiastically to clone various species.

7. Have you used matching elements within parallel construction?

   *Original:* Proposed reproductive technology projects include creating ways for sterile individuals to procreate, developing cures for genetic disease, and eugenic programs designed to improve the human species.

*Revision:* Proposed reproductive technology projects include creating ways for sterile individuals to procreate, developing cures for genetic disease, and designing eugenic programs to improve the human species.

8. Are punctuation marks used correctly?

*Original:* The potentially dire social consequences of genetic engineering, must be examined carefully, before we embrace this powerful new frightening technology.

*Revision:* The potentially dire social consequences of genetic engineering must be examined carefully before we embrace this powerful, new, frightening technology.

9. Are spelling, capitalization, and other mechanics (abbreviations, numbers, italics) correct?

*Original:* Research on Reproductive Technology is not often funded by The Government, since these innovations are so controversial.

*Revision:* Research on reproductive technology is not often funded by the government, since these innovations are so controversial.

## Manuscript Format

For this stage of revision, you need a great deal of patience and a good pair of eyes. Here is a checklist of features to note.

---

### MANUSCRIPT CHECKLIST

_____ Have you double-spaced and left one-inch margins on all sides?

_____ Are all typed words and corrections legible?

_____ Will your audience be able to tell which thoughts are yours and which are derived from sources?

_____ Are all quotations enclosed in quotation marks and properly punctuated?

_____ Have you properly documented all quotations, paraphrases, and summaries?

_____ Do you include all sources in a works cited list or references list?

---

The *MLA Handbook for Writers of Research Papers* describes particular guidelines for manuscript preparation. In Figure 2-2, we annotate Maura's final draft to show the important features of MLA manuscript format.

*SAMPLE RESPONSE ESSAY*

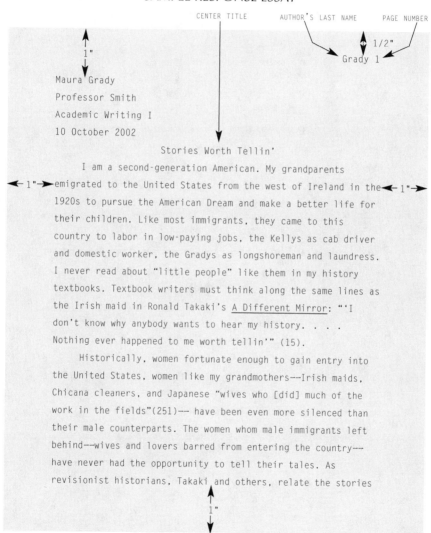

Figure 2-2

of the "little people." I hope they remember to give women a
strong voice. I want my daughters to be able to look into the
"'mirror' of history" and through the lens of the present to
see "who [women] have been and hence are" (16) and what they
have the potential to become.

Takaki tells us that more women emigrated from Japan
than China because Japan had a strong government which was
able to promote female emigration. Though this may be the
case, when I read Takaki's account of the "predominantly male
Chinese community in the United States" (248), I am reminded
that these young Chinese men were segregated in all-male
ghettos because exclusion laws prohibited them from bringing
wives to the United States and forbade them from marrying
Caucasians. Is it any wonder they turned to "prostitution,
gambling, and drunkeness" (248)? How lonely it must have been
for these men and how devastating for the wives they left
behind in China. Few of these women ever saw their loved ones
again. What hardships these impoverished women must have
endured as they struggled to raise their children. I would
like to hear these women's stories.

It seems the Japanese resolved the problem of male
isolation by negotiating the Gentlemen's Agreement and thus
paving the way for over 60,000 women to enter the United
States, "many as 'picture brides'" for men they had never met
(248). Though arranged marriages were consistent with Japanese
custom, the prospect of crossing the Pacific to wed an older
man, whom she had seen only in a picture, must have been
daunting and traumatic to a young Japanese woman. Such
arrangements still exist. An acquaintance of my father
recently "sent for" and married a Russian woman he had
selected from a catalog of picture brides. A more common
practice is for professional couples to recruit au pair girls
and nannies from other countries. Employment agencies have

1"

1"     1"

Grady 3

placed thousands in American families, sometimes as illegal
aliens in inadequate conditions earning inadequate pay. I
would like to hear these women's stories.

Despite great strides in many areas, poor women,
especially immigrants, are marginalized today. Women of color
are still in the lowest paid jobs in the nation, and female
heads of families and their children constitute the poorest of
the poor. New welfare legislation will require millions of
these women to join the workforce, yet childcare facilities
are dreadfully scarce. I would also like to hear these women's
stories.

Takaki quotes Leslie Marmon Silko's precaution:

I will tell you something about stories . . .

They aren't just entertainment.

Don't be fooled (15).

As readers, it may be difficult for some of us to step outside
the familiar histories we learned in school to enter the
stories of women whose lives are "worth tellin'." To identify
with the storyteller, we will have to cross barriers of race,
gender, and class. Our reward will be a better understanding
of history and ourselves.

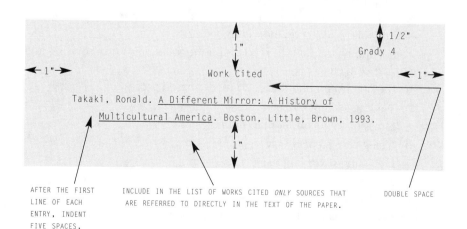

1/2"
Grady 4

1"

←1"→                    Work Cited                    ←1"→

Takaki, Ronald. <u>A Different Mirror: A History of</u>
        <u>Multicultural America</u>. Boston, Little, Brown, 1993.

1"

AFTER THE FIRST        INCLUDE IN THE LIST OF WORKS CITED *ONLY* SOURCES THAT        DOUBLE SPACE
LINE OF EACH           ARE REFERRED TO DIRECTLY IN THE TEXT OF THE PAPER.
ENTRY, INDENT
FIVE SPACES.

## INDIVIDUAL EXERCISE ON REVISING STYLE AND EDITING

1. Obtain a copy (photocopy or extra computer-generated copy) of at least two pages of a paper you have written. Select a paper written for any course, either a final draft or a rough draft. (Your instructor may elect to distribute a single essay to the entire class.)

2. Revise the draft according to the advice in this chapter, keeping in mind the following concerns:

   a. Moving from writer-based to reader-based prose
   b. Varying sentence length
   c. Stressing verbs rather than nouns
   d. Using words effectively
   e. Detecting sexist language
   f. Adding your own voice
   g. Editing for complete sentences, run-on sentences, pronoun reference, subject-verb agreement, verb tense, use of modifiers, parallel structure, punctuation, and mechanics

   Handwrite on the essay any revisions that seem necessary.

3. Submit the original version of the essay along with your revised version.

## COLLABORATIVE EXERCISE ON REVISING STYLE AND EDITING

1. In preparation for this exercise, the instructor will need to copy a short student essay (not more than two pages) for each class member. A preliminary draft will work best.

2. Form collaborative learning groups of five students each, as described in the preface, or fashion groups according to your own method.

3. Select one student to read the essay aloud. Other group members should follow along on their own copies.

4. Select another student to read aloud the following list of revising and editing concerns:

   a. Moving from writer-based to reader-based prose
   b. Varying sentence length
   c. Stressing verbs rather than nouns
   d. Using words effectively
   e. Detecting sexist language
   f. Adding your own voice
   g. Editing for complete sentences, run-on sentences, pronoun reference, subject-verb agreement, verb tense, use of modifiers, parallel

structure, punctuation, and mechanics. Discuss any revisions to the essay suggested by these editorial concerns, and have the recorder write out the changes the group agrees on.

5. Reconvene the entire class. Each group recorder should report the revisions the group made and explain why they are necessary. Try to account for differences in revisions.

## WORKS CITED

Ehrenreich, Barbara. "The Economics of Cloning." *Time* 22 Nov. 1993: 86.

Flower, Linda. "Writer-Based Prose: A Cognitive Basis for Problems in Writing." *College English* Sept. 1979: 19–37.

Lanham, Richard A. *Revising Prose.* 2nd ed. New York: Macmillan, 1987.

Neisser, Ulrich. "The Imitation of Man by Machine." *Science* 139 (1963): 193–97.

Sagan, Carl. "In Defense of Robots." *Broca's Brain.* New York: Ballantine, 1980. 280–92.

# *three*

# Composing Essays Drawing from Two or More Sources: Comparison and Contrast and Synthesis

Up to now we have focused on assignments in which the writer is working chiefly with a single reading source. Now you will tackle assignments that expect you to draw on two or more sources, such as books, journal articles, and newspaper reports. This is a complex task because you have to locate consistencies among the sources and then integrate the relevant information with your own ideas on the topic. In this chapter, we show you how to write two types of papers that draw on multiple sources:

1. An essay comparing and contrasting sources
2. A synthesis

## COMPARISON AND CONTRAST ESSAY

Writers use comparison and contrast to explore similarities and differences between two or more objects of study. With this organizational pattern, you might discuss the relationships between two authors' views on the causes of homelessness, for example, or you might attempt to persuade your readers that two authors who represent different political positions have come to synonymous conclusions on a topic.

Usually, the object of comparison and contrast is not simply to list and report similarities and differences as an end in itself. There is nothing intrinsically wrong with this pattern, but when it is your only goal, you may fall into the trap of doing too much summarizing, giving a synopsis of each author's views, and then explaining how the authors are alike and different. For maximum impact, you should take the process a step further. Strive to make some point about the two subjects you are comparing. This will be easy if, after you locate the similarities and differences, you step back and ask yourself what they represent, reveal, or demonstrate. Why are they interesting, relevant, eventful, or meaningful? What angle or point of view emerges with regard to the material? Answering these questions will help you decide how to write an assignment that shapes or expands on your ideas in an engaging way.

## Identifying Comparisons and Contrasts

When you first read the materials that you intend to compare and contrast, jot down any connections you can make between your previous knowledge and the ideas in the reading sources. As you read, annotate the two sources to highlight correspondences between them. Then do a second reading for the purpose of identifying as many similarities and differences as you can. If you have difficulty elaborating on the reading sources, refer to the suggestions in the Strategies for Elaborating on Reading Sources box on pp. 43–44. Here are some additional strategies that will help you discover how two reading sources are similar and different.

---

### ELABORATING TO UNCOVER COMPARISONS AND CONTRASTS

1. Identify points where one source author
   a. Agrees or disagrees with the other author;
   b. Says something relevant about the topic that the other author has neglected to say;
   c. Qualifies ideas stated by the other author;
   d. Extends a proposition made by the other author.
2. Validate one author's assertion with information provided by the other author.
3. Subsume similarities and differences between the sources under subordinate categories.
4. Create hierarchies of importance among ideas that are similar or different.
5. Make judgments about the relevance of one author's view in relation to the other's view.

---

A useful technique for formulating links between points of similarity and difference is webbing (see Fig. 3-1). Once you identify a point of similarity or difference, summarize the point in a short phrase and place it in a box in the center of a sheet of paper. Next, spin out the web by writing each author's ideas around this key idea node. Circle each of these ideas and connect them with lines to the key idea and, where appropriate, to each other. When you are finished webbing, you will have a visual display of the points of similarity and difference.

To illustrate the process of composing a comparison and contrast essay, let us accompany our student Kathy Tryer as she works on the following assignment:

> Write a three- to four-page essay explaining the differences between the views of Myron Magnet in "Rebels with a Cause" and Herbert Gans in "The War Against the Poor" on the topic of poor people. Write for an audience of classmates.

Magnet's article appears in the *National Review*, March 15, 1993, pages 46 to 50. The Gans selection is in Chapter 10 of this book.

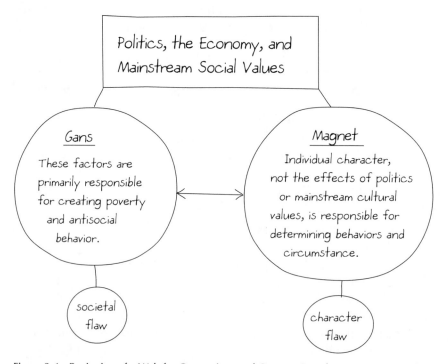

Figure 3-1    Beginning of a Web for Comparison and Contrast Based on Myron Magnet's "Rebels with a Cause" and Herbert Gans's "The War Against the Poor"

On her first reading, Kathy underlines and annotates the articles, jotting down her reactions and marking passages where one author's views relate to the other's. Then, as she reads the two pieces a second time, she examines them closely for additional points of similarity and difference while she elaborates on select passages.

### Gans, Paragraph 4

True, some poor people are indeed guilty of immoral behavior—that is, murderers, street criminals, drug sellers, child abusers.

### Kathy's Notes

Gans uses the examples of criminality and morality, as does Magnet, but in different ways. Taking great pains to clarify his own perception of morality, Gans defensively pits the abject criminality of murderers and drug sellers against the merely antisocial behavior of teenage mothers and individuals incapable of remaining employed. Here Gans attempts to soften the argument of immorality against the less severe offenders of mainstream moral standards. In contrast to Magnet, who suggests preventative tactics and never raises the issue of morality, Gans proposes a band-aid approach to the problem that is only getting worse with time.

### Gans, Paragraph 5

Then there are poor people whose anger at their condition cannot be defined as political protest. Even so, most of those labeled "undeserving" are simply poor people who for a variety of reasons cannot live up to mainstream behavioral standards, like remaining childless in adolescence, finding and holding a job, and staying off welfare. This does not make them immoral.

### Magnet, Paragraph 5

. . . For though the governmental structure of force and threat—police, judges and prisons—is a key means by which society restrains aggression and crime, it isn't the principal means. The most powerful curb is the internal inhibition society builds into each man's character, the inner voice (call it reason, conscience, superego, what you will) that makes the social contract an integral part of our deepest selves.

### Kathy's Notes

Though the examples of government and control by authority are discussed by both Magnet and Gans, Magnet suggests that the true controlling factor in human life is the internal motivations of the individual. If such motivation is misguided or absent, criminal behavior may result. Magnet argues that within impoverished cultures, built-in inhibition is absent from the character makeup of many of its individuals. This approach, which holds each man or culture responsible for its own behaviors, differs greatly from Gans's. He states that antisocial behaviors are a symptom of poverty, which in turn, is a symptom of government policies and the social attitudes and beliefs of mainstream culture. Gans never suggests that individuals within a given culture can (or should) be responsible for their own beliefs and behaviors, unless they have demonstrated an ability to do so according to mainstream moral values.

## Planning Comparison and Contrast Essays

Once Kathy has generated a series of elaborations, she does two things: She (1) selects and orders her ideas, and (2) sketches out a blueprint for the essay. Keeping in mind that her purpose is to compare and contrast the views of two authors, she reviews her elaborations, identifies the ones dealing with similarities and differences (see p. 79), and places them in categories. Kathy creates two lists: one list for resemblances between the sources and the other for differences. Another way you might do this is by marking the text wherever you've discovered similarities or differences (use symbols: = for similarities and ≠ for differences). Here are Kathy's two lists:

### Similarities:

* Both Gans and Magnet believe that poverty is a symptom of social decay.
* Both writers demonstrate that antisocial behavior may be used as a form of power, and that such behavior may be admired by certain groups or cultures.

### Differences:

* Cultural mores serve as the basis of both writer's arguments, but whereas Gans blames government policies and the attitudes of society at large, Magnet finds the absence of traditional middle-class values to blame.

* Gans blames politics, the economy, and the cultural mores of the middle class as either unfair, outmoded, or not applicable to the real-life situations faced by impoverished peoples.

* Magnet uses a historical/theoretical model to demonstrate that impoverished peoples lack the internal guidance and discipline that characterize the "social contract" adhered to by the middle and upper classes.

* Whereas Gans writes of declining morality in terms of it being a recent phenomenon, Magnet suggests that moral standards have undergone continual change, and that, historically, moral decline has always been a part of human culture.

As Kathy analyzes the similarities and differences, she asks herself two questions: (1) What do these similarities and differences demonstrate? and (2) What do they tell us about each of the two authors? Whenever you ask such questions, see if you can form some kind of a generalization from the similarities and differences. Even if your generalization has exceptions, it will still be useful.

Usually, a writer compares and contrasts reading sources to make a point or propose a thesis. As we said earlier, the writer may simply want to describe the similarities and differences, but this limited rhetorical purpose leaves little room for the writer to bring background knowledge to bear on the text. A more powerful purpose would require the writer to have a specific reason for comparing and contrasting: for example, to describe, explain, or argue a point, or to focus the essay on what the comparison reveals or demonstrates about the subject.

| *Limited Goal* | *More Powerful Goal* |
|---|---|
| Bring out similarities and differences in the subject matter. | 1. Use the comparison to describe, explain, or argue a position. |
| | 2. Show what the comparison reveals or demonstrates about the subject. |

In the essay on pp. 87–91, you will see that as Kathy lays out the similarities and differences between the two readings, she aligns herself more with Magnet than with Gans, leading up to paragraphs 5 and 6, where she argues that Magnet's analysis of poverty is more realistic and constructive than Gans's.

## Organizing the Comparison and Contrast Essay

Comparison and contrast essays are usually organized in a point-by-point format, a block arrangement, or a combination of the two.

---

### POINT-BY-POINT ORGANIZATIONAL PATTERN

**Introduction**

1. Identify the sources and the issue(s) they focus on.
2. Explain your rhetorical goal (your purpose for comparing the sources).

**Body Paragraphs**

1. Compare the sources with respect to a single characteristic.
2. Repeat step 1 for each characteristic you intend to treat.

**Conclusion**

See the techniques on p. 57.

### BLOCK ORGANIZATIONAL PATTERN

**Introduction**

1. Identify the sources and the issue(s) they focus on.
2. Explain your rhetorical goal (your purpose for comparing the sources).

**Body Paragraphs**

1. Identify and discuss the characteristics of the first source.
2. Compare the characteristics of the second source with those of the first source.

**Conclusion**

See the techniques on p. 57.

---

Notice that Kathy Tryer organizes her essay according to both patterns. Paragraphs 2 and 3 treat Magnet and Gans, respectively, in "blocks." In the remaining paragraphs (4, 5, and 6), Kathy compares both writers in point-by-point fashion.

If Kathy had used the point-by-point pattern exclusively, she would have written her essay according to the outline that follows.

### OUTLINE FOR COMPARISON ESSAY WRITTEN IN POINT-BY-POINT ARRANGEMENT

*Paragraph 1:* Introduction

#### Objectivity (Point 1)

*Paragraph 2:* Magnet's argument—a practical social and historical monograph explaining the causes of ills suffered by the poor.

Gans's argument—reactionary, reminiscent of a classic "knee-jerk" liberal response.

#### Examples (Point 2)

*Paragraph 3:* Gans—band-aid style approach to an age-old problem.

*Paragraph 4:* Magnet—doesn't suggest a solution aimed at diminishing the ways the poor are viewed negatively, but does identify the conditions needed for the advancement of the poor.

#### Rhetorical Stance (Point 3)

*Paragraph 5:* Gans's and Magnet's arguments lie at opposite ends of the spectrum. Gans claims the cause of the prevailing view of the poor is mainstream political precepts.

*Paragraph 6:* Magnet blames what he believes to be poverty's root itself: the values and character of individuals.

*Paragraph 7:* Conclusion

If Kathy had relied solely on the block pattern instead of alternating between Magnet and Gans with each point of comparison, she would have contrasted them in blocks, dealing with one author in the first block and switching to the other in the second segment. Her outline would look like the following.

### OUTLINE FOR COMPARISON ESSAY WRITTEN IN BLOCK ARRANGEMENT

*Paragraph 1:* The introduction is the same as in the point-by-point essay.

### First Block: Magnet

*Paragraph 2:* Magnet's argument—not reactionary or desperate, objective and convincing.

*Paragraph 3:* Magnet claims that antisocial behavior, poverty, and the other ills of the lower classes beget an underdeveloped "social contract." He cites examples from history, philosophy, and psychology.

*Paragraph 4:* Magnet tries to persuade his audience that the condition of the poor is due to individual, not social, circumstances.

### Second Block: Gans

*Paragraph 5:* Gans—reactionary, reminiscent of a classic "knee-jerk" liberal response.

*Paragraph 6:* Thorough in explaining his argument for social change, but he fails to convince the reader of either the problem or his proposed solution.

*Paragraph 7:* Gans's attempts to elicit an emotional response from his readers further the overall perception that his arguments are biased and one-sided.

*Paragraph 8:* Conclusion

## Drafting Comparison and Contrast Essays

After Kathy selects an organizational plan, she writes a draft of her essay. This first draft is preliminary; it is not the final, polished product. She will have an opportunity to change direction, sharpen her focus, and revise at a later date.

The box that follows lists conventions for comparison essays. As you read Kathy's essay, notice the extent to which she uses them.

---

### CONVENTIONS FOR COMPARISON ESSAYS

1. Give your readers some background about the topic.
2. Identify the sources by title and author.
3. Clearly indicate the focus or thesis of your paper.
4. Make clear to your readers what you are using as points of comparison.

(continued on the next page)

---

5. Develop each point of comparison by paraphrasing, summarizing, or quoting relevant points in the readings and bringing your prior topic knowledge and experience to bear on the text.
6. Clearly differentiate your own ideas from those of the authors of the sources.
7. Correctly document source material that is paraphrased, summarized, or quoted.

## SAMPLE COMPARISON AND CONTRAST ESSAY

Tryer 1

Kathy Tryer

Professor Kennedy

English 131

16 September 2002

Poverty's Roots--The Environment
versus the Individual: Two Views

Myron Magnet and Herbert J. Gans, both writing about poverty in America, arrive at startlingly different conclusions concerning its roots, causes, and prevention. Magnet, in "Rebels with a Cause," argues that the poor are an inevitable by-product of advanced cultures. According to Magnet, those within advanced cultures incapable of the discipline or restraint necessary for social advancement become outcast, socially immobile, and poor. Magnet supports his argument with substantive examples and draws on historical, philosophical, and psychological literature. Gans, however, in "The War Against the Poor," proposes a means to end mistreatment of the poor rather than proposing methods by which to end poverty, and places the blame for the social condition of the poor and their mistreatment squarely on the shoulders of mainstream society itself. Neither writer suggests it is possible to end poverty entirely. Magnet, though, examines poverty's underlying causes, identifies the conditions necessary for its reduction, and offers the more sensible analysis of the condition.

Magnet points out that the personal values of the poor place them outside the social order. He discusses the importance of order in society, claiming, "the achievements of civilization rest upon the social order, which rests in turn upon a mutual agreement to foreswear aggression" (50). Magnet alludes to statements made by Plato, St. Augustine, Hobbes, Burke, and Freud and points out that each of these thinkers concluded that "as men come from the hand of nature, they are instinctively aggressive, with a built-in inclination to violence" (47). The underlying purpose of social order, a relatively recent phenomenon in history, Magnet explains, "is to restrain man's instinctual aggressiveness, so that human life can be something higher than a war of all against all" (47). Social order is the principal element lacking in poor society, Magnet claims, and this problem must be traced to the individual. To elaborate, "the hardest of hard realities-- whether people commit crimes or not--comes down to a very large extent to nothing more than values and beliefs in the world within the individual," claims Magnet (48). The values and beliefs of the poor, according to Magnet, are out of step with those of the larger society, which is the direct cause of their socio-economic conditions.

Gans, however, sees things differently. He believes poverty is caused by mainstream society which, <u>by design</u>, suppresses the poor and creates a social climate hostile to the poor. He blames the economy, politics, and social policy toward the poor for their ills and for the creation of an environment conducive to their debasement. For example, he cites the economy as a culprit and claims that mainstream attitudes toward the poor were "initiated by dramatic shifts in the domestic and world economy which have turned more and more unskilled and semiskilled workers into surplus labor" (461). Individuals within the middle and upper classes,

however, view the poor unsympathetically and see them "not as
people without jobs but as miscreants who behave badly
because they do not abide by middle-class or mainstream moral
values" (461). He does allow, though, that some poor people
are involved in criminal or indecent behavior, but suggests
this is an insignificant segment of the underclass
population. To counteract the problems created by the
economy, politics, and existing social policy, Gans suggests
enormous government programs such as a "new" New Deal for the
poor, programs to find uses for stagnant or redundant private
enterprise to raise levels of employment, and for those
remaining who can't--or won't--work, a program of income
grants. "Alas," concedes Gans, "when taxpayers discover how
much cheaper it is to pay welfare than to create jobs, that
remedy may end as it has before" (462). Gans's proposals do
nothing to improve the condition of the poor, nor do they
address the underlying causes of poverty. Indeed, as he notes
above, to implement such programs might actually increase the
anger of mainstream culture toward the poor. In short, Gans
proposes a band-aid approach to solving an age-old problem.

    Magnet, while he doesn't suggest a solution aimed at
diminishing the ways the poor are viewed negatively, does
identify the conditions needed for the advancement of the
poor. Unlike Gans, Magnet does not think that "society has
so oppressed people as to bend them out of their true
nature" (48), believing instead that the plight of the poor
is oftentimes attributable to social maladjustment of the
poor themselves. "Examine the contents of their minds and
hearts and what you find is free-floating aggression, weak
consciences, anarchic beliefs, detachment from the community
and its highest values," he states (48). Moreover, the
condition of the poor is a

         predictable result of unimaginably weak
         families, headed by immature irresponsible
         girls, who are at the margin of the community,
         pathological in their own behavior, and too

often lacking the knowledge, interest and inner
resources to be successful molders of strong
characters in children. (48)

Clearly then, to "adequately socialize" the members of the
underclass who lack inner discipline and social order, their
values and morals must change.

Gans's and Magnet's arguments are in direct
opposition. Gans claims the cause of the prevailing view
and the current condition of the poor is mainstream social
and political precepts. Magnet blames the values and
character of the individual alone. Gans proposes government
intervention and an "intellectual and cultural defense"
(463) on behalf of the poor. Magnet suggests uncovering the
true basis for poverty and acting on a local level by
attempting to understand poverty-stricken individuals
themselves, of whom Gans admits "Americans accept so many
untruths" (461). Gans's band-aid approach to artificially
elevating the status of the poor through government
programs and cash subsidies will do little toward changing
mainstream society's negative view of the poor. Magnet's
more comprehensive value-oriented approach to addressing
the ills of the underclass, grounded in historical,
philosophical, and psychological precedents, has a better
chance of success.

Magnet, in suggesting a reexamination of the very
mechanism which catalyzes poverty and crime, offers a
possible solution that is far more realistic than that
submitted by Gans. Gans's emotionally charged argument
attempts to conjure enemies from inanimate entities: the
government, politics, and the economy. Magnet's proposal
provides a constructive, accountable approach to addressing
the problems of the poor. Thus, Gans's suggestions amount to
little more than a critique of mainstream American society
and an unfounded claim that American institutions are
responsible for the plight of the underclass.

```
                                              Tryer 5


                        Works Cited

Gans, Herbert. "The War Against the Poor." Dissent
      Fall 1992: 461-65.
Magnet, Myron. "Rebels with a Cause." National Review
      15 March 1993: 46-50.
```

You will notice that Kathy Tryer's paper has followed many of the guidelines we've suggested for comparison and contrast papers. No piece of writing can ever be expected to observe all the guidelines for a particular kind of writing, because each topic or issue introduces matters that require their own distinctive treatment. Nevertheless, you will note in Kathy's paper a consistent attention to detail that implies her audience's general knowledge of Magnet's and Gans's articles and their positions; a careful assessment of the information, organizational plans, and rhetorical concerns of Magnet's and Gans's articles, showing that Kathy has annotated her reading materials point by point; and an elaboration of Kathy's argument in a clear, systematic manner from her opening paragraph about the major differences between Magnet and Gans, through individual paragraphs that focus on each, to her concluding paragraph about their divergence.

Though we have presented Kathy's final draft of her paper, you should bear in mind that Kathy produced this version after several preliminary drafts of its parts and their whole. Here are some additional steps that Kathy followed when she revised her writing.

## Revising the Preliminary Draft

When you are satisfied with your preliminary draft, make arrangements to share it with your teacher or a classmate. Before you proceed any further, you need to get some feedback on what you have written so far.

## Instructor Conferences

If your instructor invites students to confer with him or her, be sure to take advantage of this opportunity. The conference will be beneficial to you if you approach it with the correct mind-set and adequate preparation. Don't expect your instructor to correct your work or simply tell you what to do. You should assume a proactive role: Set the agenda and do most of the talking. After the teacher reads your draft—preferably, you should read it to the teacher—inquire about what worked well and what fell flat. Be prepared to explain what you are trying to achieve and point out the parts of the paper you feel good about and the parts you think need work. Most important, be ready to answer the teacher's questions.

## Peer Reviews

If your teacher agrees, make arrangements to have a classmate or a friend review your preliminary draft and give you feedback. If that is not possible, set the paper aside for a few days and then review it yourself. Respond to the questions listed in the box that follows.

---

**QUESTIONS FOR HELPING A WRITER REVISE THE FIRST DRAFT OF A COMPARISON AND CONTRAST ESSAY**

1. Is the writer's rhetorical purpose clear? Explain how he or she is attempting to influence or affect readers.
2. Does the writer explain what the similarities and contrasts reveal or demonstrate, or is the writer's purpose simply to show that similarities and differences exist?
3. Does everything in the essay lead to or follow from one central meaning? If not, which ideas appear to be out of place?
4. Will the reader understand the essay, and is the writer sensitive to the reader's concerns?
   a. Does he or she provide necessary background information about the subject matter, the sources, and their titles and authors? If not, what is missing?
   b. Throughout the essay, when the writer refers to the source, does he or she supply the reader with necessary documentation?

(continued on the next page)

---

c. Does the writer provide clear transitions or connecting ideas that differentiate his or her own ideas from those in the sources?

d. Does the writer display an awareness of the authors by referring to them by using names and personal pronouns ("Smith states," "she explains") rather than personifying the source ("the article states," "it explains")?

5. Is the organizational format appropriate for a comparison and contrast essay? Is the writer using point-by-point or block arrangement?

6. Has the writer revealed the points of comparison to the reader? Are these criteria or bases for comparison clear or confusing? Explain.

7. Does the writer provide transitions and connecting ideas as he or she moves from one source to another or from one point of comparison to the next? If not, where are they needed?

8. Do you hear the writer's voice throughout the entire essay? Describe it.

9. Does the writer use an opener that catches the reader's attention?

10. Does the conclusion simply restate the main idea, or does it offer new insights?

11. Does the essay have an appropriate title?

12. What other suggestions can you give the writer for improving this draft?

## Editing the Preliminary Draft

When you are satisfied with your revision, read your paper aloud. This will enable you to catch any glaring errors. Then reread the essay line by line and sentence by sentence. Check for grammatical correctness, punctuation, spelling, mechanics, manuscript form, and typos. If you are using a word processing program with a spell checker, apply the checker to your essay. If you are especially weak in editing skills, ask a friend to read over your work.

### INDIVIDUAL EXERCISE ON COMPARISON AND CONTRAST ESSAYS

Reread Kathy Tryer's paper. Note the structure of its presentation. After an introduction, Kathy summarizes Myron Magnet's article. Then she summarizes Herbert Gans's article. Can you make any generalizations about her selective use of paraphrase and quotation? Note that she does not summarize, paraphrase, or quote from Magnet's or Gans's entire article; instead, she focuses on issues on which Magnet's argument relates specifically to Gans's. Evaluate her selection.


## SYNTHESIZING SOURCES

To synthesize is to select elements from two or more sources on a topic or interest that they share and then to organize them, along with your own ideas, under a controlling theme or concept. You read an array of materials—for example, two articles from academic journals, a chapter from a book, and a column from a newspaper—and you look for or create a controlling idea or thematic consistency. Then you combine the different pieces of information in a coherent, original paper. Your aim is to draw together a body of information from the reading sources and then to state or restate and to support an idea common to them all with a particular rhetorical purpose in mind.

Your purpose might be to define poverty. After reading various sources on poverty, you select pertinent ideas, combine them, and formulate a definition. Another purpose might be to chart the development of the Arab-Israeli controversy. As in the previous example, you read different sources, identify common elements, combine historical perspectives, and finally construct a coherent narrative account.

From the preceding examples, you can see that there is a difference between synthesis on the one hand and comparison and contrast on the other. When you compare two reading sources, you examine them with an eye to pointing out their similarities and differences. You consider the readings with regard to some target, theme, characteristic, or quality that relates them to one another. For example, you might read two journal articles on the topic of health reform and compare the authors' opposing views. The reading materials already converge on the same topic, however different their premises and conclusions may be.

When you synthesize, however, the readings you use may focus on separate, discrete topics or issues. Your task is to identify constituent elements of their interlocking materials and combine them into a single, unified piece of writing. Your aim should nonetheless go beyond a simplistic presentation of information in the sources and beyond a general statement of your reaction to the sources. Your goal is to represent different sources that will enable you to define your own thesis or idea and to support your idea with reference to those sources.

You need to begin your synthesis with an open mind about how to use your different materials. First, read the sources to obtain background information on the topic and identify its dimensions. As you do this initial reading, set two goals: to bring your own ideas to bear on the topic by elaborating on and reacting to the material and to identify common elements in the sources. To achieve the latter goal, read each source, searching for its relationships to the other sources. Next, ask yourself the questions listed in the following box.

---

**QUESTIONS FOR IDENTIFYING RELATIONSHIPS AMONG SOURCES**

1. Does the source give background information or additional information about points that are presented in other sources?
2. Does it provide additional details about points made in other sources?
3. Does it provide evidence for points made by another author?
4. Are there places where this author contradicts or disagrees with the other authors you have read?
5. Are there places where the author supports or agrees with other authors?
6. Are there cause-and-effect relationships between this source and the other sources?
7. Are there time relationships among the sources?
8. Does this source contain elements that can be compared or contrasted with those in other sources?
9. Are there other common threads running through this source and the other sources?
10. Do the authors of the sources use similar key words or phrases?
11. Are there any other ways you can categorize the ideas in the sources?

---

To illustrate the process of writing a synthesis paper, consider the following assignment:

> Drawing on Lillian B. Rubin's " 'People Don't Know Right from Wrong Anymore,' " Frances K. Goldschneider and Linda J. Waite's "Alternative Family Futures," and Robert L. Griswold's "Fatherhood and the Defense of Patriarchy," write a four- to five-page essay explaining what American families are like today. Address your essay to an audience of peers.

For this assignment, your rhetorical purpose is to explain the various ways the American family is being redefined. First, you should review the sources with an eye to what each contributes to the controlling idea, the transformation of the family. Then, you should determine how each source relates to the others. As you review each one, write down your answers to the questions that appear in the preceding box.

Once you have answered the questions and discovered the common elements among the sources, decide what ideas of your own you want to communicate to your readers. The next step is to locate in the sources information that you can use to develop each of the ideas you want to communicate. This will require you to go back to the sources. As you reread them, look for bits of information that relate to your points. Mark this content in the text or copy it into your notebook. When you have located a sufficient amount of relevant information, you can start to draft your essay. As you begin to write, you must decide whether to paraphrase, quote, or summarize each piece of supporting information. A recap of the entire process appears in the following box.

---

### STRATEGIES FOR WRITING A SYNTHESIS FOR A SPECIFIC PURPOSE

1. Read all the sources to get a general impression of the content.
2. Reread each source, elaborating on it by bringing your previous knowledge to bear on the text.
3. Determine the elements each source has in common with the other sources by asking each item in the Questions for Identifying Relationships Among Sources box (p. 95).
4. Decide what ideas of your own you want to get across to your readers.
5. Locate in the sources information that you can use to develop each of your ideas.
6. Draft your essay by quoting, paraphrasing, or summarizing relevant supporting information from the sources and by drawing on your knowledge of the basic features of writing: titles, introductions, sentences, paragraphs, transitions, and so on (see pp. 50–59).

---

When you have completed a preliminary draft of your essay, schedule a conference with your professor (see p. 92), and if your professor agrees, ask a classmate or a friend to give you suggestions for revision.

---

### QUESTIONS FOR REVISING A SYNTHESIS ESSAY

1. Does the title give you some indication of the writer's attitude toward the topic?
2. Is there an interesting lead that attracts the reader's attention?
3. Does the writer give you sufficient background information on the topic?
4. Does the writer make his or her overall purpose clear to the reader?
5. Can you locate the writer's thesis or expression of point of view?
6. As you read each paragraph, are you aware of the purpose that the writer is trying to accomplish?
7. Does the writer identify relationships among sources?
8. In each paragraph, does the writer provide sufficient support from the sources?
9. Does the writer include enough of his or her own commentary in each of the paragraphs?
10. Does the conclusion do more than simply summarize the main points of the paper?
11. Does the writer include parenthetical documentation where it is necessary and clearly differentiate among sources?
12. Is there a Works Cited page?

---

What follows is an essay by a student, Siryal Benim, written in response to the assignment on page 95.

*SAMPLE SYNTHESIS ESSAY*

```
                                                        Benim 1
     Siryal Benim
     Academic Writing I
     Professor Smith
     23 September 1999
                   Today's American Family: Where Did We Go
                   Wrong--And Is Any Recourse Possible?
              Our families today neither resemble nor function
     like those of just two decades ago. In the past, American
```

cultural norms suggested that upon finishing school, young
adults would seek employment, get married, or live with their
parents until they were prepared to do either one or both of
the above. Lillian B. Rubin, in "'People Don't Know Right
from Wrong Anymore,'" points out that the average age for
marriage was earlier than it is today, at 20.6 years for women
and 22.5 years for men (17). Indeed, the past two decades have
seen three "revolutions," or social upheavals, each popularly
termed as sexual, gender, and divorce-related. Additionally,
America and the world have weathered "shifts in the economy,
which forced increasing numbers of women into the labor force"
(Rubin 16). As a direct result of these changes, our families
and lifestyles now differ substantially from what they were
twenty years ago. While new family structures and lifestyles
are often described as "alternative," these patterns may be
adopted by default as often as by choice.

　　The traditional nuclear family is diminishing relative
to other family structures in American culture today. Apart
from finding different family systems today, such as single-
parent households, traditional roles for men, women and
children have changed as well. Men are no longer likely to be
the sole breadwinners for the family, and in some cases, may
not even be the principal wage earners. Due to the ascension
of women in the workforce and their growing parity with men in
terms of power and income, many men have difficulty facing the
new realities of economics and family. Goldschneider and
Waite, in "Alternative Family Futures" suggest, forebodingly,
that "men who still hold traditional definitions of their
appropriate adult role are increasingly having difficulty
finding wives willing to take the full burden of family
obligations left by a husband whose only responsibilities are
to work" (208). "It is also the case," they continue, "that
pressures have been building on men to become more involved in
the family and its tasks whether they want to or not" (208).

Signs of of an emerging "new fatherhood" point encouragingly toward a reaffirmation of shared values and an effort toward renewed cohesiveness among family members (Griswold 257).

Robert Griswold, in "Fatherhood and the Defense of Patriarchy," states "feminists and advocates for the men's movement hope that the new fatherhood will be a progressive step in redefining American manhood" (257). Lack of enthusiasm, however, for the so-called men's movement may suggest that men are not prepared to adopt, en masse, any such feminist-driven ideology. On the other hand, the dramatic change in men's roles over the past two decades may merely indicate the rapid deterioration of the traditional nuclear family as a cultural mainstay. Hence, we have seen over the past two decades a high rate of divorce and the rise of the new "traditional" families: family units still headed by two parents or guardians, but who are not necessarily biologically related to each other's children.

Over the last twenty years, "step" parents have become more common. Previously married individuals remarry to create new, sometimes complex family units with various step relatives. "Now, when, on the average, women live to nearly eighty and men to a little over seventy, we can marry and bear children very much later, safe in the knowledge that we'll be around to raise and nurture them as long as they need us" (Rubin 17).

In the 1990s, single-parent families, especially those headed by mothers, are subjected to increasingly demanding schedules and levels of stress. Goldschneider and Waite point out that women today need more help than ever when raising families: "Despite the number of women who take on both parental and economic roles, not all women can do so; few can parent totally alone" (202). Indeed, the viability of single-parent families became a major campaign issue in the 1992 presidential race. Political rhetoric aside, it

would seem that children in single-parent households stand
to suffer the greatest consequences when the pressures are
too great for the family to bear.

An increasing number of families opt to remain
childless. Historically, the absence of children in a family
was less often a matter of choice than it was result of
physical limitations. Modern families make this choice based
upon their own goals and the potential impact of these goals
on family life. It would seem that such decisions are
typically based on sound, rational judgments, and that they
represent a morally responsible alternative to child-rearing.

Apprehensive about marriage due to high rates of
divorce, many couples today postpone wedding plans
indefinitely. Again, due to greater life expectancy through
improved medical technology, this is a luxury our ancestors
were not afforded. Similarly, neither was effective birth
control or abortion, and unplanned pregnancies often led to
marriage. Writes Rubin, "Sometimes the young couple married
regretfully; often one partner, usually the man, was
ambivalent" (13). But regardless of circumstances, "it didn't
really matter; they did what was expected" (Rubin 13); such
was the power exerted by cultural norms just twenty years
ago. But have advances in human health practices devalued
matrimony? Has the once time-honored principle of commitment
been reduced to a mere buzzword among couples today? People
today realize that even if their first or even second
marriages don't succeed, they may take vows a third or
possibly a fourth time, until they are satisfied. Certainly,
the families of the 1990s are very different from those of
our ancestors. It remains to be determined, however, if these
changes are for better or for worse.

Perhaps today couples and families simply have more
options to choose from when making decisions. This freedom
comes with its own set of pros and cons. To debate the issue
of today's fractured family using sound-bite styled catch

Benim 5

phrases such as "family values" misses the point: values are
widely held precepts based on accepted cultural norms which
are usually grounded in history or tradition. Quite simply,
it is precisely because of the absence of any consensus in
our culture today, morally, spiritually, or otherwise, that
an understanding of what constitutes appropriate family
behavior cannot be attained. Perhaps we are now creating a
new concept of the "traditional" family that will be passed
on to subsequent generations.

Benim 6

Works Cited

Goldschneider, Frances K., and Linda J. Waite. "Alternative
    Family Futures." New Families, No Families? The
    Transformation of the American Home. Berkeley: U of
    California P, 1991. 200-205.
Griswold, Robert L. "Fatherhood and the Defense of
    Patriarchy." Fatherhood in America, A History. New York:
    Basic Books, 1993. 257-260.
Rubin, Lillian B. "'People Don't Know Right from Wrong
    Anymore.'" Families on the Fault Line. New York:
    HarperCollins, 1994.

You will notice that Siryal Benim's paper exemplifies many of our guidelines for synthesis essays. It incorporates diverse materials from three different reading sources, each of which appears to address a separate topic about the family. From these different perspectives on alternative family patterns, the role of fatherhood, and various moral points associated with these issues, Siryal discusses changes in contemporary family life. The paper argues that many currently available options make possible a variety of different family structures.

### INDIVIDUAL EXERCISE ON SYNTHESIS ESSAYS

Reread Siryal Benim's paper. Note the structure of its presentation. After an introductory statement about changes in family patterns, Siryal discusses new roles for fathers, stepparents, couples without children, late marriages, and divorce, and then draws on information variously from three sources. Read the titles of these sources in the list of works cited. What separate topic does each appear to address? Can you make any generalization about Siryal's alternating and selective use of these sources?

### COLLABORATIVE EXERCISE ON SYNTHESIS ESSAYS

1. Form collaborative learning groups of three students each, as described in the preface, or fashion groups according to your own method.
2. Assign each member a single source to trace through Siryal's paper. Ask each to comment on the focus that Siryal puts on the material from that particular source.
3. When the class reconvenes, have each group recorder explain the conclusions that individual members reached about Siryal's use of particular sources.

### WORKS CITED

Gans, Herbert. "The War Against the Poor." *Dissent* Fall 1992: 461–65.

Goldschneider, Frances K., and Linda J. Waite. "Alternative Family Futures." *New Families, No Families? The Transformation of the American Home*. Berkeley: U of California P, 1991. 200–05.

Griswold, Robert L. "Fatherhood and the Defense of Patriarchy." Fatherhood in America, A History. New York: Basic Books, 1993. 257–60.

Magnet, Myron. "Rebels with a Cause." *National Review* 15 March 1993: 46–50.

Rubin, Lillian B. " 'People Don't Know Right from Wrong Anymore.' " *Families on the Fault Line*. New York: HarperCollins, 1994.

C H A P T E R

# *f o u r*

# Essays of Argument, Analysis, and Evaluation

## ARGUMENT: AN INTRODUCTION

In the broad sense, every college paper that expresses a thesis is an "argument" because the writer's goal is to get the reader to accept his or her perspective, position, or point of view. Even if a writer devotes most of the paper to summarizing, paraphrasing, comparing, or contrasting sources, he or she can still develop an argument that promotes a distinctive point of view. The choice of materials with their emphasis and arrangement will imply a perspective and demonstrate a position.

The synthesis essay generally presents an argument in the broad sense of the word. It pertains to setting out or explaining a particular idea, attitude, or speculative point of view. A more specialized sense of the word evokes the goal of moving audiences to a particular action or persuasion. The word *argument* need not imply a quarrel or a polemic. It derives from a Greek word related to *argent*, "silver or white" (compare Ag, the chemical abbreviation for "silver"), denoting brilliance or clarity. From it comes the name of Argos, the mythological demigod with a hundred eyes. The word implies that a speaker or writer has seized upon an idea, clarified its point, and made its meaning strikingly visible.

The difference between written argument in the broad sense of getting your readers to see your point of view and argument in the narrower sense of persuading your readers to take your position is illustrated in the two thesis statements that follow. Both concern "communitarianism," a popular social movement. Although "community" was a watchword for the nineties, it remains a contested concept. Many writers are still embroiled in a controversy over whether it is more important to uphold community values or safeguard individual rights. The political philosophers and intellectuals who value identification with or membership in a community over private initiative or personal autonomy are referred to as communitarians.

### THESIS A: ARGUMENT IN THE BROAD SENSE

The ideals set forth by communitarians are undemocratic, un-American, unconstitutional, and unfair.

### THESIS B: ARGUMENT IN THE SPECIALIZED SENSE

Although the academics who espouse communitarianism tout it as the panacea for our nation's ills, the ideals they set forth are undemocratic, un-American, unconstitutional, and unfair.

The difference between thesis A and thesis B is that B has more of a prescriptive or directive edge. Writer B knows that some of her readers will not agree with her. She expects them to argue that restoration of community is a solution to America's social problems. When writer B says, "Although the academics who espouse communitarianism tout it as the panacea for our nation's ills," she anticipates her audience's opposing response. Later, in the body of her essay, she will give reasons why her view, expressed as that of "mainstream Americans," holds more weight than her opponents' views. Writer A has no opposition to worry about. She is writing a response essay to explain why she agrees with a published author's views on communitarianism. She is mainly interested in clarifying her position in relation to the author's, whereas writer B is intent on persuading her audience to agree with her own position.

---

#### ARGUMENT IN THE BROAD SENSE

1. You do not have to acknowledge explicitly your audience's (conflicting) view.
2. Your thesis is not necessarily arguable or debatable.
3. Your purpose is usually to explain or present your position. You are not intent on persuading your reader.

(continued on the next page)

## ARGUMENT IN THE SPECIALIZED SENSE

1. You anticipate conflicting views, acknowledge them, and directly address them.
2. Your thesis is issue-centered and debatable.
3. You want your readers to accept and agree with your position rather than the view of your opponents.

## Developing Support for Arguments

To develop a strong argument, you must impart a breadth and depth to its focus. Try to make the argument two-dimensional. An argument that hammers away at one central idea until it has exhausted all available evidence and concludes by restating the original proposition, as in the following, is not what you want to write.

> The ideals set forth by communitarians are undemocratic, un-American, unconstitutional, and unfair. . . . Thus we see that communitarianism is undemocratic, un-American, unconstitutional, and unfair.

Instead, the writer can pursue a rounder, perhaps more oblique path if the argument recognizes its own limitations. Two-dimensional argument explicitly acknowledges competing hypotheses, alternative explanations, and even outright contradictions.

> The ideals set forth by communitarianism are undemocratic, un-American, unconstitutional, and unfair even though its proponents tout it as the panacea for our nation's ills.

The value of this approach is that it widens the tunnel vision that repeats only one proposition. It implies that you have explored competing hypotheses and have weighed the evidence for and against each. Your reader may or may not agree with your conclusion, but he or she will certainly respect your effort to set it in a broader context.

## Using Sources in Argument Essays

This section is a discussion of writing about argument in the specialized sense of the word. Think of a controversial issue on which you have a strong opinion. Note that we use the word *issue* here rather than subject or topic. A subject or *topic* maps out a general area for discussion or inquiry. An *issue* involves some specific point or matter for contention and debate. Abortion is a topic. Whether or not women should have free choice in the matter of abortion is an issue. In your journal or notebook, jot down your views on one of the following issues or on an issue of your choice:

1. Whether we should buy American-made goods rather than imports.
2. Whether rap or heavy metal music promotes violence.
3. Whether television damages family life.
4. Whether the United States should extend the school year.
5. Whether cosmetics firms should be allowed to experiment on animals.

Next, state the primary reason you hold your position. Ask yourself two questions: (1) What underlying fact or cause is the basis for my view? and (2) Based on this reason, would someone agree or disagree with my reasoning? When you begin to think about how your reader or larger audience might react to your position, you will see how difficult it can be to construct a persuasive argument defending your views. We will return to this activity in a collaborative exercise after we have considered some strategies and techniques for fashioning strong arguments.

When you develop support for such an argument, be sure to differentiate between reasons and opinions. An *opinion* is a belief that you cannot substantiate with direct proof, whereas a *reason* carries with it the weight of logic and evidence. Students who sprinkle their compositions with the tag "in my personal opinion" are redundant because by their nature opinions are personal. The student who explains that "The school year should be lengthened because young kids usually waste away their summers anyway" is expressing an opinion about the productivity of kids on vacation. Similarly, the student who argues that "From the time I was thirteen, I worked hard at a job all summer long. Kids should work during the summer and not go to school" is also expressing an opinion. Both individuals define their points of view, but neither gives firm grounds of support. On the other hand, the student who writes

> Because our school year is 180 days and Japan's and West Germany's extends from 226 to 243 school days, Japanese and German children have more time to learn science and math. A lengthened school year will allow our students to spend as much classroom time on science and math as

students in other industrialized countries and perhaps "catch up" with the competition.

has provided a rational ground of support for his or her view. This is called a *reason*.

To make a strong argument, you need to support your position with substantial reasons. This will be easy if you have ample background knowledge of and firsthand experience with the issue. But if you know little about the issue, even if you have very strong opinions on it, you must refer to reading sources for additional information.

In some courses, your professors will stipulate the issues for you to discuss. At other times, you will be permitted to select your own topic. When this is the case, you can convert your topic into an arguable statement or issue by asking, "What is controversial about _____? What do people argue about?" Take communitarianism, the topic we introduced earlier (see p. 104). If you have thought or read about this social movement and know that the conflict is between individual claims and collective life, you will have no trouble delving beneath the surface and discovering a number of specific issues. Your background knowledge will enable you to refine the topic and come up with an innovative slant on it. If you know very little about communitarianism, however, you will have to learn more about it by carefully reading the sources your professor recommends or by conducting library research. Chapter 5 will assist you with library work.

Once you have determined what it is that people argue about, convert that information into an issue: Discuss whether the interests of communities are more important than the interests of individuals. If you prefer, state your issue as a question: Which is more sacred, communal or individual rights?

Subject or Topic → What Do People Argue About? → Issue

You may have strong opinions on the issue from the outset ("No, communal rights are far less important than individual rights"; "Yes, people should honor the common good rather than the selfish individual"), but remember that opinions are not enough. To persuade someone else, you need convincing reasons. Unless you are fully informed about the issue, you will have to consult reading sources.

As you embark upon reading the sources, keep in mind that you may uncover so much information that you will have to redefine and narrow your issue. Remember to probe both sides and read with an open mind, even if you have already taken a stand. A useful activity at this point is what Peter Elbow calls the "believing game." As you encounter views that conflict with your own, try to see them through the holder's eyes. Even if the views are absurd or directly opposite to yours, put yourself in the other person's place. As Elbow points out, "To do this requires great energy, attention, and even a kind of inner commitment. It helps to think of it as trying to get inside the head of someone who saw things this way. Perhaps even constructing such a person for yourself. Try to have the experience of someone who made the assertion" (149).

After you have read through the sources, write a clear-cut statement of your position and the conflicting view. To illustrate the process of composing an argumentative essay, we follow a student, Sarah Allyn, as she works on her paper entitled "Communitarianism Contested" (see pp. 115–20). For this essay, Sarah read four sources: Amitai Etzioni's "Morality as a Community Affair"; Christopher Little's "Communitarianism, A New Threat for Gun Owners"; Barry Jay Seltser and Donald E. Miller's "Ambivalences in American Views of Dignity"; and Michael Walzer's "Multiculturalism and Individualism."

Here is Sarah's schematic outline of the issue that she intends to write about:

<u>Issue</u>: Whether communitarianism is a panacea for the problems facing America.

| <u>My position</u>: Few mainstream Americans will consider communitarianism a worthwhile solution to America's problems. | <u>My opponent's position</u>: Communitarian principles will solve the nation's problems. |
|---|---|

Taking the two positions, Sarah composes a thesis statement that includes the main points of both sides:

Even though some of the recommendations of communitarians are laudable, few, if any, mainstream Americans will see the resurgence of "community" as a panacea for our nation's ills.

Then Sarah returns to her reading sources to locate reasons for each position. She asks herself, "Which facts, examples, pieces of evidence, and citations by reliable authorities support my views and the views of my opponents?" As Sarah discovers reasons, she jots them down in her notebook.

## Support for My Positions

1. We should keep in mind that "communitarian writers are mainly academics, some of whom enjoy close connections to the Washington political community" (Little 30).

2. Etzioni himself admits that communitarian organizations can be excessive and corrupt, for example McCarthyism and the Ku Klux Klan (36).

3. How will the "common good" prevail and communitarianism function if, as Etzioni explains, "Americans don't like to tell others how to behave"?

4. Another conflict between individuals and communities is related to the issue of personal property. Seltser and Miller remind us that "property is defined as an extension of the self" (121).

5. Little: How can communitarianism be morally advantageous when it abrogates certain rights (30)?

6. Levinson in <u>Yale Law Journal</u> argues that most Americans will uphold individual rights, even at cost to others (Little 84).

## Support for the Other Side

1. Walzer: "Individuals are stronger, more confident, more savvy, when they are participants in a common life, responsible to and for other people" (189).

2. Seltser and Miller: A common moral or ethical code is reasonable because society is formed "by a mixture of values and beliefs that both form its citizens and are in turn formed by them" (118).

3. Etzioni argues that the alternative to having the community voice sound moral principles is "state coercion or social and moral anarchy" (36).

4. Walzer: If we adopt communitarian principles, we will have "greater social and economic equality" (190).

The writer of an argumentative essay should bear in mind the likely reader of or audience for the essay. If the issue is highly controversial, the reader will probably have an opinion of his or her own about it. A writer who addresses a single reader—say, a college professor or a public official whose confidence one seeks to engage—should estimate what the reader already knows and might think about the issue.

Members of a larger audience may hold conflicting points of view. Writers who address such an audience need especially to rely on the power and conviction of their argued proofs.

---

**QUESTIONS ABOUT AUDIENCE FOR AN ARGUMENTATIVE ESSAY**

1. Am I writing for my professor, my classmates, a broader audience, or a special group of readers?
2. What do my readers already know about the issue? Will I have to explain basic concepts and provide background information for my point of view to make sense?
3. How do I want to come across to my audience—as an objective, scholarly authority, or as someone who identifies with my readers and shares their concerns?
4. Is my audience noncommittal, or have my readers already taken a stand on the issue I am discussing?

---

Answers to these questions tell writers a number of things: (1) how much effort they should expend to attract their audience's attention with the lead sentence and introduction; (2) how much background information they should provide so that their readers will thoroughly understand the issue; (3) how they will address their readers (whether they will be totally objective or use pronouns such as "I," "you," or "we"); and (4) how they will order their presentation and how much space they will devote to opposing views.

---

**WAYS TO SUPPORT YOUR REASONS**

1. Examples:
    a. Based on a similarity to something that happened in the past.
    b. Based on a similar case.
    c. Based on a hypothetical situation.
2. Relevant information:
    a. Facts.
    b. Statistics.
    c. Points of interest.

(continued on the next page)

---

3. Statements, testimony, or other relevant information from acknowledged authorities.
4. Personal experience (be sure the experience relates directly to the reason you are developing).

## INDIVIDUAL EXERCISE ON SUPPORTING ARGUMENTS

To develop full, rich, rounded arguments requires some practice. One can often get this practice by playing with controversial ideas in a creative and free-spirited way.

1. Take an idea, any idea, no matter how preposterous or absurd: for example, "Homelessness is a desirable way of life," "The U.S. government should allow all immigrants to enter this country," "Drugs should be freely available to anyone who wants them," "Communities should have the right to prohibit stores from selling questionable types of rock music," "Public schools and colleges should enforce strict dress codes." Write down the idea in your own words.
2. Write a statement about the opposite point of view.
3. Brainstorm a list of possible reasons to explain the first idea. After that, brainstorm a list of possible reasons to explain the opposite point of view.
4. Decide which reasons are most convincing for each position. Rank them in order of strength of importance.
5. Decide which position is most convincing. State that position as the main clause of an independent sentence. Recast the other position as a subordinate clause linked to the main clause by "because," "although," "despite," or the like. Finally, try to express the relationship between both clauses: What is the connecting link that brings them together?

## COLLABORATIVE EXERCISE ON SUPPORTING ARGUMENTS

1. Here we return to the activity that we initiated above in our discussion on argument in a specialized sense of the word. In your journal or notebook, jot down your views on one of the following controversial issues or on an issue of your choice:
   a. Whether we should buy American-made goods rather than imports.
   b. Whether rap or heavy metal music promotes violence.

c. Whether television damages family life.

d. Whether the United States should extend the school year.

e. Whether cosmetics firms should be allowed to experiment on animals.

Next, state the primary reason you hold your position. Ask yourself two questions: (1) What underlying fact or cause is the basis for my view? and (2) Would someone agree or disagree with my reasoning?

2. Form collaborative learning groups of five students each, as described in the preface, or fashion groups according to your own method. Share your positions and reasons with your classmates.

3. As each student explains the issue and gives his or her position and reason for holding it, the other group members should remain non-committal. In other words, if a student in your group explains why she is in favor of lengthening the school year, pretend that you have no opinion on the issue. From your neutral stance, evaluate your classmate's argument. Have you been persuaded to accept his or her view?

4. When each student's argument has been examined, come to a consensus on what characteristics made arguments either strong or weak. Have the group recorder note your group's conclusions.

5. Reconvene the entire class. Each group recorder should explain the characteristics of strong and weak arguments that the group identified.

## Organizing Argumentative Essays

As history shows, some of the principles of argument that were taught in ancient Greece and Rome have been adapted for writers today. If you were a student in ancient times, you would have been taught to set up your argument in six parts: (1) the introduction (*exordium*), (2) the statement or exposition of the case under discussion (*narratio*), (3) the outline of the points or steps in the argument (*divisio*), (4) the proof of the case (*confirmatio*), (5) the refutation of the opposing arguments (*confutatio*), (6) the conclusion (*peroratio*) (Corbett 25). Today's principles of organization are not quite so rigid or formulaic as the ones prescribed by the Ancients. Nevertheless, most modern writers of arguments use some variation of the following divisions: opening, explanation of the issue, background information, writer's thesis or point of view, presentation of and response to opposing views, reasons for writer's point of view, conclusion.

**ARRANGEMENT OF THE ARGUMENTATIVE ESSAY**

**Introductory Section**

*Opener:* Introduce the topic and interest your reader.

*Explanation of Issue:* Familiarize your reader with the controversy.

*Background:* Give information the reader needs to know fully to understand the issue at hand.

*Thesis:* Give your stand on the issue.

**Body of the Essay**

**Presentation of and Response to Opposing Views**

**Reasons for the Writer's Point of View**

| *Variation A* | *Variation B* |
|---|---|
| 1. Opposing view | 1. Reasons and various types of support for your own view |
| 2. Your response | 2. Opposing view |
| 3. Reasons and various types of support for your own view | 3. Your response |

**Conclusion**

Recap of argument.

Concluding technique.

You can arrange your reasons in several different ways. Many writers prefer to present weaker reasons first and work to a climax by saving their strongest argument until the end of the composition. This movement from weak to strong provides a dramatic effect. Other writers start the body of the essay with their opponents' view; then, in sharp contrast, they present their strongest arguments; finally, they close with their weakest points. This movement begins the essay with an energetic claim that seizes the reader's attention. Still other writers think it best to present a relatively strong argument first, saving the strongest until last; in between, they arrange the weaker ones. This movement combines the dramatic effect of the first pattern with the attention-seizing of the second. Whether you choose to acknowledge and respond to opposing views before you give reasons for your own position or after you present your case depends on the situation and the nature of your audience. There is no hard rule that says that you must arrange your essay one way or the other.

But what if your opponents' objections are especially weighty or substantial? In that case, you may want to arrange the body of your essay in a different way. Instead of, or along with, presenting the conflicting view and your position in separate, self-contained sections, you can respond to the objections in a point-by-point fashion. The box that follows shows an outline of this alternating arrangement.

---

**ALTERNATING ARRANGEMENT FOR ARGUMENTATIVE ESSAY**

**Introductory Section**

*Opener:* Introduce the topic and interest your reader.

*Explanation of Issue:* Familiarize your reader with the controversy.

*Background:* Give information the reader needs to know in order to understand fully the issue at hand.

*Thesis:* Give your stand on the issue.

**Body of the Essay**

1. Position taken in source(s) on one aspect of the controversy.
2. Writer's refutation or support of the position described in 1.
3. Position taken in source(s) on another aspect of the controversy.
4. Writer's refutation or support of the position described in 3. (This pattern continues until you have covered all the aspects of the issue that you choose to focus on.)

**Conclusion**

Recap of the argument.

Concluding technique.

---

Let us return to Sarah Allyn's argument against communitarianism. Since Sarah assumes that a number of her readers will be supportive of communitarianism, she acknowledges and refutes their arguments in paragraphs 3, 4, and 5. Then in paragraphs 6 and 7, she provides further support for her own position.

Here is Sarah's essay.

## SAMPLE ARGUMENT ESSAY

Allyn 1

Sarah Allyn

Professor Kennedy

English 131

30 September 1999

Communitarianism Contested

There exists in America today a growing sense that a breakdown in our moral fiber, an erosion of the values that helped build our nation, has all but dissolved the once mighty American spirit. From those who advocate communitarianism, a movement which seeks to enforce popular social beliefs by communal decree, perhaps this message is heard loudest. Leading proponents of communitarianism such as Harvard professor Amitai Etzioni advocate a position which presupposes such notions as "we are each other's keepers" (Etzioni 31) and "strong rights presume strong responsibilities" (Little 30). Michael Walzer, writing in the academic journal <u>Dissent</u>, claims "empowerment is, with rare exceptions, a familial, class, or communal, not an individual achievement" (Walzer 187). More than mere sloganeers, however, communitarians are working to realize a society bereft of many of the hard-fought liberties achieved in our national Constitution, which set forth to ensure liberty for all Americans. We should keep in mind, moreover, that "communitarian writers are mainly academics, some of whom enjoy close connections to the Washington political community" (Little 30). Are these the voices Americans want speaking for them?

Is the mainstream American population as willing as those from academia's privileged left wing to sacrifice

personal liberty for the greater welfare of the many? To
place their responsibility and duty to others in front of
their personal rights? To uphold the safety of others and
the liberty of the group before considering the claims of
the individual? To sacrifice one's Constitutional rights as
an American citizen--to do so in the name of a socialist
political agenda devised by academics secure enough in their
means to undertake such a radical experiment? Even though
some of the recommendations of communitarian intellectuals
are laudable, few, if any, mainstream Americans will
consider the principles of communitarianism to be a
worthwhile "answer" to our nation's ills.

　　　　As a system of organization, communitarianism is
inherently impractical. In "Multiculturalism and
Individualism," Walzer argues, "Individuals are stronger,
more confident, more savvy, when they are participants in a
common life, responsible to and for other people" (189). If
the recent failure of Communism isn't enough to disprove
Walzer's claim, consider the decline of a redundant form of
communitarianism--labor unions. Labor unions haven't
succeeded for the same reasons that any attempt to galvanize
people according to structure reminiscent of Marxist
principles would be doomed. First, in a democracy, the
majority gets what it votes for, and most likely, existing
forms of political leadership would be prepared to meet any
challenge posed by a communitarian constituency. Second,
communitarian organizations, much like labor unions, would
be extremely vulnerable to excessiveness and corruption.
"Forty years ago, for example, America experienced the
nightmare of McCarthyism. Likewise the memory of the real Ku
Klux Klan" (Etzioni 36). Consider also the disgraceful
spectacle of organized labor's relationship with organized
crime. These examples of communitarianism run awry remain
fresh in the collective American consciousness. Furthermore,
according to Prof. Sanford Levinson writing in the <u>Yale Law
Journal</u>, Americans place such a high value on their

individual rights that "one will honor them even when there
is significant social cost in doing so" (quoted in Little 84).
Lastly, and as Etzioni himself points out, "Americans do not
like to tell others how to behave" (34). For communitarianism
to function as it is intended, heavy emphasis is placed on
individuals' ability to "police" one another, a troublesome
and wholly undemocratic process.

While it may be true that "societies are defined, in
large part, precisely by the mixture of values and beliefs
that both form [their] citizens and are in turn formed by
them" (Seltser and Miller 118), creating a factional, quasi-
governmental system won't serve to advance Americans' common
moral or ethical code. Moreover, along with the complexities
inherent in forging relationships according to a
communitarian model of social behavior, decisions to
determine power accords and their regulation would be left
up to a decentralized governing body. Such potentially great
power represented without the benefit of definitive
leadership could be dangerous. In "Ambivalences in American
Views of Dignity," Barry J. Seltser and Donald E. Miller
uncover a source of conflict that opposes communitarianism's
principles. They explain that "in one important strand of
the liberal political tradition, of course, property is
defined as an extension of the self, as something of myself
that has been mixed in with the physical world and therefore
remains 'mine' in some important sense" (121). This
contradiction alone between democratic and communitarian
ideals makes the prospect of successfully managed
communitarian environments seem all the more unlikely, at
least as long as America intends to remain a democracy.

The advocates of communitarianism, in retreat, resort
to hysteria. In "Morality as a Community Affair," Etzioni,
admonishing his readers about the importance of catering to
the whims and needs of the community, and in rare form,
declares, "The alternative is typically state coercion or
social and moral anarchy" (36). While claiming the only

alternatives "to the exercise of moral voices" are either "a
police state" or "a moral vacuum in which anything goes"
(37), he neglects, however, to mention that with a few rare
exceptions in America's history, such alternatives have not
been seriously considered. This is due to the fact that
America's government, despite its tender age, has exhibited
the greatest degree of stability and success in the annals
of our planet's social order. Preying on "a strong
egalitarian and populist strain" (Walzer 186) such as is
found in America, some communitarians seem merely determined
to stress the negative aspects of our democratic society.
Advocates of multiculturalism such as Walzer believe
"greater social and economic equality" would be the end
result of the adoption of such communitarian principles
(191). He goes on to admit, however, that acting according
to multicultural principles today may bring more trouble
than hope (191). He attributes this to America's weak social
agenda, but this rationalization serves merely as an excuse.

The adoption of communitarianism in America would
necessitate a paradigm shift in our fundamental cultural
construction, from individualism to collectivism. Though
America is no longer a fledgling democracy, there is still
evidence of "rugged individualism" within our culture.
Individualism has played an important role in our national
development. And for many Americans, particularly recent
immigrants, communitarian principles may prove a barrier to
pursuing the American dream. Clearly, communitarianism,
perhaps even in its mildest form, threatens the vitality of
the American populace and poses a potential challenge to
American democracy.

Although indeed most who advocate communitarianism
champion its principles as morally advantageous, still others
disagree. Whereby "its public policy recommendations either
implicitly or expressly call for the attenuation or
even abrogation of certain rights" (Little 30), does not
communitarianism breach the moral foundations of our nation?

Disturbingly, as Little points out, "a recent issue of The
Communitarian Reporter states that the White House is
'seeking to move along communitarian lines,' a fact well
attested by the communitarian substance of many speeches and
writings of President Clinton" (31). "In fairness," Little
continues, "there are signs that Clinton is not a 'purist'
communitarian," though "nevertheless, his communitarian bent
is by definition an anti-constitutional bent" (84). Given
the dubious morality and constitutionality of
communitarianism, it is hard to account for its appeal.
Don't such radical principles actually serve the interests
of the few rather than the many?

Perhaps we ought to be, as Amitai Etzioni stated, "each
other's keepers" after all (31). Democracy is indeed an
efficient system of social checks and balances, a system
which enables Americans to determine their collective
progress or decline. We, as Americans, owe at least this
much to one another: to guard against the debasement of our
personal freedoms, to uphold our long-standing heritage of
individualism and to never relinquish our Constitutional
rights. It is our responsibility, as privileged citizens of
this great nation, to oppose the undemocratic, un-American
ideals set forth by the immoral, unconstitutional, and
unfair theories of communitarianism.

Works Cited

Etzioni, Amitai. "Morality as a Community Affair." The
    Spirit of Community: Rights, Responsibilities, and the
    Communitarian Agenda. New York: Crown, 1993. 30-38.

Allyn 7

Little, Christopher. "Communitarianism, A New Threat for
     Gun Owners." <u>American Rifleman</u> Oct. 1993: 30-31+.
Seltser, Barry Jay, and Donald E. Miller, "Ambivalences in
     American Views of Dignity." <u>Homeless Families, The
     Struggle for Dignity</u>. Urbana: U of Illinois P, 1993.
     118-23.
Walzer, Michael. "Multiculturalism and Individualism."
     <u>Dissent</u> Spring 1994: 185-91.

You will note that Sarah Allyn's paper has followed many of the guidelines we've suggested for argumentative papers. It displays a broad knowledge of ideas that support the concept of communitarian ethics and related issues; it outlines major areas of controversy on the topic, such as the status of personal liberties, factional politics, and multicultural populism; and it articulates a strong thesis that expresses a particular point of view about the issues in question. Sarah's thesis is an oppositional one that takes the source readings to task for compromising personal liberties. An argumentative thesis need not be so negative as this one. In general, a positive argument that expands one's understanding of the source materials succeeds much better than a wrangling altercation. Still, Sarah Allyn leaves no doubt that she has examined the issues and has considered how she wants her audience to respond.

Though we have presented Sarah Allyn's final draft, you should bear in mind that she produced it after several preliminary drafts of its parts and their whole. The following sections describe some additional steps that she followed when she revised her essay.

## Revising the Preliminary Draft

If possible, schedule a conference with your instructor, and if your instructor approves of it, have a classmate or a friend read over your first draft and answer the questions listed below. If no one is available, answer the questions yourself. Keep in mind the following concerns:

1. Move from writer-based to reader-based prose.
2. Vary sentence length.
3. Stress verbs rather than nouns.
4. Use words effectively.
5. Eliminate sexist language.
6. Add your own voice.

---

### QUESTIONS FOR REVISING AN ARGUMENT ESSAY

1. Does the writer organize the discussion around the discernible purpose of persuading or convincing an audience?
2. Does the writer fail to move beyond the purpose of simply synthesizing or comparing or contrasting opposing views?
3. Is the argument two-dimensional, taking into account both sides of the issue?
4. Is the argument one-sided?
5. Does the writer use the conventions (not necessarily in this order) that the reader expects to find in an argument essay?
   a. Explanation of the issue?
   b. Arguable thesis?
   c. Background information?
   d. Support for the position being argued?
   e. Mention of the conflicting position?
   f. Writer's response to the opposition?
   g. Conclusion?
6. Does the writer present reasons rather than opinions?
7. Are the reasons substantiated with evidence and support?
8. Does the writer draw on reliable sources?
9. Does the writer create a favorable, creditable impression of himself or herself?
10. Does the writer display an awareness of the audience's needs by setting a context for the reader?
   a. Giving appropriate background information?
   b. Mentioning authors and titles of sources when necessary?

(continued on the next page)

c. Supplying necessary documentation for sources?

d. Providing clear connectives that differentiate his or her ideas from those of the writers of the sources?

## Editing the Preliminary Draft

When you are satisfied with your revision, read your paper aloud. Then reread it line by line and sentence by sentence. Check for correct usage, punctuation, spelling, mechanics, manuscript form, and typos. If you are using a word processing program with a spell checker, apply the checker to your essay. If you are especially weak in editing skills, try getting a friend to read over your work.

### INDIVIDUAL EXERCISE ON ARGUMENTATIVE ESSAYS

Reread Sarah Allyn's paper. Note the structure of its presentation. After an introduction, Sarah questions whether mainstream America endorses communitarian thought; she points to shortcomings in quotations from its supporters; she cites criticism by its opponents; and she speculates upon consequences that could follow from its adoption. Evaluate the strength of her argument.

### COLLABORATIVE EXERCISE ON ARGUMENTATIVE ESSAYS

1. Form collaborative learning groups of five students each, as described in the preface, or fashion groups according to your own method.

2. Assign each member a paragraph from the body of Sarah Allyn's paper. Ask each to comment on Sarah's use of her sources, the accuracy of her summaries and paraphrases, the relevance of her quotations, and the power of her own reasoning.

3. Reconvene the entire class. Each group recorder should read the members' evaluations and respond to inquiries from the rest of the class about the effectiveness of Sarah's argument.

## ANALYSIS AND EVALUATION: AN INTRODUCTION

To analyze a text is to break it up into its elements or parts. This dissection requires the critical reading strategies that you have been using throughout this book: reading for information; form, organization, expository and stylistic features; and rhetorical concerns. Evaluation marks a further stage in the process. To evaluate a text is to assess its strengths and its weaknesses on the basis of a close analysis.

Professors assign analytical essays because they want their students to apply critical reading strategies to what they read. When they assign evaluative essays, they expect you to base your appraisal on a systematic examination of the material, not on personal opinions or reactions. Analytical and evaluative essays differ from reaction or response essays. As we saw in Chapter 2, the response essay is based on your previous knowledge of and experiences with the topic. *A reaction or response essay focuses on the content of the reading source, but an essay of analysis and evaluation examines how that content is conveyed.*

An evaluation follows from an analysis in that it requires a systematic study and assessment of the reading source. The primary difference between a bare analysis and one that requires evaluation is that the latter judges the strengths and weaknesses of the source according to criteria that are acceptable within the academic community. The analytical essay sets forth an interpretation of the source; it does not necessarily pass judgment on its quality or worth. Another difference between analysis and evaluation is that the evaluation essay has a more persuasive edge to it. It aims to get its readers to agree with its conclusions. An evaluative book review, for example, may affect its readers by inciting them to read the book.

Figure 4-1 indicates some clear-cut distinctions between reaction or response essays and essays of analysis and evaluation.

**Figure 4-1**

| Essay Type | Strategy | Goal |
|---|---|---|
| Reaction or Response (Subjective) | Draw on the knowledge and experiences you bring to the text | Express informed opinions about the subject matter |
| Analysis (Objective) | Draw on an examination of the various elements of the reading source | Interpret how the writer conveys meaning |
| Evaluation (Objective) | Draw on an examination of the various elements of the reading source and judge the elements according to a set of established criteria | Show the relative strengths and weaknesses of the work |

Keep in mind that various academic fields have their own standards for analyzing and evaluating written work. When you take courses in the social sciences, for instance, you will see that the criteria differ from those used in the humanities. Make sure that you keep track of the standards that are presented in the various fields and use them when you read and write in each area.

## WRITING AN ANALYTICAL ESSAY

### Reading the Source and Planning Your Essay

Successful analysis requires careful planning. Assignments that direct you to analyze or evaluate a text are typically harder than assignments that ask you to react, compare and contrast, or argue because they require a more detailed examination of the reading source and a closer observation of the author's writing skills. Without attentive preparation, you may generate an extended summary or reaction instead of an acceptable analysis and evaluation.

### Clarify the Assignment, Set Your Rhetorical Goal, and Consider Your Audience

When you receive your assignment, pay attention to what it asks you to do. Some assignments are open-ended and allow you to determine which aspects of the reading source you will examine. Other assignments may stipulate the parts of the text on which you should focus. For example, a professor might ask you to discuss the role of language in a particular piece or to comment on the structure of a text and explain why it is organized as it is. If you have questions about the type of analysis the assignment calls for, be sure to ask your professor before you proceed.

Once you have clarified the assignment, decide on your rhetorical purpose by asking yourself, "Why am I writing this essay? What effect do I hope to have on my audience?" For an analytical essay, your fundamental purpose should be to explain to your readers your understanding of the reading source and in so doing demonstrate how one or more characteristics of the text contribute to its meaning. For an evaluative essay, you move beyond interpretation into the realm of judgment. Your purpose is to estimate quality or worth. Rather than simply describing how a writer's evidence supports his or her argument, you explain how well the evidence serves the writer's purpose. Rather than simply stating that a writer's position has merit or not, you demonstrate how the writer's language functions. In addition to treating the text's strengths, you may point out its weaknesses.

Your audience may require some background material if your essay is to make sense to them. Ask yourself the following questions:

1. What will my readers already know about the reading source?
2. How much of the source should I summarize, and what form should the summary take?
3. Will I need to explain basic concepts and provide background for the material to make sense?
4. What overall impact do I hope to have on my readers?

If your audience is familiar with the piece, you need to provide only a minimal amount of background information. Summarize parts of the text that are crucial to your thesis. It is not necessary to provide coverage of the entire piece, but only enough to persuade your readers that you have a valid, reasonable interpretation and/or evaluation that will enlighten their understanding.

## Do a First Reading to Get a General Impression of the Text

Your first reading may leave you with little more than a general impression, an overall sense of the topic, the author's approach, and the central point. You probably won't pay much attention to other characteristics of the text unless they are highly conspicuous. At this stage, you may want to freewrite your reactions, especially if the text evokes a strong response.

## Reread and Ask Questions About Analyzing and Evaluating the Text

Analyzing and evaluating a reading source is largely a matter of asking the right questions. The second reading allows you to question, annotate, and take notes. You will work with essentially the same questions about information and content, form, organization, expository and stylistic features, and rhetorical concerns that you have been using throughout this book, but you will make them more probing and more detailed. Your objective is to delve deeper into the material. Don't trust your memory. Write answers to the questions in your journal or notebook. These answers may serve as the basis for your essay.

A typical assignment in literature courses is to analyze a short story, novel, poem, or play. Literary analysis proceeds in much the same way as other types of analysis by requiring the student to determine how form, organization, stylistic features, and rhetorical elements contribute to meaning. The additional requirement for analyzing poetry, drama, or fiction is that you must consider certain special characteristics of literary texts, the most common of which are theme, plot, characterization, setting, and point of view.

The following questions serve two functions. They help you break down the text into its principal components, and they help you develop a structure for your paper. The italicized questions are phrased in a way that encourages you to evaluate as well as interpret. Record your answers to these questions in your journal or notebook.

---

### QUESTIONS FOR ANALYZING AND EVALUATING TEXTS

**Questions About Information and Content**

1. What is the author's thesis—the central point he or she is making about the topic?
2. *Is the thesis plausible? defensible? illuminating?*
3. What other important points are made?
4. *Do the other important points follow logically from the thesis?*
5. What aspects of the topic has the author chosen to emphasize?
6. What aspects does he or she disregard?
7. *Is the author emphasizing appropriate aspects of the topic? Does he or she disregard important aspects or put too much emphasis on certain points?*
8. Does the author acknowledge and refute the views of individuals who might oppose his or her argument?
9. What types of evidence does the author use to support his or her points? (For a review of various types of evidence, see pp. 110–11).
10. *Does the author use a sufficient amount of evidence to support his or her points? Which points need more support or explanation?*
11. Do the author's conclusions follow logically from the evidence?
12. *Are there places where the reader has difficulty seeing the connection between the evidence and conclusions?*

(continued on the next page)

---

13. *Are the conclusions accurate? Do they have direct implications for readers, or do they have limited applicability and usefulness?*

### Questions About Form, Organization, and Expository and Stylistic Features

#### Form

1. Does the writer use an identifiable form? In this textbook, you have already examined certain essay types: response, comparison and contrast, and argument. Other recognizable forms of nonfiction are editorials, news stories, feature articles, biographies, autobiographies, and letters to the editor.
2. How does the form contribute to the argument?
3. *Is the form appropriate for the content? Would the writer have been better able to convey his or her message in another form?*

#### Organization

1. What is the organizational pattern: (1) time order, narration, process; (2) antecedent-consequent, cause-effect; (3) description; (4) statement-response; (5) comparison/contrast (either point-by-point or block structure); (6) example; (7) analysis/classification; (8) definition; (9) analogy; (10) argument (including position, reasons, opposition, and refutation); or (11) problem-solution?
2. *Is the organizational pattern clear and well conceived?*
3. How does the organizational pattern contribute to the meaning of the piece?
4. *Would the meaning be better represented if the parts were arranged differently, for example, if the thesis were disclosed in the introduction instead of the conclusion; if the narrative had progressed from past to present instead of present to past; if reasons were ordered from most important to least important instead of vice versa?*

#### Expository and Stylistic Features

1. What are the recognizable characteristics of the text, and how do they help convey the author's point?
2. Does the author use any memorable or significant devices that enable you to see the subject from a new perspective? To answer these

(continued on the next page)

questions, look closely at features such as language, sentence elements, images and scenes, and references and allusions.

Language

a. Does the writer's language serve to heighten and illuminate the topic, or is it merely adequate?

b. Does the writer use precise wording, vivid details, words that appeal to the senses, and words with emotional intensity?

c. Does the writer use figurative language (for example, similes, metaphors, personification) to explore the subject?

d. *Is the figurative language appropriate or confusing, inexact, or misleading?*

e. *Is the author's vocabulary unnecessarily formal or pompous? Does he or she use strange or unusual or overly technical words where common ones would do?*

Sentence Elements

a. Are you struck by rhythmic, balanced, symmetrical, or graceful sentences, or are they disorganized and awkward?

b. How do these sentences help to convey the meaning of the text?

c. *Is the author concise, or does he or she try to pack too many ideas into long, sprawling sentences?*

Images and Scenes

a. Does the writer create memorable images (mental pictures) and scenes that contribute to the meaning of the text?

b. *If the author creates images and describes scenes, do they vivify the text or are they superfluous?*

c. *What would be gained if the author included more images?*

d. *What would be lost if the images were left out?*

References and Allusions

a. Do the writer's references or allusions illuminate or add significantly to the subject matter? Take account of the writer's formal references to other written sources as well as other types of references and allusions. (An allusion, not to be mistaken for "illusion," is a reference to some literary, cultural, or historical piece of

(continued on the next page)

information, whether through direct or indirect citation, that taps the reader's knowledge or memory.)

b. *What would be lost if the references and allusions were left out?*

c. *Are the references to other written sources welcome additions to the text, or do they appear to be superfluous?*

d. *Are the other sources timely, or does the author rely on outdated information?*

## Questions About Rhetorical Concerns

1. What is the writer's persona or stance (attitude or rhetorical posture), and how does it contribute to his or her point?

2. *Is the author's persona or stance suitable, or does it detract from the piece?*

3. How does the writer's voice contribute to effectiveness?

4. *Are the voice and tone appropriate or unnecessarily pompous or formal?*

5. *Does the author come across as authoritative, creditable, and reliable, or are you left with questions about his or her background, prestige, political or religious orientation, or overall reputation?*

6. *Is the author impartial, or does he or she appear to be biased?*

7. *Does the author supply the reader with sufficient background information, or does he or she make erroneous assumptions about the reader's previous knowledge?*

## ADDITIONAL QUESTIONS FOR FICTIONAL SOURCES

### Theme

1. What theme or central idea does the author express in this piece? (The theme registers the main idea of the piece. It is comparable to the thesis in a work of nonfiction, except that it is rarely stated in one or two sentences. Like a thesis, a theme implies a subject and a verb. You would not say that "justice" is the theme of a work; rather, you would say that the theme is "justice prevails even in the face of adversity.")

2. *Does the theme make an important statement about the subject, or does it contribute only minor insights?*

(continued on the next page)

## Plot

1. What types of conflicts occur while the plot is unfolding? (The plot refers to the pattern of events, or story line. It involves a conflict of some kind, usually between a person and another person, nature, social forces, or destiny. The struggle comes to a head in a moment of crisis.)
2. When does the conflict come to a head?
3. *Does the plot evolve in a realistic way, or is it too unpredictable or even preposterous?*
4. *Does the plot focus on the problematic issues, or does it drive them into the background?*
5. *Is there enough conflict in the story, or is there so little conflict that a plot hardly exists?*

## Characterization

1. Which techniques of characterization does the author use: (a) describing characters and commenting on their actions; (b) depicting characters in action and reserving commentary; or (c) showing how actions and emotions affect characters internally, without authorial commentary?
2. *Does the author create lifelike characters or mere cardboard figures or caricatures?*
3. *Are the characters complex, or are they two-dimensional characters that lack depth?*
4. *Are the characters dynamic (that is, they are changed by their actions or experiences) or static (characters who do not appear to change at all)?*

## Setting

1. How does the setting contribute to the piece? Which elements— time, scenery, location, characters' occupations or lifestyles—are most influential?
2. *Does the author include all the elements (for example, time, locale, scenery, characters' occupations) that are needed to develop the theme, or does he or she omit crucial background information?*
3. *Does the setting advance the ideas in the text, or does it work as a foil against them?*

(continued on the next page)

### Point of View

1. From what point of view is the story told: (a) an omniscient narrator who is aware of everything that is happening; (b) a first person narrator who tells the story as he or she experiences it; or (c) a limited point of view in which the story is told in the third person but presented through the eyes of a single character?
2. *Is the point of view appropriate to the issue that the author is exploring?*
3. *Does the point of view distort the issue in any way?*
4. *How would the story change if it were told from a different vantage point—for example, if the author wrote from the perspective of a first-person narrator instead of an omniscient narrator?*

## Review Your Answers to the Questions for Analysis

After you have finished rereading and responding to the questions, pause to organize your thoughts while the answers are still fresh in your mind. As you review your notes, keep in mind that your rhetorical purpose is neither to interpret nor to evaluate the piece for your readers.

1. Look to see if a particular question has produced a lengthy, substantive response. If this is the case, you might want to go for depth rather than breadth and focus your analysis on a single, prominent feature.
2. See whether you are able to group together answers that pertain to similar categories. Grouping your answers will help you make sense of the particular issue you are dealing with.
3. Select two or more elements for your focus. Instead of zeroing in on a single, substantive response or categorizing several related responses, you can focus on two or more dominant concerns in the text.
4. Return to the relevant parts of the text to check for supporting material. Each time you make a point about a textual feature, your essay should provide textual evidence in the form of a quotation, a paraphrase, or a summary. At this juncture, go back to the reading and mark passages you might use to support your points. If you cannot find enough textual evidence, consider changing your focus.

## Deciding on an Organizational Plan

You can organize your essay in any number of ways. The important thing is to keep your rhetorical purpose in mind. Four typical patterns of organization are presented here.

1. Cause and Effect

   Here you can show how the writer's stylistic features create rich layers of meaning in the text.

   *Thesis:* In "Everyday Use," the imagery and descriptive language reinforce Alice Walker's depiction of Maggie's transformation from a backward and repressed character to a selfless and compassionate sustainer of family traditions.

   *Essay Structure:*

   1. Introductory paragraph(s).
   2. One to two paragraphs explaining how imagery reinforces the transformation.
   3. One to two paragraphs explaining how figurative language reinforces the transformation.
   4. Concluding paragraph.

2. Comparison and Contrast

   This arrangement permits you to draw specific points of comparison or difference between textual elements or themes.

   *Thesis:* Although Alice Walker's "Everyday Use" initially depicts Dee as more progressive than Maggie about reviving her cultural roots, it eventually shows that Maggie has better absorbed her family's deepest cultural values.

   *Essay Structure:*

   1. Introductory paragraph(s).
   2. One or two paragraphs comparing and contrasting Dee's expressive nostalgia for the past to Maggie's quiet sense of continuity with the past.
   3. One or two paragraphs comparing and contrasting Dee's self-absorption with Maggie's open-minded practicality.
   4. Concluding paragraph.

3. Structure of the Reading Source

   This pattern shows the complex structural organization of the reading source by following its order. You take up each feature in the sequence in which it is presented in the text.

   *Thesis:* Throughout "Everyday Use," Alice Walker reveals Dee's shortcomings and weaknesses as opposed to Maggie's understanding and inner strength.

*Essay Structure:*

1. Introductory paragraph(s).
2. Paragraph demonstrating the characters' respective strengths and weaknesses at the beginning of the story.
3. Paragraph demonstrating the characters' respective strengths and weaknesses in the middle of the story.
4. Paragraph demonstrating the characters' respective strengths and weaknesses at the end of the story.

4. Argument

   Here you can structure your analysis and interpretation along the lines of the argument essays we discussed on pp. 113–14. If your goal is simply to persuade your readers that you have found significant meaning in the text, you will be writing an argument in the broad sense, stating your position and offering reasons to support it.

   *Thesis:* Alice Walker's description and figurative language contribute significantly to her representation of continuity and tradition in a family's self-understanding.

   *Essay Structure:*

   1. Introductory paragraph(s).
   2. One or two paragraphs giving reasons why the descriptions offer significant contrasts between superficial display and genuine self-understanding.
   3. One or two paragraphs giving reasons why the figurative language reinforces significant insights into self-understanding.
   4. Concluding paragraph.

The usual structure for an evaluation essay is some variation of the format used for an argument. You can write a unidimensional argument in which you

1. State your thesis and the three or four criteria that you will use to evaluate the source.
2. Allocate one or more body paragraphs to each criterion, developing each with specific evidence from the source.

Another possibility is to construct a two-dimensional argument. This structure allows you to acknowledge points of agreement between you and the author of the reading source and at the same time assess the source's strengths and weaknesses.

1. State your thesis, agreement, and the criteria that you will use to evaluate the source's strengths and weaknesses.
2. Allocate a paragraph or two acknowledging the source's strengths, substantiating your claims with evidence.
3. Allocate paragraphs to discussing the weaknesses.

The four patterns of organization may be used individually, or they may overlap. In Chapter 12, Isaac Kramnick and R. Laurence Moore's "Is America a Christian Nation?" uses both the argument pattern and the structural organization of the reading source—Pat Robertson's "America, a Christian Nation"—that it is evaluating. Toward the beginning of their article the authors acknowledge that the principal framers of the American political system had a serious investment in religious issues: They crafted a national government that separated church from state "despite their enormous respect for religion, their faith in divinely endowed human rights, and their belief that democracy benefited from a moral citizenry who believed in God" (paragraph 4). They then summarize the arguments of Pat Robertson and others that the Constitution does not pose a wall of separation between church and state, and they evaluate Robertson's claim: "History and victories won through the course of our American past tell us that he is wrong" (paragraph 15).

## Drafting

After you have decided upon an organizational plan, you are ready to compose a preliminary draft of your essay. Remember that this will not be a final, polished draft. You will have an opportunity to revise it at a later date. Before you begin writing, consider how you want to come across to your readers. Will you subordinate your voice to the text you are analyzing by focusing on the expository features and stylistic techniques particular to the text? Or will you offer a personal interpretation, using the first-person pronoun and evoking experiences and expectations familiar to you and your audience but not necessarily to the writer of the text you are analyzing? The degree of formality or informality may be dictated by the assignment. If you are unsure about taking a particular stance, ask your professor for advice.

As you draft your essay, you may want to consult the sections on paper openers, introductions, and conclusions in Chapter 2. After you have arranged the notes that you took on the questions, convert them into body paragraphs in accordance with your organizational plan. Be sure that as you develop each paragraph, you support your points with evidence (quotations, paraphrases, or summaries) from the reading source.

A further consideration is that you adhere to the special conventions that academic writers follow when composing argumentative, analytical, and evaluative essays.

1. Use the present tense when explaining how the author uses particular procedures and writing techniques.
2. Identify the author of the source by first and last name initially and thereafter only by the last name.
3. Indent long (four or more lines) quotations in block format.

The following student essay by Philip Nekmail analyzes Alice Walker's story "Everyday Use" in this anthology (see Chapter 13). Read the story before you read Philip's essay. As you examine the student essay, bear in mind the strategies for writing an analytical essay that we have discussed, and ask whether the student writer has followed those guidelines.

### SAMPLE ESSAY OF LITERARY ANALYSIS

Nekmail 1

Philip Nekmail

Professor Smith

Academic Writing II

15 May 2003

A Daughter's Entitlement in Alice Walker's "Everyday Use"

Simple yet complex, Alice Walker's portrayal of a domestic dilemma in "Everyday Use" pits moral value judgments against contradiction. With this, the assumptions, the values, and the individuality of each character are evoked. The main characters in the story, Mama, Maggie, and Dee, though members of one family, display contradictions evident in each of their roles as well as within themselves.

Mama, the story's narrator, makes known her stature in life while describing each of her two daughters, Dee and Maggie. Her pride in Dee, though repressed, could perhaps be equated with her pity for Maggie, the less fortunate of the two girls. While her sister visits, Maggie "will stand hopelessly in corners, homely and ashamed" (629), whereas for Dee, "'no' is a word the world never learned to say to her" (629).

By her own definition, Mama is "a large big-boned woman with rough, man-working hands" (629). Simple, practical, and traditional, she is neither quick to assume, nor soon to forget her past. This aspect of her nature emerges when she and her daughters focus upon the value of the two quilts. They see the quilts from dissimilar worlds and vantage points. Dee sees them as objects of artistic value while Mama and Maggie see them as household items of economic and practical utility. Thus, Mama's own assumptions and judgments about the value of the quilts define her individuality. The two quilts may be for Mama the closest link to her past that she holds.

Dee's attitude toward the quilt as a mere art object reveals her lack of respect for the deeper meaning of the quilt as a sign of tradition. In changing her name to evoke a remote imagined past, Dee actually rejects the tradition of her immediate family past. In doing this, she offends Mama and the very principle--her heritage--which the quilts signify. Mama's practical nature is evinced in her intent to give the quilts to Maggie who will "probably be," according to Dee, "backward enough to put them to everyday use" (635). This, of course, was Mama's intent to begin with.

Maggie, the pitied, undervalued member of the family, maintains a low profile throughout the story, achieving a quiet victory over Dee in acquiring the two quilts. Maggie's assumptions concerning the quilts' value are made evident

when she tells her mother, "'She [Dee] can have them, Mama,'
she said, like somebody not used to winning anything, or
having anything reserved for her" (636). In her simplistic
nature, then, Mama is at odds with the sophisticated Dee and
in accord with simple Maggie.

A sense of entitlement, a display of arrogance, and a
flair for style are not so much the factors that denominate
the differences between Dee and her family. It is the
hypocrisy, the contradiction that is the very nature of Dee
that sets her apart. Her personality traits belie those of
her mother, for where Mama is simple, Dee is complex; where
Mama is practical, Dee is impractical, stylish, and in
disregard of the tradition her mother so values. Immediately
observable is Dee's assumption of her entitlement to
anything she pleases. Mama's refusal to grant Dee the quilt
signifies a turning point in her life, as Dee's sense of
entitlement is undoubtedly a learned behavior. It is Dee's
lack of reverence for tradition that offsets the balance she
has achieved between herself and her mother. Most central in
the story is Dee's decision to change her name. Not only
does this offend Mama, but it is also an offense to her
heritage. ". . . you was named after your aunt Dicie," Mama
says. "Dicie is my sister. She [is] named Dee" (633).

Through contrasts of simplicity and complexity,
"Everyday Use" highlights the interplay of morality and
judgment versus contradiction. The congruence of attitudes
between the mother and Maggie clashes with the hypocritical
nature of the stylish, educated Dee. Maggie's selfless
character overpowers Dee, whose disregard for family
tradition and heritage proves to be her ultimate downfall.
Through the conflict that arises over the quilts, the
uniqueness, the assumptions, and the values of each
character become evident.

Nekmail 4

Work Cited

Walker, Alice. "Everyday Use." <u>Writing in the Disciplines: A</u>
    <u>Reader for Writers</u>. 5th ed. Mary Lynch Kennedy, William
    J. Kennedy, and Hadley M. Smith. Upper Saddle River, NJ:
    Prentice Hall, 2003. 628-37.

You will notice that Philip Nekmail's essay has followed many of the guidelines we've suggested for writing analytical essays. It probes the story's organization and form for clues about the characterization of Dee and Maggie; it describes different perspectives on Dee's self-absorption and Maggie's openness as elements in the narrative's conflict; and, finally, it considers the author's point of view on Maggie's respect for tradition as the story's dominant focus.

Though we have presented the final draft of Philip's essay, you should remember that he produced this paper after several preliminary drafts, both in part and in whole. The following sections describe some additional steps that Philip followed when he revised his writing.

### Revising the Preliminary Draft

Schedule a conference with your professor (see p. 92), or if your instructor agrees, make arrangements to have a classmate or a friend review your preliminary draft and give you feedback. If that is not possible, set the paper aside for a few days and then review it yourself. Respond to the questions given in the following box.

---

**QUESTIONS FOR HELPING A WRITER REVISE THE FIRST DRAFT OF ARGUMENTATIVE, ANALYTICAL, AND EVALUATIVE ESSAYS**

1. Can you identify the writer's rhetorical purpose? Is the writer giving you an interpretation of the source and in so doing explaining how certain characteristics contribute to its meaning?

(continued on the next page)

---

2. Does everything in the draft lead to or follow from some dominant meaning? If not, which ideas seem to be out of place?

3. Do you understand the analysis, and is the writer sensitive to your concerns?

   a. Does he or she provide necessary background information about the subject and enough summary of the source as well as the title and the author? If not, what is missing?

   b. Throughout the essay when the writer refers to the source, does he or she supply you with necessary documentation?

   c. Does the writer provide clear transitions and connecting ideas that differentiate his or her own ideas from those of the author?

   d. Does the writer display an awareness of the author by referring to the author by using names and personal pronouns ("Smith states," "she explains") rather than personifying the source ("the article states," "it explains")?

4. Which organizational format does the writer use: cause and effect, comparison and contrast, argument, or the order of the source? If another pattern is used, is it appropriate for an analysis essay?

5. Has the writer made you aware of the bases for the analysis? On which characteristics of the source is the analysis focused? If the bases for the analysis are unclear, explain your confusion.

6. Does the writer support each of his or her points with direct evidence (quotations, paraphrases, summaries) from the source? If not, where are they needed?

7. Does the writer provide smooth transitions and connecting ideas as he or she moves from one point of analysis to another? If not, where are they needed?

8. Do you hear the writer's voice throughout the essay? Describe it.

9. What type of paper opener does the writer use? Is it effective? If not, why not?

10. Does the paper have an appropriate conclusion? Can you suggest an alternative way of ending the essay?

11. Is the title suitable for the piece? Can you suggest an alternative?

12. Has the writer followed academic writing conventions, such as

    a. Writing in present tense when explaining how the author uses particular procedures and techniques?

    b. Identifying the author initially by first name and last name and thereafter only by last name?

    c. Indenting long quotations in block format?

## Editing the Preliminary Draft

When you are satisfied with your revision, read your paper aloud. Then reread it line by line and sentence by sentence. Check for correct usage, punctuation, spelling, mechanics, manuscript form, and typos. If you are using a word processing program with a spell checker, apply the checker to your essay. If you are especially weak in editing skills, try getting a friend to read over your work.

### INDIVIDUAL EXERCISE ON ARGUMENTATIVE, ANALYTICAL, AND EVALUATIVE ESSAYS

Reread Philip Nekmail's paper. Note its structure. After an introduction, the writer recounts features of Mama's characterization, then of Dee's, and finally of Maggie's. Then he shows how Dee's values differ from Mama's and Maggie's. Throughout this analysis, he quotes specific words and phrases that imply the narrator's tone toward the characters. Evaluate how thoroughly Philip Nekmail has analyzed these expository and stylistic features in the fiction.

### COLLABORATIVE EXERCISE ON ARGUMENTATIVE, ANALYTICAL, AND EVALUATIVE ESSAYS

1. Form collaborative learning groups of five students each, as described in the preface, or fashion groups according to your own method.
2. Assign each member of a group a character's perspective or point of view from which to examine the story—Mama's, Dee's, Maggie's, the narrator's, the reader's. Ask each member to comment on how carefully Philip Nekmail has analyzed the story from that particular point of view.
3. At the end of the small-group session, the recorder should have an assessment of how well the student writer has analyzed each perspective.
4. Reconvene the entire class. Each group recorder should read the list of assessments. Discuss points of agreement and difference.

### WORKS CITED

Corbett, Edward. *Classical Rhetoric for the Modern Student*. 3rd ed. New York: Oxford UP, 1990.

Elbow, Peter. *Writing without Teachers*. New York: Oxford UP, 1973.

Etzioni, Amitai. "Morality as a Community Affair." *The Spirit of Community: Rights, Responsibilities, and the Communitarian Agenda*. New York: Crown, 1993. 30–38.

Little, Christopher. "Communitarianism, A New Threat for Gun Owners." *American Rifleman* Oct. 1993: 30–31.

Seltser, Barry Jay, and Donald E. Miller, "Ambivalences in American Views of Dignity." *Homeless Families, The Struggle for Dignity*. Urbana: U of Illinois P, 1993. 118–23.

Walzer, Michael. "Multiculturalism and Individualism." *Dissent* Spring 1994: 185–91.

C H A P T E R

*five*

# Writing Research Papers

## THE RESEARCH PAPER: AN INTRODUCTION

Research involves collecting information from multiple sources and then acting on that information by organizing, synthesizing, analyzing, generalizing, or applying it. Often, we connect the term "research" with scientific and medical discoveries, but it applies to systematic investigation in any discipline, including the humanities and the social sciences. Professors typically assign research papers to make you an active, independent scholar who is able, first, to locate other people's ideas and, second, to analyze and synthesize those ideas and come to an independent conclusion. In a sense, studying research methods is learning how to learn.

In Chapters 1 through 4, we have stressed that the writing process involves active engagement, careful thought, and hard work, and the same is true for research. Research involves more than just finding and recording information. A collection of facts on a topic may mean little to an audience without explanation, organization, and commentary. It is difficult even to locate appropriate sources in the library without planning and thinking about what you want to find. Writing the research paper involves those tasks as well as all the other writing processes and strategies you have learned in this book. The clerical work of compiling a list of facts is only a small part of the overall process.

Although research begins with examining other people's ideas, it can develop into a highly creative activity. Bringing together information

142

from different sources can help you come to new conclusions that are entirely your own.

## IDENTIFYING A RESEARCH TOPIC

The process you go through to identify a research topic depends upon the specificity of your assignment. If your assignment is focused, you may be able to begin searching for materials right away. Here is a focused assignment from a psychology course: "Write a three-page summary of the psychological literature on dance therapy published during the past year." This assignment tells you that you need to consult the past year's issues of psychological journals and look for articles on dance therapy. If you receive an open-ended assignment, however, you may not know where to begin the search for information. Consider the following assignment that our student Jennifer Piazza received in an upper-level psychology course entitled "Counseling: Theory and Dynamics": "Write a ten- to fifteen-page research paper that expands upon one of the topics covered in our textbook or class lectures. Use at least ten sources of information, not including the textbook."

Jennifer cannot proceed to the library before she narrows the focus of this very general assignment. She must think through the subject areas covered in class and isolate one topic, or better yet several, that might become the focus of her paper. Two of the prewriting strategies we described in Chapter 1, freewriting and brainstorming, can help identify possible research topics. Jennifer might brainstorm a list of words and phrases in response to the assignment and then read over the list and look for similarities, patterns, and connections. Alternatively, Jennifer might freewrite nonstop for ten minutes, using any cues in the assignment to generate ideas, and then search her freewriting for useful ideas. The following is an excerpt from Jennifer's freewriting.

> The chapter on counseling trauma victims was especially interesting to me. I'm currently working as a volunteer with Suicide Prevention and Crisis Services, and many of the hotline calls I answer are from people who are coping with the result of a traumatic experience. Perhaps if I did my research paper on trauma, I would learn something that would be of direct benefit to my hotline clients. But I'm not sure how I could add anything to what the textbook presented except maybe to add more details about the theory. Perhaps I could write about how current ideas about dealing with trauma are different from what was previously believed. Our textbook chapter started with Freud,

so I could research what was believed about trauma before Freud and try to show how the theory developed over time. One topic that I wish the textbook had said more about was how talking through a traumatic experience is helpful in dealing with it. I know that my hotline clients feel better after they are able to get the experience off their chest by describing it fully. In my Personal Essay class, I wrote about a particularly traumatic event in my own life: When I was four, a close relative was diagnosed with cancer and in response to the news, my family really freaked out. I was terrified to see adults in this condition, and no one fully explained to me what was going on, so I couldn't make sense of it at all. I felt a strong sense of relief when, fifteen years later, I was able to relive the experience on paper and explain my emotions. Perhaps I could do research on the therapeutic effects of "reliving" traumatic experiences in conversation or on paper.

As she rereads her freewriting, Jennifer realizes that she would like to learn more about the two topics discussed in the freewriting excerpt: the history of psychic trauma theory and current therapies for trauma, in particular the use of verbal expression as a therapeutic response to trauma. She decides to focus her initial research on these areas.

Another way of zeroing in on a research topic is to consult general subject headings in indexes (see pp. 160–163) related to your broad subject area (biology, music, psychology, and so forth). You could also ask your professor to suggest topics within his or her discipline. Follow your interests. The research and writing process will be more successful and rewarding if you identify a topic that appeals to you.

Try to come up with several alternative topics because the one you initially select may not be practical for research. For example, you might inadvertently select a topic that is treated only in scholarly literature, material that you might have difficulty understanding because of your unfamiliarity with the methodology, analytical techniques, and specialized vocabulary associated with the discipline. You might also choose a topic that requires information resources that are difficult to obtain; the books, magazines, or newspapers that you need may be unavailable in your college library. You might even identify a topic that cannot be researched because no literature exists that addresses it; not every issue in a particular discipline attracts the interest of scholars. Preliminary research may show that an initial research question is naive and must be modified accordingly. If you have several possible topics in mind before you begin to do research, you will be able to abandon those that aren't feasible.

## DEVELOPING A RESEARCH STRATEGY

Once you have defined a topic, you need a plan of attack that will guide your search for information. We call this plan your research strategy. Before you begin to look for sources, think about the goals for your research. What are you trying to accomplish and how long will it take you? What questions are you trying to answer and how will you know when you have found the answers? How will you find information on your topic? Think about these concerns before you begin your search.

Make sure that your research strategy is flexible enough to accommodate the unexpected. In practice, research often does not proceed as planned. You may need to change your goals during the research process.

### Allocate Sufficient Time for Research

As you plan a research project, make sure that you allocate sufficient time. Of course, the amount of time you need to set aside depends upon the scope of your assignment. If the instructor provides the narrowed topic and requires one or two sources, you may need just a single visit to the library and you might begin the process only a week before the paper is due. However, for an assignment that asks you to design your own topic and draw on ten or more sources, you would be wise to begin a month before the due date. You must always allow for the unexpected in research assignments. Even the most knowledgeable researchers can encounter difficulties that require more time than they had anticipated. Since Jennifer must focus her own topic and locate at least ten sources, she begins four weeks before the due date and assumes that she will make four or five visits to the library.

### Identify Research Questions

In Chapter 1, we encouraged you to become an active reader with clear goals for reading rather than a passive reader who sees the words on the page but does not process them. Similarly, you should be an active researcher who does not merely look up information but rather uses research to answer specific questions about topics. Before you begin to look for sources, try to list the questions that you hope your research will answer. Here are some of the questions that interest Jennifer concerning trauma therapy:

1. What did Freud's predecessors say about the cause of and treatment for trauma? How did Freud's theory differ? To what extent do psychologists still accept Freud's theory concerning trauma?

2. How does current psychological theory explain the impact of traumatic experiences?

3. What therapies are available for victims of psychic trauma? Which are most effective?

4. According to psychologists and communication experts (writing and speech), what role does the verbal expression of traumatic experiences play in the recovery process?

5. Do victims of psychological trauma receive adequate attention in the mental health system?

## Brainstorm a List of Terms or a Search Vocabulary

To look up information in the library, you will need to use words or phrases associated with your topic as you search the library catalog, indexes to periodicals, and reference works. Before you go to the library, brainstorm a list of words or phrases associated with your topic. Anticipate the words that might be used to describe or categorize the subject. These are the terms you will look up when you use the catalogs and indexes. Jennifer brainstorms the following list of search terms that might help her find information on trauma therapy:

1. Trauma or shock
2. Traumatic experiences
3. Freud and trauma
4. Psychology and trauma
5. Writing and trauma
6. Verbal expression (communication) and trauma
7. Trauma therapy
8. Trauma counseling
9. Post-traumatic stress disorder (or syndrome)
10. Traumatic neuroses
11. Trauma and the mental health system

Be expansive and list as many terms as you can. Then add to your list when you locate sources that suggest additional terms. You need a rich list of search terms, since it is often hard to guess which ones will give you access to the information you want.

### INDIVIDUAL EXERCISE ON RESEARCH STRATEGY

Think of research papers you have written in the past. How did you isolate a topic? What planning did you do before attempting to locate sources? How were your activities during the early stages of the research process either different from or similar to our descriptions of identifying a topic and developing a research strategy? Freewrite for ten minutes in response to these questions.

### COLLABORATIVE EXERCISE ON RESEARCH STRATEGY

1. Form collaborative learning groups of five students each, as described in the preface, or fashion groups according to your own method.
2. Decide on a topic of mutual interest that your group might want to research. Do not take more than two or three minutes to come to a consensus. (The instructor might choose to assign research topics.)
3. Working together, generate a list of research questions that pertain to your topic. Then brainstorm a list of search terms that might help you locate information on this topic.
4. Reconvene the entire class. Each group recorder should identify the group's topic, read the lists of research questions and search terms, and describe any problems that the group encountered with its particular topic.

## VIRTUAL LIBRARIES

Ten years ago, students and scholars working on research papers would typically spend many hours in academic libraries locating and reading source material. Libraries housed the actual books, periodicals, and other sources of information that researchers needed as well as the indexes and catalogs that helped the researchers locate these sources. Advances in electronic information technology that occurred over the last decade have made it possible for students and scholars to conduct much of their research without actually going to a library. Using networked computers in their dorm rooms or offices, researchers can connect to their academic libraries' electronic catalogs and to commercial periodical indexes to which their libraries subscribe. Thus, without ever entering a library, researchers can compile lists of books, periodical articles, and other sources relevant to almost any topic. In some cases, online systems provide the complete texts of sources, so students may find that they can complete all the research for relatively short projects without traveling to the library at all. As full-text periodical access grows and more book-length works become available online, it will undoubtedly become possible to conduct more extensive research from homes and offices.

The explosive growth of the World Wide Web has also affected how students and scholars conduct research. This vast collection of electronic texts, graphics, and sounds covers every imaginable topic. Most academic libraries now provide World Wide Web access, and many sources that are appropriate for academic research are available in full-text versions on the Web.

## USING ELECTRONIC RETRIEVAL SYSTEMS

Whether you are searching your college library's online catalog, an electronic version of a periodical index, or the World Wide Web, you will need to understand certain principles of online searching. Database software often gives users the impression that electronic searching is simple. The software invites users merely to type in words or phrases that describe what they are looking for and then provides lists of information sources. Despite this impression of simplicity, researchers who want to take maximum advantage of online information systems need to know how search software operates.

### How Computerized Information Retrieval Systems Function

You begin searching an electronic database by typing in a "query," which is typically several words that are related to your topic of interest. In response, the retrieval system attempts to match the query with relevant information sources in the system's database. While systems vary in their precise search strategies, most compare the specific words in queries to indexes or word lists compiled from all the information sources. Some indexes are created by subject-area professionals who read sources and then assign indexing terms that describe their contents; others are merely lists of all the words that occur in the text of the source, often ranked by frequency.

In addition to subject indexes, systems may include indexes based on a variety of bibliographic elements. While author, title, and subject are the standard indexes available for searching library catalogs, many systems index other items, such as publication date, language, personal name, geographic name, and source type (book, video, sound recording, and so forth). Often, you can examine several indexes with a single query; for example, you could search for sources on writing about trauma that were published since the year 2000. In databases that provide the full texts of magazine, journal, or newspaper articles, the words used within each article may be indexed so that you can actually search the articles' contents.

You can narrow a search by specifying a particular index, or you can broaden the search by choosing the "free-text" or "keyword" options that instruct the system to examine all available indexes for matches to the query. In many information systems, free-text searching is the default mode that is automatically offered to users, and in these cases, you must select "expert," "advanced," or "power" search options if you want to limit searches to particular indexes.

Each item in a retrieval system index points to one or more electronic "records" for individual sources that are related to the index item. A record contains a description of a source and an indication of where it can be found. In some cases, for instance when searching the World Wide Web, the record may provide a direct electronic link to the complete version of the source. (See Figure 5-1 for a schematic of these relationships.)

It is important to understand that computerized retrieval systems do not, for the most part, possess "artificial intelligence." They are merely word-matching tools and cannot make even the simplest inferences about your intentions. Don't expect the system to do any of your thinking for you. In addition, most retrieval systems cannot correct for

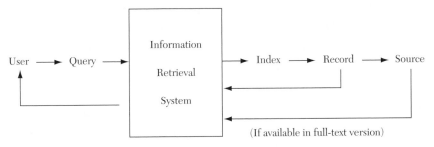

Figure 5-1

misspelling or adjust for variations in spelling. Distinctions that may seem insignificant to you, such as the difference between "first" and "1st," may be crucial when using a computerized system.

## Recall versus Relevancy

The terms *recall* and *relevancy* are used to describe how information retrieval systems respond to queries. If a system provided perfect recall, then it would, in response to a query, retrieve every source in the system's database that was related to the specified topic. If the system was perfect with regard to relevancy, then every source retrieved would be precisely the type of information specified in the query. Typically, an information search involves a trade-off between recall and relevancy. Maximizing recall will help ensure that relevant sources are not overlooked but may retrieve irrelevant material as well. Maximizing relevancy will help assure that the sources retrieved are useful but may pass over other sources that would also be of interest to the researcher.

Balancing recall and relevancy becomes particularly difficult when you are working with a very large database, such as the World Wide Web. A broad search that maximizes recall will retrieve thousands of sources, far more than you can carefully review, but searching for very specific terms may fail to retrieve the material within the database that would best serve your purposes. For example, imagine that you are writing a research paper on whether or not human cloning should be legal in the United States. If you use the term "human cloning" to search the World Wide Web, you might retrieve thousands of information sources, only some of which would be relevant to your particular topic. However, if you used a more exclusive query such as "human cloning regulation," you would probably retrieve useful sources concerning legal restrictions on cloning but might overlook more philosophical pieces on the wisdom of allowing human cloning.

With very large databases, perhaps the best strategy is to conduct four or five relatively narrow searches, trying out a range of search terms. This technique may help zero in on relevant sources but will expand recall beyond what would be achieved with a single query.

## Keyword Searching

When you are using a printed index based on an alphabetical arrangement, you need to know the initial word of a subject heading or title in order to locate it, but a computerized *keyword* search will locate one or more words in any position within the subject heading or title. For example, let's assume our student Jennifer Piazza intends to look up "trauma therapy" in a title index. Using an electronic index, she can locate all titles that include the words "trauma" and "therapy," but with a paper index she finds only titles that begin with "Trauma Therapy." It is often useful to search titles for key words or phrases since a title is a good indicator of a source's content. Keyword searching is also advantageous for subject indexes because it allows you to retrieve a reference without knowing the exact wording of the subject heading. For instance, a keyword search for "welfare reform" would retrieve the subject headings "public welfare reform," "reform, welfare," and "reform, public welfare" as well as "welfare reform" and "Welfare Reform Reconciliation Act of 1996."

A disadvantage of keyword searching is that it has the potential to draw in a great many irrelevant sources because the words in the query are matched to the index without regard to context. For instance, a keyword title search for "Grateful Dead" would retrieve the article entitled "Anti-Union Bill Dead in Committee: Autoworkers Grateful for Senator's Pivotal Vote." Some retrieval systems, however, allow you to search for exact phrases, for strings of words that appear in a particular order. For example, an exact phrase search for "Grateful Dead" would only retrieve index items in which the word "Dead" immediately followed the word "Grateful." Exact phrase searches are typically specified by placing the target words in the query within quotation marks.

### Truncation

Computerized retrieval systems often allow you to truncate or shorten search terms. Instead of typing in the search statement, "Politically Correct Movement," you might enter "Political? Correct?" The "?" or "*" are commonly used in retrieval systems as truncation symbols. This query would retrieve "Politically Correct Movement," "Political Correctness," and other variations on this terminology. It is often wise to truncate words in search statements, particularly when you are unsure of the precise indexing terms used in the database.

### Boolean Searching

By using the Boolean operators AND, OR, and NOT, you can create a very specific search request that takes full advantage of electronic searching. For example, we mentioned earlier that you can restrict a search to a particular publication year. To limit a search by subject and by year, you would use the Boolean operator AND in your search statement. Let's assume that you want information on the national debate over welfare reform that occurred in 1996. If you enter the subject heading (SH) Welfare Reform, the Boolean operator AND, and the publication year (PY) 1996, the computer will respond as shown below:

### What the Researcher Types:

(SH = Welfare Reform) AND (PY = 1996)

### How the Computer Responds to the Query:

1. Creates a list of all items that have a subject heading (SH) "Welfare Reform."
2. Creates a list of all items that have a publication year (PY) of 1996.
3. Compares List 1 and List 2 and creates a new list of all items that both have "Welfare Reform" as a subject heading *and* were published in 1996.
4. Returns to the researcher the total number of items in List 3 and, if requested, the reference for each item in List 3.

The Boolean AND sometimes confuses researchers, since they associate the word "and" with addition and thus think that the operation will increase the number of sources retrieved. The Boolean AND actually places more restrictions on searches and usually cuts down on the number of hits. The Boolean operator that is used to increase the number of sources retrieved is OR. The expression (SH = Welfare Reform) AND (SH = Occupational Training) would retrieve only articles that covered both welfare reform and job training efforts. On the other hand, the expression (SH = Welfare Reform) OR (SH = Occupational Training) would locate articles that focused just on welfare reform and articles on job training only, along with articles that covered both topics.

The Boolean operator NOT excludes specific items from the retrieval process. For example, the expression (SH = Welfare Reform) NOT (SH = Occupational Training) would identify articles on welfare reform but would exclude articles that concerned job training.

You can use Boolean operators in algebraic expressions to piece together complex search statements such as the following: ((SH = Welfare Reform) OR (SH = Occupational Training)) AND (PY = 1996).

## THE LIBRARY OR THE WORLD WIDE WEB?
## CHOOSING A RESEARCH SITE

Without a doubt, the growth of the World Wide Web has made it easier to locate certain types of information. For instance, if you play the guitar, you can, in a few minutes, find Web sites that provide product information on new and used guitars, chords for the latest songs, and a discography for your favorite guitarist. All this information might take hours to collect without the help of the Web. The Web works well in this case for several reasons. Since thousands of amateur musicians and music fans use the Web to share information, its popular music resources are vast and will probably cover any guitar, song, or guitarist that you are interested in. Also, search queries about guitars, guitar music, and guitarists are relatively easy to formulate, since they are based on straightforward names (Fender, "Voodoo Child," Jimi Hendrix) rather than descriptions of content. Finally, as an amateur guitarist, you are looking for information that is interesting or useful but may not be concerned with precise accuracy. For example, you would be satisfied with playable chord progressions that sound acceptably close to the original songs rather than completely authentic musical transcriptions.

Unfortunately, the World Wide Web does not work as well for academic researchers as it does for hobbyists. One difficulty is that books and academic journals remain the standard vehicles for scholarly communication, and these publications are not necessarily available on the Web. Thus, there is no guarantee that the Web will provide access to the important scholarly resources on any given topic. Another problem is that academic research usually involves searching by subject matter rather than by proper name, and the Web is not arranged for efficient subject searching. Given its huge size, haphazard organization, and poor indexing, it may be difficult to locate material on a particular subject even if it is, in fact, available on the Web. On the other hand, relevant information may be buried in long lists of information sources that contain the vocabulary in your search statement but are not actually useful to you. For example, if Jennifer, in her research on trauma therapy, used the query "trauma" on the Web, it might steer her to the Web page of the Discoteca Trauma, a nightclub in Barcelona, Spain.

A final difficulty is that academic researchers care very much about reliability and accuracy, but the Web has no effective quality control. Any individual or group can establish a Web page and disseminate any information that they choose, except for content that is in clear violation of the law. Some Web pages may use graphics that appear very professional but include content that is merely uninformed opinion. Of course, print sources can also contain unreliable content, but the Web has expanded tremendously the opportunity for "publishing" material that has no basis in fact. Consequently, subject searches conducted on the Web often direct the researcher to Web sites that do not provide reliable information. The issues of reliability and objectivity are further complicated by the commercial nature of many Web sites. For instance, the search term "trauma" will likely provide a great many links to the business Web pages of psychologists, psychiatrists, and social workers who specialize in trauma therapy and use the Web to advertise their services. While some of these commercial sites may provide information that is useful to a researcher, they may also be biased and manipulative. Even the standard Web search engines, the electronic retrieval systems that are used to search the Web, are produced as commercial ventures and may intentionally steer you to certain information providers who have paid the search engine companies to highlight their Web sites.

In contrast to the World Wide Web, a college library collection is developed specifically to serve the needs of academic researchers. Books, periodicals, and other materials are chosen either by librarians who specialize in collection development or by faculty members who are experts in particular fields of study. Because the collection is built systematically, an academic library collection is much more likely to include the seminal works in a particular discipline, whereas the Web does not discriminate between expert and uninformed opinion. Your library may also include special collections for certain programs of study that are highlighted at your college. Currently, relatively few books are available in full-text online versions; thus, with the exception of periodicals, most of the scholarly sources in your college library's collection are probably not available online.

Another advantage of conducting research in your college library is that you can get help from the reference librarians. The major responsibility of these information professionals is to help students and faculty members with their research questions. Reference librarians can show you how to use your own library's collection but also how to access sources that are available online from remote sites, including material on the World Wide Web. In most cases, a few minutes spent discussing your research needs with a reference librarian will be more productive than hours of surfing the Web.

A final advantage of academic libraries is that they provide the sophisticated searching tools that you will need to conduct scholarly research. In your college library, you will find a catalog of the library's holdings that will likely be available on a computerized system. In some cases, the catalog will provide electronic links to other libraries from which you can obtain material via interlibrary loan. Your library will also have electronic and print versions of periodical indexes that will help you locate information in journals, magazines, and newspapers. Whether you use electronic or print versions of catalogs and indexes, these resources allow you to conduct far more precise searches than is possible with the access tools available on the World Wide Web.

While we have stressed the advantages of using your college library and recommend you begin your research there, we do recognize the importance of the Web to researchers. Many of the same sources available in academic libraries can be accessed in electronic form over the Web, and some sources are available only online. The Web is particularly useful when you are trying to locate a specific source that you have identified in an index but that is not available in your own library. For example, as we were researching the topic of virtual reality for Chapter 7, we found a reference in an online database to an article in a journal called *Japan Echo*. Our area libraries did not have this journal in their collections, so we conducted a quick Web search and found a home page for this publication that included full-text English language copies of past issues. If you know exactly what source you are looking for, the Web may provide convenient and free access.

---

### ADVANTAGES OF THE WORLD WIDE WEB FOR RESEARCHERS

- 24-hour, 365-day availability
- continuous updating
- vast resources
- coverage of virtually all topics
- convenience, "one-stop shopping"

### ADVANTAGES OF ACADEMIC LIBRARIES FOR RESEARCHERS

- expert collection development and quality control
- systematic organization

(continued on the next page)

- careful indexing
- expert staff of reference librarians
- extensive collections of book-length sources
- commitment to scholarly inquiry and objectivity

## LOCATING INFORMATION IN AN ACADEMIC LIBRARY

If you intend to use an academic library to do research, you must first familiarize yourself with the facility. Libraries vary dramatically in how they organize their collections and how they provide access to materials. Before you attempt to do any research, get a guide or a map that shows how your campus library is organized. Make sure you know where your library's reference desk is located. Do not confuse it with the circulation desk, the place where items are checked out. The librarians at the reference desk will provide one-on-one research assistance. Your library reference department may also offer library orientation sessions, reference-skills workshops, and credit-bearing courses on information resources. Take advantage of opportunities to learn about your library early in your academic career.

### INDIVIDUAL EXERCISE ON LIBRARY ORIENTATION

Take a self-guided tour of your college library. Start by locating the reference desk. Find out what days and hours reference librarians are available and what services they provide. Find out how the collection is organized. Does your library use the Library of Congress or the Dewey decimal classification system? Are periodicals shelved with books or separately? Are other formats (recordings, microfilms, and so on) shelved separately? Are there any subject-specific (music, science, and so forth) libraries on your campus? You should be able to answer these questions based on materials that you can obtain at the reference desk. Now tour the library and make sure you can find the principal elements of the collection.

### COLLABORATIVE EXERCISE ON LIBRARY ORIENTATION

1. Form collaborative learning groups of five students each, as described in the preface, or fashion groups according to your own method.

2. Pick an area of the library that your group will investigate from the following list. Groups should not duplicate one another's choices so that as many areas as possible will be covered.

   Reference collection
   Book collection (main stacks)
   Microforms collection
   Magazine and journal collection
   Sound recordings collection
   Video collection
   Newspaper collection
   Any discipline-specific collection

3. Proceed to the library from class or arrange a time that your group can meet in the library for about an hour.

4. When you arrive at the library, work together to answer the following questions concerning your area: What resources are available? What services are available?

5. Reconvene the entire class. Each group recorder should read the group's answers to the two questions and respond to any inquiries from the class about the part of the library collection that the group investigated.

## The Library Catalog

The library catalog contains a description of each item in the collection and indexes items by subject, title, and author. Catalogs typically list not only books but also periodicals (magazines, journals, and newspapers), pamphlets, sound recordings (reel-to-reel and cassette tapes, LPs, and compact discs), sheet music, microforms (microfilm, microfiche, and microcards), motion pictures, video recordings, computer data files, images (graphics and photos), three-dimensional artifacts, and maps. Note that the central library catalog provides the titles of periodicals (*The New York Times, College English, Newsweek,* and so forth) and date range of holdings for periodicals but does not describe individual articles. On pages 160–163 we explain how to find particular periodical articles on a given subject.

In most academic libraries, the catalog is computerized and can be searched by subject, title, or author according to the principles described on pages 147–152. Your library houses computer workstations linked to the online catalog, but the catalog may also be accessible from other computer workrooms across campus or even from your dorm room. The following example (Figure 5-2) is a computer catalog entry that Jennifer located in her research on trauma therapy:

TRAMA AND RECOVERY

| | |
|---|---|
| Author: | ● Herman, Judith Lewis, 1942- |
| Title: | ● Trauma and recovery / Judith Lewis Herman; [with a new afterword by the author.] |
| Physical description: | ● xi, 290 p. ; 21 cm. |
| Publisher: | ● New York : BasicBooks, c1997. |
| Subjects: | ● Post-traumatic stress disorder. <br> ● Post-traumatic stress disorder--Treatment. |
| Notes: | ● Originally published:[New York, N.Y.]:BasicBooks,c1992. <br> ● Includes bibliographical references(p.[248]-281) and index. |
| OCLC number: | ● 36543539 |
| ISBN: | ● 0465087302 |
| System ID no: | ● ACW-2893 |
| Holdings: | ● LOCATION:General Stacks--CALL NUMBER : RC552.P67H471997 <br><br> ● c.1 Available |

| Search Author | Search Title | Search Subject | Search Keyword | Search Numbers | ILL Forms |
|---|---|---|---|---|---|

Figure 5-2   Sample Computer Catalog Entry

Notice that the sample computer catalog entry includes a "call number" for the item: RC552.P67 H47 1997. This number indicates the item's subject area and its shelving location. You are probably familiar with the Dewey decimal call numbers used in most primary and secondary schools. College libraries typically use the Library of Congress system rather than the Dewey decimal system, and the call number in Figure 5-2 is based on the Library of Congress system.

The initial parts of either Library of Congress or Dewey call numbers indicate the general subject area. The following chart lists the basic Library of Congress subject areas and the corresponding Dewey subject headings.

| *Library of Congress* | *Dewey* |
|---|---|
| A—General Works | 000—Generalities |
| B—Philosophy, Psychology, and Religion | 100—Philosophy and related disciplines |
| C—Auxiliary Sciences of History | 200—Religion |

| | |
|---|---|
| D—General and Old World History | 900—History; Geography |
| E–F—American History | |
| G—Geography; Maps; Recreation; Anthropology | |
| H—Social Sciences (Economics, Sociology) | 300—Social Sciences |
| J—Political Science | |
| K—Law | |
| L—Education | |
| M—Music | 700—The Arts |
| N—Fine Arts | |
| P—Linguistics; Languages; Literature | 400—Language<br>800—Literature |
| Q—Science | 500—Pure Science |
| R—Medicine | 600—Applied Science; Technology |
| S—Agriculture | |
| T—Technology | |
| U—Military Science | |
| V—Naval Science | |
| Z—Bibliography; Library Science | |

Books and other materials are shelved systematically by call numbers. As an example, let's consider the parts of the call number for Herman's *Trauma and Recovery:*

$$\text{RC} \quad 552.P67 \quad H47 \quad 1997$$

On the library shelves, books are alphabetized according to the letters indicating the general topic area, RC in the example above. Within each general topic area, items are arranged in ascending numerical order according to the topic subdivision, in this case 552.P67. For books, items within the subdivision are arranged alphabetically by the first letter of the author's last name and then numerically by an additional filing number. In our example, H is the first letter of Herman's name and 47 is the additional filing number. Finally, 1997 is the book's date of publication. Call numbers can get more complex than our example indicates, but the same filing and shelving principles that we just described always apply. Call numbers not only provide a shelving address for an information source but also assure that items on the same topic will be stored together. Thus, if you locate one item on your subject, you may find others shelved nearby.

## Periodical Indexes

As we mentioned in the previous section, the central library catalog lists titles of periodical holdings but does not provide information on the individual articles that these periodicals contain. The tools used to access periodical articles are developed by commercial companies that sell their indexes to academic libraries. You are probably familiar with the *Readers' Guide to Periodical Literature,* an index that is often available in high school and public libraries either in print or electronic form. The *Readers' Guide* surveys over 200 popular magazines as well as a selection of specialized journals and assigns each article to one or more subject areas. Articles are also indexed by the authors' names. The *Readers' Guide* is a good index for college researchers who want nonscholarly articles on topics of general interest. InfoTrac's *Expanded Academic Index,* an electronic retrieval tool, is another general interest index that is commonly available in college libraries. The *Expanded Academic Index* provides access to articles in over 1,000 magazines and journals and covers many of the periodicals available through the *Readers' Guide.*

Using the *Expanded Academic Index,* Jennifer enters the search term "Trauma" and finds that a number of subject headings contain this word, (see Figure 5-3). Jennifer selects the subject headings "Psychic Trauma," "Psychic Trauma in Children," and "Rape Trauma Syndrome," which seem closest to her topic. She finds that the "Psychic Trauma" subject heading has twenty topical subdivisions; she selects the "care and treatment" subdivision and views the entries. Figure 5-4 is an excerpt (one computer screen) from the twenty references listed under the "care and treatment" subheading. Jennifer peruses the lists of sources under each of the subject headings and subheadings that seems relevant. For titles that look promising, she views the complete records for the articles, which include publication information and, in some cases, the full texts of articles.

There are scores of different periodical indexes, available both in paper and electronic forms, which vary widely in topic area and in organizational structure. Whereas the *Expanded Academic Index* covers a vast range of subject areas, *PsycInfo,* another database Jennifer consults in her research on trauma therapy, focuses on literature in psychology and related disciplines. Some indexes, such as the *Readers' Guide,* are relatively

Return to: EasyTrac Expanded Academic ASAP

? Subject Guide     New Database     New Search

**Subjects containing the words:** trauma

**Trauma Care Systems**
See Trauma Centers
**Trauma Centers**
View 73 articles
See also 26 subdivisions
**Trauma Disorders, Cumulative**
See Cumulative Trauma Disorders
**Trauma Records**
View 6 articles
**Trauma Units**
See Trauma Centers
**Trauma, Physical**
See Wounds and Injuries
**Trauma, Psychic**
See Psychic Trauma
**Acoustic Trauma**
View 1 article
**American Trauma Society**
View 1 article
**Blunt Trauma**
View 59 articles
See also 15 subdivisions
**Burn Trauma**
See Burns and Scalds
**Cumulative Trauma Disorders**
View 94 articles
See also 24 subdivisions
See also 1 related subject
**Penetrating Trauma**
See Penetrating Wounds
**Psychic Trauma**
View 121 articles
See also 20 subdivisions
See also 1 related subject
**Psychic Trauma in Children**
View 41 articles
See also 13 subdivisions
**Rape Trauma Syndrome**
View 13 articles
See also 1 related subject
**Blunt Force Trauma**
See Blunt Trauma

Figure 5-3    Expanded Academic Index™.
© 1998 Information Access Company.

Return to:
Subject Guide

Expanded Academic ASAP

Citation List

New Database

New Search

**Citations 1 to 20**
**Subject:** Psychic Trauma **Subdivision:** care and treatment

☐ **Fifteen-month follow-up of eye movement desensitization and reprocessing (EMDR)**
Mark **treatment for posttraumatic stress disorder and psychological trauma.** Sandra A.
Wilson, Lee A. Becker, Robert H. Tinker.
*Journal of Consulting and Clinical Psychology* Dec 1997 v65 n6 p1047(10)
View extended citation and retrieval choices

☐ **Is EMDR being held to an unfair standard? Rejoinder to Van Ommeren (1996).** (eye
Mark movement desensitization and reprocessing)(response to article by M. Van Ommeren, Professional
Psychology: Research and Practice, vol. 27, p. 529, 1996) Ricky Greenwald.
*Professional Psychology, Research and Practice* June 1997 v28 n3 p306(1)
View abstract and retrieval choices

☐ **Need and responsiveness in the treatment of a severely traumatized patient: a**
Mark **relational perspective.** (Case Study) Mary E. Connors.
*American Journal of Psychotherapy* Wntr 1997 v51 n1 p86(16)
View abstract and retrieval choices

☐ **From fragmentation to wholeness: an integrative approach with clients who**
Mark **dissociate.** Marye O'Reilly-Knapp.
*Perspectives in Psychiatric Care* Oct-Dec 1996 v32 n4 p5(7)
View text with graphics and retrieval choices

☐ **The interpersonal dynamics and treatment of dual trauma couples.** Dennis Balcom.
Mark *The Journal of Marital and Family Therapy* Oct 1996 v22 n4 p431(12)
View abstract and retrieval choices

☐ **Treating the traumatic memories of patients with dissociative identity disorder.**
Mark Richard P. Kluft.
*American Journal of Psychiatry* July 1996 v153 n7 pS103(8)
View abstract and retrieval choices

☐ **Trauma management therapy: a preliminary evaluation of a multicomponent**
Mark **behavioral treatment for chronic combat-related PTSD.** (Post-Traumatic Stress Disorder)
B. Christopher Frueh, Samuel M. Turner, Deborah C. Beidel, Robert F. Mirabella, Walter J. Jones.
*Behaviour Research and Therapy* July 1996 v34 n7 p533(11)
View extended citation and retrieval choices

☐ **Letting go of bitterness and hate.** Mary M. Baures.
Mark *The Journal of Humanistic Psychology* Wntr 1996 v36 n1 p75(16)
View abstract and retrieval choices

Figure 5-4   Expanded Academic Index™.
© 1998 Information Access Company.

straightforward and self-explanatory, but others, such as the print version
of the *MLA International Bibliography,* can be baffling to the novice. You
may need the help of a reference librarian the first time you attempt
to use a specialized index. Other examples of periodical indexes and data-

bases include *Book Review Digest, Business Index,* ERIC (Educational Resource Information Center, a database), *Film Literature Index, General Science Abstracts, GPO Monthly Catalog* (federal publications), *Humanities Index, Index to Legal Periodicals, Medline* (health and medicine), *Music Index, National Newspaper Index, PAIS International* (Public Affairs Information Service), *Social Science Index, SPORT Discus* (athletics), and *Contemporary Women's Issues.*

Often, periodical indexes provide abstracts of articles, which are short summaries of articles' contents. Keep in mind that abstracts are intended only to help researchers decide which articles are most relevant to their interests; they are not meant to circumvent careful reading of the relevant articles. Do not rely on abstracts as information sources; they are only access tools. It is considered academically dishonest to cite an article in a research paper if you have read only an abstract and did not obtain the article's full text.

Academic libraries often provide electronic versions of periodical indexes. A major advantage of electronic indexes is that they often cover more than one year of publication. With one command to the computer, a researcher can find references to articles on a particular subject over a several-year period. With paper indexes, the same search would involve looking up the topic in index volumes for each of the desired years. Your library may devote specific computer workstations to one or several selected electronic periodical indexes or may link all its electronic indexes together so that they can all be accessed, along with the library's online catalog, from each library workstation. These services may be accessible from computer workrooms outside the library or even from your dorm room depending upon the characteristics of your college's computer system.

As more periodicals are becoming available in electronic form, many academic libraries are cutting back on the number of paper or microform periodicals in their collections and instead providing online access to periodicals. Your library may have computer workstations where students can locate periodical articles, view them in full-text versions, and print out articles of particular interest.

### INDIVIDUAL EXERCISE ON LOCATING SOURCES

Select a topic or use one assigned by your professor. Go to the library and locate two books and two periodical articles on your topic. Use a computerized access tool, either an online catalog or a CD-ROM database, to find at least one of these sources, and if possible, have the computer print out the record for the source. Photocopy the table of contents of the book or periodical, and on the photocopy, circle the chapter or article that is relevant to your topic. Submit the computer printout and the photocopies to your instructor.

## COLLABORATIVE EXERCISE ON LOCATING SOURCES

1. Form collaborative learning groups of five students each, as described in the preface, or fashion groups according to your own method.
2. Come to a consensus on a topic you would like to research, or use one assigned by your instructor.
3. Assign each group member one type of information resource: general reference, discipline-specific book, magazine, newspaper, or professional journal.
4. Proceed to the library from class or go individually outside of class time. Find a source on your topic that represents the particular type of information resource that you were assigned. Photocopy the table of contents of the book or periodical, and on the photocopy, circle the chapter or article that is relevant to your topic.
5. Reconvene your group at the next class meeting. Have each group member report on the source he or she found. Then discuss which types of resources seemed most useful for your topic and what further research would be necessary to actually write on your topic.
6. Reconvene the entire class. Each group recorder should explain the group's topic and summarize the group's discussion of sources on this topic.

## CONDUCTING RESEARCH USING THE WORLD WIDE WEB

On pages 153–156, we explained some limitations of the World Wide Web as a research tool. In general, we suggest that you begin your research in your college library or another library in your area rather than on the World Wide Web. Once you have conducted at least your preliminary research in a library, you may be able to use the Web to good advantage.

If you are using the World Wide Web as a primary research tool, you can attempt to minimize its problematic aspects by observing several principles:

1. Read all the help screens or searching tips that accompany the particular search engine you are using. Each search engine has its unique

characteristics, which you must understand if you are to take full advantage of its potential.

2. Familiarize yourself with the expert or advanced searching options. When you start up most search engines, they are configured for simple keyword searches of all available indexes. All too often, these keyword searches yield thousands of hits, most of which are not useful. In order to refine your search and take advantage of features such as Boolean operators, you may need to shift to advanced searching mode.

3. Try your query on several different search engines. Given that the Web search engines are not precise research tools, it often helps to experiment with several and find which responds best to your particular query.

4. Look for electronic sources that have comparable print versions and steer away from sources that have no print equivalents. Unsubstantiated opinion does sometimes appear in print, but as a general principle, information that finds its way into print is more reliable than that which is available only on the Web.

5. Evaluate the reliability of Web sources. As we mention on page 168, researchers should always question the reliability of any source they locate, even if it comes from an academic library. It is, however, particularly important to evaluate critically Web-based information sources. With the computer tools currently available, anyone can create a very professional-looking Web page and then stock it with content that is completely absurd. Ask yourself the following questions about Web sites:

- What is the overall goal of the Web site? Do the authors of the Web site have motives other than presenting the objective truth? For instance, does the site attempt to advocate for a particular political agenda or to sell a product?

- Is the site produced by a reputable organization? Does it provide a mailing address and phone number? Does it invite inquiries?

- Do the authors of the Web site identify themselves? Do they provide any evidence of their expertise or credibility? For example, do they possess training or experience in the topic area covered by their site? Do they demonstrate that they are aware of the standard scholarly or professional literature in the topic area?

- Do the authors distinguish between opinion and fact? Do they provide nonanecdotal evidence to substantiate their conclusions? Do they cite published sources?

- When was the site created? How often is it updated? When was it last updated?

## COLLECTING INFORMATION ON YOUR OWN: SURVEYS AND INTERVIEWS

In most cases, the bulk of the material you use in research papers will come from published sources; however, depending upon your topic and assignment, it might be appropriate to use information that you collect personally through informal interviews and surveys. For example, imagine you are writing a research paper for a psychology class on how birth order (only child, first born, last born, and so on) affects personality. The psychological literature contains numerous studies on this topic, but you might also interview selected students in your dorm who represent each of the birth order positions and use these "cases in point" in your paper as concrete illustrations of the conclusions reached in the psychological studies. You might also survey twenty or thirty students representing a range of birth orders to see if their perceptions of the relationship between birth order and personality match the research findings.

Of course, informal interviews and surveys provide only anecdotal information and are not a reliable basis for any firm conclusions. Still, anecdotes are often useful for explaining a concept to an audience or for framing an interesting introduction or closing for a research paper. Informal surveys may help you sharpen your research question or identify trends that may warrant more careful investigation. While an informal survey is not sufficient to challenge the conclusions of published studies, it can be useful to note a significant difference between informal and published research results. For instance, imagine that a student researcher conducts an informal survey in a college dorm on the interaction between birth order and personality. If the results of this informal survey differ from published conclusions, then the student might suggest in his or her paper that additional formal research should be conducted to see if the published conclusions still hold for the current college-age population.

A final advantage of conducting informal surveys and interviews is that they get students directly involved with the topics they are researching. This hands-on approach may help increase student interest, particularly for topics that seem rather dry based on the published sources alone. Even if students do not end up using any of the anecdotal information they collect in their research papers, the experience of getting actively involved with the topic will lead to a better final product.

Whenever you conduct informal interviews or surveys, keep in mind the following principles:

1. Make sure you comply with any college regulations concerning use of human subjects. While these regulations are typically used with more formal research studies, it is possible that your college does have guidelines even for informal interviews and surveys. Check with your instructor if you are unsure of your college's human subject policies.

2. Whatever your college's policies are, make sure you respect the privacy of your interview or survey subjects. Do not repeat their responses in casual conversation, and do not use subjects' actual names in your research paper unless there is a clear reason to do so and you have their permission.

3. Establish clear goals for your questions. Interview or survey questions should have one of the following goals:
   - Establishing facts
   - Recording beliefs about what is fact
   - Recording personal feelings or values

4. Try asking the same question worded in several different ways. Sometimes, a slight change in wording will prompt a different response from a subject. It is often difficult to predict what precise wording will convey your question most effectively.

5. Don't ask questions that betray a bias. For example, imagine you are surveying or interviewing first-born children to research a possible link between birth order and personality. You would indicate a bias if you asked, "In what ways did your parents and older siblings spoil you?" A more neutral question would be, "What personality characteristics distinguish you from your older siblings?"

6. Do not press anyone who seems reluctant to undergo an interview or to complete a survey. Many people do not want to discuss their personal lives, particularly when someone is taking notes on what they say.

## MODIFYING YOUR SEARCH STRATEGY

Research, by its very nature, is a creative process that exposes new approaches and gives rise to new ideas. As your research proceeds, you may find that you want to modify your topic (if the assignment allows you to define your own topic), your research schedule (you may require more trips to the library than you initially anticipated), your research questions, or your search vocabulary.

Consider how Jennifer has to modify her search strategy. Recall her initial research questions:

1. What did Freud's predecessors say about the cause of and treatment for trauma? How did Freud's theory differ? To what extent do psychologists still accept Freud's theory concerning trauma?

2. How does current psychological theory explain the impact of traumatic experiences?

3. What therapies are available for victims of psychological trauma? Which are most effective?

4. According to psychologists and communication experts (writing and speech), what role does the verbal expression of traumatic experiences play in the recovery process?

5. Do victims of psychological trauma receive adequate attention in the mental health system?

Jennifer decides to drop questions 3 and 5. She realizes that question 3 is too broad for a ten- to fifteen-page paper, since it involves surveying and evaluating all the therapeutic techniques used in working with trauma victims, and she has found from her research that a wide range of treatments is available. She eliminates question 5 because it is not addressed directly in any of the sources she has located so far. In addition, Jennifer has discovered that questions 2 and 4 fit together because recent psychological theory, particularly that grounded in research on brain physiology, highlights the therapeutic value of communication, and as a result of the reading she has done so far, she has become particularly interested in these questions. She believes that her research on question 1 may fit into an introductory section of the paper that will provide historical context.

You will likely modify your search vocabulary as your research becomes more focused. Indexes, catalogs, and specific information sources will suggest additional search terms to you, and you may decide to eliminate from your list terms that are not productive. Remember that you will need to come to the library equipped with as many search terms as you can. Indexing vocabularies vary considerably, and thus, for a given topic, you may need different search terms as you move among indexes.

## EVALUATING INFORMATION SOURCES

As you search for source material, you are constantly judging whether or not the information you find has direct relevance to your topic. Don't excerpt information that is only remotely related to your topic. As you locate and work with sources, ask yourself how they fit in with your overall goals for the research paper. To what parts of the topic do the sources pertain? What perspectives on the topic do they represent? Try to make sense of the sources as you examine each one rather than waiting until you have completed your research.

In addition to evaluating the sources' relevance to your topic, you should also judge their comparative quality. We discussed on page 154 some concerns with the reliability of sources found on the World Wide Web, but even library materials come with no absolute guarantees. Too many students have complete confidence in any source they find in a library.

As you analyze sources, it is always helpful to speculate on the author's rhetorical purpose, as we described in Chapter 1. What are the author's reasons for writing? Who is the author's intended audience? How does the author want to influence that audience? The answers to these questions will help you understand the source better and figure out whether it is appropriate for your paper. For instance, if you are writing for a science course on the future of nuclear power, you may be skeptical of information from lobby groups for the nuclear industry. If you think about writers' motives, you will be able to put their ideas in a proper perspective.

## EXCERPTING INFORMATION FROM SOURCES

The basic skills for excerpting information from library sources—paraphrasing, summarizing, and quoting—are covered in Chapter 1 of this book. Here, we will discuss the special problems associated with the sheer number of sources you are working with for a research paper. A common problem is that a researcher loses track of the exact source for an important piece of information. Each time you excerpt a passage from a source, whether you handcopy, reword, or photocopy, make sure that you carefully record a complete citation to the source. You will need to record the exact page numbers where specific pieces of text are located. When you draft your paper, you will cite the source as well as the page for each paraphrase, summary, and quotation. In the appendix, we give essential citation formats. For books, you will need to record author(s), title, publisher, city of publication, date of publication, and pages where the information you excerpted is located. For magazines and newspapers, record author(s), title of article, name of magazine, date (day, month, year), inclusive pages for entire article, and pages where the information you excerpted is located (the section number or letter is needed for multisectioned newspapers). For scholarly journals, you will need to record the same information as for magazines and newspapers as well as the volume number.

Another common difficulty is failing to distinguish adequately between paraphrases and quotations in research notes and thus including an author's exact words in the research paper without quotation marks. This is an unintentional yet serious form of plagiarism. Be very meticulous about your use of quotation marks as you take notes. Read once again our discussion of plagiarism on page 17.

There is also a danger of excerpting too much information. Some students compulsively collect every scrap of information that is remotely related to their topics, thinking that they will make sense of it all at their leisure. Don't bury yourself in paper, whether it is note cards, pages of notes, or photocopies of sources. Excerpt only what you think you might use. As we remarked earlier, research is a sense-making process. It is hard to make sense when you are overwhelmed with information.

Much has been written on how you should record the information that you excerpt from sources. Some textbooks strongly recommend index cards for research notes because cards can be grouped and regrouped easily. Of course, you can cut up pages from your research notebook or photocopies of sources and group these pieces just as you can note cards. Another alternative is to record your research notes on a computer and use word processing or outlining programs to organize the information. We recommend that you try various methods of recording excerpts and decide what works best for you. In addition to notes that record specific pieces of information or individual concepts, you should keep a separate set of notes for preliminary thesis statements, organizational plans, or other important ideas that occur to you during the process of research.

## WRITING A PRELIMINARY THESIS

After you have collected enough sources to form generalizations about your topic, work on a preliminary thesis. The purpose of the preliminary thesis is to focus and direct your research. You may have a working thesis in mind when you begin researching. If not, one may emerge as you collect information. You can generate a thesis from your research notes by (1) scanning your research notes quickly, noting any general trends, main concepts, or overall patterns; (2) freewriting for ten minutes on what you think your research might tell your reader; and

(3) reducing your freewriting to several sentences that explain what you want to say to your reader.

After scanning her research notes, Jennifer freewrites the following paragraph:

Freud's initial work on trauma led to the Seduction Hypothesis, the suggestion that hysteria resulted from the traumatic memories of sexual abuse. However, Freud abandoned this notion, and I don't want Freud to be the focus of my paper. Instead, I want to draw attention to the more current work by brain scientists that explains how trauma is etched into the human brain as an un-processed memory. The research by van der Kolk best demonstrates this concept. Then I can go on to examine the evidence which shows that allowing these traumatic memories to be fully processed, through either speaking or writing, can provide relief from the trauma. The research done by Pennebaker will be helpful here. I still need more evidence on this point, but I think I will be able to back it up.

Jennifer rereads her freewriting and condenses it into a preliminary thesis:

In our society, people are discouraged from expressing their feelings about traumatic events that happen to them and instead are encouraged to "keep your chin up." Despite this, there is increasing evidence that it is psychologically helpful to express feelings about trauma. Based on studies of the human brain, it has been established that allowing verbal analysis of traumatic experiences may allow processing of the experiences to take place and may aid in recovering from the impact of trauma.

This is still a preliminary thesis. Compare it with Jennifer's final thesis, excerpted from the final version of her research paper:

While we live in a culture where personal trauma and the lasting psychological effects of traumatic events have been and continue to be silenced, current research suggests that verbal expression of pain, grief, and other responses to trauma speeds recovery. Psychologists and physiologists who study the brain have established that traumatic experiences are encoded in memory as images that are not fully processed by the conscious mind. Verbal analysis of the traumatic event, either through speech or writing, allows processing to take place and aids in recovering from the impact of trauma.

Notice that Jennifer's final thesis is refined, more fully developed, and more coherent. The main purpose of a preliminary thesis is to focus your research activities, but sometimes you may need to depart from the initial thesis as you understand more about the topic.

## PLANNING THE RESEARCH PAPER

A research paper can follow one organizational plan or a combination of the plans we have discussed in this book. Review the major organizational plans that we presented on pages 46–50.

In many cases, a plan will occur to you as you conduct research. For instance, Jennifer has decided to write on how communicating about a traumatic event can help repair the psychological damage caused by the event. Thus, it occurs to her that a problem-solution organizational plan could work for the body of her essay.

Because research writers must juggle many sources and deal with issues in depth, they need an outline that will keep them on task and provide a framework that unifies information from various sources. Review our explanation of free-form and formal outlining on pages 48–50. A pitfall of writing research papers is becoming so bogged down in the details from sources that you fail to clarify the relationships among ideas. Your research paper will be easier to write if you draft it working from a detailed outline, and, in the end, your train of thought will likely be more evident to your audience.

As an example of a free-form outline, consider the one Jennifer develops for her research paper on trauma:

### Thesis

--Psychologists and physiologists who study the brain have established that traumatic experiences are encoded in memory as images that are not fully processed by the conscious mind. Verbal analysis of the traumatic event, either through speech or writing, allows processing to take place and aids in recovering from the impact of trauma.

### Background

--In the late nineteenth century, Charcot began to catalog the symptoms of hysteria (Herman).
--Charcot's students, Freud and Janet, determined that trauma early in life led to hysteria (Herman). Freud advanced the Seduction Hypothesis but then

abandoned it in favor of psychoanalytic theory, and Janet's ideas were forgotten (Herman).

--After World War I, trauma again came to attention of researchers in studies
of shell shock victims. Rivers encouraged those victims to talk and write about
wartime experiences (Herman).

--Later, a link was made between war-induced trauma and trauma which
resulted from domestic violence and sexual abuse (Herman).

## Current Physiological Research on Trauma

--The hormonal systems of trauma victims do not respond appropriately to
everyday stress. In these cases, small levels of stress release a flood of
hormones which lead to constant hyperarousal or numbness (van der Kolk, 1996).

--The brain responds to trauma through several distinct structures. The
amygdala attaches emotional meaning to the experience, the hippocampus
records the special dimensions of the experience and controls short-term
memory of the experience, and the prefrontal cortex analyzes and
categorizes the experience (van der Kolk, 1996).

--The information from a traumatic event goes first to the amygdala. If
the emotional impact is too severe, the message cannot proceed to the
hippocampus and prefrontal cortex for complete processing. Thus, the
experience cannot be fully contextualized and understood (van der Kolk,
1996; LeDoux, Romanski, & Xagoraris). As a result, the traumatic experience
is stored as images, not as a coherent narrative. The painful emotional
feelings may remain over time, but the individual does not have a clear
explanation for them and thus cannot cope with them.

--There is a distinction between explicit (conscious) and implict (unconscious)
memory (van der Kolk, 1996; Levinson). Traumatic experience interferes with
explicit memory but not implicit memory (van der Kolk, 1996). Thus, an implicit
(unconscious) memory of trauma remains even when no explicit (conscious)
memory exists. The victim has a feeling that something is very wrong but
cannot find words to describe the memory (van der Kolk).

## Recovering from Trauma

--Victims must first understand what makes the memories resurface (Rauch).
Then, they must find a way to describe the memories verbally and give them
meaning.

## Writing as Therapy for Trauma

--Writing can describe and give context to moments and images and help individuals make sense of incidents that initially were verbally indescribable.

--Writing has healing power and aids the immune system (Pennebaker).

--Writing provides an outlet to express the pain that our society masks in everyday life.

## Opposition and Response

--Some contemporary psychologists favor using beta-blockers to erase the memory of traumatic experience (Davis; Cahill). If this is done, the victims will never have a chance to fully process the experience, a necessary step on the road to recovery.

## WRITING FROM YOUR OUTLINE

Use your outline as a guide for drafting. Group your notes or note cards according to the points in your outline and draft the essay paragraph by paragraph. Keep in mind our advice in Chapter 2 on developing paragraphs, introductions, and conclusions. Be sure to include complete references for all source information in the first draft. It is easy to lose track of where information came from if you do not record this information initially.

As you draft your essay, you may find that you need to depart from your outline. An outline is supposed to guide your writing, but it should not be a straitjacket. If you discover new patterns or ideas in the process of writing, don't hesitate to include them in your essay.

## REVISING

---

### CHECKLIST FOR REVISING A RESEARCH PAPER

\_\_\_\_\_ Is the paper written on a sufficiently narrow topic?
\_\_\_\_\_ Can you understand the writer's research goals?
\_\_\_\_\_ Does the writer present a clear thesis?
\_\_\_\_\_ Does the writer make sense of the information from sources?

(continued on the next page)

_____ Can you discern the research paper's form (multiple-source comparison and contrast, summary of multiple sources, objective synthesis, essay of response to multiple sources, synthesis with a specific purpose, argument, analysis, or evaluation)?

_____ Is the information from sources organized according to a clear plan?

_____ Does the writer use information from sources convincingly?

_____ Are the writer's assertions substantiated with material from sources?

_____ Does the writer provide transitions among sources and among pieces of information?

_____ Is the writer's voice appropriate for this type of essay? Why or why not?

_____ Is the paper opener satisfactory? Why or why not?

_____ Does the essay have an appropriate conclusion?

_____ Is the title suitable for the piece?

_____ Can you identify the source for each piece of information?

_____ Does the paper end with a list of works cited that includes all sources referred to in the text of the paper?

## EDITING

When you are satisfied with your revision, read your paper aloud. Then reread it line by line and sentence by sentence. Check for correct usage, punctuation, spelling, mechanics, manuscript form, and typos. If you are using a word processing program with a spell checker, apply the checker to your essay. If you are especially weak in editing skills, try getting a friend to read over your work. Keep in mind the following concerns:

1. Are all your sentences complete?
2. Have you avoided run-on sentences, both fused sentences and comma splices?
3. Do pronouns have clear antecedents, and do they agree in number, gender, and case with the words for which they stand?
4. Do all subjects and verbs agree in person and number?
5. Is the verb tense consistent and correct?
6. Have you used modifiers (words, phrases, subordinate clauses) correctly and placed them where they belong?

7. Have you used matching elements within parallel construction?
8. Are punctuation marks used correctly?
9. Are spelling, capitalization, and other mechanics (abbreviations, numbers, italics) correct?

## SAMPLE RESEARCH PAPER

The final draft of Jennifer Piazza's research paper appears on the following pages. Since Jennifer is writing her paper for a psychology class, she uses the American Psychological Association (APA) manuscript and documentation style rather than the MLA style used in our previous examples of student essays. APA style is utilized in many disciplines besides psychology. The appendix to this text includes a brief guide to the APA documentation style.

<br>

Silent Expression     1 ← 1" →

Silent Expression

Jennifer R. Piazza

Professor Nelson

Counseling: Theory and Dynamics

April 24, 2003

<br>

Silent Expression     2

The world of trauma engulfs people suffering from abuse, grief, and loss of self. From world wars to domestic violence, from the death of a loved one to the occurrence of a tragic accident, from mental illness to physical disabilities, from a host of factors, trauma infiltrates lives. Yet, when trauma touches us on a personal level, we are taught that disclosing personal information is not only undesirable, it is unacceptable. The teachings come in the form of hushed words when a victim of trauma enters the

room; they are evident when people look the other way as
the widow of a spouse who committed suicide walks down the
street; and the teachings are strengthened when the media
focuses on how a victim of a traumatic event could have
prevented it. Those who contain their sorrow become the
strong and resilient, while those who display reactions to
trauma become the weak and insecure. While we live in a
culture where personal trauma and the lasting psychological
effects of traumatic events have been and continue to be
silenced, current research suggests that verbal expression
of pain, grief, and other responses to trauma speeds
recovery. Psychologists and physiologists who study the
brain have established that traumatic experiences are
encoded in memory as images that are not fully processed by
the conscious mind. Verbal analysis of the traumatic event,
either through speech or writing, allows processing to take
place and aids in recovering from the impact of trauma.

 During the late nineteenth century, Jean-Martin Charcot
studied hysteria in an attempt to bring voices to those
silenced. At that time, hysteria was thought to be a
"strange disease with incoherent and incomprehensible
symptoms" (Herman, 1992, p. 10) that originated in the
uterus and was found only in women. To explore the symptoms
of hysteria. Charcot reformed a hospital complex and
observed, described, and classified patients with hysteria.
He focused on the actual symptoms of hysteria and determined
that symptoms such as amnesia and sensory loss were
psychological. In creating a taxonomy of hysteria, Charcot
restored dignity to the topic, and after his death Charcot's
students were able to build upon the foundation he had laid.
Two of his students, Pierre Janet and Sigmund Freud, sought
to surpass Charcot's work by finding the cause of hysteria
(Herman, 1992).

 The rivalry between Janet and Freud pushed them their
separate ways. However, by utilizing what was known as the

"talking cure" (Herman, 1992, p. 12), both discovered a common cause of hysteria. Both determined that trauma precipitated neuroses and putting the traumatic experience into words was essential to moving past the trauma and dispelling neurotic symptoms. Freud discovered that everyday, trivial experiences seemed to trigger memories of childhood trauma in his patients. Freud stated that hysteria was the result of premature sexual experiences, what is known as the Seduction Hypothesis. This explanation was widely rejected by the medical and psychological establishments because of the large numbers of women from the upper levels of society who were diagnosed with hysteria. The idea that many upper-class men had sexually abused their young daughters was considered preposterous and unacceptable. Freud, unable to persevere beneath the pressure of his superiors, dismissed the Seduction Hypothesis and went on to invent psychoanalysis, which "became a study of the internal vicissitudes of fantasy and desire, dissociated from the reality of experience" (Herman, 1992, p. 14).

At the same time Freud was exploring the Seduction Hypothesis in Vienna, Janet was studying traumatic memory in France. He, like Freud, came to the conclusion that hysteria was the result of early childhood trauma. However, unlike Freud, Janet never abandoned his theory of hysteria and remained faithful to his patients. Soon after, the medical and psychological establishments accepted Freud, while Janet and his ideas of hysteria were forgotten. As a result, trauma research was halted for decades (Herman, 1992).

It was not until after World War I that trauma was once again in the forefront of research. Veterans who had undergone traumatic experiences returned from the war displaying symptoms of hysteria, or what was then called shell shock. What was considered a disease that only

afflicted women began to victimize large numbers of men who
at one time were considered glorious and brave. Viewed as
cowards and weak invalids, these men were treated poorly
until W. H. R. Rivers, following the model of Dorothea
Dix's mental health movement, began to treat these soldiers
with dignity and respect. Rivers encouraged soldiers to
write and to talk about the horrors of war, but it was not
until after the Vietnam War that "rap groups" raised
awareness of the effects war has on the individual. Rap
groups served as a place for Vietnam veterans to tell their
stories in the company of fellow veterans and psychiatrists
(Herman, 1992).

Trauma was publicized as a result of war, but the
traumas of domestic violence, abuse, and rape were hidden.
However, because both men and women displayed similar
behaviors after their own personal traumas, the distinction
between the trauma of war and the trauma of sexual assault
and abuse began to blur. As a result of the recognition of
psychological effects that occur both during and after
traumatic events, the diagnosis of post-traumatic stress
disorder (PTSD) was included in the *Diagnostic and
Statistical Manual* in 1980 (Herman, 1992). Unfortunately,
the battle fought by trauma survivors did not end when
psychologists considered post-traumatic stress disorder
legitimate. On the contrary, victims of trauma are still
being silenced, and to this day the rift still exists
between trauma survivors and those who cannot understand the
psychological and biological effects of trauma.

Dennis Charney, head of the clinical neuroscience
division of the National Center for PTSD states:

> Victims of devastating trauma may never be the
> same, biologically. It does not matter if it was
> the incessant terror of combat, torture of
> repeated abuse in childhood, or a one-time
> experience, like being trapped in a hurricane or

almost dying in an auto accident. All
uncontrollable stress can have the same biological
impact. (Butler, 1996, p. 41)

Individuals who have not experienced a major traumatic
event or chronic trauma have the natural ability to prepare
their bodies for danger. In a threatening situation, normal
individuals' stress hormones increase, and the fight or
flight response prepares them to escape the danger, either
by resisting or by running. When the danger subsides, they
return to a normal state because hormones have leveled off,
and the nervous system is no longer in a state of arousal.
It can be concluded, therefore, that normal, everyday stress
does not permanently alter an individual's neurobiology (van
der Kolk, McFarlene, & Weisaeth, 1996).

Unfortunately, this is not the case with trauma,
especially trauma that occurs on a chronic basis. According
to Bessel van der Kolk et al., "Chronic and persistent
stress inhibits the effectiveness of the stress response
and induces desensitization" (1996, p. 222). Stress
hormones in traumatized individuals are elevated because
victims of trauma are in a state of constant hyperarousal
and cannot modulate their bodies efficiently. Small
stressors have the ability to trigger the release of a
flood of hormones, which results in overreacting to
everyday events. As a result, even in normal environments,
the nervous system is always on alert. Although the
increase of hormones seems adaptive, what happens is that
when the hormones are truly needed in a dangerous
situation, they are not utilized properly. As demonstrated
by Rauch and his co-researchers, hormones such as cortisol
increase an individual's ability to numb his or her
reactions. After watching a fifteen-minute video of combat
scenes from *Platoon*, veterans with PTSD showed a drop in
pain sensitivity and a release of natural opiates. As a

result of the influx of numerous hormones at unusual times, traumatized individuals do not have the ability to reach an equilibrium; instead, they compensate by overutilizing the hormonal systems, leaving them either hyperaroused or numb (Rauch et al., 1996).

It is evident that the neurochemistry of traumatized individuals is abnormal, and it is important to understand that traumatic experiences are also stored and processed differently from normal experiences. Bessel van der Kolk et al. (1996) state that "in the course of evolution, the human brain has developed three interdependent subanalyzers; the brainstem/hypothalamus, the limbic system and the prefrontal cortex" (p. 214). The brainstem and hypothalamus are responsible for regulating internal homeostasis, and are partially dependent on the limbic system and prefrontal cortex to function properly. The limbic system, which maintains balance between the internal and external world, contains the hippocampus and the amygdala, two structures that are involved with processing traumatic events. The hippocampus records spacial dimensions of an experience and plays an important role in short-term memory; the amygdala is responsible for attaching emotional meaning to the sensory input of an experience. In other words, the hippocampus is responsible for the context of an experience, and the amygdala is responsible for the emotional weight of an experience. Finally, the prefrontal cortex analyzes the experience and categorizes it with past experiences (van der Kolk et al., 1996).

According to van der Kolk et al. (1996), all information that we receive through our five senses reaches the amygdala before it travels to the hippocampus and the prefrontal cortex. Therefore, emotional responses occur before an actual experience can be interpreted and evaluated. When experiencing a normal event, this is not a

problem because the emotional weight is too weak to outweigh
the actual experience. However, when experiencing a
traumatic event, the emotional impact is too extreme for
further processing to occur. As demonstrated in animal
studies (LeDoux, Romanski, & Xagoraris, 1989), if the
amygdala is excessively stimulated, it interferes with the
functioning of the hippocampus. If there is interference of
the hippocampus, as in the case of trauma, it is impossible
for a person to form a context for his or her experience.
Thus, integration of the traumatic memory with a wide store
of other memories never occurs (van der Kolk et al., 1996).

Because integration does not occur, it is nearly
impossible for people suffering from trauma to create a
narrative that describes their traumatic memory. Instead,
their experience exists in the form of images. Although the
traumatic experience in its entirety may be hazy and
difficult to retrieve, the images of certain moments remain
frozen, untarnished. The pictures of a traumatic event are
not organized. Traumatized victims cannot pick their mental
photo albums off a shelf and note the manner in which they
occurred. Their pictures are scattered, bent, torn. There
are no dates written on the back and no explanations as to
why the event occurred. Thus, trauma victims may dissociate
from the experience. However, it is impossible to disown an
experience without ramifications. Burying images in a box
does not allow a person to forget they exist; it just
prevents organizing them in a way that makes sense. It
distances the person from the event, until events and the
emotions are no longer intertwined. This seems like an ideal
defense mechanism: Forget it existed and it never happened.
What many people do not realize, however, is that the
emotions need an outlet, which is why many traumatized
individuals experience feelings they cannot explain. They

are consciously unable to tie past events with their present
emotional states.

This inability to be consciously aware of the
connection between events and emotions can be explained by
the theory of implicit and explicit memory. According to
van der Kolk, explicit or declarative memory is utilized
to remember a particular moment and enables an individual to
consciously tie his or her present behavior to an incident
that occurred in his or her past. It is the memory of
context and is tied closely to the hippocampus. Implicit
memory, unlike explicit memory, does not rely on the
hippocampus. It is utilized when perceptions, thoughts, and
actions are unconsciously influenced by past experiences
(van der Kolk et al., 1996). To demonstrate the difference
between explicit and implicit memory, Levinson (1965) had
surgeons state a mock crisis during surgery. Patients in the
control condition heard no message during their surgery,
while patients in the experimental condition were exposed to
negative messages, such as those suggesting that they might
not make it. The patients were later questioned about the
surgery, and results showed that those in the negative
message condition became extremely agitated when questioned,
while those in the no message condition had no such adverse
reaction. No patients were able to explicitly recall what
had been said, but the results showed that some implicit
memory had formed.

Traumatic experience interferes with explicit memory
but does not interfere with implicit memory. Interference
with explicit memory can be attributed to the fact that the
hippocampus does not function properly during traumatic
experience, due to excessive amygdala stimulation and
elevated levels of neurohormones, such as corticosteroids.
Since the hippocampus is essential for short-term memory,

any damage to the hippocampus results in a person's inability to establish context for his or her experiences. Due to damage to the hippocampus, explicit memory cannot function properly. However, implicit memory is intact (van der Kolk et al., 1996).

Without remembrance for context, trauma survivors have trouble discovering that the person they have become is a direct extension of the life-altering experience of the trauma. In other words, the conscious may not be aware of the impact of the trauma, but the unconscious always remembers, which is why sensory input can trigger feelings that cannot be explained. Because the memories of trauma are not stored in the same way that typical memories are, an individual must rely on bits and pieces of information that exist in the form of sensations, flashes of images, or perhaps a particular smell or taste. The images are intrusive and appear without conscious thought. Unable to understand and know why these sensations occur, a person cannot find words to describe his or her memories (van der Kolk et al., 1996).

Navigating through the aftermath of a traumatic event begins with an explanation as to how memories resurface; the purpose of this is so the traumatized individual understands why only feelings and fragments can be recalled rather than the entire incident. An inability to narrate a traumatic experience was examined by Rauch et al. in 1996. By playing to combat veterans and sexual abuse survivors with PTSD a tape of their most horrific memory, the three researchers were able to stimulate flashbacks. During recollection, positron emission tomography (PET) scans were used to record brain activity in these individuals. Results showed that areas of the brain's cortex involved in sensory memory were active, while Broca's area, which plays a large part in verbal articulation of experience, was inactive. When asked to recall a mundane experience, the opposite trend emerged:

The sensory areas were inactive, while Broca's area was active (Rauch et al., 1996).

   If a person is unable to verbally express his or her experience, a cohesive narrative cannot be formed during therapy. Victims may want to talk about what happened, but because Broca's area is inactive, they may be unable to. It is difficult to talk about an image or a feeling in a way that makes sense to people; thus, some trauma victims may become so frustrated at their lack of ability to communicate that they may shut down.

   For some of those trauma victims, writing is a vehicle for communication (MacCurdy, 1999). Writing is largely based on moments and images. A person can make lists of things such as colors, feelings, and sounds. A piece of paper and a pen allow a person to collect her or his thoughts; these inanimate objects, unlike most people, are not impatient, nor do they become annoyed at images that do not form a story that makes sense. Rather, an individual has the power to write as quickly or as slowly as needed. The act of writing freezes a thought or an image that a person feels at a certain point. When several images have been focused upon, a story begins to form. A person can begin to label cluttered boxes of snapshots in a way that allows processing to occur. Writers can arrange their pictures and take power over their prose until a story eventually emerges. The images are no longer uncontrollable; they are within the traumatized individual's control. The act of writing can be empowering to individuals as they try to make sense of incidents that initially seem indescribable.

   In addition to the mental healing writing provides, physical healing may also occur. Writing has been shown to enhance immune system functioning and reduce the number of physician visits (Pennebaker, Kiecolt-Glaser, & Glaser, 1988). Studies have shown that writing "increases antibody responses to the Epstein-Barr virus, and antibody response

to hepatitis B vaccinations" (Pennebaker, 1997, p. 162). It
also helps to increase t-helper cell growth (1997). Short-
term changes in autonomic activity, such as lowered heart
rate and electrodermal activity, are also produced by
disclosure. Pennebaker (1997) has concluded that "the mere
expression of trauma is not sufficient. Health gains appear
to require translating experiences into language" (p. 164).
Writing serves to translate experiences that an individual
cannot express verbally.

Writing also provides an outlet when no other outlet
exists. Our society silences victims of trauma by ignoring
their cries for help. Some believe that traumatic events
occur only to those who deserve them. By blaming the victim,
we can say with assurance that "this will never happen to
me." We live in a society that denies the presence of
trauma, despite historical evidence and personal accounts.
In school, children learn about the glorious war battles
that men fought to save the land we walk upon; we are shown
that the grieving time for the loss of a loved one is
limited to three days of mourning; we see that rape is
justified because the woman asked for it; and we understand
that abusive environments exist only in the lives of "those
people." But no one talks about the war veteran who can no
longer sleep without a gun nearby, or the family who stares
at the empty chair that their loved one used to occupy. We
don't discuss the flashbacks and constant fear a rape victim
must struggle with, nor do we talk about domestic violence
that results in a new generation of children who are taught
that violence is the answer. How can a victim of incest feel
safe enough to talk about her experience when she is shut
out time and again? How does our denial affect the child who
is abused over and over again?

Without a supportive community, trauma remains buried
beneath layers and layers of self-blame, guilt, and denial.
The process of writing serves to integrate experience and

document personal history. Memories, no matter how painful,
make us who we are. By telling the story of our lives, we
realize why we react the way we do in certain situations and
why each person is unique.

Unfortunately, some psychologists do not see the
importance of community and disclosure. Instead, they would
rather take the actual traumatic memory away by using drugs
such as propranolol. According to Davis (1998), propranolol
essentially blocks the ability to connect aversive emotions
to traumatic memories by acting as an antagonist on the
B-adrenergic receptor. During and after emotional
experience, the B-adrenergic stress hormone systems are
activated, resulting in enhanced memory for the emotional
event. In a study conducted in 1994 (see Cahill, Prins,
Weber, & McGaugh) participants were given either propranolol
or a placebo an hour before being shown a series of slides
accompanied by narratives. The emotionally neutral narrative
described a mother taking her son to visit his father, who
worked as a laboratory technician in a hospital. The
emotionally charged narrative started with the boy and
mother going to visit the boy's father at work, but in this
version, the two never made it to the lab because the boy
was struck by a car and suffered severe brain trauma. In
addition, the boy's feet were severed, but a surgical team
was able to reattach them. Participants were then given
memory tests; results showed that participants in the
emotionally neutral scenario, regardless of whether they had
received the propranolol, had similar recall. In the
emotionally charged condition, however, participants who
were given propranolol scored significantly lower than
participants who were given a placebo. The results of this
study show the profound impact beta-blockers can have in the
face of a traumatic event.

According to Davis, the next step is to use
propranolol to conduct a controlled study with trauma

Silent Expression     14

victims. In my opinion, the thought of erasing a memory from
another human being is terrifying. The neurobiology of
trauma victims may leave them speechless, but with a
supportive community and therapeutic writing, their voices
can return. Unfortunately, our society does not recognize
this. It was bad enough that we isolated victims from
society; now we isolate them from themselves.

Silent Expression     15

References

Butler, K. (1996, March/April). The biology of fear.
    *Networker,* 39-45.

Cahill, L., Prins, B., Weber, M., & McGaugh, J. L.
    (1994). B-adrenergic activation and memory for emotional
    events. *Nature, 271,* 702-704.

Davis, M. (1998). Neural systems involved in fear and
    anxiety. Symposium conducted at the University of Scranton,
    Scanton, PA.

Herman, J. L. (1992). *Trauma and recovery.* New York:
    HarperCollins.

LeDoux, J. E., Romanski, L., & Xagoraris, A. (1989).
    Indelibility of subcortical emotional memories. *Journal
    of Cognitive Neuroscience, 1,* 238-243.

Levinson, B. W. (1965). States of awareness during
    general anesthesia: Preliminary communication. *British
    Journal of Anesthesia, 37,* 544-546.

MacCurdy, M. (1999). From trauma to writing: A theoretical
    model for practical use. In C. Anderson & M. MacCurdy
    (Eds.), *Writing and healing: Toward an informed practice.*
    Urbana, IL: National Council of Teachers of English.

Silent Expression    16

Pennebaker, J. W. (1997). Writing about emotional experiences
    as a therapeutic process. *Psychological Science,*
    *8*(3), 162-165.
Pennebaker, J. W., Kiecolt-Glaser, J. K., & Glaser, R. (1988).
    Disclosure of traumas and immune function: Health
    implications for psychotherapy. *Journal of Counseling*
    *and Clinical Psychology, 56*(2), 239-245.
Rauch, S. L., van der Kolk, B. A., Fisler, R. E., Alpert,
    N. M., Orr, S. P., Savage, C. R., et al. (1996). A
    symptom provocation study of posttraumatic stress
    disorder using positron emission tomography and script-
    driven imagery. *Archives of General Psychiatry,*
    *53*, 380-387.
van der Kolk, B. A., McFarlane, A. C., & Weisaeth, L.
    (1996). *Traumatic stress.* New York: Guilford Press.

## INDIVIDUAL EXERCISE ON RHETORICAL GOALS FOR RESEARCH PAPERS

Reread Jennifer Piazza's research paper. What is her goal for writing? What is she trying to accomplish? What is the relationship between the sources of information she draws on and her own views? Freewrite for ten minutes in response to these questions.

## COLLABORATIVE EXERCISE ON RHETORICAL GOALS FOR RESEARCH PAPERS

1. Form collaborative learning groups of five students each, as described in the preface, or fashion groups according to your own method.
2. Within your group, discuss the following questions: To what extent is Jennifer Piazza's paper a report on the content of the sources she consulted? To what extent is her paper an explanation of her own conclusions about the topic? Have the recorder note the high points of your deliberations.
3. Reconvene the entire class. Each group recorder should explain the group's answers to the two questions. Then, discuss any disagreements among groups.

P A R T

*two*

# An Anthology
of Readings

# Natural Sciences and Technology

## SUBJECTS AND METHODS OF STUDY IN THE NATURAL SCIENCES AND TECHNOLOGY

### The Scientific Method

Science and technology are based on a common methodology, and thus scientific and technical researchers the world over share an approach to their work. Even though they may give conflicting answers to important questions in their disciplines, they rarely argue about the basic process of conducting scientific investigation. The specific means by which researchers discover, collect, and organize information is called the scientific method. This approach involves questioning, observing, experimenting, and theorizing. Drawing on previous knowledge and prior investigations, scientists ask questions not only about the unknown but also about phenomena that are supposedly understood. Often, they challenge commonly accepted beliefs as well as the conclusions of other scientists. Indeed, no fact or theory is exempt from legitimate inquiry. Even the most widely accepted ideas are continually reexamined. This questioning process helps make science self-correcting, since errors made by scientists can be detected and corrected by subsequent investigation.

Scientific ideas must be confirmed through observation before they are considered fact. Assertions that cannot be supported by direct observation are generally greeted with skepticism by the scientific community. For phenomena that cannot be observed readily in nature, scientists design experiments that make events stand out more clearly. As with other information derived from observations, experimental findings are continually reexamined, and experiments are considered valid only if they can be repeated with identical results by different investigators.

Scientists build theories to account for direct observations and experimental results. Theories are rules or models that explain a large body of separate facts. An example is the Bohr model of the atom, in which electrons orbit around the nucleus like moons around a planet. The Bohr model explains many basic observations made by physicists and chemists, but it is by no means the only theoretical description of the atom; quantum theory suggests an atomic model that does not include electrons in discrete orbits. Scientists often weigh competing theories that purport to explain the same facts. The other parts of the scientific method—questioning, observing, and experimenting—contribute to constructing and testing theories.

## WRITING ABOUT SCIENCE AND TECHNOLOGY

Texts concerning science and technology can be separated into two groups: (1) reports of original research, which focus on a narrow topic, and (2) summary or speculative articles, which generalize about a body of specific information. Research reports are typically written for experts in scientific or technical disciplines. Summary and speculative articles are often directed to less specialized audiences. Consider, for example, Thomas Colbridge's summary article (Chapter 8) that reviews the constitutional issues that arise from police use of thermal imaging technology and Raymond Kurzweil's speculative article (Chapter 7) in which he considers the consequences of transferring the contents of a human mind into a computer. Most of the articles in Chapters 6, 7, and 8 are summary and speculative articles written for a general audience rather than an audience of professional scientists.

### Organization

Research reports share a common rhetorical pattern. Scientists within specific disciplines have established standard methods for organizing research reports, and most journals that publish research results accept only articles written according to those formats. Summary and speculative articles, however, vary widely in rhetorical structure. Nonscientists who think the only aim of science writing is to relate established facts fail to recognize that much science writing argues a point. As you read through the next three chapters, notice that the majority of the articles are organized as arguments. For example, the title of Charles Krauthammer's article "Crossing Lines: A Secular Argument Against Research Cloning" (Chapter 6) indicates that the essay will present an argument. The pursuit of science often gives rise to intense debate over what questions should be investigated, what observations are accurate, and what theories best explain particular observations; thus, argumentative writing is common in science. In addition to argumentation, the full range of rhetorical patterns can be found in popular science writing.

Writing research reports according to a set organizational formula does have its drawbacks. In some cases, scientists may become so obsessed with fitting their work into a research report formula that they lose sight of the central goal of scientific research: an active pursuit of the truth. A similar problem sometimes surfaces in popular science writing in which the rhetorical pattern becomes more important than scientific accuracy. For example, Joseph Weizenbaum, an internationally known computer scientist, states that most essays about the societal impact of computer technology follow a set pattern. First, they survey the benefits to society of computers; then, they consider some of the potential dangers of widespread computer use; finally, they claim that those dangers can be overcome with new technology and argue for a vigorous program to expand computer development and use. Weizenbaum implies that this simplistic, problem-solution approach to writing about computers may obscure the truth. Much popular writing about controversial science and technology follows a pattern similar to the one Weizenbaum describes. To fit a set format, the science writer may ignore important facts or pass over alternative interpretations of certain facts. Consequently, analyzing rhetorical structure is an important element in comprehending science writing.

## Style

Although the tone of research report writing is almost always unemotional and authoritative, popular science writing varies considerably in tone and style. Once free from the constraints of the professional research report, scientists express emotions and personal attitudes, as do writers in other fields. As you read the article by Joshua Quittner in Chapter 8, notice that the writer uses a personal tone to discuss a technical issue: electronic information systems.

No matter what the tone, a science writer establishes authority by providing concrete evidence. Even the most eminent scientists must support their theories with verifiable observations. In Chapters 6, 7, and 8, you will find that most of the authors include objective evidence to support major assertions. That evidence often comes from scientific investigation, but it also comes from informal observations, anecdotes, and hypothetical cases. For example, in "Loving Technology" which appears in Chapter 7, Sherry Turkle lists a number of observations about children's interaction with electronic "pets" and then uses those observations as a basis for predicting how interactions between intelligent machines and humans will develop in the future. Most science writers are careful to build on evidence, even when they are writing for a general audience. Consequently, it is important for readers of science writing to identify and evaluate the evidence authors provide in support of their claims.

Nonscientists are often amazed to find that different sources may present conflicting versions of scientific "fact." The same body of experimental evidence can lead to several different notions of what the truth is. When you find that the experts disagree, try to describe precisely the various versions of the facts, and if possible, try to explain the reasons for the differences of opinion.

Sometimes, differences of opinion on scientific issues have nothing to do with scientific fact but, rather, reflect conflicting personal or social values. Science is not immune to the political and moral controversy that is part of other human activities. As you read the articles in Chapter 6 on human and animal cloning, you will see that the writers address social and moral issues. When writers do not support scientific claims with objective evidence, you should consider the moral, ideological, or emotional motivations behind their assertions.

Even nonscientists can evaluate intelligently many summary and speculative articles about science. As you read and think about the material in the next three chapters, keep in mind that many of the articles are organized as arguments and can be analyzed like other forms of argumentative writing. Also, ask yourself whether the article involves questioning, observing, experimenting, or theorizing, the basic components of the scientific method. Be sensitive to the author's tone. Look for evidence that supports the author's claims. Note the specific points on which the experts disagree, and try to account for those differences of opinion. Finally, consider the social or ethical questions that scientific advances raise. These procedures will help you read about science and technology with more understanding and better critical judgment.

### WORK CITED

Weizenbaum, Joseph. "The Impact of the Computer on Society." *Science* 176 (1972): 609–14.

# six

# Cloning

Intervention in reproductive processes is as old as civilization. Since prehistoric times, humans have selectively bred animals to enhance their usefulness: to make them pull heavier loads, produce more milk, have more offspring, and so forth. Ancient humans also tried to intervene in their own reproductive processes, for example, by trying to improve fertility through the use of amulets, rituals, and herbs. Certain cultures systematically controlled human reproduction, for instance, by putting some female babies to death to maintain a relatively high proportion of male laborers and warriors.

Modern technology provides new, dramatic ways of intervening in reproduction. Most domestic cattle now result from artificial insemination. Human couples with faulty eggs or sperm can now receive genetic material from donors that is used to create an embryo outside the womb, a "test-tube baby" that can be implanted in the mother-to-be. Surrogate mothers incubate babies for women who are able to conceive but not bear children. And now, both animal and human embryos have been successfully cloned, opening up a range of new possibilities for reproduction.

Although interventions in reproductive processes have always been controversial, recent cloning experiments on animals and humans have intensified the debate. Is cloning just another reproductive technology, or does it raise unique ethical, political, or social issues? Should we allow asexual reproduction and the genetic duplication of particular individuals? Should childless couples or singles be allowed to use cloning to obtain children to whom they are biologically related? Should individuals be allowed to produce genetic copies of themselves in a bid for "immortality"? Should we use cloning to reproduce the "best" individuals in our culture, the Einsteins and Mozarts? Should we clone endangered animal species to ensure their survival? Should we use cloning to bring back species that are already extinct?

The articles in Chapter 6 focus on controversies over human and animal cloning. In "Jennifer and Rachel," an excerpt from his book *Remaking Eden: Cloning and Beyond in a Brave New World*, Lee Silver describes the circumstances under which a human might opt for cloning and maintains that human cloning does not threaten society. In "Me, My Clone, and I (Or In Defense of Human Cloning)," Jonathan Colvin defends cloning as a means for allowing disabled individuals to realize their genetic potential. Written in response to an experiment in which scientists cloned human cells, John Conley's "Narcissus Cloned" states that cloning human embryos violates the sanctity of human life and undermines human relationships. Charles Krauthammer argues that cloning should not be used in attempts to remove genetic defects from human embryos in his article "Crossing Lines: A Secular Argument Against Research Cloning." In "Species on Ice," Karen Wright discusses how cloning and embryo transplantation technology might be used to save endangered or extinct species, while Malcolm Tait attacks those practices in "Bessie and the Gaur."

# Jennifer and Rachel

## *Lee M. Silver*

*Lee M. Silver is a professor at Princeton University who holds appointments in the departments of Molecular Biology, Ecology, and Evolutionary Biology. He is a fellow of the American Association for the Advancement of Science and an expert on the social impact of reproductive technology. This article is excerpted from Silver's book* Remaking Eden: Cloning and Beyond in a Brave New World.

## PREREADING

What have you previously read or seen in the news concerning cloning? Brainstorm a list of specifics. Now read through your list. Based on the items in your list, would you say the news media present cloning in a positive, negative, or objective light? Do they sensationalize cloning, or do they provide balanced reporting?

Jennifer is a self-sufficient single woman who lives by herself in a stylish apartment on Manhattan's Upper West Side. She has focused almost all her energies on her career since graduating from Columbia University, fourteen years earlier, and has moved steadily upward in the business world. In financial terms, she is now quite well off. In social terms, she is happy being single. Jennifer has had various relationships with men over the years, but none was serious enough to make her consider giving up her single lifestyle.

And then on April 14, 2049, the morning of her thirty-fifth birthday, Jennifer wakes up alone, in her quiet room, before the break of dawn, before her alarm is set to go off, and she begins to wonder. With her new age—thirty-five—bouncing around in her mind, a single thought comes to the fore. "It's getting late," she tells herself.

It is not marriage or a permanent relationship that she feels is missing, it is something else. It is a child. Not any child, but a child of her own to hold and to love, to watch and to nurture. Jennifer knows that she can afford to raise a child by herself, and she also knows that the firm she works for is generous in giving women the flexibility required to maintain both a family and a career. And now she feels, for the first time, that she will soon be too old to begin motherhood.

Jennifer is a decisive woman, and by the end of that day she decides to become a single mother. It is the same positive decision that hundreds of thousands of other woman have made before her. But unlike twentieth-century women, Jennifer knows there is no longer any reason to incorporate a sperm donor into the process. An anonymous sperm cell could introduce all sorts of unknown, undesirable traits into her child, and Jennifer is not one to gamble. Instead, she makes the decision to use one of her own cells to create a new life.

Jennifer is well aware that federal law makes cloning illegal in the United States except in cases of untreatable infertility. She realizes that she could get around the law through a marriage of convenience with a gay friend, who would then be declared infertile by a sympathetic physician. But she decides to do what increasing numbers of other women in her situation have done recently—take an extended vacation in the Cayman Islands.

On Grand Cayman Island, there is a large reprogenetic clinic that specializes in cloning. The young physicians and biologists who work at this clinic do not ask questions of their clients. They will retrieve cells from any willing adult, prepare those cells for fusion to unfertilized eggs recovered from any willing woman, and then introduce the embryos that develop successfully into the uterus of the same, or another, willing woman. The cost of the procedure is $80,000 for the initial cell cloning and embryo transfer, and $20,000 for each subsequent attempt at pregnancy if earlier embryos fail to implant. When the clinic first opened, the fees were twice as high, but they dropped in response to competition from newly opened clinics in Jamaica and Grenada.

Since Jennifer is a healthy fertile woman, she has no need for other biological participants in the cloning process. A dozen unfertilized eggs are recovered from her ovaries and made nucleus-free. One-by-one, each is fused with a donor cell obtained from the inside of her mouth. After a period of incubation, healthy-looking embryos are observed under a microscope, and two of these are introduced into her uterus at the proper time of her menstrual cycle. (The introduction of two embryos increases the probability of a successful implantation.) After the procedure, Jennifer stays on the island three more days to rest, then flies back to New York.

A week later, Jennifer is thrilled by the positive blue + symbol that appears on her home pregnancy test. She waits another two weeks to confirm that the pregnancy has taken with another test, and then schedules an appointment with Dr. Steven Glassman, her gynecologist and obstetrician. Dr. Glassman knows that Jennifer is a single woman, and he doesn't ask—and Jennifer doesn't tell—how her pregnancy began. The following eight and a half months pass by uneventfully, with monthly, then weekly, visits to the doctor's office. Ultrasound indicates the presence of a single normal fetus, and amniocentesis confirms the absence of any known genetic problem. Finally, on March 15, 2050, a baby girl is born. Jennifer names her Rachel. To the nurses and doctors who work in the delivery room, Rachel is one more newborn baby, just like all the other newborn babies they've seen in their lives.

Jennifer, holding Rachel in her arms, is taken to a room in the maternity ward, and shortly thereafter, the nurse on duty brings by the form to fill out for the birth certificate. Without a word, she enters Jennifer's name into the space for "the mother." She then asks Jennifer for the name of the father. "Unknown," Jennifer replies, and this is duly recorded. A day later, Jennifer is released from the hospital with her new baby girl.

Rachel will grow up in the same way as all other children her age. 10 Occasionally, people will comment on the striking similarity that exists between the child and her mother. Jennifer will smile at them and say, "Yes. She does have my facial features." And she'll leave it at that.

From time to time, Jennifer will let Rachel know that she is a 11 "special" child, without going into further detail. Then one day, when her daughter has grown old enough to understand, Jennifer will reveal the truth. And just like other children conceived with the help of repro-genetic protocols, Rachel will feel…special. Some day in the more distant future, when cloning becomes just another means of alternative reproduction, accepted by society, the need for secrecy will disappear.

Who is Rachel, and who really are her parents? There is no ques- 12 tion that Jennifer is Rachel's birth mother, since Rachel was born out of her body. But, Jennifer is not Rachel's genetic mother, based on the traditional meanings of mother and father. In genetic terms, Jennifer and Rachel are twin sisters. As a result, Rachel will constantly behold a glimpse of her future simply by looking at her mother's photo album and her mother herself. She will also understand that her single set of grandparents are actually her genetic parents as well. And when Rachel grows up and has children of her own, her children will also be her mother's children. Thus, with a single act of cloning, we are forced to reconsider the meaning of parents, children, and siblings, and how they relate to one another.

## IS CLONING WRONG?

Is there anything wrong with what Jennifer has done? The most logical 13 way to approach this question is through a consideration of whether anyone, or anything, has been harmed by the birth of Rachel. Clearly no harm has been done to Jennifer. She got the baby girl she wanted and she will raise her with the same sorts of hopes and aspirations that most normal parents have for their children.

But what about Rachel? Has she been harmed in some way so 14 detrimental that it would have been better had she not been born? Daniel Callahan, the Director of the Hastings Center (a bioethics think tank near New York City), argues that "engineering someone's entire genetic makeup would compromise his or her right to a unique iden-tity." But no such "right" has been granted by nature—identical twins are born every day as natural clones of each other. Dr. Callahan would have to concede this fact, but he might still argue that just because twins occur naturally does not mean we should create them on purpose.

Dr. Callahan might argue that Rachel is harmed by the knowledge 15 of her future condition. He might say that it is unfair for Rachel to go through her childhood knowing what she will look like as an adult, or being forced to consider future medical ailments that might befall her. But even in the absence of cloning, many children have some sense of the future possibilities encoded in the genes they got from their parents. In my own case, I knew as a teenager that I had a good chance of inheriting the pattern baldness that my maternal grandfather expressed so thoroughly. Furthermore, genetic screening already provides people with the ability to learn about hundreds of disease predispositions. And as genetic knowledge and technology become more and more sophisticated, it will become possible for any human being to learn even more about their genetic future than Rachel can learn from Jennifer's past. In American society, it is generally accepted that parents are ultimately responsible for deciding what their children should, or should not, be exposed to. And there's no reason to expect that someone like Jennifer would tell Rachel something that was not in her best interest to know.

Just because Rachel has the same genes as Jennifer does not mean 16 that her life will turn out the same way. On the contrary, Rachel is sure to have a different upbringing in a world that has changed significantly since her mother's time. And there is no reason why she can't chart her own unique path through life. Furthermore, when it comes to genetic predispositions, they are just that and nothing more. Although their genetically determined inclinations may be the same, mother and daughter may choose to follow those inclinations in different ways, or not at all.

It might also be argued that Rachel is harmed by having to live up 17 to the unrealistic expectations that her mother will place on her. But there is no reason to believe that Jennifer's expectations will be any more unreasonable than those of many other parents who expect their children to accomplish in their lives what the parents were unable to accomplish in their own. No one would argue that parents with such tendencies should be prohibited from having children. Besides, there's no reason to assume that Jennifer's expectations will be unreasonable. Indeed, there is every reason to believe Rachel will be loved by her mother no matter what she chooses to do, as most mothers love their children.

But let's grant that among the many Rachels brought into this 18
world, some *will* feel bad that their genetic constitution is not unique.
Is this alone a strong enough reason to ban the practice of cloning? Before answering this question, ask yourself another: Is a child having
knowledge of an older twin worse off than a child born into poverty? If
we ban the former, shouldn't we ban the latter? Why is it that so many
politicians seem to care so much about cloning but so little about the
welfare of children in general?

Some object to cloning because of the process that it entails. The 19
view of the Vatican, in particular, is that human embryos should be
treated like human beings and should not be tampered with in any way.
However, the cloning protocol does *not* tamper with embryos, it tam-
pers only with *unfertilized* eggs and adult cells like those we scratch off
our arms without a second thought. Only after the fact does an embryo
emerge (which could be treated with the utmost respect if one so
chooses).

There is a sense among some who are religious that cloning leaves 20
God out of the process of human creation, and that man is venturing
into places he does not belong. This same concern has been, and will
continue to be, raised as each new reprogenetic technology is incorporated into our culture, from in vitro fertilization twenty years ago to genetic engineering of embryos—sure to happen in the near future. It is
impossible to counter this theological claim with scientific arguments....

Finally, there are those who argue against cloning based on the 21
perception that it will harm society at large in some way. The *New York
Times* columnist William Safire expresses the opinion of many others
when he says, "Cloning's identicality would restrict evolution." This is
bad, he argues, because "the continued interplay of genes...is central
to humankind's progress." But Mr. Safire is wrong on both practical and
theoretical grounds. On practical grounds, even if human cloning became efficient, legal, and popular among those in the moneyed classes
(which is itself highly unlikely), it would still only account for a fraction
of a percent of all the children born onto this earth. Furthermore, each
of the children born by cloning to different families would be different
from one another, so where does the identicality come from?

On theoretical grounds, Safire is wrong because humankind's 22
progress has nothing to do with unfettered evolution, which is always
unpredictable and not necessarily upward bound. H. G. Wells recognized this principle in his 1895 novel *The Time Machine*, which portrays the natural evolution of humankind into weak and dimwitted, but

cuddly little creatures. And Kurt Vonnegut follows this same theme in *Galápagos*, where he suggests that our "big brains" will be the cause of our downfall, and future humans with smaller brains and powerful flippers will be the only remnants of a once great species, a million years hence.

Although most politicians professed outrage at the prospect of 23 human cloning when Dolly [the first cloned sheep] was first announced, Senator Tom Harkin of Iowa was the one lone voice in opposition. "What nonsense, what utter utter nonsense, to think that we can hold up our hands and say, 'Stop,' " Mr. Harkin said. "Human cloning will take place, and it will take place in my lifetime. I don't fear it at all. I welcome it."

As the story of Jennifer and Rachel is meant to suggest, those who 24 want to clone themselves or their children will not be impeded by governmental laws or regulations. The marketplace—not government or society—will control cloning. And if cloning is banned in one place, it will be made available somewhere else—perhaps on an underdeveloped island country happy to receive the tax revenue. Indeed, within two weeks of Dolly's announcement, a group of investors formed a Bahamas-based company called Clonaid (under the direction of a French scientist named Dr. Brigitte Boisselier) with the intention of building a clinic where cloning services would be offered to individuals for a fee of $200,000. According to the description provided on their Web page (http://www.clonaid.com), they plan to offer "a fantastic opportunity to parents with fertility problems or homosexual couples to have a child cloned from one of them."

Irrespective of whether this particular venture actually succeeds, 25 others will certainly follow. For in the end, international borders can do little to impede the reproductive practices of couples and individuals.

## SURREPTITIOUS CLONING

In democratic societies, people have the right to reproduce and the 26 right to *not* reproduce. This last "right" means that men and women cannot be forced to conceive a child against their will. Until now, it has been possible to exercise this particular right by choosing not to engage in sexual intercourse, and not to provide sperm or eggs for use in artificial insemination or IVF [in vitro fertilization]. But suddenly, human cloning opens up frightening new vistas in the realm of reproductive choice, or lack thereof. Suddenly, it becomes possible to use the genetic material of others without their knowledge or consent.

Let's reconsider the Jennifer and Rachel scenario in the light of re- 27
productive choice. At first glance, it might seem that nothing is amiss
here because Jennifer obviously gave her consent to be cloned. But reproductive choice has been interpreted traditionally to mean that people
have the right not to be genetic parents against their will. Does this mean
that Jennifer should have asked her own parents for permission to create
a clone—her identical twin and their child—before proceeding? Actually,
all of *your* genes, as well, came from *your* mother and father. Does this
mean that your parents have the right to tell you how to use them?

At least Jennifer gave her consent to be cloned. But what are we 28
to make of a situation in which someone is cloned without his or her
knowledge, let alone consent? It takes only a single living cell to start
the cloning procedure, and that cell can probably be obtained from almost any living part of the human body. There are various ways in
which cells could be stolen from a person. I will illustrate one here with
what I will call the Michael Jordan scenario.

Let's move to the near future. The year is 2009, and Jordan has 29
now retired as a professional basketball player. He goes into his doctor's
office for his annual checkup, during which a blood sample is taken into
a standard tube. Jordan's sample, along with others, is given over to a
medical technician, who has been waiting for this moment since Jordan
scheduled his appointment a month before. After closing the lab door
behind her, she opens the tube of Jordan's blood and removes a tiny
portion, which is transferred to a fresh tube that is quickly hidden in
her pocket. The original tube is resealed, and no one will ever know
that it has been tampered with.

At the start of her lunch break, the technician rushes the tube of 30
blood to her friend at a private IVF clinic on the other side of town.
The small sample is emptied into a laboratory dish, and there Jordan's
white blood cells are bathed in nutrients and factors that will allow
them to grow and multiply into millions of identical cells, each one
ready for cloning. The cells are divided up into many portions, which
are frozen in individual tubes for later use.

And then the word goes out on the street. For a $200,000 fee, you 31
can have your very own Michael Jordan child. Would anyone buy? If
not a Michael Jordan child, would they be interested in a Tom Cruise, a
Bill Clinton, or a Madonna (the singer, not the saint)?

It's important to understand that what most people want more 32
than anything else is to have their *own* child, not someone else's child,
no matter who that someone else might be. And if cloning someone

else is an option, then cloning oneself is also an option. So what possible reason could exist for choosing a genetically unrelated child?

Perhaps heartless mothers will want a clone of someone famous in   33 the belief that they will prosper on the income that a clone could make, or the fame that he would bring. But it would require an enormous investment in time and money to raise a child over many years before there was even a chance of a payback. Clones of Michael Jordan would likely be born with the potential to become outstanding athletes, and clones of Tom Cruise or Madonna might have the same artistic talent as their progenitors. But the original Jordan, Cruise, and Madonna owe their success even more to hard work than genetic potential.

Clones might not have the same incentive to train and exert them-   34 selves even if—and perhaps because—unscrupulous parents and promoters try to force them in a specified direction against their will. And while one Madonna clone might attract fame and attention, the next dozen will almost certainly be ignored. It is hard to imagine that many potential parents would be willing to take this gamble, with the wait being so long and the chances of success so small.

There will probably always be some infertile couples or individuals   35 who will want to clone simply for the opportunity to raise a child who is likely to be beautiful or bright, without any desire to profit from the situation themselves. These people will be able to reach their reproductive goals by cloning someone—who is not famous—*with* their consent. In the future, cell donors could be chosen from a catalog in the same way that sperm and egg donors are chosen today.

In contrast, cloning surreptitiously will almost certainly be   36 frowned upon even by those who accept other uses of the cloning technology. And those who participate will run the risk of serious litigation on the basis of infringing upon someone else's reproductive rights. This is not to say, however, that surreptitious cloning will never occur. On the contrary, if something becomes possible in our brave new reproductive world, someone will probably do it, somewhere, sometime.   ❀

### READING FOR INFORMATION

1. What factors led Jennifer to decide to have herself cloned?
2. Why must Jennifer travel to the Cayman Islands for the cloning procedure?
3. Paraphrase Silver's description of the cloning process that Jennifer undergoes.

4. What is the biological relationship between Jennifer and Rachel? Between Rachel and Jennifer's parents?

5. In what ways will Rachel's and Jennifer's lives differ, even though the two individuals are genetically identical?

6. What might be the motive for "surreptitious cloning"?

7. Why does Silver think that relatively few people will want to raise clones of famous, talented individuals?

## READING FOR FORM, ORGANIZATION, AND EXPOSITORY FEATURES

1. Why does Silver begin his piece with an extended scenario?

2. Where does Silver respond to the views of those who oppose human cloning? Is that response successful?

3. Why does Silver choose to discuss "surreptitious cloning" at the end of the piece?

4. Would you characterize this as a piece of academic writing? Why, or why not? What types of sources and authorities does Silver cite?

## READING FOR RHETORICAL CONCERNS

1. How do Silver's credentials affect your reading of his essay?

2. What assumptions does Silver make about the general public's response to cloning? Why has he written this piece, and what is his attitude toward his readers?

3. What is Silver's rhetorical purpose? What does he want to get across to his readers?

4. Where does Silver indicate his own attitude toward Jennifer's use of cloning technology?

## WRITING ASSIGNMENTS

1. In a 500-word essay, summarize the potential benefits and dangers of human cloning that are discussed in Silver's article. Write for an audience of nonscientists.

2. Write a 1,000-word essay that attacks or defends Silver's suggestion that Jennifer's decision to use cloning technology is reasonable.

3. Using Silver's article as a springboard, discuss the extent to which various segments of our society (scientists, the general public, elected officials, and so forth) should be involved in decisions about human cloning. Write at least 1,000 words.

# Me, My Clone, and I (Or In Defense of Human Cloning)

## *Jonathan Colvin*

*Jonathan Colvin is a freelance technical writer.*

### PREREADING

Assume the role of a supporter of human cloning. What is the strongest reason you could give in support of that practice? Answer this question in ten minutes of free writing.

Clone. To many people the word has sinister overtones; it's a disturbing amalgam of flesh and technology. A recent poll revealed that 88 percent of Canadians believe that human cloning should be illegal, and most governments are moving to concur.

Interested in this near-unanimous sentiment, I carried out my own impromptu survey of friends and strangers. Most said they agreed with the prohibition of human cloning. But when I asked them to explain exactly why they thought it should be illegal, the poll became much more revealing.

Many mumbled about the dangers of "cloning Hitler" or creating a subclass of slaves. Others brought up the specter of basketball teams full of identical seven-foot-tall players. A smaller, more thoughtful percentage believed it would be unnatural or the ultimate in narcissism. In general, however, public attitudes toward human cloning seem to be based on a diet of science-fiction B-movies and paperbacks.

But should human cloning be feared as the next Frankenstein's monster of genetic engineering?

While undoubtedly fascinating, few people would perceive identical twins to be the least bit sinister. And yet identical twins are in fact natural clones, formed from the same egg and sharing the same

Colvin, Jonathan. "Me, My Clone, and I (Or In Defense of Human Cloning)." *The Humanist,* May 2000: 39+. Reprinted by permission of the author.

genotype. If natural clones are not to be feared, why should we fear the deliberate ones?

Many of the attitudes concerning human cloning are reminiscent  6
of the arguments against in vitro fertilization in the 1960s, when accusations of "playing God" and interfering with nature were common. Today, however, "test tube" babies are celebrated for their own individuality and as people in their own right. Exactly, say opponents of cloning. Babies born in vitro are unique individuals; clones are photocopies of people who already exist. What will happen to individuality if we can stamp out copies of ourselves like so many cookies on a tray?

Interestingly, many of those who make this argument also tend to  7
emphasize nurture over nature and deny that our genes determine ourselves—whether it be IQ, athletic ability, or our favorite ice cream flavor. But these arguments contradict each other. For if nurture triumphs over nature, then a clone will be an individual as unique as any other, determined for the most part by the environment in which she or he was reared.

Perhaps the most weighty argument against cloning is that by  8
eliminating the mixing of genes that occurs during conventional reproduction, human biodiversity will be diminished and human evolution will cease. It is the serendipitous mixing of genes that produces the Einsteins and Mozarts of the world; take away this process and surely the potential for new genius will cease. However, the fact is that human biological evolution for all intents and purposes has become insignificant compared to cultural evolution.

At this point, it is appropriate that I reveal the source of my inter-  9
est in this subject. For the truth is, I wish to clone myself. Before my gate is stormed by villagers wielding branding irons, let me explain why.

I am thirty-two years old and have cystic fibrosis, an inherited ge-  10
netic disease that prohibits those who suffer from it from conceiving children and usually kills by the mid-thirties. My dream is to clone myself, repair my clone's genetic defect, and give him the opportunity to fulfill the potential that has been denied to me by a cruel quirk of nature.

Perhaps my clone will climb Mount Everest, singlehandedly sail  11
around the world, or simply marry and raise a family without the fear that his children will be prematurely fatherless and his wife a widow. The clone will not be me, but perhaps he will be who I could have been.

My body, my self. Surely also my DNA, my self.  12

With the coming genetic revolution, we will be directing our own  13
evolution rather than relying on a natural (and sometimes disastrous)

lottery to do it for us. And surely cloning will remain an esoteric and unusual method of reproduction, with most people choosing to do it the old-fashioned (and far more pleasurable) way. But should government be able to tell me what I can or cannot do with what is, after all, an intrinsic part of what and who I am?

Criminalizing an activity may be easier than answering the thorny 14 philosophical questions raised by it. But before government rushes to outlaw my dream, it should at least seriously consider whether the opposition to human cloning is based on real dangers.    ✤

## READING FOR INFORMATION

1. What does Colvin conclude from his impromptu survey on attitudes toward cloning?
2. According to Colvin, what was the initial public response to "test tube" babies?
3. Why does Colvin state that a human clone would be "an individual as unique as any other"?
4. What does Colvin believe is the most significant argument against cloning? What is his response to that argument?
5. Why does Colvin believe that he should have the right to clone himself?

## READING FOR FORM, ORGANIZATION, AND EXPOSITORY FEATURES

1. Describe the organizational strategy of Colvin's piece.
2. Why does Colvin delay his thesis until the ninth paragraph of an essay that totals only fourteen paragraphs? Is this strategy successful?
3. Why did Colvin choose to include only ten words in paragraph 12?
4. What is the effect of the questions that end paragraphs 4 and 5?

## READING FOR RHETORICAL CONCERNS

1. How does Colvin's status as a victim of a genetic disease affect the success of his argument?
2. How are Colvin's assumptions about the general public's response to cloning similar to those of Silver?
3. How does Colvin want the reader to view government regulation of citizens' personal lives? Is he successful in achieving that effect?
4. How does Colvin respond to the viewpoints of those who oppose human cloning? Is his response effective?

## WRITING ASSIGNMENTS

1. In a 1,000-word essay, summarize Colvin's argument and then either attack or defend it.

2. Should disabled individuals have more access to reproductive technologies than those who are not handicapped? Compose a 750-word essay that explains your answer.

3. Draw on Colvin's article to write a 1,000-word essay of personal response that evaluates whether you should have the right to "be all that you can be."

# Narcissus Cloned

## *John J. Conley*

*John J. Conley, S.J., is a professor of philosophy at Fordham University.*

### PREREADING

Is human cloning immoral? Explain your answer in ten minutes of freewriting.

The recent experiment in human cloning in Washington, 1 D.C., has provoked moral unease in the public. Both specialists and laypersons sense that this new technology is fraught with ethical and political peril. The discussion of the ethics of human cloning, however, rarely moves from intuitive praise and blame to careful analysis of the moral values—more frankly, the disvalues—presented by this practice. The discussion also reveals the moral impoverishment of our culture's categories for dealing with biotechnological challenges because the key ethical issues are often obscured by a bland subjectivism that reduces moral values to the simple desire of the parent or researcher.

Here I will sketch out the moral debits of the practice of cloning 2 and criticize the narrow types of moral reasoning that have prevented our society from collectively facing the incipient ethical and political dangers in this practice.

First, human cloning violates respect for the life of each human ₃
being, which is due from the moment of conception. While empirical science as such cannot determine the nature and extension of the person, it
is indisputable that conception marks the radical beginning of the personal history of each human being. Many of the physical characteristics
that clearly influence our interpersonal relations, such as gender, height
and somatic constitution, are clearly shaped in the moment of conception. Contemporary genetic research continues to reveal how profoundly
other more "spiritual" traits of the person, such as intelligence and emo-
tive temperament, are molded by one's conceptive history. The insistence
that respect for human life begin at the time of conception is not a sectar-
ian doctrine. Until quite recently, it formed the keystone of medical
ethics, as witnessed by the influential doctor's oath designed by the World
Medical Association in the aftermath of World War II: "I will maintain
the utmost respect for human life from the moment of conception."

Current experimentation in human cloning deliberately conceives ₄
a human being for the sake of research and then designates this human
embryo for destruction. It is true that this pre-embryo represents a
human being in an extremely primitive state of development. Nonetheless, this minute being remains clearly human (it can belong to no other
species), uniquely human (due to its singular corporeal occupation of
space and time) and, if placed in the proper environment, a being with
an internal capacity to develop the distinctly human faculties of intellect and will.

The fabrication and destruction of human embryos may appear a ₅
minor assault on life in a U.S. society numbed by 1.5 million abortions a
year and Dr. Jack Kevorkian's house calls. The acid test of whether we
corporately esteem human life, however, is not found primarily in our
treatment of powerful adults. Rather, it emerges in our treatment of the
vulnerable, like these fragile human beings at the dawn of gestation.

Second, the practice of cloning undermines one of the key values ₆
of social interaction: human diversity. Emmanuel Levinas, a contemporary French philosopher, argues that the central challenge in interpersonal contact is accepting the other person precisely as other, as
something more than the mirror image of oneself. One of the oddest of
the recent arguments in favor of human cloning went something like
this: Childbearing will be easier for the parents if they can raise siblings
hatched from the same egg, since the parents will always be dealing
with children having the identical genetic code. (We could even save on

the clothing bills.) It is hard to see how the family will benefit from becoming a hall of mirrors. The moral apprenticeship of family life consists precisely in the recognition of differences among siblings and the parents' recognition that their children are not simply the projection of their plans and wishes.

The possible reduction of human difference in a regime of routine 7 cloning raises troubling political issues. Just who or what will constitute the model for the clonable human? Which race? Which physical composition? Which emotional temperament? Which kind of intelligence and at what level? The development of earlier biotechnologies, such as amniocentesis and eugenic abortion, has already begun to homogenize the human population.

Several sources indicate that up to 90 percent of fetuses with 8 Down's Syndrome are currently aborted in the United States. The tendency to eliminate those ticketed as "disabled" contradicts the gains of the disability rights movement, which correctly urges us to respect and include those who are different because of physical or mental anomalies. Certain enthusiasts for cloning appear to dream Narcissus-like of a uniform humanity created in their own idealized image, an amalgam of Einstein and the Marlboro Man. Our aesthetic values, which focus so frequently on the unique timbre of a human voice or the difference between two human faces, would fade in such a monocolor regime. One can only marvel at the moral dexterity of our generation, which valiantly defends everything from the whale to the snail-darter lest bio-diversity be lost, yet calmly greets our growing destruction of the human other through eugenic technology.

Third, the practice of cloning undermines the integrity of human 9 love. Human beings, until quite recently, have usually been conceived in the conjugal embrace of their parents. In marital intercourse, the two values of union between the spouses and the procreation of the family's children remain indissoluble. It is the same act unifying the couple and bringing forth the nascent child. Cloning, however, stands to radicalize the divorce between conjugal union and procreation already introduced by in vitro fertilization. A third person, the scientist in the laboratory, invades the once-intimate drama of the generation of children.

I have long been haunted by the remark of Louise Brown, the first 10 child successfully conceived in vitro, when the doctor who had artificially conceived her died. Louise was plunged into grief. She told the press: "I feel that I have lost the person who made me"—as if the role once reserved to God and parent had now passed to the scientist in the white coat. The ancient setting of procreation, the sacramental embrace of spouses, is abandoned in favor of the fertile/sterile laboratory.

The initial experiment in human cloning indicates how radically 11 procreation has been divorced from conjugal union. The sperm and egg, provided by anonymous donors, were deliberately fused to fabricate a human embryo that would deteriorate within several days. It is true that in the future married couples struggling with infertility might resort to cloning technology. Even in this case, however, the wedge between unitive and procreative values remains. The intimate union between the conjugal gift of love and life remains severed.

The language employed by journalists to describe these new means 12 of generation also indicates the sea change wrought by cloning and related techniques. "Procreation" becomes "reproduction." "The glimmer in my parents' eyes" becomes "the product of conception." "The act of love" becomes "reproductive technology." The reduction of the child, once the immediate evidence of romance, to a product of the laboratory suggests the assault on the integrity of human love implicit in this practice.

Cloning's infringements on the basic goods of life, love, and other- 13 ness ultimately challenge human dignity itself. Immanuel Kant argues that human dignity entails the recognition that other human beings are ends in themselves, worthy of respect, rather than means to the ends of individual persons or society as a whole. Widespread cloning, however, would radically reduce humans to a eugenic mean. The human embryo would lose all claim to moral respect and legal protection by serving as an object of scientific curiosity or as an aid, easily discarded, to human fertility. In such a eugenic regime, human beings would increasingly be valued only for possessing certain socially desirable traits rather than for the simple fact that they exist as humans. By reducing the human person to an object stripped of intrinsic worth, routine cloning could threaten the ensemble of human rights itself.

The task of developing a moral response to the advent of human 14 cloning is rendered all the more problematic by the superficial debate our society is currently conducting on this issue. Whether on the editorial page of *The New York Times* or on Phil and Oprah's television screen, the discussion tends to obscure the key moral problems raised by this practice. Certain popular types of reasoning prevent, rather than assist, the careful debate we deserve on this issue.

One common approach is the Luddite condemnation of all ge- 15 netic engineering. Jeremy Rifkin, the most visible critic of the cloning experiment, exemplifies this approach. This position argues that the moral and political risks of genetic engineering are so grave that we should simply censure and, where possible, ban all such technology. References to Pandora's Box, Frankenstein, and the Third Reich decorate this blanket condemnation of all scientific intervention into human gestation. Such a categorical critique of biotechnology refuses to discern the different moral values present in the quite varied operations of genetic technology. While human cloning quite clearly appears to distort basic human goods, other therapeutic interventions can legitimately heal infertility and help an individual struggling with a genetic malady. Moral panic cannot ground a nuanced discernment of these disparate technological interventions.

Another approach, frequently offered by the proponents of cloning, 16 contends that the current experiments are simply "scientific research." Since they are just research, they should not be the object of moral critique. In other words, the Pope & Co. should chill out. This aura of value-free science seriously constricts the scope of the moral enterprise. The object of moral judgment is any human action, i.e., any act of human beings rooted in intellect and will. Moral scrutiny of scientific action is eminently justified inasmuch as such action is patently the result of rational deliberation and choice. The effort to sequester human cloning from ethical judgment, like the earlier attempt to "take morality and politics out of fetal tissue research," simply blinds us to the moral values at stake.

Perhaps the most common reasoning used to justify human 17 cloning is the subjectivist approach. As the editors of *The New York Times* argued, the producers of the material for cloning—I presume they mean the parents—should be the only ones to decide how the product is to be used. A thousand callers on radio talk shows claimed that "Father (or mother) knows best" and that no one could judge the clients and doctors who resort to this practice. Several proponents piously argued that these researchers sincerely wanted to help infertile couples. Such noble motives exempted them from moral censure.

In such a subjectivist perspective, the only relevant moral value is 18 the motive of the parties concerned, and the only virtue is unqualified tolerance for the desire of the scientist or the parent. Such subjectivism systematically averts its gaze from the action of cloning itself, and the question of whether or how this practice destroys human goods can never be raised. Moral scrutiny of this action is suffocated under a sentimental veil of compassion or, worse, under the steely curtain of private property rights.

The subjectivists legitimately highlight the psychological plight of 19 infertile couples who desire to bear children. They suppress, however, the salient ethical issue of which means, under what conditions, can properly be used to remedy this problem of infertility. An ancient moral and legal tradition rightly censures the buying and selling of infants as a just solution. There is a growing moral consensus that the violent battles over legal custody, not to mention the destruction of surplus embryos, have revealed the moral disvalues of surrogate mothering. Sentimental appeals to the pain of infertile couples "open to life" easily mask the ethical dangers of technologies that attempt to remedy infertility by the calculated manipulation and destruction of human lives.

The accompanying political debate must squarely question 20 whether this practice promotes or vitiates the common good. Conducting such a trenchant debate, however, is problematic in a society that increasingly perceives moral judgments as the arbitrary product of emotion or preference.

## READING FOR INFORMATION

1. What is Conley's opinion on the public debate over cloning humans?
2. When does Conley believe that life begins?
3. What is Conley's opinion on abortion? Where is that opinion indicated?
4. Outline Conley's three main reasons for opposing cloning.
5. Outline the three popular responses to cloning humans that Conley criticizes.
6. What does Conley mean by the "subjectivist" position? What disturbs Conley about that position?

## READING FOR FORM, ORGANIZATION, AND EXPOSITORY FEATURES

1. What is the purpose of Conley's second paragraph?
2. Outline the main elements in Conley's argument. How does Conley signal the boundaries between those elements?
3. What is Conley's opening strategy?

## READING FOR RHETORICAL CONCERNS

1. What does the "S.J." title that follows Conley's name indicate? How might that affiliation influence his views on reproductive technology?
2. In the first paragraph, how does Conley describe his purpose in writing?
3. How does Conley treat the arguments of those he disagrees with?

## WRITING ASSIGNMENTS

1. In a 1,000-word essay, summarize and respond to Conley's argument against cloning humans.

2. Write a 1,000-word argumentative essay that supports or takes issue with Conley's assertion that "the subjectivists legitimately highlight the psychological plight of infertile couples who desire to bear children. They suppress, however, the salient ethical issue of which means, under what conditions, can properly be used to remedy this problem of infertility."

3. Write a 1,000-word analysis of Conley's rhetorical purpose and technique. Describe his goals, his intended audience, and the techniques he uses to influence that audience.

# Crossing Lines: A Secular Argument Against Research Cloning

## *Charles Krauthammer*

*Charles Krauthammer is a syndicated columnist and a contributing editor of* The New Republic. *He is a medical doctor and a member of the President's Council on Bioethics.*

### PREREADING

What have you read or heard about stem-cell research? What have you read or heard about the use of cloning technology to develop treatments for human diseases? Freewrite for ten minutes in response to these questions.

### THE PROBLEM

You were once a single cell. Every one of the 100 trillion cells in your body today is a direct descendent of that zygote, the primordial cell formed by the union of mother's egg and father's sperm. Each one is genetically identical (allowing for copying errors and environmental

Krauthammer, Charles. "Crossing Lines: A Secular Argument Against Research Cloning." *New Republic* 29 April 2002: 20+. Reprinted by permission of Dr. Charles Krauthammer.

damage along the way) to that cell. Therefore, if we scraped a cell from, say, the inner lining of your cheek, its DNA would be the same DNA that, years ago in the original zygote, contained the entire plan for creating you and every part of you.

Here is the mystery: Why can the zygote, as it multiplies, produce every different kind of cell in the body—kidney, liver, brain, skin— while the skin cell is destined, however many times it multiplies, to remain skin forever? As the embryo matures, cells become specialized and lose their flexibility and plasticity. Once an adult cell has specialized—differentiated, in scientific lingo—it is stuck forever in that specialty. Skin is skin; kidney is kidney. 2

Understanding that mystery holds the keys to the kingdom. The Holy Grail of modern biology is regenerative medicine. If we can figure out how to make a specialized adult cell dedifferentiate—unspecialize, i.e., revert way back to the embryonic stage, perhaps even to the original zygotic stage—and then grow it like an embryo under controlled circumstances, we could reproduce for you every kind of tissue or organ you might need. We could create a storehouse of repair parts for your body. And, if we let that dedifferentiated cell develop completely in a woman's uterus, we will have created a copy of you, your clone. 3

That is the promise and the menace of cloning. It has already been done in sheep, mice, goats, pigs, cows, and now cats and rabbits (though cloning rabbits seems an exercise in biological redundancy). There is no reason in principle why it cannot be done in humans. The question is: Should it be done? 4

Notice that the cloning question is really two questions: (1) May we grow that dedifferentiated cell all the way into a cloned baby, a copy of you? That is called reproductive cloning. And (2) may we grow that dedifferentiated cell just into the embryonic stage and then mine it for parts, such as stem cells? That is called research cloning. 5

Reproductive cloning is universally abhorred. In July 2001 the House of Representatives, a fairly good representative of the American people, took up the issue and not a single member defended reproductive cloning. Research cloning, however, is the hard one. Some members were prepared to permit the cloning of the human embryo in order to study and use its component parts, with the proviso that the embryo be destroyed before it grows into a fetus or child. They were a minority, however. Their amendment banning baby-making but permitting research cloning was defeated by 76 votes. On July 31, 2001, a bill outlawing all cloning passed the House decisively.... 6

## THE PROMISE

This is how research cloning works. You take a donor egg from a woman,   7
remove its nucleus, and inject the nucleus of, say, a skin cell from another
person. It has been shown in animals that by the right manipulation you
can trick the egg and the injected nucleus into dedifferentiating—that
means giving up all the specialization of the skin cell and returning to its
original state as a primordial cell that could become anything in the body.

In other words, this cell becomes totipotent. It becomes the   8
equivalent of the fertilized egg in normal procreation, except that instead of having chromosomes from two people, it has chromosomes
from one. This cell then behaves precisely like an embryo. It divides. It
develops. At four to seven days, it forms a "blastocyst" consisting of
about 100 to 200 cells.

The main objective of cloning researchers would be to disassem-   9
ble this blastocyst: Pull the stem cells out, grow them in the laboratory,
and then try to tease them into becoming specific kinds of cells, say,
kidney or heart or brain and so on.

There would be two purposes for doing this: study or cure. You   10
could take a cell from a person with a baffling disease, like Lou Gehrig's,
clone it into a blastocyst, pull the stem cells out, and then study them in
order to try to understand the biology of the illness. Or you could begin
with a cell from a person with Parkinson's or a spinal cord injury, clone it,
and tease out the stem cells to develop tissue that you would reinject
into the original donor to, in theory, cure the Parkinson's or spinal cord
injury. The advantage of using a cloned cell rather than an ordinary stem
cell is that, presumably, there would be no tissue rejection. It's your own
DNA. The body would recognize it. You'd have a perfect match.

(Research cloning is sometimes called therapeutic cloning, but   11
that is a misleading term. First, because therapy by reinjection is only
one of the many uses to which this cloning can be put. Moreover, it is
not therapeutic for the clone—indeed, the clone is invariably destroyed
in the process—though it may be therapeutic for others. If you donate a
kidney to your brother, it would be odd to call your operation a therapeutic nephrectomy. It is not. It's a sacrificial nephrectomy.)

The conquest of rejection is one of the principal rationales for re-   12
search cloning. But there is reason to doubt this claim on scientific
grounds. There is some empirical evidence in mice that cloned tissue
may be rejected anyway (possibly because a clone contains a small
amount of foreign—mitochondrial—DNA derived from the egg into

which it was originally injected). Moreover, enormous advances are being made elsewhere in combating tissue rejection. The science of immune rejection is much more mature than the science of cloning. By the time we figure out how to do safe and reliable research cloning, the rejection problem may well be solved. And finally, there are less problematic alternatives—such as adult stem cells—that offer a promising alternative to cloning because they present no problem of tissue rejection and raise none of cloning's moral conundrums.

These scientific considerations raise serious questions about the 13 efficacy of, and thus the need for, research cloning. But there is a stronger case to be made. Even if the scientific objections are swept aside, even if research cloning is as doable and promising as its advocates contend, there are other reasons to pause.

The most obvious is this: Research cloning is an open door to re- 14 productive cloning. Banning the production of cloned babies while permitting the production of cloned embryos makes no sense. If you have factories all around the country producing embryos for research and commerce, it is inevitable that someone will implant one in a woman (or perhaps in some artificial medium in the farther future) and produce a human clone. What then? A law banning reproductive cloning but permitting research cloning would then make it a crime not to destroy that fetus—an obvious moral absurdity.

This is an irrefutable point and the reason that many in Congress 15 will vote for the total ban on cloning. Philosophically, however, it is a showstopper. It lets us off too early and too easy. It keeps us from facing the deeper question: Is there anything about research cloning that in and of itself makes it morally problematic?

## OBJECTION I: INTRINSIC WORTH

For some people, life begins at conception. And not just life—if life is 16 understood to mean a biologically functioning organism, even a single cell is obviously alive—but personhood. If the first zygotic cell is owed all the legal and moral respect due a person, then there is nothing to talk about. Ensoulment starts with Day One and Cell One, and the idea of taking that cell or its successor cells apart to serve someone else's needs is abhorrent.

This is an argument of great moral force but little intellectual in- 17 terest. Not because it may not be right. But because it is unprovable. It rests on metaphysics. Either you believe it or you don't. The discussion ends there.

I happen not to share this view. I do not believe personhood be- 18 gins at conception. I do not believe a single cell has the moral or legal standing of a child. This is not to say that I do not stand in awe of the developing embryo, a creation of majestic beauty and mystery. But I stand in equal awe of the Grand Canyon, the spider's web, and quantum mechanics. Awe commands wonder, humility, appreciation. It does not command inviolability. I am quite prepared to shatter an atom, take down a spider's web, or dam a canyon for electricity. (Though we'd have to be very short on electricity before I'd dam the Grand.)

I do not believe the embryo is entitled to inviolability. But is it en- 19 titled to nothing? There is a great distance between inviolability, on the one hand, and mere "thingness," on the other. Many advocates of research cloning see nothing but thingness. That view justifies the most ruthless exploitation of the embryo. That view is dangerous.

Why? Three possible reasons. First, the Brave New World Factor: 20 Research cloning gives man too much power for evil. Second, the Slippery Slope: The habit of embryonic violation is in and of itself dangerous. Violate the blastocyst today and every day, and the practice will inure you to violating the fetus or even the infant tomorrow. Third, Manufacture: The very act of creating embryos for the sole purpose of exploiting and then destroying them will ultimately predispose us to a ruthless utilitarianism about human life itself.

## OBJECTION II: THE BRAVE NEW WORLD FACTOR

The physicists at Los Alamos did not hesitate to penetrate, manipulate, 21 and split uranium atoms on the grounds that uranium atoms possess intrinsic worth that entitled them to inviolability. Yet after the war, many fought to curtail atomic power. They feared the consequences of delivering such unfathomable power—and potential evil—into the hands of fallible human beings. Analogously, one could believe that the cloned blastocyst has little more intrinsic worth than the uranium atom and still be deeply troubled by the manipulation of the blastocyst because of the fearsome power it confers upon humankind.

The issue is leverage. Our knowledge of how to manipulate human 22 genetics (or atomic nuclei) is still primitive. We could never construct ex nihilo a human embryo. It is an unfolding organism of unimaginable complexity that took nature three billion years to produce. It might take us less time to build it from scratch, but not much less. By that time, we as a species might have acquired enough wisdom to use it wisely. Instead, the human race in its infancy has stumbled upon a genie infinitely too complicated to create or even fully understand, but understandable enough to command and perhaps even control. And given our demonstrated unwisdom with our other great discovery—atomic power: As we speak, the very worst of humanity is on the threshold of acquiring the most powerful weapons in history—this is a fear and a consideration to be taken very seriously.

For example, female human eggs seriously limit the mass produc- 23 tion of cloned embryos. Extracting eggs from women is difficult, expensive, and potentially dangerous. The search is on, therefore, for a good alternative. Scientists have begun injecting human nuclei into the egg cells of animals. In 1996 Massachusetts scientists injected a human nucleus with a cow egg. Chinese scientists have fused a human fibroblast with a rabbit egg and have grown the resulting embryo to the blastocyst stage. We have no idea what grotesque results might come from such interspecies clonal experiments.

In October 2000 the first primate containing genes from another 24 species was born (a monkey with a jellyfish gene). In 1995 researchers in Texas produced headless mice. In 1997 researchers in Britain produced headless tadpoles. In theory, headlessness might be useful for organ transplantation. One can envision, in a world in which embryos are routinely manufactured, the production of headless clones—subhuman creatures with usable human organs but no head, no brain, no consciousness to identify them with the human family.

The heart of the problem is this: Nature, through endless evolu- 25 tion, has produced cells with totipotent power. We are about to harness that power for crude human purposes. That should give us pause. Just around the corner lies the logical by-product of such power: human-animal hybrids, partly developed human bodies for use as parts, and other horrors imagined—Huxley's Deltas and Epsilons—and as yet unimagined. This is the Brave New World Factor. Its grounds for objecting to this research are not about the beginnings of life, but about the ends; not the origin of these cells, but their destiny; not where we took these magnificent cells from, but where they are taking us.

## OBJECTION III: THE SLIPPERY SLOPE

The other prudential argument is that once you start tearing apart blas- 26 tocysts, you get used to tearing apart blastocysts. And whereas now you'd only be doing that at the seven-day stage, when most people would look at this tiny clump of cells on the head of a pin and say it is not inviolable, it is inevitable that some scientist will soon say: Give me just a few more weeks to work with it and I could do wonders.

That will require quite a technological leap because the blastocyst 27 will not develop as a human organism unless implanted in the uterus. That means that to go beyond that seven-day stage you'd have to implant this human embryo either in an animal uterus or in some fully artificial womb. Both possibilities may be remote, but they are real. And then we'll have a scientist saying: Give me just a few more months with this embryo, and I'll have actual kidney cells, brain cells, pancreatic cells that I can transplant back into the donor of the clone and cure him. Scientists at Advanced Cell Technology in Massachusetts have already gone past that stage in animals. They have taken cloned cow embryos past the blastocyst stage, taken tissue from the more developed cow fetus, and reimplanted it back into the donor animal.

The scientists' plea to do the same in humans will be hard to ig- 28 nore. Why grow the clone just to the blastocyst stage, destroy it, pull out the inner cell mass, grow stem cells out of that, propagate them in the laboratory, and then try chemically or otherwise to tweak them into becoming kidney cells or brain cells or islet cells? This is Rube Goldberg. Why not just allow that beautiful embryonic machine, created by nature and far more sophisticated than our crude techniques, to develop unmolested? Why not let the blastocyst grow into a fetus that possesses the kinds of differentiated tissue that we could then use for curing the donor?

Scientifically, this would make sense. Morally, we will have crossed 29 the line between tearing apart a mere clump of cells and tearing apart a recognizable human fetus. And at that point, it would be an even smaller step to begin carving up seven- and eight-month-old fetuses with more perfectly formed organs to alleviate even more pain and suffering among the living. We will, slowly and by increments, have gone from stem cells to embryo farms to factories with fetuses in various stages of development and humanness, hanging (metaphorically) on meat hooks waiting to be cut open to be used by the already born.

We would all be revolted if a living infant or developed fetus were 30 carved up for parts. Should we build a fence around that possibility by prohibiting any research on even the very earliest embryonic clump of cells? Is the only way to avoid the slide never to mount the slippery slope at all? On this question, I am personally agnostic. If I were utterly convinced that we would never cross the seven-day line, then I would have no objection on these grounds to such research on the inner cell mass of a blastocyst. The question is: Can we be sure? This is not a question of principle; it is a question of prudence. It is almost a question of psychological probability. No one yet knows the answer.

## OBJECTION IV: MANUFACTURE

Note that while, up to now, I have been considering arguments against 31 research cloning, they are all equally applicable to embryonic research done on a normal—i.e., noncloned—embryo. If the question is tearing up the blastocyst, there is no intrinsic moral difference between a two-parented embryo derived from a sperm and an egg and a single-parented embryo derived from a cloned cell. Thus the various arguments against this research—the intrinsic worth of the embryo, the prudential consideration that we might create monsters, or the prudential consideration that we might become monsters in exploiting post-embryonic forms of human life (fetuses or even children)—are identical to the arguments for and against stem-cell research.

These arguments are serious—serious enough to banish the insou- 32 ciance of the scientists who consider anyone questioning their work to be a Luddite—yet, in my view, insufficient to justify a legal ban on stem-cell research (as with stem cells from discarded embryos in fertility clinics). I happen not to believe that either personhood or ensoulment occurs at conception. I think we need to be apprehensive about what evil might arise from the power of stem-cell research, but that apprehension alone, while justifying vigilance and regulation, does not justify a ban on the practice. And I believe that given the good that might flow from stem-cell research, we should first test the power of law and custom to enforce the seven-day blastocyst line for embryonic exploitation before assuming that such a line could never hold.

This is why I support stem-cell research (using leftover embryos 33 from fertility clinics) and might support research cloning were it not for one other aspect that is unique to it. In research cloning, the embryo is created with the explicit intention of its eventual destruction. That is a given because not to destroy the embryo would be to produce a cloned child. If you are not permitted to grow the embryo into a child, you are obliged at some point to destroy it.

Deliberately creating embryos for eventual and certain destruc- 34 tion means the launching of an entire industry of embryo manufacture. It means the routinization, the commercialization, the commodification of the human embryo. The bill that would legalize research cloning essentially sanctions, licenses, and protects the establishment of a most ghoulish enterprise: the creation of nascent human life for the sole purpose of its exploitation and destruction.

How is this morally different from simply using discarded embryos from in vitro fertilization (IVF) clinics? Some have suggested that it is not, that to oppose research cloning is to oppose IVF and any stem-cell research that comes out of IVF. The claim is made that because in IVF there is a high probability of destruction of the embryo, it is morally equivalent to research cloning. But this is plainly not so. In research cloning there is not a high probability of destruction; there is 100 percent probability. Because every cloned embryo must be destroyed, it is nothing more than a means to someone else's end.

In IVF, the probability of destruction may be high, but it need not necessarily be. You could have a clinic that produces only a small number of embryos, and we know of many cases of multiple births resulting from multiple embryo implantation. In principle, one could have IVF using only a single embryo and thus involving no deliberate embryo destruction at all. In principle, that is impossible in research cloning.

Furthermore, a cloned embryo is created to be destroyed and used by others. An IVF embryo is created to develop into a child. One cannot disregard intent in determining morality. Embryos are created in IVF to serve reproduction. Embryos are created in research cloning to serve, well, research. If certain IVF embryos were designated as "helper embryos" that would simply aid an anointed embryo in turning into a child, then we would have an analogy to cloning. But, in fact, we don't know which embryo is anointed in IVF. They are all created to have a chance of survival. And they are all equally considered an end.

Critics counter that this ends-and-means argument is really obfuscation, that both procedures make an instrument of the embryo. In cloning, the creation and destruction of the embryo is a means to understanding or curing disease. In IVF, the creation of the embryo is a means of satisfying a couple's need for a child. They are both just means to ends.

But it makes no sense to call an embryo a means to the creation of a child. The creation of a child is the destiny of an embryo. To speak of an embryo as a means to creating a child empties the word "means" of content. The embryo in IVF is a stage in the development of a child; it is no more a means than a teenager is a means to the adult he or she later becomes. In contrast, an embryo in research cloning is pure means. Laboratory pure.

And that is where we must draw the line. During the great debate 40
on stem-cell research, a rather broad consensus was reached (among
those not committed to "intrinsic worth" rendering all embryos inviolable) that stem-cell research could be morally justified because the
embryos destroyed for their possibly curative stem cells were derived
from fertility clinics and thus were going to be discarded anyway. It was
understood that human embryos should not be created solely for the
purpose of being dismembered and then destroyed for the benefit of
others. Indeed, when Senator Bill Frist made his impassioned presentation on the floor of the Senate supporting stem-cell research, he included among his conditions a total ban on creating human embryos
just to be stem-cell farms.

Where cloning for research takes us decisively beyond stem-cell 41
research is in sanctioning the manufacture of the human embryo. You
can try to regulate embryonic research to prohibit the creation of Brave
New World monsters; you can build fences on the slippery slope, regulating how many days you may grow an embryo for research; but once
you countenance the very creation of human embryos for no other purpose than for their parts, you have crossed a moral frontier.

Research cloning is the ultimate in conferring thingness upon the 42
human embryo. It is the ultimate in desensitization. And as such, it
threatens whatever other fences and safeguards we might erect around
embryonic research. The problem, one could almost say, is not what
cloning does to the embryo, but what it does to us. Except that once
cloning has changed us, it will inevitably enable further assaults on
human dignity. Creating a human embryo just so it can be used and
then destroyed undermines the very foundation of the moral prudence
that informs the entire enterprise of genetic research: the idea that
while a human embryo may not be a person, it is not nothing. Because
if it is nothing, then everything is permitted. And if everything is permitted, then there are no fences, no safeguards, no bottom.    ✿

### READING FOR INFORMATION

1. What is "the mystery" that Krauthammer refers to in the first sentence of
   paragraph 2?
2. What is the goal of regenerative medicine?
3. What is the distinction between reproductive cloning and research
   cloning?
4. According to Krauthammer, what do most Americans think about reproductive cloning?

5. Describe how research cloning might be used to develop treatments for diseases.

6. Summarize the argument Krauthammer presents against research cloning in paragraphs 14 and 15.

7. Summarize the argument Krauthammer presents against research cloning in paragraphs 21 to 25.

8. Summarize the argument Krauthammer presents against research cloning in paragraphs 26 to 30.

9. Summarize the argument Krauthammer presents against research cloning in paragraphs 31 to 41.

10. What are "Huxley's Deltas and Epsilons" that Krauthammer refers to in paragraph 25?

11. Why does Krauthammer support stem-cell research but not research cloning?

## READING FOR FORM, ORGANIZATION, AND EXPOSITORY FEATURES

1. How does Krauthammer use subheadings to signal the parts of his argument?

2. What is the relationship between the content under the subheading "Objection I: Intrinsic Worth" and the content under the next three subheadings?

3. Krauthammer uses two sentence fragments in paragraph 20. Comment on his decision to use sentence structures that are technically incorrect. Is this decision consistent with his other stylistic choices?

4. What do you think is Krauthammer's target audience? What aspects of the article seem to be designed for that particular audience?

## READING FOR RHETORICAL CONCERNS

1. Krauthammer does not provide a compact thesis statement at the outset of the article but rather in his last paragraph. Comment on that strategy.

2. To what extent does Krauthammer draw on his expertise as a medical doctor to support his argument against research cloning?

3. In paragraphs 14 and 15, Krauthammer presents an argument against research cloning that he believes is "irrefutable." What is his rationale for continuing the essay after delivering what he considers to be a decisive blow against research cloning?

4. To what extent does Krauthammer acknowledge and examine the arguments of his opponents?

## WRITING ASSIGNMENTS

1. Draw on Krauthammer's article to write a 500-word objective explanation of the goals of research cloning.

2. In a 1,000-word essay, either attack or support Krauthammer's assertion that research cloning should be banned. Make sure that you summarize the principal points in Krauthammer's argument.

3. Write a 750-word essay of personal response in which you balance Krauthammer's objections to research cloning with the concerns of people who suffer from terminal and disabling illnesses.

# Species on Ice

### *Karen Wright*

*Karen Wright is a science writer whose work has appeared in* Discover, Science, *and* Scientific American.

## PREREADING

What efforts are you aware of to save endangered species? Freewrite for ten minutes in response to this question.

The tabby crouched on the cage's platform is fiercely attentive, as if he's not sure whether he's the hunter or the hunted. Something's different about this cat: His big blue eyes are a little too close together, his nose a bit long, and his limbs on the rangy side—even for a tom. Among the dozens of friendly felines romping in a nearby corridor, this one stands out, as nervous and haughty as the last cat on Earth.

Actually, Jazz is the first of his kind, an endangered African wildcat born almost two years ago from a frozen embryo that was implanted in an ordinary house cat. Acting as midwife was Betsy Dresser, director of the Audubon Center for Research of Endangered Species, on the bayou near New Orleans. Dresser is a leading advocate of efforts to protect rare animals by cloning and other advanced reproductive techniques. Her controversial aim is to provide a last-ditch, high-tech redoubt for species that might otherwise vanish when their habitats do.

"We're a safety net for these species," explains Dresser. "I feel like   3
I'm in the emergency room of the conservation movement."

Some conservationists say that such singular feats of assisted re-   4
production are unlikely to yield meaningful results for species survival.
But no one disputes the fact that Dresser's compound is ground zero
for such feats or that her new wildcat is the most conspicuous example
yet. Jazz began as a twinkle in Dresser's eye back in the 1980s, when
she first began considering the concept of frozen zoos—collections of
sperm, embryos, and tissue samples from imperiled animals stored in
tanks of liquid nitrogen. With technological advances, the frozen cells
might someday be used to re-create populations of species that face extinction. Dresser knew that in order to effect such recoveries biologists
would have to get humble surrogates to gestate embryos of exotic
species. Using mothers of the endangered species could be impractical,
if not impossible. The advantage of using surrogate mothers is that
"you'd be able to make more babies because you're not using the endangered mothers themselves," she says.

The principle of interspecies surrogacy was first demonstrated in   5
the 1970s, when an Asian mouflon lamb was born to a domestic wool
sheep. In the early 1980s, Dresser and her colleagues at the Cincinnati
Zoo coaxed a rare African antelope called a bongo from a doe of a more
plentiful species, the eland. A few years later, the Cincinnati team shepherded the birth of a gaur, an endangered Asian ox, by a Holstein cow.
In 1994, Dresser announced the live birth of a threatened Indian desert
cat, delivered by a house cat that had been implanted with a fresh embryo. Jazz represents the next stage in Dresser's vision: living, purring
proof that frozen embryos can remain viable after thawing and can develop normally in the womb of another species.

Because egg cells, unlike sperm, don't freeze well, Dresser needs   6
fresh eggs to make her frozen embryos. But collecting fresh eggs or embryos from rare wild females is tricky, so scientists are developing a new
cloning technology as an alternative. In ordinary cloning, the nucleus of
an egg cell is replaced with the nucleus from a body cell of the animal to
be cloned. A jolt of electricity then prompts the egg to begin dividing,
after which it is implanted in a surrogate mother. To get around the problem of collecting eggs from endangered mothers, conservation cloning
would have to involve two added twists: The egg cells, as well as the

surrogate mothers, would be of a different species than the animal being cloned. Earlier this year, scientists at Advanced Cell Technology in Worcester, Massachusetts, announced the birth of the first such chimeric clone, a gaur calf that was produced from a skin-cell nucleus injected into the egg of, and nurtured in the womb of, an ordinary cow. The calf appeared healthy at birth but died from a bacterial infection two days later.

Meanwhile, Dresser's own attempts to clone bongos and wildcats 7 in surrogate species have failed, and Chinese ventures to clone giant pandas are foundering as well. When scientists at Advanced Cell Technology cloned the gaur, they worked on 692 eggs to get one live birth.

That's not surprising, says David Wildt, head of reproductive sci- 8 ences at the National Conservation and Research Center. Cloning and other assisted reproductive technologies won't save the panda or any other endangered species unless conservationists also develop detailed knowledge of each species' biology, he says.

"It's easier to highlight these one-shot wonders than it is to ad- 9 dress the huge need for basic knowledge of the reproductive biology of endangered species," he says. For example, artificial insemination has become critical to the captive breeding of pandas, black-footed ferrets, and cheetahs, but only after years of research on the reproductive mechanisms unique to each animal. Success in one species doesn't translate easily to any other. Fifteen years ago, Wildt hoped he could quickly adapt the breeding methods that had become routine in cattle to cheetahs. "We learned that cheetahs are not cows," he says.

Wildt and other critics fear that cloning encourages a false sense 10 of hope and complacency where immediate action is needed. "There's a total misperception about what these reproductive services can offer," he says. He worries that surrogate programs like Dresser's, which tend to focus on species that are related to such well-studied mammals as cows and cats, divert attention away from the most threatened species and the preservation of their habitats. "The point is that there's 40,000 vertebrate species out there being ignored."

Dresser says that by working with domesticated species and their 11 relatives now, she can expand the reach of the program later. She plans to take her techniques out of the Audubon Center compound to the field, implanting bongo embryos in wild eland in Kenya, for example, so the offspring will learn to fend for themselves in natural surroundings.

In the meantime, some members of the conservation community 12 may become more accepting of the center's approach. In an April [2001] talk at the American Museum of Natural History, research scientist Phil

Damiani of Advanced Cell Technology emphasized the potential of frozen zoos for preserving the diversity of a dwindling species' gene pool. Instead of a two-by-two Noah's ark approach, genome banks could store tissue samples from thousands of individuals of each species. "I had people coming up and saying, 'We never really looked at cloning in that respect,'" says Damiani. "They take a second look at it when they realize we're not talking about creating a genetic bottleneck."

But Dresser says that the idea of keeping a species alive in a nitro- 13 gen tank rather than in the wild will never be appealing. It's a grimly pragmatic solution to the problem of encroaching humanity—realpolitik for the biosphere. "Some people say, 'If this is the way we have to save them, then I'd rather they went extinct,'" she says. "I don't agree with that at all."    ✿

## READING FOR INFORMATION

1. What is "interspecies surrogacy"?
2. Describe how Dresser uses "frozen zoos" and "interspecies surrogacy" to help protect endangered wild animal populations.
3. How successful have past efforts been to clone endangered species?
4. Summarize David Wildt's viewpoint on cloning endangered species.
5. Why does Wildt believe that Dresser's efforts are counterproductive?
6. What specific endangered species are mentioned in the article? Are these species you were aware of?

## READING FOR FORM, ORGANIZATION, AND EXPOSITORY FEATURES

1. What is Wright's organizational plan? How does she signal that plan to her readers?
2. For the most part, Wright quotes David Wildt directly rather than paraphrasing or summarizing his remarks. Why do you think Wright made this decision?
3. What is Wright's opening strategy? Is it effective? Why, or why not?
4. Characterize the style of Wright's article.

## READING FOR RHETORICAL CONCERNS

1. What is Wright's goal in writing? How does she achieve that goal?
2. What do you think is Wright's viewpoint on cloning endangered species? In what way does she indicate that viewpoint?

3. Do you think it is significant that Wright concludes with a statement from Dresser rather than a statement from Wildt?

4. What are Dresser's and Wildt's professional qualifications? Do those qualifications indicate that Dresser and Wildt are experts on preserving endangered species?

## WRITING ASSIGNMENTS

1. Write a 750-word essay in which you summarize the debate between Dresser and Wildt.

2. Write a 1,000-word essay in which you argue in favor of either Dresser's or Wildt's position on cloning endangered species. Make sure you take your opposition into account.

3. Write a 750-word essay of personal response in which you evaluate the balance between protecting endangered animal species and meeting the needs of human society.

# Bessie and the Gaur

## *Malcolm Tait*

*Malcolm Tait is the managing editor of* The Ecologist.

### PREREADING

Do you think that, in general, scientists serve the best interests of society? Freewrite for ten minutes in response to that question.

Maybe it's a symptom of twothousanditis, the condition 1 brought on by excessive attention paid to a particular number with no significance whatsoever other than tidiness, but this year has seen an extraordinary rash of stories relating to the science of the future: genetics. Wherever you look, there's a new challenge to medical and human ethics—children's gender genetically manipulated in Spain

This article first appeared in the December 2000 issue of *The Ecologist*, Vol. 30, No. 9, www.theecologist.org. Reprinted with permission.

to bypass inherited disease; genetic information required by insurance companies; a baby genetically chosen with cells that might save his dying sister; the human genome under the microscope; even a UFO-cult with the funds, alleged ability, and necessary loopholes to try cloning the first human. It's as if someone at the beginning of the year opened the Pandora's box marked "Frankenstein," and the doctor's influence came pouring out.

Mankind has always enjoyed testing its own limits, of course, and there's nothing it likes better than a good ethical argument—talk radio and TV chat shows wouldn't survive without it—but we've entered a moral maze this year that has heads spinning.    2

As ever, the arguments boil down to one key confrontation: the needs of the planet versus the rights of the individual. The topic—genetics—may be comparatively new, but it's the same old argument. The world has more people than it can cater for: Yes, but if science can help my childless marriage, why shouldn't I have the right to take advantage of it? Excessive vehicle use causes global warming and ultimately destruction: Yes, but I need my car to get my children to school. The long-term prospects would appear to be disastrous: Yes, but I need a short-term solution.    3

However, there's one of this year's genetic developments that has nothing to do with human rights, nothing to do, despite appearances to the contrary, with animal rights, and everything to do with scientific experimentation dressed up as benefit. Last month, a cow named Bessie from Iowa was due to give birth to a gaur, an endangered ox-like animal from Asia. The process was achieved by injecting gaur cells, complete with their DNA, into hollowed-out cow eggs, then electrically fusing the eggs and DNA together. Of the 81 successfully developed eggs that were implanted into cattle, eight resulted in pregnancy, three managed not to miscarry, and two turned into embryos which were removed for monitoring. Only Bessie soldiered on. . . .    4

Already there are plans afoot for more work along similar lines. The bucardo, a Pyrenean mountain goat, became extinct in January [2000], when the last of its kind was put out of its lonely misery by a falling tree. Cells were taken from the corpse, and the Massachusetts-based company Advanced Cell Technology is planning to clone the creature back to life. The panda is next on the list for rejuvenation, and there's talk of trying to bring back the Tasmanian tiger, a wolf-like animal that lost its last grip on survival in the 1930s. Even the mammoth, for crying out loud, is being looked at for a possible comeback. The    5 makers of next year's second sequel to Jurassic Park will be able to keep their marketing funds firmly in their back pockets.

Now, the mammoth may be a bit pie-in-the-sky—the DNA that  6 we've got from an ancient frozen carcass is patchy, to say the least—but there's no doubt that the thought of bringing back the bucardo, an extinct species, certainly stimulates the imagination. It's a fascinating scientific gimmick, a perfect example of doing something because we can. We should leave it at that.

But we won't. Already there is talk of this process being a mar-  7 velous aid to conservation, a boon to the world's endangered species, a solution to the perennial problem of man's cohabitation with beast. This is tripe, for the cloning of endangered species is as far removed from the spirit and psychology of conservation as we've ever been since man first noticed he was killing off the birds and beasts.

Conservation is a precarious affair, because its failure is finite. It  8 has, quite literally, a deadline. Sometimes that deadline is easy to see, other times it's not. In the 1980s, it was realized that whales were struggling in their relationship with man, and new laws and consumption restrictions were put into place. By the early 1990s, the plight of the elephant came to life and [was] reasonably successfully dealt with. We've recently discovered that the troubled tiger is in even more danger than we'd previously thought. Wheels are beginning to turn. Yet for every headline species that captures the heart, there are many, many more that don't make it. Most of the world first heard of Miss Waldron's Red Colobus monkey this year, for example, when it was announced that it had become extinct. A sense of simultaneous gain and loss.

Extinction, of course, is part of evolution, and had man's footprint  9 not covered the lands and seas, the world would still have continued its course of saying farewell to species whose day had gone. The fact is, however, that man has not just accelerated that process, but is continuing to do so at a rate that doesn't allow the surviving species to adjust to their new ecosystems. Conservation isn't just about saving a particular species, it's about reducing our destructive impact on natural processes that are in increasing danger of being unable to sustain themselves, and ultimately, therefore, of sustaining us.

There's too much at stake, for nature and for ourselves, to take  10 conservation lightly. But conservation takes time and money. It requires careful management and planning, and involves apparent sacrifices. It demands that the long-term view takes precedence over, or is at least built into, the short term. If conservation is going to work, mankind has to want so much that it hurts.

## SLIPPERY SLOPE

Which brings us back to Bessie. Suddenly, for the first time ever, we've got an alternative to conservation. It's only a tiny crack at present, but science will want to widen it. What's the point in putting all that effort into looking after ecosystems if we've got the ability to clone everything back into existence? Just think of what we can achieve—we can carry on crashing through the planet, doing what we want, and whenever some species starts to totter as a result, we've got the technology to see it through the hard times. Of course, no biotech company would put it like that at present—it would appear as scientific coldheartedness and therefore be commercial suicide—but the option will be there. Cloning endangered species is a classic case of science no longer being used for prevention, but for apparent cure. It is lazy science. However much its supporters may protest that cloning will only ever be used to complement conservation, to step in when conservation has failed, the day will come when the financial benefits of, say, clearing a forest will outweigh the costs of cloning the endangered species within. Someone will be prepared to pay for it, and the rot will have begun.

But what will we then do with these phoenix-like creatures? If their habitat is no more, where will we put them? Perhaps we will create reservations for them—but to save space, we'll need to make sure we only hang on to the species which benefit ourselves. We'll need to recreate habitats that suit them, and if our new cloned versions require special diets, or develop viruses or illnesses that their originals never encountered, then we can genetically modify their surroundings to suit. Any imperfections that are built in, we can decode and correct. In short, who needs Nature's ecosystems when we can create our own?

This may seem a far-fetched future, but it is in fact perfectly in line with the way mankind has always been—except that he's now taking a bigger step than ever before. From his earliest days, he has used whatever tools are available to him to conquer nature and reshape it into his own likeness. He has recorded his kills by scratching them into a rock; when he realized hunting was too difficult, he herded instead; he has carved his image into every known material; he has put creatures into cages to look at, or taken them on as pets; he has hunted them for fun. Why would anyone think he wouldn't instinctively want to go that one further step—albeit a mightier one than ever—and restructure nature to suit his precise needs?

## PASSING THE BUCK

None of this is to say that genetic scientists and those who fund them 14 are necessarily power-mad, corrupt seekers of world domination. Science is the discipline of discovery, of finding out, of increasing knowledge. Thus it is that, generally, each new step forward is taken with the honest and sincere desire to benefit man. Yet it's curious how often genetic scientists, nudging the process onward, tend to see their own work in isolation and distinct from the overall movement.

"The prospect of human cloning causes us grave misgivings," 15 writes Ian Wilmut, co-cloner with Keith Campbell in 1996 of Dolly the sheep, in his book *The Second Creation.* "It is physically too risky, it could have untoward effects on the psychology of the cloned child, and in the end we see no medical justification for it. For us, the technology that produced Dolly has far wider significance."

Wilmut is fully convinced of the benefits of his own work, knows 16 that he has paved the way for future cloning, yet is distancing himself from any responsibility for it. It's rather like the work in the 1930s on splitting the atom and harnessing its energy—everyone involved could see possible positive benefits in their own specific research, but relied on everyone else not to see the potential for harm.

Which is why, ultimately, we should none of us be fooled. The 17 cloning of endangered or extinct animals is an extraordinary feat, and one which, if continued, will inevitably lead to yet more and more extraordinary feats.

It is the latest stage in man's attempts to control his world, and 18 like Frankenstein's monster, it may one day lead to its creator's own destruction.

So let's drop the pretense right now. Let's honestly admit to our- 19 selves what we're getting into. Cloning is a brand new chapter in the history of mankind, but it has nothing, absolutely nothing, to do with conservation. ❖

## READING FOR INFORMATION

1. Explain Tait's reference to "twothousanditis" in the first sentence of the essay.

2. Explain the "key confrontation" that Tait outlines in paragraph 3.

3. What endangered and extinct species that are candidates for cloning are mentioned in Tait's article?

4. If endangered and extinct species are cloned, how does Tait think they will be integrated into the environment?

5. Who are Ian Wilmut and Keith Campbell?

6. What connection does Tait make between cloning and splitting the atom?

7. To what extent does Tait believe that cloning will aid animal conservation efforts?

## READING FOR FORM, ORGANIZATION, AND EXPOSITORY FEATURES

1. Describe Tait's tone, and give specific examples that support your answer.

2. How does Tait attempt to engage his audience?

3. Which paragraphs contain Tait's thesis statement?

4. Why does Tait end his article with three short paragraphs?

## READING FOR RHETORICAL CONCERNS

1. In paragraph 15, Tait quotes cloning pioneer Ian Wilmut. What is Tait's attitude toward Wilmut's statement? Do you think Tait is fair to Wilmut?

2. Do you think Tait excludes or includes scientists in his target audience? Explain your answer.

3. Tait refers to Frankenstein at the beginning and end of his article. What is he trying to achieve with those references? Is he successful?

## WRITING ASSIGNMENTS

1. Write a 750-word essay of personal response on whether or not we can trust scientists to serve the best interests of the public. Draw on material from Tait's article.

2. Write a 750-word essay of personal response on how to balance, in Tait's words, "the needs of the planet versus the rights of the individual."

3. Write a 1,000-word essay that either attacks or defends Tait's argument.

## SYNTHESIS WRITING ASSIGNMENTS

1. Imagine how it would be to have a younger brother or sister who was cloned from one of your cells. Write a 1,000-word essay that comments

on the desirability of living with a clone sibling. Draw on at least two articles from Chapter 6 to support your commentary.

2. Design a scenario that illustrates the complex controversies over child custody that can develop when parents use cloning for reproduction. Write a 1,000-word essay in which you describe your scenario and weigh the various ethical considerations that the scenario involves.

3. Write a 1,250-word essay that argues for or against the legalization of human cloning. Make use of sources from Chapter 6 to support your viewpoint.

4. Synthesize material from Chapter 6 readings to describe, in a 1,250-word essay, how human and animal cloning technology might change our society. Evaluate these potential changes.

5. Imagine that in the future you and your partner are unable to conceive a child through either sexual intercourse or in vitro fertilization. Write a 1,000-word essay of personal reflection in which you explain why you would or would not resort to cloning in an effort to have a child.

6. Draw on articles by Silver, Colvin, and Conley to discuss, in a 1,000-word essay, the pros and cons of cloning humans.

7. Use material from Chapter 6 readings to write a 1,500-word essay that analyzes the presentation of cloning technology in one or more science fiction movies, such as *Jurassic Park*, *Multiplicity*, and *The Boys from Brazil*.

CHAPTER

*seven*

# Human/Machine Interaction

Most Americans are accustomed to relationships with machines. For example, we talk to our cars, feel betrayed when they break down, and sometimes grieve when they are hauled to the junkyard. As a nation, we spend more time in front of televisions than we do with family and friends. Video games have captivated a generation of adolescent males, and many of their parents spend workdays in front of computer screens. The development of virtual-reality systems that emulate the real world may signal a new era in our relationship with machines, wherein circuitry may be an important source of "life" experiences.

Technology is often described as a double-edged sword that can work to our benefit or detriment, depending upon how it is applied. Some commentators argue that our relationship to machinery and electronics will provide us with greater control over our lives; others claim it will alienate us from human experience. Those viewpoints and others are presented in the sources in this chapter. "We Are Not Special," an excerpt from Rodney A. Brooks's book *Flesh and Machines: How Robots Will Change Us*, claims that humans are biological "machines" that are no different, in essence, than machines constructed of plastic and metal. Steve Mann writes about how he uses a wearable computer system to enhance his natural abilities in "Cyborg Seeks Community." The potential for intimacy between humans and intelligent machines is explored in Sherry Turkle's "Loving Technology." In "Live Forever," Raymond Kurzweil predicts the consequences of beings able to transfer the contents of a human mind into a computer. Clifford Stoll argues that technology cuts us off from contact with other humans in an excerpt from his book *High Tech Heretic.* Jeff Barbian's "The Gist Generation" claims that using computerized systems has made humans intellectually lazy. Finally, David Brooks, in "Time to Do Everything but Think," maintains that wireless communication cuts humans off from fully experiencing the real world.

# We Are Not Special

## *Rodney A. Brooks*

*Rodney Brooks is professor of computer science and engineering, and serves as director of the Artificial Intelligence Lab at M.I.T. This selection is excerpted from his recent book* Flesh and Machines: How Robots Will Change Us.

### PREREADING

> Imagine a robot that looked and acted exactly like a human. Should that robot be treated as a human? Freewrite in response to this question for ten minutes.

If we accept evolution as the mechanism that gave rise to us, 1 we understand that we are nothing more than a highly ordered collection of biomolecules. Molecular biology has made fantastic strides over the last fifty years, and its goal is to explain all the peculiarities and details of life in terms of molecular interactions. A central tenet of molecular biology is that *that is all there is.* There is an implicit rejection of mind-body dualism, and instead an implicit acceptance of the notion that mind is a product of the operation of the brain, itself made entirely of biomolecules. We will look at these statements in more detail later in the chapter. So every living thing we see around us is made up of molecules—biomolecules plus simpler molecules like water.

All the stuff in people, plants, and animals comes from trans- 2 cription of DNA into proteins, which then interact with each other to produce structure and other compounds. Food, drink, and breath are also taken into the bodies of these organisms, and some of that may get directly incorporated into the organism as plaque or other detritus. The rest of it either reacts directly with the organism's biomolecules and is broken down into standard components—simple biomolecules or elements that bind to existing biomolecules—or is rejected and excreted. Thus almost everything in the body is biomolecules.

Biomolecules interact with each other according to well-defined laws. As they come together in any particular orientation, there are electrostatic forces at play that cause them to deform and physically interact. Chemical processes may be initiated that cause one or both of the molecules to cleave in interesting ways. With the totality of molecules, even in a single cell, there are chances for hundreds or thousands of different intermolecular reactions. It is impossible then to know or predict exactly which molecules will react with which other ones, but a statistical model of the likelihood of each type of reaction can be constructed. From that we can say whether a cell will grow, or whether it provides the function of a neuron, or whatever. 3

The body, this mass of biomolecules, is a machine that acts according to a set of specifiable rules. At a higher level the subsystems of the machine can be described in mechanical terms also. For instance, the liver takes in certain products, breaks them down, and recycles them. The details of how it operates can be divined from the particular bioreactions that go on within it, but only a few of those reactions are important to the liver itself. The vast majority of them are the normal housekeeping reactions that are in almost every cell in the body. 4

The body consists of components that interact according to well-defined (though not all known to us humans) rules that ultimately derive from physics and chemistry. The body is a machine, with perhaps billions of billions of parts, parts that are well ordered in the way they operate and interact. We are machines, as are our spouses, our children, and our dogs. 5

Needless to say, many people bristle at the use of the word "machine." They will accept some description of themselves as collections of components that are governed by rules of interaction, and with no component beyond what can be understood with mathematics, physics, and chemistry. But that to me is the essence of what a machine is, and I have chosen to use that word to perhaps brutalize the reader a little.... The particular material of which we are made may be different. Our physiology may be vastly different, but at heart I am saying we are 6 much like the robot Genghis, although somewhat more complex in quantity but not in quality. This is the key loss of specialness with which I claim mankind is currently faced.

And why the bristling at the word "machine"? Again, it is the deep-seated desire to be special. To be more than mere. The idea that we are machines seems to make us have no free will, no spark, no life. But people seeing robots like Genghis and Kismet do not think of them as clockwork automatons. They interact in the world in ways that are remarkably similar to the ways in which animals and people interact. To an observer they certainly seem to have wills of their own.

When I was younger, I was perplexed by people who were both religious and scientists. I simply could not see how it was possible to keep both sets of beliefs intact. They were inconsistent, and so it seemed to me that scientific objectivity demanded a rejection of religious beliefs. It was only later in life, after I had children, that I realized that I too operated in a dual nature as I went about my business in the world.

On the one hand, I believe myself and my children all to be mere machines. Automatons at large in the universe. Every person I meet is also a machine—a big bag of skin full of biomolecules interacting according to describable and knowable rules. When I look at my children, I can, when I force myself, understand them in this way. I can see that they are machines interacting with the world.

But this is not how I treat them. I treat them in a very special way, and I interact with them on an entirely different level. They have my unconditional love, the furthest one might be able to get from rational analysis. Like a religious scientist, I maintain two sets of inconsistent beliefs and act on each of them in different circumstances.

It is this transcendence between belief systems that I think will be what enables mankind to ultimately accept robots as emotional machines, and thereafter start to empathize with them and attribute free will, respect, and ultimately rights to them. Remarkably, to me at least, my argument has turned almost full circle on itself. I am saying that we must become less rational about machines in order to get past a logical hangup that we have with admitting their similarity to ourselves. Indeed, what I am really saying is that we, all of us, overanthropomorphize humans, who are after all mere machines. When our robots improve enough, beyond their current limitations, and when we humans look at them with the same lack of prejudice that we credit humans, then too we will break our mental barrier, our need, our desire, to retain tribal specialness, differentiating ourselves from them. Such leaps of faith have been necessary to overcome racism and gender discrimination. The same sort of leap will be necessary to overcome our distrust of robots.

## RESISTANCE IS FUTILE

If indeed we are mere machines, then we have instances of machines 12 that we all have empathy for, that we treat with respect, that we believe have emotions, that we believe even are conscious. That instance is us. So then the mere fact of being a machine does not disqualify an entity from having emotions. If we really are machines, then in principle we could build another machine out of matter that was identical to some existing person, and it too would have emotions and surely be conscious.

Now the question is how different can we make our Doppel- 13 gänger from the original person it was modeled upon. Surely it does not have to be precisely like some existing person to be a thinking, feeling creature. Every day new humans are born that are not identical to any previous human, and yet they grow to be a unique emotional, thinking, feeling creature. So it seems that we should be able to change our manufactured human a little bit and still have something we would all be willing to consider a human. Once we admit to that, we can change things some more, and some more, and perhaps eventually build something out of silicon and steel that is still functionally the same as a human, and thus would be accepted as a human. Or at least accepted as having emotions.

Some would argue that if it was made of steel and silicon, then as 14 long as people did not know that, they might accept it as human. As soon as the secret was out, however, it would no longer be accepted. But that lack of acceptance cannot be on the basis that it is a machine, as we are already supposing that we are machines. Indeed, the many arguments that abound about why a machine can never have real emotions, or really be intelligent, all boil down to a denial of one form or another, that we are machines, or at least machines in the conventional sense.

So here is the crux of the matter. I am arguing that we are ma- 15 chines and we have emotions, so in principle it is possible for machines to have emotions as we have examples of them (us) that do. Being a machine does not disqualify something from having emotions. And, by straightforward extension, does not prevent it from being conscious. This is an assault on our specialness, and many people argue that it cannot be so, and argue that they need to make the case that we are more than machines.

Sometimes they are arguing that we are more than conventional computers. This may well be the case, and I have not, so far, taken any position on this. But I *have* taken a position that we are machines.    ❖    16

## READING FOR INFORMATION

1. Drawing on paragraphs 1 through 5, summarize Brooks's explanation of why he views humans as "machines."
2. Why does Brooks say that humans recoil from thinking of themselves as machines?
3. How does Brooks explain that he is able to believe that his children are machines but still interact with them as a human parent?
4. In what ways does Brooks think that humans are prejudice against robots? How does he think humans could overcome that prejudice?
5. What does Brooks mean in paragraph 11 when he says that we "over-anthropomorphize" humans?
6. Paraphrase Brooks's explanation in paragraph 12 of why he believes a machine could have emotions.
7. What is a Doppelgänger, a noun Brooks uses in paragraph 13?

## READING FOR FORM, ORGANIZATION, AND EXPOSITORY FEATURES

1. Why does Brooks use the subheading "Resistance Is Futile"?
2. Comment on the choices Brooks made with regard to paragraph length.
3. In what places does Brooks use topic sentences to indicate the logical connections among the various parts of his argument?

## READING FOR RHETORICAL CONCERNS

1. Comment on the logic that serves as the underpinning for Brooks's argument.
2. In what way does Brooks establish his authority?
3. What assumptions does Brooks make about his audience?

## WRITING ASSIGNMENTS

1. Write a 500-word summary of Brooks's argument that humans are machines and that it is theoretically possible to build a machine that has human emotions and self-consciousness. Make sure you capture the logic of Brooks's argument.

2. Write a 1,000-word essay that either supports or takes issue with Brooks's assertion that humans are machines.

3. Write a 1,000-word essay that either supports or takes issue with Brooks's assertion that humans hold unreasonable prejudices against machines.

# Cyborg Seeks Community

### Steve Mann

*Steve Mann is a professor of electrical and computer engineering at the University of Toronto and an inventor of wearable computer systems.*

## PREREADING

Read the first paragraph of Mann's article. What is your response to the image of himself that Mann presents in the paragraph? Freewrite for ten minutes in response to this question.

People find me peculiar. They think it's odd that I spend most    1
of my waking hours wearing eight or nine Internet-connected
computers sewn into my clothing and that I wear opaque wrap-around
glasses day and night, inside and outdoors. They find it odd that to sustain wireless communications during my travels, I will climb to the
hotel roof to rig my room with an antenna and Internet connection.
They wonder why I sometimes seem detached and lost, but at other
times I exhibit vast knowledge of their specialty. A physicist once said
he felt that I had the intelligence of a dozen experts in his discipline;
a few minutes later, someone else said they thought I was mentally
handicapped.

Despite the peculiar glances I draw, I wouldn't live any other way.    2
I have melded technology with my person and achieved a higher state
of awareness than would otherwise be possible. I see the world as
images imprinted onto my retina by rays of light controlled by several
computers, which in turn are controlled by cameras concealed inside
my glasses.

Every morning I decide how I will see the world that day. Sometimes I give myself eyes in the back of my head. Other days I add a sixth sense, such as the ability to feel objects at a distance. If I'm going to ride my bicycle, I'll want to feel the cars and trucks pressing against my back, even when they are a few hundred feet away.

Things appear different to me than they do to other people. I see some items as hyperobjects that I can click on and bring to life. I can choose stroboscopic vision to freeze the motion of rotating automobile tires and see how many bolts are on the wheels of a car going over 60 miles per hour, as if it were motionless. I can block out the view of particular objects—sparing me the distraction, for example, of the vast sea of advertising around me.

I live in a videographic world, as if my entire life were a television show. And many people assume that by living my life through the screen, I do exactly what television leads us to do—tune out reality. In fact, WearComp has quite the opposite effect: Visual filters help me concentrate on what is important, heightening my sensitivity and setting my imagination free. I do of course have occasion to remove my computational prostheses, as when I sleep, shower, or splash around in the ocean.

In addition to having the Internet and massive databases and video at my beck and call most of the time, I am also connected to others. While I am grocery shopping, my wife—who may be at home or in her office—sees exactly what I see and helps me pick out vegetables. She can imprint images onto my retina while she is seeing what I see. I hope to add to the population of similarly equipped people; last fall at the University of Toronto, I taught what I believe to be the world's first course for cyborgs.

Much of my passion has been fueled by a desire to restore some balance of privacy in a world where individuals are increasingly affronted by government surveillance and corporate encroachments. In fact, one goal of my work was to challenge the notion of totalitarian video surveillance—the now-common practice of a corporate or governmental establishment wishing to know everything about everyone in the establishment while revealing nothing about itself. Many department stores, for example, use large numbers of hidden cameras and yet prohibit customers from taking pictures.

I attempted to draw attention to this phenomenon of unreciprocated video surveillance in *Shooting Back*, a documentary I made during my day-to-day life in several different countries over a period of many years. Whenever I found myself in a store or some other establishment with electronic eyes perusing the premises, I asked its management why they were taking pictures of me without my permission. They would typically ask me why I was so paranoid and tell me that only criminals are afraid of cameras. Of course I was covertly recording this response using my own hidden eyetap video camera. Then I would pull an ordinary camcorder out of my satchel and give them a chance to explain their position for the record. (The camcorder was simply a prop, of course, as the eyetap camera had been capturing the scene.) The same people who claimed that only criminals were afraid of cameras had an instantly paranoid (and sometimes violent) reaction to my camcorder. *Shooting Back* was, I believe, the first documentary to be transmitted in real time to the World Wide Web while it was shot. (Selected portions of *Shooting Back* may be viewed at http://wearcam.org/ shootingback.html.)

## AHEAD OF MY TIME

Growing up during the 1960s and early 1970s, I always seemed to be 9 creating things before their time. I grew up in Hamilton, Ontario—a city on the western tip of Lake Ontario about 100 kilometers from Toronto. I came by this inclination naturally; during the early 1950s, my father had built what was perhaps the first wearable radio. (He had pursued radio as a hobby since his childhood.) He had taught me quite a bit about electronic circuits by the time I started kindergarten. As a young child, I removed the head from a portable battery-powered dictating machine and replaced it with the head from a high-fidelity audio cassette deck. From this cassette transport mechanism, I built a system that enabled me to listen to music while walking around. While many people scoffed at this invention, I found it nice to be able to drown out background music while shopping, to assert my own idea of personal space, and to defend myself from theft of my solitude by the department stores with their Muzak.

In my teens I founded a concept of mediated reality, which I 10 called "light-space." The goal of lightspace was to experience an altered perception of visual reality by exploring a large range of possible forms of illumination while observing a scene or object from different viewpoints. My work with lightspace led to the invention of my wearable computer. My desire to create photographic instruments that would function as true extensions of my mind and body—and my desire to control these photographic instruments in new ways—created a need for the ability to program complex sequences of events.

I began to take this matter seriously, building a digital computer 11 from a large number of electronic components salvaged from an old telephone switching computer. I did much of this experimentation in the basement of a television repair shop where I spent much of my childhood as a volunteer, fixing TV sets. In this shop I built up a great deal of knowledge about electronic circuits.

The result of my early efforts was, in the early 1970s, a family of 12 wearable computers I called "WearComp0." Sometimes I took these cumbersome prototypes outside in search of spaces dark enough to explore the altered perception of visual reality I could create using portable battery-powered light sources. People would cross the street to avoid me, not knowing what to make of what must have looked to them like an alien creature. The rig was physically a burden, weighing as much or more than I did. After wearing one of these encumbrances from sundown (when it got dark enough to use them) to sunrise, my feet would be swollen, blistered and bleeding.

I continued to refine WearComp0 and its evolutionary successor, 13 WearComp1. After much tinkering, I came up with WearComp2—my first system that truly qualified as a wearable computer in the sense that it was not just a special-purpose device. WearComp2 was field programmable, with a full-function input device (a keyboard and joystick for cursor control both built into the handle of an electronic flashgun), text and graphical displays, sound recording and playback (crude, home-brew analog-to-digital and digital-to-analog converters), and a wireless data connection to provide links to other computers. I completed this system in 1981, before most of the world realized that computers could be portable, much less wearable.

Though an advance over my earlier prototype, WearComp2 was 14 still a burden to lug. I wanted to reduce its bulk and make it look more normal. This goal led me in 1982 to experiment with building components directly into clothing. I learned how to make flexible circuits that could be embedded into ordinary fabric. This work enabled me to make versions of WearComp that were not only more comfortable to walk around in but also less off-putting to others.

In spite of these advances, my life as a cyborg remained mostly 15 solitary. I did connect quite literally (by serial data cable) with an understanding woman during my freshman year at McMaster University in my hometown of Hamilton. We faced unusual challenges in this configuration, such as having to choose which public restroom to use when we were joined. Thinking back, I imagine we must have made a comical sight, trying to negotiate doorways without snagging the cable that tethered us together.

Such relationships were rare, and it was seldom that I could get [16] others to wear my seemingly strange contraptions. Many people were unable to get past my technological shell, which they apparently found more than a little odd. Still, multimediated reality had provided me with a unique vision of the world, and by the mid-1980s I had a following of people on the fringes of society who shared (or at least appreciated) my vision. I was invited to shoot pictures for album covers and hair ads. By 1985, I began to realize that it wasn't just the finished photographs people wanted; they also seemed to enjoy watching me take the pictures. Often I would be shooting in large warehouses, with audiences of hundreds of people. I began to realize that I had become a cyborg performance artist. By the end of the 1980s, however, I found myself yearning to return to my more substantive childhood passions for science, mathematics, and electrical engineering.

While at McMaster, I added biosensors to the WearComp so that [17] it could monitor my heart rate (as well as the full EKG waveform) and other physiological signals. I also invented the "vibravest"—a garment studded with radar transceivers and vibrating elements. Wearing this vest made objects at a distance feel as if they were pressing against my body. I could close my eyes and walk down the hallway, confident that any wall or other obstacle would be felt as warning vibrations on the appropriate side of the vest. By sparing myself from the cognitive load of processing all that visual information, I found I was able to think more clearly.

In 1991, I brought my inventions to MIT as a PhD student. As a [18] cyborg, uprooting myself from Canada was a formidable task, since I had installed my cyberbody in Canada over a period of many years. Going to MIT was a sudden move of my extended self.

First, I secretly climbed up onto the rooftops of buildings around [19] the city to put in place the wireless data communications infrastructure I had brought with me from Canada. I had to quickly deploy my base stations at the top of elevator shafts or anywhere else I could find warm dry places. This way, whenever I wanted an Internet connection, these gateways would be ready to send the data to me, no matter where I was—even if I was in a basement or riding on the subway.

Although I kept in touch with my family through cyberspace, my [20] first two years at MIT were lonely times IRL—in real life. I was, after all, the only person there with a wearable computer. Then in 1993, at the request of a fellow student, a local engineer named Doug Platt built a wearable system. I was no longer the only cyborg at MIT.

It took some years to get other cyborgs at MIT, thus enabling the 21 beginnings of a sense of community. Although I never succeeded in getting a large community outfitted with my high-speed packet radio systems, the cellular telephones that began to emerge provided another answer to the problem of connectivity.

By the end of 1995, my work was attracting serious academic in- 22 terest. I was asked to write an article about my work for *IEEE Computer*, a publication of the Institute of Electrical and Electronics Engineers' Computer Society. I also proposed an academic symposium on wearables and was referred to T. Michael Elliott, executive director of the Computer Society. I figured that such a conference would legitimize the field, which until then had consisted in many people's minds of "Steve, that crazy guy running around with a camera on his head." Elliott was enthusiastic about the idea and in 1996 the Computer Society responded with an overwhelming "yes." This marked a turning point in my acceptance by my professional peers.

More than 700 people attended this first IEEE-sponsored sympo- 23 sium on wearable computing, held in Cambridge, Mass., in October 1997. A gala "Wearables" event the following day drew 3,000 people. In that same year I received my doctorate from MIT in wearable computing. This was a gratifying culmination: I had turned a childhood hobby and passion into an MIT project, the topic of a conference, and a PhD dissertation.

This past year I returned to Canada to pursue my work at the Uni- 24 versity of Toronto. Why Toronto? I had lived there in the mid-1980s, and the city had seemed very "cyborg-friendly." I had sensed there a cosmopolitan diversity as well as a genuine warmth and openness that contrasted with the more cyborg-hostile and tense atmosphere of some large U.S. cities.

## WEARING WELL

Although I spent many years developing WearComp in relative isolation, 25 I welcome efforts to commercialize wearable computers. At the vanguard is Xybernaut, based in Fairfax, Virginia. Xybernaut's latest model is being manufactured by Sony, indicating that the Japanese electronics giant has an interest in what some believe will become the Walkman of computing. Last May, Xybernaut organized its own conference on wearable computing (and invited me to give the keynote address). I may also begin to license some embodiments of my original WearComp, as well as many of my more recent innovations, to companies who want to manufacture commercial systems. I think it will be especially important to make the cyborg outfit less cumbersome—something that's long been a goal of mine. My latest version is quite sleek, and looks just like ordinary bifocal eyeglasses, with the eyetap point hidden along the cut line. Even when fully rigged, I can still play an acceptable game of squash.

I realize that some people see me and my invention as a potential 26 threat—like the Borg of *Star Trek* fame: "You will be assimilated." Clearly, there are important philosophical issues to be explored. Not only is there the danger of the technology being used to monitor people to make them into obedient productive cyborgs, but there is also the potential that people will become too dependent on this technology. My goal as a responsible inventor and engineer, however, has always been to encourage the development and manufacture of wearable computers as a means of personal, not institutional, empowerment. That will make worthwhile all the obstacles and challenges I have faced during my more than 20 years of developing this technology.

I hope that if I bring WearComp to market, anyone who wishes to 27 will eventually be able to become a cyborg. We'll live in a collaborative computer-mediated reality that will allow us to no longer need to distinguish between cyberspace and the real world. And then this cyborg will have lots of company. ✤

## READING FOR INFORMATION

1. Describe in brief the function of Mann's wearable computer system.
2. In what ways was Mann's childhood unusual?
3. What was the purpose of Mann's video documentary *Shooting Star*?
4. In what ways does Mann feel that wearable technology can increase his level of privacy?
5. Describe several of Mann's inventions.
6. Why did Mann place communication devices on various rooftops in the city where he lived?
7. What is Mann's vision of the future of wearable computers?

## READING FOR FORM, ORGANIZATION, AND EXPOSITORY FEATURES

1. What is the organizational plan of Mann's piece?
2. How does Mann attempt to interest the reader in wearable computers?

3. Describe Mann's writing style. Is his style what you would expect from a computer expert? Explain your answer.

## READING FOR RHETORICAL CONCERNS

1. In his first paragraph, Mann describes why most people who meet him think he is "peculiar." As you read the initial paragraphs of the article, did Mann seem peculiar to you? Did your view of him change as you read the rest of the article? Explain your answers.
2. To what extent does Mann's article present an argument?
3. Is Mann directing his piece to a general audience or only to those who might consider becoming cyborgs?

## WRITING ASSIGNMENTS

1. Write a 500-word description of Mann's wearable computer systems for an audience that knows little about computers.
2. Based on your own experiences, write a 750-word essay in response to Mann's viewpoint that technology is often used to intrude on personal privacy.
3. Write a 1,000-word essay in which you draw on the content of Mann's article to weigh the pros and cons of becoming a cyborg.

# Loving Technology

## *Sherry Turkle*

*Sherry Turkle is Abby Rockefeller Mauzé Professor in the Program in Science, Technology, and Society at MIT and the founder and current director of the MIT Initiative on Technology and Self. She is the author of* Psychoanalytic Politics: Jacqes Lacan and Freud's French Revolution, The Second Self: Computers and the Human Spirit, *and* Life on the Screen: Identity in the Age of the Internet.

## PREREADING

Think of a machine with which you have a "relationship," perhaps a car, a computer, or an electronic "pet." In what ways, if any, do you treat that machine as if it were more than just a collection of metal and plastic? Freewrite for ten minutes in response to this question.

Reprinted with the permission of Sherry Turkle. This article appeared in *Technos*, Fall 2001.

One of the questions posed by the recent Stephen Spielberg movie *A.I.: Artificial Intelligence* is whether a humanoid robot could "really" be developed, with the focus on the reality of the new machine. I am going to turn that question around. There is an unstated question that lies behind much of our historic preoccupations with the computer's capabilities. That question is not what computers can do or what will the computer be like in the future, but instead, what will we be like? What kind of people are we becoming as we develop increasingly intimate relationships with machines?

In this context, the central character of the story on which *A.I.* is based is not the "reality" of the boy, the nonbiological son, but of his adoptive, biological mother—this mother whose response to a machine who asks for her nurturance is the desire to nurture the machine; whose response to a creature who reaches out to her is to feel attachment and horror and confusion.

The question for the mother is, "What kind of relationship is it appropriate to have with a machine?" I want to suggest that in terms of the "reality" of the film, that question is not science fiction but is current and urgent, and in this sense totally "real."

It is current and urgent, and not because AI [artificial intelligence] designers have yet built machines that are "really" intelligent . . . but because they have built machines that can bypass this essentialist question of what is innate in the machine and go straight to doing things that cause us to treat them as sentient, even emotional. So, even today we are faced with relational artifacts that—even when they are as simple as digital pets and dolls, the simple robotic creatures that are marketed to children—have people responding to them in ways that have something in common with the mother in the film. When a robotic creature makes eye contact, follows your gaze, and gestures towards you, what you feel is the evolutionary button being pushed to respond to that creature as a sentient and even caring other. I will come back to this.

## FIRST, A LITTLE HISTORY

Let me step back a moment to a historical view of twentieth-century thinking about how we develop our notions of what is alive and what is not.

When the Swiss developmental psychologist Jean Piaget interviewed children in the 1920s and 1930s about which objects were alive and which were not, he found that children honed their definition of life by developing increasingly sophisticated notions about motion, the world of physics. In contrast, when I began to study the nascent computer culture in the early 1980s, children argued about whether a computer was alive through discussions about its psychology. Did the computer know things on its own, or did it have to be programmed? Did it have intentions, consciousness, feelings? Did it cheat? Did it know it was cheating? Faced with intelligent machines, children took a new world of objects and imposed a new world order. To put it too simply, motion gave way to emotion and physics gave way to psychology as criteria for aliveness.

By the 1990s, that order had been strained to the breaking point.   7 Children spoke about computers as just machines but then described them as sentient and intentional. They talked about biology, evolution. They said things like, *The robots are in control but not alive, would be alive if they had bodies, are alive because they have bodies, would be alive if they had feelings, are alive the way insects are alive but not the way people are alive; the simulated creatures are not alive because they are just in the computer, are alive until you turn off the computer, are not alive because nothing in the computer is real; the Sim creatures are not alive but almost alive, they would be alive if they spoke, they would be alive if they traveled, they're not alive because they don't have bodies, they are alive because they can have babies, would be alive if they could get out of the game and onto America Online.*

There was a striking heterogeneity of theory here: Children cycled   8 through different theories to far more fluid ways of thinking about life and reality to the point that my daughter, upon seeing a jellyfish in the Mediterranean, said, "Look, Mommy, a jellyfish; it looks so realistic"; and visitors to Disney's Animal Kingdom in Orlando complained that the biological animals that populated the theme park were not "realistic" enough compared to the animatronic creatures across the way at Disney World.

## FEELINGS

Most recently, there is a new development in the story. A new kind of   9 computational object, a production of artificial intelligence, is raising new questions about what kinds of relationships seem appropriate to have with machines.

There are robot cats for lonely elders; at the MIT AI lab, Bit, a  10
robot infant, now on the market as My Real Baby®, makes baby
sounds and even baby facial expressions, shaped by mechanical muscu-
lature under its artificial skin. Most significant, this computationally
complex doll has baby "states of mind." Bounce the doll when it is
happy, and it gets happier. Bounce it when it is grumpy, and it gets
grumpier. At the MIT Media Lab, Rosalind Picard's research group are
developing affective computers, machines that are programmed to assess their users' emotional states and respond with emotional states of
their own. In the case of the robotic doll and the affective machines,
the user is confronted with a relational artifact. It demands that the
user attend to its psychology.

During the more than two decades in which I have explored  11
people's relationships with computers, I have used the metaphor of
"computer as Rorshach"—the computer as a screen that allowed people to project their thoughts and feelings, their very different cognitive styles. With relational artifacts, the Rorschach model of a
computer/human relationship breaks down. People are learning that
to relate successfully to a computer you have to assess its emotional
"state"; people are learning that when you confront a computational
machine, you do not ask how it "works" in terms of any underlying
process, but take the machine "at interface value," much as you would
another person. Perhaps most important, a first generation of children
are learning that artifacts have a life cycle and that they need care,
even emotional nurturance.

To grow and be healthy, even the first popular relational artifacts,  12
the very primitive Tamagotchis® (little screen creatures), need to be
fed, they need to be cleaned, and amused. Furbies® (a cuddly owl-like
creature) simulate learning and loving. Furbies arrive in the child's life
speaking "Furbish." They "learn" to speak English. They play hide and
seek. They communicate with each other and join together in song.
They say, "I love you."

In my research on children and Furbies, I have found that when  13
children play with these new objects, they want to know their "state,"
not to get something "right" but to make the Furbies happy. Children
want to understand Furby language, not to "win" in a game over a
Furby, but to have a feeling of mutual recognition. Children are not
concerned with how Furbies "work" or what they "really" know, but are
very concerned with the toys' health and well-being. In sum, a new

generation of objects push on our evolutionary buttons to respond to certain forms of interactivity by experiencing ourselves as being with a kindred "other."

Historically, in my studies of children and computer toys, children  14 described the lifelike status of machines in terms of their cognitive capacities (the toys could "know" things, "solve" puzzles). In my studies on children and relational artifacts, I have found that children describe these new toys as "sort of alive" because of the quality of their emotional attachments to the Furbies and because of their fantasies about the idea that the Furby might be emotionally attached to them. So, for example, when I ask the question, "Do you think the Furby is alive?" children answer not in terms of what the Furby can do, but how they feel about the Furby and how the Furby might feel about them.

> *Ron (6):* Well, the Furby is alive for a Furby. And you know, some-  15
> thing this smart should have arms. It might want to pick up some-
> thing or to hug me.
>
> *Katherine (5):* Is it alive? Well, I love it. It's more alive than a Tam-  16
> agotchi because it sleeps with me. It likes to sleep with me.
>
> *Jen (9):* I really like to take care of it. So, I guess it is alive, but it  17
> doesn't need to really eat, so it is as alive as you can be if you don't
> eat. A Furby is like an owl. But it is more alive than an owl because
> it knows more and you can talk to it. But it needs batteries, so it
> is not an animal. It's not like an animal kind of alive.

Children talk about "an animal kind of alive and a Furby kind of  18 alive." Will they also talk about a "people kind of love" and a "computer kind of love"?

## WHAT IS "REAL"?

We are in a different world from the old "AI debates" of the 1960s to  19 1980s in which researchers argued about whether machines could be "really" intelligent. The old debate was essentialist; the new objects sidestep such arguments about what is inherent in them and play instead on what they evoke in us. When we are asked to care for an object, when the cared-for object thrives and offers us its attention and concern, we experience that object as intelligent, but more important, we feel a connection to it. So, my goal here is not to enter a debate about whether objects "really" have emotions, but to reflect on what relational artifacts evoke in the user.

How will interacting with relational artifacts affect people's way of 20 thinking about themselves, their sense of human identity, of what makes people special? Children have traditionally defined what makes people special in terms of a theory of "nearest neighbors." So, when the nearest neighbors (in children's eyes) were their pet dogs and cats, people were special because they had reason. The Aristotelian definition of man as a rational animal made sense, even for the youngest children. But when, in the 1980s, it seemed to be the computers that were the nearest neighbors, children's approach to the problem changed. Now, people were special not because they were rational animals but because they were emotional machines. So, in 1983, a 10-year-old told me, "When there are robots that are as smart as the people, the people will still run the restaurants, cook the food, have the families, I guess they'll still be the only ones who'll go to church." He rendered unto the machines the domains of reason; he rendered unto the people the realms of emotionality and sociability.

Now, in a world where machines present themselves as emotional 21 and sociable, what is left for us?

The media reported a comment on AIBO®, Sony's household en- 22 tertainment robot, that startled me in what it might augur for the future of person-machine relationships: "[AIBO] is better than a real dog. . . . It won't do dangerous things, and it won't betray you. . . . Also, it won't die suddenly and make you feel very sad."

Mortality has traditionally defined the human condition. A shared 23 sense of mortality has been the basis for feeling a commonality with other human beings, a sense of going through the same life cycle, a sense of the preciousness of time and life, of its fragility. Loss (of parents, of friends, of family) is part of the way we understand how human beings grow and develop, and bring the qualities of other people within themselves. The possibilities of engaging emotionally with creatures that will not die, whose loss we will never need to face, presents dramatic questions that are based on current technology—not issues of whether the technology depicted in *A.I.* could "really" be developed.

## BY ANY OTHER NAME

The question, "What kinds of relationships is it appropriate to have with 24 machines?" has been explored in science fiction, including *A.I.*, and in technophilosophy. But the sight of children and, for that matter, the elderly exchanging tendernesses with robotic pets brings technophilosophy down to earth. It concretizes it in a new, more urgent posing of the question of what kinds of relationships are appropriate to have with a machine. In the end, the question is not just whether our children will come to love their toy robots more than their parents, but what will loving itself come to mean?

When I began studying popular responses to the idea of AI in the 25 late 1970s, the dominant models of AI were based on models of information processing, of symbols, of top-down instructions. At the time, I found that people tended to respond to the field with a kind of romantic reaction, saying, for example, that simulated thinking might be thinking, but simulated thinking could never be thinking, and simulated love could never be love. People's sense of personal identity often became focused on whatever they defined as "not cognition" or "beyond information."

Models of AI changed from those information-processing ideas. 26 By the late 1980s and early 1990s, AI models that looked to the brain and nervous system for their underlying images, models that looked to the behavior of insects and simple creatures, began to dominate the field. (They had been popular in the early days of AI, had gone out of favor, and were now in a period of restoration.) These more biological and behavioral models provoked a very different response. Once AI suggested that its creatures would be unpredictable and nondeterministic, they met the romantic reaction to artificial intelligence with their own "romantic machines." AI started to encourage a language of nature as a computer and of the computer as part of nature. It encouraged a way of thinking in which traditional distinctions between the natural and artificial, the "real" and simulated, might dissolve. Children described computers, machines, and people as made of the same stuff: "Just yucky computer cy-dough-plasm." By the 1990s, we were in the midst of an evolving cyborg consciousness.

Let me put this history somewhat differently: When, in the heyday 27 of information-processing AI, Marvin Minsky justified the AI enterprise with the quip, "The mind is a meat machine," the remark often was cited with irritation, even disgust. History has shown us that much of what seemed unacceptable about Minsky's words had to do with the prevailing images of what kind of meat machine the mind might be. The images were mechanistic and deterministic. But today's AI models suggest an artificiality made up of biologically or psychologically resonant components. With a changed image of machines, the idea that the mind could be one became far less problematic.

Walt Whitman said, "A child goes forth every day/And the 28 first object he look'ed upon/That object he became." We make our technologies, and our technologies make and shape us. We are not going to be the same people we are today on the day we are ever faced with "loving" machines.    ✿

## READING FOR INFORMATION

1. Paraphrase the question Turkle poses in paragraph 1.
2. If you have not seen the film *A.I.: Artificial Intelligence,* ask a classmate to explain its plot.
3. What is the meaning of the word "sentient" that Turkle uses in paragraph 4?
4. Summarize the confusion between what is real and what isn't that Turkle describes in paragraph 8.
5. What is a Tamagotchi? A Furby?
6. Summarize how children respond to Furbies as described by Turkle in paragraphs 13 through 18.
7. In what sense does Turkle believe that the debate over artificial intelligence changed in the 1990s?
8. Summarize Turkle's comments in paragraph 27 on viewing the mind as a machine.

## READING FOR FORM, ORGANIZATION, AND EXPOSITORY FEATURES

1. Comment on Turkle's use of subheadings.
2. Paragraphs 2, 5, 18, and 21 are only one or two sentences long. Comment on how Turkle uses short paragraphs.
3. Describe Turkle's organizational plan.
4. What conventions of academic writing are exhibited in Turkle's article?

## READING FOR RHETORICAL CONCERNS

1. What is Turkle's goal in writing?
2. What is the basis of Turkle's authority on her topic?
3. Where does Turkle draw conclusions?

## WRITING ASSIGNMENTS

1. In paragraph 3, Turkle poses the following question: "What kind of relationship is it appropriate to have with a machine?" Write a 750-word essay of personal response that answers Turkle's question.

2. Write a 1,000-word essay that draws on Turkle's article and attempts to define "criteria for aliveness" (paragraph 6).

3. In a 1,000-word essay, compare and contrast Turkle's and Rodney Brooks's views on the potential for developing machines that exhibit emotion.

# Live Forever

## *Raymond Kurzweil*

*Raymond Kurzweil is responsible for a number of significant innovations in computer technology, including the first print-to-speech reading machine for the blind. He is the author of* The Age of Spiritual Machines: When Computers Exceed Human Intelligence.

### PREREADING

What is your response to the idea behind Kurzweil's title, "Live Forever"? Does immortality seem desirable to you? Freewrite for ten minutes in response to those questions.

Within 30 years, we will be able to scan ourselves—our intelligence, personalities, feelings and memories—into computers. Is this the beginning of eternal life? 1

Thought to Implant 4: OnNet, please. 2

Hundreds of shimmering thumbnail images mist into view, spread fairly evenly across the entire field of pseudovision. 3

Thought: Zoom upper left, higher, into Winston's image. 4

Transmit: It's Nellie. Let's connect and chat over croissants. Rue des Enfants, Paris in the spring, our favorite table, yes? 5

Four-second pause. 6

Background thought: Damn it. What's taking him so long? 7

Receive: I'm here, ma chère, I'm here! Let's do it! 8

The thumbnail field mists away, and a cafe scene swirls into place.  9
Scent of honeysuckle. Pâté. Wine. Light breeze. Nellie is seated at a
quaint table with a plain white tablecloth. An image of Winston looking
twenty and buff mists in across from her. Message thumbnails occasionally blink against the sky.

Winston: It's so good to see you again, ma chère! It's been months!  10
And what a gorgeous choice of bodies! The eyes are a dead giveaway,
though. You always pick those raspberry eyes. Tres bold, Nellita. So
what's the occasion? Part of me is in the middle of a business meeting in
Chicago, so I can't dally.

Nellie: Why do you always put on that muscleman body, Winston?  11
You know how much I like your real one. Winston morphs into a man in
his early 50s, still overly muscular.

Winston: (laughing) My real body? How droll! No one but my  12
neurotechnician has seen it for years! Believe me, that's not what you
want. I can do much better! He fans rapidly through a thousand images,
and Nellie grimaces.

Nellie: Damn it! You're just one of Winston's MIs! Where is the
real Winston? I know I used the right connection!

Winston: Nellie, I'm sorry to have to tell you this. There was a  13
transporter accident a few weeks ago in Evanston, and . . . well, I'm
lucky they got to me in time for the full upload. I'm all of Winston that's
left. The body's gone.

When Nellie contacts her friend Winston through the Internet  14
connection in her brain, he is already, biologically speaking, dead. It is
his electronic mind double, a virtual reality twin, that greets Nellie in
their virtual Parisian cafe. What's surprising here is not so much the notion that human minds may someday live on inside computers after
their bodies have expired. It's the fact that this vignette is closer at hand
than most people realize. Within 30 years, the minds in those computers may just be our own.

The history of technology has shown over and over that as one  15
mode of technology exhausts its potential, a new, more sophisticated
paradigm emerges to keep us moving at an exponential pace. Between
1910 and 1950, computer technology doubled in power every three
years; between 1950 and 1966, it doubled every two years; and it has recently been doubling every year.

By the year 2020, your $1,000 personal computer will have the  16
processing power of the human brain—20 million billion calculations

per second (100 billion neurons times 1,000 connections per neuron times 200 calculations per second per connection). By 2030, it will take a village of human brains to match a $1,000 computer. By 2050, $1,000 worth of computing will equal the processing power of all human brains on earth.

Of course, achieving the processing power of the human brain is 17 necessary but not sufficient for creating human-level intelligence in a machine. But by 2030, we'll have the means to scan the human brain and re-create its design electronically.

Most people don't realize the revolutionary impact of that. The 18 development of computers that match and vastly exceed the capabilities of the human brain will be no less important than the evolution of human intelligence itself some thousands of generations ago. Current predictions overlook the imminence of a world in which machines become more like humans—programmed with replicated brain synapses that re-create the ability to respond appropriately to human emotion, and humans become more like machines—our biological bodies and brains enhanced with billions of "nanobots," swarms of microscopic robots transporting us in and out of virtual reality. We have already started down this road: Human and machine have already begun to meld.

It starts with uploading, or scanning the brain into a computer. 19 One scenario is invasive: One very thin slice at a time, scientists input a brain of choice—having been frozen just slightly before it was going to die—at an extremely high speed. This way, they can easily see every neuron, every connection and every neurotransmitter concentration represented in each synapse-thin layer.

Seven years ago, a condemned killer allowed his brain and body to 20 be scanned in this way, and you can access all 10 billion bytes of him on the Internet. You can see for yourself every bone, muscle, and section of gray matter in his body. But the scan is not yet at a high enough resolution to recreate the interneuronal connections, synapses, and neurotransmitter concentrations that are the key to capturing the individuality within a human brain.

Our scanning machines today can clearly capture neural features 21 as long as the scanner is very close to the source. Within 30 years, however, we will be able to send billions of nanobots—blood cell-size scanning machines—through every capillary of the brain to create a complete noninvasive scan of every neural feature. A shot full of nanobots will someday allow the most subtle details of our knowledge, skills, and personalities to be copied into a file and stored in a computer.

We can touch and feel this technology today. We just can't make the nanobots small enough, not yet anyway. But miniaturization is another one of those accelerating technology trends. We're currently shrinking the size of technology by a factor of 5.6 per linear dimension per decade, so it is conservative to say that this scenario will be feasible in a few decades. The nanobots will capture the locations, interconnections, and contents of all the nerve cell bodies, axons, dendrites, presynaptic vesicles, neurotransmitter concentrations, and other relevant neural components. Using high-speed wireless communication, the nanobots will then communicate with each other and with other computers that are compiling the brain-scan database.

If this seems daunting, another scanning project, that of the human genome, was also considered ambitious when it was first introduced twelve years ago. At the time, skeptics said the task would take thousands of years, given current scanning capabilities. But the project is finishing on time nevertheless because the speed with which we can sequence DNA has grown exponentially.

Brain scanning is a prerequisite to Winston and Nellie's virtual life—and apparent immortality.

In 2029, we will swallow or inject billions of nanobots into our veins to enter a three dimensional cyberspace—a virtual reality environment. Already, neural implants are used to counteract tremors from Parkinson's disease as well as multiple sclerosis. I have a deaf friend who can now hear what I'm saying because of his cochlear implant. Under development is a retinal implant that will perform a similar function for blind people, basically replacing certain visual processing circuits of the brain. Recently, scientists from Emory University placed a chip in the brain of a paralyzed stroke victim who can now begin to communicate and control his environment directly from his brain.

But while a surgically introduced neural implant can be placed in only one or at most a few locations, nanobots can take up billions or trillions of positions throughout the brain. We already have electronic devices called neuron transistors that, noninvasively, allow communication between electronics and biological neurons. Using this technology, developed at Germany's Max Planck Institute of Biochemistry, scientists were recently able to control from their computer the movements of a living leech.

By taking up positions next to specific neurons, the nanobots will 27 be able to detect and control their activity. For virtual reality applications, the nanobots will take up positions next to every nerve fiber coming from all five of our senses. When we want to enter a specific virtual environment, the nanobots will suppress the signals coming from our real senses and replace them with new, virtual ones. We can then cause our virtual body to move, speak, and otherwise interact in the virtual environment. The nanobots would prevent our real bodies from moving; instead, we would have a virtual body in a virtual environment, which need not be the same as our real body.

Like the experiences Winston and Nellie enjoyed, this technology 28 will enable us to have virtual interactions with other people—or simulated people—without requiring any equipment not already in our heads. And virtual reality will not be as crude as what you experience in today's arcade games. It will be as detailed and subtle as real life. So instead of just phoning a friend, you can meet in a virtual Italian bistro or stroll down a virtual tropical beach, and it will all seem real. People will be able to share any type of experience—business, social, romantic, or sexual—regardless of physical proximity.

The trip to virtual reality will be readily reversible, since, with 29 your thoughts alone, you will be able to shut the nanobots off or even direct them to leave your body. Nanobots are programmable in that they can provide virtual reality one minute and a variety of brain extensions the next. They can change their configuration and even alter their software.

While the combination of human-level intelligence in a machine 30 and a computer's inherent superiority in the speed, accuracy, and sharing ability of its memory will be formidable—this is not an alien invasion. It is emerging from within our human-machine civilization.

But will virtual life and its promise of immortality obviate the fear 31 of death? Once we upload our knowledge, memories, and insights into a computer, will we have acquired eternal life? First, we must determine what human life is. What is consciousness, anyway? If my thoughts, knowledge, experience, skills, and memories achieve eternal life without me, what does that mean for me?

Consciousness—a seemingly basic tenet of "living"—is perplexing 32 and reflects issues that have been debated since the Platonic dialogues. We assume, for instance, that other humans are conscious, but when we consider the possibility that nonhuman animals may be conscious, our understanding of consciousness is called into question.

The issue of consciousness will become even more contentious 33 in the twenty-first century because nonbiological entities—read: machines—will be able to convince most of us that they are conscious. They will master all the subtle cues that we now use to determine that humans are conscious. And they will get mad if we refute their claims.

Consider this: If we scan me, for example, and record the exact 34 state, level, and position of my every neurotransmitter, synapse, neural connection, and other relevant details, and then reinstantiate this massive database into a neural computer, then who is the real me? If you ask the machine, it will vehemently claim to be the original Ray. Since it will have all of my memories, it will say, "I grew up in Queens, New York, went to college at MIT, stayed in the Boston area, sold a few artificial intelligence companies, walked into a scanner there, and woke up in the machine here. Hey, this technology really works."

But there are strong arguments that this is really a different per- 35 son. For one thing, old biological Ray (that's me) still exists. I'll still be here in my carbon, cell-based brain. Alas, I (the old biological Ray) will have to sit back and watch the new Ray succeed in endeavors that I could only dream of.

But New Ray will have some strong claims as well. He will say that 36 while he is not absolutely identical to Old Ray, neither is the current version of Old Ray, since the particles making up my biological brain and body are constantly changing. It is the patterns of matter and energy that are semi-permanent (that is, changing only gradually), while the actual material content changes constantly and very quickly.

Viewed in this way, my identity is rather like the pattern that water 37 makes when rushing around a rock in a stream. The pattern remains relatively unchanged for hours, even years, while the actual material constituting the pattern—the water—is replaced in milliseconds.

This idea is consistent with the philosophical notion that we 38 should not associate our fundamental identity with a set of particles, but rather with the pattern of matter and energy that we represent. In other words, if we change our definition of consciousness to value patterns over particles, then New Ray may have an equal claim to be the continuation of Old Ray.

One could scan my brain and reinstantiate the new Ray while I 39 was sleeping, and I would not necessarily even know about it. If you then came to me, and said, "Good news, Ray, we've successfully reinstantiated your mind file so we won't be needing your old body and brain anymore," I may quickly realize the philosophical flaw in the argument that New Ray is a continuation of my consciousness. I may wish New Ray well, and realize that he shares my pattern, but I would nonetheless conclude that he is not me, because I'm still here.

Wherever you wind up on this debate, it is worth noting that data 40 do not necessarily last forever. The longevity of information depends on its relevance, utility, and accessibility. If you've ever tried to retrieve information from an obsolete form of data storage in an old obscure format (e.g., a reel of magnetic tape from a 1970s minicomputer), you understand the challenge of keeping software viable. But if we are diligent in maintaining our mind file, keeping current backups and porting to the latest formats and mediums, then at least a crucial aspect of who we are will attain a longevity independent of our bodies.

What does this super technological intelligence mean for the fu- 41 ture? There will certainly be grave dangers associated with twenty-first-century technologies. Consider unrestrained nanobot replication. The technology requires billions or trillions of nanobots in order to be useful, and the most cost-effective way to reach such levels is through self-replication, essentially the same approach used in the biological world, by bacteria, for example. So in the same way that biological self-replication gone awry (i.e., cancer) results in biological destruction, a defect in the mechanism curtailing nanobot self-replication would endanger all physical entities, biological or otherwise.

Other salient questions are: Who is controlling the nanobots? 42 Who else might the nanobots be talking to?

Organizations, including governments, extremist groups, or even a 43 clever individual, could put trillions of undetectable nanobots in the water or food supply of an entire population. These "spy" nanobots could then monitor, influence, and even control our thoughts and actions. In addition, authorized nanobots could be influenced by software viruses and other hacking techniques. Just as technology poses dangers today, there will be a panoply of risks in the decades ahead.

On a personal level, I am an optimist, and I expect that the cre- 44 ative and constructive applications of this technology will persevere, as I believe they do today. But there will be a valuable and increasingly vocal role for a concerned movement of Luddites—those anti-technologists inspired by early nineteenth-century weavers who in protest destroyed machinery that was threatening their livelihood.

Still, I regard the freeing of the human mind from its severe phys- 45 ical limitations as a necessary next step in evolution. Evolution, in my view, is the purpose of life, meaning that the purpose of life—and of our lives—is to evolve.

What does it mean to evolve? Evolution moves toward greater 46 complexity, elegance, intelligence, beauty, creativity, and love. And God has been called all these things, only without any limitation, infinite. While evolution never reaches an infinite level, it advances exponentially, certainly moving in that direction. Technological evolution, therefore, moves us inexorably closer to becoming like God. And the freeing of our thinking from the severe limitations of our biological form may be regarded as an essential spiritual quest.

By the close of the next century, nonbiological intelligence will be 47 ubiquitous. There will be few humans without some form of artificial intelligence, which is growing at a double exponential rate, whereas biological intelligence is basically at a standstill. Nonbiological thinking will be trillions of trillions of times more powerful than that of its biological progenitors, although it will be still of human origin.

Ultimately, however, the earth's technology-creating species will 48 merge with its own computational technology. After all, what is the difference between a human brain enhanced a trillion-fold by nanobot-based implants and a computer whose design is based on high-resolution scans of the human brain and then extended a trillion-fold?

This may be the ominous, existential question that our own chil- 49 dren, certainly our grandchildren, will face. But at this point, there's no turning back. And there's no slowing down.    ✸

## READING FOR INFORMATION

1. What point is Kurzweil trying to make in the scenario he presents in paragraphs 2 through 14?

2. Summarize Kurzweil's description in paragraphs 17 through 22 of the technology that may be used in the future to duplicate an actual human brain within a computer.

3. What are nanobots?

4. Summarize Kurzweil's description in paragraphs 25 through 29 of the technology that may be used in the future to provide humans with the ability to slip in and out of virtual reality at will.

5. Summarize Kurzweil's explanation in paragraphs 34 through 40 of the ways in which an electronic download of a human's brain would be similar to and different from the original.

6. What dangers of nanobot technology does Kurzweil mention in paragraphs 42 and 43?

7. Explain "evolution" as Kurzweil defines it in paragraphs 45 and 46.

## READING FOR FORM, ORGANIZATION, AND EXPOSITORY FEATURES

1. Explain Kurzweil's opening strategy. Does it work?

2. What is the organizational plan for Kurzweil's article?

3. Is the vocabulary Kurzweil uses to describe computer technology appropriate for an audience that does not have special expertise? Use examples to explain your answer.

## READING FOR RHETORICAL CONCERNS

1. Why do you think the editors of *Psychology Today* were interested in printing Kurzweil's article?

2. How does Kurzweil attempt to lend authority to his predictions?

3. How does Kurzweil want his readers to feel about the concept of downloading human intelligence? Does he achieve that effect? Why, or why not?

4. Does Kurzweil address the views of those whose predictions for the future of human-machine interaction differ from his own?

## WRITING ASSIGNMENTS

1. Write a detailed 750-word summary of Kurzweil's predictions for the future.

2. Does Kurzweil's description of what he terms a "human-machine civilization" appeal to you? Write a 1,000-word essay of personal response in answer to that question. Include a brief explanation of the human-machine civilization that Kurzweil envisions.

3. Write a 1,000-word scenario set in the future that explores the consequences of the technology that Kurzweil predicts will be developed.

# Isolated by the Internet

## *Clifford Stoll*

*Clifford Stoll is an astronomer, an expert on computer security, and the author of* The Cuckoo's Egg *and* Silicon Snake Oil: Second Thoughts about the Information Highway. *The article that follows is taken from Stoll's book* High Tech Heretic.

### PREREADING

Think of the ways you use the Internet to contact other people. Do you believe technology improves the quality of your social interactions? Freewrite for ten minutes in response to that question.

For all my grinching about the soul-deadening effects of the  1
Internet, most Internet users speak positively about it. One friend tells how she found a support group for an obscure medical condition. Another tells me that his modem provides an escape from a dull world, providing a rich mixture of fantasy and role playing. One soon-to-be-married couple writes how they met through postings to a Usenet news group. And one computer programmer confesses that although she's extremely shy in person, in her electronic chat room, she becomes a feisty, enchanting contessa. Meanwhile, wired families keep in touch via email, and new friendships blossom thanks to online special interest groups. Isolated hobbyists sign onto Web sites to exchange information and help each other. Surely the electronic virtual community is a positive social development.

Well, not necessarily. According to Carnegie Mellon University  2
psychologists Robert Kraut and Vicki Lundmark, there are serious negative long-term social effects, ranging from depression to loneliness. The result of a concerted research effort, their findings were surprising, since this research was funded by high-tech firms like AT&T, Apple Computer, Lotus, Intel, and Hewlett-Packard. Their report, "The Internet Paradox—A Social Technology That Reduces Social Involvement

and Psychological Well-Being?" appeared in the September 1998 issue of the *American Psychologist*.

Kraut and Lundmark had asked how using the Internet affects 3 connections between people. They looked at both the extent and the depth of human links, and tried to understand how the Internet affected these connections. Deep social ties are relationships with frequent contact, deep feelings of involvement, and broad content. Weak ties have superficial and easily broken bonds, infrequent contact, and narrow focus. Weak ties link us to information and social resources outside our close local groups. But it's the strong social ties that buffer us from stress and lead to better social interactions.

Hardly surprising that strong personal ties come about when 4 you're in close proximity to someone . . . it's been that way for millennia. Suddenly, along comes the Internet, reducing the importance of distance and letting you develop new relationships through chat rooms, email, news groups, and Web pages.

To learn about the social effects of the Internet, Kraut and Lund- 5 mark followed ninety-six families of various backgrounds for two years. They provided computers, software, modems, accounts, and training; in all, some 256 individuals entered the study, and two thirds of them completed it. The software allowed full Internet use but recorded how much time was spent in various online activities. Each participant answered questionnaires before they went online, after a year, and after two years of Internet use.

The researchers measured stress, loneliness, and depression using 6 standardized psychological tests like the UCLA Loneliness Scale and the Center for Epidemiologic Studies Depression Scale. Participants would agree or disagree with statements like "I feel everything I do is an effort," "I enjoy life," "I can find companionship when I want it," "There is someone I could turn to for advice about changing my job or finding a new one." Kraut and Lundmark then measured each participant's social circle and distant social network during the two-year study.

After following the study group, the psychologists found an aver- 7 age increase in depression by about 1 percent for every hour spent online per week. Online activity resulted in increased loneliness as well. On the average, subjects began with sixty-six members in their nearby social circle. For every hour each week spent online, this group shrank by about 4 percent.

Depression. Loneliness. Loss of close friendships. This is the 8 medium that we're promoting to expand our global community?

It's true that many online relationships developed as well, but 9
most represented weak social ties rather than deep ones: a woman who
exchanged mittens with a stranger, a man who exchanged jokes with a
colleague he met over a tourist Web site. A few friendships blos-
somed—one teenager met his prom date online—but these were rari-
ties. And even though such friendships were welcomed when they
happened, there was an overall decline in real-world interaction with
family and friends.

The overwhelming majority of online friendships simply aren't 10
deep. Online friends can't be depended on for help with tangible favors: small loans, baby-sitting, help with shopping, or advice about jobs
and careers. One participant "appreciated the email correspondence
she had with her college-aged daughter, yet noted that when her
daughter was homesick or depressed, she reverted to telephone calls to
provide support."

Kraut and Lundmark concluded that "greater use of the Internet 11
was associated with small but statistically significant declines in social
involvement as measured by communication within the family and the
size of people's local social networks, and with increases in loneliness
and depression. Other effects on the size of the distant social circle, social support, and stress did not reach standard significance levels but
were consistently negative." Paradoxically, the Internet is a social technology used for communication, yet it results in declining social involvement and psychological well-being.

What's important to remember is that their research wasn't a col- 12
lection of casual claims, but "an extremely careful scientific study," said
Tora Bikson, a senior scientist at Rand Corporation. "It's not a result
that's easily ignored." Despite a decade of concerns, it's the first time
that professional psychologists have done such a longitudinal study.

"We were shocked by the findings, because they are counterintu- 13
itive to what we know about how socially the Internet is being used,"
said Dr. Kraut, who hypothesized that Internet use is "building shallow
relationships, leading to an overall decline in feeling of connection to
other people."

Not surprisingly, computer makers scoffed: One Intel psychologist 14
replied that "This is not about the technology, per se; it's about how it is
used. It points to the need for considering social factors in terms of how
you design applications and services for technology." In other words,
technology is just a neutral tool and social technologists will solve this
problem. Uh, right.

According to computer scientists James Katz and Philip Aspden, 15 there's no reason to be pessimistic about the social effects of Internet use. They telephoned six hundred Internet users to survey the social effects of computer use. Their 1997 report, "A Nation of Strangers," argues that the Internet augments existing communities. It's a medium for creating friendships and to stay in touch with family members. They cheerily suggest that some two million new meetings have taken place thanks to the Internet. Katz and Aspden happily conclude that "The Internet is creating a nation richer in friendships and social relationships."

Unfortunately, Katz and Aspden used a biased system of self- 16 reporting, a phone survey in which those called judged themselves on whether they had gained or lost friends. Hardly anyone's going to tell a stranger on the phone, "Oh, I've lost friends because I spend too much time online." Also, while Katz and Aspden tallied all social ties made over the Internet, they didn't probe into the possible loss of strong local ties. Since they didn't ask about the depth, nature, or quality of online "friendships," naturally their phone survey delivered a happily optimistic conclusion.

Psychologists point out that the best predictor of psychological 17 troubles is a lack of close social contacts. There's a surprisingly close correlation between social isolation and such problems as schizophrenia and depression. Long hours spent online undercut our local social support networks; this isolation promotes psychological troubles.

Kraut and Lundmark's work points to a serious problem looming 18 for wired generations: Will the proliferation of shallow, distant social ties make up for the loss of close local links?

Stanford psychology professor Philip Zimbardo has part of the an- 19 swer. Since the mid-1970s, he's studied the psychology of shyness. In 1978, Dr. Zimbardo found that some 40 percent of undergraduates said, "I think of myself as shy." By 1988, this number had reached 45 percent. And by 1995, some 50 percent of undergrads saw themselves as shy; some research suggests that 60 percent of the population now suffers from shyness.

Why this epidemic of shyness? At a 1997 conference, Professor 20 Zimbardo pointed to several reasons, many connected to technology. Television and computing make us more passive . . . and passivity feeds into shyness. Now that many family members have separate televisions, watching TV is no longer a communal experience, but rather an isolated, nonsocial nonencounter. One report suggested that parents, busy from work which they've brought home, spend only six to eight minutes a day talking with their children.

"The electronic revolution of emails and faxes means the medium 21 has finally become the message," said Professor Zimbardo. "With more virtual reality overtaking real reality, we're losing ordinary social skills, and common social situations are becoming more awkward."

Yep, for better or worse, the only way to learn how to get along 22 with others is to spend plenty of time interacting with people. Email, telephones, and faxes all prevent us from learning basic skills of dealing with people face to face. These electronic intermediaries dull our abilities to read each other's gestures and facial expressions, to express our feelings, to strike up conversations with strangers, to craft stories, to tell jokes.* Those weaned on computer communications won't learn basic social rules of conversation. How to interrupt. How to share time with another. How to speak to an audience. When to be quiet.

In the past, shyness has been passed off as a trivial problem that 23 children grow out of. "Although we think of shy people as passive and easily manipulated, at the same time there is a level of resentment, rage, and hostility," Zimbardo warned. I wonder if that explains some of the anger pervading the anonymous chat rooms and postings to Usenet news groups.

The notion that people can become addicted to the Internet was 24 scoffed at by professional psychologists. It was considered to be a joke in the same way that alcoholism, compulsive gambling, and obsessive shopping were thought laughable in the 1950s. After all, you can just stop. Only recently have a few psychologists asked questions about the seductive nature of the Internet and the type of person likely to become hooked. They're finding that the clinical definitions of established addictions fit the profiles of plenty of people who spend their lives online.

Psychologist Kimberly Young was among the first to investigate 25 clinical cases of Internet addiction. She tells of a Pennsylvania college student she calls Steve who's online sixty to seventy hours a week. Steve's a wizard in the Multi-User Dungeons; Internet fantasy games best known as MUDs.

"MUDs are like a religion to me, and I'm a god there. I'm re- 26 spected by all the other MUDders. . . . Even when I'm not playing, I wonder if there will be more newbies for me to kill that night or which other guys will be playing. I am in control of my character and my

---

*Once, people told stories—you'd pay attention to the homegrown comedian who knew how to tell a joke. Joke telling meant timing, inflection, and expression. Now, thanks to jokes passed by email and Internet forums, stale comedy routines constantly circulate online. People who can't tell jokes won't shut their mouths.

destiny in this world. My character is a legend and I identify with him."
Yet when Steve's not online, he's held back by low self-esteem. Shy and
awkward around people, he's uncomfortable around women and believes he doesn't fit in at school. "When I'm playing the MUDs, I'm not
feeling lonely or mopey. I'm not thinking about my problems. . . . I want
to stay on the MUDs as long as I possibly can."

Where once Steve would have work within the real world and 27
slowly learn how to deal with people, today he is able to turn to the Internet for solace and escape.

Compounding the withdrawal of individuals from their close social 28
circle, technology also blurs the line between work and play. Thanks to
telephones, pagers, and cell phones, work seeps into our private time,
forcing shallow, impersonal communication into quiet hours and intimate moments. Email reaches our desktops and laptops; even our wrist-
watches have alarms and electronic reminders. At home, on the road, or
on the golf course, we can't escape an electronic bombardment.

Walking in Yosemite Park, I met a hiker with all the latest parapher- 29
nalia hanging from his belt: pager, GPS locator, and electronic altimeter.
Amid the quiet of the sugar pines, his cell phone squawked and I over-
heard one side of his conversation with some New York advertising firm:
"Tell both clients that I won't be able to make Monday's meeting," he told
an unseen secretary. "I'll get them a proposal when I'm over this cold."

Here's a guy who's brought the stress of his office into the tran- 30
quillity of the forest. He's never lost and always in reach. At the same
time, he's utterly lost and out of touch.*

Office work tags along with homes equipped with fax machines. 31
On the street, drivers and pedestrians dodge each other while talking
over cell phones. In cafes, nerds type on laptops. Office managers bring
their work home on floppy disks. The telecommuter merely represents
one milestone in the blurring of home and office.

As work sneaks into playtime, play just isn't as much fun. Used to 32
be that only students brought classwork home; increasingly, everyone
has homework, everyone's on call. Our home provides little refuge from
the stress of the outside world.

This isn't just the fault of technology—so many people want high- 33
tech careers and professions that they willingly latch onto jobs which

---

*In response to the noise and interruptions, one Japanese symphony hall has installed special
transmitters to disable all cell phones and pagers in the audience. I hadn't realized it before, but
one of the joys of speleology is that none of my caving partners can be reached a hundred feet
under the ground.

demand twenty-four-hour availability. And so we find the Webmaster who's on call all night, just in case the file server crashes. The high school teacher who answers students' email all evening. The gardener who polishes her Web site when she comes home. For them, home is simply an extension of their workplace.

For children, home computers, instructional videotapes, and edu- 34 cational television extend the school into their home. Forget the innocence of childhood: Our kids are increasingly programmed as academic automatons.

The Internet is widely promoted as an aid for speed, profit, pro- 35 ductivity, and efficiency. These business goals simply aren't the aims of a home. Maybe there's such a thing as kitchen productivity, but efficiency doesn't make much sense in my living room, and exactly who considers profits in their bedroom?

At home, our goals might include tranquillity, reflection, and 36 warmth . . . hardly the image brought up by the phrase "home computing." With houses increasingly wired for communications, electronic messages invade our home life. It's not just the telemarketers who disrupt dinner with sales and surveys. Rather, our private space is increasingly available to the outside world, whether it's a call from the boss, tonight's business news on the TV, or an email message about a business meeting.

Nor are the goals of business those of a school. Productivity 37 doesn't map onto a sixth-grade class in pre-algebra. It's absurd to speak of increasing the efficiency of an instructor teaching a third-grade student how salt melts ice. Will a 200-MHz computer educate a child twice as fast as a 100-MHz computer?

The way we communicate constrains how we interact. Computer 38 networks provide chat rooms in which emotions must fit into eighty columns of ASCII text, punctuated by smiley faces. No longer need my correspondent begin a letter with a gratuitous "Dear Cliff." Rather, the header of the email describes recipient, sender, and subject. Any pretense of politeness is erased by the cold efficiency of the medium.

One survey reports that office workers typically receive 190 mes- 39 sages per day. Yet computer network promoters tell us that we need ever faster links and constantly more connectivity. Will I get more work done today if I receive three hundred messages rather than two hundred?

Instead of encouraging me to concentrate on a single job, the con- 40 stant stream of electronic messages makes me constantly flip from one task to another. Computers are great at doing this, but people aren't. Promoters of electronic work-places may speak glowingly of living asynchronous lives, but most of my work requires concentration, thinking, and organization . . . hardly promoted by a river of electronic messages.

Getting a high-speed link to the Internet causes Web pages to 41 load faster. At first glance, you'd think that this would reduce the amount of time that students would spend online. Hardly. As connection speeds increase, college students spend more time surfing the Web and less time writing, studying, or whatever they don't want to do. Same's true for office workers—an Internet link is a license to goof off.

As Robert Kraut and Vicki Lundmark's study reveals, email en- 42 hances distant communications while degrading local interactions. It perniciously gives us the illusion of making friends with faraway strangers while taking our attention away from our friends, family, and neighbors.

In the past, people in trouble relied on close, nearby friends for 43 support. Today, plenty of people turn to online support groups or chat rooms. Professor Mary Baker of Stanford reports that while she was expecting, she exchanged five email messages a day with a friend across the country . . . a woman she'd never met. Yet email pen pals can hardly provide the social support of a nearby friend or family member—if Professor Baker had to rush to the hospital, she could hardly get a ride from her email friend.

Today, it's natural enough to look to the Internet for a community, 44 since our real neighborhoods have been relentlessly undercut by television, automobiles, and urban renewal. Yet as more and more people turn to the Internet, our real communities receive even less human investment.

For the effect of instant electronic communications is to isolate us 45 from our colleagues next door. I met two computer jocks at a television station who spent their free time playing an Internet game with each other. Even though they sat five feet from each other, they'd communicate via email and rarely so much as glanced at each other.

Professor Zimbardo tells me that sometimes he sticks his head 46 into the office of a friend down the hall, with nothing more important than to say, "Hi!" "On several occasions, my greeting has been received with the shock of 'What's so important that you're invading my personal space? Why are you interrupting my productivity?' "

The price of computing at home—as in school and at work—is far 47 more than the cost of the hardware. The opportunity cost is our time, and it is taken out of our individual lives and our very real neighborhoods. The time you spend behind the monitor could be spent facing another person across a table or across a tennis court. Disguised as efficiency machines, digital time bandits steal our lives and undermine our communities.    ✿

## READING FOR INFORMATION

1. In paragraphs 3 through 13, Stoll describes research on Internet communication that was conducted by Kraut and Lundmark. Explain briefly the results of their research.
2. In paragraph 15, Stoll describes research on Internet communication that was conducted by Katz and Aspden. Explain briefly the results of their research.
3. Why does Stoll believe that Katz and Aspden's research is problematic?
4. In paragraphs 19 through 24, Stoll describes research on social skills that was conducted by Philip Zimbardo. Explain briefly the results of his research.
5. In paragraphs 24 through 27, Stoll describes research on Internet addiction that was conducted by Kimberly Young. Explain briefly the results of her research.
6. What are the functions of the "pager, GPS locator, and electronic altimeter" that Stoll mentions in paragraph 29?
7. In what ways does Stoll believe that electronic communication devices intrude on home life?
8. In what ways does Stoll believe that access to electronic messages affects productivity in the workplace?

## READING FOR FORM, ORGANIZATION, AND EXPOSITORY FEATURES

1. Describe Stoll's opening strategy.
2. Describe Stoll's style of writing. Do you find Stoll's style appealing or irritating? Explain your answer.
3. Comment on Stoll's use of examples. Does he need to use as many examples as he does? Are his examples effective?

## READING FOR RHETORICAL CONCERNS

1. Write a one- or two-sentence summary of Stoll's thesis.
2. What assumptions does Stoll make about his audience?
3. What is the primary support that Stoll provides for his thesis?
4. Where does Stoll summarize and respond to the viewpoints of his opponents? Does he respond effectively to his opponents?

## WRITING ASSIGNMENTS

1. Write a 1,000-word argument that draws support from your own experience with electronic communication to either defend or attack Stoll's thesis.
2. In a 750-word essay, explain and respond to Stoll's closing words: "The time you spend behind the monitor could be spent facing another person across a table or across a tennis court. Disguised as efficiency machines, digital time bandits steal our lives and undermine our community."
3. Electronic communication via the Internet increases dramatically the opportunities for human-to-human contact and improves the social lives of millions. Attack or defend this statement in a 750-word essay that draws on Stoll's article.

# The Gist Generation

## *Jeff Barbian*

*Jeff Barbian is the associate editor of* Training *magazine.*

### PREREADING

In what ways do you depend upon your memory in everyday life? Freewrite in response to this question for ten minutes.

I have an ongoing argument with James—a fellow journalist 1 and former boss of mine. He contends that within the context of the history of civilization, the need for human memory recall is now at an all-time low. The culprit, he says, is high technologies like the Internet, which give us such timesavers as email, the World Wide Web, and well-paid IT workers.

At most, our only burdens of memorization consist of a handful of 2 passwords that are master keys to our automated memories—memories that merge with the main vein of the Global Village. Who we know and what we need to know are patterned into a galaxy of 1s and 0s that materialize at the flex of a fingertip.

We simply have little incentive—or necessity—to commit our personal and professional lives to memory, says James. With the fountainhead of the Web, the rigors of mental absorption are relaxed and the circuitous routes of research simplified (which incidentally, James would say, goes for cars with Global Positioning Systems that tell us when to turn). The positive result is akin to freeing RAM space from our brains and the subsequent illusion of more time to spend on important pursuits.  3

For my part, I'm not convinced that we humans have developed the mental savvy to cash in on our plug-in memories. For one, James's contention raises the well-worn debate of the quantity of time versus the quality of time. I'm sure few would argue that the Internet for many has been a boon to procrastination and a feeling that what we absorb is disposable and dispensable, since it's all only a download away. And while it's hard to argue the conveniences of instant sports updates, immediate news, online shopping, downloadable music, and the colossal garage-sale universe of eBay, the Web too easily leads us into the marshy weeds of fluff when it comes to intellectual pursuits.  4

With the commonness of email—where the rules of grammar are relaxed and spell checks cover our butts, I also suspect our collective writing skills have taken a turn for the worse.  5

We are the Gist Generation. We have acquired a taste for hit-and-run, cut-and-paste knowledge. We expect a home page or email correspondence to give us the gist and only the gist—time is money and you're a click away from an iconographic trash can, so get to the point.  6

What we get is an iffy illusion of learning—like a one-hour PBS special on the big cats of Africa—the Web is wonderful at filling nutshells of knowledge that rarely overflow with substantial scholarship.  7

I would even argue that when engaged in online learning, it's hard to resist the urge to coast through each course on cruise control and merely focus on the gist.  8

Several years out of college, I find that I'm nostalgic for the fusty aromas of a library. I miss textbooks, with their publisher's stamp of approval and meaty pages of detail. Textbooks carry an air of integrity, whereas the Web, even in its most reliable moments, is forever pitching products throughout its infinite pages. It's like sprinting through an art gallery. Here you are trying to research the Roman Empire while baby billboards lure you to the lowest airfares to Italy or super deals on Andiamo luggage.  9

At the end of the day, perhaps it doesn't matter what we absorb. As David Halberstam of *The New York Times* wrote, "Memory is often  10 less about the truth than about what we want it to be." I suspect this holds true for learning.   ❀

## READING FOR INFORMATION

1. According to Barbian's friend James, how do certain new technologies decrease the need for humans to remember things?
2. How does Barbian think the Internet will affect humans' intellectual pursuits? Give specific examples.
3. Why does Barbian miss libraries and textbooks?
4. In what ways does Barbian think the commercial aspects of the Internet affect its value as a research tool?

## READING FOR FORM, ORGANIZATION, AND EXPOSITORY FEATURES

1. Explain Barbian's title.
2. Comment on Barbian's decision to write primarily in the first person.
3. What is Barbian's organizational plan?

## READING FOR RHETORICAL CONCERNS

1. What is Barbian's goal in writing? What impact does he want to have on his readers?
2. Barbian presents himself as somewhat old-fashioned. How does this affect the success of his argument?
3. Who do you think is Barbian's target audience? How does he try to accommodate that audience?

## WRITING ASSIGNMENTS

1. Is it worth trying to memorize information about the world when so much is available online? Write a 500-word essay of personal response in answer to that question.
2. Write a 1,000-word essay that explains what Barbian means by the "Gist Generation" and discusses the extent to which you and your contemporaries are part of it.
3. Write a 750-word essay in which you compare and contrast the Internet and a library as sources of information. Incorporate material from Barbian's article into your essay.

# Time to Do Everything but Think

## *David Brooks*

*David Brooks is the author of* Bobos in Paradise.

### PREREADING

> Based on your own observations and experience, how do you think wireless communication, including cell phones, has affected everyday life? Freewrite for ten minutes in response to this question.

Somewhere up in the canopy of society, way above where normal folks live, there will soon be people who live in a state of perfect wirelessness. They'll have mobile phones that download the Internet, check scores, and trade stocks. They'll have Palm handhelds that play music, transfer photos, and get Global Positioning System readouts. They'll have laptops on which they watch movies, listen to baseball games, and check inventory back at the plant. In other words, every gadget they own will perform all the functions of all the other gadgets they own, and they will be able to do it all anywhere, any time.

Wireless Woman will do a full day's work on the beach in her bikini: Her personal digital assistant comes with a thong clip so she can wear it on her way to the piña colada stand. Her phones beep, her pagers flash red lights; when they go off, she looks like a video arcade. Wireless Man will be able to put on his performance underwear, hop in his SUV, and power himself up to the top of a Colorado mountain peak. He'll be up there with his MP3 device and his carabiners enjoying the view while conference-calling the sales force and playing MegaDeath with gamers in Tokyo and Sydney. He'll be smart enough to have enough teeny-tiny lithium batteries on hand to last weeks, and if he swallows them they'd cure depression for life. He's waiting for them to develop a laptop filled with helium that would actually weigh less than nothing, and if it could blow up into an inflatable sex doll, he'd never have to come down.

So there he sits in total freedom on that Rocky Mountain peak. 3
The sky is blue. The air is crisp. Then the phone rings. His assistant
wants to know if he wants to switch the company's overnight carrier. He
turns off his phone so he can enjoy a little spiritual bliss. But first,
there's his laptop. Maybe somebody sent him an important email. He
wrestles with his conscience. His conscience loses. It's so easy to check,
after all. . . .

Never being out of touch means never being able to get away. But 4
Wireless Man's problem will be worse than that. His brain will have
adapted to the tempo of wireless life. Every 15 seconds there is some
new thing to respond to. Soon he has this little rhythm machine in his
brain. He does everything fast. He answers emails fast and sloppily.
He's bought the fastest machines, and now the idea of waiting for something to download is a personal insult. His brain is operating at peak
RPMs.

He sits amid nature's grandeur and says, "It's beautiful. But it's *not* 5
*moving*. I wonder if I got any new voice mails." He's addicted to the
perpetual flux of the information networks. He craves his next data fix.
He's a speed freak, an info junkie. He wants to slow down, but can't.

Today's business people live in an overcommunicated world. 6
There are too many Web sites, too many reports, too many bits of information bidding for their attention. The successful ones are forced to
become deft machete wielders in this jungle of communication. They
ruthlessly cut away at all the extraneous data that are encroaching upon
them. They speed through their tasks so they can cover as much ground
as possible, answering dozens of emails at a sitting and scrolling past
dozens more. After all, the main scarcity in their life is not money; it's
time. They guard every precious second, the way a desert wanderer
guards his water.

The problem with all this speed, and the frantic energy that is 7
spent using time efficiently, is that it undermines creativity. After all,
creativity is usually something that happens while you're doing something else: When you're in the shower your brain has time to noodle
about and create the odd connections that lead to new ideas. But if your
brain is always multitasking or responding to techno-prompts, there is
no time or energy for undirected mental play. Furthermore, if you are
consumed by the same information loop circulating around everyone
else, you don't have anything to stimulate you into thinking differently.
You don't have time to read the history book or the science book that

may actually prompt you to see your own business in a new light. You don't have access to unexpected knowledge. You're just swept along in the same narrow current as everyone else, which is swift but not deep.

So here's how I'm going to get rich. I'm going to design a placebo 8 machine. It'll be a little gadget with voice recognition and everything. Wireless People will be able to log on and it will tell them they have no messages. After a while, they'll get used to having no messages. They'll be able to experience life instead of information. They'll be able to reflect instead of react. My machine won't even require batteries.    ❀

## READING FOR INFORMATION

1. Describe the types of wireless communication that Brooks refers to in his article.
2. In what ways does Brooks suggest that people have become "addicted" to wireless communication?
3. What is Brooks's attitude toward the business community's use of electronic communication?
4. Why does Brooks believe that information technology has had an adverse effect on creativity?

## READING FOR FORM, ORGANIZATION, AND EXPOSITORY FEATURES

1. Comment on the effectiveness of Brooks's portraits of "Wireless Woman" and "Wireless Man."
2. What is the effect of the series of short sentences at the beginning of paragraph 3?
3. What is Brooks's closing strategy? Do you believe it is effective? Explain your answer.

## READING FOR RHETORICAL CONCERNS

1. Describe the tone of Brooks's article. What is your response to that tone?
2. How do you think Brooks wants readers to respond to his article? Does he hope to change their behavior in any way? Explain your answer.

## WRITING ASSIGNMENTS

1. Write a 750-word essay in which you analyze Brooks's portrayal of wireless communication and assess the extent to which it is accurate.

2. Brooks asserts that Americans suffer from information overload. In a 1,000-word essay, explain Brooks's assertion and respond to it based on your own observations.

3. Write your own "Wireless Woman" and "Wireless Man" portraits that reflect your own views on the impact of wireless communication.

## SYNTHESIS WRITING ASSIGNMENTS

1. Draw on at least four of the articles in this chapter to develop a 1,250-word essay that projects the future of human/machine interactions.

2. The "Wireless Man" described by David Brooks has some similarities to the "cyborg" described by Steve Mann. Write a 1,000-word essay that draws on Brooks and Mann to explain the positive and negative aspects of life as a "wired" human being.

3. Draw on at least four of the articles in this chapter to develop a 1,250-word argument on what human rights should be accorded to robots and other forms of artificial intelligence that possess humanlike thought and emotions.

4. Some commentators have called virtual reality the "LSD of the 1990s." Use the articles in this chapter to write a 1,000-word response to that characterization of virtual reality.

5. Draw on the readings in this chapter to critique the portrayal of relationships between humans and machines in a work of science fiction you have read or seen (for example, a film such as *The Matrix*). What issues does the science fiction address? Are they the same issues that are raised in the nonfiction articles in this chapter?

6. Try to imagine a future in which humans and machines interact in the ways the articles in this chapter suggest they might. How would this future differ from the present? What would life be like for human beings? Would the human species have to change to live happily in that environment? Write a 1,000-word essay in response to these questions. You might organize your essay around a comparison between the present and the future.

# *eight*

# Crime-Fighting Technology: Balancing Public Safety and Privacy

Modern technology has created challenges to civil liberties that the framers of the Constitution did not envision. Audio and visual surveillance, monitoring of electronic communications, duplication of private or copyrighted computer files, DNA fingerprinting, and a host of other innovations make it much easier for government agencies, employers, and anyone else who takes an interest in our activities to find out what we are doing and thinking. When these technologies are employed to reduce crime, they often receive support from the public. Since the attacks on the World Trade Center and the Pentagon on September 11, 2001, many Americans want the police and military to use any means available to reduce the risk of terrorism. On the other hand, Americans are quick to assert their personal rights, particularly their right to privacy. Although invasive technologies do assist police investigations, some commentators wonder if, by opting for technological quick fixes, we enter into a Faustian bargain that will eventually result in the loss of important constitutional rights.

The readings in this chapter focus on how our constitutional rights to privacy and to protection from illegal searches might be affected by technological innovations. Journalist Francis X. Clines describes Mosaic-2000, a computer program designed to identify students who might be prone to commit violent acts, and "Rooting Out the Bad Seeds?" by Kelly Patricia O'Meara highlights the dangers to civil liberties posed by the Mosaic-2000 technology. In his article "Kyllo v. United States: Technology v. Individual Privacy," FBI agent Thomas Colbridge discusses the implications of a recent Supreme Court decision regarding the use of thermal imaging technology to detect indoor marijuana growing operations. In "DC's Virtual Panopticon," Christian Parenti describes the expansion of video surveillance in DC in the wake of the September 11 events. Wendy Kaminer, the author of "Trading Liberty for Illusions," also focuses on the response to September 11 and argues that Americans should not surrender civil liberties in exchange for a false sense of security. In "Invasion of Privacy," Joshua Quittner maintains that the benefits of modern technological advances are worth the reduction of individual privacy that comes with them.

# Computer Project Seeks to Avert Youth Violence

### *Francis X. Clines*

*Francis X. Clines, a prominent journalist, has been on the staff of* The New York Times *since 1958.*

## PREREADING

What do you know about the Columbine High School shootings that took place in Littleton, Colorado? If you are unfamiliar with that incident, ask a friend for information or do some quick online research. Write down the basic facts in the case.

Spurred by the deadly rampage at Columbine High School, the federal Bureau of Alcohol, Tobacco and Firearms is working with a threat-evaluation company to develop a computer program to help school administrators spot troubled students who might be near the brink of violence.    1

When the national pilot program, known as Mosaic-2000, begins testing at more than 20 schools in December, its technique of confidentially vetting and rating potentially violent students on a scale of 1 to    2

10 will come not a moment too soon for Steve Dackin, principal of Reynoldsburg High School.

"Columbine forever changed things for all of us," Dackin said of ₃ the school in Littleton, Colorado, where two students shot thirteen people to death before killing themselves in April [1999].

Dackin knocked on wood in his office as he explained that his ₄ school, like most in the nation, had been spared gun violence yet had suffered very real waves of post-Columbine panic and concern for safety that must now be dealt with through safeguard programs like Mosaic.

"I see this as being a useful tool," Dackin said of the program, ₅ which is based on systems now variously employed by Yale University and federal courthouses to evaluate the potential for violence of individuals who make threats.

The Ohio chapter of the American Civil Liberties Union has criti- ₆ cized the pilot program as a "technological Band-Aid" driven by profiteering in parental fears. "We are understandably hesitant about any program designed to classify students or anyone else in society as potentially dangerous based on supposedly credible data fed into a black box," said Raymond Vasvari, legislative director of the Ohio ACLU.

But the Ohio attorney general, Betty Montgomery, who favors the ₇ pilot project, noted that school administrators must already maintain confidential files on troubled students who might veer toward violence. Mosaic, she said, will be a wonderful additional tool based on a wide range of objective experience. Far from Big Brother, she said, Mosaic is nothing more than highly useful software—a "three-ring notebook" to help worried school officials delve better into an existing area of responsibility.

"It brings together the shared experiences of many experts plus an ₈ evaluative piece," Ms. Montgomery said. "It says, 'Look, we've gone back and spoken to X number of people who have committed these crimes, and these are the risk factors we feel are present in their lives. It collects these risk factors based on actual cases and organizes them in a way so we can have a consistent approach.'"

Mosaic programs, which are based on carefully worded questions ₉ about student behavior based on case histories of people who have turned violent, are designed by Gavin de Becker, Inc., a private software company in California. They are intended to help officials discern a real threat amid the innocuous, if frightening, outbursts that regularly cause concern. For the last ten years, the company has tailored risk-assessment programs for special law-enforcement concerns like threats of domestic violence and threats to the safety of members of the Supreme Court and the governors of eleven states, according to the company.

"I think it's a wonderful tool that has a great deal of potential, and 10 I hope it's properly used by the schools," said Andrew Vita, associate director for field operations of the Bureau of Alcohol, Tobacco and Firearms, who found the Mosaic approach useful in investigating bombings at abortion clinics.

"We are trying to get some of our focus and resources up front of 11 violence, in violence prevention, violence avoidance," Vita said. He noted that his bureau was also developing a program with the Department of Education to train school officials to cope with another area of concern underlined at Columbine—homemade explosives in schools.

The Mosaic school program promises to provide questions care- 12 fully crafted from case histories by two hundred experts in law enforcement, psychiatry and other areas. A variety of concerns beyond alarming talk or behavior will be included, from the availability of guns to a youngster's abuse of dogs and cats.

The questions allow a range of answers, from a student who has 13 "no known gun possession," for example, to one who has "friends with gun access." Not all the questions might be effectively answered by administrators who control the software, officials conceded. But they said the more that were, the greater the credibility of the rating would be in the hands of principals facing the responsibility of deciding when to step in and call for help from specialists.

Dackin . . . said Mosaic's immediate virtue would be in producing 14 detailed documentation of its evaluation of a troubled student so that doubting parents could no longer challenge an administrator's judgment as too subjective. But Mosaic, he stressed, will at best be a useful instrument, with the school community's ultimate safeguard being in making sure that all students feel fully involved in school.

"It's easy to put up metal detectors," Dackin said, "but harder to 15 create a system where students feel connected."

The program, which is still being formulated, is to be tested from 16 grades one through twelve, with the main focus being in high schools. All the sites have not been determined. It will involve only students who give cause for special concern, school and law-enforcement officials emphasize. "We certainly wouldn't want to develop any kind of tool for labeling students in any way," Vita said.

[Reynoldsburg] school officials expressed confidence that the con- 17 fidentiality of student records required by law would not be breached by Mosaic. They emphasized that the software would not be connected to any central data program.

"It sounds okay, so long as you don't wind up labeling kids," said 18 Shelly Darby, who works at the Sun Tang Luck restaurant and is the mother of a second-grader. . . .

"There's kind of scary stuff out there," Ms. Darby said. "But there 19 can be a real fine line between a kid out to get attention and a really troubled kid."

She drew an empathetic nod from Aron Ross, the assistant super- 20 intendent of schools in Reynoldsburg, a city of 35,000 just east of Columbus [Ohio].

"A few dramatic, sad incidents have spawned hysteria," he ex- 21 plained, describing a nightmarish week of baseless rumors and count- less alarms that caused midnight checks on school lockers after the Columbine killings. And through repeated meetings with anxious par- ents, Ross said, the question remains: What else can we do so it doesn't happen here?

"School people in my situation must respond to this new reality di- 22 rectly," he said. "It used to be a platitude, but no longer, about creating an environment where students and teachers are safe and feel safe."

The de Becker company describes itself as a specialist in high- 23 stakes assessments. On its Internet site (www.gdbinc.com), the com- pany has posted a detailed series of explanations and reassurances about the school software. "School administrators would use Mosaic- 2000," the company asserts, "only in situations that reach a certain threshold (e.g., a student makes a threat, brings a weapon to school, teachers or students are concerned a student might act out violently)."

The system "merely brings organization and expert opinion to a 24 process every principal already has," the company says.

The company has not determined the overall cost of the program, 25 but Ms. Montgomery, the attorney general, described it as "very afford- able" at less than $ 10,000 for the high school.

The Mosaic systems are "very well thought out and valuable 26 tools," said James Perrotti, chief of police at Yale University, which for five years has used the Mosaic-2000 program to assess threats received by professors and students.

Perrotti, one of the experts helping to shape the Mosaic-2000 27 questions, said the system had offered effective warning about poten- tially violent situations that were nipped in the bud. "It's not a real pre- dictor but it's the next best thing."

Vita, the federal firearms official, says school officials need Mosaic 28
and other tools to deal with an ever more complex threat in which relatively good students with access to guns may erupt because they feel
victimized by bullies or by the school system.

"They're the hard ones for the school administrators to identify," 29
Vita said. "It's easy to pick out the gang members with tattoos. It's these
other people that kind of surprise administrators, and these are the
ones they really need to identify."   ✤

## READING FOR INFORMATION

1. What is Mosaic-2000, and how does it function?
2. Give some examples of the questions that are included in the Mosaic-
   2000 database.
3. What age range is the Mosaic-2000 system designed for?
4. Who would have access to the data that Mosaic-2000 contains?
5. Summarize briefly the views of Ohio attorney general Betty Montgomery
   on the advantages of the Mosaic-2000 system over traditional methods of
   monitoring troubled students.
6. What criticisms of Mosaic-2000 are described in Clines's article?
7. What impact did the Columbine High School killings have on the way
   school officials, law enforcement authorities, and parents view issues of
   school safety?

## READING FOR FORM, ORGANIZATION, AND EXPOSITORY FEATURES

1. Describe the purpose of Clines's first paragraph.
2. In what ways is Clines's paragraph structure characteristic of journalistic
   writing rather than academic writing?
3. How does Clines's documentation of source material differ from what
   one would find in a piece of academic writing?

## READING FOR RHETORICAL CONCERNS

1. What is Clines's goal in writing?
2. Is there any indication in the article of what Clines thinks about the
   Mosaic-2000 system? Explain your answer.
3. Describe the expertise of the authorities Clines draws on. Did he draw
   on authorities that were appropriate for his topic? Explain your answer.

## WRITING ASSIGNMENTS

1. Write a 500-word summary of the viewpoints of Mosaic-2000 supporters, including Ohio attorney general Betty Montgomery, Bureau of Alcohol, Tobacco and Firearms agent Andrew Vita, Yale University chief of police James Perrotti, and high-school principal Steve Dackin.

2. Write a 750-word description of what you know from personal experience or the experience of your acquaintances about school safety in your hometown.

3. Using Clines's article and your own knowledge, explain in a 1,000-word essay how the Columbine High School killings affected American public education.

# Rooting Out the Bad Seeds?

### *Kelly Patricia O'Meara*

*Kelly Patricia O'Meara is an investigative reporter for* Insight on the News.

### PREREADING

What does the term *criminal profiling* mean? Freewrite in response to this question for ten minutes. If you have never heard the term before, speculate on what you think it might mean.

To ensure that America's youth enjoy good mental health, psy- 1
chologists have been deployed to learning institutions to diagnose behavioral problems and distribute psychotropic drugs such as Ritalin. *Insight's* groundbreaking articles on this issue have excited commentary from *The New York Times* to *Time* and *Newsweek*. But, as with the gunmen at Columbine High School in Littleton, Colorado, or the six-year-old shooter in Flint, Michigan, crimes continue to occur in schools despite the growing network of prescription drugs and psychobabble. For parents who are becoming just a little crazed about all this psychological evaluation of their children, the newest initiative to weigh

and record the state of mind of every student in the public schools may put them over the edge.

Mosaic-2000, a "method" designed to identify potentially violent children, is being tested at random in high schools throughout the country. The problem for those wary of educators caught up in such psychological experiments is that parents will not have a clue about what soon could amount to criminal profiling of every child; nor will they know where, beyond the immediate school officials, the information obtained from their children is sent or how it might affect their future.

It is about as easy to contact Gavin de Becker, Inc., the California-based consulting company specializing in personal security, as it has been to get White House officials to produce missing emails. The designer of the Mosaic-2000 system is in hiding and does not respond directly to questions. Its Web site, however, purports to provide a detailed explanation of its brainchild, and *Insight* has reviewed carefully its descriptions and claims.

This would-be electronic mind reader isn't the first of its kind. Mosaic computer-profiling systems have been used for years by several federal law-enforcement agencies, including the Secret Service, the U.S. Marshals Service, and the Bureau of Alcohol, Tobacco and Firearms, or BATF. Contrary to media reports, the BATF is not "involved in Mosaic other than assisting de Becker in the preliminary screening," according to Jeff Roehm, chief of public information for that agency. Roehm explains: "We had a couple of folks who sat on the panel and shared their expertise in law enforcement. They helped in fleshing out the questions that may be asked, but de Becker is a private company offering it to schools."

BATF is just one of the law-enforcement agencies that played a major role in developing criminal profiling of kids through Mosaic-2000. According to de Becker, Gil Garcetti, the Los Angeles County district attorney; Richard Devine, the state's attorney for Cook County, Illinois; and Donald W. Ingwerson, superintendent of the Los Angeles County Office of Education, are the "three leaders who partnered to facilitate the development and testing of the new system for evaluating threats in schools."

So what did the best and brightest in law enforcement come up with to help their partners seek out and identify the next Columbine shooter?

The Mosaic-2000 is described on the de Becker Web site as a   7
"computer-assisted method for helping evaluate situations involving
students who make threats and might act out violently." But it is not a
test that students are asked to take. Children are questioned by school
or law-enforcement officials and the information fed into the Mosaic
system (the children are not told who will evaluate the information or
how it will be analyzed). The system then produces a report on the
child being evaluated for criminal tendencies.

The computer-assisted system already has divined questions as   8
well as possible replies. After a subject's answers are run through the
computer, they are rated on a scale of one (low potential for violence) to
ten (high potential for violence). School officials or law officers then
make a "threat assessment" of the student.

Critics say the worst potential problems with Mosaic-2000 are en-   9
capsulated in what the company stresses never would occur. For instance, de Becker says, Mosaic-2000 is "not a computer program. It will
not share information about the students (at least in the field tests), student names will be automatically deleted from the system after the evaluation process is complete, and because Mosaic-2000 helps evaluate
situations and not students, it does not explore any demographic questions such as age, gender, ethnicity, socioeconomic situations, et cetera."
In other words, students are not being evaluated—"situations" are evaluated. The information that is fed into the system about the "situation" is
not shared with anyone, and there is no record of the "assessment."

If that is the case, say critics, what is the purpose of all this? And   10
why are parents who become aware of the Mosaic system refused a list
of the questions it poses? The most important element of the system,
the questions, are carefully guarded and simply unobtainable for independent evaluation. "We don't know if this thing is fish or fowl. We
don't know how the information is going to be used," Ted Deeds, chief
operating officer of the Law Enforcement Alliance of America, a
Virginia-based coalition of law-enforcement officials, victims, and citizens united for justice, tells *Insight*. "First, if the data does work, what
the hell do you do with it? Will the schools segregate the potentially
violent students, isolate them, carry out more locker checks, or send
them into counseling? What's the review mechanism? They all say it's
not a profiling of the student, but we're not convinced."

Struggling to find a rationale for Mosaic-2000, Deeds comes up   11
only with more questions: "How do you train personnel for using such a

system? How does one know that the answer is truthful and whether the kid understands the questions being asked? No one has addressed these questions. Remember, we're dealing with kids, not adults. Parents would be insane to allow their children to be put into this kind of database—it could show up for the next 20 years. Does anyone really believe that this information won't be used by other law-enforcement agencies? Just look at the Social Security number, which we were promised would never be used for general identification. We've seen these promises before. This isn't anything new; the spin is just a little different."

Officials participating in the trial program immediately are defensive and provide conflicting views of Mosaic-2000. Aaron Ross, assistant superintendent of Reynoldsburg School District in suburban Ohio, tells *Insight*, "We're trying to use the system, but we haven't found anyone to test. That's the good news." Questioned about Mosaic-2000 as a form of profiling for potentially violent students, Ross suddenly is emphatic. "Some people," Ross declares, "have said to me that Mosaic-2000 is profiling. That is just stupid. This system doesn't profile kids. It's just twenty questions. It's a piece of software that contains twenty questions that ask the investigating officer, principal, or counselor about a specific situation. What Mosaic-2000 permits that would not otherwise be available is [the gathering of] information that is organized into twenty categories that are relevant to risk assessment when the situation arises." 12

"The principal," Ross continues, "can make a decision with the additional information that has been delivered by Mosaic-2000 with greater confidence in determination of the risk. It's a nice system. It takes the information from the answers provided by the student and organizes them into relevant categories. There is no rating of kids or situations. In fact, it can be completely anonymous. The point of the program is to help the investigator. When he's done, the notes will be thrown away." 13

Ross harbors doubts, nevertheless. "I have no idea if someone is keeping a record of this information. The same can be said, however, of every other piece of information we keep on our students—grades, test scores, and disciplinary actions. The bottom line is that we have a situation around the country where kids are getting killed. We're always looking for tools to help in unusual situations—to make schools safe." 14

Although claiming to be more than willing to provide *Insight* with a copy of Mosaic's twenty questions, Ross says he does not have them 15 and is unaware of how they could be obtained short of requesting them directly from de Becker. (De Becker has not returned *Insight*'s calls or email requests.) Bob Benjamin, communications director for Devine, the Cook County, Illinois, state's attorney, one of the three leaders who partnered to come up with the system, says he is aware of Mosaic-2000 but, like Ross, does not have a copy of the profiling questions—even though Mosaic-2000 is being tested in three suburban Chicago high schools.

"This system," explains Benjamin, "is a consequence of what hap- 16 pened at Columbine. What we're trying to find out is who is in such personal trouble that they might do something that may endanger another student or themselves. I don't think parental consent is necessary before the test is given. Everyone involved wants to see how this program will work. . . . The tests are ongoing and it will take time to assess the system."

Everyone concerned with this project agrees that Mosaic-2000 17 was born out of the tragedy that occurred last year at Columbine High School and that its purpose is to identify the potential for violent behavior in schoolchildren. But according to data released by the Bureau of Justice Statistics, or BJS, and the National Center for Education Statistics, or NCES, schools are safer now than they have been in years. In fact, according to a recent BJS/NCES report, "a child is more likely to be a victim of a violent crime in their community or at home than at school."

In 1996 (the most recent data available), there were 255,000 inci- 18 dents of nonfatal but serious violent crime at school, but that figure nearly triples to 671,000 incidents concerning children away from school. The data further show a "decline in school crime and a reduction in the percentage of students carrying weapons to school." The data for the 1996–97 school year show that "10 percent of all public schools reported at least one serious violent crime to the police or a law-enforcement representative. Forty-seven percent of public schools reported less-serious violent or nonviolent crimes, and the remaining 43 percent of public schools reported none of these crimes."

It is precisely this kind of information that has critics questioning 19 the need for Mosaic-2000 as well as its methodology. "We've heard them say that they aren't going to use this information for anything," says Deeds. "So why are they taking it? The federal government likes to flush money away, but most of the time they do it with some purpose."

As a civil libertarian concerned about law enforcement, Deeds is 20 both knowledgeable and aware of the slippery slope. "Let's face it, the federal government has been profiling people for years," he says. "It's exactly like what happened with the National Instant Check System, or NICS. They said they weren't going to keep the records of the people who passed the firearms check, but they have. The people who cleared the system are not criminals, yet they remain in the system like they are. This administration keeps records on 99.9 percent of the people who aren't criminals. Remember Filegate? The administration was using secret or classified data on their Republican opponents. They've proved what they're about and they seem willing to do anything to push their political agendas."

It is unclear what Mosaic-2000 is about and whether the informa- 21 tion it collects on students will be shared with other agencies. But it isn't difficult for many in law enforcement to see it moving in that direction, especially because it is based on controversial profiling systems already in use by federal law-enforcement officials. Of such concerns de Becker writes in his Web site, "The first step toward understanding Mosaic-2000 is to recognize that it will not fit neatly into methods you may have encountered in the past. Though similar approaches are used in several sciences (most notably as part of medical diagnoses and decision-making), few people have encountered Artificial Intuition."

Apparently, de Becker is suggesting the computer-assisted system 22 has a kind of sixth sense. Of course, critics say that relying on this sort of "evaluation" amounts to kookery and increases the possibility of labeling innocent kids. Such worries may not be too big a leap, considering that some law-enforcement officials have been labeling as extremists motorists who display political or religious views on bumper stickers. For instance, according to a December 1999 article in the *FBI Law Enforcement Bulletin* titled "Vehicle Stops Involving Extremist Group Members," if motorists "sport bumper stickers with antigovernment or progun sentiments . . . and show other extremist signs such as presenting a copy of the Constitution, a Bible, or political literature," law enforcement is trained to handle the situation with caution.

The Constitution? A Bible? No wonder civil libertarians are com- 23 plaining about profiling. ❀

### READING FOR INFORMATION

1. Does O'Meara's description of how Mosaic-2000 functions differ in any respects from Clines's description? Explain your answer.

2. Working from paragraph 9, explain de Becker's rationale for claiming that Mosaic-2000 does not endanger students' privacy.

3. What is Ted Deeds's concern about how Mosaic-2000 data will be used?

4. What is the basis for O'Meara's claim that school officials provide conflicting information about Mosaic-2000?

5. How many questions are in the Mosaic-2000 database?

6. Why is O'Meara unable to get copies of the Mosaic-2000 questions?

7. What do data from the Bureau of Justice Statistics and the National Center for Educational Statistics indicate about the level of safety in schools?

8. What examples of criminal profiling are presented in O'Meara's article other than Mosaic-2000?

## READING FOR FORM, ORGANIZATION, AND EXPOSITORY FEATURES

1. Explain O'Meara's title.

2. Does O'Meara provide a thesis statement?

3. Describe the function of paragraph 6.

4. Describe and comment on O'Meara's closing strategy.

## READING FOR RHETORICAL CONCERNS

1. Based on the first paragraph, what is O'Meara's attitude toward efforts by public school officials to monitor and treat students' psychological problems?

2. Explain the tone and function of paragraph 3. What does the paragraph imply?

3. Who do you think is O'Meara's target audience? How does she intend to affect that audience?

## WRITING ASSIGNMENTS

1. Drawing on O'Meara, write a 500-word summary of the potential problems with the Mosaic-2000 system.

2. Imagine that you are the principal of the high school you attended and write a 500-word defense of using the Mosaic-2000 system.

3. Imagine that you are the student government president of the high school you attended and write a 500-word attack on using the Mosaic-2000 system.

# Kyllo v. United States: Technology v. Individual Privacy

## Thomas D. Colbridge

*Thomas Colbridge is an FBI agent and a legal instructor at the FBI Academy.*

### PREREADING

Do police officials need expanded powers to help them combat drug dealers? Freewrite for ten minutes in response to this question.

Few issues evoke as much passionate debate as police use of new technologies to combat crime. As noted in a previous article regarding thermal imaging (1), the introduction of any advanced crime-fighting device into law enforcement's arsenal of weapons raises public concern about the erosion of constitutional rights. The specter of "Big Brother" looms large in the public mind. The debate is an honest one, raising basic issues regarding the proper balance between the personal privacy of individuals and the government's obligation to enforce the law and ensure public safety. Recently, the U.S. Supreme Court decided another skirmish in this ongoing philosophical battle in the case of *Kyllo v. United States* (2), involving police use of thermal imaging. 1

This article discusses the Court's holding in the Kyllo case and its restrictions on police use of thermal-imaging devices (3). The article also explores major themes developed by federal courts when assessing the impact of new police technologies on traditional Fourth Amendment search law. 2

### FOURTH AMENDMENT SEARCH

The Fourth Amendment to the Constitution of the United States prohibits unreasonable searches (4). The drafters of the Constitution never defined the concepts of "unreasonable" and "search" as used in the 3

Colbridge, Thomas. "Kyllo v. United States: Technology v. Individual Privacy." *FBI Law Enforcement Bulletin* (October 2001): 25+.

Fourth Amendment. The Supreme Court struggled with these constitutional definitions for many years. Finally, in 1967 in the famous case of *Katz* v. *United States* (5), the Supreme Court formulated the modern definition of a search for purposes of the Constitution. The Court said that a Fourth Amendment search occurs whenever the government intrudes into an individual's reasonable expectation of privacy (6). Supreme Court Justice Harlan, in a concurring opinion, established a useful two-prong test to determine if a reasonable expectation of privacy exists: (1) Do individuals have an actual (subjective) expectation that their activities will remain private? and (2) Is their subjective expectation of privacy one that society is willing to accept as reasonable (objectively reasonable)? (7) If the answer to both questions is yes, then a reasonable expectation of privacy exists, and any governmental invasion of that expectation is a search for Fourth Amendment purposes.

However, the Fourth Amendment does not prohibit all government searches, only unreasonable ones. Assuming the government does conduct a search as defined in *Katz*, is it reasonable or unreasonable? Unlike the question of whether a search has occurred, which can be difficult, the question of the reasonableness of the search is straightforward. If the search is conducted under the authority of a search warrant, or one of the recognized exceptions to the warrant requirement, the search is reasonable for Fourth Amendment purposes (8).

## THERMAL-IMAGING TECHNOLOGY

Thermal imaging is not a new technology. It has been used by both the military and law enforcement for years. The public is accustomed to seeing thermal images of battlefields on the nightly news and thermal images of the streets on popular police reality television programs.

All objects with a temperature above absolute zero emit infrared radiation, which is invisible to the naked eye. The warmer an object is, the more infrared radiation it emits. The thermal imager detects this infrared radiation and converts it into a black-and-white picture. The hotter areas (i.e., those areas emitting more infrared radiation) appear lighter in the picture; the cooler areas appear darker. The device does not measure the actual temperature of objects, only the relative temperatures of the surfaces of objects scanned. It emits no rays or beams that penetrate the object viewed. Law enforcement has found several uses for the device, including locating bodies, tracking fleeing persons, and detecting possible indoor marijuana-growing operations. Using the thermal imager in the battle against indoor marijuana-growing operations brought Danny Kyllo and the thermal imager to the attention of the U.S. Supreme Court.

## THE KYLLO CASE

The facts of the Kyllo case are typical of these types of investigations. An agent of the U.S. Bureau of Land Management developed information that Kyllo might be growing marijuana inside his home. Among the information he gathered were the facts that Kyllo's ex-wife, with whom he still was apparently living, was arrested the previous month for delivery and possession of a controlled substance; that Kyllo told a police informant that he could supply marijuana; and that other individuals suspected of drug trafficking lived in the same triplex occupied by Kyllo and his ex-wife. The agent subpoenaed Kyllo's utility records and concluded that his utility use was abnormally high. Finally, at the request of the investigator, a member of the Oregon National Guard scanned Kyllo's home using a thermal imager. The scan was made at approximately three o'clock in the morning from the streets in front of and behind the Kyllo residence. No search warrant authorizing the scan was sought. The scan revealed what investigators believed to be abnormally high amounts of heat coming from Kyllo's home. Investigators concluded that the facts of the case gave them probable cause to believe Kyllo was growing marijuana in his house. Investigators applied for and obtained a warrant to search Kyllo's home, using the results of the thermal scan as part of their probable cause. The search revealed marijuana plants, weapons, and drug paraphernalia.

After his indictment for manufacturing marijuana (9), Kyllo moved to suppress the evidence gathered in his home on several grounds, including the use of the thermal imager without a search warrant. Kyllo argued that targeting his home with a thermal imager was an unreasonable Fourth Amendment search because there was no warrant authorizing it, and the government could not justify the lack of a search warrant under one of the warrant exceptions. The trial court denied his motion and Kyllo was convicted. The case was appealed to the U.S. Court of Appeals for the Ninth Circuit.

### The Circuit Court's View

The U.S. Court of Appeals for the Ninth Circuit heard the Kyllo case three times before it reached a final conclusion. The Ninth Circuit's struggle to decide this case is a reflection of the divergence of opinion that had developed in the courts regarding the warrantless thermal scanning of a home. It also is an interesting study of the difficulty that courts have in dealing with the impact of advancing technology on Fourth Amendment privacy issues.

The first time the Ninth Circuit considered Kyllo's appeal, it made 10 no decision regarding the constitutionality of a warrantless scan of a home with a thermal imager. Instead, it sent the case back to the trial court for additional hearings on the capabilities of the thermal imager (10). The trial court found that the imager used by police in this case recorded no intimate details of life inside Kyllo's home; did not invade any personal privacy inside the home; could not penetrate walls or windows to reveal human activities or conversations; and recorded only heat escaping from the house (11). On that basis, the trial court decided that the thermal scan did not invade a reasonable expectation of privacy and therefore was not a search within the meaning of the Fourth Amendment. It again refused to suppress the evidence. The case went back to the Ninth Circuit for a second time.

This time, a three-judge panel of the Ninth Circuit decided that 11 the warrantless thermal scan of Kyllo's home was an unconstitutional search (12). The court adopted the view that using a thermal imager to target a private home is a Fourth Amendment search, requiring probable cause and authorization of a search warrant or one of the exceptions to the warrant requirement (13). Its decision was clearly a minority view among federal circuit courts at the time (14). However, the Ninth Circuit's debate over the issue was not finished. In July 1999, the court withdrew this opinion (15) and decided to reconsider the issue.

On its third and final consideration of this case, the Ninth Cir- 12 cuit reversed itself and held that a thermal scan of a residence is not a search under the Fourth Amendment (16). It joined the majority of other federal circuit courts (17) in deciding that Kyllo had no actual (subjective) expectation of privacy in the "waste heat" (18) radiating from the surface of his home because he made no effort to conceal the emissions. Even if he could demonstrate an actual expectation of privacy in the escaping heat, the court reasoned that privacy expectation was not objectively reasonable. The court said that the crucial question to be answered in judging the impact of new technologies on privacy issues is whether the technology used to enhance the senses of the police officer is "so revealing of intimate details as to raise constitutional concerns" (19). This court decided thermal imaging was not so revealing. To resolve the conflicting views among federal circuit courts regarding the constitutionality of residential thermal scans, the U.S. Supreme Court agreed to hear the case (20).

## The Supreme Court's View

The Supreme Court disagreed with the majority of the federal circuit 13 courts. In a 5 to 4 decision, it ruled that targeting a home with a thermal imager by police officers is a search under the Fourth Amendment (21) and therefore requires probable cause and a search warrant unless the government can forego the warrant under one of the Court's recognized exceptions to the warrant requirement (22).

The majority and dissenting opinions in this case reflect the diffi- 14 culty courts in general have resolving the tension between individual privacy and governmental use of technology to combat crime. Several themes emerged in the opinion that echoed arguments made in previous rulings involving police use of emerging technologies.

The first theme involves the area that actually was searched. The 15 majority opinion argued that the surveillance in this case was of the interior of a private home. The Court made it clear that the interior of a home indeed is still a castle. It said, "'[A]t the very core' of the Fourth Amendment 'stands the right of a man to retreat into his own home and there be free from unreasonable governmental intrusion'" (23). While the Court often has held that naked-eye surveillance of the exterior of a home and its curtilage by the police is not objectionable as long as police have a lawful vantage point from which to see the home (24), this case involved more. Using the thermal imager, the majority felt, police were able to explore details of the interior of Kyllo's house that they could not have gotten otherwise without going inside (25).

The dissent disagreed. It distinguished between technology per- 16 mitting "through-the-wall surveillance," a search it admitted is presumptively unconstitutional (26), and "off-the-wall surveillance," a search it assumed to be constitutional (27). The thermal imager in this case, according to the dissent, passively measured heat emissions from the exterior surfaces of Kyllo's home. There was no penetration into the interior of the residence by the police or by rays or beams emitted by the imager. The dissent argued that police simply gathered information exposed to the public from the outside of Kyllo's home.

A second theme discussed by the Court is the public availability of 17 the technology used. This issue was raised in 1986 in the Dow Chemical Company (28) case. In that case, the Supreme Court noted in passing that "[I]t may well be, . . . that surveillance of private property by using highly sophisticated surveillance equipment not generally available to the public . . . might be constitutionally proscribed absent a warrant" (29). It was significant to the majority in the Kyllo case that thermal-imaging technology is not widely available to the general public (30).

While the dissent did not specifically disagree (31), it criticized 18 the majority for not providing guidance regarding how much use constitutes general public use. It is difficult to discern from the opinion why public availability is important or how important it actually is. It may be a recognition on the part of the Court that as technology makes its way into everyday life, it becomes more difficult for individuals to claim a reasonable expectation to be shielded from its impact.

A third theme that emerges in this case is the debate over the na- 19 ture and quality of the information supplied to the police by the thermal imager. The Court framed its discussion of this issue in terms of whether or not the technology enabled police to gather information regarding "intimate details" (32) of human activities in the home. This debate also arose in the Dow Chemical Company case. The issue there was the government's use of an aerial mapping camera to photograph a Dow Chemical plant to look for environmental violations. In its opinion, the Court said, ". . . [b]ut the photographs here are not so revealing of intimate details as to raise constitutional concerns" (33). The obvious corollary of that statement is that technology in the hands of the government that reveals intimate details of in-home activities does raise constitutional concerns.

The Kyllo majority rejected the government's contention that be- 20 cause the imager used in this case did not provide exacting detail regarding activities inside Kyllo's home, it should not be of constitutional concern. As the majority opinion put it, "In the home, our cases show all details are intimate details because the entire area is held safe from prying government eyes" (34). The majority reasoned, for example, that the imager used in this case might reveal when a person inside the home regularly took a bath each night. Several previous Supreme Court cases were cited to support this view. In *United States v. Karo* (35), where government agents simply detected the presence of a can of ether in a private residence by monitoring a beeper placed in the can, the Court found that the agents had conducted an unconstitutional search. In *Arizona v. Hicks* (36), an officer lawfully inside a home moved a record player to see its serial number. The Court said that was an unlawful search because it went beyond what the officer could see in plain view. In both cases, the information gathered by the police was relatively insignificant, but because it was information about the inside of a home, the majority felt it was intimate enough to warrant protection from the government.

The dissent argued that the thermal scan here provided scant detail regarding the exterior of Kyllo's home and certainly no information concerning its interior. In the dissent's view, the only information gathered by police was an indication that some areas of Kyllo's roof and outside walls were hotter than others. That kind of information, the dissent argued, is unworthy of Fourth Amendment protection because anyone can tell the warmth of a home's walls and roof by looking at evaporation or snowmelt patterns on the roof, and because most people do not care if the amount of heat escaping from their homes is made public (37). 21

These major themes are important for law enforcement for two reasons. The first reason is practical—the Kyllo case will have an immediate impact on the use of thermal imaging in criminal investigations. The second reason is less immediate but more far-reaching. The Supreme Court has given law enforcement important clues regarding the government's future use of technology to gather criminal evidence (38). 22

## Limitations on the Use of the Thermal Imager

The most immediate impact of the Kyllo case is the elimination of the thermal imager as an investigative tool in residential indoor marijuana-growing cases. The majority opinion makes it clear that using a thermal imager to surveil a home is a search under the Fourth Amendment, requiring a search warrant supported by probable cause or justified by one of the search warrant exceptions. If officers have probable cause to believe marijuana is being grown inside a house (or any premises where there is a reasonable expectation of privacy), they will get the warrant and search, not get a warrant and conduct a thermal scan. Consequently, thermal imagers have been rendered superfluous in indoor residential marijuana-growing investigations. 23

However, the thermal imager still is a valuable tool for use where there is no expectation of privacy or when police are excused from the warrant requirement. For example, using the device to search for fleeing fugitives in an open field, where there is no expectation of privacy, is permissible. In addition, using the thermal imager to target even a private residence still is arguably permissible in emergency situations where the search warrant requirement is excused (39). For example, if 24 faced with a dangerous barricaded subject or a hostage situation and officers decide an entry is necessary, no warrant would be necessary to thermally scan a premises as long as officers have reasonable suspicion to believe a threat to life exists (40). Of course, if time permits, officers always should seek a warrant before entering a private area.

## LARGER IMPLICATIONS OF KYLLO

Law enforcement officers have sworn to uphold the Constitution of the   25 United States and of their respective states. The oath includes the obligation to assess their actions in light of ever-changing interpretations of the law by the courts. That assessment must include the increasing use of sophisticated technology to ferret out crime.

In *Kyllo*, the Supreme Court provided some guidance to law en-   26 forcement regarding when its use of technology unreasonably infringes personal privacy. In light of *Kyllo*, law-enforcement officers should ask themselves certain questions before using sophisticated devices in their investigations.

### What Is Being Targeted?

*Kyllo* confirms the familiar proposition that anytime police invade a   27 reasonable expectation of privacy, it is a Fourth Amendment search requiring a warrant or an exception to the warrant requirement. That is true whether the invasion is physical or technological as in the Kyllo case. If the target of the technological surveillance is the interior of a home, the Supreme Court has made it clear that there is an expectation of privacy, and it is reasonable (41). The same conclusion must be reached where the target of the surveillance is the interior of a commercial building inaccessible to the public. Where the target is the exterior of a premises, there likely is no expectation of privacy as long as police have a lawful vantage point from which to conduct their technological surveillance, and the results of the surveillance reveal nothing regarding the interior of the premises.

Similarly, if the thermal imager is used to search a person (as op-   28 posed to search for a person in an area where there is no expectation of privacy), a reasonable expectation of privacy must be assumed. For example, using a thermal imager, it is theoretically possible to detect the presence of objects concealed under a person's clothing. Such a use of the thermal imager is a Fourth Amendment search and must comply with the constitutional requirements.

## What Information Is Gathered?

It is clear from the *Kyllo* decision that the Supreme Court is concerned 29 about the collection by the police of what it calls "intimate details" or "private activities occurring in private areas" (42). The Court did not define what details are intimate and private and what details are not, and wants to avoid deciding the issue on a case-by-case basis. Instead, the Court opted for a rule that within the confines of a home, "all details are intimate details" (43) and protected by the Fourth Amendment. Consequently, if officers are considering using a device that will enable them to gather any information regarding the interior of a home (or any area in which there is a reasonable expectation of privacy) from outside, they must comply with the provisions of the Fourth Amendment.

## Is the Device Generally Available to the Public?

As noted above, the Supreme Court often limits its reservations regard- 30 ing police use of technological devices to those devices not generally available to the public. It did so in its opinion in the Dow Chemical Company (44) case and in *Kyllo* (45). It is unclear how important this consideration is to the Court. The implication seems to be that individuals cannot claim a reasonable expectation of privacy against technological intrusions that are widely known to occur and happen on a regular basis. The Court in *Kyllo* acknowledged that. It said, "[I]t would be foolish to contend that the degree of privacy secured to citizens by the Fourth Amendment has been entirely unaffected by the advance of technology. For example . . . the technology enabling human flight has exposed to public view (and, hence, we have said, to official observation) uncovered portions of the house and its curtilage that once were private" (46).

Does that mean if thermal imagers become commonplace the 31 Court will permit police to routinely scan the interior of homes without warrants? Probably not, for two reasons. The Court has long distinguished between police surveillance of the exterior of homes and the interior of homes: "We have said that the Fourth Amendment draws a firm line at the entrance to the house, [citation omitted]. That line, we think, must be not only firm but also bright . . ." (47). Given the strong language in the *Kyllo* opinion, it is unreasonable for police to assume that governmental intrusions into private areas are permissible simply because everyone is doing it. In addition, private (nongovernmental) and commercial use of new technologies does not raise constitutional concerns. The Constitution was written to limit the authority of the government, not private citizens (48). Consequently, the Supreme Court will not question the use of a thermal imager by an insulation company to demonstrate homeowners' need to insulate their homes, but put the same thermal imager into the hands of the police investigating a crime, and a multitude of weighty legal issues will arise. When assessing the Fourth Amendment implications of using technological devises to gather information about the interior of premises, officers should not rely on the fact that the device is widely available.

### Why Is the Device Being Used?

Using technology to gather evidence of criminal activity obviously raises 32 Fourth Amendment concerns. However, criminal investigation is not always the goal. Often, technology is employed by the government for the broader purpose of public safety. The most obvious example is the use of X-ray and magnetic screening devices at airports and government office buildings. Courts have long recognized that such warrantless searches are permissible because they are administrative in nature, not criminal, and are not very intrusive. They serve the valid governmental purpose of securing public safety rather than gathering evidence of criminal activity (49). So long as the technological search is narrowly limited to serve only that public safety purpose, it will pass constitutional muster.

### Where and When Is the Device Being Used?

Another factor courts consider when assessing police use of technology 33 is where and when the device is used. If the device is used in public areas, such as airports and public buildings, where people are aware of its presence, courts generally have fewer constitutional reservations regarding its use. Under those conditions, people can make a choice to enter the screening area or not. If they choose to enter, some courts have reasoned that they have consented to be searched by the device in use (50). If the device is used in the dead of night, as happened in the Kyllo case, consent obviously is impossible.

### CONCLUSION

Historically, modern technology in the hands of the police has raised 34 well-founded fears in the public mind concerning the erosion of privacy rights. The police, however, have an obligation to protect the public safety through whatever constitutional means are available to them. Criminal elements are quick to adopt the latest technological gadgets in order to stay one step ahead of the police. Police quickly must respond in kind. The tension between these two legitimate interests has created some of the most difficult issues faced by U.S. courts.

In *Kyllo* v. *United States*, the U.S. Supreme Court drew a bright 35 line around the home and announced a rule that warrantless police use of technology stops at the front door. Simply put, the Court stated that if police use technology from outside the home to gather information they could not otherwise obtain without going inside, they have conducted a search within the meaning of the Constitution, which must be supported by a warrant or a recognized exception to the warrant requirement.

While the Kyllo case dealt specifically with thermal-imaging tech- 36 nology, it has much larger implications. Law-enforcement officers have an obligation to assess all technological devices in their arsenal in light of the lessons delivered in this case.

## ENDNOTES

1. Thomas D. Colbridge, "Thermal Imaging: Much Heat but Little Light," *The FBI Law Enforcement Bulletin*, December 1997, 18–24.
2. 121 S. Ct. 2038 (2001).
3. While the Kyllo case dealt with a thermal imaging device, the legal principles discussed in this article apply equally to the Forward Looking Infrared Radar (FLIR) device, an adaptation of the thermal imager for use on aircraft.
4. U.S. Const. Amend IV: "The right of the people to be secure in their persons, houses, papers, and effects against unreasonable searches and seizures shall not be violated. . . ."
5. 389 U.S. 347 (1967)
6. Id.
7. Supra note 5 at 361 (J. Harlan, concurring).
8. Supra note 5 at 357. The exceptions to the search warrant requirement recognized by the Supreme Court are the consent search (*Schneckloth* v. *Bustamonte*, 412 U.S. 218 [1973]); the search incident to arrest (*U.S.* v. *Robinson*, 414 U.S. 218 [1973]); the emergency search or exigent circumstances search (*Warden* v. *Hayden*, 387 U.S. 394 [1967]); the motor vehicle search (*Carroll* v. *U.S.*, 267 U.S. 132 [1925]); the inventory search (*South Dakota* v. *Opperman*, 428 U.S. 364 [1976]); certain administrative searches of regulated businesses (*New York* v. *Berger*, 482 U.S. 691 [1987]); and "special needs" searches (*Veronia School District 47 J* v. *Acton*, 515 U.S. 646 [1995]).
9. 21 U.S.C. 841(a)(1).
10. *United States* v. *Kyllo*, 37 F.3d 526 (9th Cir. 1994).
11. *United States* v. *Kyllo*, No. CR 92-051-FR (D.Or. March 15, 1996).
12. *United States* v. *Kyllo*, 140 F.3d 1249 (9th Cir. 1998).
13. Id. at 1255.
14. The U.S. Court of Appeals for the Tenth Circuit held in 1995 that a thermal scan of a home was a search: *United States* v. *Cusumano*. 67 F.3d 1497 (10th Cir. 1995), vacated on other grounds, 83 F.3d 1247 (10th Cir. 1996). Two states also had adopted

this minority view: *State* v. *Young*, 867 P.2d 593 (Wash. 1994) and *State* v. *Siegel*, 934 P.2d 176 (Mont. 1997).

15. *United States* v. *Kyllo*, 184 F.3d 1059 (9th Cir. July 29, 1999).

16. *United States* v. *Kyllo*, 190 F.3d 1041 (9th Cir. 1999).

17. See *United States* v. *Ishmael*, 48 F.3d 850 (5th Cir. 1995); *United States* v. *Myers*, 46 F.3d 668 (7th Cir. 1995); *United States* v. *Pinson*, 24 F.3d 1056 (8th Cir. 1994); *United States* v. *Robinson*, 62 F.3d 1325 (11th Cir. 1995).

18. Supra note 16 at 1046.

19. Supra note 16 at 1047 (quoting *Dow Chemical Co.* v. *United States*, 476 US 227 (1986) at 238).

20. *Kyllo* v. *United States*, 530 U.S. 1305 (2000).

21. *Kyllo* v. *United States*, 121 S. Ct. 2038 at 2043.

22. Supra note 8 lists the exceptions to the search warrant requirement.

23. Kyllo, 121 S. Ct. at 2043 quoting *Silverman* v. *United States*, 365 U.S. 505 (1961) at 511.

24. *California* v. *Ciraolo*, 476 U.S. 207 (1986); *Florida* v. *Riley*, 488 U.S. 445 (1989).

25. Kyllo, 121 S. Ct. at 2043.

26. Kyllo, 121 S. Ct. at 2048 (J. Stevens, dissenting), citing *Payton* v. *New York*, 445 U.S. 573 (1980).

27. Kyllo, 121 S. Ct. at 2048, (J. Stevens, dissenting), citing *California* v. *Ciraolo*, supra note 24; *Florida* v. *Riley*, supra note 24; *California* v. *Greenwood*, 486 U.S. 35 (1988); *Dow Chemical Co.* v. *United States*, supra note 19; and *Air Pollution Variance Board of Colorado* v. *Western Alfalfa Corporation*, 416 U.S. 861 (1974).

28. Supra note 19.

29. Dow Chemical Company, 476 U.S. at 238 (1986).

30. Kyllo, 121 S. Ct. at 2043.

31. The dissent did point out in a footnote that thousands of thermal imagers had been manufactured and are available for rental by anyone. See Kyllo, 121 S. Ct. at 2050, note 5. (J. Stevens, dissenting).

32. Kyllo, 121 S. Ct. at 2045.

33. Dow Chemical Company, 476 U.S. at 238 (1986).

34. Kyllo, 121 S. Ct. at 2045 (emphasis in original).

35. 468 U.S. 705 (1984).

36. 480 U.S. 321 (1987).

37. Kyllo, 121 S. Ct. at 2048 (J. Stevens, dissenting).

38. Regarding certain technology in development, the Court offered more than clues. In a footnote, the majority specifically named surveillance devices under development and implied they would raise Fourth Amendment concerns. Those technologies are the Radar-Based Through-the-Wall Surveillance System, Handheld Through-the-Wall Surveillance, and a Radar Flashlight enabling officers to detect people through interior building walls. See Kyllo, 121 S.Ct. at 2044, footnote 3.

39. See *United States* v. *Johnson*, 9 F.3d 506 (6th Cir. 1993).

40. See *Terry* v. *Ohio*, 392 U.S. 1 (1968); *United States* v. *Menard*, 95 F.3d 9 (8th Cir. 1996).

41. Kyllo, 121 S. Ct. at 2043. Of course, even inside the home, there is no expectation of privacy regarding matters that individuals choose to expose to the public: *Katz* v. *United States*, 389 U.S. 347 at 351 (1967), and cases cited at supra note 27.

42. Kyllo, 121 S. Ct. at 2045.

43. Kyllo, 121 S. Ct. at 2045.

44. Supra note 29.

45. Supra note 30.

46. Kyllo, 121 S. Ct. at 2043.

47. Kyllo, 121 S. Ct. at 2046, citing *Payton* v. *New York*, 445 U.S. 573 (1980).

48. *United States* v. *Jacobson*, 466 U.S. 109 (1984); *United States* v. *Knoll*, 16 F. 3rd 1313 (2nd Cir.), cert. denied 115 S. Ct. 574 (1994).

49. *United States* v. *Bulalan*, 156 F. 3rd 963 (9th Cir. 1998); *United States* v. *John Doe, aka Geronimo Pizzaro-Calderon*, 61 F.3d 107 (1st Cir. 1995); *United States* v. *$124,570 U.S. Currency*, 873 U.S. 1240 (9th Cir. 1989).
50. *United States* v. *DeAngelo*, 584 F.2d 46 (4th Cir. 1978), cert. denied 440 U.S. 935 (1979); *United States* v. *Miner*, 484 F.2d 1075 (9th Cir. 1973).  ✿

## READING FOR INFORMATION

1. Summarize the definition of privacy that emerged from *Katz* vs. *United States*.
2. Summarize how thermal imagers function.
3. Summarize briefly the events that led up to Kyllo's arrest.
4. Explain briefly the basis for each of the three separate opinions on the Kyllo case that were issued by the U.S. Court of Appeals for the Ninth Circuit.
5. Summarize the basis for the majority opinion of the Supreme Court on the Kyllo case.
6. Summarize the basis for the dissenting opinions of the Supreme Court on the Kyllo case.
7. In the wake of the Kyllo decision, what options remain for police use of thermal imagers?
8. Summarize briefly what Colbridge believes are the implications of *Kyllo* for police searches that do not involve thermal imaging.

## READING FOR FORM, ORGANIZATION, AND EXPOSITORY FEATURES

1. Characterize Colbridge's use of language.
2. Comment on Colbridge's use of section headings to divide his article.
3. Explain Colbridge's extensive use of endnotes.
4. Does Colbridge's conclusion capture the essence of the Supreme Court's ruling in the Kyllo case? Explain your answer.

## READING FOR RHETORICAL CONCERNS

1. Who do you imagine is the target audience for *The FBI Law Enforcement Bulletin*, the publication in which Colbridge's article appears?
2. How does Colbridge establish his authority?
3. What is Colbridge's goal in writing?
4. How does Colbridge's job as an FBI agent complicate his role as author of an article on the Kyllo case?

## WRITING ASSIGNMENTS

1. Write a 500-word summary of the most important elements in the case against Kyllo and in the Supreme Court's ruling in *Kyllo* v. *United States*.

2. Write a 1,000-word essay that defends or attacks the Supreme Court's ruling in *Kyllo* v. *United States*.

3. In the movie *E.T.*, government agents use high-power listening devices to monitor conversations taking place within private homes in a neighborhood where they suspect children might be hiding an alien creature. Do you think the audio monitoring in *E.T.* would pass the standards for police searches set forth in *Kyllo*? Defend your answer in a 750-word essay.

# DC's Virtual Panopticon

### *Christian Parenti*

*Christian Parenti is the author of* Lockdown America: Police and Prisons in the Age of Crisis.

## PREREADING

In your everyday life, under what circumstances are you photographed by surveillance video cameras? Freewrite for ten minutes in response to that question.

The future is bearing down on Washington, DC. In recent  1
weeks the District's police have begun constructing a centrally monitored, citywide closed-circuit television (CCTV) surveillance system—the first of its kind in the nation. Eventually, the Metropolitan Police Department (MPD) plans to link 1,000 cameras to watch streets, public schools, the DC Metro transit system, federal facilities, and even part of a Georgetown business improvement district. The nucleus of this system, made up of thirteen $15,000-apiece cameras, is already in place, mounted high on buildings, sending live wireless feed to the

*DC's Virtual Panopticon* by Christian Parenti from the June 3, 2002 issue of *The Nation*. Reprinted with permission from the June 3, 2002 issue of *The Nation*.

MPD's $7 million, NASA-style Joint Operations Command Center. In this room filled with video monitors, computers, and communications gear, surveillance images are recorded and logged by the police, Secret Service, FBI, and at times other agencies. Departmental brass say the Command Center and camera network are a response to the attacks of September 11, part of an effort to "enhance public safety" by fighting terrorism and crime. And they claim widespread public support for the project: Recent opinion polls show 60 to 80 percent approval ratings for increased surveillance of streets and public space.

"We've started with important federal locations, but we've already   2
had numerous requests from nearby neighborhoods. People are like, 'Hey, we've got crime; we need some cameras over here,'" says Kevin Morison, communications director for the MPD. He predicts that "community extensions" will be the next phase of the surveillance system.

Once the full camera network is operative, police will be able to   3
read license plates and track cars as they move through the city, zoom in on individuals, read newsprint from hundreds of feet away, and send real-time images to the laptops of the department's 1,000 patrol cars. According to local press reports, engineers are even working to equip some of the cameras with night vision. They could also be outfitted with biometric facial-recognition software for comparing faces on the street against mug shots in the department's database. But so far, the police say they won't use biometrics, in part because facial recognition is still a very imperfect technology.

In preparation for the big linkup, both the school system and the   4
Metro are retooling and are connecting their surveillance systems. The school system started installing cameras at middle and high schools after the Columbine killings in 1999. The Metro has used cameras since the tunnels opened in the late 1970s, but the new Metro surveillance gear will include recorders and be linked by fiber optics into a centralized control station. Eventually the whole system will be connected to the Joint Operations Command Center. "It makes sense," explains Polly Hanson, deputy chief of the DC Metro Police. "When there are emergencies or demonstrations, we coordinate with the MPD anyway. This technical upgrade and connection seemed like a natural fit." Since September 11, the Metro has received $49 million in federal antiterrorist funding and has overhauled surveillance in fourteen key stations; completing the whole job will take several years.

As soon as news of the emerging DC surveillance network broke   5
in late February [2002], civil libertarians began raising questions.

Particularly problematic in the eyes of many is the fact that the system was created without any written guidelines or community consultation. The outcry has forced DC Police Chief Charles Ramsey to promise a set of written parameters for the camera system's operation. But details of the surveillance plans remain a mystery.

"We still have a lot of unanswered questions," says Johnny Barnes, 6 executive director of the Washington American Civil Liberties Union. Despite meetings with the police brass, Barnes and the ACLU still want to know: Who will monitor the video? When will the system be complete? How long will the tapes be kept and by whom? What agencies will get access to the tapes? And what steps will be taken to prevent video voyeurism or racist and anti-homeless profiling? Nor are the ACLU's concerns merely hypothetical: Already, police in Detroit and DC have used CCTV to stalk personal foes, political opponents, and young women.

Other critics go even further, arguing that written regulations and 7 police consultations with the ACLU do little more than legitimize a dangerous and unnecessary surveillance network. "Police guidelines are very frequently violated and can always be changed," says Mara Verheyden-Hilliard, a cofounder of, and attorney with, the Partnership for Civil Justice (PCJ). "Instead of signing off on this new system, we think it needs to be abolished. We believe there's a very strong legal case for the elimination of these cameras. People have the right to traverse the streets and parks of DC without being under the scrutiny of Chief Ramsey and the FBI."

Though one does not have a total right to privacy while walking on 8 the street—we accept that being looked at is the price of being in public—people do have a Fourth Amendment protection against unreasonable searches. And it could be argued by the PCJ or others that when police watch a person with high-powered, interconnected, and intelligent cameras that are linked to criminal-history databases, they are in effect conducting an unwarranted and possibly unconstitutional search. The PCJ also worries that if allowed in DC, such camera networks will proliferate across the country.

Perhaps the most disturbing feature of the DC surveillance network is its past political uses. District police first hooked up their camera surveillance and high-tech Joint Ops Center in 1999 when thousands of activists protested at NATO's fiftieth-anniversary summit. The gear was again deployed in April 2000 to monitor activists and control crowds during mass protests against the joint World Bank and

International Monetary Fund meeting. And the same system spied on protesters during the contested inauguration of George W. Bush in 2001.

"Americans have the right to protest with some level of anonymity, 10 but this system and the other uses of surveillance are stripping people of that right," says Verheyden-Hilliard. "After the inauguration we talked with numerous people who don't normally go to demonstrations, but who went to protest Bush and the stolen election—many of them were shocked and really intimidated by the police militarism and intense surveillance." Many protesters agree that such intensive surveillance has a politically chilling effect.

Veteran activist and videographer Mark Liiv, of Whispered Media, 11 says excessive police surveillance is always "creepy" but that in DC it was particularly so. "At the IMF protests, everyone in the convergence center felt really sketched out. There were lots of cameras on the streets but also guys on rooftops. Some were filming, some were snipers—a bullet backing every camera," says Liiv.

"There's definitely a performative aspect to police surveillance. If 12 you shoot video of the cops doing surveillance, they make a really big deal of getting up in your face and letting you know that you're being filmed. If there are all these high-powered cameras on buildings, why the guys in the street, if not to psych us out and breed paranoia?"

According to material handed over in court to the Partnership for 13 Civil Justice, the DC police even used their surveillance system to observe the superorderly, rather mainstream Million Family March in October 2000. And along with powerful cameras mounted on buildings, the DC police have equipped their helicopters with wireless surveillance video that also feeds the screens monitored at the high-tech Command Center. For a more close-up view from within the crowds of demonstrators, the MPD contracts with a private "script to screen" video firm called SRB Productions. Advertised as "100 percent minority and woman-owned," SRB has worked for everyone from the *Oprah Winfrey Show* to the Navy. As a hireling of the DC police, the firm conducts surveillance of demonstrations using its commercial television equipment, according to an SRB spokesperson. It also mixed a montage video of protest highlights for Chief Ramsey's viewing.

Neither the PCJ nor any other civil libertarians have yet filed 14 a lawsuit demanding that the new camera network be dismantled or that the surveillance of demonstrations be halted. PCJ is still waiting on Freedom of Information Act requests, and litigation may follow.

Unfortunately, PCJ's legal argument that the DC surveillance actually constitutes an illegal search, however compelling, will probably not hold up in today's law-and-order courts.

The DC officialdom's interest in cameras closely parallels events 15 from a decade ago in Britain—the nation that now has the highest CCTV density in the world. In fact, Chief Ramsey is full of praise for the cameras of Britain. But recent history from across the Atlantic can also be read as a political warning.

During the early 1990s British media were gripped by a moral 16 panic that fixated on the double threat of crime and terrorism. When it was all over, Britain was covered with cameras. The cycle started in 1990 when the IRA resumed its "mainland campaign" with a bomb at the London Stock Exchange, followed by a mortar attack on a Cabinet meeting at No. 10 Downing Street in 1991. A bombing in April 1992 left London's financial district with three dead, ninety-one injured, and more than $1.2 billion in damages. The next year another massive "dump-truck bomb" in the same general area killed one and injured dozens. Later, the IRA bombed central Manchester and launched a mortar assault on Heathrow airport.

In response, the police erected a "Ring of Steel" security cordon 17 around central London, involving vehicle barriers, traffic bans, random armed checkpoints, and hundreds of new electronic eyes in the form of CCTV.

Amid this buildup, two 10-year-old boys abducted and killed a 18 toddler named Jamie Bulger. The kidnapping was caught on grainy surveillance film and endlessly looped on British television. All of this helped cast video surveillance as the public safety tool du jour. Now Britain has more than 2.5 million surveillance cameras; London alone is wired with 150,000.

But contrary to what the boosters say—here and in Britain—the 19 record on CCTV is mixed. In London cameras have indeed been correlated with declining crime rates, but now crime is on the rise again despite surveillance. And no terrorists were ever caught using CCTV. Leading British criminologists have found one clear trend: CCTV does lead to racial profiling. One large study by the well-known British criminologists Clive Norris and Gary Armstrong found that black people were twice as likely as whites to be watched for "no obvious reason."

Surveillance cameras are already spreading across the United States 20 well beyond DC. A survey done last year by the International Association of Chiefs of Police found that 80 percent of police departments use CCTV, while another 10 percent are planning to do so. A 1998 study by the New York Civil Liberties Union counted 2,397 surveillance cameras, many private but some controlled by the police, all "trained on public streets, sidewalks, buildings, and parks in Manhattan." When asked for an explanation, then-Mayor Rudy Giuliani waved the group away, saying, "They . . . raise questions about everything." Even more disturbing is the increased use of hidden or disguised CCTV cameras in Gotham.

In Oakland, California, more than seventy surveillance cameras 21 watch the civic center, and a private force of blazer-clad security personnel ushers away homeless sleepers and skateboarding youth. A duplicate system exists around San Francisco's Yerba Buena Center for the Arts, where the rules include everything from no lying down to no kite flying to no bike riding. Santa Rosa, California, also has cameras watching its Courthouse Square and "Transit Mail" with the explicit intent of discouraging the presence of homeless people and youth.

Scores of other towns have similar small-scale systems. Worcester, 22 Massachusetts, has CCTV around its parks. Virginia Beach uses CCTV to monitor the pedestrian crowds of its boardwalk. Similar arrangements exist on Mobile, Alabama's Dauphin Street, site of the local Mardi Gras. More cameras (paid for with money confiscated during drug busts) watch Mobile's Government Plaza, the park near its adjacent convention center, and the traffic corridors that feed into downtown streets. In Los Angeles, police are using motion-sensing cameras to combat graffiti around government buildings.

One thing is clear in most of these cases. Jeffrey Rosen of George 23 Washington School of Law sums it up well: "Surveillance cameras are technologies of classification and exclusion." This can take the form of social prejudice, as when people of color, the homeless, or youth are excessively monitored and driven from public space. Or, as in the case with intensive surveillance of demonstrations in DC, the "exclusions" can be more overtly political.  ❦

### READING FOR INFORMATION

1. Describe the basic operational features of the video surveillance system that District of Columbia police are developing.
2. What areas in Washington will be under surveillance?
3. What are some of the examples Parenti gives to illustrate the quality of the video images that will be obtained with the new system?

4. Explain ACLU representative Johnny Barnes's concerns about the new video monitoring system.

5. Explain PCJ attorney Mara Verheyden-Hilliard's concerns about the new video monitoring system.

6. How has video surveillance been used in the past to monitor political protests in Washington?

7. Why does Parenti think that the courts will rule that the DC video surveillance system is constitutional?

8. What is the status of video surveillance in England?

9. What point does Parenti make in his final paragraph?

## READING FOR FORM, ORGANIZATION, AND EXPOSITORY FEATURES

1. What is the effect of Parenti's opening sentence?

2. Why does Parenti choose, for the most part, to quote authorities directly rather than to paraphrase their ideas?

3. Does Parenti have a thesis statement? Explain your answer.

## READING FOR RHETORICAL CONCERNS

1. Describe the authorities that Parenti cites in his article.

2. What is Parenti's viewpoint on the new DC video surveillance system? Where is that viewpoint indicated?

3. Does Parenti give a fair explanation of arguments both for and against the video surveillance system?

## WRITING ASSIGNMENTS

1. Imagine that you live in Washington, DC. Would you object to the new video surveillance system as an infringement on your privacy, or would you support it as an enhancement to your safety? Write a 750-word essay in response to this question.

2. Draw on Colbridge's and Parenti's articles to write a 1,000-word essay that compares and contrasts the level of privacy that you think people should have in their homes to the level of privacy you think they should have while driving cars and walking on the street.

3. Write a 1,000-word essay that compares and contrasts the video surveillance system that is being developed in DC with that described in George Orwell's *1984*.

# Trading Liberty for Illusions

## *Wendy Kaminer*

*Wendy Kaminer is a lawyer and has written several books, including* Sleeping with Extra-Terrestrials: The Rise of Irrationalism and the Perils of Piety.

### PREREADING

How have the events of September 11, 2001, affected your own views about crime detection efforts? Freewrite for ten minutes in response to that question.

Only a fool with no sense of history would have been sanguine    1
about the prospects for civil liberties after the September 11 attack. Whenever Americans have felt frightened or under siege, they have responded by persecuting immigrants, members of suspect ethnic groups, or others guilty only of real or apparent sympathy for unpopular ideologies. Our most revered, or at least respected, presidents have been among the worst offenders: John Adams supported the Alien and Sedition Acts, which criminalized opposition to the government (and was used to imprison his political foes); Abraham Lincoln suspended habeas corpus and presided over the arrests of thousands of people for crimes like "disloyalty" (which sometimes consisted of criticizing the president); Woodrow Wilson imprisoned Eugene Debs for speaking out against America's entry into the First World War; Franklin Roosevelt famously and shamefully interned Japanese-Americans during World War II. Liberty was trampled by all of these measures, while security was enhanced by none of them.

But the cruelty and folly of imprisoning people for their political    2
views or their ethnicity is usually acknowledged only in hindsight. During World War II some people no doubt felt safer knowing that their Japanese-American neighbors were interned. The Supreme Court ruled at the time that the internment was justified on national security

grounds. People felt safer last fall when the Bush administration swept up and detained over one thousand immigrants in the wake of the September 11 attack, even though the vast majority of them had no apparent connection to terrorism. History shows that frightened people tend to assume that restrictions on liberty make them safe. They support repressive measures instinctively in the expectation that other people will be targeted by them, and ask questions only decades later.

Consider the false promise of many electronic surveillance measures, like facial-recognition systems. A recent report by the American Civil Liberties Union reveals that the widely publicized facial-recognition system used on the streets by police in Tampa, Florida, "never identified even a single individual contained in the department's database of photographs." Instead, "the system made many false positives, including such errors as confusing what were to a human easily identifiable male and female images." The ACLU report was based on a review of police logs obtained through Florida's open-records law.    3

Technological inaccuracies like these were coupled with human errors and abuses of discretion. A facial-recognition system can only be as good as its database in identifying terrorists or other violent criminals, and in Tampa the photographic database was not limited to known criminals: It included people the police were interested in questioning in the belief that they might have "valuable intelligence." Under guidelines like this, ordinary law-abiding citizens who venture out in public might find themselves setting off alarms in facial-recognition systems (should they ever work properly).    4

Whether or not your photograph is in the database, your privacy is likely to be invaded by a facial-recognition system. Cameras scan crowds and, as the ACLU observes, in Britain, where electronic surveillance is becoming routine, camera operators are apt to focus disproportionately on racial minorities or while away the hours peering up women's skirts. In Michigan, according to a report by the *Detroit Free Press*, police used a database to stalk women and intimidate other citizens.    5

Considering the ways facial-recognition systems have been used and abused so far, it's fair to say that they constitute a threat—to privacy, liberty and even physical safety—not a promise of security. But we are beginning to use them more, not less. Several cities have decided to deploy the kind of system that failed so miserably in Tampa, and of course, facial recognition is being touted as an important airport security tool. Airports in cities including Boston, Providence, and Palm    6

Beach are installing facial-recognition systems. Meanwhile, precautions that might actually enhance security, like screening all checked bags and carry-ons, are as far from implementation as ever.

Why do a majority of Americans tolerate and support invasive or    7
repressive faux security measures? I suspect we're simply too frightened and uninformed to challenge them. People who want or need to continue flying, for example, can't bear to devote much thought to the continuing inadequacies of airport security; instead they take comfort in whatever false promise of security they're offered. So, the problem for civil libertarians isn't the tendency of people to trade liberty for security. It's their tendency to trade liberty for mere illusions of security. Liberty would benefit greatly from a logical, pragmatic approach to safety. In our frightened, irrational world, freedom may be threatened most by wishful thinking.     ✤

## READING FOR INFORMATION

1. Paraphrase the first sentence of Kaminer's article.
2. According to Kaminer, how, in the past, have Americans responded when they felt threatened?
3. How does facial-recognition technology function?
4. According to Kaminer, how successful has facial recognition been in reducing crime?
5. What specific dangers of facial-recognition technology does Kaminer identify?
6. Why, according to Kaminer, do Americans accept "invasive or repressive faux security measures"?

## READING FOR FORM, ORGANIZATION, AND EXPOSITORY FEATURES

1. Describe Kaminer's opening strategy.
2. Describe Kaminer's organizational plan.
3. Comment on the length of Kaminer's piece.

## READING FOR RHETORICAL CONCERN

1. Characterize Kaminer's attitude toward the government.
2. What is Kaminer's intended audience? What assumptions does she make about her audience?
3. How do you think police officers would respond to Kaminer's article?

## WRITING ASSIGNMENTS

1. Write a 1,000-word essay that weighs the pros and cons of using facial-recognition technology to monitor the general public.

2. Write a 1,000-word essay of response to Kaminer's assertion that "freedom may be threatened most by wishful thinking."

3. Write a 1,000-word essay that compares and contrasts facial-recognition technology with one or more of the other infringements on personal freedom that are mentioned in Kaminer's first and second paragraphs.

# Invasion of Privacy

## *Joshua Quittner*

*Joshua Quittner, a journalist, is a frequent contributor to* Newsday *and* Wired. *Among the books he has co-authored with Michelle Slatalla are* Masters of Deception: The Gang That Ruled Cyberspace, Flame War, *and* Speeding the Net: The Inside Story of Netscape, How It Challenged Microsoft and Changed the World.

## PREREADING

Based on your own experience and that of your family and friends, are you confident in the safety of credit cards, ATM cards, phone cards, and other electronic records that control "private" business? Is the convenience of these computerized transactions worth any potential for loss or invasion of privacy?

For the longest time, I couldn't get worked up about privacy: my right to it; how it's dying; how we're headed for an even more wired, underregulated, overintrusive, privacy-deprived planet. 1

I mean, I probably have more reason to think about this stuff than the average John Q. All Too Public. A few years ago, for instance, after I applied for a credit card at a consumer-electronics store, somebody got hold of my name and vital numbers and used them to get a duplicate 2 card. That somebody ran up a $3,000 bill, but the nice lady from the fraud division of the credit-card company took care of it with steely digital dispatch. (I filed a short report over the phone. I never lost a cent. The end.)

I also hang out online a lot, and now and then on the Net someone 3 will impersonate me, spoofing my email address or posting stupid stuff to bulletin boards or behaving in a frightfully un-Quittner-like manner in chat parlors from here to Bianca's Smut Shack. It's annoying, I suppose. But in the end, the faux Quittners get bored and disappear. My reputation, such as it is, survives.

I should also point out that as news director for Pathfinder, Time 4 Inc.'s mega info mall, and a guy who makes his living on the Web, I know better than most people that we're hurtling toward an even more intrusive world. We're all being watched by computers whenever we visit Web sites; by the mere act of "browsing" (it sounds so passive!) we're going public in a way that was unimaginable a decade ago. I know this because I'm a watcher too. When people come to my Web site, without ever knowing their names, I can peer over their shoulders, recording what they look at, timing how long they stay on a particular page, following them around Pathfinder's sprawling offerings.

None of this would bother me in the least, I suspect, if a few years 5 ago, my phone, like Marley's ghost, hadn't given me a glimpse of the nightmares to come. On Thanksgiving weekend in 1995, someone (presumably a critic of a book my wife and I had just written about computer hackers) forwarded my home telephone number to an out-of-state answering machine where unsuspecting callers trying to reach me heard a male voice identify himself as me and say some extremely rude things. Then, with typical hacker aplomb, the prankster asked people to leave their messages (which to my surprise many callers, including my mother, did). This went on for several days until my wife and I figured out that something was wrong ("Hey . . . why hasn't the phone rung since Wednesday?") and got our phone service restored.

It seemed funny at first, and it gave us a swell story to tell on our 6 book tour. But the interloper who seized our telephone line continued to hit us even after the tour ended. And hit us again and again for the next six months. The phone company seemed powerless. Its security folks moved us to one unlisted number after another, half a dozen times. They put special PIN codes in place. They put traces on the line. But the troublemaker kept breaking through.

If our hacker had been truly evil and omnipotent, as only fictional ₇ movie hackers are, there would probably have been even worse ways he could have threatened my privacy. He could have sabotaged my credit rating. He could have eavesdropped on my telephone conversations or siphoned off my email. He could have called in my mortgage, discontinued my health insurance, or obliterated my Social Security number. Like Sandra Bullock in *The Net*, I could have been a digital untouchable, wandering the planet without a connection to the rest of humanity. (Although if I didn't have to pay back school loans, it might be worth it. Just a thought.)

Still, I remember feeling violated at the time and as powerless as a ₈ minnow in a flash flood. Someone was invading my private space—my family's private space—and there was nothing I or the authorities could do. It was as close to a technological epiphany as I have ever been. And as I watched my personal digital hell unfold, it struck me that our privacy—mine and yours—has already disappeared, not in one Big Brotherly blitzkrieg but in Little Brotherly moments, bit by bit.

Losing control of your telephone, of course, is the least of it. After ₉ all, most of us voluntarily give out our phone number and address when we allow ourselves to be listed in the *White Pages*. Most of us go a lot further than that. We register our whereabouts whenever we put a bank card in an ATM machine or drive through an E-Z Pass lane on the highway. We submit to being photographed every day—twenty times a day on average if you live or work in New York City—by surveillance cameras. We make public our interests and our purchasing habits every time we shop by mail order or visit a commercial Web site.

I don't know about you, but I do all this willingly because I appre- ₁₀ ciate what I get in return: the security of a safe parking lot, the convenience of cash when I need it, the improved service of mail-order houses that know me well enough to send me catalogs of stuff that interests me. And while I know we're supposed to feel just awful about giving up our vaunted privacy, I suspect (based on what the pollsters say) that you're as ambivalent about it as I am.

Popular culture shines its klieg lights on the most intimate corners ₁₁ of our lives, and most of us play right along. If all we really wanted was to be left alone, explain the lasting popularity of Oprah and Sally and Ricki tell-all TV. Memoirs top the best-seller lists, with books about incest and insanity and illness leading the way. Perfect strangers at cocktail parties tell me the most disturbing details of their abusive upbringings. Why?

"It's a very schizophrenic time," says Sherry Turkle, professor of 12 sociology at the Massachusetts Institute of Technology, who writes books about how computers and online communication are transforming society. She believes our culture is undergoing a kind of mass identity crisis, trying to hang on to a sense of privacy and intimacy in a global village of tens of millions. "We have very unstable notions about the boundaries of the individual," she says.

If things seem crazy now, think how much crazier they will be 13 when everybody is as wired as I am. We're in the midst of a global interconnection that is happening much faster than electrification did a century ago and is expected to have consequences at least as profound. What would happen if all the information stored on the world's computers were accessible via the Internet to anyone? Who would own it? Who would control it? Who would protect it from abuse?

Small-scale privacy atrocities take place every day. Ask Dr. Denise 11 Nagel, executive director of the National Coalition for Patient Rights, about medical privacy, for example, and she rattles off a list of abuses that would make Big Brother blush. She talks about how two years ago, a convicted child rapist working as a technician in a Boston hospital riffled through 1,000 computerized records looking for potential victims (and was caught when the father of a nine-year-old girl used caller ID to trace the call back to the hospital). How a banker on Maryland's state health commission pulled up a list of cancer patients, cross-checked it against the names of his bank's customers, and revoked the loans of the matches. How Sara Lee bakeries planned to collaborate with Lovelace Health Systems, a subsidiary of Cigna, to match employee health records with work-performance reports to find workers who might benefit from antidepressants.

Not to pick on Sara Lee. At least a third of all Fortune 500 com- 15 panies regularly review health information before making hiring decisions. And that's nothing compared with what awaits us when employers and insurance companies start testing our DNA for possible imperfections. Farfetched? More than two hundred subjects in a case study published last January in the journal *Science and Engineering Ethics* reported that they had been discriminated against as a result of genetic testing. None of them were actually sick, but DNA analysis suggested that they might become sick someday. "The technology is getting ahead of our ethics," says Nagel, and the Clinton administration clearly agrees. It is about to propose a federal law that would protect medical and health-insurance records from such abuses.

But how did we arrive at this point, where so much about what we 16 do and own and think is an open book?

It all started in the 1950s, when, in order to administer Social Se- 17 curity funds, the U.S. government began entering records on big mainframe computers, using nine-digit identification numbers as data points. Then, even more than today, the citizenry instinctively loathed the computer and its injunctions against folding, spindling, and mutilating. We were not numbers! We were human beings! These fears came to a head in the late 1960s, recalls Alan Westin, a retired Columbia University professor who publishes a quarterly report *Privacy and American Business*. "The techniques of intrusion and data surveillance had overcome the weak law and social mores that we had built up in the pre–World War II era," says Westin.

The public rebelled, and Congress took up the question of how 18 much the government and private companies should be permitted to know about us. A privacy bill of rights was drafted. "What we did," says Westin, "was to basically redefine what we meant by 'reasonable expectations of privacy'"—a guarantee, by the way, that comes from the Supreme Court and not from any constitutional "right to privacy."

The result was a flurry of new legislation that clarified and defined 19 consumer and citizen rights. The first Fair Credit Reporting Act, passed in 1970, overhauled what had once been a secret, unregulated industry with no provisions for due process. The new law gave consumers the right to know what was in their credit files and to demand corrections. Other financial and health privacy acts followed, although to this day no federal law protects the confidentiality of medical records.

As Westin sees it, the public and private sectors took two very dif- 20 ferent approaches. Congress passed legislation requiring that the government tell citizens what records it keeps on them while insisting that the information itself not be released unless required by law. The private sector responded by letting each industry—credit-card companies, banking, insurance, marketing, advertising—create its own guidelines.

That approach worked—to a point. And that point came when 21 mainframes started giving way to desktop computers. In the old days, information stored in government databases was relatively inaccessible. Now, however, with PCs on every desktop linked to office networks and then to the Internet, data that were once carefully hidden may be only a few keystrokes away.

Suddenly someone could run motor-vehicle-registration records 22 against voting registrations to find six-feet-tall Republicans who were arrested during the past year for drunk driving—and who own a gun. The genie was not only out of the bottle, he was also peering into everyone's bedroom window. (Except the windows of the very rich, who can afford to screen themselves.)

"Most people would be astounded to know what's out there," says 23 Carole Lane, author of *Naked in Cyberspace: How to Find Personal Information Online.* "In a few hours, sitting at my computer, beginning with no more than your name and address, I can find out what you do for a living, the names and ages of your spouse and children, what kind of car you drive, the value of your house, and how much taxes you pay on it."

Lane is a member of a new trade: paid Internet searcher, which al- 24 ready has its own professional group, the Association of Independent Information Professionals. Her career has given her a fresh appreciation for what's going on. "Real privacy as we've known it," she says, "is fleeting."

Now, there are plenty of things you could do to protect yourself. 25 You could get an unlisted telephone number, as I was forced to do. You could cut up your credit card and pay cash for everything. You could rip your E-Z Pass off the windshield and use quarters at tolls. You could refuse to divulge your Social Security number except for Social Security purposes, which is all that the law requires. You'd be surprised how often you're asked to provide it by people who have no right to see it.

That might make your life a bit less comfortable, of course. As in 26 the case of Bob Bruen, who went into a barbershop in Watertown, Massachusetts, recently. "When I was asked for my phone number, I refused to give them the last four digits," Bruen says. "I was also asked for my name, and I also refused. The girl at the counter called her supervisor, who told me I could not get a haircut in their shop." Why? The barbershop uses a computer to record all transactions. Bruen went elsewhere to get his locks shorn.

But can we do that all the time? Only the Unabomber would seri- 27 ously suggest that we cut all ties to the wired world. The computer and its spreading networks convey status and bring opportunity. They empower us. They allow an information economy to thrive and grow. They make life easier. Hence the dilemma.

The real problem, says Kevin Kelly, executive editor of *Wired* 28 magazine, is that although we say we value our privacy, what we really want is something very different: "We think that privacy is about information, but it's not—it's about relationships." The way Kelly sees it, there was no privacy in the traditional village or small town; everyone knew everyone else's secrets. And that was comfortable. I knew about you, and you knew about me. "There was a symmetry to the knowledge," he says. "What's gone out of whack is we don't know who knows about us anymore. Privacy has become asymmetrical."

The trick, says Kelly, is to restore that balance. And not surprisingly, he and others point out that what technology has taken, technology can restore. Take the problem of "magic cookies"—those little bits of code most Web sites use to track visitors. We set up a system at Pathfinder in which, when you visit our site, we drop a cookie into the basket of your browser that tags you like a rare bird. We use that cookie in place of your name, which, needless to say, we never know. If you look up a weather report by keying in a zip code, we note that (it tells us where you live or maybe where you wish you lived). We'll mark down whether you look up stock quotes (though we draw the line at capturing the symbols of the specific stocks you follow). If you come to the *Netly News*, we'll record your interest in technology. Then, the next time you visit, we might serve up an ad for a modem or an online brokerage firm or a restaurant in Akron, Ohio, depending on what we've managed to glean about you. 29

Some people find the whole process offensive. "Cookies represent a way of watching consumers without their consent, and that is a fairly frightening phenomenon," says Nick Grouf, CEO of Firefly, a Boston company that makes software offering an alternative approach to profiling, known as "intelligent agents." 30

Privacy advocates like Grouf—as well as the two companies that control the online browser market, Microsoft and Netscape—say the answer to the cookie monster is something they call the Open Profiling Standard. The idea is to allow the computer user to create an electronic "passport" that identifies him to online marketers without revealing his name. The user tailors the passport to his own interests, so if he is passionate about fly-fishing and is cruising through L.L. Bean's Web site, the passport will steer the electronic-catalog copy toward fishing gear instead of, say, Rollerblades. 31

The advantage to computer users is that they can decide how much information they want to reveal while limiting their exposure to intrusive marketing techniques. The advantage to Web site entrepreneurs is that they learn about their customers' tastes without intruding on their privacy. 32

Many online consumers, however, are skittish about leaving any footprints in cyberspace. Susan Scott, executive director of TRUSTe, a 33 firm based in Palo Alto, California, that rates Web sites according to the level of privacy they afford, says a survey her company sponsored found that 41 percent of respondents would quit a Web page rather than reveal any personal information about themselves. About 25 percent said when they do volunteer information, they lie. "The users want access, but they don't want to get correspondence back," she says.

But worse things may already be happening to their email. Many 34 office electronic-mail systems warn users that the employer reserves the right to monitor their email. In October software will be available to Wall Street firms that can automatically monitor correspondence between brokers and clients through an artificial-intelligence program that scans for evidence of securities violations.

"Technology has outpaced law," says Marc Rotenberg, director of 35 the Washington-based Electronic Privacy Information Center. Rotenberg advocates protecting the privacy of email by encrypting it with secret codes so powerful that even the National Security Agency's supercomputers would have a hard time cracking it. Such codes are legal within the United States but cannot be used abroad—where terrorists might use them to protect their secrets—without violating U.S. export laws. . . .

Rotenberg thinks we need a new government agency—a privacy 36 agency—to sort out the issues. "We need new legal protections," he says, "to enforce the privacy act, to keep federal agencies in line, to act as a spokesperson for the federal government and to act on behalf of privacy interests."

*Wired*'s Kelly disagrees. "A federal privacy agency would be disas- 37 trous! The answer to the whole privacy question is more knowledge," he says. "More knowledge about who's watching you. More knowledge about the information that flows between us—particularly the meta information about who knows what and where it's going."

I'm with Kelly. The only guys who insist on perfect privacy are hermits like the Unabomber. I don't want to be cut off from the world. I have nothing to hide. I just want some measure of control over what people know about me. I want to have my magic cookie and eat it too.  ❀

## READING FOR INFORMATION

1. According to Quittner, what are some (name at least five) of the ways that we regularly surrender our privacy?

2. What examples does Quittner provide of potentially dangerous invasions of privacy?

3. What evidence does Quittner give to support his assertion that Americans don't really want to be left alone?

4. Why did some Americans react negatively to the introduction of the Social Security number in the 1950s?

5. How, according to Quittner, has the shift from large mainframe computers to desktop PCs affected privacy?

6. In response to the computer revolution, what steps did the federal government take to protect citizens' privacy? What steps did the private sector take?

7. According to Carole Lane, what information can you locate on the Web about a given individual, beginning with only a name and address?

8. What are "magic cookies"?

9. Explain the controversy over encryption technology.

## READING FOR FORM, ORGANIZATION, AND EXPOSITORY FEATURES

1. Quittner begins with a series of anecdotes. How do these anecdotes work together as an opening to his piece?

2. Based on the first ten paragraphs of the article, how would you characterize Quittner's writing style? Is this style appropriate, given the nature of the piece he is writing?

3. Describe Quittner's organizational plan.

## READING FOR RHETORICAL CONCERNS

1. What in the article indicates Quittner's intended audience?

2. Identify the two sections of the essay in which Quittner states his own opinion.

3. Paraphrase Quittner's proposal for balancing privacy concerns and access to technology.

4. In what way is Quittner's article confessional?

## WRITING ASSIGNMENTS

1. Write a 1,000-word essay that objectively describes how modern technology has eroded personal privacy. Draw on Quittner's article for examples.

2. In paragraph 10, Quittner asserts that ". . . I do all this [surrender privacy] willingly because I appreciate what I get in return: the security of a safe parking lot, the convenience of cash when I need it, the improved service of mail-order houses that know me well enough to send me

catalogs of stuff that interests me . . . while I know we're supposed to feel just awful about giving up our vaunted privacy, I suspect (based on what the pollsters say) that you're just as ambivalent about it as I am." In a 1,000-word essay, explain Quittner's assertion and respond to it based on your own views.

3. Do you think Quittner's views are consistent with constitutional guarantees of civil liberties? Defend your view in a 1,000-word essay.

## SYNTHESIS WRITING ASSIGNMENTS

1. In a 1,000-word essay, compare and contrast Quittner's and Kaminer's attitudes toward the development of advanced surveillance technology and its effect on individual rights.

2. Many private citizens and law-enforcement officers maintain that if you have done nothing wrong, then you have nothing to fear from surveillance of your activities or searches of your home or car. Respond to that belief in a 1,250-word essay that draws on at least three readings from this chapter.

3. Are the amendments to the Constitution sufficient to protect our individual rights, given recent advances in surveillance technology? Answer this question in a 1,250-word essay that draws on at least three of the articles in this chapter.

4. Under what circumstances, if any, do we have to give up our right to privacy? Answer this question in a 1,250-word essay that draws on at least three of the articles in this chapter.

5. Do the events of September 11, 2001, justify employing technology that may violate individual privacy? Answer this question in a 1,250-word essay that draws on at least three of the articles in this chapter.

6. Write a 1,250-word essay that distinguishes between types of high-tech evidence that should be admitted in court and types that should be excluded. Cover all the varieties of crime-fighting technology that are described in this chapter.

7. How far has technology taken us along the path Orwell predicted in *1984*? In response to this question, write a 1,250-word essay that draws on at least three of the articles in this chapter.

8. In the first paragraph of his article, Colbridge points out that it is difficult to maintain the "proper balance between the personal privacy of individuals and the government's obligation to enforce the law and ensure public safety." Draw on at least two other articles to write a 1,250-word response to Colbridge's statement.

# Social Sciences

## SUBJECTS AND METHODS OF STUDY IN THE SOCIAL SCIENCES

Anthropology, economics, education, political science, psychology, sociology, and geography are called social sciences because they use the process of scientific inquiry to study various aspects of society, such as human behavior, human relationships, social conditions, conduct, and customs. Social scientists begin their inquiry by asking questions or identifying problems related to particular phenomena. In Chapter 9, Pauline Irit Erera asks, "What Is A Family?" In Chapter 10, Jeremy Seabrook asks, "What Are 'Class' and 'Inequality'?" The social scientists posing those questions identify possible causes of the phenomena they are studying and then form a hypothesis based on certain assumptions they have made. They next try to verify the hypothesis by making a series of careful observations, assembling and analyzing data, and determining a clear pattern of response. If the data verify their hypothesis, they will declare it confirmed. Many social scientists conduct investigations in the "field," testing their hypotheses in actual problem situations by making onsite observations, interviewing, conducting case studies and cross-sectional and longitudinal studies, collecting surveys and questionnaires, examining artifacts and material remains, studying landscapes and ecology. Patrick James McQuillan derives "A Day in the Life of Rafael Jackson" (Chapter 11) from an ethnographic research study he conducted in an urban high school. Other social scientists, such as experimental psychologists, work under carefully controlled conditions in laboratory settings.

## SPECIAL TYPES OF SOCIAL SCIENCE WRITING

When researchers complete their studies, they present their findings in official reports, organized in accordance with the scientific method (see the introductory section on the natural sciences). A format commonly found in research articles is introduction with background and problem statement; method; results; discussion; summary. An abstract (a brief summary of the article) may precede the study. Usually, the study begins with a literature review in which the writer recapitulates previous research. Social scientists regard this acknowledgment of their predecessors' work and of divided opinion about it to be crucial to the development of any new thesis or interpretation. Often, when they publish their work, they designate it as a "proposal" or a "work in progress" because they have not yet arrived at conclusions that they are willing to consider final. They view this kind of publication as a means of receiving feedback or peer review that will enable them to continue with new insights and perspectives. They believe that a community of scholars cooperating within a complex system of checks and balances will ultimately arrive at some statement of truth.

Advanced social science courses teach students how to evaluate these formal reports of research findings. Meanwhile, all students should be familiar with less specialized forms of writing in the social sciences, such as summaries of research; reviews of the literature; case studies; proposals; position papers; presentation of new theories and methods of analysis; and commentaries, reviews, analyses, critiques, and interpretations of research.

For examples of various types of social science writing, consult the following sources:

> *Review of the literature:* Robert L. Barret and Bryan E. Robinson's "Children of Gay Fathers," Chapter 9; Wade F. Horn's "Promoting Marriage as a Means for Promoting Fatherhood," Chapter 9; Pauline Irit Erera's "What Is A Family?" Chapter 9.
>
> *Case study:* Barret and Robinson's "Children of Gay Fathers," Chapter 9; Patrick James McQuillan's "A Day in the Life of Rafael Jackson," Chapter 11.
>
> *Theory:* Shelby Steele's "Educating Black Children," Chapter 11.

*Position paper:* Herbert Gans's "The War Against the Poor Instead of Programs to End Poverty," Chapter 10.

*Interpretation of research:* Larry E. Frase and William Streshly's "Myth 5: Self-esteem Must Come First—Then Learning," Chapter 11.

*Proposal:* David Popenoe's "Seven Tenets for Establishing New Marital Norms," Chapter 9.

## PERSPECTIVES ON SOCIAL SCIENCE TOPICS

In this anthology, we present reading selections on social science topics by journalists and other popular writers as well as by social scientists. These writers treat the same subject matter, but their approaches differ. Take, for example, Dirk Johnson, whose *New York Times* article, "White Standard for Poverty," appears on pages 445–48, and Leon Botstein whose *International Herald Tribune* article, "High School, an Institution Whose Time Has Passed," appears on pages 472–75. These writers do not use special modes of social science writing, nor do they rely heavily on other sources or write for specialized readers. Still, their writing is very important for social scientists because it reflects the very stuff of everyday life that social scientists study. Also consider Barbara Ehrenreich's "Serving in Florida" from her popular book, *Nickel and Dimed: On (Not) Getting By in America.* Ehrenreich treats an issue that social scientists find extremely important as a barometer of public feeling.

## SOCIAL SCIENCE WRITERS' ORGANIZATIONAL PLANS

Social science writers rely on a variety of organizational plans: time order, narration, process; antecedent-consequent, cause-effect; description; statement-response; comparison and contrast; analysis, classification; definition; problem-solution. You will find that some plans appear more frequently than others. Given the nature of the inquiry process, social scientists use the statement-response, problem-solution, question-answer plans with some regularity. Notice that in Jeremy Seabrook's "What Are 'Class' and 'Inequality'?" (Chapter 10), the title indicates a question that will be answered. Also popular is the antecedent-consequent plan, because it enables writers to analyze and explain the causes of behaviors and events. Notice how Bempechat structures "Challenging Our Assumptions" (Chapter 11) according to this plan. Also examine the selection by Leonce Gaiter in Chapter 10.

When you are reading social science writing, look for overlapping organizational plans. Very few social science writers rely on only one; they use networks of different plans, often intermeshing them in a single piece.

## AUTHORS' LITERARY TECHNIQUES

Did you ever wonder why some writers are clear and easy to understand and others are pedantic and inaccessible? Clear writers process their information and ideas in an organized and modulated sequence, and they articulate their thinking in crisp, uncluttered prose. Pedantic and inaccessible writers often presume that their readers know a great deal of specialized terminology that allows them to dispense with explanations, examples, and illuminating details. Writers make themselves understood by defining new terms, concepts, and specialized vocabulary; providing examples, scenarios, and illustrations; and using figurative language.

You will find that many of the selections in this unit are replete with specialized vocabulary; moreover, familiar terms are often given new, specialized meanings. Take, for example, the various definitions of "family" in Chapter 9. As you read, pay close attention to the different ways writers handle vocabulary. Some use specialized words with impunity, assuming that their readers have sufficient background knowledge for comprehension. Others provide helpful contexts that give clues to verbal meaning. Still others supply definitions of specialized vocabulary. Definitions may take the form of explanations of causes, effects, or functions; synonyms; negations; analogies; descriptions; and classifications. Some definitions are brief, like the following from Pauline Irit Erera's "What Is A Family?"

> Only half of American children live in families that the Census Bureau defines as the traditional nuclear family: a married couple living with their biological children and no one else (Vobejda, 1994). (p. 350)

Others are long, extended definitions, such as Herbert Gans's definition of "undeserving poor" in "The War Against the Poor Instead of Programs to End Poverty" (Chapter 10).

Another technique social science writers use to make specialized subjects more accessible to nonspecialized readers is to provide concrete examples and illustrations. Notice the extended examples provided by Steele and McQuillan, and other effective examples found in the writing of Gaiter, Browne, Ehrenreich, and Bempechat.

Writing in the social sciences, then, commands a wide variety of approaches, organizational plans, styles, authorial perspectives, and literary techniques. Although the selections in this chapter do not always exemplify wholly academic social science writing, they do suggest the range of types, modes, and styles in that discourse. Writers in the social sciences often vary their own range from the extreme impersonality of technical reports to the impassioned concern of urgent social issues. The social sciences, after all, study people and their interaction in society. The diversity of the social sciences, therefore, is as broad as the diversity of people and institutions they examine.

# nine

## The Changing American Family

Drawing on research in sociology, psychology, and social psychology, the seven readings in this chapter focus on the dramatic challenges confronting American families. Our traditional views of families come into question as families are being transformed and redefined by forces such as single parenting, divorce, maternal employment, delayed childbearing, adult independent living, and homosexual parenting couples. As the authors in this chapter point out, the American family is both vulnerable and resilient in the face of these forces.

In the opening piece, "Brave New Family," a lesbian mother, Kimberly Mistysyn, describes a family arrangement in which her son, Kyle, is growing up with two moms and two dads. In the second selection, "Children of Gay Fathers," Robert L. Barret and Bryan E. Robinson discuss the ramifications of homosexual parents for children's development. Next, Pauline Irit Erera traces the rise and fall of the traditional family in "What Is A Family?" Central to Erera's discussion is a defense of diverse, nontraditional families.

Alarmed by the dissolution of the nuclear family, David Popenoe, in "Seven Tenets for Establishing New Marital Norms," recommends a new set of social norms that will safeguard certain elements of the traditional family. In a similar vein, James Q. Wilson weighs the costs and benefits of cohabitation as an alternative to marriage and concludes that living together is less advantageous than being married. In the next selection, Wade F. Horn focuses on the problem of the increasing number of father-absent households. According to Horn, a revitalization of marriage is the chief means of strengthening father-child relationships. Judith Stacey rounds out the chapter with her prophetic "Toward Revels or a Requiem for Family Diversity." Stacey maintains that alternative families are here to stay. In the future we can expect to see even more disruption of the traditional family, for families will become more rather than less diverse.

# Brave New Family

## *Kimberly Mistysyn*

*Kimberly Mistysyn is an American-born Canadian mother, partner, and writer. She is the co-editor of* The Bent Guide to Gay/Lesbian Canada 1995–96.

### PREREADING

What kind of image does the title conjure up for you? Who would be the members of a "brave new family"? Of what does such a family consist? Respond in your journal.

Once upon a time, the only acceptable form of family consisted of one male breadwinner, one female housekeeper, and two or more children, with at least one of them being male. As the family format evolved to reflect our changing economy and society, this previous model became the "ideal" family. Increasing change has brought about a high rate of divorce and separation; the discovery of the dysfunctional dynamic in families that endeavor to mirror, on the surface, the ideal family; and the ever-growing liberation of gays, lesbians, bisexuals, transsexuals, and transgendered individuals has forever changed the definition of the ideal family structure. The number of parents or their gender can no longer define the ideal family. Love, 1

From *Home Fronts: Controversies in Nontraditional Parenting* (pp. 185–86), ed. Jess Wells. Copyright 2000 by Jess Wells. Los Angeles, CA: Trade Paperback Original published by Alyson Publications. Reprinted by permission of the author, Kimberly Lei Mistysyn.

support, understanding, trust, and communication are now the only acceptable defining characteristics for a family. Our laws are constantly changing to allow individuals without blood ties or the legal marriage link to consider themselves members of a family they created. This new millennium will see these brave new families continue to evolve and challenge society's rules and regulations. Ours is one such brave new family, consisting of two gay moms, two gay dads, and our son. Let us tell you about our son's world.

Kyle was planned a year in advance. We chose not to go the expensive route of buying sperm and instead broached the idea of sperm donation with the dads, David and Clarke. The plan was pretty simple. I had already been charting my cycle and was taking folic acid. Clarke and David are an intergenerational couple; David, being the younger of the two, was our actual choice for "sperm donor cum laude." We wanted primary custody to our potential bundle of joy, and we hoped the dads would play an active role. As soon as the baby was born we wanted David to sign an affidavit giving up his legal rights to our child, thereby allowing Cynthia, the non-bio mom, to adopt our child. To cement the deal, we all signed, with witnesses in tow, a nonlegal document outlining our mutual agreement to these terms and additional concerns should something happen to me during childbirth. We all went into this with our eyes wide open—love, trust, and communication being the crucial elements.

Babymaking was exciting, funny, nerve-racking, and, thankfully, quick. Cynthia sterilized the artichoke-heart jars by the dozen (actually eating their previous contents as well), the dads were at our beck and call with the fresh sperm, and the syringe was engaged with great pomp and ceremony. By the second month I had conceived. We told the dads of our success by giving them a gift-wrapped pregnancy predictor test with the confirmation displayed.

Our happiness knew no bounds as we prepared for a completely natural home birth with midwife and family members present. The dads attended all our visits with the midwife as well as our prenatal classes. And, as is usually the case with best laid plans, our son was born in a hospital—after an induction, an epidural, and an emergency C-section with only Cynthia and David allowed in the room. Kyle's due date had originally coincided with National Coming Out Day, but he decided that would be a bit too perfect and he aimed for our Canadian Thanksgiving weekend instead. He does, however, have a pink birthstone.  ✿

## READING FOR INFORMATION

1. According to Mistysyn, what are the defining characteristics of a family?
2. In your own words, explain why the family arrangement that Mistysyn describes works.

## READING FOR FORM, ORGANIZATION, AND EXPOSITORY FEATURES

1. Describe the contrast that Mistysyn expresses in the first paragraph.
2. Personal narratives depend on detail for their effectiveness. Which details make this writing come alive for you?

## READING FOR RHETORICAL CONCERNS

1. What feeling, view, incident, or phenomenon motivated Mistysyn to write this narrative?
2. What is Mistysyn's rhetorical purpose? What does she hope to get across to the reader by telling her story?

## WRITING ASSIGNMENTS

1. Write a brief essay in which you agree or disagree with Mistysyn's statement, "The number of parents or their gender can no longer define the ideal family."
2. Mistysyn discusses the advantages of a four-parent family. What might become of the disadvantages? Write an essay in which you compare the advantages to the disadvantages.

# Children of Gay Fathers

## *Robert L. Barret and Bryan E. Robinson*

*Bob Barrett is a professor of counseling at the University of North Carolina at Charlotte, a psychologist, a gay father, and a grandfather of five. His current writings include* Gay Fathers: Encouraging the Hearts of Gay Dads and Their Families, *coauthored with Bryan E. Robinson;* Counseling Gay Men and Lesbians, *coauthored with Colleen Logan; and* Ethical Issues in HIV-Related Psychotherapy *with Jon Anderson.*

*Bryan E. Robinson, a professor of counseling, special education, and child development at the University of South Carolina, has authored over twenty-five books and more than one hundred articles. His most recent books include* Gay Fathers: Encouraging the Hearts of Gay Dads and Their Families, *coauthored with Bob Barrett;* Don't Let Your Mind Stunt Your Growth, *and* A Guidebook for Workaholics, Their Partners and Children and the Clinicians Who Treat Them.

### PREREADING

Comment on your familiarity with the issue of homosexual parenting. Did the idea of a gay man choosing to be an active parent and visible father ever occur to you? Why, or why not? Freewrite your response.

The children of gay fathers are like children from all families. 1 Some are academically talented, some struggle to get through school, some are model students, and some are constantly in trouble. In thinking about the children of gay fathers, it is essential to recognize that many of them have experienced the divorce of their parents, others have grown up in single-parent homes, and still others have been caught in major crossfire between their parents, grandparents, and perhaps their community over the appropriateness of gay men serving in the father role. Much of any distress that one sees in a child living with a gay father may in fact be the result of the divorce or other family tensions. Legitimate concerns about the impact of living with a gay father include the developmental impact of the knowledge that one's father is gay, reasonable worries about the timing of coming out to children, and creating sensitivity to how the children will experience society's generally negative attitudes towards homosexuality.

Coming out to children is usually an emotion-laden event for gay fathers. The disclosure of one's homosexuality creates anxiety about rejection, fear of hurting or damaging the child's self-esteem, and grieving over the loss of innocence. Some gay fathers never accomplish this task and remain deeply closeted, citing legal and emotional reasons (Bozett, 1980, 1981; Humphreys, 1979; Spada, 1979). Recent publications report the intricacies of this question (Corley, 1990). Those who never disclose their homosexuality often lead deeply conflicted lives and present parenting styles that are characterized by psychological distance (Miller, 1979). Those who do come out to their children do so in the desire to be more of a whole person as a father. As they try to merge their gayness with the father role, they encounter a different kind of conflict: deciding how open to be about their sexual relationships and how much exposure to the gay community to offer their children (Robinson & Barret, 1986).

Fathers report that the first concern they have about coming out is the well-being and healthy adjustment of their children. Many gay fathers seek the help of counselors or specialists in child development as they decide when and how to tell their children about their homosexuality. Research studies indicate that fathers and children report that they are closer after self-disclosure about the father's sexual orientation (Bozett, 1980; Miller, 1979). Bigner and Bozett (1989) studied the reasons that gay fathers give for coming out to their children. Among the most cited were wanting their children to know them as they are, being aware that children will usually discover for themselves if there is frequent contact, and the presence of a male lover in the home.

Gay fathers may come out indirectly by showing affection to men in front of their children or by taking them to gay community events. Others choose to come out verbally or by correspondence (Maddox, 1982). Factors in disclosure are the degree of intimacy between the father and his children and the obtrusiveness of his gayness (Bozett, 1988). By and large, the research suggests that children who are told at an earlier age have fewer difficulties with the day-to-day issues that accompany their father's homosexuality (Bozett, 1989).

The parenting styles of gay fathers are not markedly different from those of other single fathers, but gay fathers try to create a more stable home environment and more positive relationships with their children than traditional heterosexual parents (Bigner & Jacobsen, 1989a; Bozett, 1989). One study found that homosexual fathers differed from their heterosexual counterparts in providing more nurturing and in having less traditional parenting attitudes (Scallen, 1981). Another study of gay fathers found no differences in paternal involvement and amount of intimacy (Bigner & Jacobsen, 1989b). In general, investigators have found that gay fathers feel an additional responsibility to provide effective fathering because they know their homosexuality causes others to examine their parenting styles more closely (Barret & Robinson, 1990). This is not to say that no risk is involved in gay fathering. Miller (1979) found that six daughters of the gay fathers in his study had significant life problems. Others have reported that the children of gay fathers must be prepared to face ridicule and harassment (Bozett, 1980; Epstein, 1979) or may be alienated from their agemates, may become confused about their sexual identity, and may express discomfort with their father's sexual orientation (Lewis, 1980). Most researchers have concluded that being homosexual is compatible with effective parenting and is not usually a major issue in parental relationships with children (Harris & Turner, 1986).

As Chip reveals (Figure 9-1), dealing with the outside world is a task that gay fathers and their children must master. Gay families live in a social system that is generally uncomfortable with homosexuality and that certainly does not overtly support gay parenting. One reality for gay fathers is figuring out how to interact successfully with the world of schools, after-school activities, PTAs, churches, and their children's social networks. Many gay fathers see no choice other than to continue living relatively closeted lives (Bozett, 1988; Miller, 1979). Others, fearing the damage that exposure may bring to their children and/or possible custody battles involving their homosexuality, live rigidly controlled lives and may never develop a gay identity. Those who are more open about their gayness struggle to help their children develop a positive attitude toward homosexuality while simultaneously cautioning them about the dangers of disclosure to teachers and friends. Teaching their children to manage these two tasks is a major challenge for gay fathers (Morin & Schultz, 1978; Riddle, 1978). Accomplishing this task when there are virtually no visible role models frequently leaves these fathers and their children feeling extremely isolated.

Bozett (1988) identified several strategies that these children use as they experience both their own and the public's discomfort with their

## CASE STUDY—CHIP SPEAKS

My name is Chip and I'm seventeen and in twelfth grade. When we first moved to Indianapolis, I learned my dad was gay. I was twelve. I didn't really think much about it. There was a birthday coming up and Dad said we were going to go out and buy a birthday card. He went out, drove around the block and then parked in front of our house. Then he took me to the park and told me the facts of life. He asked me if I knew what it meant to be gay. I told him, "Yeah, it means to be happy and enjoy yourself." Then he started to explain to me about being homosexual. I really didn't know what it was at that point, until he explained it to me.

It's an accepted part of my life now. I've been growing up with it almost five years. When he invites another guy into the house it's OK. I don't bring other kids home then. One of my friends is extremely homophobic and he lets that fact be known. I wouldn't dare risk anything or it would be like "goodbye" to my friend. My other two friends, I don't know how they would react. So I have to be careful about having certain friends over. To me it's blatantly obvious. Having been exposed to so many gay people, I know what to look for and what I'm seeing. Sometimes it's kind of hard because people make fun of gay people. And, if I stick up for their rights, then I get ridiculed. So I just don't say anything at school. It's kind of hard sometimes.

The good thing is that you get a more objective view of people in general, being raised by someone who's so persecuted by society. You begin to sympathize with anyone who is persecuted by society. You tend not to be as prejudiced. You need to appreciate people for what they are personally, not just in terms of color, religion, or sexual preference. That's the best thing. The hardest thing is hearing all those people making cracks or jokes on TV or at school and not being really able to do anything about it. Because he's my dad after all, it makes me kind of sad. I never feel ashamed or embarrassed, but I do feel a little pressured because of this. One time a friend of mine made a joke about gay people. I just played it off like I thought it was funny, but I didn't. You have to pretend you think the same thing they do when you don't. That makes me feel like a fraud.

When my dad puts his arm around another man, the first thing I think is, "I could never do that." It makes me a little bit uncomfortable, but I'm not repulsed by it. There are times I wish he wouldn't do it, but other times I'm glad he can have the freedom to do it. When he first

(continued on the next page)

came out to me, the only question I asked him was, "What are the chances of me being gay?" He couldn't answer it. But today, to the best of my knowledge, I'm not gay. I like chasing after girls.

Sometimes I feel like I'm keeping a big secret. My dad had a holy union with a man once. My friends had big plans and we were all going out on the day of the big event. And I couldn't go and couldn't explain why. Things like that have happened a number of times. I can't go and I can't tell why. They start yelling at me and get mad. They'll get over it; it's none of their business.

As fathers go, mine tends to be a little nicer—almost a mother's temperament. A friend of mine's father doesn't spend much time with him. They just seem to have stricter parents than mine. I don't know if that's just because of his personality in general or if it's because he's gay. He's a very emotional person; he cries easily. I love him. He's a good dad. He's more open than other dads. He doesn't let me get away with a lot. He tends to be more worried about me and a girl together than some other fathers are about their sons—more worried about my having sex. Whenever I go out on a date, he always says something like, "Don't do anything I wouldn't do," only he doesn't say it jokingly. Sometimes he's just overly cautious.

If I could change my dad and make him straight, I wouldn't do it. It might make things easier for me in some ways, but I wouldn't have grown up the way I have. Being exposed to the straight world and gay world equally has balanced me out more than some of the other people I know. The only things I'd want to change is society's treatment of him. (Barret & Robinson, 1990, pp. 14–15)

(*Note:* Chip's dad died of AIDS two years after this interview took place.)

Figure 9-1

gay fathers. The children of gay fathers in his study used boundary control, nondisclosure, and disclosure as they interacted with their fathers and the outside world. For example, some children limited or attempted to control the content of their interactions with their father. One father we talked with (Barret & Robinson, 1990) reported that he had offered to introduce his teenaged daughter to some of his gay friends in the hope that she would see how normal they were. Her reply was a curt "Dad, that will never happen!" Another father told of trying to reconcile with his son but being rebuffed by the comment, "I don't want to hear anything about your personal life. I can't handle it." Such boundary control limits the ability of the relationship to grow. Other ways that children control boundaries are by not introducing their friends to their fathers or by carefully managing the amount of time they spend together, as Chip reveals in his interview.

Some children do learn to let their friends know carefully about their father's homosexuality. These disclosures have a potential for both increased intimacy and rejection. Helping children discriminate when and how to inform their friends is a critical challenge of gay parenting. As children grow up, these issues may become more complex, as families struggle to involve gay fathers in events such as weddings, graduations, and birth celebrations, where the presence of the gay father and his partner may raise questions. 8

Children of gay fathers do sometimes worry that their sexual orientation may become contaminated by their father's homosexuality. Either they or their friends may begin to question whether they are gay as well. Those children who do disclose their father's homosexuality report being harassed by the use of such terms as *queer* and *fag*. Naturally, this concern is greatest during their teenage years (Riddle & Arguelles, 1981). Obviously, the children of gay fathers need to consider carefully the consequences of disclosure. Keeping this aspect of their lives secret may have the same negative impact on their development as isolation, alienation, and compartmentalization does on gay men. 9

This is not to say that the responses of social support networks are universally negative. Many children with gay fathers report that their friends are both curious and supportive. It is important to recognize that coming out is a process rather than a discrete event. Fathers, children, and their friends need time to move into the process and to examine their own feelings and attitudes so that acceptance and understanding replace confusion and fear. One child of a gay father said: 10

> At first, I was really angry at my dad. I couldn't figure out how to tell my friends what was going on, so I said nothing. My dad and I had terrible fights as he put pressure on me to say it was OK. I thought what he was doing was sinful and embarrasing. But over time, I began to realize that he is the same dad he has always been, and now we are closer than ever. My friends have also got used to the idea and like to spend time with him, too.

## STATE OF RESEARCH ON CHILDREN OF GAY FATHERS

In reviewing the impact of gay fathering on children, it is important to 11
acknowledge that most children who live with gay fathers are also the
products of divorce and may show the psychological distress that typically accompanies the experience of marital dissolution. All too often,
the emotional distress of children with gay parents is solely attributed to
the parents' sexual orientation and is not seen as a complex mixture of
family dynamics, divorce adjustment, and the incorporation of the parents' sexual coming out.

Only two studies have directly addressed the children of gay fa- 12
thers (Green, 1978; Weeks, Derdeyn, & Langman, 1975). In both studies, the researchers gave psychological tests to the children. The
findings from this testing have been used to support the notion that a
parent's homosexuality has little bearing on the child's sexual orientation. Children showed clear heterosexual preferences or were developing them. Green concluded that "The children I interviewed were able
to comprehend and verbalize the atypical nature of their parents'
lifestyles and to view their atypicality in the broader perspective of the
cultural norm" (p. 696). Our interviews with children have also supported this finding (Barret & Robinson, 1990). Still, the problem is that
the observations of Weeks and his colleagues (1975) are based on the
clinical assessment of only two children, and the Green study (1978)
observed only the children of lesbian mothers and the children of parents who had experienced sex-change surgery. None of the parents in
that sample were classified as gay fathers. The findings of these two
studies and others of lesbian mothers (e.g., Goodman, 1973; Hoeffer,
1981; Kirkpatrick, Smith, & Roy, 1981) are frequently generalized to include the gay father's children, even though important differences exist
between transsexuals and gay men as well as between gay men and
lesbians.

## CONCLUSIONS

The profile we use to understand and describe gay fathers and their 13
children is far from conclusive. Clearly, the literature has improved,
after 1982, in its use of comparison groups and a more diverse, nationwide sampling. Still, until researchers can obtain larger, more representative samples and use more sophisticated research designs, caution
must be exercised in making sweeping generalizations about gay fathers

and their families. Meanwhile, it is possible to speculate from some limited data that, although not fully developed, provides an emerging picture of the children of gay fathers:

1. They are like all kids. Some do well in just about all activities; some have problems; and some are well adjusted.
2. They live in family situations that are unique and must develop strategies to cope with these situations.
3. They need help sorting out their feelings about homosexuality and their anxieties about their own sexual orientation.
4. They may be isolated and angry and may have poor relationships with their fathers.
5. They are in little danger of sexual abuse and unlikely to "catch" homosexuality.
6. Many of them adjust quite well to their family situation and use the family as a means to develop greater tolerance of diversity.
7. Some of them become involved in the human rights movement as they promote gay rights.
8. Their relationships with their fathers have a potential for greater honesty and openness.

## REFERENCES

Barret, R., & Robinson, B. (1990). *Gay fathers*. New York: Free Press.

Bigner, J., & Bozett, F. (1989). Parenting by gay fathers. *Marriage and Family Review, 14*, 155–175.

Bigner, J., & Jacobson, R. (1989a). Parenting behaviors of homosexual and heterosexual fathers. *Journal of Homosexuality, 18*, 173–186.

Bigner, J., & Jacobsen, R. (1989b). The value of children to gay and heterosexual fathers. *Journal of Homosexuality, 18*, 163–172.

Bozett, F. (1980). Gay fathers: How and why they disclose their homosexuality to their children. *Family Relations: Journal of Applied Family and Child Studies, 29*, 173–179.

Bozett, F. (1981). Gay fathers: Evolution of the gay father identity. *American Journal of Orthopsychiatry, 51*, 552–559.

Bozett, F. (1988). Social control of identity of gay fathers. *Western Journal of Nursing Research, 10*, 550–565.

Bozett, F. (1989). Gay fathers: A review of the literature. *Journal of Homosexuality, 18*, 137–162.

Corley, R. (1990). *The final closet: The gay parent's guide to coming out to their children*. Miami: Editech Press.

Epstein, R. (1979, June). Children of gays. *Christopher Street*, 43–50.

Goodman, B. (1973). The lesbian mother. *American Journal of Orthopsychiatry, 43,* 283–284.

Green, R. (1978). Sexual identity of 37 children raised by homosexual or transsexual parents. *American Journal of Psychiatry, 135,* 692–697.

Harris, M., & Turner, P. (1986). Gay and lesbian parents. *Journal of Homosexuality, 18,* 101–113.

Hoeffer, B. (1981). Children's acquisition of sex-role behavior in lesbian-mother families. *American Journal of Orthopsychiatry, 51,* 536–544.

Humphreys, L. (1979). *Tearoom trade.* Chicago: Aldine.

Kirkpatrick, M., Smith, C., & Roy, R. (1981). Lesbian mothers and their children. *American Journal of Orthopsychiatry, 51,* 545–551.

Lewis, K. (1980). Children of lesbians: Their point of view. *Social Work, 25,* 200.

Maddox, B. (1982, February). Homosexual parents. *Psychology Today,* 62–69.

Miller, B. (1979, October). Gay fathers and their children. *The Family Coordinator, 28,* 544–551.

Morin, S., & Schultz, S. (1978). The gay movement and the rights of children. *Journal of Social Issues, 34,* 137–148.

Riddle, D. (1978). Relating to children: Gays as role models. *Journal of Social Issues, 34,* 38–58.

Riddle, D., & Arguelles, M. (1981). Children of gay parents: Homophobia's victims. In I. Stuart & L. Abt (Eds.), *Children of separation and divorce.* New York: Van Nostrand Reinhold.

Robinson, B., & Barret, R. (1986). *The developing father.* New York: Guilford Press.

Scallen, R. (1981). *An investigation of paternal attitudes and behaviors in homosexual and heterosexual fathers.* Doctoral dissertation, California School of Professional Psychology, San Francisco, CA. (*Dissertation Abstracts International, 42,* 3809B).

Spada, J. (1979). *The Spada report.* New York: Signet Books.

Weeks, R. B., Derdeyn, A. P., & Langman, M. (1975). Two cases of children of homosexuals. *Child Psychiatry and Human Development, 6,* 26–32.

## READING FOR INFORMATION

1. Why do Barret and Robinson mention repeatedly that most children of gay fathers have experienced their parents' divorce? Why is that an important consideration?

2. Why is it that some gay fathers never disclose their sexuality to their children?

3. List the three strategies that children of gay fathers use when they have to interact with the outside world.

4. Summarize what the research reveals about the effect of parents' homosexuality on their children.

5. According to Barret and Robinson, why must we exercise caution in making generalizations about gay fathers and their children?

## READING FOR FORM, ORGANIZATION, AND EXPOSITORY FEATURES

1. Underline and identify the various types of data, research findings, and authorities Barret and Robinson cite to support their view.

2. Which features of Barret and Robinson's writing are particularly scholarly or "academic"?

3. Compare Barret and Robinson's writing style with that of Chip in the case study. How are the two styles similar or different?

4. Notice how Barret and Robinson conclude the selection. Explain whether or not you think the ending is effective.

## READING FOR RHETORICAL CONCERNS

1. What is Barret and Robinson's rhetorical purpose? What is the central point they want to communicate to their readers?

2. Why do you think the authors include the case study of Chip? What is the effect on the reader? What would be gained or lost if the case study were left out?

3. Why do you think Barret and Robinson refer to Chip only once? Why don't they analyze or respond to Chip's story?

## WRITING ASSIGNMENTS

1. Write a brief summary of the barriers that gay parents and their children must overcome.

2. For an audience who has not read "Children of Gay Fathers," write an essay in which you discuss the problems that children of gay fathers face and explain how these children turn out.

3. Go to the library and research the topic of homosexual parenting. Write a three- to four-page paper answering questions like the following: How do gay men and lesbians become parents? Are the numbers of homosexual families increasing? What is the reaction of conservative groups to gay parenting? What are the views of the gay community?

# What Is A Family?

### *Pauline Irit Erera*

*Pauline Irit Erera, Associate Professor at the University of Washington School of Social Work, has written extensively about family diversity, focusing on step-, foster, and lesbian families, and on noncustodial fathers. This selection is from her recent book,* Family Diversity: Continuity and Change in the Contemporary Family.

## PREREADING

Respond to the title "What Is A Family?" by writing out your definition for family. Share your definition with the other students in your class.

Families have always come in various forms, reflecting social  1
and economic conditions and the cultural norms of the times. However, since the 1960s, the increasing diversity among families in the United States and most other Western nations has been especially striking. At a dizzying pace, the traditional, two-parent, heterosexual family has given way to a variety of family arrangements. Today, most adults no longer live in a coresident nuclear family (Hill, 1995). The first-married, heterosexual family we have cherished since at least Victorian times is but one of numerous alternative family structures (Csikszentmihalyi, 1997).

In 1998, just 26 percent of American households were composed  2
of married couples with children. This was down from 45 percent in the early 1970s (University of Chicago National Opinion Research Center, 1999). Only half of American children live in families that the Census Bureau defines as the traditional nuclear family: a married couple living with their biological children and no one else (Vobejda, 1994). Furthermore, family arrangements differ considerably according to race and ethnicity. Although about 56 percent of white American children live in

a traditional nuclear family, only about 26 percent of African American children and 38 percent of Hispanic children do (Vobejda, 1994).

In this [reading] I examine alternative constructions of what a family is. I trace the rise and decline of the traditional family, outline the subsequent increase in family diversity, and examine reactions to family diversity as expressed in the debate about "family values." I also discuss the continuing influence of the traditional family model. Finally, I consider the strengths and promise of family diversity, and set forth the perspectives that inform the analysis of the families in this book.

## DEFINING FAMILIES

The family is not simply a social institution. It is an ideological construct laden with symbolism and with a history and politics of its own. As Jagger and Wright (1999) put it, "The groupings that are called families are socially constructed rather than naturally or biologically given" (p. 3). In studying families, we need to keep clear the distinctions between the institutionalized family, the ideology of the family, and the lives of actual families. Although social and economic forces shape family life, our understanding of family is shaped by the evolving patterns of the actual families around us. Furthermore, conceptions of what constitutes a family are necessarily rooted in time and place. White, Western, two-parent families have generally been regarded, explicitly or implicitly, as the model or template against which we compare all families, regardless of culture, ethnicity, race, or class. This parochial view distorts our understanding of diverse families by considering them deviations from the norm (Smith, 1995; Thorne, 1982).

One early definition of the family was that offered by the anthropologist George Peter Murdock (1949), based on his survey of 250 ethnographic reports:

> The family is a social group characterized by common residence, economic cooperation, and reproduction. It includes adults of both sexes, at least two of whom maintain a socially approved sexual relationship, and one or more children, own or adopted, of the sexually cohabiting adults. (p. 1)

Murdock identified the basic family unit found in about one quarter of the societies he surveyed as "a married man and woman with their offspring" (p. 1), which he termed a nuclear family. Another quarter of the societies were predominantly polygamous, with families based on plural marriages of a spouse, hence, in his view, constituting two or more nuclear families. In the remaining half surveyed, the families were extended in that the nuclear family resided with the bride's or the groom's parents and/or other relatives. Murdock, reflecting the prevailing orthodoxy of the times, concluded that the nuclear family was universal and inevitable, the basis for more complex family forms.

Given the diversity of families and the political debates about   6
them, a single, all-encompassing definition of "family" is impossible to achieve. Families are defined in a variety of ways depending on the purposes and circumstances (Smith, 1995; Sprey, 1988). Although traditionalists have held blood ties or consanguinity to be a defining characteristic of the family, others argue that we should define families according to the attachments and intimacy that individuals have toward significant people in their lives. This latter definition shifts the focus from the family's structure or legal status to the nature and meaning of relationships (Dowd, 1997).

Diverse families challenge our definition and perceptions of what   7
a family is. These families also "challenge gender roles and influence gender typing by what they say and what they do" (Dowd, 1997, p. 110). They force us to reconsider our conceptions of what a mother, father, parent, and sibling are. Is a family defined by genes and blood relationships? Shared residence? Is it a group of people who provide one another social, emotional, and physical support, caring, and love? Does a family necessarily involve two adults? Are these adults necessarily of the opposite sex? Must families be based on marriage? Can a child have two or more mothers or fathers? Is a parent more "real" by virtue of biological or legal status? Does a family have to share a common residence, economic cooperation, and reproduction to be a family? Such questions are the subject of heated debates about the family and "family values."

## THE RISE AND DECLINE OF THE TRADITIONAL FAMILY

### The Heyday of the Traditional Family

The 1950s saw a surge in family formation associated with the end of   8
the depression and World War II. Although few Americans ever enjoyed family lives as harmonious, wholesome, or predictable as the ones portrayed in those beloved fifties television sitcoms, such programs symbolized a definition of ideal family life that was widely shared in that decade. Three fifths of U.S. households in that period fit the model

of the nuclear family structure, with its breadwinner-husband and homemaker-wife, of their pop culture icons. The economy was booming and even many working-class men earned enough to support such families. Yet this upsurge in marriage and childbearing proved to be a short-lived experiment. Starting in the 1960s, fertility rates began to decline, and the trend to early marriage was reversed (Silverstein & Auerbach, 1999).

Family life in the 1950s was hardly ideal. Families were not as well  9 off economically as they would become by the end of the 1960s; African Americans in particular had higher rates of poverty than they do now. Women, minorities, lesbians, gays, and nonconforming groups were subject to discrimination, and family problems got little attention or social assistance (Coontz, 1997).

In some ways, the decline of the 1950s family grew out of the  10 trends and contradictions of the fifties themselves. The main reason for family change was the breakdown of the postwar social compact between government, corporations, and workers. The 1950s were years of active government assistance to families. Government-backed home mortgages financed many of the new family homes, and the minimum wage was set high enough to support a family of three above the poverty level. Large numbers of workers joined unions, received pensions and health benefits, and worked a relatively short workweek. Corporations and the wealthy were taxed at high rates to support high levels of spending on veterans benefits and public works (Coontz, 1997).

## Family Diversity in the 1960s and 1970s

The affluence and optimism that explains the family behavior of the  11 postwar generation were challenged by America's new economic problems, whose impact was felt at the family level in the form of inflation and lower real earnings. Public policies aggravated these problems by cutting taxes for corporations and the wealthy while cutting spending for services, public works, and investments in human capital (Coontz, 1997). This meant that families had to modify the socially valued form of the family to try to protect their socially valued lifestyle: the standard of living to which they had become accustomed. Economic pressures made women's employment more a matter of necessity than of choice (Coontz, 1997). Today's politicians are being disingenuous when they advocate a return to the 1950s family while opposing the kinds of social and political supports that helped make it possible (Coontz, 1997).

Along with the economic shifts in the late 1950s and early 1960s  12
came technological developments and social movements that also contributed to the stunning increase in family diversity. The example of
African Americans' struggle to secure civil rights inspired other minorities and marginalized groups—women, gay men and lesbians, the disabled—to fight for their rights. The 1960s and 1970s became an era of
diversity and identity politics as a host of "others" sought recognition
and liberation from the constraints of discriminatory laws, social policies, and negative stereotypes. Foremost among those claiming their
rights were women.

The struggle for women's liberation was advanced by the availabil-  13
ity of the birth control pill and other methods that gave women control
over reproduction. These changes generated an increased acceptance
of sexual behavior not necessarily linked with marriage, for women as
well as for men (Riley, 1997). While white feminists began to claim the
right to control and limit their fertility through the use of contraception
and abortion, women of color started claiming the right to have their
fertility not be controlled by forced contraception and sterilization
(Hargaden & Llewellin, 1996). By 1973, many women in the United
States and other industrialized countries were able to prevent pregnancies, had access to legal abortion, and could end unwanted pregnancies
before birth (Riley, 1997).

The movement for gender equality led to increased employment  14
opportunities for women, while at the same time declining wage rates
for unskilled male workers made them less desirable marriage partners.
Although paid far less than their male counterparts, an increasing number of women were now employed and financially independent. Consequently, more women who were unhappy in their marriages were able
to divorce (Coontz, 1997; Riley, 1997). The changing roles of women,
their increasing participation in the labor force, and their economic independence had undercut the economic basis of marriage (Lichter &
McLaughlin, 1997). With divorce becoming more available, community
norms regarding divorce, single parenthood, and nonmarital childbearing began to change. More people were themselves the product of diverse families, and were more accepting of divorce, single parenthood,
and women's right to live independently.

Single-parent families were in many respects the pioneers of fam-  15
ily diversity, paving the way for the recognition of other families. The
growing acceptance of divorced, single-parent families facilitated the
emergence of yet another form of single parenthood: that resulting not

from divorce but from women electing to give birth while remaining single. Women increasingly saw motherhood without marriage as offering greater satisfaction and security than a marriage of questionable stability (Mann & Roseneil, 1999). Increasingly, women chose to cohabit rather than formally marry, to postpone marriage and childbearing, and to live alone. Still others chose to give birth, adopt, or foster children as single parents. Many women, defying the stigma attached to childless women, elected not to have children at all, thus creating a new family configuration: childless families by choice.

With fewer unwanted pregnancies and fewer unwanted births, [16] and with more white, single mothers keeping their babies as had African American mothers in the past, fewer white babies were available for adoption (Riley, 1997). The decline in the number of babies placed for adoption precipitated an increased interest in international adoptions as an alternative. Because these adoptions often involved children who were racially and/or ethnically different from their adoptive parents, the adoption could not be kept secret as had been the practice in the past. The growing acceptance of adoptive families, in turn, facilitated a greater acceptance of stepfamilies and other families not related by blood.

With the increasing numbers and visibility of single-parent, step-, [17] and adoptive families, the gay liberation movement opened the way for the emergence of gay and lesbian families. Some gay men and lesbians were divorced and had custody of the children, becoming in the process single-parent families. Others chose to give birth to a child within the lesbian/gay relationship.

Another factor contributing to family diversity since the 1970s, and [18] especially to foster families and grandmother-headed families, has been a dramatic increase in the imprisonment of women and mothers, a legacy of the war on drugs with its harsh sentencing policies. Most of the women in prison are there for drug-related offenses, often because of the activities of a male partner. This, together with the growing number of women, especially women of color, infected by HIV (the human immunodeficiency virus) has contributed to an increasing number of children whose mothers are not able to parent them. In addition, many children, and especially African American children, are removed from homes considered unfit and placed in foster care, sometimes with relatives. Increasingly, grandmothers are assuming responsibility for raising their grandchildren.

Finally, innovations in reproductive technology have vastly opened [19] up the possibilities for people to create new kinds of families, further challenging conventional definitions of family. New reproductive technologies (NRTs) include donor insemination, embryo freezing and transfer, ovum extraction, and *in vitro* fertilization (IVF). The first test-tube baby, conceived through *in vitro* fertilization, was born in England in 1978, and the first surrogate birth, in which an embryo was transferred to a woman with no genetic connection to it, took place in 1986. In 1992, a postmenopausal grandmother gave birth to her own granddaughter in South Africa, having served as a surrogate for her daughter's embryo.

To protect marriages, the law in most jurisdictions recognizes hus- 20 bands of inseminated women as the "real" fathers (Benkov, 1997) while denying parental rights to donors (Bartholet, 1993). Although NRTs reflect a preference for biological reproduction over social parenting through adoption, fostering, or informal care of relatives (McDaniel, 1988), social parenting has become a powerful force in family diversity. NRTs were originally administered to support traditional nuclear families, and were denied to unmarried women. However, as they became increasingly available through for-profit laboratories seeking to expand their markets, they were offered to single women, including lesbians. To date, about one million children have been conceived in laboratories in the United States (Benkov, 1997). The NRTs have undermined the cultural norm that blood relations are the *sine qua non* of families, and that nonbiological members are not "real" family members. Families created through reproductive technologies, similar to adoptive-foster families, and to some extent like stepfamilies, defy the notion that biological conception has to be the basis for family formation. This disjunction between reproduction and parenting, between the biological and social aspects of parenting, alters the meaning of parenthood, kinship, and family (Benkov, 1997; Gross, 1997; Stacey, 1996).

## Families in the 1980s and 1990s: The Backlash Against Family Diversity

The 1980s and 1990s were, in many respects, a period of regression in 21 the United States with respect to civil rights and policies supporting diversity. The family became, and continues to be, a battleground over contending visions of what a family ought to be. Voices on the right blame changes in the family for a wide range of social problems, while voices on the left look to the family to provide the basis for a more communitarian society. At one extreme, we hear claims that the family is obsolete, a reactionary institution destined to disappear. At the other, conservatives strive to uphold "family values," advocating a return to the conventional family arrangements enshrined in midcentury television sitcoms (Csikszentmihalyi, 1997). Across the political spectrum, invoking "family values" is a way of idealizing the traditional nuclear family to the exclusion of other family forms (Jagger & Wright, 1999).

Family values proponents offer a simple and dangerous misdiag- 22 nosis of what they consider wrong in America—the "family breakdown" thesis (Stacey, 1998). Family breakdown—namely the high divorce rates, the decline of the two-parent married family, and the increase in family diversity—has been blamed for everything from child poverty, declining educational standards, substance abuse, high homicide rates, AIDS (acquired immune deficiency syndrome), infertility, and teen pregnancy to narcissism and the Los Angeles riots (Coontz, 1997; Jagger & Wright, 1999; Wright & Jagger, 1999). Family breakdown is in turn attributed to a generalized decline in family values, which is often blamed on a lack of commitment to marriage, an acceptance of female-headed families as a way of life, feminism, the sexual revolution, and gay liberation (Beca Zinn, 1997; Coontz, 1997). Hence women's desire for personal fulfillment is described by conservatives as an egotistic abandonment of parental obligations that sacrifices the well-being of children (Council on Families in America, 1996). Ironically, the current emphasis on family self-sufficiency and the pressure on single mothers to be self-supporting are in direct conflict with conservatives' traditional preference for full-time mothers (Wright & Jagger, 1999).

In keeping with the family breakdown thesis, political discourse in 23 the 1990s blamed single motherhood for the perpetuation of an "underclass" in British and American society. Although there is little consensus among scholars about the underclass, or whether it exists at all, under the label of the underclass debate, researchers returned to old questions about the relationship between family structure, race, and poverty. In the 1960s and early 1970s, the discussion focused on how poor families adapted to poverty; current discussions, in contrast, are primarily concerned with the failure of women-headed families to lift themselves and their children out of poverty (Jarrett, 1994). For example, American conservative Charles Murray, who played a prominent role in blaming single motherhood for poverty and violence, argued (in Wright & Jagger, 1999) that more young women were choosing unwed motherhood because the sexual revolution had destigmatized it and the welfare system was rewarding it. Though welfare costs have always been a very small portion of the federal budget, single-parent families were also held responsible for a "crisis" of the welfare state (Beca Zinn, 1997; Mann & Roseneil, 1999; Wright & Jagger, 1999).

Although single mothers were being attacked, they suffered high 24 rates of poverty, a legacy of social policies that especially disadvantages women and children. Welfare benefits to impoverished single mothers and their children in the United States declined markedly from the 1970s to the 1990s, and in 1996, the federal welfare entitlement was abolished in favor of a drastically limited employment-based program. The attacks on welfare were, in effect, attacks against struggling and vulnerable families (Stacey, 1996).

The attack on single mothers is partly a backlash against feminism, 25 an attempt to restore fathers to their "rightful role." It is also motivated by concerns over how women are exercising their agency and their freedom of choice to become mothers or not. Instead of viewing disadvantaged women as committed, responsible mothers who assume custody and care of their children, the rhetoric portrays them as oppressors of the fathers. The fathers, on the other hand, who are at least as responsible for the creation of poor single-parent families, are often viewed as the victims. If they pay child support, they are heralded as responsible fathers, even though the child support is usually insufficient to meet the expense of raising the children, and even though they generally forgo the daily responsibilities of caring for the children. This rhetoric justifies reductions in government assistance to single mothers and their children, making their situations even worse (Mann & Roseneil, 1999).

## THE FAMILY VALUES AGENDA

Family values proponents define the family as an institution comprising 26 people related by blood and marriage that performs specific social functions. The majority of family values advocates use "the family" to mean a heterosexual, conjugal, nuclear, domestic unit, ideally one with a male breadwinner, female homemaker, and their dependent offspring—a version of the 1950s television Ozzie-and-Harriet family, sometimes updated to include employed wives and mothers (Stacey, 1998). This prescriptive definition of what constitutes a proper family obscures racial, class, and sexual diversity in domestic arrangements, as well as masking the inequities within the traditional family (Stacey, 1998). Pluralism, so commonly recognized in other aspects of American society, has yet to be fully accepted when it comes to the family (Klee, Schmidt, & Johnson, 1989).

A striking feature of our contemporary family politics is the chasm 27 between behavior and ideology. Most family values enthusiasts still judge our "brave new families" by a fifties standard to which only a minority of citizens would wish to return (Stacey, 1998). In a 1999 national survey, for example, only a third of the respondents thought that parents should stay together just because they have children (University of Chicago National Opinion Research Center, 1999).

Support for "traditional family values" serves political purposes. It 28 provides a rationale for family surveillance and intervention, focuses attention on individual moral solutions to social problems rather than costly public solutions, and offers a simple alternative to dealing with the real complexities of social change. The new call for family values represents an effort to reduce collective responsibility and increase the dependency of family members on one another (Wright & Jagger, 1999).

Pro-family values stories are appearing in the press, in popular 29 magazines, on radio and television talk shows, and in scholarly journals. During the late 1980s, a network of research and policy institutes, think tanks and commissions, began mobilizing to forge a national consensus on family values and to shape the family politics of the "new" Democratic Party. Central players were the Institute for American Values and the Council on Families in America, whose goal is to restore the privileged status of lifelong, heterosexual marriage.

The Council on Families in America (1996) urges marriage coun- 30 selors, family therapists, and family life educators to approach their work "with a bias in favor of marriage" and to "link advocacy for children to advocacy for marriage" (p. 311). It advocates a revision of the federal tax code "to provide more favorable treatment for married couples with children" (p. 313), and advocates a "bias in favor of marriage-with-children in the allocation of subsidized housing loans and public housing" (p. 314).

Marriage has become increasingly fragile with the increase in 31 women's employment and their reduced economic dependency on men. It has also become less obligatory, particularly for women. In all cultures and eras, stable marriage systems have rested upon coercion—overt or veiled—and on inequality. Proposals to restrict access to divorce and parenting implicitly recognize this. Without coercion, divorce and single motherhood will remain commonplace. It seems a poignant commentary on the benefits to women of modern marriage that even when women retain chief responsibility for supporting children, raising them and caring for them, when they earn much less than men with similar "cultural capital," and when they and their children suffer major economic loss after divorce, so many regard divorce as the lesser evil.

Rather than examining and solving the problems of traditional 32 marriages that so often end up in divorce, advocates of family values aim to coerce women to stay in marriages by erecting barriers to divorce. They wish to restore fault criteria to divorce proceedings and impose new restrictions, like mandatory waiting periods and compulsory counseling. Claiming that divorce and unwed motherhood inflict devastating harm on children, they seek to revive the social stigma that once marked these "selfish" practices. They advocate restricting adoption to married couples, and they oppose welfare payments to unmarried mothers. However, in their staunch advocacy of marriage, they avoid examining what might be lacking in a traditional marriage, especially for women, or questioning why so many women choose to divorce or not to marry.

What is primarily at stake in the debate over the family is the rela- 33 tionship between the sexes. Advocates of family values assign responsibilities to families without explicitly acknowledging the burdens that family life places on women or the gender conflicts resulting from unequal roles. At the same time, they place most of the blame for family problems on "deviant" women, especially those who raise children alone.

### The Significance of Family Structure

Contrary to the claims of family values advocates, there is no empirical 34 basis for granting privileged status to the heterosexual, nuclear, two-parent family (Acock & Demo, 1994; Dowd, 1997; Silverstein & Auerbach, 1999). Few social scientists would agree that a family's structure is more important than the quality of the relationships between parents and children. Revisionists employ academic sleights of hand to evade this consensus. For example, they rest claims on misleading comparison groups and on studies that do not use any comparison groups at all. In fact, most children from both divorced or nondivorced families turn out reasonably well; and when other parental resources—like income, education, self-esteem, and a supportive social environment—are roughly similar, signs of two-parent privilege largely disappear. Most research indicates that a stable, intimate relationship with one responsible, nurturing adult is a child's surest path to becoming a nurturing adult as well (Furstenberg & Cherlin, 1991). As Dowd (1997) points out, "Dysfunctional families come in all shapes and sizes; so do healthy families" (p. xv). There is no question that two responsible, loving parents generally can offer children more than one parent can. However, three or four might prove even better. Putting the case against the essential significance of structure, Dowd (1997) concludes,

> Children need love, care, and parenting. Structure neither produces nor insures that those things will be present. We need to put children first, structure second. It makes no sense to punish children or separate them from their families as the consequence of structure that they had no hand in creating and that are unconnected to their well-being. (p. xix)

### The "Essential Father"

With many mothers no longer at home full time, and in the absence of 35 universal child care and policies to help families integrate work and caregiving, the conservative stance taps into widespread anxiety about "who will raise the children" (Silverstein & Auerbach, 1999). Attacks on single-parent families are also based on claims that families without fathers cannot socialize sons into civilized manhood (Charles Murray, in Wright & Jagger, 1997). These concerns about the well-being of children, and especially boys, represent a reaction against the women's movement, the perceived loss of male privilege, and the gay liberation movement (Silverstein & Auerbach, 1999). As expressed by the Council on Families in America (1996), "The explosion of never-married motherhood in our society means that fathers are increasingly viewed as superfluous, unnecessary, and irrelevant" (pp. 302–303). Men have lost their position at the center of family life. With marriage losing its normative force and with increasing numbers of women working, men have seen their economic ascendancy over the family being eroded, and most are expected to share at least some of the domestic tasks. The conservative concern about the necessity of the "essential father" can be seen as an effort to reestablish male dominance by rescuing the traditional family based on traditional gender roles (Silverstein & Auerbach, 1999).

Conservatives have it backward when they argue that the collapse 36 of traditional family values is at the heart of our social decay. The losses in real earnings and in breadwinner jobs, the persistence of low-wage work for women, global economic restructuring, and corporate greed have wreaked far more havoc on Ozzie-and-Harriet land than have the combined effects of feminism, the sexual revolution, gay liberation, the counterculture, narcissism, and every other value flip of the past half-century. There is no going back to the "good old 1950s," when breadwinner-husbands had unpaid homemaker wives who tended dependent children and the household full time. The modern family has been decisively replaced by the postmodern family of working mothers, high divorce rates, and diverse family arrangements (Coontz, 1997; Stacey, 1998). Nevertheless, the traditional family continues to cast its shadow over other family forms.

## THE HEGEMONY OF THE TRADITIONAL FAMILY

The overpowering strength of the paradigm of the first-married, het- 37
erosexual family lingers even though this family style has long since lost its place as the most prevalent (Glick, 1989). Despite the diversity, society's institutions continue to support a single family structure that is no longer applicable to the majority of families. As Dowd (1997) states,

> We as a society, through law, support nuclear marital families in significant material and ideological ways. We provide resources including financial support, fringe benefits, tax breaks, and housing. We facilitate the use of reproductive technology or adoption for favored families. We define our vision of family, ideologically and practically...by limiting recognition of non-marital families. (p. 4)

The supremacy and the idealization of the traditional family model 38
are expressed in laws, policies, and institutional practices, attitudes, and behaviors. Nuclear families have historically provided a model of normalcy for which family specialists, such as psychologists, social workers, family researchers and theorists, have based their ideals (Adams & Steinmetz, 1993). Increased social tolerance for diversity has, to some extent, modified the notion that nuclear families offer an exemplary family structure. Nevertheless, social policies and attitudes still favor the traditional family. This puts enormous pressures on diverse families to play down their uniqueness and to act like the traditional family, as if this is the only "right" kind of family, irrespective of the differences in structure and style. Despite its demographic decline, "The image of this idealized form [of the traditional nuclear family] persists in the social consciousness and remains the standard against which all other configurations are compared" (Allen & Baber, 1992, p. 379).

Viewed against a template of the first-married, heterosexual fam- 39
ily, other family structures tend to fall into two broad stereotypical categories: the deviant and the variant. A deviant stereotype is assigned to
families that seem much too different to be regarded as a variation of
the first-married, heterosexual family. In the past, this included the
single-parent family, and now includes lesbian and gay families, teenage
single-parent families, and childless families, among others. Deviant
implies not only that these families are different, but that they are bad
or wrong in some way. Therefore, "deviant" families need somehow to
prove their legitimacy.

The variant family stereotype views diverse families more posi- 40
tively, considering them more or less like first-married, heterosexual
families, but with a difference. Families considered variant usually have
two parents of the opposite sex who reside with children in the same
household; notable examples are adoptive and stepfamilies. Although
lacking the negative connotation of deviance, this positive stereotype is
also problematic. It establishes unrealistic expectations based on the
model of the traditional nuclear family. Because such families are not
quite the same when measured against the template, they may be left
feeling that they are falling short in some respects. The stereotypes
exert pressures on families to try to function in the same mold as the
traditional family, or to "pass" in order to gain the legitimacy and resources reserved for traditional families. The appeal of assimilation is
especially attractive for those families that most resemble a traditional
family. "Passing," however, creates tensions between the actual and idealized lifestyles of family members. As Eheart and Power (1995) found
in their study of adoptive families, "failure occurs when families live
stories that differ in acceptable ways from their expectations of what
their family life should be like" (p. 211). It engenders a falsehood that
may lead family members to experience a sense of failure, shame, and
identity confusion. At the same time, it restricts their creativity, flexibility, and uniqueness (Biddle, Kaplan, & Silverstein, 1998). In contrast,
when families manage to let go of myths of the ideal family life, their
lives are experienced as appropriate and fitting.

It is therefore not surprising that with the exception of stepfami- 41
lies and single-parent families, families...have rarely been examined
as family structures in their own right. To the extent that they have
been considered at all, it has been from a particular academic or practice perspective. Foster families, viewed as nuclear families temporarily hosting an additional child, are examined from the standpoint of

child welfare; gay and lesbian families, under gender or women's studies; and grandmother-headed families, within gerontology or race and gender studies. Furthermore, these families are often characterized as lacking something. Single-parent families are deemed deficient for lack of a father. Grandparents raising grandchildren are discounted because they are old, are not the parents, and are frequently people of color and poor. Gay and lesbian families are not considered as families at all because the partners are of the same sex and because they are not married. The refusal to acknowledge them as families is a denial that their relationships count, regardless of their stability, duration, or quality.

Family theories do not sufficiently account for families in their di- 42 versity. New perspectives are needed that value family plurality and resilience (Demo & Allen, 1996; McAdoo, 1998). As Weitzman (1975) noted a quarter of a century ago, in a diverse society, a single family form cannot fit the needs of all. Rather than shaping concepts of the family from a single mold, we must recognize the diversity and fluidity of family and household arrangements, and acknowledge change in families as a sign of strength.

Acock, A. C., & Demo, D. H. (1994). *Family diversity and well-being*. Thousand Oaks, CA; Sage.

Adams, B. N., & Steinmetz, S. K. (1993). Family theory and methods in the classics. In P. G. Boss & W. J. Doherty (Eds.), *Sourcebook of family theories and methods: A contextual approach* (pp. 71–94). New York: Plenum.

Allen, K. R., & Baber, K. M. (1992). Starting the revolution in family life education: A feminist vision. *Family Relations, 41*, 378–384.

Bartholet, E. (1993). *Family bonds: Adoption and the politics of parenting*. Boston: Houghton Mifflin.

Beca Zinn, M. B. (1997). Family, race, and poverty. In A. S. Skolnick & J. H. Skolnick (Eds.), *Family in transition* (9th ed., pp. 316–329). New York: HarperCollins.

Becvar, R. J., Ray, W. A., & Becvar, D. S. (1996). A modest/immodest proposal: Reciprocal foster families. *Contemporary Family Therapy, 18*(2), 257–265.

Benkov, L. (1997). Reinventing the family. In A.S. Skolnick & J.H. Skolnick (Eds.), *Family in transition* (9th ed., pp. 354–379). New York: HarperCollins.

Biddle, C., Kaplan, S.R., & Silverstein, D. (1998). *Kinship: Ties that bind*. Available at: http://www.adopting.org/silveroze/html/kinship.html.

Coontz, S. (1997). *The way we really are: Coming to terms with America's changing families*. New York: Basic Books.

Council on Families in America. (1996). Marriage in America: A report to the nation. In D. Popenoe, J. Bethke-Elshtain, & D. Blankenhorn (Eds.), *Promises to keep: Decline and renewal of marriage in America* (pp. 293–317). Lanham, MD: Rowman & Littlefield.

Csikszentmihalyi, M. (1997). *Finding flow: The psychology of engagement with everyday life*. New York: Basic Books.

Demo, D. H., & Acock, A. C. (1996). Family structure, family process, and adolescent well-being. *Journal of Research on Adolescence, 6*(4), 457–488.

Demo, D. H., & Allen, K. R. (1996). Diversity within lesbian and gay families: Challenges and implications for family theory and research. *Journal of Social and Personal Relationships, 13*(3), 415–434.

Dowd, N. E. (1997). *In defense of single-parent families*. New York: New York University Press.

Eheart, B. K., & Power, M. B. (1995). Adoption: Understanding the past, present, and future through stories. *Sociological Quarterly, 36*(1), 197–216.

Furstenberg, F. F., Jr., & Cherlin, A. J. (1991). *Divided families: What happens to children when parents part*. Cambridge, MA: Harvard University Press.

Glick, P. C. (1989). Remarried families, stepfamilies, and stepchildren: A brief demographic analysis. *Family Relations, 38*, 24–27.

Gross, E. R. (1992). Are families deteriorating or changing? *Affilia, 7*(2), 7–33.

Gross, H. E. (1997). Variants of open adoptions: The early years. *Marriage and Family Review, 25*(1–2), 19–42.

Hargaden, H., & Llewellin, S. (1996). Lesbian and gay parenting issues. In D. Davies & C. Neal (Eds.), *Pink therapy: A guide for counselors and therapists working with lesbian, gay and bisexual clients* (pp. 116–130). Buckingham, England: Open University Press.

Hill, M. S. (1995). When is a family a family? Evidence from survey data and implications for family policy. *Journal of Family and Economic Issues, 16*(1), 35–64.

Jagger, G., & Wright, C. (1999). Introduction: Changing family values. In G. Jagger & C. Wright (Eds.), *Changing family values* (pp. 1–16). London: Routledge.

Jarrett, R. L. (1994). Living poor: Family life among single parent, African-American women. *Social Problems, 41*(1), 30–49.

Klee, L., Schmidt, C., & Johnson, C. (1989). Children's definitions of family following divorce of their parents. In C. A. Everett (Ed.), *Children of divorce: Developmental and clinical issues* (pp. 109–127). New York: Haworth.

Lichter, D. T., & McLaughlin, D. K. (1997). Poverty and marital behavior of young women. *Journal of Marriage and the Family, 59*(3), 582–595.

Mann, K., & Roseneil, S. (1999). Poor choices? Gender, agency and the underclass debate. In G. Jagger & C. Wright (Eds.), *Changing family values* (pp. 98–118). London: Routledge.

McAdoo, H. P. (1998). African-American families: Strengths and realities. In H. I. McCubbin, E. A. Thompson, A. I. Thompson, & J. A. Futrell (Eds.), *Resiliency in African-American families* (pp. 17–30). Thousand Oaks, CA: Sage.

McDaniel, S. A. (1988). Women's roles, reproduction, and the new reproductive technologies: A new stork rising. In N. Mandell & A. Duffy (Eds.), *Reconstructing the Canadian family: Feminist perspectives* (pp. 175–206). Toronto, Ontario: Butterworths.

Murdock, G. P. (1949). *Social structure*. New York: Free Press.

Riley, N. (1997). American adoptions of Chinese girls: The socio-political matrices of individual decisions. *Women's Studies International Forum, 20*(1), 87–102.

Risman, B. J. (1998). *Gender vertigo: American families in transition*. New Haven, CT: Yale University Press.

Silverstein, L. B., & Auerbach, C. F. (1999). Deconstructing the essential father. *American Psychologist, 54*(6), 397–407.

Smith, T. E. (1995). What a difference a measure makes: Parental-separation effect on school grades, not academic achievement. *Journal of Divorce and Remarriage, 23*(3–4), 151–164.

Sprey, J. (1988). Current theorizing on the family: An appraisal. *Journal of Marriage and the Family, 50*(4), 875–890.

Stacey, J. (1996). *In the name of the family: Rethinking family values in the postmodern age.* Boston: Beacon.

Stacey, J. (1998). *Brave new families: Stories of domestic upheaval in late twentieth century America* (Rev. ed.). New York: Basic Books.

Thorne, B. (1982). Feminist rethinking of the family: An overview. In B. Thorne & M. Yalom (Eds.), *Rethinking the family: Some feminist questions* (pp. 1–24). New York: Longman.

Tilly, C., & Albelda, R. (1994). It's not working: Why single mothers can't work their way out of poverty. *Dollars and Sense, 196*, 8–10.

University of Chicago National Opinion Research Center, (1999, November 24). *The emerging 21st century American family.* Available at: http://www.norc.uchicago.edu/new/homepage.htm.

Vobejda, B. (1994). Study alters image of "typical" family. *Seattle Times.* Available at: http://seattletimes.nwsource.com.

Weitzman, L. J. (1975). To love, honor, and obey? Traditional legal marriage and alternative family forms. *Family Coordinator, 24*(4), 531–547.

Wright, C., & Jagger, G. (1999). End of century, end of family? Shifting discourses of family "crisis." In G. Jagger & C. Wright (Eds.), *Changing family values* (pp. 17–37). London: Routledge.  ❀

## READING FOR INFORMATION

1. Explain what Erera means when she says, "The main reason for family change was the breakdown of the postwar social compact between government, corporations, and workers" (paragraph 10).

2. Make a list of the various complaints about single mothers. Explain how Erera defends the single moms against each attack.

3. Summarize Erera's argument against proponents of family values.

4. Does Erera view fathers as "essential" to the well-being of children? Why, or why not?

5. Explain the distinction Erera makes between deviant and variant families.

## READING FOR FORM, ORGANIZATION, AND EXPOSITORY FEATURES

1. Use the section of Chapter 4 devoted to argument to explain how Erera has fashioned an "argument in a specialized sense" (i.e., a two-dimensional argument).

2. What devices or aids help the reader follow Erera's argument?

3. What types of sources does Erera draw upon, and what functions do those sources serve?

## READING FOR RHETORICAL CONCERNS

1. Toward the beginning of the selection, Erera provides a number of alarming statistics. What purpose do they serve?

2. What is the function of the questions in paragraph 7?

3. How do you think readers will be affected by Erera's argument? After reading the selection, would you support her position? Why, or why not?

## WRITING ASSIGNMENTS

1. After reading the selection, respond to the question, "What is a family?" Compare your post-reading response to the definition you wrote for your prereading. Write a brief essay comparing and/or contrasting the two definitions.

2. How do the statistics in paragraph 2 compare to your experience? Is your family included in the 26 percent of American households with married couples and children? Write an essay that describes your family.

3. Interview an individual or couple who are representative of one of the nontraditional structures or lifestyles—single-parent families, lesbian and gay families, teenage single-parent families, childless families, grandmother-headed families, foster families—that Erera discusses. Ask the interviewee(s) to explain what he or she sees as the advantages and disadvantages of the particular lifestyle. Then write an essay in which you compare your interviewee's explanations with those presented by Erera. Draw your own conclusions.

4. Using Erera's explanation of the family breakdown thesis and her description of the attack on single mothers as a base, conduct some research on separated, divorced, never married, and widowed single-parent families. Drawing on the section "Synthesizing Sources" in Chapter 3, write an essay addressed to your classmates explaining the rewards and difficulties of single parenting today.

# Seven Tenets for Establishing New Marital Norms

## *David Popenoe*

*David Popenoe is Professor of Sociology at Rutgers University, New Brunswick, New Jersey, and co-director of the National Marriage Project. He has written numerous scholarly and popular articles and a number of books, including* Life Without Father: Compelling New Evidence that Fatherhood and Marriage are Indispensable for the Good of Children and Society, Disturbing the Nest: Family Change and Decline in Modern Societies, *and* Housing and Neighborhoods. *This selection is from* Promises to Keep: Decline and Renewal of Marriage in America, *a volume he edited with Jean Bethke Elshtain and David Blankenhorn.*

### PREREADING

Do you think that society needs new marital norms? Are our current expectations for marital behavior outdated? Respond in your journal.

I propose as a remedy for society's confusion over marital gender-role expectations, a pattern of late marriage followed, in the early childrearing years, by what one could call a "modified traditional nuclear family." The main elements of this pattern can be summarized as follows. (I recognize, of course, that this pattern—being a set of normative expectations—is not something to which everyone can or should conform.)

1. Girls as well as boys should be trained according to their abilities for a socially useful paid job or career. It is important for women to be able to achieve the economic, social, and psychic rewards of the

workplace that have long been reserved for men. It is important for society that everyone be well educated and that they make an important work contribution over the course of their lives.

2. Young people should grow up with the expectation that they 3 will marry only once and for a lifetime and that they will have children. Reproduction is a fundamental purpose of life, and marriage is instrumental to its success. Today, close to 90 percent of Americans actually marry, and about the same percentage of American women have children. Although these figures have been dropping, the social expectation in these respects is currently quite well realized. Lifetime monogamy is not so well realized, however, with the divorce rate now standing at over 50 percent.

3. Young adults should be encouraged to marry later in life than 4 is common now, with an average age at time of marriage in the late twenties or early thirties (the average ages currently are twenty-six for men and twenty-four for women). Even later might be better for men, but at older ages than this for women who want children, the "biological clock" becomes a growing problem.[1]

From society's viewpoint, the most important reasons why people 5 should be encouraged to marry relatively late in life is that they are more mature, they know better what they want in a mate, they are more established in their jobs or careers, and the men have begun to "settle down" sexually (partly due to a biological diminution of their sex drive). Age at marriage has proven to be the single most important predictor of eventual divorce, with the highest divorce rates found among those who marry in their teenage years.[2] But we must also recognize that both women and men want to have time, when they are young, to enjoy the many opportunities for personal expression and fulfillment that modern, affluent societies are able to provide.

We should anticipate that many of these years of young adulthood 6 will be spent in nonmarital cohabitation, an arrangement that often makes more sense than the alternatives to it, especially living alone or continuing to live with one's family of origin. I am not implying, much less advocating, sexual promiscuity here, but rather serious, caring relationships which may involve cohabitation.

4. From the perspective of promoting eventual family life, however, the downside to late age of marriage is that people live for about a 7 decade or more in a nonfamily, "singles" environment which reinforces their personal drive for expressive individualism and conceivably

reduces their impulse toward carrying out eventual family obligations, thus making the transition to marriage and childrearing more difficult.[3] To help overcome the anti-family impact of these years, young unmarried adults should be encouraged to save a substantial portion of their income for a "family fund" with an eye toward offsetting the temporary loss of the wife's income after marriage and childbirth.

5. Once children are born, wives should be encouraged to leave   8 the labor market and become substantially full-time mothers for a period of at least a year to eighteen months per child. The reason for this is that mother-reared infants appear to have distinct advantages over those reared apart from their mothers. It is desirable for children to have full-time parenting up to at least age three, but after eighteen months—partly because children by then are more verbal—it is appropriate for fathers to become the primary caretakers, and some men may wish to avail themselves of the opportunity. At age three, there is no evidence that children in quality group care suffer any disadvantages (in fact, for most children there are significant advantages). Once children reach that age, therefore, the average mother could resume working part-time until the children are at least of school age, and preferably in their early to middle teen years, at which point she could resume work full-time. Alternatively, when the children reach the age of three the father could stay home part-time, and the mother could resume work full-time.

For women, this proposal is essentially the strategy known as "se-   9 quencing."[4] The main difficulty with it, as sociologist Phyllis Moen has noted, "is that child-nurturing years are also the career-nurturing years. What is lost in either case cannot be 'made up' at a later time."[5] Yet I would argue that it is possible to "make up" for career loss, but impossible to make up for child-nurturing loss. To make it economically more possible for a family with young children to live on a single income, we should institute (in addition to the "family fund") what virtually every other industrialized society already has in place—parental leave and child allowance programs. And, to help compensate women for any job or career setbacks due to their time out of the labor force, we should consider the development of "veterans benefits" type programs that provide mothers with financial subsidies and job priorities when they return to the paid work force. In general, women must be made to feel that caring for young children is important work, respected by the working community.

6. According to this proposal, the mother and not the father ordi- 10 narily would be the primary caretaker of infants. This is because of fundamental biological differences between the sexes that assume great importance in childrearing, as discussed above. The father should be an active supporter of the mother-child bond during this period, however, as well as auxiliary homemaker and care provider. Fathers should expect to spend far more time in domestic pursuits than their own fathers did. Their work should include not only the male's traditional care of the house as a physical structure and of the yard and car, but in many cases cooking, cleaning, and child care, the exact distribution of such activities depending on the individual skills and talents of the partners. And, as noted above, after children reach age eighteen months it may be desirable for the father and not the mother to become the primary caretaker. This means that places of employment must make allowances for substantial flex-time and part-time job absence for fathers as well as for mothers.

7. It should be noted that there is some balancing out of domes- 11 tic and paid-work roles between men and women over the course of life. Under current socioeconomic conditions, husbands, being older, retire sooner than their wives. Also, in later life some role switching occurs, presumably caused in part by hormonal changes, in which women become more work-oriented and men become more domestic.[6] Given current male-female differences in longevity, of course, the average woman can expect to spend an estimated seven years of her later life as a widow.

Later marriage, together with smaller families, earlier retirement, 12 and a longer life in a society of affluence, provide both men and women in modern societies an historically unprecedented degree of freedom to pursue personal endeavors. Yet what David Gutmann has called the "parental imperative"[7] is also a necessary and important part of life, and during the parental years expressive freedom for adults must be curtailed in the interest of social values, especially the welfare of children.

Male breadwinning and female childrearing have been the pattern 13 of social life throughout history, albeit not always in quite so extreme a form as found in modern societies over the past century and a half. Except perhaps for adult pair-bonds in which no young children are involved, where much social experimentation is possible, it is foolhardy to think that the nuclear family can or should be entirely scrapped. When children become a part of the equation, fundamental biological and social constraints come into play—such as the importance of mothers to young children—and central elements of the nuclear family are dismissed at society's peril. Rather than strive for androgyny and be continuously frustrated and unsettled by our lack of achievement of it, we would do much better to more readily acknowledge, accommodate, and appreciate the very different needs, sexual interests, values, and goals of each sex. And rather than the unisex pursuit of "freedom with a male bias," we should be doing more to foster a culture in which the traditional female values of relationship and caring are given a higher priority and respect.

In a much modified form, then, traditional marital gender roles 14 are necessary if the good of society—and of individuals—are to be advanced.

1. The late age of marriage is one of the many ways in which this marriage pattern differs significantly from that of the 1950s; in 1957, the average woman who married was still a teenager!
2. Teresa Castro Martin and Larry L. Bumpass, "Recent Trends in Marital Disruption," *Demography* 26, no. 1 (1989): 37–51.
3. Alice S. Rossi, "Life Span Theories and Women's Lives," *Signs: Journal of Women in Culture and Society* 6 (1980): 4–32; Linda J. Waite, Frances K. Goldscheider, and Christina Witsberger, "Nonfamily Living and the Erosion of Traditional Family Orientations among Young Adults," *American Sociological Review* 51, no. 4 (1986): 541–54.
4. Arlene Rossen Cardozo, *Sequencing* (New York: Collier Books, 1986); Felice N. Schwartz, *Breaking with Tradition: Women, Management, and the New Facts of Life* (New York: Warner, 1992).
5. Phyllis Moen, *Women's Two Roles: A Contemporary Dilemma* (New York: Auburn House, 1992), 133.
6. David Gutmann, *Reclaimed Powers: Toward a New Psychology of Men and Women in Later Life* (New York: Basic Books, 1987).
7. David Gutmann, "Men, Women, and the Parental Imperative," *Commentary* 56, no. 5 (1973): 59–64. 🏵

## READING FOR INFORMATION

1. What reasons does Popenoe give for marrying in one's late twenties or thirties?

2. Is Popenoe for or against nonmarital cohabitation? Explain.

3. What is the function of the "family fund," parental leave, child allowance programs, and "veterans' benefits"?

## READING FOR FORM, ORGANIZATION, AND EXPOSITORY FEATURES

1. Describe the organizational features that make this selection easy to follow.
2. What is the function of the last three paragraphs?

## READING FOR RHETORICAL CONCERNS

1. Explain Popenoe's rhetorical purpose. What impact do you think he wants to have on his readers?
2. How do the endnotes serve Popenoe's purpose? How do they affect the impact of his argument?

## WRITING ASSIGNMENTS

1. Select any one of the seven tenets and write an essay agreeing or disagreeing with Popenoe's position.
2. Write an essay in which you summarize the division of labor patterns Popenoe proposes, and give your views about whether or not this type of shared parenting will work.

# Cohabitation Instead of Marriage

## *James Q. Wilson*

*James Q. Wilson served as the Shattuck Professor of Government at Harvard University and the James Collins Professor of Management and Public Policy at UCLA. He is the author or co-author of fourteen books, including* Moral Judgement, Moral Sense, American Government, Bureaucracy, Thinking About Crime, Varieties of Police Behavior, Political Organizations, *and* Crime and Human Nature *(co-authored with Richard J. Herrnstein). This selection is from his 2002 book,* The Marriage Problem: How Our Culture Has Weakened Families.

## PREREADING

In your view, is marriage a prerequisite to living with a partner? Why do you think increasing numbers of people are deciding to live together rather than marry? Respond to these questions in your journal.

If marriage is designed to help solve a society's need to main-   1
tain family, and if modern societies such as ours have created
ways of raising children that are independent of family life, then family
life ought not to be very important. If a child can be raised by a nanny
or a day-care center, if its education can be left in the hands of public
and private schools, if its physical well-being can be entrusted to police
officers and social workers, then marriage does not offer much to the
father and mother. And if the couple has no wish for children, then
marriage offers nothing at all. Perhaps men and women can simply decide to live together—to cohabit—without any formalities that define a
"legal" marriage.

But cohabitation creates a problem that most people will find hard   2
to solve. If people are free to leave cohabitation (and they must be, or it
would be called a marriage instead), then in many cases, neither the
man nor the woman has any strong incentive to invest heavily in the
union. Marriage is a way of making such investments plausible by
telling each party that they are united forever, and if they wish to dissolve this union that they will have to go through an elaborate and possibly costly legal ritual called divorce. Marriage is a way of restricting
the freedom of people so that investing emotionally and financially in
the union makes sense. I can join my money with yours because, should
we ever wish to separate, we would have to go through a difficult
process of settling our accounts. That process, divorce, makes merged
accounts less risky. If a cohabiting couple has a child, its custody can be
decided by one parent taking it. If we marry, however, the custody of
the child will be determined by a judge, and so each of our interests in
its custody will get official recognition. This fact makes it easier for us to
have a child.

And love itself is helped by marriage. If we cohabit and I stop lov-   3
ing you, I walk away. This means that you have less of an incentive to
love me, since your affection may not be returned by me for as long as
you would like and hence your love might be wasted. But if we promise
to live together forevermore (even though we know that we can get a
divorce if we are willing to put up with its costs), each of us is saying
that since you have promised to love me, I can afford to love you.

Cohabiting couples in the United States tend to keep separate   4
bank accounts and divide up the expenses of their life together. And
this financial practice signals a potential social burden. While married
couples with unequal incomes are less likely to get a divorce than those

with more equal ones, cohabiting ones with unequal incomes are likely to split apart. If our money is kept in separate accounts, then your having more (or less) money than I makes a difference. If it is kept in merged accounts, then nobody observes differences in income.

Cohabitation ordinarily does not last very long; most such unions 5 in America break up (sometimes with a split, sometimes with a marriage) within two years. Scholars increasingly regard cohabitation as a substitute to being single, not an alternative to marriage. And a good thing, since people seem to bring different expectations to the former than to the latter. When high-school seniors were followed into their early thirties, women who highly valued having a career and men who greatly valued leisure were more likely to cohabit than were people with the opposite views. Women seemed to think that cohabitation helps their careers, men to think it helps them spend more time with "the boys." Neither view makes much sense, since cohabitation not only does not last very long, most people think cohabiting couples are doing something odd. Like it or not, the couple living together will discover in countless ways that society thinks they should either get married or split apart. And society's opinion makes sense. As Linda Waite and Maggie Gallagher put it,

> ...marriage makes you better off, because marriage makes you very important to someone. When you are married you know that someone else not only loves you, but needs you and depends on you. This makes marriage a contract like no other.

Until recently, cultures set rules for marriage that were not only de- 6 signed to protect the child but to achieve a variety of other goals as well. A family was a political, economic, and educational unit as well as a child-rearing one. It participated in deciding who would rule the community and (except in wandering hunter-gatherer groups) control or have privileged access to land that supplied food and cattle. Until the modern advent of schools, families educated their children, not with books, but by demonstrating how to care for other children, perform certain crafts, and mind cattle and agricultural fields. These demonstrations sometimes took the form of games and sometimes depended simply on show-and-tell, but a child's life in either event was governed by the need to demonstrate, year by year, that it had learned how to watch, carry, feed, hunt, fish, and build. These tutorial, educational, and economic families were linked together in kinship groupings that constituted the whole of the small society—often no more than two hundred people, and sometimes even fewer—that lived together in a settlement.

These social functions did not prevent married men and women 7 from caring for each other, even in arranged marriages. Affection existed, though of course it was sometimes interrupted by quarrels and beatings. This affection and the companionship it entailed were valuable supports to family life, but they were not until recently the chief, much less the sole, grounds for maintaining the union.

Today, the family has lost many of these functions. Politically, the 8 family has been replaced by the voting booth and the interest group, economically by the office and the factory, and educationally by the school and the Internet. Modernity did not simply produce these changes: Capitalism did not change the family (the family first changed in ways that made capitalism possible), and schools did not make families less relevant (families changed in ways that made schools more valuable). In later chapters we shall see how these complex alterations occurred.

But for now it is important to observe that the family now rests al- 9 most entirely on affection and child care. These are powerful forces, but the history of the family suggests that almost every culture has found them to be inadequate to producing child support. If we ask why the family is, for many people, a weaker institution today than it once was, it is pointless to look for the answer in recent events. Our desire for sexual unions and romantic attachments is as old as humankind, and they will continue forever. But our ability to fashion a marriage that will make the union last even longer than the romance that inspired it depends on cultural, religious, and legal doctrines that have slowly changed. Today people may be facing a challenge for which they are utterly unprepared: a vast, urban world of personal freedom, bureaucratized services, cheap sex, and easy divorce.

Marriage is a socially arranged solution for the problem of getting 10 people to stay together and care for children that the mere desire for children, and the sex that makes children possible, does not solve. The problem of marriage today is that we imagine that its benefits have been offset by social arrangements, such as welfare payments, community tolerance, and professional help for children, that make marriage unnecessary. But as we have already seen, the advantages of marriage—personal health, longer lives, and better children—remain great. The advantages of cohabitation are mostly illusory, but it is an illusion that is growing in its appeal.    ❀

## READING FOR INFORMATION

1. What does Wilson say about the longevity of cohabitation?
2. Do women and men cohabit for the same reasons?
3. According to Wilson, the family has lost many of its traditional functions. What has been lost?
4. Summarize Wilson's explanation of the problem of marriage today.

## READING FOR FORM, ORGANIZATION, AND EXPOSITORY FEATURES

1. What effect does Wilson achieve with the sequence of "If…then" constructions in the first paragraph?
2. How would you describe the overall organizational structure of the selection? What other organizational patterns do you notice in the various paragraphs?

## READING FOR RHETORICAL CONCERNS

1. Explain Wilson's rhetorical purpose. What is the main point he is trying to get across?
2. Notice that Wilson draws heavily on one particular source. How strong would his argument be if he did not use that source to bolster his case?

## WRITING ASSIGNMENTS

1. Write an essay in which you compare and contrast a marriage contract and a cohabitation arrangement.
2. Write an essay in response to Wilson's definition of marriage as "a socially arranged solution for the problem of getting people to stay together and care for children" (paragraph 10). If you wish, you may draw upon other sources in this chapter.

# Promoting Marriage as a Means for Promoting Fatherhood

## Wade F. Horn

*Wade F. Horn is the assistant secretary for Children and Families for the U.S. Department of Health and Human Services. He also served as president of the National Fatherhood Initiative and as the U.S. Commissioner for Children, Youth, and Families. He has co-authored several books on parenting, including* The Better Homes and Gardens New Father Book *and* The Better Homes and Gardens New Teen Book.

### PREREADING

Read the first two paragraphs of the selection and speculate on the reasons for the dramatic increase in father-absent households. Record your response in your journal.

### INTRODUCTION

The most disturbing and consequential social trend of our time is the   1
dramatic increase over the past four decades in the number of children living in father-absent households. In 1960, the total number of children living absent their biological fathers was less than 10 million. Today, that number stands at nearly 25 million, more than one-third of all children in the United States.[1]

The situation is getting worse, not better. By some estimates,   2
60 percent of children born in the 1990s will spend a significant portion of their childhoods in a father-absent home.[2] For the first time in our nation's history, the average expectable experience of childhood now includes time spent living without one's own father.

This is not good news, especially for children. Almost 75 percent   3
of American children living in single-parent families will experience

poverty before they turn eleven years old, compared to only 20 percent of children in two-parent families.[3] Moreover, violent criminals are overwhelmingly males who grew up without fathers, including up to 60 percent of rapists,[4] 75 percent of adolescents charged with murder,[5] and 70 percent of juveniles in state reform institutions.[6]

Children living in a father-absent home are also more likely to be suspended or expelled from school,[7] or to drop out,[8] develop an emotional or behavioral problem requiring psychiatric treatment,[9] engage in early and promiscuous sexual activity,[10] develop drug and alcohol problems,[11] commit suicide as an adolescent,[12] and be a victim of child abuse or neglect.[13] On almost any measure one can imagine, children who grow up absent their fathers do worse compared to those who live with their two, married parents.[14] In the realm of social science, there are few statements one can make with certitude, but here is one: When fatherhood falters, children suffer.

Fortunately, America seems to be awakening from its three-decade denial about the importance of fathers to families and children. A recent Gallup poll indicates that nearly 80 percent of Americans agree, "The most significant family or social problem facing America is the physical absence of the father from the home."[15] The question is no longer whether fatherlessness matters. The new question is, what can be done about it?

## Child Support Enforcement

The historic answer to the problem of fatherlessness has been child support enforcement. This, of course, is not without merit. Any man who fathers a child ought to be held financially responsible for that child. But as important as child support enforcement may be, it is unlikely by itself to substantially improve the well-being of children for several reasons.

First, having a child support order in place is no guarantee that child support will actually be paid. Some men—the true "deadbeat dads"—can pay, but don't. Others, however, are undereducated and underemployed and have little ability to pay child support. Indeed, 20 percent of all nonresident fathers earn less than $6,000 annually.[16] These fathers are not so much "deadbeat" as "dead broke." Trying to extract child support from such men has been likened to the proverbial attempt to get blood from a turnip.

Second, while receipt of child support has consistently been found to be associated with improvements in child outcomes, the magnitude of the effects tend to be small. That's because the average level of child support paid to custodial mothers is quite modest, only about $2,500 per year.[17] Such a modest amount of additional income, although certainly helpful, is unlikely to substantially improve the life trajectory of most children.

Third, an exclusive emphasis on child support enforcement may 9 drive many low-income, nonresident fathers farther away from their children. As word circulates within low-income communities that cooperating with paternity establishment, but failing to comply with subsequent child support orders, may result in imprisonment or revocation of one's driver's license, many marginally employed fathers may choose to disappear rather than face the possibility of such harsh consequences. Hence, the unintended consequence of tough child support enforcement policies may be to decrease, not increase, the number of children growing up with an actively involved father, proving once again that no good deed goes unpunished.

Finally, an exclusive focus on child support enforcement ignores 10 the many noneconomic contributions that fathers make to the well-being of their children. If, however, we want fathers to be more than cash machines for their children, we will need to encourage their work as nurturers, disciplinarians, mentors, moral instructors, and skill coaches, and not just as economic providers. To do otherwise is to effectively downgrade fathers to, in the words of social historian Barbara Dafoe Whitehead, "paper dads."

### Visitation

Some people, dissatisfied with the results of using child support en- 11 forcement as the primary strategy for dealing with today's crisis of fatherlessness, advocate enhanced visitation as the mechanism for improving the well-being of children. Indeed, there is evidence that positive involvement by non-custodial fathers enhances child well-being. For example, a recent meta-analysis of sixty-three studies by Paul Amato and Joan Gilbreth found that children who reported feeling close to their noncustodial fathers and had fathers who engaged in authoritative parenting—that is, they listened to their children's problems, gave them advice, provided explanations for rules, monitored their academic performance, helped with their homework, engaged in mutual projects, and disciplined them—were significantly more likely to do well at school and show greater psychological health compared to children whose noncustodial fathers mostly engaged them in recreational activities, such as going out to dinner, taking them on vacations, and buying them things.[18] Hence, positive father involvement by nonresident fathers does count.

Unfortunately, other research has found that nonresident fathers [12] are far less likely than in-the-home dads either to have a close relationship with their children or to engage in authoritative parenting.[19] One reason for this, as Amato and Gilbreth point out, is the constraints inherent in traditional visitation arrangements. Because their time with their children is often severely limited, many nonresident fathers strive to make sure their children enjoy themselves when they are with them. As a result, nonresident fathers tend to spend less time than in-the-home fathers helping their children with their homework, monitoring their activities, and setting appropriate limits, and more time taking them to restaurants or the movies, activities that are not associated with enhanced child outcomes. In essence, many nonresident, but visiting, fathers transform into "treat dads." As such, while visitation by nonresident fathers is certainly to be encouraged, the context of visitation reduces the likelihood that nonresident fathers will engage in behavior most associated with enhanced child well being.

## Cohabitation

If, some argue, enhanced visitation is not the answer, perhaps cohabita- [13] tion is. In fact, cohabitation is one of the fastest growing family forms in the United States today. In 1997, 4.13 million couples were cohabiting outside of wedlock, compared to fewer than a half million in 1960.[20] Of these cohabiting couples, 1.47 million, or about 36 percent, have children younger than eighteen residing with them, up from 21 percent in 1987. For unmarried couples in the twenty-five to thirty-four age group, almost half have children living with them.[21] Indeed, it is estimated that nearly half of all children today will spend some time in a cohabiting family before the age of sixteen.[22]

Strengthening cohabitation as a means of strengthening father- [14] hood has found new impetus in recent research by Sara McLanahan and Irwin Garfinkel, who studied "fragile families"—low-income, non-married couples who have had a child out-of-wedlock. Preliminary analysis of data from two cities, Oakland, California, and Austin, Texas, suggests that at the time a child is born out-of-wedlock, more than half of these couples are cohabiting.[23] Consequently, the argument goes, interventions should be aimed at strengthening this "fragile family" (so named to emphasize that these families are at greater risk of breaking up and living in poverty compared to more traditional families) and encouraging "team parenting."

Other research, however, suggests that cohabitation is unlikely to produce lifetime dads for children. First of all, cohabitation is a weak family form. Cohabiting couples break up at much higher rates than married couples.[24] Furthermore, only four out of ten couples who have a child while cohabiting ever go on to get married, and those that do are more likely to divorce than couples who wait until after marriage to have children.[25] Overall, three-quarters of children born to cohabiting parents will see their parents split up before they reach age sixteen, compared to only about one-third of children born to married parents.[26]

The fact that children born to cohabiting couples are likely to see their dads eventually transform into occasional visitors is worrisome for several reasons. First, research on disruptions in early attachment figures suggests children may fare worse when their father is involved early in their life only to disappear than they would fare if they never established a relationship with their father in the first place. If so, encouraging cohabitation may actually be making a bad situation worse.

Second, many men in cohabiting relationships are not the biological father of the children in the household, or at least are not the biological father of all the children in the household. By one estimate, 63 percent of children in cohabiting households are born not to the cohabiting couple, but to a previous union of one of the adult partners, most often the mother.[27] This is problematic in that cohabitation involving biologically unrelated children substantially increases the risk of physical and sexual child abuse.[28] Thus, not only is cohabitation unlikely to deliver a lifetime father to a child, it also brings with it an increased risk for child abuse.

Neither child support enforcement, increased visitation, nor cohabitation is the answer—but that doesn't mean there is no answer.

While it is becoming increasingly popular to speak of the importance of fathers to the well-being of children, it is still out of fashion to speak of the importance of marriage to the well-being of fatherhood. Yet research has consistently found that, over time, nonmarried fathers tend to become disconnected, both financially and psychologically, from their children.[29] Robert Lerman and Theodora Ooms, for example, found that whereas six of ten unwed fathers were visiting their children at least once a week during the first two years of their children's lives, by the time the children were 7.5 years old, that number dropped to only two of ten.[30] Overall, 40 percent of children living absent their fathers have not seen their fathers in more than a year. Of the remaining 60 percent, only one in five sleeps even one night per month in the father's home. Remarriage, or, in cases of unwed fatherhood, marriage to someone other than the child's mother, makes it especially unlikely that a noncustodial father will remain in contact with his children.[31]

Marriage, on the other hand, is a much more effective glue for [20] binding fathers to their children. Indeed, an analysis of a national probability sample of over thirteen thousand households found the most important determinant of whether a father lived with his children was marital status at the time of the child's birth. Fully 80 percent of fathers who were married to the mother at the time of the child's birth were living with all their biological children, compared to only 23 percent of unwed fathers.[32] Given that about 40 percent of all first marriages end in divorce, marriage is not a certain route to a lifetime father. It is, however, a more certain route than any other.

Nevertheless, discussing marriage as the ideal or even preferred [21] family structure is difficult for several reasons. First, marriage is a deeply personal issue. One can safely assume that at least 40 percent of adults in any given audience are divorced. Many others will either have parents who are divorced, a spouse who is from a divorced family, or children who are divorced. When adults touched by divorce hear others suggest that marriage is the "best" or "ideal" situation, they often interpret this as a personal rebuke. No one likes to be told that his or her situation is somehow "second best."

Second, some have bought into the notion of "family relativism"; [22] the idea that all family structures are inherently equal, with no differential consequences for children (or adults) except for the greater propensity of single parent families to be poor. Indeed, this argument goes, if we solve the economic disadvantage of single-parent households, there will be no ill effects of growing up in a home without two married parents.

Third, some simply don't like marriage. They either see marriage [23] promotion as a thinly veiled strategy for withdrawing support from single mothers or as a means for reasserting male privilege and dominance over women. To such folks, marriage promotion is not just foolish, but downright dangerous.

The empirical literature is quite clear, however, that children do [24] best when they grow up in an intact, two-parent, married household. We know, for example, that children who grow up in a continuously married household do better at school, have fewer emotional problems, are more likely to attend college, and are less likely to commit crime or develop alcohol or illicit drug problems.[33] That these results are not simply due to differences in income is attested to by the fact that children reared in stepfamilies, which have household incomes nearly equivalent to continuously married households, do not fare any better than children reared in single-parent households. On some measures they may even do worse.[34]

The empirical evidence also is quite clear that adults—women as well as men—are happier, healthier, and wealthier than their single counterparts. Moreover, married adults report having more satisfying sex than nonmarried adults, and married men show an earnings boost that is not evident in cohabiting relationships.[35] In regards to fatherhood, married fathers are, on average, more likely to be actively engaged in their children's lives and, perhaps just as important, are more accessible to them.

Of course, some married households, especially those in which domestic violence and child abuse are present, are horrible places for both children and adults. But contrary to the stereotypes perpetuated by the media and some advocacy groups, the reality is that domestic violence and child abuse are substantially less likely to occur in intact, married households than in any other family arrangement. The truth is the most dangerous place for women and children is a household in which mom is cohabiting with a man who isn't biologically related to the children.[36]

Given that marriage is so important to the well-being of children, adults, and communities, how do we overcome our reluctance to talk about it? Syndicated columnist William Raspberry suggests the answer: Put children back at the center of things.

Adults have spent far too much time arguing among themselves about the virtues of marriage and far too little time helping our children understand why marriage is important and how to form and sustain healthy marriages. Yet national surveys consistently show that young people, far from rejecting marriage as an ideal, desperately want to avoid the serial marriages and high divorce rates of their elders.[37] It is time for us to give our children what they want.

Accomplishing this is not as simple as pointing young couples to the altar and insisting they marry. We do not need more bad marriages. What we need is more healthy, mutually satisfying, equal-regard marriages. To attain that, young couples will need help in acquiring the knowledge and skills necessary to form and sustain healthy marriages. That requires a new commitment of both public and private resources aimed at providing meaningful premarital education to couples contemplating marriage, marital enrichment to those couples who are already married, and outreach to couples in troubled marriages.

It is not, however, just children and young adults in the middle [30] class who want stable marriages. Data from the Fragile Families Initiative suggests that at the time of the child's birth, two-thirds of low-income, unwed couples want—and expect—to get married.[38] The problem is that many, if not most, of these low-income couples do not go on to get married. That, however, may be as much our fault as theirs, for our reluctance even to bring up the topic sends the not-so-subtle message that marriage is neither expected nor valued. When we are afraid even to say the "m"-word, the wonder is not that so few ever get married, but that some actually do.

## CONCLUSION

Marriage cannot be the only answer to strengthening father–child rela- [31] tionships. Not all marriages are made in heaven. Some nonresident fathers are terrific dads. Some male cohabiting partners provide children with valuable economic and social resources. And when nonresident fathers are capable of providing financial support for their children but do not, laws and policies should seek to right this wrong. Nevertheless, if what we really care about is the well-being of children, rather than the desires of adults, the inescapable conclusion is this: Children want and need their fathers as well as their mothers, and fathers are most likely to be positively involved in their children's lives if they are married to the mother. Saying so may not give much comfort to those adults who worship at the altar of self-fulfillment, but it surely gives a greater measure of hope to children who hunger for their dads.

The views expressed in this chapter do not necessarily represent [32] the views of the Administration for Children and Families, the United States Department of Health and Human Services, or the United States government.

## NOTES

1. Wade F. Horn, *Father Facts*, 3rd ed. (Gaithersburg, Md.: The National Fatherhood Initiative, 1998).
2. Frank F. Furstenberg, Jr., and Andrew J. Cherlin, *Divided Families: What Happens to Children When Parents Part* (Cambridge: Harvard University Press, 1991).
3. National Commission on Children, *Just the Facts: A Summary of Recent Information on America's Children and Their Families* (Washington, D.C., 1993).
4. Karl Zinsmeister, "Crime Is Terrorizing Our Nation's Kids," *Citizen* (August 20, 1990): 2.
5. Dewey Cornell et al., "Characteristics of Adolescents Charged with Homicide," *Behavioral Sciences and the Law* 5 (1987): 11–23.

6. M. Eileen Matlock et al., "Family Correlates of Social Skills Deficits in Incarcerated and Nonincarcerated Adolescents," *Adolescence* 29 (1994): 119–130.

7. Deborah Dawson, "Family Structure and Children's Well-Being: Data from the 1988 National Health Survey," *Journal of Marriage and Family* 53 (August 1991): 573–584.

8. Sara McLanahan and Gary Sandefur, *Growing Up with a Single Parent: What Hurts, What Helps* (Cambridge: Harvard University Press, 1994), 58–59.

9. Ronald J. Angel and Jacqueline L. Angel, "Physical Comorbidity and Medical Care Use in Children with Emotional Problems," *Public Health Reports* 111 (1996): 140–145.

10. Christina Lammers et al., "Influences on Adolescents' Decision to Postpone Onset of Sexual Intercourse: A Survival Analysis of Virginity Among Youths Aged 13 to 18 Years," *Journal of Adolescent Health* 26 (2000): 42–48.

11. John P. Hoffman and Robert A. Johnson, "A National Portrait of Family Structure and Adolescent Drug Use," *Journal of Marriage and the Family* 60 (August 1998): 633–645.

12. Judith Rubenstein et al., "Suicidal Behavior in Adolescents: Stress and Protection in Different Family Contexts," *American Journal of Orthopsychiatry* 68 (1998): 274–284.

13. Catherine M. Malkin and Michael E. Lamb, "Child Maltreatment: A Test of Sociobiological Theory," *Journal of Comparative Family Studies* 25 (1994): 121–130.

14. For a complete review of this literature see Horn, *Father Facts*.

15. George Gallup, "Report on Status of Fatherhood in the United States," *Emerging Trends* 20 (September 1998): 3–5.

16. Irwin Garfinkel, Sara S. McLanahan, Daniel R. Meyer, and Judith A. Seltzer, *Fathers Under Fire: The Revolution in Child Support Enforcement* (New York: Russell Sage Foundation, 1998).

17. U.S. Bureau of the Census, *Child Support for Custodial Mothers and Fathers: 1997* (Washington, D.C., 2000).

18. Paul R. Amato and Joan G. Gilbreth, "Nonresident Fathers and Children's Well-Being: A Meta-Analysis," *Journal of Marriage and the Family* 61 (August 1999): 557–573.

19. Susan D. Steward, "Disneyland Dads, Disneyland Moms? How Nonresident Parents Spend Time with Absent Children," *Journal of Family Issues* 20 (July 1999): 539–556.

20. Lynne Casper and Ken Bryson, *Household and Family Characteristics: March 1997* (Washington, D.C.: U.S. Bureau of the Census).

21. Wendy Manning and Daniel T. Lichter, "Parental Cohabitation and Children's Economic Well-Being." *Journal of Marriage and the Family* 58 (November 1996): 998–1010.

22. Larry Bumpass and Hsien-Hen Lu, *Trends in Cohabitation and Implications for Children's Family Contexts in the U.S.*, CDE Working Paper No. 98-15 (Center for Demography Ecology, University of Wisconsin-Madison, 1999).

23. *Dispelling Myths About Unmarried Fathers*, Fragile Families Research Brief, Number 1 (Bendhelm-Thoman Center For Research and Child Well-Being Princeton University and Social Indicators Survey Center, Columbia University, May 2000).

24. Bumpass and Lu, *Trends in Cohabitation*.

25. Kristin A. Moore, "Nonmarital Childbearing in the United States," in *Report to Congress on Out-of-Wedlock Childbearing* (Washington, D.C.: U.S. Department of Health and Human Services, September, 1995), vii.

26. David Popenoe and Barbara Dafoe Whitehead, *Should We Live Together? What Young Adults Need to Know About Cohabitation Before Marriage* (New Brunswick, NJ: The National Marriage Project, 1999), 7.

27. Deborah R. Graefe and Daniel T. Lichter, "Life Course Transitions of American Children: Parental Cohabitation, Marriage, and Single Motherhood," *Demography* 36 (May 1999).

28. Robert Whelan, *Broken Homes and Battered Children: A Study of the Relationship Between Child Abuse and Family Type* (London, England: Family Education Trust, 1993), 29, table

12; see also Martin Daly and Margo Wilson, "Evolutionary Psychology and Marital Conflict: The Relevance of Stepchildren," in David M. Buss and Neil Malamuth, ed., *Sex, Power, Conflict: Evolutionary and Feminist Perspectives* (New York: Oxford University Press, 1996), 9–28; Leslie Margolin, "Child Abuse by Mothers' Boyfriends: Why the Over-Representation?" *Child Abuse and Neglect* 16 (1992): 541–551.

29. E. G. Cooksey and P. H. Craig, "Parenting From a Distance: The Effects of Paternal Characteristics on Contact Between Nonresidential Fathers and Their Children," *Demography* 35 (1998): 187–200.

30. Robert Lerman and Theodora Ooms, *Young Unwed Fathers: Changing Roles and Emerging Policies* (Philadelphia: Temple, 1993), 45.

31. Linda S. Stephens, "Will Johnny See Daddy This Week?" *Journal of Family Issues* 17 (July 1996): 466–494.

32. L. Clarke, E. C. Cooksey, and G. Verropoulou, "Fathers and Absent Fathers: Sociodemographic Similarities in Britain and the United States," *Demography* 35 (1998): 217–228.

33. Linda J. Waite and Maggie Gallagher, *The Case for Marriage: Why Married People Are Happier, Healthier and Better Off Financially* (New York: Doubleday, 2000).

34. Nicholas Zill, Donna Ruane Morrison, and Mary Jo Coiro, "Long-Term Effects of Parental Divorce on Parent–Child Relationships, Adjustment, and Achievement in Young Adulthood," *Journal of Family Psychology* 7 (1993): 91–103.

35. Steven Stack and J. Ross Eshleman, "Marital Status and Happiness: A 17-Nation Study," *Journal of Marriage and the Family* 60 (May 1998): 527–536; see also Maggie Gallagher, *The Abolition of Marriage* (Washington, D.C.: Regnery, 1996); Linda J. Waite, "Does Marriage Matter?" *Demography* 32 (1995): 483–501.

36. Waite and Gallagher, *The Case for Marriage*, 150–160.

37. David Popenoe and Barbara Dafoe Whitehead, *The State of Our Unions, 1999* (New Brunswick, NJ: National Marriage Project, 1999).

38. *Dispelling Myths About Unmarried Fathers.*

## READING FOR INFORMATION

1. Why does an exclusive focus on child support enforcement downgrade fathers to the position of "cash machines"?

2. Explain why enhanced visitation will not necessarily encourage nonresident dads to become further involved with their children.

3. Why is cohabitation unlikely to result in more positive father involvement?

4. Summarize Horn's claims as to why marriage is the most "effective glue for binding fathers to their children."

## READING FOR FORM, ORGANIZATION, AND EXPOSITORY FEATURES

1. In the first section of the article, Horn draws heavily on scholarship, incorporating information from fifteen different sources. What effect does this strategy have on the reader?

2. Construct an outline that depicts the organization of Horn's argument. You may wish to consult the arrangements for argument essays in Chapter 4.

3. Cite the paragraphs in which Horn anticipates conflicting views, acknowledges them, and directly addresses them.

## READING FOR RHETORICAL CONCERNS

1. How does Horn's background prepare you for his argument?
2. Consider where the material was originally published? How does that information contribute to your understanding of the selection? Explain.

## WRITING ASSIGNMENTS

1. Write an essay in which you agree or disagree with Horn's claim that when it comes to the topic of absentee fathers, people are reluctant to talk about marriage.
2. Collaborative assignment. Break into three groups, each of which is responsible for researching one of the solutions to the problem of fatherlessness—child support enforcement, enhanced visitation rights, and cohabitation—and determining whether or not the particular solution will be more effective than Horn's recommendations with regard to stable marriages. After evaluating the arguments and evidence offered for each solution, each group will write an essay and report its findings to the class.

# Toward Revels or a Requiem for Family Diversity?

## *Judith Stacey*

*Judith Stacey, a professor of sociology at the University of Southern California, has written extensively on the family. Her books include* Balancing Act: Marriage, Motherhood, and Employment among American Women, Brave New Families: Stories of Domestic Upheaval in Late Twentieth-Century America, *and* In the Name of the Family: Rethinking Family Values in the Postmodern Age.

### PREREADING

Read the introductory statement, the *U.S. News and World Report* 1983 projection of what families will be like in the year 2033. In small groups, discuss (1) the extent to which the projection describes families today and (2) the accuracy of the scenario for families in 2033. Each group reports to the class. The class then comes to some consensus about the future of the family.

On a spring afternoon half a century from today, the Joneses are gathering to sing "Happy Birthday" to Junior.

There's Dad and his third wife, Mom and her second husband, Junior's two half brothers from his father's first marriage, his six stepsisters from his mother's spouse's previous unions, 100-year-old Great-Grandpa, all eight of Junior's current "grandparents," assorted aunts, uncles-in-law and stepcousins.

While one robot scoops up the gift wrappings and another blows out the candles, Junior makes a wish—that he didn't have so many relatives.

The family tree by the year 2033 will be rooted as deeply as ever in America's social landscape, but it will be sprouting some odd branches.

—*U.S. News & World Report*, 1983

Seventeen years ago, *U.S. News & World Report* ("When   1
'family' will have a new definition," 1983) posed the same impossible challenge to an assortment of social scientists that has been assigned me—to project the future trajectory of family change into the
next half century. I open with the magazine's synthesis of that earlier
collective crystal-ball exercise to simplify my present, more solitary one.
Our world today has traveled one-third of the distance to the year 2033.
Perhaps by assessing the ways in which contemporary family patterns
and meanings compare with the kind of kinship formation those 1983
forecasters predicted would have become normative by then, I can prepare a more prophetic one.

However bold and visionary those social scientists may have felt,   2
the presumptions governing the contours of Junior's imaginary kindred
that they projected should strike their counterparts today as almost
quaintly traditionalist. Indeed, what now seems odd about their portrait
of a modal twenty-first-century family is how innocently conventional,
parochial, and ethnocentric it already appears. The trajectory they predicted seems to presume a linear progression from the practices of serial marriage, divorce, and remarriage that have become increasingly
normative among primarily white, Euro-American, middle-class heterosexuals. The kindred they chose to conjure are the presumptively
white, Anglo-Saxon, protestant Joneses, after all, who gather to celebrate the birth of one of their patronymically christened "Junior" heirs
in a technologically well-equipped abode. Apparently all Junior's relatives either live within easy reach or enjoy sufficient affluence to afford
long-distance travel to attend birthday celebrations for even a step-
cousin. Curiously, too, all the assembled guests are related by birth,
marriage, or divorce. Junior appears to have no chosen kin or friend
that he or the party's hosts take to be as intimate or valued as even distant relatives. The social forecasters gave no indication that any of Junior's relatives might be lesbian, gay, or in any way "queer." He has
neither adoptive nor foster kin. None of his adult relatives seems to be a
single parent or to cohabit.

Indeed, the social scientists seem to have presumed that well into   3
the twenty-first century "dad" and "mom" would remain singular and
unproblematic concepts. They felt no cause to specify whether the
"dad" would be a sperm dad or a social father, or whether "mom" would
be a birth mom, a gestational mom, a custodial mom, or a co-mom.
They mentioned no surrogates, paraparents, godparents, or guardians.

They made no reference to progeny conceived with the assistance of reproductive technology nor alluded to the specter of cloning. No workplace demands prevented a relative from attending, nor did ill health, death, custody disputes, or incarceration threaten to diminish the number or joy of Junior's assembled kin. In short, even though we have not yet traversed half the distance to the family future that prominent social scientists envisioned in 1983, the branches that our families are sprouting now are already much "odder" and far more diverse than they then dared to imagine.

Equally quaint today appears the social scientists' confidence that "the family tree" will remain so "firmly rooted," not to speak of so harmoniously extended. Few of those scholars' contemporary counterparts seem as sanguine about the character or security of family ties. Note how many anxious titles adorn books about U.S. family life that were published in the 1990s—*Brave New Families* (Stacey, 1990). *Embattled Paradise* (Skolnick, 1991). *Fatherless America* (Blankenhorn, 1995), *No Man's Land* (Gerson, 1993), *Families on the Fault Line* (Rubin, 1994), *Declining Fortunes* (Newman, 1993), *Promises to Keep* (Popenoe, Elshtain, & Blankenhorn, 1996), *Life Without Father* (Popenoe, 1996), *Balancing Act* (Spain & Bianchi, 1996), *Divorce Culture* (Whitehead, 1997), *The Abolition of Marriage* (Gallagher, 1996), *Divided Families* (Furstenberg & Cherlin, 1991), *The Way We Really Are* (Coontz, 1997), *The Minimal Family* (Dizard & Gadlin 1991), and *The Neutered Mother, the Sexual Family and Other Twentieth Century Tragedies* (Fineman, 1995). Note, too, the incessant outpouring of jeremiads about family crisis, instability, and decline that flourished in the media and the political arena as the twentieth century expired. Despite the fact that the right-wing "profamily" movement had already played a prominent part in the Reagan "revolution," the social scientists queried in 1983 seem to have believed that the movement's impact on future family forms would be inconsequential. Clearly, they did not anticipate how rapidly campaigns for "family values" would proliferate across the ideological spectrum, let alone that within a decade, some social scientists themselves would be spearheading a secular "cultural crusade" for family values with vast influence on public discourse and politics.[1]

---

[1] I discuss the use and abuse of social science by secular family-values crusaders at length in Stacey (1996).

## BEST- AND WORST-CASE FUTURES FOR FAMILY DIVERSITY

As the twenty-first century begins, are we on the road to repressive
Gilead or to a family diversity jubilee? Will the backlash against plural-
ist family patterns and values triumph, or will birthday celebrations in
the year 2033 draw a multiracial, gender-bending, rainbow blend of
"natural," social, adoptive, legal, fictive, para- and "queer" kin? Will our
society adapt to postmodern family conditions by taking measures to realize more of the democratic potential of the forms of family diversity
they generate and to mitigate the disruptive harms they inflict? Or will
we continue to pursue the politics of nostalgic denial and displacement
that fuel our retreat from collective responsibility for family welfare, ex-
acerbate postindustrial conflicts between family and work, and inflict
harm on the majority of actual families?

Present indicators are decidedly contradictory. On the one hand,
the climate of political reaction and the triumph of the global market
furnish abundant road signs of a route to Gilead. Campaigns for family
values continue to achieve victories, like DOMA and the advent of
"covenant marriage." Moreover, assaults on welfare; tax cuts that continue to widen the gap between rich and poor families; the erosion of secure, living-wage jobs for undereducated men; and escalating rates of
incarceration for men of color are turning marriage into a form of class
and race privilege, just as it was in Atwood's (1985) imaginary Gilead.
Conditions like these guarantee that marital instability will continue, regardless of family values. Even if the current move to curb divorces
gains force, as seems possible, it is unlikely to increase dramatically the
proportion of marriages that remain intact physically and emotionally, as
well as legally. Couples can be prevented from obtaining legal divorces,
but only a blatantly coercive regime like Gilead or the Taliban in
Afghanistan can do much to prevent desertion, flight, or "no-fault" sepa-
rations. Consequently, the rate of de facto marital dissolution is likely to
remain high, fluctuating, I would conjecture, around the current range
of 45 percent to 60 percent. Indeed, the fact that marrying couples now
face even odds on achieving conjugal endurance until death do them
part is perhaps about as much as one should expect within a marriage
system that is based on the principles of romantic love, monogamy, companionship, and the free choice of individuals. After all, few cultures
have ever expected the conjugal relationship to meet as many needs for
intimacy and gratification as ours does, let alone to do so under such
contradictory conditions and with such poor social support.

Clearly, the present climate gives scant cause to expect a turn to the kind of humane realism and economic democracy that would nurture the more democratic implications of the postmodern family condition. Nonetheless, the prospects for placing those disruptive genies—particularly the global economy and reproductive technology—back in their lamps strike me as even dimmer. Many of the same economic exigencies that fuel the reaction will also ensure that maternal employment is here to stay, and the backlash against welfare mothers actively, promotes this situation. Likewise, reproductive technology is not going to disappear, and whereas donor insemination is actually a low-tech, readily available process, the state cannot readily regulate women's access to voluntary sperm donors. Indeed, even the current political outcry to curb research that might achieve human cloning is apt to prove no more effective than spitting in wind. Test-tube babies themselves no longer seem to belong to the realm of science fiction.

Similarly, despite the backlash, struggles for gender equity and gay rights are unlikely to cease. For one thing, most women "can't go home again" (Stacey, 1986) even if they wanted to, and substantial numbers do not want to, not even if they had husbands who could afford to support them. Most postindustrial women want to combine parenting with paid work, and want men to pull their load in both domains (Hochschild 1989; Presser, 1995). Hence, we can confidently anticipate that women will continue to struggle for relief from the gymnastic "balancing act" between family and work demands and from the "stalled revolution" of shared domestic labor (Hochschild 1989; Spain & Bianchi, 1996). Demands for affordable, acceptable child care; paid family leaves; flextime; and paternal involvement in child rearing are more likely to increase than to disappear.

Moreover, there are millions of lesbian and gay parents and families. I find it difficult to imagine that they or their successors will acquiesce in a return to the closet or to family purgatory. On the contrary, one of the few progressive arenas of family reform that I feel comfortable predicting during this reactionary era will be the gradual legalization of same-sex marriage and of gay and lesbian custody rights. Although the majority of citizens—58 percent in a 1996 *Newsweek* poll ("Support for Clinton's stand on gay marriage," 1996)—still oppose same-sex marriage, the trend in public opinion surveys has been moving rapidly in the progressive direction. To gain some perspective on contemporary public-disapproval ratings for gay marriage, it is instructive to remember the history of the legalization of interracial marriage. It was not until 1967 that the U.S. Supreme Court ruled that state bans on interracial marriages were unconstitutional. Nonetheless, five years later, when the Gallup Organization began to survey white attitudes toward such marriages, only 25 percent of the whites who were polled expressed their approval, and even 30 years after the *Loving v. Virginia* decision, the white approval rating was only 61 percent (Holmes, 1997). In contrast, a higher percentage of heterosexuals already claim to support same-sex marriage than the proportion of whites who supported interracial marriage five years after it became the law of the land.

## TOMORROWLAND

Is the glass that holds the fate of postmodern family fortunes half empty 10 or half full? The very week of the antigay conference at Georgetown, the Southern Baptists voted to boycott the Walt Disney Company—the corporation that was once thought to be synonymous with mainstream family values. The denomination took this action to protest the corporation's recent "gay-friendly" policies, such as its provision of domestic-partner benefits to employees and sponsorship of *Ellen*, the first television sitcom to feature a lesbian lead character. The Southern Baptists' action represents a paradigmatic instance of the contentious contemporary politics of family values. If the future of family diversity were to hinge on the fate of the denomination's contest with Disney's "tomorrowland," I would readily lay odds that new branches will continue to sprout on the nation's family trees. How comfortably these branches will be embraced or how widely scorned is much more difficult to guess.

    Which branches will enjoy a place at the table when our Juniors 11 gather to celebrate their birthdays in the year 2033? The future of family diversity depends on how we pursue the politics of family values today.

Atwood, M. (1985). *The handmaid's tale*. New York: Ballantine Books.

Blankenhorn, D. (1995). *Fatherless America: Confronting our most urgent social problem*. New York: Basic Books.

Coontz, S. (1997). *The way we really are*. New York: Basic Books.

Dizard, J. E., & Gadlin, H. (1991). *The minimal family*. Amberst, MA: University of Massachusetts Press.

Fineman, M. (1995). *The neutered mother, the sexual family and other twentieth century tragedies*. New York: Routledge.

Furstenberg, F. F., Jr., & Cherlin, A. (1991). *Divided families.* Cambridge, MA: Harvard University Press.

Gallagher, M. (1996). *The abolition of marriage: How we destroy lasting love.* Washington, DC: Regenery.

Gerson, K. (1993). *No man's land: Men's changing commitments to family and work.* New York: Basic Books.

Hochschild, A., with Machung, A. (1989). *The second shift: Working parents and the revolution at home.* New York: Viking Press.

Holmes, S. A. (1997, June 15). A rose-colored view of race. *New York Times*, p. E4.

Newman, K. (1993). *Declining fortunes: The withering of the American dream.* New York: Basic Books.

Popenoe, D. (1996). *Life without father.* New York: Free Press.

Popenoe, D., Elshtain, J. B., & Blankenhorn, D. (Eds.). (1996). *Promises to keep: Decline and renewal of marriage in America.* Lanham, MD: Rowman & Littlefield.

Presser, H. B. (1995). Are the interests of women inherently at odds with the interests of children or the family? A Viewpoint. In K. Oppenheim Mason & A.-M. Jensen (Eds.), *Gender and family change in industrialized countries* (pp. 297–319). Oxford, England: Clarendon Press.

Rubin, L. (1994). *Families on the fault line: America's working class speaks about the family, the economy, race, and ethnicity.* New York: HarperCollins.

Skolnick, A. (1991). *Embattled paradise: The American family in an age of uncertainty.* New York: Basic Books.

Spain, D., & Bianchi, S. (1996). *Balancing act: Marriage, motherhood, and employment among American women.* New York: Russell Sage Foundation.

Stacey, J. (1990). *Brave new families: Stories of domestic upheaval in late twentieth century America.* New York: Basic Books.

Whitehead, B. D. (1997). *The divorce culture.* New York: Alfred A. Knopf.

## READING FOR INFORMATION

1. What are Stacey's views on the current movement to curb divorces?

2. What does Stacey foresee as the future of new reproductive technologies?

3. Why is Stacey optimistic about the legalization of same sex marriage?

## READING FOR FORM, ORGANIZATION, AND EXPOSITORY FEATURES

1. Explain the function of the opening paragraph for *U.S. News and World Report.* How would the impact of Stacey's article change if she had forecast the future of the family without using this passage?

2. Paraphrase Stacey's answers to the questions she poses in paragraph 5.

3. Do you agree or disagree with Stacey's claim that women "can't go home again" (paragraph 8)?

## READING FOR RHETORICAL CONCERNS

1. What do you see as Stacey's rhetorical purpose? Why has she written this piece, and what does she want to get across to her audience?

2. How would you describe Stacey's tone? What does that tone suggest about the author?

## WRITING ASSIGNMENTS

1. From your point of view, what will Junior's birthday party be like in the year 2033? Write an essay in which you predict the future of the family. You may draw on Stacey's article or other selections in this chapter.

2. Search your college library holdings for one of the books on U.S. family life that Stacey mentions in paragraph 4. Read the book and write an essay in which you summarize and evaluate the author's argument.

3. Stacey mentions certain measures for strengthening the family: covenant marriages and the Defense of Marriage Act. Conduct research on one of these measures and summarize your findings in a brief essay.

## SYNTHESIS WRITING ASSIGNMENTS

1. Use Erera's arguments in "What Is A Family?" to write a defense of the family arrangements described in Mistysyn's "Brave New Family" and Barret and Robinson's "Children of Gay Fathers."

2. In "What Is A Family?" Erera explains how new reproductive technologies have enabled people to create various forms of alternative, nontraditional families. How do you think cloning might affect marriage and the family? After reading the selections in Chapter 6, write an essay explaining your position.

3. Of all the statements Popenoe makes in "Seven Tenets for Establishing Marital Norms," which would Erera find most problematic? Identify the statement and write an essay in which you speculate how Erera would respond to it.

4. In your view, is cohabitation a true testing ground for marriage, or is it simply "playing house"? Write an essay in response to this question and support your position by drawing on the selections in this chapter.

5. Write an essay in which you compare and contrast Popenoe's and Horn's arguments as to why marriage is the preferred family arrangement.

6. Writing about reproductive technologies, Stacey predicts, "Indeed, even the current political outcry to curb research that might achieve human cloning is apt to prove no more effective than spitting in the wind."

Drawing on the articles in Chapter 6, agree or disagree with Stacey's view.

7. Drawing upon the selections in this chapter, write an argument essay in which you defend your position with regard to the future of the American family.

# *t e n*

# Social Class and Inequality

The selections in Chapter 10 examine ideas about social class from different perspectives and offer explanatory principles for the unequal distribution of income, power, and prestige. The authors discuss class conflict, examine factors that profoundly affect the existence and continuance of poverty, and offer solutions for dealing with these persistent problems. The evidence these authors supply has political, psychological, cultural, and moral ramifications as well as social consequences.

In the first selection, "What Are 'Class' and 'Inequality'?" Jeremy Seabrook situates social class in a global historical context and explains how the concept of "class" has been redefined as "inequality." Patricia Clark Smith, in "Grandma Went to Smith, All Right, But She Went from Nine to Five: A Memoir," and Leonce Gaiter, in "The Revolt of the Black Bourgeoisie," illustrate through personal experiences how individuals can be made to feel out of place because of their social, economic, or racial background. Patricia Clark Smith discusses the pain she and her family experienced when they were unjustly stereotyped on the basis of their economic status. In a similar vein, Gaiter argues that middle- and upper-class blacks suffer discrimination when they are lumped with economically and socially deprived blacks instead of being treated as individuals.

Next, Herbert J. Gans debunks the concept of "underclass" and similar stereotypes, and in "The War Against the Poor Instead of Programs to End Poverty" offers an intellectual and cultural defense of poor people. In "White Standard for Poverty," Dirk Johnson gives us a glimpse of two faces of poverty in the Native American population and warns us against imposing white standards of poverty on Indians. The final selection in this chapter is "Serving in Florida," Barbara Ehrenreich's account of her experiences as a low-wage worker trying to survive on six to seven dollars an hour as a server in restaurants in Key West, Florida.

# What Are "Class" and "Inequality"?

## *Jeremy Seabrook*

*Jeremy Seabrook is the author of more than thirty books. His most recent books are the* No-Nonsense Guide to Class, Caste, & Hierarchies, *from which this selection is taken,* Children from Other Worlds, Love in a Different Climate, *and* Colonies of the Heart. *He has contributed to numerous journals and newspapers, and currently writes for* The Statesman *in Calcutta.*

### PREREADING

Write a response to the question posed by the title of the selection. What do you see as the difference between social class and inequality?

All societies are stratified, in one way or another, in hierarchies of power and wealth. The few egalitarian exceptions, of indigenous and tribal peoples, have been destroyed or degraded by contact with the modern world. Privilege has many methods of self-preservation, not least physical force, but sometimes through a mystical appeal to the special intellectual or spiritual powers the privileged claim to possess. Some societies are built on slavery, most upon the oppression of those who perform the most vital labor of that society. Throughout history, there have been struggles of the oppressed against their

By Jeremy Seabrook, from *The No-Nonsense Guide to Class, Caste, & Hierarchies,* © 2002. Reprinted by permission of New Internationalist Publications, Ltd.

"superiors," although even when the "natural" order has been over-thrown, it has rarely been long before new powerful groups established their own supremacy, their own lineage, their own religion or power over others.

At the time of the Industrial Revolution social classes became    2
more sharply antagonistic, as older mystiques legitimating social stratifi-cation decayed, and the rich confronted the poor in stark antagonism. Social class, in its contemporary understanding, was defined primarily in Europe. The United States, with its egalitarian origins in reaction against the feudal order of Europe, saw itself as liberated from archaic categories of aristocracy and the lower orders. It was only later that the profound inequalities of slavery were addressed, and while the idea of class remained foreign to the U.S. tradition, institutionalized social in-justice has persisted. Today this is discussed in terms of "inequality" rather than of opposing social classes. The modern idea of class was born in Europe, became an obsession in Britain, and was denied in the United States.

## GLOBAL INEQUALITY

According to the United Nations *Human Development Report*,[1] the    3
world's richest 20 percent receive 86 percent of the world's gross prod-uct; the middle 60 percent, 13 percent; while the poorest 20 percent re-ceive one percent. The ratio between the incomes of the top and bottom fifth of humanity is seventy-four to one. In 1960 it was thirty to one.

But there is another story, which perhaps helps to explain why    4
these often quoted, extreme inequalities are not only tolerated by the peoples of the world, but regarded as part of the natural order of things; why, in other words, there is so little pressure to resist the continuously growing economic injustice in the world.

Datamonitor UK also notes that there are nearly 4 million people    5
(that is, 8 percent of the population over sixteen years of age) who have liquid assets of between $45,000 (£30,000) and $300,000 (£200,000).[2] The numbers in this group have been growing by 12 percent a year for the past five years. Their wealth consists of cash or shares, before the value of any property or pension funds they hold is taken into account.

A survey based on fieldwork from the Office for National Statistics    6
found that at the end of 1999, 26 percent of the British population was living in poverty, measured in terms of low income and multiple

deprivation of necessities. This pattern is repeated (with minor variations) in all industrialized countries.

## GLOBAL RICH

There exists a global rich class, made up of inheritors of wealth, but increasingly of celebrities; entrepreneurs; the makers of spectacular fortunes; the new rich of Information Technology, life sciences, and... other recent technological windfalls; sports and media stars; musicians; and show people. There is also a fast-growing and powerful global middle class. This serves, in one way or another, the process of the creation of surplus value, or profit, often for big transnational corporations and the bureaucracies that support them. These people are a significant force in the world. Their role is twofold. They offer a model to the aspiring poor, and they help police poverty; for privilege, even modest privilege, may expand and grow only if the gap between rich and poor is

---

### WEALTH AND POVERTY

- 1.3 billion people lack access to clean water: 1.2 billion live on less than a dollar a day: 840 million are mainourished.
- More than 20,000 people die each day from hunger-related diseases.
- The assets of the world's 200 richest individuals more than doubled between 1994 and 1998 to over $1 trillion.
- The richest three people in the world have assets greater than the combined output of the 48 poorest countries.
- In the 1990s, 55 countries experienced real per capita income decrease.
- There are around 7 million millionaires in the world, half of them in the United States.
- 12 of the 20 richest people in the world are Americans.
- Independent market analysis research from Datamonitor in Britain,[2] states that the number of millionaries in Britain is growing at the rate of 17 percent a year; and by 2001 there were 74,000 millionaires.
- Data from the UK's Office for National Statistics stated that 1999–2000 saw the highest gap between rich and poor yet recorded. The poorest fifth of households had 6 percent of national income after tax, while the share held by the top fifth rose from 44 to 45 percent.

maintained, or increased, as is the case in almost every country in the world.

*Inequality* is an abstraction. Its great advantage to the rich is that   8
it replaces earlier concepts of class. These were embodied in real living figures of flesh and blood and their relationship to each other. Inequality is a statistical term in which the participants appear only as victims or beneficiaries. If human beings have any part to play in remedies for inequality, these will be highly qualified experts and professionals. Ordinary people are absent from inequality; in class relationships the people are omnipresent.

## GROWING INEQUALITY

The U.N. *Human Development Report* tells only part of the story, for   9
the 60 percent in the middle who receive the 13 percent of income are by no means a homogeneous group. Their inclusion as a single entity is misleading, for it implies that only the bottom 20 percent are poor—those living on less than a dollar a day. But *three billion* people live on less than two dollars a day and far more than that on less than five dollars a day. So the figures that lump together 60 percent need to be broken down to give a clearer picture, not only of the extremes—which are shocking enough—but also of the inequalities hidden by the bulging middle.

These figures are widely published, accessible, and in whatever   10
form they are presented, they lead to the same conclusion. Growing inequality is continuously monitored by international institutions and by academic establishments within countries. There is no attempt to conceal or justify this process. It is just the way things are.

This acceptance of inequality is at odds with a world which con-   11
stantly advertises its miracles of technology, its mastery of the secrets of nature, its capacity for transforming the lives of the people. The global economy creates the impression of a busy, restless, can-do culture sweeping with irresistible force across the face of the earth. Nothing, it seems, can withstand the impact of the communications revolution, the conquest of space, breakthroughs in medicine, the mapping of the human genome, and all the other promises of emancipation for humanity. Why are governments and international institutions apparently impotent when confronted by the widening divide between rich and poor? In a world where everything is possible, why should this central issue present such a difficult problem?

Why do the poor accept an arbitrary withholding from them of the 12
necessities of life, when the rich take for themselves a disproportionate
share of the wealth of the world? This question requires an understanding of the history—and continuing existence—of class relationships and
their reconfiguration in the wake of globalization. For social classes
have not been eliminated by the treacherous continuum of inequality,
but have been remade, often in ways which make them obscure to the
participants. The story (and it is a story) is a simple one; yet it consists
of layers of complexity and *complicatedness*, which sometimes make it
difficult to follow the thread.

## WHY CLASS BECAME CRUCIAL

Class stratification means the division of society into unequal strata or 13
groups. The differences between them express social relationships and
constitute the social identity of the members of each group. Some mobility between classes is usually possible. Caste, on the other hand, as-
cribes a position to people usually through birth, and it is more difficult
for individuals to move beyond the inherited position in the caste hierarchy. There are elements of both class and caste in most societies.

Discussions of class in industrial society have been colored by 14
philosopher Karl Marx, who reduced class interests to two—the owners
of capital and those who have nothing but their labor power to sell. It is
the objective of the former to make profit out of the surplus value produced by the workers. The relationship is exploitative, antagonistic, and
according to Marx, highly unstable. It must lead to conflict, which will
end either in the triumph of the workers or in the ruin of the contending classes—the famous choice between socialism and barbarism.

The word *class,* meaning the economic and social position of 15
groups of people, is of fairly recent origin. Its present-day use dates
from the mid-eighteenth century. Its roots are in the Latin *classis,* referring to the six orders the Romans were divided into for the purposes
of taxation. Before the idea of class became significant in the West, concepts of *rank* and *station* described the social position of individuals. In
Britain, the word *order*—dating from around 1300—indicated the collective position of groups of people.

In the medieval world, society was divided into *estates*. They com- 16
prised three legal classifications—the nobility, the clergy, and the common people. Class came into usage in France, partly as a consequence
of the work of the *Encyclopedistes*, a group of eighteenth-century

## THE 20 RICHEST PEOPLE IN THE WORLD, 2000

Lists are produced each year of the wealthiest people; each list has a slightly different order but the same names crop up with astonishing regularity.

| | | Value (US $ billions) | Country | Age | Source of wealth |
|---|---|---|---|---|---|
| 1 | Gates, Bill | 58.7 | US | 45 | Microsoft |
| 2 | Buffett, Warren | 32.3 | US | 70 | investments |
| 3 | Allen, Paul | 30.4 | US | 48 | Microsoft |
| 4 | Ellison, Larry | 26.0 | US | 56 | Oracle computers |
| 5 | Albrecht, Theo & Karf | 25.0 | Germany | — | supermarkets |
| 6 | Prince Alaweed Bin Talal | 20.0 | Saudi Arabia | 44 | investments |
| 7 | Walton, Jim | 18.8 | US | 53 | Wal-Mart |
| 8 | Walton, John | 18.7 | US | 55 | Wal-Mart |
| 9 | Walton, Robson | 18.6 | US | 57 | Wal-Mart |
| 10 | Walton, Alice | 18.5 | US | 52 | Wal-Mart |
| 11 | Walton, Helen | 18.5 | US | 81 | Wal-Mart |
| 12 | Quandt, Joanna | 17.8 | Germany | 74 | BMW |
| 13 | Ballmer, Steve | 16.6 | US | 45 | Microsoft |
| 14 | Thomson, Kenneth | 16.4 | Canada | 77 | publishing |
| 15 | Bettencourt, Liliane | 15.6 | France | 75 | L'Oréal |
| 16 | Anachutz, Philip | 15.3 | Sweden | 75 | Ikea |
| 18 | Redstone, Sumner | 12.6 | US | 78 | Viacom |
| | Li Ka Ly | 12.6 | Hong Kong | 73 | diversified |
| 20 | Kirch, Leo | 12.0 | Germany | 74 | media |

*Forbes 500.*

French intellectuals who attempted to assemble all the knowledge available to the modern world. This led them to systematic classification of plants, animals, and minerals, and phenomena of the natural world. It was then a short step to apply the methodology to the social and economic position of individuals in society. In Britain, the philanthropist Jonas Hanway was the first to refer to the "lower classes of people" in 1772. The economist Adam Smith, in his *Wealth of Nations* (1776), used the word class in a general sense, but when he spoke of the division of labor, with its different functions, he spoke of "the ranks and conditions" of people in society.

The concept of *class* fitted in with changes brought about by industrial society, and it gained wide currency with early industrialism in the first half of the nineteenth century. The medieval idea of estates had suggested an organic relationship. Classes, although mutually dependent, were also antagonistic; it was Marx who elevated this clash into his fateful theory of irreconcilable interests between *bourgeoisie* and *proletariat*. Marx specifically stated that class was an expression of a relationship to the means of production—the capitalists who owned the mills, mines, and factories and the workers who had nothing but their labor power to sell.

The origins of the word proletariat are in the Latin *proletarii*. This referred to the poorest classes, those whose only resources lay in their offspring. The word found its way into French in the eighteenth century but occurred in its modern sense in English only in 1853, when it was used disparagingly of the lowest classes.

*Bourgeois* has a more complicated history. From Latin *burgus* and German *Burg*, meaning a town under the protection of a castle, it came to mean citizen in medieval France, as opposed to peasant or noble. The word was used in France to indicate the mercantile middle class (those involved in trade and commerce) from the seventeenth century. Before the revolution, the nobility used the word as a term of contempt towards those whose money they certainly did not despise. Both words—*bourgeois* and *proletarian*—still have an alien sound to English speakers.

### WHAT'S IN A NAME?

In Britain, definitions of class continued to be influenced by older ideas of rank, despite the social upheaval of industrialization. The lower orders, the laboring classes, and the middling ranks of society existed alongside the aristocracy and gentry. As the stratification of industrial society became more rigid, these definitions settled into the now familiar classification of upper, middle, and working *class*.

The discrepancy in these categories was pointed out by philosopher and social critic Raymond Williams.[3] He wrote, "Most people in Britain think of themselves as 'middle class' or 'working class.' But the first point to make is that these are not true alternatives. The alternatives to 'middle' are 'lower' and 'upper'; the alternative to 'working' is 'independent' or 'propertied.' The wonderful muddle we are now in springs mainly from this confusion, that one term has a primarily social, the other a primarily economic reference."

"Middle" suggests simply a position in society. "Working" sug- 22 gests a function. This helps, perhaps, to explain why a working class has become virtually invisible in the contemporary Western world. In the United States in particular, but increasingly in Europe also, this is a category in which people decreasingly recognize themselves. U.S. politicians regularly refer to the middle classes and sometimes to working people, but mention of a working class is said to turn people off.

The idea of a growing middle class expresses a relationship not so 23 much to the means of production, as to *other people*. It introduces an element of *status*, which derives from sociologist Max Weber's efforts to define more clearly the complexity of expanding industrial society towards the end of the nineteenth century, a time when the wider range of economic possibilities blurred the easy classification of capitalists and workers. For Weber, class is multidimensional, and includes both the relationship to the means of production and to the means of consumption. Class becomes more diffuse and complex.

In the United States, the idea of working class, although it figured 24 in politics, was virtually absent from academic discussion until the Great Depression in the mid-twentieth century. It is a paradox that the most advanced capitalist society dispensed with categories which Marx and most European commentators regarded as vital to discussion of social relationships in industrial societies. Status replaced class as the key indicator on the continuum of rich and poor in the United States. Status was acquired through power rather than power through status: The American belief that anyone can rise from humble origins to become President of the United States continued to exercise a powerful hold over the imagination even when it had clearly become myth (most U.S. Presidents have come from wealthy, often highly privileged backgrounds).

Even so, the United States promised freedoms that would wipe 25 out European hierarchies. It offered greater opportunities to get rich and to consume than were available to the majority in Europe. In the United States, moreover, the proportion of people in the industrial sector never reached levels seen in early industrial Britain. The growth of middle-class occupations stifled the emergence of a dominant working-class consciousness.

---

### THE UNITED STATES AND THE MYSTERY
### OF THE DISAPPEARING WORKING CLASS

The working class has been believed, ever since Marx, to be insepara-
ble from working-class organization. From the relative weakness of such
movements in the United States (although of course there were many
activists and struggles) it has been concluded that the working class
scarcely exists. In a country marked by continuous diversity of migra-
tion, other struggles and identities have taken priority—people have
seen themselves as black, Jewish, Irish, Italian, Hispanic before they
see themselves as working class. In 2001, more than 30.5 million Americans were born outside the country—more than 11 percent of the population. The ideology of the Americanization of immigrants has been a
more powerful unifying force than perceptions of class, especially to
those who saw the United States as a destination, a haven from poverty
and persecution elsewhere.

---

## RICH AS ROCKEFELLER

In the period since the Second World War, the positional aspect of sta- 26
tus has supplanted the functional aspect of class for many (former
working-class) people in Europe as well as in the United States. Sociologist Vance Packard suggested people were ceasing to identify themselves as members of this or that social class, but were creating a new
sense of belonging through objects of consumption.[4] Communities of
shared tastes and lifestyles were being defined against those of different
(lower or higher) patterns of expenditure. Status, in contemporary society, is close to station in preindustrial hierarchies, with the important
difference that station implies socially fixed positions, while status-
oriented society is extremely mobile. The jackpot winner, the singer
with the hit record, the TV star, and the successful entrepreneur can
surround themselves with the trappings of luxury as fast as they can buy
them.

In preindustrial society, it was acknowledged that "birth" or 27
"breeding" distinguished those at the top of the social pyramid. The
upper classes were separated from the "lower orders" by the "middling
rank" of society. In status-conscious societies, objects of conspicuous
consumption are identified with forms of honor, which formerly clus-
tered around other characteristics—inherited position, property, military prowess. The contemporary iconography of high status is more

open—anyone who can afford it can go through the obligatory shopping list of ornate villas with tight security, champagne and caviar, diamonds, yachts, Rolls Royce cars, Armani suits, and accessories bearing the "correct" brand-name.

Before industrialization, social belonging was a function simply of 28 position in society. It was only with the Industrial Revolution that a working class—or proletariat, as Marx called it—emerged. The fact that the *function* of this class is its principal characteristic suggests that industrial labor was a profoundly disruptive force. It was destined not only to disturb social hierarchies which had persisted since the feudal times of the Middle Ages (c800–1300) but also to overshadow the antagonism which had grown between the old aristocracy of landed classes and the class of entrepreneurs who were, by the end of the eighteenth century, knocking at the doors of political power and privilege.

## FOREVER FEUDAL

Feudalism was essentially a caste system and is significant because it 29 still characterizes many agrarian societies in the world. It lays the groundwork for the structures of class, caste, and hierarchies that exist today. To find out about it, we step back in time to the Middle Ages in England.

The word *feudal* comes from the same root as the German word 30 *Viehl*, meaning cattle, reflecting an earlier nomadic society in which cattle were the principal source of wealth. The king stood at the apex above a strongly hierarchical system of landed dependency. Lords obtained land for past services (mainly military) and in expectation of similar future loyalty. The *vassal* was the personal follower of his immediate lord. Lords granted land to their vassals not in ownership, but in *usufruct*, which means they had access to the produce of that land. This was granted originally on a personal basis, but eventually became hereditary. The land held by a vassal was the expression of an invisible bond to his superior. Lords had power to hold their own courts, a power derived ultimately from the king. This secular hierarchy was paralleled by a religious one of bishops and priests and monks—the second "estate" of the three great estates that constituted medieval society.

Feudalism was eroded in the late Middle Ages by the growth of 31 towns and the rise of a money-based rather than a land-based economy. It became impracticable for lords to retain knights in their service

waiting for the call of war. The knights commuted their military obligations for money; and eventually money replaced land as a symbol of
power. Similarly, the emancipation of *villeins* (*serfs* or tied peasants cultivating a lord's land) grew, and tenure by service gave way to tenure by
rent—the lord's fields were tilled by hired laborers.

The Black Death wiped out surplus labor; it became impossible 32
legally to bind labor to the soil. Villeins escaped from their own lords to
become laborers for hire. Lords became landlords, and villeins landless
laborers. Although birth remained the principal determinant of status,
the growth of mercantilism—merchants and trading—and manufacturing led to a steady accession of the particularly talented into higher
ranks of society, usually by means of royal and political patronage. But
until the industrial era, the sense of hierarchy persisted: the superior,
middle, and lower ranks in society.

## PRIVILEGE PREVAILS

Privilege in every society spins myths to legitimize its power or its mo- 33
nopoly over resources. Ruling castes or classes perpetuate themselves
by a mystical appeal to antiquity, lineage, divine sanction, or breeding,
which justify their right to rule. Historian Walter Bagehot[5] claimed
that the nobility preserves a country from too great a worship of
money and that reverence for rank is less base than reverence for
money. In 1835, after the passage of the 1832 Reform Bill, British
Prime Minister Benjamin Disraeli wrote, "For nearly five centuries
the hereditary Peerage...has formed an active and powerful branch
of our legislature.... No statesman can doubt that the peculiar character of the hereditary branch of our legislature has mainly contributed
to the stability of our institutions, and to the order and prosperous security which that stability has produced. Nor can we forget that the
hereditary principle has at all times secured a senate for this country
inferior in intelligence to no political assembly on record...."[6] He
refers to "an ancient people, who have made inheritance the pervading principle of their social polity, who are proud of their old families
and fond of their old laws."

An idealized version of hierarchical relationships reinforced the 34
British idea of its own past; this took root, paradoxically, in the psyche
of the industrial bourgeoisie, who made their fortunes out of manufacture. Historian Martin Wiener[7] speaks of the "consolidation of a 'gentri-
fied' bourgeois culture, particularly the rooting of pseudo-aristocratic

attitudes and values in upper-middle class educated opinion." Wiener sees this as harmful to economic efficiency and a cause of the relative economic decline of Britain. However that may be, it is remarkable that whatever the disdain for financial gain on the part of the old nobility, they managed to salvage a great deal of their material advantage, as well as their power and honor, in the generations after the Industrial Revolution.

In the end, the interests of the nobility merged with those of the 35 new moneyed middle class; a compromise born of expediency, especially when confronted by a rising working class. The heritage of the old rich was maintained by the wealth of the new, a marriage of convenience.

In our time, this has yielded to a more overt stratification by 36 money, exemplified by pop stars and sports heroes—people like Madonna or Magic Johnson—where money and talent create a new class of celebrities, which is honored and admired—and plays a significant role in reconciling the poor to their status. These people have, in some measure, replaced the aristocracy and monarchy. The decline in reverence for the royal family in Britain reflects this change: Positions derived from birth no longer inspire the respect commanded by wealth from the intensive marketing of talent, youth, and glamour. The Spice Girls pop group, five women who answered a newspaper advertisement in the early 1990s, had personal fortunes by 2001 of at least $33 million (£22 million) each. This rise of exceptional individuals is of course familiar in the United States, where people were founding their own plutocratic—wealth makes them powerful—dynasties, while British entrepreneurs aped the aristocracy.

Not that the old ruling class has become impoverished. Among 37 the richest people in the world, the Queen of England, the Sultan of Brunei, and the King of Saudi Arabia are still present, along with Bill Gates and other representatives of spectacular contemporary enterprise. The wealth of the Duke of Westminster amounts to $5.6 billion (£3.75 billion). If the private assets of the Queen are included, she is probably among the twenty richest people in the world.

The Rich List, compiled each year by the London *Sunday Times*, 38 recorded an increase between 1999 and 2000 of almost $47 billion (£31 billion) in the wealth of the thousand richest people in Britain. Of these, "only" 258 inherited their millions, compared with two-thirds in 1989. Whether wealth is old or new is rather academic in a world in which inequality is growing so spectacularly.

1. *United Nations Development Report*, UNDP/OUP 2000.
2. Datamonitor, United Kingdom, 2001.
3. *The Long Revolution*, Raymond Williams, Chatto and Windus, 1961.
4. *The Status Seekers*, Vance Packard, 1959, Bedford/St Martin's Press, 1995.
5. *The English Constitution*, Walter Bagehot, 1904 (cited in *The English Ruling Class*, W. L. Guttsman, Weidenfeld and Nicholson, 1969).
6. "A Vindication of the English Constitution" in *Whigs and Whiggism: Political Writings*, Benjamin Disraeli, London, 1913.
7. *English Culture and the Decline of the Industrial Spirit 1850–1980*, Martin Wiener, Penguin, 1985. ✤

## READING FOR INFORMATION

1. What is Seabrook's explanation for people's tolerance for the extreme inequalities that exist in the world?
2. Explain what Seabrook means when he says, "For social classes have not been eliminated by the treacherous continuum of inequality, but they have been remade, often in ways which make them obscure to the participants" (paragraph 12).
3. Explain the difference between the following concepts: class and caste; status and station; bourgeoisie and proletariat?
4. Who are the "global rich," and how have they replaced the aristocracy and the monarchy?

## READING FOR FORM, ORGANIZATION, AND EXPOSITORY FEATURES

1. How would you describe the overall organization of the selection? Which patterns of organization are used in the various sections of the piece?
2. Mark the passages that contain histories or etymologies of words and explain what this information adds to Seabrook's argument.
3. What is the function of the boxed material? Does it add or detract from the essay?
4. What effect does the final sentence have on the reader?

## READING FOR RHETORICAL CONCERNS

1. How would you describe Seabrook's rhetorical purpose? What are the most essential points he wants to get across to his audience?
2. Who is Seabrook's intended audience? Do you think his argument has appeal to readers from other nations? Why, or why not?
3. What is Seabrook's background? Is he a creditable authority on the topic of class?

## WRITING ASSIGNMENTS

1. Drawing on Seabrook's article, write a brief essay describing the social class to which you belong.

2. Explain the origin of class in contemporary society by writing a summary of the history of class from feudal times to the present.

3. Write an essay in which you compare and contrast the conception of class in the UK and the United States.

4. For an audience of students who have not read Seabrook's article, explain why there is such a growing divide between the rich and the poor today.

# Grandma Went to Smith, All Right, But She Went from Nine to Five: A Memoir

## *Patricia Clark Smith*

*Patricia Clark Smith teaches in the Department of English at the University of New Mexico. She is the author of* Talking to the Land, Changing Your Story, Western Literature in a World Context *(co-edited with Davis, Harrison, Johnson, and Crawford), and As* Long as the Rivers Flow: The Stories of Nine Native Americans.

### PREREADING

In your journal, speculate about the meaning of the title. Located in Northampton, Massachusetts, Smith is one of the seven private colleges that make up what was once called "the seven sister schools" or "the women's Ivy League." What do you think the author means when she says her grandmother went to Smith from nine to five? Freewrite your response.

The area marked "Property of Smith College" on Northampton town plats comprises the nearest sizable green space to the house where my family lived until I turned seven, in the same

1

By Patricia Clark Smith, from *Working Class Women in the Academy*, by Michelle M. Tokarczyk and Elizabeth A. Fay, eds., © 1993. Reprinted by permission of University of Massachusetts Press.

upstairs apartment where my mother was born.* That house, 53 Old South Street, was torn down in the mid-1950s, but I like knowing that my mother and I came to consciousness in the same set of rooms, that our eyes first learned to distinguish squares of sunlight shifting across the same kitchen floor, the same tree shadows on the wall.

The Smith campus, too, my mother and I both knew early in our lives. But here there is a difference between my mother's experience and my own, for she explored that place only after she was big enough to go there with her gang of neighborhood kids. Her mother, the grandmother I called Nana, seldom took her there. Smith land and Smith events have traditionally been open to townspeople, but Nana was Quebec-born, with a few years of grade school education, not the sort of Northampton resident likely to assume the college was accessible to her. Besides, even though my mother was her only child, Nana had little leisure for long walks with a toddler. Walks were what Nana took on her way upstreet from our house on the flats to go shopping, to go to Mass, or to go to work; walks were what she took to the bus stop, en route to visit relatives or to nurse them. She and my grandfather, who died when my mother was in her late teens, both came from sprawling and often hapless families, hers French Canadian and Micmac, his Irish. Both sides were riddled with tuberculosis, alcoholism, infant failure-to-thrive—the classic diseases of the poor. The stunning exception, the one success in my mother's family, was one of my grandfather's brothers, who made his way upward through ward politics to a term as mayor of Northampton in the thirties; his success was short, and apparently, unlike T.B., it was not catching within families.

For Nana, Smith College was primarily the place where she worked intermittently throughout her life cleaning dormitory bathrooms and hallways. It is easy to see why she did not think of the Smith campus as an arena for leisure or pleasure, as a place to take a baby. My mother was the first in our family to see the grounds of Smith as in some way a part of her turf. She played there as a child; as a grown woman, she ventured into the art gallery, attended public lectures and foreign films, though always with a sense that Smith was special, its delights not her birthright, but privileges graciously extended to her.

As for me, her daughter, I cannot remember a time before the Smith campus was a familiar presence to me. I knew it first through my body, through bare feet and skinned knees, by way of the dirt lodged in

*"Plats" are maps of sections of cities: "green space" is the city planning term for undeveloped open land. "Upstreet" and "slate sink" are colloquial to western Massachusetts.

the creases of my palms and caked beneath my fingernails, dirt Nana scrubbed off with gritty Boraxo in our slate sink. I learned to walk, and later to ice skate, on the campus; my first bullfrogs hunkered on the margin of the lily pool by Lyman Plant House.

And Smith was where I first understood metaphor, not in any 5 freshman English class, but in the woods at the western edge of the campus heavy in early spring with the rich smell of leaf mold, soaked through by melting snow, where I hunkered down to inspect a jack-in-the-pulpit. On walks there, my parents taught me the wonderfully satisfying names of things: rose-breasted grosbeak, Solomon's seal, nuthatch, dogtooth violet, lady's slipper.

Within the boundaries of the campus, the Mill River widened out 6 and briefly changed its name to Paradise Pond, though Nana said it was really still the same old Mill River. The Paradise Pond skating rink was kept glossy and clear of snow by the Kingsmen. Smith patois for the male groundskeepers and maintenance men. No question of Kingspersons in those days. There were cooks and chambermaids, all women. And there were Kingsmen. *Kingsman* is said to derive from Franklin King, an early president of Smith, whose name at full length was also given to the colonaded neo-Georgian dormitory where Nana worked as a maid. A *chambermaid*.

For me and other Northampton kids whose relatives did service 7 work at the college, *Kingsman* and *chambermaid* were words of double meaning. They meant the ordinary jobs held down by familiar adults. But the words also evoked the quaintly dressed people in the illustrations of Mother Goose books, the world of Humpty Dumpty and Old King Cole and the four-and-twenty blackbirds. When I entered Smith, the information booklet for freshmen commented upon the nice aptness of calling gardeners and janitors *Kingsmen*, for "they help put Smith back together again," no matter what maintenance problems might arise. I don't remember any mention in that booklet of chambermaids, only an oral explanation during some orientation session that those women were not to be tipped and were to be treated with courtesy. There was little danger of anyone tipping them, of course; as for the courtesy, I came to Smith knowing Nana's stories. And I had done some time by then as a waitress myself.

I grew up in a politically progressive family, where unions and 8 strikes were common table talk. But as a little kid, I like most of my friends had no notion of the class assumptions evident in cutely calling working people Kingsmen. It seemed only one more odd conjunction of language, one I might some day figure out—and there were so many of those adult puns and euphemisms to puzzle over. My dad's step-father, the only grown man I saw regularly during the war years, would chuck me under the chin and pinch my nose, and ask if I wanted to hear the story of Goldilocks and the Three Beers; when my brother Mike was born, and I asked my mother why Pop Noffke called Mike's tiny penis an "erector set," she said it was because the first erector sets were made at the Gilbert factory where Pop worked as a janitor (no "Kingsmen" in the Holyoke mills, to be sure), and Pop loved erectors sets, and he loved baby Mike.... She trailed off. *Kingsmen* was probably that sort of mystery.

The adult world was full of such secrets, of mysterious imports  9 and double meanings. I took for granted the significance of names, words, multiple identities, even if often I could not guess what the significance might be, whether the doubling of meaning were portentous or playful.

But I knew one thing from an early age: There was some acute  10 difference between being a chambermaid in the way Nana was and the apple-checked girls dressed in ruffled aprons and mob caps in the Mother Goose book. In a folklore course at Smith. I discovered the Opies' *Oxford Dictionary of Nursery Rhymes*, where I read avidly about the politics, sex, and class wars secreted in those texts. At four, at seven, I knew only that the chambermaids in the bright pictures seemed spunky, healthy, young, and largely cheerful, even when threatened by blackbirds and crosspatch mistresses. But then, as Nana once remarked when I asked her about the connection between her job and the pictures, those maids didn't have to scrub toilets. In the pastoral vision of the illustrators, maids milked bonny cows; they hung out clothes, they stood prettily all-in-a-row. It was different with Nana.

It is a soft spring evening in 1948. I come upon Nana sitting in her  11 rocker in the darkened kitchen, rubbing her thick ankles. She is crying. I am five; I am terrified. In all the world, she is my steadiest point, steady and beautiful, like her name: Julia Larock Dunn.

*What, Nana, what?* I ask.

*Oh, those girls*, she says, and I know she means the students who live at Franklin King House. But what have those girls done?

*They called me a bitch*, she says, *right to my face!*

She sees I don't know the word, and now she's sorry she's used it, but I press her: *They called you what?*

*A bitch*, she says. *A she-dog. Like Lady*. And she names the mongrel next door, a very doggy-smelling dog with dangling teats.

I cannot believe this. I am sobbing, and now she is holding me, rocking me, singing to me in her gravelly Quebecois: *Allouette, je te plumarais*. Little skylark, I will pluck your wings. Don't cry; everything is all right.

Two kinds of bitch, two kinds of chambermaids, and the Mill and  12
Paradise the same flowing water; many of my first confusions of language centered around Smith.

In the April after I turned seven, Nana felt poorly one evening,  13
but not yet so poorly that I could not go in to kiss her goodnight. In her room I whispered to her the prayer she taught me, one she perhaps picked up from the Irish in-laws, a prayer I now know is called "The White Paternoster," and is recited in the British Isles as a charm against ghosts:

> Four posts round my bed.
> Four angels o'er my head.
> Matthew, Mark, Luke, and John.
> Bless the bed I lie upon.

And I spoke the names of all whom I wished to bless. By the time my father waked me in the morning, the ambulance had come and gone with Nana. I ran home from school breathlessly that noon, willing myself to hear from the backstairs landing the sounds of her stumping about the kitchen, singing along with the radio tuned to "The Franco-American Hour." I prayed now not for Evangelists to guard me, but to smell tomato soup, baking apples, a chicken roasting, to find everything somehow in place.

Instead, there was only Aunt Anna, trembling, telling me with a  14
terrible false smile that Nana was all gone, that Nana was with the angels now.

For a few years after, I would sometimes wake in the darkness of  15
my room, after an evening when I had gone to bed sad or afraid, to feel a rough hand gripping my thumb beneath the covers. In time, these tactile visitations frightened and disturbed me more than they comforted me, and one night I asked Nana aloud to go away. She did.

I never told anyone of those experiences, and never heard from  16
anyone a comparable story until I read Chapter Four of *Moby Dick*, with Ishmael's (and Melville's I'd bet) memory of the ghostly hand. I was at Smith by then, and I cried after reading that passage, looking out

my dormitory window across the darkened quadrangle toward Franklin King House.

The day after Nana's funeral, the gas company property manager 17 called on us to serve an eviction notice. The company owned the house, and they had allowed Nana to continue her lease on grudging sufferance, as she was the widow of a gas inspector, we were only a gas-company's widow's survivors. And so Aunt Anna moved to Florence to share a tiny house with three cheerful maiden ladies, as they called themselves, who worked beside her at Pro Brush, and we moved, my father, my pregnant mother, my baby brother, and I, to Hampshire Heights, a low-income veterans' housing project newly built at the edge of Northampton on land carved out of woodlots and farms. In the space of a few weeks, we had become a nuclear family.

The Heights spilled over with 1950s energy, alive, raw-edged, very 18 hopeful, a little dangerous. Many of the fathers, five years after the war's end, were still shaken, given to fits of depression or sudden explosive rage. We kids accepted anger as an adult male norm, the way fathers were. When I think back on our mothers, I remember them pregnant. Kids were everywhere at the Heights; you could not be granted a lease unless you had at least two. The oldest tier was all my age, seven and eight. Most of us had come to the project from wartime homes like mine, homes shared with grandparents, aunts, uncles. Families composed only of parents and children seemed to many of us small, unripe, ingrown, scarily lacking in extra sources of support and comfort, and we older kids bonded fiercely in a large nomadic tribe that transcended gender and ethnicity. We roamed parking bays and clothesline yards, playing hide and seek among wet flapping sheets; we explored woods and fields, each of us in charge of at least one younger sibling. They trailed behind us on foot, or we pulled them in wagons or sleds. We coached them on how to slide under barbed-wire fences, while one of us stood guard to make sure the lethargic bull was preoccupied in a far corner of his pasture; we carried them across the stepping stones of the brook to the Piney Woods, where we built forts of resinous boughs; we took them to the free Christmas production of Humperdinck's *Hansel and Gretel* at Smith, hissing them silent, holding them when they cried at the witch; we warned them away from the construction constantly underway around the project: *Billy Ouimet, Tony Perfito, Mikey Clark. I see you, get over here right now or you'll get a licking!*

Our bond was the stronger because by moving to Hampshire 19 Heights we had become suddenly identifiably lumped together as low-income working-class kids. We older Heights kids rejoiced out loud at how brave, how smart, how strong we were; as it turns out, we seem to have been all those things. Those of us now in our mid-forties who belonged to that first generation of Heights children keep splendid oral histories, and I know of few stories of failure among us.

In our grade school classrooms, it would have been hard for an out- 20 sider to pick out us Heights kids. But kids themselves unfailingly know who is who, and on the walks home we needed to band together, fighting, flailing against taunts: *Heights kids: Project kids!* After school it was simply easier not to try to venture beyond our own group, however welcoming other kids who lived outside the project might initially seem.

Joanie lived in a pretty ranch house in the Gleason Road addition 21 just across Jackson Street from the Heights. Joanie said her mom would let us come over until more ranch houses got built on Gleason Road, when Joanie would have more playmates of her own sort. We knew well enough not to report these remarks to our own proud families. And it was tempting to play over at Joanie's house. The best climbing tree in the neighborhood grew there, left over from the time when it was all farmland, a venerable apple tree with sturdy perches we gave names to: the Baby Seat (a foot off the ground); the Lookout (the topmost fork).

I lay stretched out on a middle limb, dreaming, my whole body 22 banked by sweet apple blossoms. That afternoon I was the last Heights kid left over at Joanie's. Suddenly from up in the Lookout, Joanie began her soft chant: *Ev*ery kid on this *A*pple tree is coming to my BIRTHday party *ex*CEPT PAT CLARK . . . and YOU KNOW WHY. And from various nooks around the tree, out of the massed blossoms and sticky new leaves, the refrain came from the mouths of hidden children: YAH, *yah*, HAH *hah*, YOU *live at* HAMP*shire Heights!*

I dropped ten feet to the ground and landed running, yelling up at 23 the whole beautiful tree, *Who cares? Who cares? Who cares about you and your stinking party?* As I ran through the front yard, I glimpsed Joanie's mom and her gentle, Polish-speaking grandma at the big picture window. Her mother's face was set; her grandma waved at me, looking sad. I did not wave back.

Well, who cared, indeed? I cared. Since then, the parties I have 24 attended stretch in a long line from that party I was not invited to, right to the present: high school proms, college mixers, graduate school sherry hours, faculty receptions, museum trustees' dinners in honor of scholarly books to which I've contributed. And I never have, I never will, attend one such function without looking surreptitiously around,

checking it out, figuring out who's here, who's here who's like me, trying
to spot my kind: *Who's here who wasn't born knowing how to do this?*

Always, I am looking for the Heights kids.

When I was ten, my father was transferred, and we moved straight 25
from Hampshire Heights to an old farmhouse on the outskirts of Portland, Maine, where I lived until I graduated from high school. Those
years don't need chronicling here, except for the last summer before I
entered Smith, the college I chose because it was the one I knew. And
because, though now I cannot recall her ever saying she hoped I would
grow up to go to Smith, I wanted to give Nana a Smith girl who knew
what Julia Larock was worth. My parents were pleased, but they were
also fearful, afraid I might not succeed, afraid I would and alter into
some unknowable stranger. I remember two stories from that summer,
one told by my mother, the other by my father.

The quote under my mother's Northampton High School year- 26
book picture, from Thomas Hood, reads "And she had a face like a
blessing." And so she did; high-cheekboned and radiant, she smiles
shyly there on the page. Other old snapshots show her slender and
graceful, even in a shapeless 1930s tanktop swim suit; she is dressed for
a dance with an orchid in her hair, à la Rita Hayworth.

One afternoon that last summer while we were shelling peas she 27
told me a story about herself newly out of high school and enrolled at
McCarthy's Business School in downtown Northampton, thrilled one
October Saturday because she had a date with a college man, a student
at Amherst. At the last moment she tucked into the picnic basket one of
her favorite books, *The Poetical Works of John Greenleaf Whittier.*

I know that book well, and I love it still, uncritically, not just 28
"Snowbound," but the ballads of shipwreck, heroism, love gone astray.
Sweet Maude Muller among her hayricks, whom the wimpy judge rejects as a possible wife, and Kathleen's wonderfully wicked stepmother,
getting in her licks in the class wars:

> There was a lord of Galway
> A mighty lord was he,
> And he did wed a second wife,
> A maid of low degree.
> But he was old, and she was young,
> And so in evil spite,
> She baked the black bread for his kin
> And fed her own with white.

No worse than batches of Keats or Yeats, or whatever my mom's 29 date was reading—D. H. Lawrence, I bet. On the grass by Paradise Pond, that boy pounced not on my mom but on her book; *What's this? Oh, my god, Whittier!* And he read snatches of it out loud, roaring with laughter, his hands greasy from the fried chicken, laughing at Maude and Kathleen, at Mom. When she cried and the picnic was ruined, he called her a bad sport.

My mother told this story without pointing any moral, just as a sad 30 little tale about how things don't always pan out. But by the time I heard this story, I had some idea myself why they might not: college man from Boston suburb, business school townie. I carried the story with me to Smith: I can still hear the cold water running in the sink, the shelled peas pinging down into the colander, as my mother imitated that boy's voice, the way he held the book out of her reach. I think of him every time a college bookstore announces the readers for a poetry series that devalues the lyrical, the narrative, and awards the avant-garde; I think of him every time I hear a teacher criticize a student's taste: "You mean you *like* 'O Captain, My Captain'?"; eyebrow raised, faint smile.

My father also had a story for me that summer of 1960, and his are 31 never told as anything *but* moral exempla.

Late August on the beach of Prout's Neck. I am holding so much 32 joy and fear and expectancy inside this summer, my whole self feels like a brimming cup I am trying not to spill. But now in a voice heavy with import my father commands me to walk with him down the shimmery waterline toward the private beaches of the big Victorian resort inns. It is low tide, and the beach is very wide, strewn with wavey parallel lines of kelp and shells, pebbles and bones, plastic beach-bottle floats, bits of glass buffed to opalescence, all the old garbage the sea keeps trying to refine.

My mother winces, mutters, "Just get away as soon as you can," 33 and I realize she is guessing better than I can what's coming. And indeed I could not have guessed. What my father wishes to tell me is not about the burden on me as the first to go to college, or even his usual sermon about how though I must certainly *go* to college, I will lose family and soul if I turn into "one of those girls too proud to wipe her own arse." Instead he relates a twisted picaresque epic of the easy sexual conquests he and his buddies made at Smith and Mount Holyoke; about how many girls he knew in high school ended up seduced and abandoned by callous college boys. (Underneath his picture in *his*

Holyoke High yearbook they wrote "The girls really fall for the charm of Joe 'Clicker' Clark and the sweet strains of his Hawaiian guitar.") He explains earnestly that (1) college girls are loose, and all townie men know that; (2) college boys believe that all townie girls are loose, and they may well be right; (3) it will be easy for anyone to spot me for what I am, and so therefore (4)....

But I don't stay for (4). I run back along the beach, crying *please,* 34 *Dad, no,* rubbing at my ears as if that could erase the sounds I have heard, but it is too late. His words reinforce my deepest fears: I am overreaching by going to Smith, condemning myself to a life of being neither duck nor swan, with no true allies, infinitely vulnerable to the worst each "sort" can say about or do to one another in these class wars I've been witness to my whole life.

I gained much from Smith, eventually. But my first years were be- 35 wildering, marked more often than they might have been by shame and despair. I lost my freshman scholarship in a dismal welter of C's and D's, though my adviser kept pointing out that I'd entered with soaring College Board scores, hoping perhaps that I'd suddenly say, Oh yeah, now I remember, I'm a good student.

But too many other things compelled my attention. Spellbound. I 36 wandered the campus and the streets I had known as a child, not a college town to me but a landscape of myth whose significance I found it impossible to impart even to the classmates closest to me. I hung out around Franklin King House, too shy to ask the people now working there if they had known Nana. I saw my Heights friends when I could, but they were working, getting ready to be married; I'd met the man I would marry myself. And I was supposed to be studying.

The great gift that first year came through the accident of being 37 placed in a dormitory with a recent reputation as "debutante house" with a lowering scholastic average which the housing office tried to stack with freshmen on scholarship. My classmates tended to be politically left, socially dim, good at friendship, spirited debate, and high nonsense. The seniors caucused about us; we were so hopeless, there would be little point staging freshmen mixers on our behalf. We grinned at each other. It was like the Heights. We had each other. We still do.

Those women got me through. What one of us didn't know, some- 38 one else was sure to. In the house dining room set with linen and candles, I learned from them how to manage a knife and fork, how to approach soup. Someone's Canadian graduate student fiancée smuggled

Enovid down to blue-lawed Massachusetts; someone else could make thrift-shop hems hang well; all of us shared the stories of where we'd come from, told one another how good we were, supported one another through and beyond the time when we found, as we almost all did, the classes and teachers who mattered, the work we really wanted to do. For me, that took the better part of three years.

As a freshman, I would stay awake all night talking, or devouring 39 books that weren't assigned, while forgetting to study for a biology exam on mitosis. I memorized great swatches of poetry, and yet the trick of the five-part essay eluded me, and I could not seem to avoid the marginal comment of *overly personal response* on papers for my English professors. The first teacher to grant me a B at Smith remarked to another student that he thought it remarkable I was so perceptive, given that I came of "poor stock." And for those first two years, given that background, I was a listless language student. My dad forced me to take Spanish instead of the French I loved because Spanish was the "language of the future," and because, as he puts it, French was spoken only by "fancy diplomats," and "your own relatives who still don't have a pot to piss in." *Aren't you glad?* he asks me, now that I have lived in New Mexico for nearly twenty years. *No,* I say. I'd have learned Spanish here, where I need it. But in that time, in Northampton, at once so strange and so familiar, so haunted with my ghosts, what I required most was to reaffirm my own roots.

My sophomore year, allowed to return on loans, I resolved to dig 40 in and do well. In a creative writing class, I tried to write about my family, my life, not Northampton, not Old South Street or Hampshire Heights, not yet, but about Maine, about summers waitressing or working at Sebago-Moc, hand-stitching the uppers for pricey moccasins such as no Algonquian ever wore; about practicing with my .22 on chunks of paper pulp floating down the Presumpscott River below our house; about my brother coming home bloodied, proud of decking the drunk who tried to mug him at the Riverside Roller Rink.

My British teacher, pale and anorexically thin, wears huge geo- 41 metric earrings, nail polish in odd shades of green and fuchsia. My stories come back with C+'s and B−'s, sparse comments in her minuscule handwriting—"inappropriate diction." When I describe Richard Widmark's wiping out a machine gun nest with three grenades, she notes "one would be sufficient surely." She reads to us from D. H. Lawrence, Mary McCarthy, never talking about our own stories, and I never get to say it took three grenades because the Japanese kicked the first two out of their foxhole. When I show up timidly at her office hour one day, she asks sharply, "Are you fishing for a change of grade?"

I say no, stuttering, I just want to do better next time. "Give that here, then," she sighs, and she takes from me the story about my brother's fight, the one that contains the description of the Widmark movie. Her fingers are almost translucent in the light through the gothic window of her office. The silence is very long.

"This, here," she says at last, and her blue fingernail taps a sentence where a father is ranging about a "nefarious sod who couldn't find his own arse with both hands." This character, she says, would not use this language.

"How come?" I ask. I truly do not know what she means; is it the profanity? Does she think someone who says "arse" wouldn't use a word like "nefarious"? But she thinks I am being insolent. Or just dumb, hopelessly dumb. She sighs again. If I don't see the point, she says, she doesn't see how she can very well convey it to me. So I don't try to explain about the grenades, about the rolling silver and vulgar eloquence of working-class Irish. I leave her office diffusely ashamed and angry, still not sure of how I've failed. But whatever that failing is, I think it will surely keep me from being a writer.

My friends kept me together. And there came at last the meaningful classes, Daniel Aaron's American literature, most dramatically, with a syllabus miraculously advanced for 1962; not just Thoreau and Melville, but Chopin, Norris, Harold Frederick's Irish immigrants, Cather's and Jewett's country people, Dreiser's working men and women. And there was Aaron himself, assuring me that I could write: Aaron, upon my shyly mentioning Nana, displaying interest and pleasure: *That's really wonderful, you know: Tell me about it. What dorm...?* I cried after I left his office that day from sheer relief, the relief of validation.

When I read the autobiographical accounts in Ryan and Sackrey's *Strangers in Paradise: Academics from the Working Class*, what surprises me is how little they speak of what that experience has meant for them as teachers of their own working-class students. Most of us, I think, carry a sense of not fully belonging, of being pretenders to a kingdom not ours by birthright. In the year I came up for tenure at UNM, I dreamed of leaving the university before I could be asked to leave, taking a job as a waitress in what I call in a poem "my sad downtown that was always waiting." Some teachers bury their sad downtowns deep inside them; they strive to be more punctilious, academic, "objective," more "Ivy League" than most of the professors who actually taught me at Smith or Yale.

But for most of us, I think, our pasts are a strength, a means of 47 connecting with our own students' lives, with literature itself, a talisman to carry into any classroom to remind us of the multiplicity of histories, of the stories we study in that room in addition to the printed ones, the stories that together with the books make up the real text of our class. At a state university in the southwest, those stories are especially multiple.

D has been my problem child in my Whitman and Dickinson 48 course—a body builder, often late, annoyingly macho. A good month into our work on Whitman, after much talk of gender, sexuality, biography, he suddenly exclaims, "Hey, wait a minute: Was Whitman queer?" He cannot, he claims, "seem to feel all this emotion you guys feel when you read poetry." In desperation, trying to help him find a paper topic, I suggest he try *Specimen Days* instead of the poems. I steel myself to read his paper.

But D's paper is a stark account of his childhood as an MIA's son, a 49 fatherless kid trying to figure out how to be a man, manly. It is about using his high school graduation gift money on a fruitless trip to Saigon to look for clues about his father, and his determination now to get on with his own life. And his paper is about the reawakening of all his old questions in reading Whitman's descriptions of released Union prisoners of war. D's paper ends by saying, *I love Walt now, but I hate him too. Because he has made me remember. And he wants to be my father.*

C is in the same class, a Pueblo Indian, a shy, attentive single 50 mother living too far from the close-knit community where she was raised. We're on Emily now—my home-girl, from Amherst, Hampshire County, in the state of Massachusetts. I've told the class how I didn't even know she was dead until I was eight or so, because every time we drove down Amherst's main street, my folks would point and say, "There's Miss Dickinson's house."

Last Friday was a beautiful October day when we were all getting 51 a little overdosed on death kindly stopping and looks of agony, and I suggested we just read together the nature poems that often don't get taught because they don't require much teacherly help or comment. It was a wonderful hour of hummingbirds like revolving wheels, leaves unhooking themselves from trees, and the frog who wears mittens at his feet. I smile to myself, remembering the bullfrogs of Smith. C nodded and nodded as we read.

Today, Monday, C comes up after class, and asks, "Did you know 52 I'm Frog Clan?"

No, I didn't. But I do now.

She tells me she brought Dickinson's frog poems home with her over the weekend to show her clan elders back at the pueblo. "They liked them," she says, and adds, grinning, "Frog people are supposed to be good talkers."

I say I think Dickinson would have loved knowing that.

Yeah, she agrees. She's been having trouble writing her paper, but she got the draft done this weekend at home. It felt good, she says: "It was kind of like taking Emily home to meet my folks, you know what I mean?"

Yeah, I do. I do.   ✿

## READING FOR INFORMATION

1. In your own words, explain why "Kingsmen" and "chambermaid" had double meanings for Clark Smith when she was a child. Can you recall words that had double meanings for you when you were younger?

2. Relate how Clark Smith and the other Hampshire Heights kids experienced class bigotry. How did you react to their experiences?

3. Do you think the stories that Clark Smith's parents told her reveal their fears about their daughter attending college? Of what was each parent fearful? Do you think their fears were justified?

4. In your own words, recount examples of the class prejudice Clark Smith experienced in college. Do you think prejudice exists in colleges today? Explain.

5. Paraphrase what Clark Smith means by "sad downtowns." How do we know that Clark Smith celebrates her "sad downtowns" instead of burying them?

## READING FOR FORM, ORGANIZATION, AND EXPOSITORY FEATURES

1. Clark Smith's article is an example of autobiographical writing. Explain how her narrative style differs from the styles of other writers in this anthology.

2. Autobiographies usually contain some sense of introspection. Underline passages in which Clark Smith looks into her own mind or feelings or analyzes herself. What do these passages tell you about the author?

3. What is the function of paragraphs 48–52?

## READING FOR RHETORICAL CONCERNS

1. Do you think that Clark Smith is simply relating her memoirs to the reader, or is her purpose more complex? What impact does she want to have on her audience?

2. Does Clark Smith draw more on feelings or on facts? What would be gained or lost if the expressions of feeling were left out?

3. Where was this piece originally published? What does that information contribute to your understanding of the author?

4. Underline passages that reveal Clark Smith's tone. How would you characterize it?

## WRITING ASSIGNMENTS

1. Have you had any experiences that are similar to Clark Smith's? When you were growing up, were you ever involved in "class wars"? When did you first become conscious of social class, social stratification, or economic inequality? Write a two- to three-page narrative essay recounting your experiences.

2. After her conference with the creative writing teacher, Clark Smith says, "I leave her office diffusely ashamed and angry, still not sure of how I've failed. But whatever that failing is, I think, it will surely keep me from being a writer" (paragraph 44). Write an essay in which you explore your own feelings about learning to write. Compare and contrast your experiences as a novice writer with those of Clark Smith. Did you have teachers who dampened your enthusiasm for writing? Did you ever have a teacher who validated your experiences?

3. All three women in Clark Smith's narrative—Nana, Clark Smith's mother, and Clark Smith herself—experienced pain because of other people's insensitivity. Write an essay comparing and contrasting each woman's experiences and the way each woman coped.

# The Revolt of the Black Bourgeoisie

## *Leonce Gaiter*

*Leonce Gaiter lives in Los Angeles and writes frequently about social issues. His essays have appeared in* The Washington Post, The New York Times, The Los Angeles Times, The New York Times Magazine, FEED, salon.com, *and elsewhere.*

### PREREADING

Answer the following questions in your journal before reading the selection: What is your image of members of the black middle class? Where did you acquire that image—from your own experiences, from African-American friends, or from the popular media? Do you know more about working-class and poor blacks than about middle- and upper-class blacks? Why is this so? Respond to these questions in ten to fifteen minutes of freewriting.

At a television network where I once worked, one of my 1 bosses told me I almost didn't get hired because his superior had "reservations" about me. The job had been offered under the network's Minority Advancement Program. I applied for the position because I knew I was exceptionally qualified. I would have qualified for the position regardless of how it was advertised.

After my interview, the head of the department told my boss I 2 wasn't really what he had in mind for a Minority Advancement Program job. To the department head, hiring a minority applicant meant hiring someone unqualified. He wanted to hire some semiliterate, hoop-shooting former prison inmate. That, in his view, was a "real" black person. That was someone worthy of the program.

I had previously been confronted by questions of black authentic- 3 ity. At Harvard, where I graduated in 1980, a white classmate once said to me, "Oh, you're not really a black person." I asked her to explain. She could not. She had known few black people before college, but a lifetime of seeing black people depicted in the American media had taught her that real black people talked a certain way and were raised in certain places. In her world, black people did not attend elite colleges. They could not stand as her intellectual equals or superiors. Any African-American who shared her knowledge of Austen and Balzac— while having to explain to her who Douglass and Du Bois were—had to be *willed* away for her to salvage her sense of superiority as a white person. Hence the accusation that I was "not really black."

But worse than the white majority harboring a one-dimensional vi-    4 sion of blackness are the many blacks who embrace this stereotype as our true nature. At the junior high school I attended in the mostly white Washington suburb of Silver Spring, Md., a black girl once stopped me in the hallway and asked belligerently, "How come you talk so proper?" Astonished, I could only reply, "It's proper*ly*," and walk on. This girl was asking why I spoke without the so-called black accent pervasive in the lower socioeconomic strata of black society, where exposure to mainstream society is limited. This girl was asking, Why wasn't I impoverished and alienated? In her world view, a black male like me couldn't exist.

Within the past year, however, there have been signs that blacks    5 are openly beginning to acknowledge the complex nature of our culture. Cornel West, a professor of religion and the director of Afro-American Studies at Princeton University, discusses the growing gulf between the black underclass and the rest of black society in his book *Race Matters*; black voices have finally been raised against the violence, misogyny, and vulgarity marketed to black youth in the form of gangsta rap; Ellis Cose's book *The Rage of a Privileged Class*, which concentrates on the problems of middle- and upper-income blacks, was excerpted as part of a *Newsweek* magazine cover story: Bill Cosby has become a vocal crusader against the insulting depiction of African-Americans in "hip-hop generation" TV shows.

Yes, there are the beginnings of a new candor about our cul-    6 ture, but the question remains. How did one segment of the African-American community come to represent the whole? First, black society itself placed emphasis on that lower caste. This made sense because historically that's where the vast majority of us were placed: It's where American society and its laws were designed to keep us. Yet although doors have opened to us over the past 20 years, it is still commonplace for black leaders to insist on our community's uniform need for social welfare programs, innercity services, job skills training, etc. Through such calls, what has passed for a black political agenda has been furthered only superficially; while affirmative action measures have forced an otherwise unwilling majority to open some doors for the black middle class, social welfare and Great Society–style programs aimed at the black lower class have shown few positive results.

According to 1990 census figures, between 1970 and 1990 the 7 number of black families with incomes under $15,000 rose from 34.6 percent of the black population to 37 percent, while the number of black families with incomes of $35,000 to $50,000 rose from 13.9 percent to 15 percent of the population, and those with incomes of more than $50,000 rose from 9.9 percent to 14.5 percent of the black population.

Another reason the myth of an all-encompassing black underclass 8 survives—despite the higher number of upper-income black families— is that it fits with a prevalent form of white liberalism, which is just as informed by racism as white conservatism. Since the early 1970s, good guilt-liberal journalists and others warmed to the picture of black down-trodden masses in need of their help. Through the agency of good white people, blacks would rise. This image of African-Americans maintained the lifeline of white superiority that whites in this culture cling to, and therefore this image of blacks stuck. A strange tango was begun. Blacks seeking advancement opportunities allied themselves with whites eager to "help" them. However, those whites continued to see blacks as inferiors, victims, cases, and not as equals, individuals or, heaven forbid, competitors.

It was hammered into the African-American psyche by media- 9 appointed black leaders and the white media that it was essential to our political progress to stay or seem to stay economically and socially deprived. To be recognized and recognize oneself as middle or upper class was to threaten the political progress of black people. That girl who asked why I spoke so "proper" was accusing me of political sins—of thwarting the progress of our race.

Despite progress toward a more balanced picture of black Amer- 10 ica, the image of black society as an underclass remains strong. Look at local news coverage of the trial of Damian Williams and Henry Watson, charged with beating the white truck driver Reginald Denny during the 1992 South-Central L.A. riots. The press showed us an African-print-wearing cadre of Williams and Watson supporters trailing Edi M. O. Faal, Williams's defense attorney, like a Greek chorus. This chorus made a point of standing in the camera's range. They presented themselves as the voice of South-Central L.A., the voice of the oppressed, the voice of the down-trodden, the voice of the city's black people.

To anyone watching TV coverage of the trial, all blacks agreed 11
with Faal's contention that his clients were prosecuted so aggressively
because they are black. Period. Reporters made no effort to show opposing black viewpoints. (In fact, the media portrait of the Los Angeles
riot as blacks vs. whites and Koreans was a misrepresentation. According to the Rand Corporation, a research institute in Santa Monica,
blacks made up 36 percent of those arrested during the riot; Latinos
made up 51 percent.) The black bourgeoisie and intelligentsia remained largely silent. We had too long believed that to express disagreement with the "official line" was to be a traitor.

TV networks and cable companies gain media raves for programs 12
like "Laurel Avenue," an HBO melodrama about a working-class black
family lauded for its realism, a real black family complete with drug
dealers, drug users, gun toters, and basketball players. It is akin to the
media presenting "Valley of the Dolls" as a realistic portrayal of the
ways of white women.

The Fox network offers a differing but equally misleading portrait 13
of black Americans, with *Martin*. While blue humor has long been a
staple of black audiences, it was relegated to clubs and records for
*mature* black audiences. It was not peddled to kids or to the masses.

Now the blue humor tradition is piped to principally white audi- 14
ences. If TV was as black as it is white—if there was a fair share of black
love stories, black dramas, black detective heroes—these blue humor
images would not be a problem. Right now, however, they stand as images to which whites can condescend.

Imagine being told by your peers, the records you hear, the pro- 15
grams you watch, the "leaders" you see on TV, classmates, prospective
employers—imagine being told by virtually everyone that in order to be
your true self you must be ignorant and poor, or at least seem so.

Blacks must now see to it that our children face no such burden. 16
We must see to it that the white majority, along with vocal minorities
within the black community (generally those with a self-serving political
agenda), do not perpetuate the notion that African-Americans are invariably doomed to the underclass.

African-Americans are moving toward seeing ourselves—and de- 17
manding that others see us—as individuals, not as shards of a degraded
monolith. The American ideal places primacy on the rights of the individual, yet historically African-Americans have been denied those
rights. We blacks can effectively demand those rights, effectively demand justice only when each of us sees him or herself as an individual

with the right to any of the opinions, idiosyncrasies, and talents accorded any other American. &#10058;

## READING FOR INFORMATION

1. In your own words, recount Gaiter's experience of how people stereotype black males.
2. Summarize the evidence that Gaiter presents in support of his contention that blacks have begun to critique and offer a more balanced view of black America.
3. Paraphrase two reasons for "the myth of an all-encompassing black underclass."
4. Give specific examples of how the media perpetuate this myth.

## READING FOR FORM, ORGANIZATION, AND EXPOSITORY FEATURES

1. Gaiter opens the article with three personal anecdotes. Why do you think he begins the selection in that way?
2. Give examples of the various types of evidence—facts, statistics, references to authorities—that Gaiter uses to support his position.
3. What technique does Gaiter use to conclude the article?

## READING FOR RHETORICAL CONCERNS

1. Do you think Gaiter is addressing all readers of *The New York Times Magazine* or focusing on a particular group? What leads you to that conclusion?
2. What impact do you think Gaiter wants to have on his audience? How does he want to change their views? Would that impact change if Gaiter were white? Explain.
3. How would you characterize Gaiter's tone? What does the tone suggest about the author?

## WRITING ASSIGNMENTS

1. What do you think of Gaiter's characterization of white liberals in paragraph 8? Do white people see all blacks, even successful blacks, "as inferiors, victims, cases, and not as equals, individuals or, heaven forbid, competitors"? Write a brief essay in response.
2. Write an essay exploring the relationship between Gaiter's argument and Herbert Gans's criticism of stereotypes in paragraphs 33 and 34 of his

article "The War Against the Poor Instead of Programs to End Poverty" (pp. 438–39).

3. a. Form collaborative groups of five students each, as described in the preface, or fashion groups according to your own method.

   b. Have a member of each group videotape two or three segments of a television series that features African Americans. Play the tape for the other members of the group. Each group member should take notes on instances of stereotyping, either the types of stereotyping Gaiter discusses or other versions.

   c. Members should take turns reporting to their group on the instances of stereotyping they found. The group recorder takes notes.

   d. Each group should work collaboratively to write a single brief essay evaluating the television show's depiction of blacks.

   e. One member of each group should read the essay aloud to the rest of the class.

   f. After all the essays are read, the class should discuss similarities and differences in the ways African Americans are portrayed by the media.

# The War Against the Poor Instead of Programs to End Poverty

## *Herbert J. Gans*

*Herbert Gans is a professor of sociology at Columbia University. He has written numerous articles and books on the subject of poverty, including* The Urban Villagers, The Levittowners, People and Plans, Popular Culture and High Culture, Deciding What's News, The War against the Poor, *and* Making Sense of America.

### PREREADING

Before you read the article, take a few minutes to write a response to the title. Do you think we are making a serious effort to end poverty in the United States? Can you think of why we might be accused of engaging in a war against the poor instead of a battle to improve their condition?

Reprinted by permission of *Dissent* Magazine and Herbert J. Gans from the Fall, 1992 issue of *Dissent* Magazine.

While liberals have been talking about resuming the War on Poverty, elected officials are doing something very different: waging a war on the poor. Even the riot that took place in Los Angeles in early May [1992] did not interrupt that war, perhaps because the riot was a mixture of protest, looting, and destruction.

The war on the poor was initiated by dramatic shifts in the domestic and world economy, which have turned more and more unskilled and semiskilled workers into surplus labor. Private enterprise participated actively by shipping jobs overseas and by treating workers as expendable. Government has done its part as well, increasingly restricting the welfare state safety net to the middle class. Effective job-creation schemes, housing programs, educational and social services that serve the poor—and some of the working classes—are vanishing. Once people become poor, it becomes ever harder for them to escape poverty.

Despite the willingness to help the poor expressed in public opinion polls, other, more covert, attitudes have created a political climate that makes the war on the poor possible. Politicians compete with each other over who can capture the most headlines with new ways to punish the poor. However, too many of their constituents see the poor not as people without jobs but as miscreants who behave badly because they do not abide by middle-class or mainstream moral values. Those judged "guilty" are dismissed as the "undeserving poor"—or the underclass in today's language—people who do not deserve to escape poverty.

True, *some* people are indeed guilty of immoral behavior—that is, murderers, street criminals, drug sellers, child abusers.

Then there are poor people whose anger at their condition expresses itself in the kind of nihilism that cannot be defined as political protest. Even so, most of those labeled "undeserving" are simply poor people who for a variety of reasons cannot live up to mainstream behavioral standards, like remaining childless in adolescence, finding and holding a job, and staying off welfare. This does not make them immoral. Because poor adolescents do not have jobs does not mean they are lazy. Because their ghetto "cool" may deter employers does not mean they are unwilling to work. Still, the concept of an underclass lumps them with those who are criminal or violent.

Why do Americans accept so many untruths about the poor and remain unwilling to accept the truth when it is available? The obvious answer is that some of the poor frighten or anger those who are better off. But they also serve as a lightning rod—scapegoats—for some problems among the better off. Street criminals rightly evoke fears about personal safety, but they and the decidedly innocent poor also generate widespread anger about the failure of government to reduce "urban" and other problems.

Among whites, the anger is intertwined with fears about blacks and 7 "Hispanics," or the newest immigrants, reflecting the fear of the stranger and newcomer from which their own ancestors suffered when they arrived here. (Few remember that at the start of the twentieth century, the "Hebrews" then arriving were sometimes described as a "criminal race"—as the Irish had been earlier in the nineteenth century.)

The hostility toward today's welfare recipients is a subtler but 8 equally revealing index to the fears of the more fortunate. This fear reflects a historic belief that people who are not economically self-sufficient can hurt the economy, although actual expenditures for welfare have always been small. Welfare recipients are also assumed to be getting something for nothing, often by people who are not overly upset about corrupt governmental or corporate officials who get a great deal of money for nothing or very little.

Welfare recipients possibly provoke anger among those concerned 9 about their own economic security, especially in a declining economy. Welfare recipients are seen as living the easy life while everyone else is working harder than ever—and thus become easy scapegoats, which does not happen to the successful, who often live easier lives.

The concern with poor unmarried mothers, especially adoles- 10 cents, whose number and family size have in fact long been declining, epitomizes adult fears about the high levels of sexual activity and the constant possibility of pregnancy among *all* adolescent girls. In addition, the notion of the "undeserving poor" has become a symbol for the general decline of mainstream moral standards, especially those celebrated as "traditional" in American society.

Ironically, however, the "undeserving poor" can be forced to up- 11 hold some of these very standards in exchange for welfare, much as some Skid Row homeless still get a night's dinner and housing in exchange for sitting through a religious service. The missionaries in this case are secular: social workers and bureaucrats. But the basic moralistic expectations remain the same, including the demand that the poor live up to values that their socioeconomic superiors preach but do not always practice. Thus, social workers can have live-in lovers without being married, but their clients on welfare cannot. Members of the more fortunate classes are generally free from moral judgments altogether; no one talks about an undeserving middle class or the undeserving rich.

The war on the poor is probably best ended by job-centered economic growth that creates decent public and private jobs. Once poor people have such jobs, they are almost automatically considered deserving, eligible for a variety of other programs to help them or their children escape poverty. 12

The most constructive way to supply such jobs would be an updated New Deal that repairs failing infrastructures, creates new public facilities (including new databases), and allows the old ones to function better—for example, by drastically reducing class size in public schools. Equally important are ways of reviving private enterprise and finding new niches for it in the global economy. Without them, there will not be enough well-paying jobs in factories, laboratories, and offices—or taxes to pay for public programs. Such programs are already being proposed these days, by Bill Clinton and in the Congress, but mainly for working-class people who have been made jobless and are now joining the welfare rolls. 13

Last but not least is a new approach to income grants for those who cannot work or find work. The latest fashion is to put welfare recipients to work, which would be a good idea if even decent entry-level jobs for them could be found or created. (Alas, when taxpayers discover how much cheaper it is to pay welfare than to create jobs, that remedy may end as it has before.) 14

Also needed is a non-punitive, universal income grant program, which goes to all people who still end up as part of the labor surplus. If such a program copied the European principle of not letting the incomes of the poor fall below 60 to 70 percent of the median income—in the United States, welfare recipients get a fifth of the median on average—the recipients would remain integral members of society, who could be required to make sure their children would not become poor. (Such a solution would also cut down the crime rate.) 15

However, even minimal conventional antipoverty programs are politically unpopular at the moment. The 1992 Democratic presidential candidates paid little attention to the poor during the primaries, except, in passing, in New York City and, then again, after Los Angeles. The future of antipoverty programs looks no brighter than before. 16

The time may be ripe to look more closely at how nonpoor Americans feel about poverty, and try to reduce their unwarranted fear and 17 anger toward the poor—with the hope that they would then be more positive about reviving antipoverty efforts.

The first priority for reducing that anger is effective policies 18 against drugs and street crime, though they alone cannot stem all the negative feelings. Probably the only truly effective solution is a prosperous economy in which the anger between all groups is lessened; and a more egalitarian society in which the displacement of such anger on the poor is no longer necessary, and the remaining class conflicts can be fought fairly.

This ideal is today more utopian than ever, but it ought to be kept 19 in mind. Every step toward it will help a little. Meanwhile, in order to bring back antipoverty programs, liberals, along with the poor and others who speak for the poor, could also try something else: initiating an intellectual and cultural defense of the poor. In a "sound bite": to fight *class* bigotry along with the racial kind.

Anti-bigotry programs work slowly and not always effectively, but 20 they are as American as apple pie. Class bigotry is itself still a novel idea, but nothing would be lost by mounting a defense of the poor and putting it on the public agenda. Ten such defenses strike me as especially urgent:

1. *Poverty is not equivalent to moral failure.* That moral undesir- 21 ables exist among the poor cannot be denied, but there is no evidence that their proportion is greater than among the more fortunate. "Bums" can be found at all economic levels. However, more prosperous miscreants tend to be less visible; the alcoholic co-worker can doze off at his desk, but the poor drunk is apt to be found in the gutter. Abusive middle class parents may remain invisible for years, until their children are badly hurt, but violent poor parents soon draw the attention of child-welfare workers and may lose their children to foster care.

Troubled middle-class people have access to experts who can 22 demonstrate that moral diagnoses are not enough. The abusive mother was herself abused; the school dropout has a learning disability; the young person who will not work suffers from depression. Poor people, on the other hand, rarely have access to such experts or to clinical treatment. For the poor, the explanations are usually moral, and the treatment is punitive.

2. *"Undeservingness" is an effect of poverty.* Whatever else can be 23 said about unmarried mothers on welfare, school dropouts, and people unwilling to take minimum-wage dead-end jobs, their behavior is almost always *poverty-related*.

This is, of course, also true of many street criminals and drug sell- 24
ers. Middle-class people, after all, do not turn into muggers and street
drug dealers any more than they become fifteen-year-old unmarried
mothers.

People who have not been poor themselves do not understand 25
how much of what the poor do is poverty-related. Poor young women
often do not want to marry the fathers of their children because such
men cannot perform as breadwinners and might cope with their economic failures by battering their wives. Although a great deal of publicity is given to school dropouts, not enough has been said about the peer
pressure in poor, and even working-class, neighborhoods that discourages doing well in school.

3. *The responsibilities of the poor.* Conservatives, often mute 26
about the responsibilities of the rich, stress the responsibilities of the
poor. However, poor people sometimes feel no need to be responsible
to society until society treats them responsibly. Acting irresponsibly becomes an angry reaction to, even a form of power, over that society.
Those whose irresponsibility is criminal deserve punishment and the
clearly lazy deserve to lose their benefits. But who would punish an unmarried mother who goes on welfare to obtain medical benefits that a
job cannot supply? Is she not acting responsibly toward her child? And
how well can we judge anyone's responsibility without first knowing
that choices, responsible and irresponsible, were actually open? Being
poor often means having little choice to begin with.

4. *The drastic scarcity of work for the poor.* Many Americans, in- 27
cluding too many economists, have long assumed that there are always
more jobs than workers, that the properly eager can always find them,
hence the jobless are at fault. This is, however, a myth—one of many
Ronald Reagan liked to promote when he was president. The facts are
just the opposite. Decent jobs that are open to the poor, especially to
blacks, were the first to disappear when our deindustrialization began.
This helps to explain why so many poor men have dropped out of the
labor force, and are no longer even counted as jobless.

Incidentally, the myth that the unemployed are unwilling to work is 28
never attached to the rising number of working- and middle-class jobless.
But, then, they are not yet poor enough to be considered undeserving.

5. *Black troubles and misbehavior are caused more by poverty than* 29
*by race.* Because the proportion of blacks who are criminals, school
dropouts, heads of single-parent families, or unmarried mothers is higher
than among whites, blacks increasingly have to face the outrageous

438 Social Class and Inequality

indignity of being considered genetically or culturally undesirable. The plain fact is that the higher rates of nearly all social problems among blacks are the effects of being poor—including poverty brought about by discrimination. When poor whites are compared with poor blacks, those with social problems are not so different, although black proportions remain higher. Even this difference can be attributed to income disparity. Black poverty has been worse in all respects and by all indicators ever since blacks were brought here as slaves.

6. *Blacks should not be treated like recent immigrants.* Black job- 30 seekers sometimes face the additional burden of being expected, both by employers and the general public, to compete for jobs with recently arrived immigrants. This expectation calls on people who have been in America for generations to accept the subminimum wages, long hours, poor working conditions, and employer intimidation that are the lot of many immigrants. Actually, employers prefer immigrants because they are more easily exploited or more deferential than native-born Americans. To make matters worse, blacks are then blamed for lacking an "immigrant work ethic."

7. *Debunking the metaphors of undeservingness.* Society's word- 31 smiths—academics, journalists, and pundits—like to find, and their audiences like to hear, buzzwords that caricature moral failings among the poor; but it should not be forgotten that these terms were invented by the fortunate. *Not only is there no identifiable underclass, but a class "under" society is a social impossibility.* Welfare "dependents" are in that condition mainly because the economy has declared them surplus labor and because they must rely on politicians and officials who determine their welfare eligibility.

Such metaphors are never applied to the more affluent. There are 32 no hard-core millionaires, and troubled middle-class people will never be labeled an under-middle class. Women who choose to be financially dependent on their husbands are not described as spouse-dependent, while professors who rely on university trustees for their income are not called tenure-dependent.

8. *The dangers of class stereotypes.* Underclass and other terms 33 for the undeserving poor are class stereotypes, which reinforce class discrimination much as racial stereotypes support racial discrimination. The many similarities between class and racial stereotypes still need to be identified.

Stereotypes sometimes turn into everyday labels that are so taken 34 for granted that they turn into self-fulfilling prophecies—and then cause particular havoc among the more vulnerable poor. For example, boys from poor single-parent families are apt to be punished harder for minor delinquencies simply because of the stereotype that they are growing up without paternal or other male supervision. Once they, and other poor people, are labeled as undeserving, public officials who are supposed to supply them with services feel justified in not being as helpful as before—though depriving poor people of an emergency rent payment or food grant may be enough to push them closer to homelessness or street crime.

The recent display of interest in and appeals for affirmative action 35 along class lines—even by conservatives like Dinesh D'Souza—suggests that the time may be ripe to recognize, and begin to fight, the widespread existence of class discrimination and prejudice. The confrontation has to take place not only in everyday life but also in the country's major institutions, politics, and courts. The Constitution that is now interpreted as barring racial discrimination can perhaps be interpreted to bar class discrimination as well.

9. *Blaming the poor reduces neither poverty nor poverty-related* 36 *behavior.* Labeling the poor as undeserving does not attack the causes of street crime, improve the schools of poor children, or reduce adult joblessness. Such labels are only a way of expressing anger toward the poor. Blaming the victim solves nothing except to make blamers feel better temporarily. Such labeling justifies political ideologies and interests that oppose solutions, and thus increases the likelihood that nothing will be done about poverty—or crime.

10. *Improving reporting and scholarship about the poor.* Most 37 poverty news is about crime, not poverty. How many reporters ever ask whether economic hardship is part of the crime story? The government's monthly jobless rate is reported, but not the shortage of jobs open to the poor. Likewise, the percentage of people below the poverty rate is an annual news story, but the actual income of the poor, often less than half the poverty line, or about $6,000 a year, is not mentioned.

The "spins," both in government statistics and in journalism, carry 38 over into scholarship. Millions were spent to find and measure an underclass, but there is little ethnographic research to discover why the poor must live as they do. Researchers on homelessness look at mental illness as a cause of homelessness; they do not study it as a possible *effect!*

There are also innumerable other studies of the homeless, but too 39 few about the labor markets and employers, housing industry and landlords, and other factors that create homelessness in the first place.

The Americans who feel most threatened by the poor are people 40 from the working class, whom journalists currently call the middle class. They are apt to live nearest the poor. They will suffer most, other than the poor themselves, from street crime, as well as from the fear that the poor could take over their neighborhoods and jobs. Indeed, as inexpensive housing and secure jobs requiring little education become more scarce, the people only slightly above the poor in income and economic security fear that their superior status will shrink drastically. Viewing the poor as undeserving helps to maintain and even widen that status gap.

No wonder, then, that in the current economic crisis, the journal- 41 ists' middle class and its job problems are the big story, and the poor appear mainly as the underclass, with candidates ignoring poverty. The political climate being what it is, this may even be unavoidable. Indeed, if the winner's margin in the coming elections comes from that middle class, the candidate must initiate enough economic programs to put *its* jobless back to work and to solve its health care, housing, and other problems.

That winner should be bold enough to make room in the program 42 for the poor as well. Poverty, racial polarization, crime, and related problems cannot be allowed to rise higher without further reducing morale, quality of life, and economic competitiveness. Otherwise, America will not be a decent, safe, or pleasant place to live, even for the affluent. ✿

## READING FOR INFORMATION

1. Summarize how the economy, the government, and the political climate have participated in the war against the poor.
2. Paraphrase Gans's objections to the concept of "underclass" (paragraphs 33 and 34).
3. Discuss why people who are better off are frightened and angered by the poor. Do you agree with Gans's explanation?
4. List Gans's solutions for ending the war on the poor. Do you think they are workable?
5. What is the ideal way of reducing the anger directed against the poor?
6. In your own words, explain which of Gans's ten defenses against class bigotry are the most workable.
7. React to Gans's forecast for the future.

## READING FOR FORM, ORGANIZATION, AND EXPOSITORY FEATURES

1. Explain Gans's overall organizational plan. What other organizational patterns does he use?
2. What is the function of paragraphs 11, 21, 22, and 32?
3. Describe the features of the article that help the reader to follow Gans's train of thought.
4. Why do you think Gans concludes the article as he does? What effect did the conclusion have on you as a reader?

## READING FOR RHETORICAL CONCERNS

1. What do you think prompted Gans to write this article?
2. Do you think Gans provides his readers with enough background to support his premise about the war against the poor? What additional information would be useful?
3. What impact does Gans want to have on his audience? Do you think he is successful?

## WRITING ASSIGNMENTS

1. Write a two- to three-page essay explaining why you agree or disagree with Gans's observation that "the Americans who feel most threatened by the poor are people from the working class" (paragraph 40).
2. Write an essay in which you argue for or against Gans's claim that Americans need to fight against class bigotry as well as racial discrimination and prejudice.
3. For a two-week period, keep a written record of how poor people are treated in a daily newspaper or a daily news broadcast. Then, use your notes to write an essay explaining whether or not the media stereotype poor people as undeserving.

# When Shelter Feels Like a Prison

## *Charmion Browne*

*Charmion Browne is a senior at Cornell University.*

### PREREADING

In an article published in *The New York Times* on March 24, 2002, Jennifer Egan writes, "Today, families make up 75 percent of New York's homeless-shelter population, with more than 13,000 children having slept in city shelters and temporary apartments most nights this winter" (34). Egan goes on to say, "In an era regarded as generally prosperous, the numbers are staggering: Between 900,000 and 1.4 million children in America are homeless for a time in a given year" (34–35). Were you aware that children make up a large percentage (up to 40 percent) of the nation's homeless population? Respond in your journal.

During my early childhood I lived in four or five different   1
homeless shelters in New York City. It's a good thing my mother found employment when she did; otherwise I, too, might have been like one of the homeless children in the city today, left without even a shelter to live in because of overcrowding. Last week some of these children were sent to an unused jail in the Bronx—and then removed when lead paint was found there—because the city could find nowhere else for them to live.

From a house to a shelter to a former jail—not the most desirable   2
pathway to take in life. I only had to deal with having to write down an address in school that was never going to be my own, living in a "house" where I had an extended family of one-hundred strangers, being cramped in a room as small as a bathroom with three other families besides my own, with no sense of privacy—ever. Some homeless children in New York can now add to their childhood memories the time they had no place else to live but a former jail.

Charmion Browne, "When Shelter Feels Like a Prison." *The New York Times*, 18 August, 2002, Sec. 4: WK13.

My mother had financial difficulties as a single mother taking care 3 of my brother and me on her own. She worked very hard to move us from a small one-bedroom apartment to a two-bedroom apartment. We finally did move into that bigger apartment when I was around 8, but after living there a week we discovered that the place was infested with centipedes and we had to move out before my mother could find us another apartment. So we ended up in a shelter. I think my mother thought it was only going to be a temporary situation until she could find someplace else to go.

On that first night without a home, I fell asleep as we waited in 4 line at the department of homeless services to find out which shelter would take us. There were no more seats available and we were there for over five hours before my mother even got to talk to someone. We then had to wait another two hours before a van came to pick us up and take us to the shelter in downtown Manhattan where we would be spending the next two months.

It still puzzles me how so many beds could fit in the room we 5 stayed in. There were four bunk beds crammed into one tiny room. I shared a top bunk with my brother, with my mother sleeping below. Every time we wanted to get to our bed, we had to jump across someone else's bed. Since we had been the last to arrive at the shelter, we had no choice; we got the bed farthest back in the room.

My brother and I learned quickly that there were unspoken rules 6 for living in these places. In a way, living there was like living in a kind of prison. You had to fit in fast or someone would take advantage of you. There weren't any curtains in the bathrooms and everyone on the floor—100 or more people—had to use the same facility. My mother quickly picked up the habit of waking us at 4 a.m. to make sure we took a shower before anyone else awakened. Later, we learned that if you didn't start lining up for meals at least two hours before the kitchen was open, you might as well forget about eating. We had to watch our things at all times, because if you weren't careful someone might take your things and you'd never see them again.

I was in high school when I finally accepted the fact that I was 7 homeless. Until that point I was in complete denial. During those miserable times, my brother and I learned how to become expert liars. We never let our friends in school know where we were living. In some cases we were lucky enough not to be going to the local school, so no one ever walked home with us. If the shelter was near our school or one of our friends caught us coming out of the "bums" building, as the kids in the neighborhood used to call it, then we would tell them our mother worked there and we had to meet her there after school. It is difficult enough to fit in when you are a kid, and worse yet when you can never invite anyone home to visit because you don't have a home.

Being in those shelters, though, helped me to see that the biggest 8 cause of homelessness is not lack of money to pay rent. There were a lot of broken families in these shelters: broken by drugs, alcohol abuse, divorce, AIDS, early pregnancy, lack of education and, most important, lack of information about how to get out of these troubles. Many of the kids I knew at the shelter really wanted to change their circumstances, but few of them did—few of them knew how. There weren't many social workers around, and even when they were around and noticed a problem, they rarely followed up. The children in these situations need a listening ear, someone to turn to consistently.

Sure, having a bed to sleep on is better than having no bed at all. 9 But sleeping on a bed in a shelter that was once a jail doesn't help ease the psychological burden of being homeless in the first place. I understand that Mayor Michael Bloomberg's administration is trying to make sure that the new shelter in the Bronx is safe, but is it working to make it seem less prison-like? A line for food, cramped space, no privacy—sounds a lot like a prison to me. The only difference now is that the city is calling a homeless shelter what it really is. ✿

## READING FOR INFORMATION

1. What event prompted Browne to write this piece?
2. In your own words, explain why living in a homeless shelter is like living in a prison.

## READING FOR FORM, ORGANIZATION, AND EXPOSITORY FEATURES

1. Explain how the opening paragraph informs the reader of the direction Browne will take in the remainder of the selection.
2. Describe the type of evidence Browne uses to support her position. Is the evidence effective?

## READING FOR RHETORICAL CONCERNS

1. Describe Browne's purpose. What is she trying to get across to the readers of *The New York Times*?

2. How would you characterize Browne's tone of voice? Is it appropriate for her rhetorical purpose?

## WRITING ASSIGNMENTS

1. In response to Charmion Browne's article, write a letter to the editor of *The New York Times.*

2. In "Serving in Florida," Barbara Ehrenreich provides insights into the problem of homelessness when she discusses the acute shortage of affordable housing for extremely low-income families. Write an essay in which you draw upon Barbara Ehrenreich as well as other authors in Chapter 10 to explain Charmion Browne's childhood of homelessness.

# White Standard for Poverty

## *Dirk Johnson*

*Dirk Johnson is a journalist who has written for* Newsweek *and* The New York Times. *He is a five-time winner of* The New York Times *Publisher's Award and author of* Biting the Dust: The Wild Ride *and* Dark Romance of the Rodeo.

## PREREADING

Before reading this short selection, comment on the economic conditions of Native Americans. Answer the following questions in your journal: To which social class do many Native Americans belong? Do you think there is much poverty on Indian reservations? What is your understanding of the expression "white standard for poverty"? Do you think white people's standard of poverty is different from that of Indians? Freewrite your response.

The rough dirt path to the Navajo sheep camp meanders be-     1
tween ancient dunes and slabs of sandstone rising in huge, shattered plates. A few rare trees, planted next to a hogan, or *cha*

*ha'oh*—a summer shade house made of branches—stick up from an ocean of low greasewood. In some places, the skin of the earth has been peeled away by scouring sandstorms and washed clean by pummeling summer rain.

This is some of the rawest land on the Navajo reservation, a place ₂ where water must be hauled in barrels by pick-up from Tuba City, some 40 miles away, and where two elderly women, Dorothy Reed and Jeanette Lewis, survive by raising sheep and cows.

By most measures, American Indians are the poorest ethnic group ₃ in the country. On some reservations, unemployment exceeds 80 percent. Of the ten poorest United States counties in the last census, four were Indian lands in South Dakota. On the Navajo lands, unemployment ranges from 30 percent to 40 percent, and shacks are more common than houses.

Income among Indians has not grown for the past decade. Some ₄ experts say those figures mask real progress, however, since a baby boom among Indians in the last generation has sharply increased the number of young people. Nearly 20 percent of Indians are younger than ten, twice the national rate.

To be sure, welfare payments account for a great share of the ₅ money on some reservations. And yet, tribal leaders say, there are two faces of poverty in Indian Country.

Rates of Indian suicide and alcoholism far exceed the national averages. Some reservations now have street gangs, a new phenomenon. ₆ And domestic violence continues to be a serious problem.

And yet, many Indian people are poor, but hardly broken. "It's important not to impose the non-Indian values of poverty on Indians," ₇ said David Lester of the Council of Energy Resource Tribes. "There are worse things than being poor. Don't get me wrong—nobody likes suffering. But money is just not the measure of success."

Many of them value the traditional ways more than modern contrivances, and no federal program could persuade them to follow a new ₈ way, even if it seemed easier.

"In the beginning, the earth was made for us by Changing ₉ Woman," said Mrs. Reed, referring to a Navajo deity. "My grandfather used to tell me that you were supposed to make a living from the earth and the sheep."

This is part of the Indian Country economy largely missing from ₁₀ government charts and graphs on employment and production: traditional Navajos who raise their own food, or wait by the roadside to sell herbs they have picked from the hills or wood they have gathered or rugs they have woven by hand.

Many of them barter goods and services: a coat in exchange for a 11 car battery, babysitting in exchange for repair work.

Some have never seen the inside of a bank. In some areas, the In- 12 dian economy has stagnated because banks are unwilling to count reservation homes as collateral, since the land is held in a trust. They will, however, lend money for trailers, since they can be repossessed and hauled away.

When Navajos run low on money, they sometimes drive or hitch- 13 hike to the pawnshops in the dusty town of Gallup, New Mexico, where they plop saddles and blankets and pieces of jewelry on the counter as collateral for high-interest loans. Often they are later unable to come up with the cash required to retrieve their belongings, which are then declared "dead pawn," and sold, frequently to prosperous tourists stopping off Interstate 40 in search of an Indian souvenir.

The Navajo women had been up since dawn, in a one-room house 14 with bare sheetrock walls, with the front facing, to greet the sunrise, as tradition decrees it. There was fry bread for breakfast. Both wore the traditional attire for elderly Navajo women: velveteen blouse closed at the neck with a turquoise clasp, long tiered satin dresses, socks and inexpensive running shoes known by the young ones as "sani sneakers"— grandma sneakers.

On this morning, some of their children and grandchildren had ar- 15 rived to help round up some stray cows. As in many Navajo families, their children had become educated and moved to town, living in houses with plumbing and electricity. But they come back often and help out with some money when they can.

Mrs. Reed's son, Willie, won a scholarship to attend an Eastern 16 prep school, and then earned bachelor's and master's degrees from Stanford University. With his education, he could have landed a high-paying job and taken a home in the city, with air-conditioning and cable television and home-delivered pizza. Instead, he returned to a tiny house on the reservation and now teaches science at a Navajo high school. ❀

## READING FOR INFORMATION

1. What do you think David Lester means when he says, "It's important not to impose the non-Indian values of poverty on Indians" (paragraph 7)?

2. Describe in your own words the "hidden" or unpublished side of the Indian economy.

3. What types of wealth do Dorothy Reed and Jeanette Lewis possess? Do you think white Americans value those types of wealth?

## READING FOR FORM, ORGANIZATION, AND EXPOSITORY FEATURES

1. What characteristics of Johnson's piece reveal that it was written for a newspaper? Explain how it differs from other selections in this chapter.

2. Underline examples of the types of evidence (facts, statistics, references to authorities, personal experiences) Johnson uses. Do you think that evidence is effective? Explain.

## READING FOR RHETORICAL CONCERNS

1. How did you react to this article? Explain the effect it will have on the readers of *The New York Times*.

2. How would you describe Johnson's tone? How does it differ from Patricia Clark Smith's in "Grandma Went to Smith"?

## WRITING ASSIGNMENTS

1. Drawing on Johnson's article, your own experience, and other selections you have read, write an essay in which you explain why some people prefer modest traditional ways to modern technology and contrivances. Write for classmates who have not read Johnson's article.

2. Some sociologists and economists report that although most Native Americans are still very poor, in recent years some have improved their economic standing. Visit the library and search for recent magazine and newspaper articles dealing with the economy of Native Americans. How do your findings compare with Johnson's? Write an essay in which you synthesize the information you locate.

# Serving in Florida

## *Barbara Ehrenreich*

*Barbara Ehrenreich has contributed articles to many magazines and written twelve books, including* The Worst Years of Our Lives, Blood Fires, Fear of Falling, *and* Nickel and Dimed: On (Not) Getting By in America, *from which this selection was taken.*

### PREREADING

This selection is a chapter in Barbara Ehrenreich's book, *Nickel and Dimed: On (Not) Getting By in America.* From 1998 to 2000, Ehrenreich went undercover and became a low-wage worker in order to experience firsthand what it is like to survive on six to seven dollars an hour. Before Ehrenreich embarked on the project, she set three rules for herself: that in her search for jobs she would not rely on her education or former occupation; that she would accept the highest paying job she was given; and that she would lower her expenses by taking the cheapest housing she could find. Over the course of the project, Ehrenreich took jobs in Key West, Florida; Portland, Maine; and Minneapolis, Minnesota.

In this selection Ehrenreich relates her experiences as a server, first at the Hearthside Restaurant where she worked from 2:00 p.m. to 10:00 p.m. for $2.43 per hour plus tips, and then at Johnny's Restaurant. She also worked briefly as a housekeeper in the hotel attached to Johnny's.

What is the lowest paid job you ever held? Take 10 to 15 minutes to write a journal entry explaining what it entailed. In small groups, share your experience with your classmates.

I still flinch to think that I spent all those weeks under the surveillance of men (and later women) whose job it was to monitor my behavior for signs of sloth, theft, drug abuse, or worse. Not that managers and especially "assistant managers" in low-wage settings like 1 this are exactly the class enemy. Mostly, in the restaurant business, they are former cooks still capable of pinch-hitting in the kitchen, just as in hotels they are likely to be former clerks, and paid a salary of only about $400 a week. But everyone knows they have crossed over to the other side, which is, crudely put, corporate as opposed to human. Cooks want to prepare tasty meals, servers want to serve them graciously, but managers are there for only one reason—to make sure that money is made for some theoretical entity, the corporation, which exists far away in Chicago or New York, if a corporation can be said to have a physical existence at all. Reflecting on her career, Gail tells me ruefully that she swore, years ago, never to work for a corporation again. "They don't cut you no slack. You give and you give and they take."

Managers can sit—for hours at a time if they want—but it's their job    2
to see that no one else ever does, even when there's nothing to do, and this is why, for servers, slow times can be as exhausting as rushes. You start dragging out each little chore because if the manager on duty catches you in an idle moment he will give you something far nastier to do. So I wipe, I clean, I consolidate catsup bottles and recheck the cheesecake supply, even tour the tables to make sure the customer evaluation forms are all standing perkily in their places—wondering all the time how many calories I burn in these strictly theatrical exercises. In desperation, I even take the desserts out of their glass display case and freshen them up with whipped cream and bright new maraschino cherries; anything to look busy. When, on a particularly dead afternoon, Stu finds me glancing at a *USA Today* a customer has left behind, he assigns me to vacuum the entire floor with the broken vacuum cleaner, which has a handle only two feet long, and the only way to do that without incurring orthopedic damage is to proceed from spot to spot on your knees.

On my first Friday at Hearthside there is a "mandatory meeting for    3
all restaurant employees," which I attend, eager for insight into our overall marketing strategy and the niche (your basic Ohio cuisine with a tropical twist?) we aim to inhabit. But there is no "we" at this meeting. Phillip, our top manager except for an occasional "consultant" sent out by corporate headquarters, opens it with a sneer: "The break room—it's disgusting. Butts in the ashtrays, newspapers lying around, crumbs." This windowless little room, which also houses the time clock for the entire hotel, is where we stash our bags and civilian clothes and take our half-hour meal breaks. But a break room is not a right, he tells us, it can be taken away. We should also know that the lockers in the break room and whatever is in them can be searched at any time. Then comes gossip; there has been gossip; gossip (which seems to mean employees talking

among themselves) must stop. Off-duty employees are henceforth barred from eating at the restaurant, because "other servers gather around them and gossip." When Phillip has exhausted his agenda of rebukes, Joan complains about the condition of the ladies' room and I throw in my two bits about the vacuum cleaner. But I don't see any backup coming from my fellow servers, each of whom has slipped into her own personal funk; Gail, my role model, stares sorrowfully at a point six inches from her nose. The meeting ends when Andy, one of the cooks, gets up, muttering about breaking up his day off for this almighty bullshit.

Just four days later we are suddenly summoned into the kitchen at   4
3:30 P.M., even though there are live tables on the floor. We all—about ten of us—stand around Phillip, who announces grimly that there has been a report of some "drug activity" on the night shift and that, as a result, we are now to be a "drug-free" workplace, meaning that all new hires will be tested and possibly also current employees on a random basis. I am glad that this part of the kitchen is so dark because I find myself blushing as hard as if I had been caught toking up in the ladies' room myself: I haven't been treated this way—lined up in the corridor, threatened with locker searches, peppered with carelessly aimed accusations—since at least junior high school. Back on the floor, Joan cracks, "Next they'll be telling us we can't have *sex* on the job." When I ask Stu what happened to inspire the crackdown, he just mutters about "management decisions" and takes the opportunity to upbraid Gail and me for being too generous with the rolls. From now on there's to be only one per customer and it goes out with the dinner, not with the salad. He's also been riding the cooks, prompting Andy to come out of the kitchen and observe—with the serenity of a man whose customary implement is a butcher knife—that "Stu has a death wish today."

Later in the evening, the gossip crystallizes around the theory that   5
Stu is himself the drug culprit, that he uses the restaurant phone to order up marijuana and sends one of the late servers out to fetch it for him. The server was caught and she may have ratted out Stu, at least enough to cast some suspicion on him, thus accounting for his pissy behavior. Who knows? Personally, I'm ready to believe anything bad about Stu, who serves no evident function and presumes too much on our common ethnicity, sidling up to me one night to engage in a little nativism directed at the Haitian immigrants: "I feel like I'm the foreigner here. They're taking over the country." Still later that evening, the drug in question escalates to crack. Lionel, the busboy, entertains us for the rest of the shift by standing just behind Stu's back and sucking deliriously on an imaginary joint or maybe a pipe.

The other problem, in addition to the less-than-nurturing man-    6
agement style, is that this job shows no sign of being financially viable.
You might imagine, from a comfortable distance, that people who live,
year in and year out, on $6 to $10 an hour have discovered some survival stratagems unknown to the middle class. But no. It's not hard to
get my coworkers talking about their living situations, because housing,
in almost every case, is the principal source of disruption in their lives,
the first thing they fill you in on when they arrive for their shifts. After a
week, I have compiled the following survey:

> Gail is sharing a room in a well-known downtown flophouse for $250 a
> week. Her roommate, a male friend, has begun hitting on her, driving
> her nuts, but the rent would be impossible alone.

> Claude, the Haitian cook, is desperate to get out of the two-room apart-
> ment he shares with his girlfriend and two other, unrelated people. As
> far as I can determine, the other Haitian men live in similarly crowded
> situations.

> Annette, a twenty-year-old server who is six months pregnant and aban-
> doned by her boyfriend, lives with her mother, a postal clerk.

> Marianne, who is a breakfast server, and her boyfriend are paying $170 a
> week for a one-person trailer.

> Billy, who at $10 an hour is the wealthiest of us, lives in the trailer he
> owns, paying only the $400-a-month lot fee.

> The other white cook, Andy, lives on his dry-docked boat, which, as far as
> I can tell from his loving descriptions, can't be more than twenty feet
> long. He offers to take me out on it once it's repaired, but the offer
> comes with inquiries as to my marital status, so I do not follow up on it.

> Tina, another server, and her husband are paying $60 a night for a room
> in the Days Inn. This is because they have no car and the Days Inn is in
> walking distance of the Hearthside. When Marianne is tossed out of her
> trailer for subletting (which is against trailer park rules), she leaves her
> boyfriend and moves in with Tina and her husband.

> Joan, who had fooled me with her numerous and tasteful outfits (hostesses
> wear their own clothes), lives in a van parked behind a shopping center at
> night and showers in Tina's motel room. The clothes are from thrift shops.[1]

[1] I could find no statistics on the number of employed people living in cars or vans, but according
to a 1997 report of the National Coalition for the Homeless, "Myths and Facts about Homelessness," nearly one-fifth of all homeless people (in twenty-nine cities across the nation) are employed in full- or part-time jobs.

It strikes me, in my middle-class solipsism, that there is gross im-  7
providence in some of these arrangements. When Gail and I are wrapping silverware in napkins—the only task for which we are permitted to
sit—she tells me she is thinking of escaping from her roommate by
moving into the Days Inn herself. I am astounded: how she can even
think of paying $40 to $60 a day? But if I was afraid of sounding like a
social worker, I have come out just sounding like a fool. She squints at
me in disbelief: "And where am I supposed to get a month's rent and a
month's deposit for an apartment?" I'd been feeling pretty smug about
my $500 efficiency, but of course it was made possible only by the
$1,300 I had allotted myself for start-up costs when I began my low-
wage life: $1,000 for the first month's rent and deposit, $100 for initial
groceries and cash in my pocket, $200 stuffed away for emergencies. In
poverty, as in certain propositions in physics, starting conditions are
everything.

There are no secret economies that nourish the poor; on the con-  8
trary, there are a host of special costs. If you can't put up the two
months' rent you need to secure an apartment, you end up paying
through the nose for a room by the week. If you have only a room, with
a hot plate at best, you can't save by cooking up huge lentil stews that
can be frozen for the week ahead. You eat fast food or the hot dogs and
Styrofoam cups of soup that can be microwaved in a convenience store.
If you have no money for health insurance—and the Hearthside's nig-
gardly plan kicks in only after three months—you go without routine
care or prescription drugs and end up paying the price. Gail, for example, was doing fine, healthwise anyway, until she ran out of money for
estrogen pills. She is supposed to be on the company health plan by
now, but they claim to have lost her application form and to be beginning the paperwork all over again. So she spends $9 a pop for pills to
control the migraines she wouldn't have, she insists, if her estrogen supplements were covered. Similarly, Marianne's boyfriend lost his job as a
roofer because he missed so much time after getting a cut on his foot
for which he couldn't afford the prescribed antibiotic.

My own situation, when I sit down to assess it after two weeks of  9
work, would not be much better if this were my actual life. The seductive thing about waitressing is that you don't have to wait for payday to
feel a few bills in your pocket, and my tips usually cover meals and gas,
plus something left over to stuff into the kitchen drawer I use as a bank.
But as the tourist business slows in the summer heat, I sometimes leave
work with only $20 in tips (the gross is higher, but servers share about

15 percent of their tips with the busboys and bartenders). With wages included, this amounts to about the minimum wage of $5.15 an hour. The sum in the drawer is piling up but at the present rate of accumulation will be more than $100 short of my rent when the end of the month comes around. Nor can I see any expenses to cut. True, I haven't gone the lentil stew route yet, but that's because I don't have a large cooking pot, potholders, or a ladle to stir with (which would cost a total of about $30 at Kmart, somewhat less at a thrift store), not to mention onions, carrots, and the indispensable bay leaf. I do make my lunch almost every day—usually some slow-burning, high-protein combo like frozen chicken patties with melted cheese on top and canned pinto beans on the side. Dinner is at the Hearthside, which offers its employees a choice of BLT, fish sandwich, or hamburger for only $2. The burger lasts longest, especially if it's heaped with gut-puckering jalapeños, but by midnight my stomach is growling again.

So unless I want to start using my car as a residence, I have to find a 10 second or an alternative job. I call all the hotels I'd filled out housekeeping applications at weeks ago—the Hyatt, Holiday Inn, Econo Lodge, HoJo's, Best Western, plus a half dozen locally run guest houses. Nothing. Then I start making the rounds again, wasting whole mornings waiting for some assistant manager to show up, even dipping into places so creepy that the front-desk clerk greets you from behind bullet-proof glass and sells pints of liquor over the counter. But either someone has exposed my real-life housekeeping habits—which are, shall we say, mellow—or I am at the wrong end of some infallible ethnic equation: Most, but by no means all, of the working housekeepers I see on my job searches are African Americans, Spanish-speaking, or refugees from the Central European post-Communist world, while servers are almost invariably white and monolingually English-speaking. When I finally get a positive response, I have been identified once again as server material. Jerry's—again, not the real name—which is part of a well-known national chain and physically attached here to another budget hotel, is ready to use me at once. The prospect is both exciting and terrifying because, with about the same number of tables and counter seats, Jerry's attracts three or four times the volume of customers as the gloomy old Hearthside.

Picture a fat person's hell, and I don't mean a place with no food. 11 Instead there is everything you might eat if eating had no bodily consequences—the cheese fries, the chicken-fried steaks, the fudge-laden desserts—only here every bite must be paid for, one way or another, in human discomfort. The kitchen is a cavern, a stomach leading to the lower intestine that is the garbage and dishwashing area, from which issue bizarre smells combining the edible and the offal: creamy carrion, pizza barf, and that unique and enigmatic Jerry's scent, citrus fart. The floor is slick with spills, forcing us to walk through the kitchen with tiny steps, like Susan McDougal in leg irons. Sinks everywhere are clogged with scraps of lettuce, decomposing lemon wedges, water-logged toast crusts. Put your hand down on any counter and you risk being stuck to it by the film of ancient syrup spills, and this is unfortunate because hands are utensils here, used for scooping up lettuce onto the salad plates, lifting out pie slices, and even moving hash browns from one plate to another. The regulation poster in the single unisex rest room admonishes us to wash our hands thoroughly, and even offers instructions for doing so, but there is always some vital substance missing— soap, paper towels, toilet paper—and I never found all three at once. You learn to stuff your pockets with napkins before going in there, and too bad about the customers, who must eat, although they don't realize it, almost literally out of our hands.

The break room summarizes the whole situation: There is none, 12 because there are no breaks at Jerry's. For six to eight hours in a row, you never sit except to pee. Actually, there are three folding chairs at a table immediately adjacent to the bathroom, but hardly anyone ever sits in this, the very rectum of the gastroarchitectural system. Rather, the function of the peri-toilet area is to house the ashtrays in which servers and dishwashers leave their cigarettes burning at all times, like votive candles, so they don't have to waste time lighting up again when they dash back here for a puff. Almost everyone smokes as if their pulmonary well-being depended on it—the multinational mélange of cooks; the dishwashers, who are all Czechs here; the servers, who are American natives—creating an atmosphere in which oxygen is only an occasional pollutant. My first morning at Jerry's, when the hypoglycemic shakes set in, I complain to one of my fellow servers that I don't understand how she can go so long without food. "Well, I don't understand how *you* can go so long without a cigarette," she responds in a tone of reproach. Because work is what you do for others; smoking is what you do for yourself. I don't know why the antismoking crusaders have never grasped the element of defiant self-nurturance that makes the habit so endearing to its victims—as if, in the American workplace, the only thing people have to call their own is the tumors they are nourishing and the spare moments they devote to feeding them.

Now, the Industrial Revolution is not an easy transition, espe- 13
cially, in my experience, when you have to zip through it in just a couple of days. I have gone from craft work straight into the factory, from
the air-conditioned morgue of the Hearthside directly into the flames.
Customers arrive in human waves, sometimes disgorged fifty at a time
from their tour buses, peckish and whiny. Instead of two "girls" on the
floor at once, there can be as many as six of us running around in our
brilliant pink-and-orange Hawaiian shirts. Conversations, either with
customers or with fellow employees, seldom last more than twenty seconds at a time. On my first day, in fact, I am hurt by my sister servers'
coldness. My mentor for the day is a supremely competent, emotionally uninflected twenty-three-year-old, and the others, who gossip a little among themselves about the real reason someone is out sick today
and the size of the bail bond someone else has had to pay, ignore me
completely. On my second day, I find out why. "Well, it's good to see
*you* again," one of them says in greeting. "Hardly anyone comes back
after the first day." I feel powerfully vindicated—a survivor—but it
would take a long time, probably months, before I could hope to be accepted into this sorority.

I start out with the beautiful, heroic idea of handling the two jobs 14
at once, and for two days I almost do it: working the breakfast/lunch
shift at Jerry's from 8:00 till 2:00, arriving at the Hearthside a few minutes late, at 2:10, and attempting to hold out until 10:00. In the few
minutes I have between jobs, I pick up a spicy chicken sandwich at the
Wendy's drive-through window, gobble it down in the car, and change
from khaki slacks to black, from Hawaiian to rust-colored polo. There is
a problem, though. When, during the 3:00–4:00 o'clock dead time, I finally sit down to wrap silver, my flesh seems to bond to the seat. I try to
refuel with a purloined cup of clam chowder, as I've seen Gail and Joan
do dozens of time, but Stu catches me and hisses "No *eating!*" although
there's not a customer around to be offended by the sight of food making contact with a server's lips. So I tell Gail I'm going to quit, and she
hugs me and says she might just follow me to Jerry's herself.

But the chances of this are minuscule. She has left the flop-house 15
and her annoying roommate and is back to living in her truck. But,
guess what, she reports to me excitedly later that evening, Phillip has
given her permission to park overnight in the hotel parking lot, as long
as she keeps out of sight, and the parking lot should be totally safe since
it's patrolled by a hotel security guard! With the Hearthside offering
benefits like that, how could anyone think of leaving? This must be

Phillip's theory, anyway. He accepts my resignation with a shrug, his main concern being that I return my two polo shirts and aprons.

Gail would have triumphed at Jerry's, I'm sure, but for me it's a  16 crash course in exhaustion management. Years ago, the kindly fry cook who trained me to waitress at a Los Angeles truck stop used to say: Never make an unnecessary trip; if you don't have to walk fast, walk slow; if you don't have to walk, stand. But at Jerry's the effort of distinguishing necessary from unnecessary and urgent from whenever would itself be too much of an energy drain. The only thing to do is to treat each shift as a one-time-only emergency: You've got fifty starving people out there, lying scattered on the battlefield, so get out there and feed them! Forget that you will have to do this again tomorrow, forget that you will have to be alert enough to dodge the drunks on the drive home tonight—just burn, burn, burn! Ideally, at some point you enter what servers call a "rhythm" and psychologists term a "flow state," where signals pass from the sense organs directly to the muscles, bypassing the cerebral cortex, and a Zen-like emptiness sets in. I'm on a 2:00–10:00 P.M. shift now, and a male server from the morning shift tells me about the time he "pulled a triple"—three shifts in a row, all the way around the clock—and then got off and had a drink and met this girl, and maybe he shouldn't tell me this, but they had sex right then and there and it was like *beautiful*.

But there's another capacity of the neuromuscular system, which  17 is pain. I start tossing back drugstore-brand ibuprofens as if they were vitamin C, four before each shift, because an old mouse-related repetitive-stress injury in my upper back has come back to full-spasm strength, thanks to the tray carrying. In my ordinary life, this level of disability might justify a day of ice packs and stretching. Here I comfort myself with the Aleve commercial where the cute blue-collar guy asks: If you quit after working four hours, what would your boss say? And the not-so-cute blue-collar guy, who's lugging a metal beam on his back, answers: He'd fire me, that's what. But fortunately, the commercial tells us, we workers can exert the same kind of authority over our painkillers that our bosses exert over us. If Tylenol doesn't want to work for more than four hours, you just fire its ass and switch to Aleve.

True, I take occasional breaks from this life, going home now and  18 then to catch up on email and for conjugal visits (though I am careful to "pay" for everything I eat here, at $5 for a dinner, which I put in a jar), seeing *The Truman Show* with friends and letting them buy my ticket. And I still have those what-am-I-doing-here moments at work, when I get so homesick for the printed word that I obsessively reread the six-page menu. But as the days go by, my old life is beginning to look exceedingly strange. The emails and phone messages addressed to my former self come from a distant race of people with exotic concerns and far too much time on their hands. The neighborly market I used to cruise for produce now looks forbiddingly like a Manhattan yuppie emporium. And when I sit down one morning in my real home to pay bills from my past life, I am dazzled by the two- and three-figure sums owed to outfits like Club Body Tech and Amazon.com.

Management at Jerry's is generally calmer and more "professional" 19 than at the Hearthside, with two exceptions. One is Joy, a plump, blowsy woman in her early thirties who once kindly devoted several minutes of her time to instructing me in the correct one-handed method of tray carrying but whose moods change disconcertingly from shift to shift and even within one. The other is B.J., aka B.J. the Bitch, whose contribution is to stand by the kitchen counter and yell, "Nita, your order's up, move it!" or "Barbara, didn't you see you've got another table out there? Come *on*, girl!" Among other things, she is hated for having replaced the whipped cream squirt cans with big plastic whipped-cream-filled baggies that have to be squeezed with both hands—because, reportedly, she saw or thought she saw employees trying to inhale the propellant gas from the squirt cans, in the hope that it might be nitrous oxide. On my third night, she pulls me aside abruptly and brings her face so close that it looks like she's planning to butt me with her forehead. But instead of saying "You're fired," she says, "You're doing fine." The only trouble is I'm spending time chatting with customers: "That's how they're getting you." Furthermore I am letting them "run me," which means harassment by sequential demands: You bring the catsup and they decide they want extra Thousand Island; you bring that and they announce they now need a side of fries, and so on into distraction. Finally she tells me not to take her wrong. She tries to say things in a nice way, but "you get into a mode, you know, because everything has to move so fast."[2]

I mumble thanks for the advice, feeling like I've just been stripped 20 naked by the crazed enforcer of some ancient sumptuary law: No

---

[2]In *Workers in a Lean World: Unions in the International Economy* (Verso, 1997), Kim Moody cites studies finding an increase in stress-related workplace injuries and illness between the mid-1980s and the early 1990s. He argues that rising stress levels reflect a new system of "management by stress" in which workers in a variety of industries are being squeezed to extract maximum productivity, to the detriment of their health.

chatting for *you*, girl. No fancy service ethic allowed for the serfs. Chatting with customers is for the good-looking young college-educated servers in the downtown carpaccio and ceviche joints, the kids who can make $70–$100 a night. What had I been thinking? My job is to move orders from tables to kitchen and then trays from kitchen to tables. Customers are in fact the major obstacle to the smooth transformation of information into food and food into money—they are, in short, the enemy. And the painful thing is that I'm beginning to see it this way myself. There are the traditional asshole types—frat boys who down multiple Buds and then make a fuss because the steaks are so emaciated and the fries so sparse—as well as the variously impaired—due to age, diabetes, or literacy issues—who require patient nutritional counseling. The worst, for some reason, are the Visible Christians—like the ten-person table, all jolly and sanctified after Sunday night service, who run me mercilessly and then leave me $1 on a $92 bill. Or the guy with the crucifixion T-shirt (SOMEONE TO LOOK UP TO) who complains that his baked potato is too hard and his iced tea too icy (I cheerfully fix both) and leaves no tip at all. As a general rule, people wearing crosses or WWJD? ("What Would Jesus Do?") buttons look at us disapprovingly no matter what we do, as if they were confusing waitressing with Mary Magdalene's original profession.

I make friends, over time, with the other "girls" who work my 21 shift: Nita, the tattooed twenty-something who taunts us by going around saying brightly, "Have we started making money yet?" Ellen, whose teenage son cooks on the graveyard shift and who once managed a restaurant in Massachusetts but won't try out for management here because she prefers being a "common worker" and not "ordering people around." Easy-going fiftyish Lucy, with the raucous laugh, who limps toward the end of the shift because of something that has gone wrong with her leg, the exact nature of which cannot be determined without health insurance. We talk about the usual girl things—men, children, and the sinister allure of Jerry's chocolate peanut-butter cream pie—though no one, I notice, ever brings up anything potentially expensive, like shopping or movies. As at the Hearthside, the only recreation ever referred to is partying, which requires little more than some beer, a joint, and a few close friends. Still, no one is homeless, or cops to it anyway, thanks usually to a working husband or boyfriend. All in all, we form a reliable mutual-support group: If one of us is feeling sick or overwhelmed, another one will "bev" a table or even carry trays for her. If one of us is off sneaking a cigarette or a pee, the others will do their best to conceal her absence from the enforcers of corporate rationality.[3]

But my saving human connection—my oxytocin receptor, as it 22 were—is George, the nineteen-year-old Czech dishwasher who has been in this country exactly one week. We get talking when he asks me, tortuously, how much cigarettes cost at Jerry's. I do my best to explain that they cost over a dollar more here than at a regular store and suggest that he just take one from the half-filled packs that are always lying around on the break table. But that would be unthinkable. Except for the one tiny earring signaling his allegiance to some vaguely alternative point of view, George is a perfect straight arrow—crew-cut, hardworking, and hungry for eye contact. "Czech Republic," I ask, "or Slovakia?" and he seems delighted that I know the difference. "Vaclav Havel," I try, "Velvet Revolution, Frank Zappa?" "Yes, yes, 1989," he says, and I realize that for him this is already history.

My project is to teach George English. "How are you today, 23 George?" I say at the start of each shift. "I am good, and how are you today, Barbara?" I learn that he is not paid by Jerry's but by the "agent" who shipped him over—$5 an hour, with the agent getting the dollar or so difference between that and what Jerry's pays dishwashers. I learn also that he shares an apartment with a crowd of other Czech "dishers," as he calls them, and that he cannot sleep until one of them goes off for his shift, leaving a vacant bed. We are having one of our ESL sessions late one afternoon when B.J. catches us at it and orders "Joseph" to take up the rubber mats on the floor near the dishwashing sinks and mop underneath. "I thought your name was George," I say loud enough for B.J. to hear as she strides off back to the counter. Is she embarrassed? Maybe a little, because she greets me back at the counter with "George, Joseph—there are so many of them!" I say nothing, neither nodding nor smiling, and for this I am punished later, when I think I am ready to go and she announces that I need to roll fifty more sets of silverware,

[3]Until April 1998, there was no federally mandated right to bathroom breaks. According to Marc Linder and Ingrid Nygaard, authors of *Void Where Prohibited: Rest Breaks and the Right to Urinate on Company Time* (Cornell University Press, 1997), "The right to rest and void at work is not high on the list of social or political causes supported by professional or executive employees, who enjoy personal workplace liberties that millions of factory workers can only dream about.... While we were dismayed to discover that workers lacked an acknowledged right to void at work, [the workers] were amazed by outsiders' naïve belief that their employers would permit them to perform this basic bodily function when necessary.... A factory worker, not allowed a break for six-hour stretches, voided into pads worn inside her uniform; and a kindergarten teacher in a school without aides had to take all twenty children with her to the bathroom and line them up outside the stall door while she voided."

and isn't it time I mixed up a fresh four-gallon batch of blue-cheese dressing? May you grow old in this place, B.J., is the curse I beam out at her when I am finally permitted to leave. May the syrup spills glue your feet to the floor.

I make the decision to move closer to Key West. First, because of the drive. Second and third, also because of the drive: Gas is eating up $4–$5 a day, and although Jerry's is as high-volume as you can get, the tips average only 10 percent, and not just for a newbie like me. Between the base pay of $2.15 an hour and the obligation to share tips with the busboys and dishwashers, we're averaging only about $7.50 an hour. Then there is the $30 I had to spend on the regulation tan slacks worn by Jerry's servers—a setback it could take weeks to absorb. (I had combed the town's two downscale department stores hoping for something cheaper but decided in the end that these marked-down Dockers, originally $49, were more likely to survive a daily washing.) Of my fellow servers, everyone who lacks a working husband or boyfriend seems to have a second job: Nita does something at a computer eight hours a day; another welds. Without the forty-five-minute commute, I can picture myself working two jobs and still having the time to shower between them.

So I take the $500 deposit I have coming from my landlord, the $400 I have earned toward the next month's rent, plus the $200 reserved for emergencies, and use the $1,100 to pay the rent and deposit on trailer number 46 in the Overseas Trailer Park, a mile from the cluster of budget hotels that constitute Key West's version of an industrial park. Number 46 is about eight feet in width and shaped like a barbell inside, with a narrow region—because of the sink and the stove—separating the bedroom from what might optimistically be called the "living" area, with its two-person table and half-sized couch. The bathroom is so small my knees rub against the shower stall when I sit on the toilet, and you can't just leap out of the bed, you have to climb down to the foot of it in order to find a patch of floor space to stand on. Outside, I am within a few yards of a liquor store, a bar that advertises "free beer tomorrow," a convenience store, and a Burger King—but no supermarket or, alas, Laundromat. By reputation, the Overseas park is a nest of crime and crack, and I am hoping at least for some vibrant multicultural street life. But desolation rules night and day, except for a thin stream of pedestrians heading for their jobs at the Sheraton or the 7-Eleven. There are not exactly people here but what amounts to canned labor, being preserved between shifts from the heat.

In line with my reduced living conditions, a new form of ugliness 26 arises at Jerry's. First we are confronted—via an announcement on the computers through which we input orders—with the new rule that the hotel bar, the Driftwood, is henceforth off-limits to restaurant employees. The culprit, I learn through the grapevine, is the ultraefficient twenty-three-year-old who trained me—another trailer home dweller and a mother of three. Something had set her off one morning, so she slipped out for a nip and returned to the floor impaired. The restriction mostly hurts Ellen, whose habit it is to free her hair from its rubber band and drop by the Driftwood for a couple of Zins before heading home at the end of her shift, but all of us feel the chill. Then the next day, when I go for straws, I find the dry-storage room locked. It's never been locked before; we go in and out of it all day—for napkins, jelly containers, Styrofoam cups for takeout. Vic, the portly assistant manager who opens it for me, explains that he caught one of the dishwashers attempting to steal something and, unfortunately, the miscreant will be with us until a replacement can be found—hence the locked door. I neglect to ask what he had been trying to steal but Vic tells me who he is—the kid with the buzz cut and the earring, you know, he's back there right now.

I wish I could say I rushed back and confronted George to get his 27 side of the story. I wish I could say I stood up to Vic and insisted that George be given a translator and allowed to defend himself or announced that I'd find a lawyer who'd handle the case pro bono. At the very least I should have testified as to the kid's honesty. The mystery to me is that there's not much worth stealing in the dry-storage room, at least not in any fenceable quantity: "Is Gyorgi here, and am having 200—maybe 250—catsup packets. What do you say?" My guess is that he had taken—if he had taken anything at all—some Saltines or a can of cherry pie mix and that the motive for taking it was hunger.

So why didn't I intervene? Certainly not because I was held back 28 by the kind of moral paralysis that can mask as journalistic objectivity. On the contrary, something new—something loathsome and servile— had infected me, along with the kitchen odors that I could still sniff on my bra when I finally undressed at night. In real life I am moderately brave, but plenty of brave people shed their courage in POW camps, and maybe something similar goes on in the infinitely more congenial milieu of the low-wage American workplace. Maybe, in a month or two more at Jerry's, I might have regained my crusading spirit. Then again, in a month or two I might have turned into a different person altogether—say, the kind of person who would have turned George in.

But this is not something I was slated to find out. When my 29
monthlong plunge into poverty was almost over, I finally landed my
dream job—housekeeping. I did this by walking into the personnel office of the only place I figured I might have some credibility, the hotel
attached to Jerry's, and confiding urgently that I had to have a second
job if I was to pay my rent and, no, it couldn't be front-desk clerk. "All
*right*," the personnel lady fairly spits, "so it's *housekeeping*," and
marches me back to meet Millie, the housekeeping manager, a tiny, fre-
netic Hispanic woman who greets me as "babe" and hands me a pamphlet emphasizing the need for a positive attitude. The pay is $6.10 an
hour, and the hours are nine in the morning till "whenever," which I am
hoping can be defined as a little before two. I don't have to ask about
health insurance once I meet Carlotta, the middle-aged African American woman who will be training me. Carlie, as she tells me to call her, is
missing all of her top front teeth.

On that first day of housekeeping and last day—although I don't yet 30
know it's the last—of my life as a low-wage worker in Key West, Carlie
is in a foul mood. We have been given nineteen rooms to clean, most of
them "checkouts," as opposed to "stay-overs," and requiring the whole
enchilada of bed stripping, vacuuming, and bathroom scrubbing. When
one of the rooms that had been listed as a stay-over turns out to be a
checkout, she calls Millie to complain, but of course to no avail. "So
make up the motherfucker," she orders me, and I do the beds while she
sloshes around the bathroom. For four hours without a break I strip
and remake beds, taking about four and a half minutes per queen-sized
bed, which I could get down to three if there were any reason to. We
try to avoid vacuuming by picking up the larger specks by hand, but
often there is nothing to do but drag the monstrous vacuum cleaner—it
weighs about thirty pounds—off our cart and try to wrestle it around
the floor. Sometimes Carlie hands me the squirt bottle of "Bam" (an
acronym for something that begins, ominously, with "butyric"—the rest
of it has been worn off the label) and lets me do the bathrooms. No service ethic challenges me here to new heights of performance. I just
concentrate on removing the pubic hairs from the bathtubs, or at least
the dark ones that I can see.

I had looked forward to the breaking-and-entering aspect of 31
cleaning the stay-overs, the chance to examine the secret physical existence of strangers. But the contents of the rooms are always banal and
surprisingly neat—zipped-up shaving kits, shoes lined up against the

wall (there are no closets), flyers for snorkeling trips, maybe an empty wine bottle or two. It is the TV that keeps us going, from Jerry to Sally to *Hawaii Five-0* and then on to the soaps. If there's something especially arresting, like "Won't Take No for an Answer" on Jerry, we sit down on the edge of a bed and giggle for a moment, as if this were a pajama party instead of a terminally dead-end job. The soaps are the best, and Carlie turns the volume up full blast so she won't miss anything from the bathroom or while the vacuum is on. In Room 503, Marcia confronts Jeff about Lauren. In 505, Lauren taunts poor cheated-on Marcia. In 511, Helen offers Amanda $10,000 to stop seeing Eric, prompting Carlie to emerge from the bathroom to study Amanda's troubled face. "You take it, girl," she advises. "I would for sure."

The tourists' rooms that we clean and, beyond them, the far more   32 expensively appointed interiors in the soaps begin after a while to merge. We have entered a better world—a world of comfort where every day is a day off, waiting to be filled with sexual intrigue. We are only gate-crashers in this fantasy, however, forced to pay for our presence with backaches and perpetual thirst. The mirrors, and there are far too many of them in hotel rooms, contain the kind of person you would normally find pushing a shopping cart down a city street—bedraggled, dressed in a damp hotel polo shirt two sizes too large, and with sweat dribbling down her chin like drool. I am enormously relieved when Carlie announces a half-hour meal break, but my appetite fades when I see that the bag of hot dog rolls she has been carrying around on our cart is not trash salvaged from a checkout but what she has brought for her lunch.

Between the TV and the fact that I'm in no position, as a first   33 dayer, to launch new topics of conversation, I don't learn much about Carlie except that she hurts, and in more than one way. She moves slowly about her work, muttering something about joint pain, and this is probably going to doom her, since the young immigrant housekeepers—Polish and Salvadoran—like to polish off their rooms by two in the afternoon, while she drags the work out till six. It doesn't make any sense to hurry, she observes, when you're being paid by the hour. Already, management has brought in a woman to do what sounds like time-motion studies, and there's talk about switching to paying by the room.[4] She broods, too, about all the little evidences of disrespect that

---

[4]A few weeks after I left, I heard ads on the radio for housekeeping jobs at this hotel at the amazing rate of "up to $9 an hour." When I inquired, I found out that the hotel had indeed started paying by the room, and I suspect that Carlie, if she lasted, was still making the equivalent of $6 an hour or quite a bit less.

come her way, and not only from management. "They don't care about us," she tells me of the hotel guests; in fact, they don't notice us at all unless something gets stolen from a room—"then they're all over you." We're eating our lunch side by side in the break room when a white guy in a maintenance uniform walks by and Carlie calls out, "Hey you," in a friendly way, "what's your name?"

"Peter Pan," he says, his back already to us.                                        34

"That wasn't funny," Carlie says, turning to me. "That was no kind 35 of answer. Why did he have to be funny like that?" I venture that he has an attitude, and she nods as if that were an acute diagnosis. "Yeah, he got a attitude all right."

"Maybe he's a having a bad day," I elaborate, not because I feel 36 any obligation to defend the white race but because her face is so twisted with hurt.

When I request permission to leave at about 3:30, another house- 37 keeper warns me that no one has so far succeeded in combining house-keeping with serving at Jerry's: "Some kid did it once for five days, and you're no kid." With that helpful information in mind, I rush back to number 46, down four Advils (the name brand this time), shower, stooping to fit into the stall, and attempt to compose myself for the on-coming shift. So much for what Marx termed the "reproduction of labor power," meaning the things a worker has to do just so she'll be ready to labor again. The only unforeseen obstacle to the smooth transition from job to job is that my tan Jerry's slacks, which had looked reasonably clean by 40-watt bulb last night when I hand washed my Hawaiian shirt, prove by daylight to be mottled with catsup and ranch-dressing stains. I spend most of my hour-long break between jobs attempting to remove the edible portions of the slacks with a sponge and then drying them over the hood of my car in the sun.

I can do this two-job thing, is my theory, if I can drink enough 38 caffeine and avoid getting distracted by George's ever more obvious suffering.[5] The first few days after the alleged theft, he seemed not to understand the trouble he was in, and our chirpy little conversations had continued. But the last couple of shifts he's been listless and un-shaven, and tonight he looks like the ghost we all know him to be, with

---

[5]In 1996 the number of persons holding two or more jobs averaged 7.8 million, or 6.2 percent of the workforce. It was about the same rate for men and for women (6.1 versus 6.2). About two-thirds of multiple jobholders work one job full-time and the other part-time. Only a heroic minor-ity—4 percent of men and 2 percent of women—work two full-time jobs simultaneously (John F. Stinson Jr., "New Data on Multiple Jobholding Available from the CPS," *Monthly Labor Review*, March 1997).

dark halfmoons hanging from his eyes. At one point, when I am briefly immobilized by the task of filling little paper cups with sour cream for baked potatoes, he comes over and looks as if he'd like to explore the limits of our shared vocabulary, but I am called to the floor for a table. I resolve to give him all my tips that night, and to hell with the experiment in low-wage money management. At eight, Ellen and I grab a snack together standing at the mephitic end of the kitchen counter, but I can only manage two or three mozzarella sticks, and lunch had been a mere handful of McNuggets. I am not tired at all, I assure myself, though it may be that there is simply no more "I" left to do the tiredness monitoring. What I would see if I were more alert to the situation is that the forces of destruction are already massing against me. There is only one cook on duty, a young man named Jesus ("Hay-Sue," that is), and he is new to the job. And there is Joy, who shows up to take over in the middle of the shift dressed in high heels and a long, clingy white dress and fuming as if she'd just been stood up in some cocktail bar.

Then it comes, the perfect storm. Four of my tables fill up at 39 once. Four tables is nothing for me now, but only so long as they are obligingly staggered. As I bev table 27, tables 25, 28, and 24 are watching enviously. As I bev 25, 24 glowers because their bevs haven't even been ordered. Twenty-eight is four yuppyish types, meaning everything on the side and agonizing instructions as to the chicken Caesars. Twenty-five is a middle-aged black couple who complain, with some justice, that the iced tea isn't fresh and the tabletop is sticky. But table 24 is the meteorological event of the century: ten British tourists who seem to have made the decision to absorb the American experience entirely by mouth. Here everyone has at least two drinks—iced tea *and* milk shake, Michelob *and* water (with lemon slice in the water, please)—and a huge, promiscuous orgy of breakfast specials, mozz sticks, chicken strips, quesadillas, burgers with cheese and without, sides of hash browns with cheddar, with onions, with gravy, seasoned fries, plain fries, banana splits. Poor Jesus! Poor me! Because when I arrive with their first tray of food—after three prior trips just to refill bevs—Princess Di refuses to eat her chicken strips with her pancake and sausage special since, as she now reveals, the strips were meant to be an appetizer. Maybe the others would have accepted their meals, but Di, who is deep into her third Michelob, insists that everything else go back while they work on their starters. Meanwhile, the yuppies are waving me down for more decaf and the black couple looks ready to summon the NAACP.

Much of what happens next is lost in the fog of war. Jesus starts going under. The little printer in front of him is spewing out orders faster than he can rip them off, much less produce the meals. A menacing restlessness rises from the tables, all of which are full. Even the invincible Ellen is ashen from stress. I take table 24 their reheated main courses, which they immediately reject as either too cold or fossilized by the microwave. When I return to the kitchen with their trays (three trays in three trips) Joy confronts me with arms akimbo: "What *is* this?" She means the food—the plates of rejected pancakes, hash browns in assorted flavors, toasts, burgers, sausages, eggs. "Uh, scrambled with cheddar," I try, "and that's—" "*No*," she screams in my face, "is it a traditional, a super-scramble, an eye-opener?" I pretend to study my check for a clue, but entropy has been up to its tricks, not only on the plates but in my head, and I have to admit that the original order is beyond reconstruction. "You don't know an eye-opener from a traditional?" she demands in outrage. All I know, in fact, is that my legs have lost interest in the current venture and have announced their intention to fold. I am saved by a yuppie (mercifully not one of mine) who chooses this moment to charge into the kitchen to bellow that his food is twenty-five minutes late. Joy screams at him to get the hell out of her kitchen, *please*, and then turns on Jesus in a fury, hurling an empty tray across the room for emphasis.

I leave. I don't walk out, I just leave. I don't finish my side work or pick up my credit card tips, if any, at the cash register or, of course, ask Joy's permission to go. And the surprising thing is that you *can* walk out without permission, that the door opens, that the thick tropical night air parts to let me pass, that my car is still parked where I left it. There is no vindication in this exit, no fuck-you surge of relief, just an overwhelming dank sense of failure pressing down on me and the entire parking lot. I had gone into this venture in the spirit of science, to test a mathematical proposition, but somewhere along the line, in the tunnel vision imposed by long shifts and relentless concentration, it became a test of myself, and clearly I have failed. Not only had I flamed out as a housekeeper/server, I had forgotten to give George my tips, and, for reasons perhaps best known to hardworking, generous people like Gail and Ellen, this hurts. I don't cry, but I am in a position to realize, for the first time in many years, that the tear ducts are still there and still capable of doing their job.

When I moved out of the trailer park, I gave the key to number 46 to 42
Gail and arranged for my deposit to be transferred to her. She told me
that Joan was still living in her van and that Stu had been fired from
the Hearthside. According to the most up-to-date rumors, the drug he
ordered from the restaurant was crack and he was caught dipping into
the cash register to pay for it. I never found out what happened to
George.  ✥

## READING FOR INFORMATION

1. Explain why affordable housing is the principal problem for low-wage
   workers.
2. Paraphrase the passage (paragraph 18) in which Ehrenreich contrasts
   her life as a low-wage worker with her middle-class life.
3. Did any of the working conditions Ehrenreich describes shock you? Give
   some examples.
4. In your own words, explain why Ehrenreich did not intervene on behalf
   of the dishwasher, George.
5. Ehrenreich describes a number of humiliations she was subjected to as a
   low-wage worker. Cite some examples.

## READING FOR FORM, ORGANIZATION, AND EXPOSITORY FEATURES

1. Ehrenreich breathes life into her story by including rich, vivid detail. Divide the class into small groups, each of which is responsible for a certain
   number of pages of the text. Identify details and explain why they are
   effective.
2. Reread paragraph 11 and comment on the effectiveness of the imagery
   Ehrenreich uses to describe Jerry's Restaurant.
3. What function do Ehrenreich's footnotes serve?
4. Throughout the selection, Ehrenreich uses humor to convey some serious thoughts to the reader. Cite five to ten examples.

## READING FOR RHETORICAL CONCERNS

1. Whom do you think Ehrenreich visualizes as her audience? What role
   does she assume in relation to these readers?
2. How would you describe Ehrenreich's tone: complacency? moral outrage? or something in between? Explain.

## WRITING ASSIGNMENTS

1. Write an essay in which you compare and contrast your work experiences with those of Ehrenreich and her coworkers. Consider questions such as the following:

   What types of obstacles did you have to overcome?

   How were you treated by your boss?

   Did you get along with your coworkers?

   Was your workplace environment satisfactory and safe?

   Did you experience any type of class bigotry or discrimination?

   Were your working conditions reasonable?

2. Ehrenreich's experiences take place from 1998 to 2000, years of unprecedented prosperity in the United States. What does this say about the growing economic chasm between the rich and the poor that Seabrook and other writers discuss in this chapter? Respond in essay form.

3. In "The War Against the Poor Instead of Programs to End Poverty," Herbert Gans writes, "People who have not been poor themselves do not understand how much of what the poor do is poverty-related" (paragraph 25). What insights did you gain from Ehrenreich's experiences? Write an essay in response.

## SYNTHESIS WRITING ASSIGNMENTS

1. Relating the story of her mother growing up near Smith College in Northhampton, Massachusetts, Patricia Clark Smith writes:

   She played there as a child; as a grown woman, she ventured into the art gallery, attended public lectures and foreign films, though always with a sense that Smith was special, its delights not her birthright, but privileges graciously extended to her. (paragraph 3)

   Write an essay on class and inequality in which you use Jeremy Seabrook's selection to explain why Clark Smith's mother would consider Smith College's offerings "not her birthright."

2. Writing about the children in the low-income housing project in which she grew up in the 1950s, Clark Smith reflects on the topic of family:

   Most of us had come to the project from wartime homes like mine, homes shared with grandparents and children, aunts, uncles. Families composed only of parents and children seemed to many of us small, unripe, ingrown, scarily lacking in extra sources of support and comfort, and we older kids bonded fiercely in a large nomadic tribe that transcended gender and ethnicity.

What do Clark Smith's experiences reveal about nuclear families? Were they as widespread as some of the writers in Chapter 9 would have us believe?

3.  Conduct research on the Personal Responsibility and Work Opportunity and Reconciliation Act (PRWORA) that Congress enacted as part of welfare reform in 1996. Your objective is to determine whether or not Herbert Gans's forecast, written in 1992, was accurate:

    The latest fashion is to put welfare recipients to work, which would be a good idea if even decent entry-level jobs for them could be found or created. (Alas, when taxpayers discover how much cheaper it is to pay welfare than to create jobs, that remedy may end as it has before.) (paragraph 14)

    Write an essay in which you assess the extent to which the reform has made a long-term difference in lifting poor people, especially women, out of poverty.

4.  At the end of her book, *Nickel and Dimed*, Barbara Ehrenreich writes:

    When someone works for less pay than she can live on—when, for example, she goes hungry so that you can eat more cheaply and conveniently— then she has made a great sacrifice for you, she has made you a gift of some part of her abilities, her health, and her life. The "working poor," as they are approvingly termed, are in fact the major philanthropists of our society. They neglect their own children so that the children of others will be cared for; they live in substandard housing so that other homes will be shiny and perfect; they endure privation so that inflation will be low and stock prices high. To be a member of the working poor is to be an anonymous donor, a nameless benefactor, to everyone else. (221)

    Drawing on "Serving in Florida" and other selections in this chapter, write an essay in response to Ehrenreich's statement.

5.  Drawing on the selections in this chapter, write an essay explaining why poverty and class divisions exist in the United States today. Write for an audience who has not read this chapter.

6.  How widespread are the class discrimination and prejudice that Gans discusses in "The War Against the Poor Instead of Programs to End Poverty"? Use the selections by Leonce Gaiter, Patricia Clark Smith, and Dirk Johnson to write an essay in response.

7.  Show how Ehrenreich's "Serving in Florida" communicates the exploitation, prejudice, discrimination, and injustice that are discussed by the other writers in this chapter. Write an essay addressed to your classmates.

C  H  A  P  T  E  R

# *eleven*

# Rethinking School

The seven selections in Chapter 11 examine problems in American public education. The chapter covers a number of issues, all of which deal with the academic performance of students in our schools. Most of the authors in this chapter argue that the United States is faced with a dire educational crisis; however, other authors maintain that the problems in education are less alarming and mostly solvable.

The first two selections question the structure and curriculum of middle schools and high schools. In "High School, an Institution Whose Time Has Passed," Leon Botstein argues that the American high school no longer serves its purpose. He proposes doing away with middle school and junior high school so that students would begin secondary education at twelve and graduate at sixteen. Patrick James McQuillan also raises questions about the value of a high-school education. In "A Day in the Life of Rafael Jackson," he provides a vignette of a high-school senior who appears to learn very little in school.

The next four authors focus on academic expectations. In an essay entitled "Educating Black Children," Shelby Steele argues that black students will succeed only if the black community encourages and enforces the highest standards of accountability and academic excellence. Janine Bempechat extends this argument to American society at large. She insists that parents need to make a radical shift in their attitudes about schooling. They need to concern themselves less with raising children's self-esteem and ensuring their well-roundedness and more with holding them to rigorous standards of academic excellence. Martin

Gross focuses on one indicator of the lack of rigor in American schools: their lax homework policies; and Larry E. Frase and William Streshly examine another indicator: the myth that high self-esteem is a prerequisite for learning.

The chapter ends with David C. Berliner and Bruce J. Biddle's contention that American education is not so deficient as critics claim. In "Manufacturing a Crisis in Education," they challenge those who insist that American schools are failing our youth.

# High School, an Institution Whose Time Has Passed

## *Leon Botstein*

*Leon Botstein is president of Bard College in Annandale-on-Hudson, New York, and music director of the American Symphony Orchestra. He has written extensively on the subject of education. In his book* Jefferson's Children: Education and the Promise of American Culture, *Botstein discusses the need for fundamental changes in education, including a redefinition of the American high school. His most recent book is* Music and Its Public: Habits of Listening and the Crisis of Musical Modernism in Vienna, 1870–1914.

### PREREADING

Take 10 to 15 minutes to write a response in which you agree or disagree with the claim stated in Botstein's title, that high school is "an institution whose time has passed."

The national outpouring after the Littleton shootings has 1 forced us to confront something we have suspected for a long time: The American high school is obsolete and should be abolished.

In the last month, high-school students present and past have 2 come forward with stories about cliques and the artificial intensity of a

This article first appeared in *The New York Times*. Reprinted with permission.

world defined by insiders and outsiders, in which the insiders hold sway because of superficial definitions of attractiveness, popularity, and sports prowess.

Indeed, a community's loyalty to the high-school system is often based on the extent to which varsity teams succeed. High school administrators and faculty members are often former coaches, and the coaches themselves are placed in a separate, untouchable category. The result is that the culture of the inside elite is not contested by the adults in the school. Individuality and dissent are discouraged.

But the rules of high school turn out not to be the rules of life. Often, the high-school outsider becomes the more successful and admired adult. The definitions of masculinity and femininity go through sufficient transformation to make the game of popularity in high school an embarrassment.

Given the poor quality of recruitment and training for high-school teachers, it is no wonder that the curriculum and the enterprise of learning hold so little sway over young people.

When puberty meets education and learning in the modern United States, the victory of puberty masquerading as popular culture and the tyranny of peer groups based on ludicrous values meet little resistance.

By the time those who graduate from high school go on to college and realize what really is at stake in becoming an adult, too many opportunities have been lost and too much time has been wasted. Most thoughtful young people suffer the high-school environment in silence, and in their junior and senior years mark time waiting for college to begin.

But the primary reason high school doesn't work anymore, if it ever did, is that young people mature substantially earlier in the late twentieth century than they did when the high school was invented. For example, the age of first menstruation has dropped at least two years since the beginning of this century and, not surprisingly, sexual activity has begun earlier in proportion. An institution intended for children in transition now holds back young adults well beyond the developmental point for which high school was originally designed.

Furthermore, whatever constraints on the presumption of adulthood existed decades ago have fallen away. Information and images, as well as the real and virtual freedom of movement we associate with adulthood, are now accessible to every fifteen-year-old and sixteen-year-old.

Secondary education must be rethought. Elementary school 10 should begin at age four or five and end with the sixth grade. We Americans should entirely abandon the concept of the middle school and junior high school. Beginning with the seventh grade, there should be four years of secondary education that we may call high school. Young people should graduate at 16, not 18.

They could then enter the real world of work or national service, 11 in which they would take a place of responsibility alongside older adults. They could stay at home and attend junior college, or they could go away to college.

At sixteen, young Americans are prepared to be taken seriously 12 and to develop the motivations and interests that will serve them well in adult life. They need to enter a world in which they are not in a lunchroom with only their peers, estranged from other age groups and cut off from the game of life as it is really played.

There is nothing utopian about this idea—it is immensely practical 13 and efficient, and its implementation is long overdue. We need to face biological and cultural facts and not prolong the life of a flawed institution that is out of date.    ❀

## READING FOR INFORMATION

1. How do you react to Botstein's claim that in high school "individuality and dissent are discouraged"? Explain why you agree or disagree.
2. Paraphrase Botstein's reasons for why high school doesn't work anymore. Can you think of additional explanations?
3. Explain why high school "holds back" young adults.

## READING FOR FORM, ORGANIZATION, AND EXPOSITORY FEATURES

1. Construct a graphic overview that depicts the organizational structure of the selection.
2. What is the function of paragraph 10?
3. Underline the evidence Botstein uses to support his position. Do you think the evidence is effective? Explain.

## READING FOR RHETORICAL CONCERNS

1. Explain Botstein's rhetorical purpose. What impact does he hope to have on his readers?

2. Is Botstein's argument one-sided, or does he concede alternative viewpoints? Explain.

3. Describe Botstein's tone.

## WRITING ASSIGNMENTS

1. Do you consider high school "a world described by insiders and outsiders" (paragraph 2)? Was there a sense of equality in the high school you attended, or were there a number of social cliques? Did certain groups have more status than others? Did the hierarchy reflect social class?

2. In your experience, do high-school juniors and seniors simply go through the motions, biding their time until they can graduate, or are most students working hard in order to get into top-ranked colleges?

3. Write an essay in which you agree or disagree with Botstein's proposal for abolishing middle school and junior high school, and graduating students at sixteen.

# A Day in the Life of Rafael Jackson

## *Patrick James McQuillan*

*Patrick James McQuillan is Assistant Professor in the School of Education at the University of Colorado. He is the author of* Reform and Resistance in Schools and Classrooms: An Ethnographic View of the Coalition of Essential Schools *and* Educational Opportunity in an Urban American High School: A Cultural Analysis, *from which this selection is taken.*

## PREREADING

The following selection is from a five-year ethnographic research study of Russell High School, an urban school in a city called Eastown. McQuillan followed two classes of students from their first day of high school to graduation. Here he offers a vignette of one day in the life of a lower-tracked senior.

In your journal, recall what a typical day in your senior year of high school was like for you.

Rafael Jackson, an African American, was a Russell High se- 1
nior who I met while observing his zoology class for a few days.
While an Eastown student, Rafael attended three different high
schools. He entered Russell High in ninth grade because his Nelson
Heights neighborhood was "zoned" for Russell. He was suspended that
year and required to transfer to Archibald High. During his sophomore
year he transferred to Travis High. Later that year his family moved,
and he enrolled in a school outside Eastown. When his family returned
to Eastown, he re-enrolled in Travis. Because he "bunked" [skipped]
school so often, he had recently been transferred back into Russell.
Since Rafael had failed all his courses at Travis—because he skipped
classes and school so often, not because he lacked intelligence—he was
placed in a number of Russell's lowest track classes, A-level. Despite his
record, Rafael had good relations with most Russell teachers and, because of his placement in mainly lower-track classes and his persuasive
abilities, he found school easy.

In certain respects, Rafael was an atypical Russell student. While 2
the school's population was highly mobile, few students transferred to
different high schools six times. Although Russell's suspension rates
were high, Rafael was suspended more than most students. He also frequently skipped class. Yet in other ways, his experiences were typical.
The classes he attended were like many I observed. In some, teachers
expected students to work, and they did. In others, teachers expected
students to work, and students did what they could to avoid working.
And in others, teachers expected little of students. Moreover, passive
learning and teacher-centered instruction were commonplace. Although
Rafael spent an inordinate amount of time roaming the hallways, other
students did as well. While Rafael was a skilled negotiator with teachers
and administrators, other students seemed equally adept at convincing
faculty and administrators to reconsider decisions they had made.

My day with Rafael began before the official start of school, hang- 3
ing out in the hallways with his "buddies" and his girlfriend. When the
homeroom bell rang, Rafael's girlfriend went to her homeroom, but he
and his friends stayed in the hallways on the school's second floor.
(Rafael liked the second floor because "the principals are always on the
first floor.") During this time a faculty member noticed the group, approached them, and told them to go to their homerooms. As he did, a
young woman walked past. Although the students had begun to move
as the teacher approached, when he said nothing to the young woman,

they stopped walking. When the teacher reached them and said to leave, one of Rafael's friends asked, "Why? You didn't make her leave or check for a pass." The teacher explained that this was because she was on her way somewhere but that they were just hanging around. Another of Rafael's friends interjected, "So if I'm walking, I can do whatever the fuck I want?" The teacher then told the student he would submit a report to the office for disciplinary action regarding his remark, and he left. After this incident another teacher told the group to report to homeroom. In apparent compliance, Rafael and his friends dispersed; shortly thereafter, they met in a deserted corridor on the third floor, never reporting to homeroom.

When homeroom ended, Rafael and I went to his first period 4 class, zoology. We arrived a few minutes late. Before the class began any formal work, Rafael told the teacher he had no pencil. She replied, "I would have bet my paycheck on it." Rafael then got a pencil from a friend, quickly placed it in his pocket, pulled it out as though it had been there the entire time, and said, "See, I've got it." He then asked the class, "Anybody got any paper?" While a student passed a piece to Rafael, the teacher took attendance and commented, "Well, let's see, we have seventeen absent today [ten in attendance]. That's not too bad, and it's not even a test day." While erasing the board, which was covered in Spanish, the teacher remarked, "Next year, they'll outlaw this stuff" (a reference to bilingual education). Rafael responded, "What, writing? Good, I hate it."

The teacher then began a review for an upcoming exam by asking, 5 "What have we been studying?" Two or three students quickly answered, "Mollusks." She continued, "What are some examples?" Students responded, "Snails," "Octopuses," and so on. One student answered most questions, pronouncing "cephalopods," "gastropods," and "echinoderm" with ease. Seven students participated in the review. One girl did math homework, and two students sat passively.

Occasionally, the teacher explored tangents related to students' 6 questions. When one asked why humans don't hibernate, she said there was evidence to suggest humans have hibernation-like behavior: "When we have light hit our eyes, we secrete hormones that make us active." She added that scientists were exploring whether humans could learn to hibernate and use that ability in conjunction with extended space travel. Slipping back into the review, the teacher discussed "crepdula fornicata," snails that stack on top of each other and change gender over time. Throughout the review, the teacher told students she was using the upcoming exam as a guide. The exam would therefore be much like the review.

For the last few minutes of class, the teacher discussed Rafael's 7 chronic lateness with him. She said that each time Rafael was late, he lost ten points from his exam grade, adding, "You'll have to get a hundred [on the upcoming exam] to get a seventy." When the conversation ended, Rafael told me that the last time this occurred the teacher threatened the same but later said, "Make up a good story for why you're late and I won't take off any points." And she didn't.

As class ended, it was announced over the intercom that the home 8 economics teacher was absent. Therefore, her cooking class, Rafael's third period, would meet in a different room. Because the notice came as students gathered their belongings to leave, Rafael couldn't hear the room number. Unshaken, he smiled, "Another reason to be late." During break Rafael talked with friends near his locker. One student was the center of attention. He had cut the corners from a $20 bill and pasted them on a $1 bill. It looked impressive and he planned to pass it as a twenty. He said banks would refund his money for the defective bill because it still had the serial number. He'd just tell the bank his little brother had done it.

Rafael and I were two or three minutes late for his second period 9 class, as were most students, many of whom arrived after us. That day, eleven students were in class. Walking to his seat, Rafael kissed one girl and waved to another across the room. The teacher then told the class they would have a dictation quiz today. While the teacher explained the quiz, Rafael conversed with the girl who had kissed him, discussing aspects of their schoolwork as well as social lives. When the teacher asked Rafael to sit down, he immediately grabbed a chair, brought it next to the girl, and continued the discussion, telling the teacher, "I'm helping her with her work." The teacher replied, "Let's get through the dictation quiz, and then you can get back to helping her. That's fair, isn't it?"

As the class readied for the quiz, a student asked, "Is this tied to 10 *Cold Cash?*" a book the class was reading. The teacher answered, "Yeah, I guess so. It has young people involved with music in it." The teacher added that the dictation would include four sets of homonyms: to, too, two; right, write; by, buy; there, their, they're. He also said there would be some "tough" words—"publish," "corporation," and "lyrics." Before beginning the quiz, he told the class, "Don't use abbreviations." A student asked, "Why not?" He responded, "Because I want you to spell it out." The student replied, "That's stupid!" Without responding to the comment, the teacher explained that the dictation would deal with quotes, apostrophes, capitals, and end points. He added, "There will be no commas, so don't use any. If you do, it'll be minus five points." Just as the teacher began dictating, Rafael asked to borrow a pencil from him.

In administering the quiz, the teacher first read quickly through the entire selection to familiarize students with it: 11

> Mitch and Larry (Hint: If you itch when Mitch comes in sight, you'll know how to spell Mitch.) spent July trying to write lyrics for the two boys' songs. Those guys tried to sell two songs by themselves. Right at the summer's end Wildcat Publishing Corporation decided to buy them. It was the thrill of their young lives. Do you suppose other companies will want their tunes?

He then read through the selection more slowly. After a third reading, the teacher told the class, "Watch capital letters, punctuation, end marks, and apostrophes. Remember, no commas." When the teacher completed the third recitation, most of the class had finished the dictation. As Rafael turned in his paper, the teacher took a quick look and remarked, "When I said, 'When you see Mitch you get an itch,' it was a clue." Rafael returned to his seat and made some corrections. 12

As a few remaining students finished the dictation, the teacher read the selection a fourth time to a student with limited-English proficiency. He also returned a student's paper and told him he had used capitals improperly. During this time, Rafael worked on U.S. history homework, explaining to me he was doing this because his history teacher promised him a state university sweatshirt if he got a perfect score on an upcoming quiz. 13

As a few students continued working on the dictation, the teacher commented, "If you're trying to find out how to spell 'lyrics,' don't just look for 'l' followed by one vowel but try a few different vowels." While the teacher helped students still completing the dictation, Rafael discussed his next class, cooking, with me—saying he liked it because he could "have fun" and there were mostly girls in the class. With nothing to do, Rafael began writing on his desk. Turning to a student sitting in the back of class staring blankly, he asked, "You've been to two classes in a row. Are you going to next period too?" The student replied, "Yeah." Rafael responded, "Wow! A record! It's too cold to bunk anyway." Rafael and this student then struck up a brief conversation. As 14 this occurred, another student completed a math assignment and three students shared a newspaper. With assistance from the teacher, two limited-English students kept working on their dictation.

After talking with his friend for a few minutes, Rafael turned to me and said that after being at Russell for three months, skipping class was easy: "It's not even a challenge to bunk. I stay in the basement and sit there all period, just chillin', watchin' everybody walk by. I know where to bunk, when to bunk, and how to bunk. But I can't bunk Mrs. Ries' class [his other English teacher]. She's a 'bulletin watcher.' She'll catch you."[1] As Rafael grew bored, he decided to go to the lavatory. When he asked for a pass, the teacher told him he could go, but he would have to serve fifteen minutes of detention (a school policy intended to reduce the number of students roaming the halls during classes by discouraging them from leaving class to use the lavatory.) Nonetheless, Rafael left. Walking to the lavatory, I asked if he planned to serve the detention that afternoon. He responded, "No . . . well, maybe I will. My girlfriend may have to stay." While we were out of the room, the period ended.

During break, we headed to Rafael's locker. On the way, Rafael discussed how he had a "magical way around Russell High," how he could do pretty much whatever he wanted. He boasted, "I've got those teachers wrapped around my little finger. I know how to talk to them." When he got to his locker and opened it, a stack of papers fell onto the floor and a book nearly dropped out. I commented on how packed it was, and Rafael explained, "I share it with six or seven other guys. You should see it when we've all got jackets in here." (At this time the lockers at Russell High were in such poor condition that the school assigned students no lockers. Nonetheless, many claimed those still in working condition, often sharing them with friends.)

Third period was cooking class. Since the teacher was absent, the class met in a regular classroom instead of the "home ec" room. In typical fashion Rafael arrived late but armed with an excuse, he couldn't hear the announcement in his zoology class. This time no excuse was needed. There was no teacher. In fact, when Rafael and I arrived, three students approached me thinking I was a substitute, and told me why they couldn't stay in class that period. Shortly thereafter, the substitute found the room and signed a flurry of passes for students asking to leave the room. Rafael and I took seats to one side of the room.

For the nine students who remained, the substitute passed out the day's assignment, a copy of a workbook page entitled, "Television

Schedules." A listing from a viewer's guide of TV specials for Monday and Tuesday nights was at the top of the page. The directions read: "In the box below is information on television specials. Use the information to answer the questions." The questions read

1. What time does *Greatest Heroes of the Bible* begin on Monday?
2. On what channel is *Bobby Vinton's Rock and Rollers* playing?
3. Would you watch *The Immigrants* on Monday night if you had to work on Tuesday night from 4 P.M. to 11 P.M.? Explain your answer.

Two questions required students to list the time a program began and its channel. To answer the third question students had to realize they could watch the first half of *The Immigrants* on Monday but would miss the second half because of work.

The second part of the worksheet had another section from a tele- 19 vision viewers' guide. The directions read: "In the box below is part of a television schedule for a Monday night. Answer the questions and fol-low the directions under the box." The questions read

1. What time does *Financial News* begin?
2. On what channel is *Gunsmoke* playing? When does *Gunsmoke* end?
3. What time does the *Mickey Mouse Club* end?
4. Would you watch *Bionic Woman* if your favorite show is *Adam-12*? Explain your answer. [You could only watch half of *Bionic Woman*, since it was an hour program and the second half overlapped with *Adam-12*.]
5. Which program is meant to make you laugh: *Mod Squad, Gunsmoke*, or *Bewitched*? [Next to *Bewitched* the guide noted "comedy."]
6. Place a check to the left of each program that is for children.

Rafael went right to work on the assignment, completed it, and 20 shared it with friends so they could fill out theirs. Throughout the pe-riod, class was calm. After completing the worksheet, some students read. One worked on her geometry homework. Others talked among themselves. Occasionally, students in the hallway stuck their heads in the room to look for friends. If they saw any, they usually greeted them and left. By the middle of the period, most students were conversing with one another. This continued until the period ended.

Rafael and I then went to the cafeteria for "first lunch." We ate 21 with his girlfriend. Walking to Rafael's fourth period class, we passed the principal talking with a cafeteria worker. He looked perturbed. The cafeteria worker was walking beside him holding a one-dollar bill with twenties pasted onto the corners and saying, "I don't know where it came from. Someone found it in her cash drawer." Rafael smiled, "I know where it came from."

When we got to Rafael's history class, we were again late, but the 22 teacher had not arrived either. Some students used the extra time to study for a quiz they would have that day. Others were entertained by a young man who performed a mock strip-tease in the front of the room. Five minutes after the bell, the teacher arrived and told the seventeen students they would have a five-question quiz. Flipping through the pages of his textbook, the teacher announced

> Question one, fill-in-the blank: A feeling of extreme loyalty to one's nation, what is the term? Number two: The short period of U.S. history after the War of 1812 when all sections of the country supported the president—the "era of good what?" Number three: Name given to tariff to keep out foreign products? Number four: Law natives are supposed to use in dealing with one another? And number five: President Monroe's warning to Europe not to interfere in the western hemisphere or establish colonies there is known as the "blank" Doctrine. Fill in the blank. I have a bonus question: Who is the principal of Russell High? I'll guarantee not everyone gets it right. Half-credit for the first name. I'll give credit for the first name and last initial.

After collecting the quizzes, the teacher told students to take out 23 their homework and exchange it with a neighbor. He then read the answers to the homework, and students graded each other's work. The first questions were fill-ins. For instance, "Britain sold its goods in so many places that it became know as the [blank] of the world." (Answer: "workshop.") The next questions were matching and included John Quincy Adams ("His father was also president"), Henry Clay ("He was known as the 'Great Compromiser'"), and Robert Fulton ("He invented the steamboat"). After students graded one another's homework, that score, combined with their quiz score, which the teacher graded during the homework review, established one's grade-for-the-day. The teacher then told each student what he or she had earned for that class. Throughout these activities, ten students participated in the teacher-directed activities. Two read newspapers, three chatted quietly among themselves, and two others appeared to be sleeping.

Next, the teacher told the class, "Open your texts to the map on 24 page 227. What states comprise the northeast?" Students responded: "Massachusetts!" "New York!" "Connecticut!" He then asked, "What states make up the West?" Students again shouted out answers. While this occurred, a young woman walked into the room to talk with a friend. The teacher told her to leave. After talking briefly with the friend, she left. Shortly thereafter, another student entered the room to get a set of keys from a friend. Five minutes later, he returned them.

After completing the map exercise, the teacher had students iden- 25 tify symbols on the map that represented products produced by various states. He asked, "What states produced rice?" and, "What states produced cotton?" He then told the class, "Now you have to compare two charts. This is the tough one. How many times greater is the production of cotton [it was 47 million bales] than wool [21 million bales]? How do you find out how many times greater?" A student replied, "Subtract." The teacher said, "You divide." After telling the class there would be another quiz tomorrow and identifying the section of the text it would cover, the teacher asked me to cover the final ten minutes of class and left the room. Some students started playing cards. The girl who had been asked to leave the room earlier because she wasn't in the class returned and sat with her friend. Students wandered in and out. One young man appeared to sleep through it all.

When the period ended, Rafael returned to his locker, met his 26 girlfriend, and walked her to class. Nonetheless, he arrived at his next class on time, his second English class, taught by Mrs. Ries, the "bulletin watcher." The class was writing short stories. Rafael had already written most of his, although the teacher told him it still needed an ending. Looking at her comments on his draft, it was apparent she had spent some time correcting Rafael's story. Mrs. Ries even suggested that those having trouble with their story might check with Rafael because he had already written most of his and had done a good job. Although she complimented Rafael on his work, he didn't enjoy the class. "This class is boring," he told me. When I asked why, he explained, "She makes us work all the time." Throughout the class most students worked on English-related projects. Some checked Rafael's work, others completed a capitalization worksheet, and others worked directly with the teacher on their stories.

When the bell rang for Rafael's final class, wood shop, he told me 27 he wouldn't be going because he had been "kicked out of class for awhile." This was because in one class there was a disruption and the teacher took Rafael out in the hall and yelled at him. Rafael explained, "You know when someone's yelling at you, how you feel like yelling back? Well, I did." Consequently, an assistant principal removed him from shop for a few days so both he and the teacher could cool off. Instead, Rafael reported to an assistant principal's office during last period. On this day the assistant principal wasn't in, and since none of his friends were in the office, Rafael left to wander the hallways. As we walked he remarked, "This is what I do all the time sixth period." "But what about when you *had* shop?" I asked. He answered, "I still did it." For much of the period we sat in two broken chairs stashed under a stairwell in the school basement. Rafael talked with friends and a few janitors who passed by. While there, Rafael said, "You know, sometimes I sit here all day and do nothing. Sometimes I go to sleep. Don't nobody come down here. That's how easy it is, man."

When Rafael got bored hanging out in the basement, we strolled 28 the corridors. Whenever we came to a section of the building administrators might patrol, Rafael stopped before entering and asked anyone passing by, "Is it clear?" At one point Rafael saw an assistant principal walk onto a floor, so he asked a student coming from that floor, "Which way did he go?" Later, Rafael saw a student trying to sneak past the main corridor and told him, "It's clear. Go ahead." As the student started down the hallway, Rafael imitated the principal's deep, guttural voice and boomed, "Hey, where are you going?!" The student immediately stopped, only to turn and see Rafael laughing.

Throughout the period, we returned to the assistant principal's of- 29 fice to see whether any of Rafael's friends were there. On one occasion Rafael encountered a friend, talked with him for a few minutes, and then left. We also went to the gym and watched a gym teacher and student shoot baskets. After a brief stay in the gym, we once again walked the corridors. When Rafael heard the principal's voice in a hallway we were approaching, he turned into the nearest stairwell and ran up to the next floor. On one visit to the assistant principal's office, as Rafael looked through the door to see who was there, a secretary opened the door and surprised him. Rafael immediately turned to the nearest locker and pretended to be opening it. The secretary passed by and said nothing.

Late in the period, Rafael turned down a hallway monitored by 30 the assistant principal who had removed him from shop. Since the assistant principal clearly saw Rafael, he could not turn around. Under his breath he muttered, "Ah fuck, I'm busted," but continued walking toward the administrator. Along the way he devised an excuse: "I'll just say I'm going to guidance." When we got to the assistant principal, he used this excuse and the assistant principal told him to hurry and not to linger in the hallway.

With the end of the day nearing, Rafael headed to his girlfriend's 31 classroom to see whether she was there so they could walk home together. Because posters covered the windows on both doors to the room, Rafael couldn't tell whether she was there. Yet he was certain that a girl he knew well, Susan Husted, would be in class since he had already seen her that day. With this certainty in mind, Rafael opened the classroom door and asked, "Is Susan Husted here? Mr. Hartnett [an assistant principal] wants to see her." As the teacher dismissed Susan from class, Rafael signaled to his girlfriend that he'd be in the hallway after class. After leaving the room, Susan thanked Rafael for getting her out of class. Rafael waited in the hallway until the bell rang. When his girlfriend came out of the room, they said good-bye to me and left school together.

## EPILOGUE

Rafael never served his fifteen minutes of detention for using the lava- 32 tory during class, and his zoology teacher never deducted any points from his exam grade for tardiness. Rafael passed all his courses that year and graduated, although he had one close call. For the first three quarters, he received grades of E, F, and F in one course. Combining an improved fourth quarter performance with some persuasive talking, Rafael convinced his teacher to give him a D for the year so that he graduated. Rafael then joined the army and served two-and-a-half years. During this time Rafael said three different sergeants called him "nigger" and he ended up fighting all three. While the army never disciplined him for these actions (although Rafael said the sergeants were reprimanded), after the third incident he went AWOL and left the army. He was given a dishonorable discharge.

Returning to Eastown, Rafael held three different jobs over the 33 next year and a half. He also began living with his high-school girlfriend, and together they had two daughters. In my last encounters with Rafael he was collecting unemployment, had no job prospects, and was supplementing his unemployment income through relatively minor but nonetheless illegal activities. Rafael's girlfriend was receiving welfare benefits and working toward her GED.

## ANALYSIS

This vignette of a school day with Rafael Jackson sought to raise one 34
question that is essential to this study, but which is too rarely asked: Of
what worth was this education? Why should Rafael value this opportunity?[2] In one class he analyzed a TV guide, in another he did a one-
paragraph transcription. When he had trouble in shop, he was removed
to spend time with the assistant principal. These were three of six major
courses. In zoology and history, knowledge largely entailed factual recall, and students relied on few skills other than memorization. Moreover, the institutional rewards offered Rafael, course credits, required
little effort. In zoology the teacher used the upcoming exam as the basis
for a review, thereby informing students of exam questions beforehand.
During a dictation quiz the teacher provided students with hints regarding errors they might make ("There will be no commas"). Rafael's
history quiz included bonus points for correctly identifying the name of
Russell's principal. In wood shop he did nothing, and in home economics he did virtually nothing. Perhaps as a consequence of seldom being
asked to do anything he couldn't already do with ease, when asked to do
something intellectually challenging and significant, writing a short
story in English, he disliked the class. Although but one day in Rafael's
education, it would be absurd to claim that such conditions constituted
"educational opportunity"—at least not an education "worth wanting"
(Howe, 1993, 1997).

Futhermore, in terms of behaviorist assumptions, institutional 35
sanctions were inconsistently enforced, which further throws into question the logic of relying so extensively and unreflectively on negative reinforcement to direct school life. While Rafael violated numerous
classroom and school rules, he experienced no negative sanctions. During homeroom, he and friends dodged a teacher who confronted them
in the hallway, merely moving to another floor. An English teacher assigned Rafael a fifteen-minute detention for leaving class to use the
restroom, but he never served that. Although his zoology teacher said
she would subtract ten points from Rafael's test grade each time he was
late, she never followed through on the threat. Rafael was supposed to
report to the assistant principal's office during shop, but since the assistant principal was elsewhere, Rafael wandered the hallways. When he
happened upon the assistant principal that period, he had a ready excuse
that worked. And in one class Rafael's grades for the first three quarters—two Fs and an E—could have prevented him from graduating; yet

he got a D for the course because he turned himself around in the fourth quarter and was rewarded for "trying hard" (Jackson, 1968: 34).

As the value of the education offered Rafael seemed dubious and [36] his academic work offered few challenges or rewards, he approached school with indifference. He regularly arrived late to class and showed little interest in course work. The classes he enjoyed, home economics and history, were attractive for nonacademic reasons, the opportunity to socialize with a number of young women, and the possibility of winning a sweatshirt. Although his English teacher held him up for emulation, he was neither excited nor engaged in this class. For Rafael, school was a place to be with friends; accordingly, his interests centered on socializing. School work had little meaning. It was more a trial to be endured (or better, avoided) than a source of insight, growth, or empowerment (Carlson, 1992; Sizer, 1984; Steinberg, et al., 1996).

Still, in some respects, watching Rafael on this day revealed a [37] measure of power, mastery, and satisfaction—all of which were tied to his ability to manipulate the institution. Rafael's actions were strategic, weighing options and taking good chances in a system with many points of vulnerability. In his own words, Rafael had a "magical way around Russell": "I know when to bunk, where to bunk, and how to bunk. . . . I've got those teachers wrapped around my little finger." Rafael enacted his informal power in ways that were ultimately debilitating. Rafael, too, succeeded in not learning.

This glimpse into the life of Rafael Jackson also offers another [38] view of control and order at Russell High. Despite popular images of violence, chaos, and overcrowding[3] in urban schools, Rafael's day was sedate; more accurately, it was boring. In most classes, work was trivial. Seldom were students asked to do something they didn't already know how to do. This kept life orderly, but again, order came with a price. As Linda McNeil found at two schools where administrators stressed discipline and control, "the strategies for instruction were quite similar: Control students by making work easy" (1986: 184). At Russell High this was routine. Teachers didn't focus on control and order; they preserved it instinctively and unthinkingly. The teacher who left class plans for the substitute in Rafael's cooking class knew how to maintain control: Give students something as simple as a TV viewer's guide to interpret. When Rafael wanted to talk to a young woman in class, the teacher instantly accommodated him: "Let's get through the dictation quiz, and then you can get back to helping her. Now that's fair, isn't it?" When a student in that class called the teacher's rationale "stupid," the comment was totally ignored. Rafael's history teacher came to class late and left early. But he kept work simple, and students were not disruptive. Because Rafael had a run-in with his shop teacher, to preserve peace, an assistant principal removed him from the class. Students, teachers, and administrators had struck their compromises. It was all routine and unquestioned; but it wasn't educational.[4]

## NOTES

1. Lacking credits needed to graduate, Rafael had to take two English courses as a senior.
2. Further, given their family backgrounds and low levels of personal capital, many Russell students had a limited sense of the opportunities offered by formal education. The value of a high-school education may therefore have been even that much more dubious for them. This day in the life of Rafael Jackson certainly suggests why this may be so.
3. Most of Rafael's classes had fewer than twenty students in them, some as few as ten. This was typical at Russell. Although union guidelines set the maximum number of students in any single class at twenty-six, because students were absent so often, most teachers regularly dealt with a dozen or fifteen students in their classes.
4. Although I focus on the degree to which work was kept simple as a way to maintain order in the classroom and school, a complementary influence was also at work. That is, many faculty saw students as incapable of doing advanced work. Basic skills were a necessary prerequisite to students undertaking more challenging work (Page, 1987b: 451).

## REFERENCES

Carlson, Dennis. 1992. *Teachers and Crisis*. New York: Routledge.

Howe, Kenneth. 1993. "Equality of Educational Opportunity and the Criterion of Equal Educational Worth." *Studies in Philosophy and Education* 11: 329–37.

———. 1997. *Understanding Equal Educational Opportunity*. New York: Teachers College Press.

Jackson, Philip. 1968. *Inside Classrooms*. Chicago: University of Chicago Press.

McNeil, Linda. 1986. *Contradictions of Control*. New York: Routledge.

Page, Reba. 1987b. "Lower-Track Classes at a College-Preparatory High School: A Caricature of Educational Encounters." In G. Spindler and L. Spindler (eds.), *Interpretive Ethnography of Education at Home and Abroad*. London: Erlbaum Associates, pp. 178–202.

Sizer, Theodore. 1984. *Horace's Compromise*. Boston: Houghton Mifflin.

———. 1992. *Horace's School*. Boston: Houghton Mifflin.

Steinberg, Laurence, Sanford Dornbusch, and Bradford Brown. 1996. *Beyond the Classroom: Why School Reform Has Failed and What Parents Can Do*. New York: Simon and Schuster.

## READING FOR INFORMATION

1. Summarize Rafael's teachers' expectations.
2. Review the number of times Rafael came late or skipped class. Were tardiness and class-cutting problems in your high school? Explain.
3. In your own words, explain the strategies Rafael used to wrap the teachers around his little finger.

## READING FOR FORM, ORGANIZATION, AND EXPOSITORY FEATURES

1. What is the function of paragraphs 32 to 38? How do they relate to the rest of the selection?
2. Evaluate McQuillan's evidence. Is it sufficient?
3. What is the effect of the final sentence?

## READING FOR RHETORICAL CONCERNS

1. After reading the biographical sketch and the information about McQuillan in the prereading exercise, what is your assessment of his credibility as a critic of American high schools?
2. Does McQuillan supply the reader with sufficient background information for his analysis and evaluation of Rafael's "day in high school"?

## WRITING ASSIGNMENTS

1. Flesh out the notes you took for the prereading exercise, then write an essay in which you compare and contrast your high-school day with Rafael's. Draw conclusions about educational opportunities in American schools.
2. McQuillan writes, "For Rafael, school was a place to be with friends; accordingly, his interests centered on socializing. School work had little meaning. It was more a trial to be endured (or better, avoided) than a source of insight, growth, or empowerment" (paragraph 36). How would Leon Botstein respond to this evaluation?
3. Use McQuillan's analysis, along with other selections in this chapter, to write an essay in response to the question, "What worth is Rafael's education?" State and defend your position.

# Educating Black Students

## *Shelby Steele*

*Shelby Steele has written extensively on race relations, multiculturalism, and affirmative action. He received the National Book Critics' Circle Award for his book* The Content of Our Character: A New Vision of Race in America *and an Emmy Award for his documentary* Seven Days in Bensonhurst.

### PREREADING

Read the first paragraph of the selection. In your journal, speculate about what Steele is calling the real problem with the education of America's black children.

The problems surrounding the education of America's black     1
youth are usually presumed to follow from either racism or
poverty, or both. America's terrible racial history adds a compelling
logic to this presumption, and no doubt poverty remains a profound
problem even if racism is far less a problem than it once was. But I believe that something very different from these two familiar difficulties is
undermining the academic development of today's black youth. Allow
me to begin with a speculation.

Suppose America decided that black people were poor in music     2
because of deprivations due to historical racism. Clearly their improvement in this area would be contingent on the will of white America to
intervene on their behalf. Surely well-designed interventions would enable blacks to close the musical gap with whites. Imagine that in one
such program a young, reluctant, and disengaged Charlie Parker is
being tutored in the saxophone by a college student.

The tutor learns that Parker's father drank too much and aban-     3
doned the family, and that his mother has had an affair with a married
man. Young Charlie is often late to his tutorial sessions. Secretly the
tutor comes to feel that probably his real purpose is therapeutic,

Reprinted from *Education in the Twenty-First Century*, edited by Edward P. Lazear, with the permission of the publisher, Hoover Institution Press. Copyright 2002 by the Board of Trustees of the
Leland Sanford Junior University.

because the terrible circumstances of Charlie's life make it highly unlikely that he will ever be focused enough to master the complex keying system of the saxophone or learn to read music competently. The tutor says as much in a lonely, late-night call to his own father, who tells him in a supportive tone that in this kind of work the results one works for are not always the important ones. If Charlie doesn't learn the saxophone, it doesn't mean that he isn't benefiting from the attention. Also, the father says, "What pleases me is how much you are growing as a human being."

And Charlie smiles politely at his tutor but secretly feels that the tutor's pained attentions are evidence that he, Charlie, must be inadequate in some way. He finds it harder to pay attention during his lessons. He has also heard from many that the saxophone—a European instrument—really has little to do with who he is. He tells this to the tutor one day after a particularly poor practice session. The tutor is sympathetic because he, too, has recently learned that it is not exactly esteem-building to impose a European instrument on an African-American child.

Finally Charlie stops coming to the program. The tutor accepts this failure as inevitable. Sadly, he realizes that he had been expecting it all along. But he misses Charlie, and for the first time he feels a genuine anger at his racist nation, a nation that has bred such discouragement into black children. The young tutor realizes that surely Charlie could have been saved had there been a program to intervene earlier in his life. And for the first time in his life the tutor understands the necessity for political involvement. He redoubles his commitment to an America that works "proactively" to transform and uplift its poor, and that carries out this work with genuine respect for cultural differences.

The following fall, back at college, he says in amazement to his favorite history professor, "Can you imagine? Teaching saxophone to a poor black kid from Kansas City?"

Of course the true story of Charlie Parker is quite different from this. Though he did grow up poor, black, and fatherless in the depression, he also became the greatest improvisational saxophone player in the history of music. When he died far too young at the age of thirty-five, he had already changed Western music forever.

Why was Charlie Parker, along with thousands and thousands of other blacks (few of whom were geniuses on a par with him), so successful at the high and complex art form of jazz despite suffering the same litany of deprivations that is today used to explain the weak academic performance of black students? Throughout the 1990s, the academic gap between blacks and whites widened, when every objective circumstance suggested that it should have narrowed. Worse, several studies, including one by the American College Board, tell us that this gap is wider between middle-class blacks and whites than it is between poor blacks and whites. This refutes the conventional wisdom that has always seen economic deprivation as the culprit in poor academic performance among blacks.

No other student group in America (and possibly the entire world) has been more studied and had its academic weaknesses more analyzed than black American students. No group has had more special programs created on its behalf or more educational theories generated in its name. And today there is no student group whose performance is more fretted over than black students. There is even an unspoken assumption that this group's performance is an indication of the moral health of the society.    9

Yet the general picture of black academic performance is nothing less than terrible. Black students at every age and grade level generally perform worse than all other groups on virtually every academic measure—test scores, grades, school attendance levels, drop-out rates, suspension rates, and so on. Black college students have the lowest collective grade point average and the highest collective drop-out rate of all student groups. And throughout the 1990s the notorious academic gap between black and white students (SAT scores are one obvious measure) only widened, despite the fact that it had been narrowing a little during the 1970s and 1980s.    10

It is the relentlessness, the seeming insistence on academic weakness in black students, that mystifies. I think at least part of the explanation for this can be seen in the story of the real Charlie Parker—a man who came from an area of life where black performance has always been superb rather than terrible.    11

I believe the real Charlie Parker had two profound advantages over his fictional counterpart. The first was that the America he lived in did not care at all about his musical development. During the depression there were no programs or tutors devoted to black musical development. In this void of indifference there was nothing between Charlie and his saxophone. Maybe he heard the music of a great musician such as Lester Young or Ben Webster and was deeply moved. However he came to the alto saxophone, the disinterest of the society in his playing allowed him to relate directly to the business of making music. There    12 was no subtext for him to decipher as he worked at the instrument, no intimations of guilt in the larger society toward him, and no sense that his achievement might have a social and political significance. He was simply a young boy with an instrument who wanted to make music. As his commitment to the instrument deepened, he had no trouble setting himself to the hard work and long hours of practice that mastery required.

The second great advantage was evident after Charlie became 13 very good on his instrument. Wanting to show off his new talent, he sat in on a jam session with a visiting band—a common practice among black musicians then and now. After he played long enough for the professionals to get a measure of his skills, the drummer dislodged a cymbal from his drum set and threw it at Charlie. Like the infamous hook in the theater, it was the sign to get off stage and go back to the "woodshed," the metaphorical crucible in which musicians develop their craft. So Charlie's second great advantage was that he belonged to a community in which only excellence was acceptable—a community that enforced excellence as an impersonal standard. The drummer was not humiliating Charlie so much as pointing to the bar of excellence. These two advantages—the disinterest of the larger society and an impersonal devotion to excellence in his own community—made Charlie's economic deprivations virtually irrelevant to his achievement. In this "clean" environment his deprivation was only a prod; it excused him from nothing.

But does this mean that the social program and the tutor were ac- 14 tual disadvantages for the fictional Charlie? I think so. The tutor let his idea of Charlie's deprivations move him to an unexamined faith that concern was the true ingredient missing from Charlie's life. If the tutor could show concern, if America could overcome its intractable indifference toward blacks and become concerned about their uplift, if people could consider mentoring, if educational funding could be more equitably distributed, if. . . . The mistake in this faith is that it makes the concern of others the agent of black social transformation. In this faith blacks are conceived as essentially inert people so overcome by deprivation that only the concerned intervention of others can transform them into self-sufficient people. Others act; blacks are acted upon. This is a profound mistake with a litany of terrible consequences for blacks. It encourages this people coming up from three centuries of oppression to trade away agency over their own advancement in order to gain the help of others. Worse, it encourages them to argue their own weakness in order to qualify for such help. It puts them in the same position as the fictional Charlie—looking to a "tutor" who is inept and self-absorbed rather than to their own talents and energies.

What is agency? It is ultimate responsibility combined with pos- 15 session. You have agency over something—a life, a problem, an education—when you have the freedom that allows you to be responsible for it and when you accept that this responsibility belongs to you whether or not others support you.

Many families in America want their children to become well edu- 16 cated, and they are willing to do what is necessary to agent that goal. They read to them in early childhood. They ask for their thoughts in frequent and pleasant conversations. They take them places and teach them to respond to the larger world. And then, having consciously nurtured their child's mind, having understood this to be an important part of parenting, they try to arrange schooling that will continue this process, schooling that is safe and challenging. If the local public school does not offer this, they will go elsewhere to find it. They will move to a better school district or pay for a private school or even try home schooling because they understand that a poor local school does not excuse them from the responsibility of providing a good education for their children. Circumstances can surely limit what even the most responsible family can achieve, but no family is ever really excused from the responsibility of imaginatively fighting difficult circumstances. President Clinton, of course, showed this kind of agency when he sent his daughter to a private school. As the responsible agent of his daughter's education, he simply chose an elite private education over a poor public one in the schools of Washington, D.C. I would have done the same thing. Agency involves determination and commitment. The real Charlie Parker withstood the ire of his neighbors who complained of his constant practicing. President Clinton withstood the political fallout that came to him as a Democratic President seemingly scorning the public schools when it came to his own daughter.

A recent study from the Manhattan Institute (Education Freedom 17 Index) found that academic achievement was higher in states where more "educational freedom" prevailed. In states such as Arizona and Minnesota, where there are many charter schools to choose from and where home schooling is allowed, SAT and NAEP (National Assessment of Educational Progress) scores were significantly higher than in states such as Hawaii and West Virginia, where charter schools and home schooling are discouraged or heavily regulated. Could it be that the more "educationally free" states encourage their parents to be the responsible agents of their children's educations? Or maybe the demand for more agency by parents in some states leads to freer educational policies.

The point is that there is an indisputable relationship between 18 agency and excellence, and that black America—as with all other communities—performs well wherever it sees itself as the responsible agent and performs poorly wherever it doesn't. Agency is a call to the will, a demand that we find the will even if our circumstances are bleak, even if great sacrifices are required. Because agency is so demanding, it has to be supported by an entire constellation of values that today would be called "traditional," a commitment to excellence, hard work, delayed gratification, initiative, risk-taking, et cetera. Among other things these values organize and focus the will. Agency is not really possible without them. Or conversely, agency always makes these values necessary.

It is certainly true that poverty and racism can affect how well a 19 group performs in a given area. But it is also true that poverty and even racism do not prevent a group from achieving excellence when it takes agency over an area and begins to live by the values that allow the will to be applied. Charlie Parker was one of thousands of black Americans who made a living in music even while segregation was pervasive. Obviously this does not mean that segregation was a benign or tolerable institution. It merely points to the relationship between group agency and group performance. American minority groups that have taken agency over their educational performance—Jews and many Asian-American groups are obvious examples—have done in education what blacks have done in music. They have excelled.

The first sign that a group (race, ethnic group, tribe, nationality, 20 gender, region, etc.) has taken agency over an area is that it impersonally enforces a rigorous standard of excellence. Somehow the group decides that its future or even its survival depend on its performance in a given area. Soon it begins to esteem individuals who perform well in those areas. This does not mean that others are devalued, only that those who perform well are seen as special carriers of group pride and honor. Achievement is reinforced by the group bestowing special esteem on its high-performing members. And in group lore this high performance is presumed to result from a special genius that is unique to the group. Thus, Charlie Parker's musical greatness was seen to come from a special black genius, and he was rewarded with much esteem from his group.

When a group takes agency in an area, it evolves an "identity" leg- 21
end or mythology that in effect says, "we do such-and-such very well"—
"we sing well," "we are smart," "we know business," et cetera. The
group presumes itself excellent in the area it takes agency over and then
rewards individuals for manifesting this excellence that is now said to
be inherent to the group. People grow up in the knowledge that their
group excels in certain areas and that their membership (identity) in
the group may give them special potential in these areas.

Of course, once this self-fulfilling prophecy is set in motion, the 22
group will likely become excellent in the area it has taken agency over.
And from this achievement it also begins to build very real expertise in
this area that can be continually refined and passed on within the
group. So there is a movement from agency to a priori faith to achievement to evolving expertise.

In some cases excellence no doubt shows itself before the group 23
takes agency. Maybe there were many superb black singers before the
group claimed an inherent excellence in this area. But this is only a
chicken-or-egg argument. Agency—a level of responsibility in which
the group proudly and fearlessly enforces impersonal standards of excellence in an area as a statement of group identity—must happen for a
group to perform competitively in an area over time.

Group identities are constructed out of agency by what a group 24
takes responsibility for and by the degree of that responsibility. Despite
poverty and intractable segregation, the real Charlie Parker succeeded
because he developed his talent in an area that was at the center of his
group's identity. The extraordinary power of this identity-agency paradigm is evident today in the multibillion-dollar rap music industry, an
industry created and sustained by the very same deprived inner-city
blacks who perform so terribly in school.

Of course, group identities are not shaped in a vacuum. In Parker's 25
day music was open to blacks but neurosurgery was not. Music could be
learned and practiced without a higher education; medicine could not
be. Oppressed minorities, in effect, have always negotiated with a hostile
larger society over where they could invest the group identity by taking
agency. In today's world this negotiation is no longer necessary. In America groups can take agency anywhere they wish. They can remold their
identity at will. Individuals can select wider circles of identity than the
traditional groups they are born into and take agency wherever they see
possibility. Today's America is a fluid society with little restriction on the
assumption of agency beyond the individual imagination.

This said, I believe this identity-agency paradigm still affects the 26
performance profile of black Americans. Group identity is very strong
in this group, which means that the group's taking or rejecting of agency
is more determining of performance than it might be in other groups.
Black America now practices identity politics more intensely than any
other group in American life. Conforming to the group's selection of
agency wins one an esteemed identity; nonconformity puts one's group
identity in great jeopardy. So it is no accident that the academic performance of black students is so weak today. The group has not taken
agency over the academic development of its children in the way that it
has taken agency over their development in other areas. One remarkable indication of this is the fact that excellent black students from
middle school to college are often taunted as "white wannabes." This
constitutes nothing less than a tragic irony: The esteemed identity goes
to the weak black student and is denied to the high-achieving black student. The excellent student is denied a feeling of belonging and esteem
from his group. He is made to suffer isolation and alienation for his academic excellence.

I must add here that wider America has also not taken agency over 27
the academic development of black children. No one has. For the last
thirty-five years, neither black America nor wider America enforced
rigorous standards of academic excellence for black youth. Less and less
has been asked of black students, and weaker and weaker performance
has been allowed to count for them—social promotion in K–12 and
lower standards for college admission than for other groups. The struggle by universities across the country to keep affirmative action is also,
inadvertently, a struggle to keep admission standards lower for blacks,
to continue the practice of asking less of them than of others. No group
in American society has been more betrayed by American education
over the past thirty-five years than black American young people. It is
now clear that the primary device for treating their academic weakness
has been to grant them a license to academic mediocrity. I have written
elsewhere about the peculiar symbiosis of black anger and white guilt
that this blindness to simple human need was born of. Suffice it to say
here (in a bit of an oversimplification) that whites have had to prove
themselves innocent of racism by supporting programs of lowered expectations and double standards for blacks. Blacks understandably developed a sense of entitlement that became a part of their group
identity. What happened quite unintentionally is that both groups took
agency for black weakness rather than for black strength. Both groups

needed the weakness more than the strength in their symbiotic trading. Without black weakness how could America redeem its moral authority from its shameful history of racism? And, if blacks were strong academically, how could they get the programs and money that are a proxy for historical justice? Untold billions of government and private dollars have been spent since the 1960s in the name of black disadvantage. Millions of careers have developed and flourished. Black academic success would end the flow of these dollars and destroy the rationale for these careers.

So when educators sit down to consider how to improve the 28 achievement of black students, they are dealing with a group that is, at the very least, ambivalent about taking agency over the education of its young people—this despite all its vociferous claims to the contrary. In fact, this group inadvertently protects the academic weakness and mediocrity of its youth as a way of sustaining its entitlement. It uses group identity more to punish academic excellence than to punish academic weakness. The weak achiever is the true black; the high achiever is a white wannabe.

Educators today must understand that the group identity of their 29 black students—as currently constructed—is very likely a barrier to the educational disciplines that high academic achievement requires. It may be impossible for educators to entirely overcome a barrier this profound. Group identity is strong in all people and stronger still in blacks. And as long as wider America continues to use black weakness as the occasion to pay off an historical debt, the incentive lies with weakness rather than with strength.

Still, the challenge for today's educators is to do what the black 30 identity is currently failing to do: to enforce for black students at all levels a strict and impersonal accountability to the highest standards of excellence. The challenge is to stand before that poor black student from a single-parent home and a drug-infested neighborhood and ask more than is asked of his wealthy white counterpart in a suburban private school. This is agency. This is the difference between the fictional and the real Charlie Parker.  ❁

### READING FOR INFORMATION

1. In your own words, explain the advantages that the real-life Charlie Parker had over those of his fictional counterpart.
2. Paraphrase Steele's definition of *agency*.

3. Explain the relationship between agency and excellence.

4. Why is group identity so strong among black Americans?

## READING FOR FORM, ORGANIZATION, AND EXPOSITORY FEATURES

1. How does Steele structure his argument? Construct a graphic overview of the selection.

2. How does the analogy with Charlie Parker strengthen Steele's argument? What would be lost if the example of Parker was left out?

3. Underline the various points where Steele asks questions. What function do these questions serve?

## READING FOR RHETORICAL CONCERNS

1. Whom do you think Steele visualizes as his audience? Is he writing to fellow blacks or to all Americans?

2. How would you characterize Steele's voice? What does it suggest about him?

3. Does Steele come across as authoritative, credible, and reliable, or are you left with questions about his orientation?

## WRITING ASSIGNMENTS

1. For an audience who has not read the selection, explain the identity-agency paradigm and relate it to the education of America's black youth.

2. Write an essay in which you agree or disagree with Steele's claims that blacks and Americans in general have too many negative suppositions about black students.

3. Using the "Questions for Analyzing and Evaluating Texts" in Chapter 4, write an essay evaluating Steele's argument.

# Challenging Our Assumptions

## *Janine Bempechat*

*Janine Bempechat, Assistant Professor at the Harvard Graduate School of Education, studies parents' influence on their school children, and academic achievement and motivation in ethnically diverse low-income children.*

### PREREADING

Read the epitaph and write whether you agree or disagree with the mother. Should fourth graders be given homework?

My children spend five hours in school every day. They work very hard while they are there, and believe me, it's stressful. The last thing they need is homework. They need to come home and relax. They have to have a life outside of school.

*—Mother of fourth-grade twins*

As an educational researcher and parent of two school-age children, I find this mother's perspective troubling. Regrettably, we find ourselves entering the millennium with our children's competence in mathematics, science, and technology increasingly at risk. Our youngsters' proficiency in mathematics and science sits at alarmingly low levels relative to that of their peers in most other industrialized nations. What's more, this is old news. We have known since the early 1980s that North American primary and secondary school students lag well behind their Japanese, Taiwanese, and Chinese counterparts in math and science achievement. More recently, large-scale studies of over forty industrialized nations have added fuel to the underachievement fire. We now know that, relative to their peers in France, Germany, England, and many other nations, our students consistently rank in the bottom fourth in all disciplines of mathematics, including algebra, geometry, functions, and probability. This is simply not a good time to let down our collective educational guard.

You may ask, Why should we be so worried? After all, as the 2 wealthiest nation, the United States enjoys the highest standard of living in the world. Do not be lulled into a false sense of security. The reality is that when our children come of age to contribute to this wealth, all indications are that they will be ill prepared. Economic survival, at an individual and societal level, depends on technologically relevant skills, and we have been and continue to be coming up short, so to speak.

Where academic achievement is concerned, we are a second-rate 3 nation, and we need to get back on track. This is a call to action for parents. We need to help our children and our nation get through this educational crisis. I believe that the "school reform movement," which means different things to different players, has failed to address the one issue that is in need of urgent attention—our wanting attitudes about academic achievement. We need a radical shift, not only in curricula, teacher training, and public school management but also in our attitudes about schooling and learning. If we are serious about improving academic achievement, we need to resolve our ambivalence about academic excellence. In particular,

- We need to worry less about self-esteem and more about competence.
- We need to expect much more from our children.
- We need to challenge our children to confront difficulty.
- We need to teach our children that disciplined effort makes all the difference in learning.
- We need to take our children's education much more earnestly.
- We need to rein in our commitment to extracurricular activities.

I know that much of what I say goes against the grain of what 4 many educators and psychologists believe about healthy psychological and social development. And I know that what I believe may sound shocking and mean spirited, but hear me out. I too am a parent of school-age children, and I want nothing more than for them to be happy and to feel good about themselves. Yet I believe that we are far too concerned with our children's happiness and self-esteem, to the detriment of their ability to cope with difficulty and setbacks. From my perspective in this debate, self-esteem is overrated, and the collective hysteria over whether children have enough of it has taken on a life of its own, one that was never anticipated by educational researchers study its development. Why is this?

The demographic, societal, and economic changes that took place from the 1960s through the 1990s led to great increases in the percentage of children who are at risk for school failure and other problem behaviors, such as drug and alcohol abuse and precocious sexuality. Poverty, single parenthood, parents with low levels of education, and limited English proficiency are factors that have contributed, either singly or in combination, to childhood psychological and social difficulties of epidemic proportions. A great many youngsters are living with and through issues that are far beyond their years, such as teen pregnancy and parenthood.

The response of many psychologists, educators, and community workers has been to place children's salvation in increasing their self-esteem. The thinking, apparently, is that if we can get kids to feel better about themselves, we can chip away at the problems that threaten their development into healthy and productive citizens. Increasing self-esteem has become the benchmark of intervention programs, and virtually everyone who works with children, whether or not those children live troubled lives, works to ensure that they have high self-esteem.

The problem is that, in the service of this elusive goal, we have embraced assumptions that are undermining our very efforts to help children *genuinely* feel better about themselves. For example, doing poorly in school understandably threatens self-esteem; being held back in school has a negative influence on self-esteem. However, rather than throwing our considerable knowledge behind programs that provide remediation (a dirty word in some education circles), we have instead embraced lower standards and "social promotion," a truly failed policy that has led to students who are functionally illiterate being graduated from high school.

Our intent is good, but that does not excuse us from letting down generations of children. High self-esteem is not a gift that we can wrap and offer up as a birthday present. When we make it easy to attain goals that would otherwise be difficult for anyone to attain, we are doing a terrible disservice to the children who most need our help.

I know from my personal experiences and my work with children in classrooms that we cannot and *should not* orchestrate our children's experiences to ensure happiness. Many parents seem desperate to protect their children from challenges, setbacks, and failure. They fear that these unpleasant experiences and the resulting feelings of sadness, frustration, and anger might undermine their children's self-esteem. In the long run, it is *precisely* these unpleasantries that allow for the greatest growth and maturity.

We do no one, least of all our children, any favors when we try to 10
shield them from difficulty. It is in the face of difficulty and challenge
that children learn to cope with the kinds of obstacles that everyone
eventually encounters. If children only experience success that comes
easily, they are certain to fall apart at the first sign of failure. The first
failure may come in the fourth grade, when they begin reading for understanding rather than reading for content. Or it may come in the
transition to middle school, when they lose the closeness of learning
from one teacher in the company of the same peers. Or it may come
in high school, when schools become much larger and increasingly
impersonal.

The first failure may even come in college or graduate school or 11
the first job—in this sense it doesn't matter when. What matters is that
it *will* happen, despite our efforts as loving and caring parents to prevent it. We will have unwittingly sent our children out into the world
unprepared to bounce back from trying experiences. In other words,
we will have robbed them of critical early opportunities to develop
strategies that will foster resilience in the face of failure.

I am not proposing that we let our children wallow in quicksand. I 12
am suggesting that we view discouraging experiences, theirs as well as
our own, as opportunities to demonstrate how to cope with disappointment—as teachable moments, if you will. Goodness knows, none of us
has to stage unpleasant experiences; they occur in daily life. We get lost
driving to a new place. We rearrange our schedule to wait at home for
the service person who never shows up. We stay up very late to prepare
for a meeting that is canceled at the last minute. We find out that we
unwittingly offended a good friend. How we react to daily challenges
speaks volumes to our children about how to deal with ourselves and
others when things do not go our way.

In order to give our children the opportunities to experience and 13
cope with challenges, we need to raise our expectations and standards
for their academic achievement. Barring the assignment of projects that
are inappropriate for their age, children are capable of doing much,
much more than we give them credit for. Complaining to teachers that
assignments are too hard and take too long to do serves no purpose
other than to undermine the teacher's efforts to teach and our children's efforts to learn. Children learn nothing from easy assignments.
That they don't does not bother me nearly as much as what they may
come to *believe* as a result of easy assignments. For example, some students can come to believe that school is a breeze, that they are really

smart. Worse still, others can come to believe that the only reason the teacher gives them easy work is because he or she feels they are "stupid" and could not possibly complete more involved assignments.

Both beliefs are dangerous. In the first case, children are lulled 14 into a false sense of intellectual security. Eventually they will encounter schoolwork that will be hard to do, and they will have no choice but to believe they are not smart enough to master it. Their balloon of high confidence is bound to burst, with very trying consequences. Previously unencountered struggles may very well leave them baffled, demoralized, and at a loss for what to do next. In the second case, the consequences for learning are disastrous: children are drawn into believing that they lack the ability to master more interesting and challenging schoolwork. If they believe they are "dumb," then there is no point in investing effort in learning. This is indeed a very high price for students to pay for *our* desire that they not be challenged or stressed in school. They cannot possibly acquire the skills they need, at the level at which they need them, unless we give them homework and other assignments that push them to reason, analyze, and synthesize information in new and creative ways.

## THE NEED FOR HOMEWORK

And so, beginning with kindergarten, all children need to have appro- 15 priately challenging homework to do after school. Homework is critical because it is the training ground for the development of qualities that we all want so much to see in our children: responsibility, diligence, persistence, and the ability to delay gratification. Children need time, and lots of it, in which to nurture these personal qualities. With very few exceptions, we cannot possibly expect students to develop these strengths of character overnight. It is the nature of childhood that youngsters are egocentric and demanding. None of us would expect a two-year-old to share her toys willingly and to wait patiently for her turn at the swings. Yet we do expect this kind of behavior from a five-year-old about to enter kindergarten. This transformation in children's behavior between two and five years of age does not happen magically. All of us can attest to the energy and time it takes over thousands of experiences, big and small, to mold the impatient and unreasonable two-year-old into the relatively composed five-year-old. And so it is with the "habits of mind" of which I speak. We cannot possibly expect children entering middle school to be efficient learners if they have had minimal exposure to homework throughout elementary school. They too need those thousands of experiences, big and small, to develop the endurance, persistence, and willingness to tolerate uncertainty that are expected of them by the time they enter the sixth grade. These skills do not emerge spontaneously—they evolve over time and as a result of a lot of effort on the part of parents and their children.

## THE NEED FOR DISCIPLINED EFFORT

For many children, effort is akin to a double-edged sword. On the one 16 hand, they know that they need to try in order to do well, but on the other hand, if they *have* to try, it means they are not smart. Rather than being a tool that can enhance their abilities, effort becomes a pure and simple condemnation of their abilities. We need to get children to see that *disciplined* effort can indeed enhance their abilities and make them "smarter." It is through struggle that students deepen their understanding of material, and an ever-deepening understanding gives them the insights that lead to higher-order thinking skills, including the ability to evaluate and think critically.

Children's beliefs about how smart they are do not take firm hold 17 until the fourth or fifth grade. The early elementary school years (kindergarten through second grade), then, are the prime years in which we can teach children strategies for coping with difficulty and confusion. We need to capitalize on these years to present children with learning experiences that foster resilience in the midst of difficulty and setbacks. Doing so will not guarantee that a child will become a highly confident student, but it will give many children a leg up on learning how to confront disappointment and failure.

## THE NEED TO VALVE SCHOLARSHIP

Despite the political rhetoric, we are a nation that does not value aca- 18 demic excellence. Our winning quarterbacks get far more accolades than do our exemplary student writers and mathematicians. In fact, missing a practice session or, heaven forbid, a game is a grave offense that carries with it punitive consequences of a most serious nature, including being benched for a few games. Yet somehow it has become increasingly acceptable to many parents that their children miss school, not for illness but to take or lengthen a family vacation. In addition, many parents see no problem in acknowledging that everyone needs to take a "mental health" day every now and again—a day to sit back, cool off, and refresh oneself. Thus some children miss a day of school here and there over the course of an academic year.

I would love to take a mental health day myself. Goodness knows, 19 writing this article has taken a lot out of me. A few days off would have done me a world of good. But I have not taken a day off, not because I am an exemplary person but because I have an obligation to my editor, who has an obligation to the people in her publishing group and company. If I am late, everyone else is late.

Certainly no real harm or long-lasting intellectual damage will 20 arise from children's missing a few days of school here and there. However, inasmuch as I have an obligation to my editor, my children have obligations to their teachers, and my husband and I feel strongly that they need to know this. For example, one day in mid-February, waking up to a cold and cloudy Boston day, my seven-year-old daughter announced that she was not going to school because she was tired. "Tough," I said. "Why should you have the day off when everyone else has to be there? And what about Mrs. Jones? Maybe she doesn't feel like teaching you today, but she will because she has to—it's her job. I bet a bunch of kids also don't feel like going to school today, but they'll all be there, along with you." And off she went, mumbling something about grown-ups and unfairness.

Our children can't have it both ways, and neither can we. We sim- 21 ply cannot espouse the singular importance of education to our children while noting times at which it turns out not to be so important. I have no doubt that such inconsistency leaves many children confused about how committed their parents really are to their schooling.

In this context, I am convinced that youngsters today are involved in far 22 too many activities outside of school. Gone are the days when children came home, did their homework, and played in the street until dinnertime. This is largely a sign of the times. Sadly, we no longer live in a society where we can happily send our children out to play with the caveat that they be home by 6:00 P.M. Concerns for our children's safety have given rise to an incredible increase in scheduled activities, many of which occur on school nights. Factor in part-time jobs for our teenagers, and you can see how a given day can be broken up into too many events that compete with schoolwork.

Why are we allowing this? For right or wrong, we live in a society 23 that values well-roundedness. We want our children to develop their talents across a range of skills and abilities, to be good students, to have friends, to be involved in sports and music, and to express their artistic creativity. We believe that helping our children develop their skills in all these areas will enhance their self-esteem; we believe this so strongly that we view children who are "only good in school" as problematic, and describe them disparagingly as nerds, geeks, and brainiacs.

For many parents, involvement in extracurricular activities is 24 sometimes more about their own self-esteem than their child's. And so, when confronted with worsening grades in school, many parents are loathe to do what comes naturally to others: pull their children out of extracurricular activities. Increasingly, I see parents viewing involvement in outside activities not as privileges but as essential elements for enhancing self-esteem and maintaining the commitment they need to demonstrate on college applications. And, surprisingly, some parents are finding support among their children's teachers and school counselors.

For example, my colleague Nancy found herself completely un- 25 dermined by her twelve-year-old daughter's social studies teacher, Mr. Jackson. Her daughter Janie went from a B to a C in this course, and Nancy reiterated the family's rule that forbids participation in extracurricular activities when report cards grades are lower than a B. Nancy explained that she would not allow Janie to play spring softball so that she would have more time to devote to her studies. Her daughter, bitterly disappointed, mentioned this in passing to Mr. Jackson, who openly disagreed with her mother. He believed very strongly that students should participate in sports. "School isn't everything," he said. To help Janie out, he awarded her an undeserved B so that she could get around her family's rule and play softball.

I have no doubt that Mr. Jackson believed he was acting in Janie's 26 best interests. Unfortunately, his "benevolence" in the service of her self-esteem did her much more harm than good. His actions trivialized her family's standards for her school performance. More seriously, he held Janie to a much lower standard than he did the other students, an act that is patently unfair to her and everyone else. Her B is not the same as everyone else's B; in other words, she knows that her teacher was willing to accept substandard work from her but not from others. Is that because he thought she could not do the work? Janie will never really know. But her high-school transcript will show that she was a member of the varsity softball team for four years.

## THE NEED TO ADDRESS COLLEGE ADMISSIONS STANDARDS

Our concerns over well-roundedness have not evolved in a vacuum. [27]
College admissions and financial aid policies have been complicit in
the collective hysteria over well-roundedness. It is not enough anymore to be an exemplary student and to serve the community ad-
mirably. Any hope of our children getting into the best colleges rests
on their demonstrating their competence in a variety of domains. So
the pressure is on to be a top student, a record-holding athlete, a
competition-winning musician, and an integral member of the community's soup kitchen.

Prestigious admissions and scholarships are going to our "well- [28]
rounded" students, which of course puts the pressure on us as parents
to make sure our children are not left in the dust. We scurry around to
give them opportunities that we think will look good on their application. We rise at 4:00 A.M. to get to the rink for her hour of practice time,
drive him and half a dozen of his buddies to two soccer practices and
one game each week, drop her off at her part-time job, get him to the
nursing home for his three-hour shift as a volunteer, and so on, and so
on. In their zeal to attract well-rounded students, many colleges, especially the top-tier schools, unwittingly shut out many exemplary students. I cannot pretend to know how we can work our way out of this
cycle. I believe that institutions of higher learning need to revisit and
refine their beliefs about the kind of college applicant best suited to
make important contributions to society and to the communities in
which they will live, work, and raise their children.

Some colleges may have begun to adopt a more reasonable ad- [29]
mission policy by targeting or "angling" their search for students. In
other words, at some schools, recruitment officers are asked to identify exemplary prospective students who can fill a particular need,
whether in the orchestra, student newspaper, or one or more of the
college's athletic teams. To the extent that a shift in college admissions
practices may be under way, it is a change that does not necessarily
stem from concerns over students' well-being, but rather from a desire to maintain a school's standing in a particular area for which it is
known.

## THE NEED TO RETHINK SCHOOLING

I know of very few educators who would advocate a "back to basics" ap- [30]
proach that would maximize the development of the *academic* child

and minimize the development of the *whole* child, and that is not the approach I am advocating. The proverbial pendulum cannot be allowed to swing back *that* far. Yet, given the current state of educational underachievement in our nation, we need to rethink the ways in which we factor schooling into our children's daily lives. We need to swing the pendulum back to some reasonable middle ground, one that acknowledges that children need opportunities to grow and express themselves in a variety of ways and in a context that places academic achievement firmly at the top of every family's list of priorities. I have no doubt that we can turn things around and get our children, and our nation, back on track.  ❀

## READING FOR INFORMATION

1. Bempechat argues that educators and parents give too much emphasis to raising children's self-esteem. Summarize her argument.
2. In your own words, explain Bempechat's views on homework.
3. What is Bempechat's position on after-school activities?
4. What is Bempechat's criticism of college admissions policies?

## READING FOR FORM, ORGANIZATION, AND EXPOSITORY FEATURES

1. Explain how Bempechat uses the opening paragraph to present a rationale for her argument.
2. Describe the organizational features that make the text easy to follow.
3. Explain the function of paragraph 3.
4. Cite the passages where Bempechat brings in personal experience. What effect do these stories have on the reader? What would be lost if they were left out?

## READING FOR RHETORICAL CONCERNS

1. Is Bempechat writing to a particular group of people? How did you come to that conclusion?
2. Do you think Bempechat gives sufficient weight to opposing views? Why, or why not?
3. How would you describe Bempechat's tone of voice: as objective, sympathetic, or judgmental? Explain.
4. Explain how Bempechat's background gives credibility to her argument.

## WRITING ASSIGNMENTS

1. Create a graphic overview of the selection and use it to summarize Bempechat's argument for students who have not read "Challenging Our Assumptions."

2. What were your family's views toward extracurricular activities? Did they view after-school activities as a privilege or an essential part of your education? Were you allowed to engage in after-school activities regardless of your grades, or did your family impose standards for school performance? Using your own experience and Bempechat's article as a base, write an essay in which you agree or disagree that "we need to rein in our commitment to extracurricular activities" (paragraph 3).

3. Write an essay in which you agree or disagree with Bempechat's view that children's academic achievement should be at the top of every family's priorities.

4. Reread paragraphs 18–20. With whom do you side: the mother who allows her child to take a "mental health" day or the mother who is reluctant to let her child miss a day of school? Write a brief essay explaining your position.

# Homework

### *Martin L. Gross*

*Martin L. Gross is the best-selling author of* The Government Racket, A Call for Revolution, The Tax Racket, The End of Sanity: Social and Cultural Madness in America, The Brain Watchers, The Doctors, The Psychological Society, *and* The Conspiracy of Ignorance: The Failure of American Public Schools, *from which this selection is taken.*

## PREREADING

A rule of thumb for college studying is two hours of homework for each hour of class work. A student taking fifteen credits should spend thirty hours per week on homework—for example, six hours per night. How much time do you spend on homework each night and for the entire week? Respond in your journal.

How much homework do Americans students do?    1
Too little.    2

The most conclusive studies have been made by the NAEP evalu-    3
ators, who questioned students taking their nationwide tests. Judging
from these studies, which were done in both 1984 and 1996, homework
is in a sorry state and shows no sign of improving. Among nine-year-
olds, little homework is assigned or done. Twenty-six percent did none.
Four percent did not do the homework assigned by teachers. Fifty-
three percent did less than an hour a day. In rounded averages, the typical fourth grade student appears to have perhaps thirty minutes of
homework a night.

That amount increases as the child ages, but not considerably. In    4
the thirteen-year-old group, most of whom are in the eighth grade in
middle school, 22 percent were assigned no homework, which is rather
shocking. Thirty-seven percent had less than an hour; while 35 percent
were given an hour or more. It appears that these typical middle school
students were given an average of only forty-five minutes a night of
study at home.

The figures are similar for seventeen-year-olds. The most disturb-    5
ing aspect of the survey is that 23 percent of high school seniors had no
homework at all, while another 13 percent of fun-loving students didn't
do what was assigned. That makes 36 percent of students who are totally out of the homework-studying loop. *Another 28 percent, or a total
of almost two-out-of-three seniors, had less than an hour's homework. If
one suspected that America's secondary schools are hopelessly lax, this
is final proof.*

Is it important? Apparently it is vital.    6

Across the board, the more homework given and completed, the    7
higher the NAEP test scores, which proves the strong correlation between homework and performance. Among high school seniors, the average NAEP reading score for those who did no homework was 273.
For those who did less than an hour, it was 288, some fifteen points
higher. And for those who did one to two hours of homework, the average score rose to 295. The score escalated even higher, to 307, for students who did more than two hours of homework a night. A nose in the
textbook—at home—is obviously the route to school success.

What are students doing instead of homework?    8

Exactly what parents know and everyone else can guess. *They are    9
watching television, a total of twenty-one hours a week, some four times
the amount given over to homework.*

While parents vocally claim to be interested in their children's 10
school performance, they are obviously unwilling to do anything about
it. The typical American parent permits excessive television watching
instead of insisting that children do their assigned homework and pressing lax school officials to assign still more. Since homework and test
results are so closely related, one would think that status-striving American parents would at least put a partial lock box on the family—or the
student's own—television set.

Reading assignments in high school are just as lax as homework. 11
One study reported that seniors are asked to read only ten pages of text
each evening, for all their classes *combined*. The NAEP study showed
that outside reading is also a prime casualty of lax schools and compulsive television watching, taking up much less than two hours *a week*, a
reflection of the visual, not literary, era in which children live.

Teachers have to take the blame for inadequate homework assign- 12
ments—a symbol of their laxity.

But why do they assign so little? One reason is the general ethos of 13
American middle and high schools, where rigor is considered to be unwarranted, outmoded, authoritarian, even perhaps injurious to the supposedly fragile student psyche. Another reason is that some teachers
feel it is too much trouble to read and grade the papers.

Still other teachers are afraid to assign too much homework lest 14
they stand out from the more permissive faculty and make students dis-
like them. Perhaps the greatest deterrent to homework is that many
teachers were poor or mediocre students as youngsters and found homework an onerous task. Why inflict it on their students, they now ask?

The lax homework policy may also result from the Establishment's 15
educational philosophy that "enough is enough." A Texas professor of
education, writing in the *High School Journal*, admits that homework
can improve a youngster's grades and knowledge. But, he warns, it will
cut into the student's "leisure time and the autonomous pursuit of individual interests." As if there's not already enough of that around to sat-
isfy a generation, or two.   �

## READING FOR INFORMATION

1. How did you react to the National Assessment of Educational Progress
   statistics in paragraphs 3, 4, and 5? Does your experience bear them out?
2. Paraphrase Gross's answer to the question he poses in paragraph 6: "Is
   [homework] important?"

3. In your own words, explain what Gross means when he says teachers have to take the blame for assigning so little homework.

## READING FOR FORM, ORGANIZATION, AND EXPOSITORY FEATURES

1. What effect does Gross achieve by asking the questions in paragraphs 1, 6, 8, and 13?
2. Underline the types of evidence Gross uses to support his argument. Do you find the evidence convincing?
3. How does the last sentence affect the reader?

## READING FOR RHETORICAL CONCERNS

1. Describe Gross's rhetorical purpose.
2. Is Gross's argument one-sided, or does he discuss alternate viewpoints? Explain.
3. Underline words that reveal Gross's tone. How would you describe the tone?

## WRITING ASSIGNMENTS

1. Divide the class into small groups and have each group member survey ten first-year students about their experiences doing homework in their senior year of high school. Ask the students questions, such as

   How many pages of reading were you assigned each night?
   In total, how many hours of homework did you do each night?
   What did you do after school besides homework?

   Have the students in each group combine their data. Then pool the group data. Using the results of the survey, write an essay in which you agree or disagree with the conclusions Gross draws in his article.
2. Use the strategies presented in Chapter 4 to write a critical evaluation of Gross's argument.
3. Write an essay in which you compare and contrast Gross's views with those of one of the other authors in Chapter 11.

# Myth 5: Self-esteem Must Come First—Then Learning

## *Larry E. Frase and William Streshly*

*Larry E. Frase, a professor of educational administration in the College of Education at San Diego State University, has written numerous articles and twenty-two books, including* School Management by Wandering Around, Maximizing People Power in Schools, Teacher Compensation and Motivation, Creating Learning Places for Teachers, Too, *and coauthored* Top Ten Myths in Education: Fantasies Americans Love to Believe, *from which this selection is taken.*

*William A. Streshly, professor and chair for the Department of Administration, Rehabilitation, and Postsecondary Education at San Diego State University, spent thirty years in public school administration. He is coauthor of* Avoiding Legal Hassles, Teacher Unions and Total Quality Education, *and* Top Ten Myths in Education: Fantasies Americans Love to Believe, *from which this selection is taken.*

### PREREADING

Do you think students need to have high self-esteem in order to learn, or is this assumption a myth? Respond in your journal.

### INTRODUCTION

Wherever we've turned these past thirty years we found book after book and program after program espousing the virtues of high self-esteem, and the need for public schools to teach it. Education lectures are packed with it. It seems to be a mantra of the National Education Association (NEA). Parent organizations wildly seek ways to help children feel good about themselves. When interviewing teachers and administrators, we frequently hear that high student self-esteem is the number-one goal and must precede all else. We challenge this notion.

## THE MYTH

The myth is that students must feel good about themselves before they  2
can learn. Supporters of this myth defend it with religious fervor. This
conviction is not without reason. No one we know defines a successful
life as one where the person feels lousy about him or herself. Feeling
good is nice; it is the way we want to feel. But to think that students
must feel good about themselves before they can learn is silly, myopic
thinking. We have never observed a student or adult who felt good
about being illiterate or ignorant. Sound funny? Only in a perverted
sense, as illustrated by Billy's friend in the cartoon.

The following are just a few examples of the faddish silliness peo-  3
ple have about self-esteem:

- A Native American teacher in a southern Arizona school district we
  audited shared her wisdom with us: "You know, these children [i.e.,
  Native American] can't learn much. My job is just to love them."
- In schools across our nation, fifth- and sixth-grade girls are asked to
  make a list of eight qualities they like about themselves. Each good
  quality is written on a paper petal to form a flower, then a photo of
  each girl is placed in the center of her own flower. Teachers, parents,
  and administrators in these school districts say this activity is necessary, since self-esteem is requisite to learning the basics, even though
  the activity is divorced from a larger lesson and cognitive gains.
- Educators in Large City School District, Texas; Inglewood, California;
  Washington, D.C.; and many other cities with high concentrations of
  African American and Hispanic teachers told us that "these poor kids
  are so oppressed they are not ready to learn; our first job is to show
  them love and help them feel good about themselves."
- Critics of today's bilingual education programs say that the underlying
  belief that Hispanic students must develop their self-esteem before
  they can learn is silly, whereas bilingual education proponents say
  doing otherwise is unwise and potentially debilitating.
- The feel-good efforts in California have failed. Companies spend huge
  sums of money to teach the state's high-school graduates simple basic
  skills. Meanwhile, California universities are providing remedial mathematics and English to thousands of students, all of whom graduated
  in the top third of their high school classes. The education system believed that self-confidence and high self-esteem are the best ways to
  enhance confidence, and that this would improve scholastic achievement and good citizenship in general.

- The self-esteem myth was summarized by one of our graduate students, a teacher in administrative training: "If a child comes to school without getting a good night's sleep, it is okay if he sleeps in class. He feels better when he wakes up. After all, the child has problems at home that render the three Rs less important."

## THE REALITY

Feeling good about yourself is a wonderful *by-product* of learning, not the *cause* of it. It happens naturally and without external inducement. It happens when we achieve, when we do something well.    4

The wonderful news is that many students want stronger teaching    5
and standards. The beleaguered and low-achieving Chicago schools are adopting higher standards. New York is in the process of beefing up its standards by requiring all high school students to pass a battery of college-preparatory Regents tests rather than the much less stringent Regents Competence Test (RCT). Many students want tougher tests. New York City students' reactions to tougher tests have been positive. A freshman recently said, "We are the class of 2000; at least we know that when we graduate, we deserve to graduate." Another said, "This [the Regents test] is a better test. The RCT feels like you're back in kindergarten." In a national study, students told the Public Agenda Organization (1997) that higher standards are not enough; they want "more attentive, demanding teachers." Further, they say that they

- admire students who do well in school;
- want more of a challenge to get their diploma ("we can glide; grades are given to us");
- believe there are too many disruptive students in class, that discipline is lax or nonexistent;
- want, like most adults desire, to be taught how to work hard;
- want better teachers, and more attention from teachers would help them achieve higher standards (63 percent said this); 23 percent think that this would help them most;
- want interesting, engaging teachers who have a special knack for getting them to do their best;
- respect the demands and consistency from drill sergeant-type teachers; and
- want students to be more respectful of teachers.

Parents, too, want their children to learn. A Los Angeles–based 6
reporter for the *New York Times* recently told of a Mexican national
couple who came to Los Angeles with their family to work in sweat-
shops so that their children could learn English and receive a fine education. After finding that the schools would not teach their children
English, they refused to allow their children to attend school. They
wanted their children to learn English (Callaghan, 1997). They were
not alone. Seventy other poor immigrant families joined them in February 1996, insisting that their children be allowed out of the bilingual
program and that they be taught English in English. These and many
more Latino parents backed a California ballot initiative designed to
end bilingual education for most children in the state. They feared that
bilingual education programs were keeping their children from learning
English in favor of maintaining and establishing their self-esteem. After
twenty-five years, bilingual education has very few defenders among
Latino parents. In a recent *Los Angeles Times* poll, 83 percent of Latino
parents in Orange County said they wanted their children to be taught
in English as soon as they started school. These parents know that unless their children become literate in English, their poverty cycle will
not end. Only 17 percent said they favored having their children taught
in their native language.

The reality is that the dropout rate for Hispanics aged sixteen to 7
twenty-four is 30 percent, nearly double that of whites and blacks. A recent study in New York City showed that 90 percent of the students
who started bilingual education in the sixth grade were unable to pass
an English-language test after three years of bilingual instruction. Yet
English as a second language and non-English-speaking students are
required to enroll in bilingual programs. The folly here is that a law was
recently passed that requires immigrants from Caribbean nations who
speak or understand a Creole language and score in the bottom 40 percent on an English-language test to be instructed in bilingual education. Had these children stayed in their Caribbean home, they would
have been instructed in English.[1]

Totally contrary to the self-esteem enthusiasts, higher percentages 8
of African American students, educators, and parents believe that academics are "extremely important" in finding a job than do non–African
American students. Black and white parents are very adamant about the
importance of academic achievement to their children. When asked
what the priority for schools should be, 80 percent of black parents and
66 percent of white parents chose raising academic standards and

achievement over integration (Farkas and Johnson, 1998). We maintain that after twenty-five years of research there is virtually no substantive evidence that high self-esteem must come first before academic learning can occur. We believe that teachers, and for that matter all adults, should respect student psyches, but self-esteem is not requisite to learning. Contrarily, learning enhances self-esteem. Purveyors of this myth actually agree, albeit unwittingly (Maeroff, 1998),[2] when they conclude that learning and overcoming challenges result in higher self-esteem.

In fact, the highly touted $735,000 California Task Force on self-esteem came to the conclusion that the relationship between self-esteem and learning is weak. Hold on to your seat: A common finding is that high self-esteem is often linked to low performance. The deeply seated belief that America's history of racial oppression resulted in low self-esteem for African Americans is also false. African American self-esteem is as high as and sometimes higher that that of whites (Rothman, 1989). The author tells us that we live in a time of irrationality; widely refuted but firmly seated beliefs continue. For example, the idea that violence is committed by people of low self-esteem is essentially false. In fact, people committing violence tend to have higher self-esteem than those who do not. Roy Baumeister's (1996) research shows that violence is more commonly committed by people with unrealistically high self-esteem. He warned that certain forms of high self-esteem are correlated to narcissism and seem to increase violence, and that unabated efforts to enhance self-esteem may be counterproductive, dangerous, and may literally end up doing considerable harm. The reality is that people develop legitimate self-esteem when they achieve something good and worthwhile, not until then. 9

Harold Stevenson (1992) studied education in Asia and in the United States for ten years. One of his many research findings is that although Asian students performed far better than American students, American students felt much greater satisfaction about their school achievement. He also found that 70 percent of the Chinese students said education was very important. Only 10 percent of American students mentioned education; they valued money and things. Similarly, Asian parents said that the most important thing for their kids is to work hard and do well in school. American parents said doing well in school is just one among a number of things—kids should be popular and good in sports. 10

The trend is clear—and not related to "self-esteem." American parents and students also lack faith in the efficacy of hard work in school. 11

Asian parents believed that their students needed to work hard through the twelfth grade before they could predict achievement on college entrance tests. American parents said that the prediction could be made in the sixth grade. In other words, Americans believed that ability, not work, was what counted. They hold schooling in "low" esteem. When asked the most important factor in math performance, 70 percent of the Japanese and 60 percent of the Taiwanese students said "studying hard." Only a little more than 20 percent of American students mentioned work, and 55 percent attributed success to having a good teacher. If they did not do well in school, it was due to poor schools or poor teaching.

A study by Nathan Caplan (1992) supports Stevenson and offers 12 powerful evidence to support the efficacy of hard work. He found that poor Indo-Chinese refugee students with little or no English-language skills, who had lost months and years of schooling during their escape from Asia and their time in relocation camps, went to schools in poor, innercity areas. Nevertheless, 27 percent achieved an *A* average and more than 50 percent a *B* average. Half of them scored in the top 25 percent in mathematics. These families clear the table after dinner, and the students do their homework and help each other. They exert effort.

The reality is that all industrialized countries scoring higher than 13 the United States hold students accountable for their learning. Self-esteem is not the issue.

These findings and common sense tell us that the "can do," work 14 hard ethic is missing in too many schools and families. We suggest achievement is what fosters high self-esteem. For example, name the two events that occurred to you in high school that you felt best about. The vast majority of people name an achievement, accomplishing something. Few, if any, name a touchy-feely activity. We bet the teachers involved in your event enforced standards, wanted you to do well, told you to do well, and acted as though they cared more about your learning than your self-esteem. Ours did.

## THE SOLUTION

The solution is obvious. Focus schools on the product: learning. Happy 15 kids and high self-esteem are natural—they result from achieving. Here are the key ingredients:

- Announce that the product of one's school district is learning, and then run the schools to achieve that end.

- Focus schools, administrators, and teachers on ensuring that only high-quality instruction occurs in the schools.
- Focus schools on doing what they can to provide highly effective learning environments, and rid the pathways to learning of road blocks.
- Teach parents and educators that hard work is good and necessary, that struggle is not a bad word, and that good things come with effort.
- Teach parents that they have the primary responsibility to require their children to do homework and hold *them* accountable for their success and failures.
- Teach parents, educators, and students that high self-esteem is the result of achievement, not the cause of it—that doing a worthwhile task or job well results in good feelings.

The solution is for schools to disabuse themselves and their communities of the myth that self-esteem must come first. Next, they must accept the empirically and scientifically proven wisdom that hard work leads to achievement and feeling good is a wonderful natural by-product. 16

## NOTES

1. For an interesting discussion see D. Ravitch (1997), "First Teach Them English," *New York Times*, vol. 146, no. 50,906, section A, p. 21.
2. For a review of unwitting agreement with our position and the folly of proposed myth, see Maerhoff (1998) wherein he claims, and rightly so, that students with low self-regard may resist learning. He then proceeds to tell stories about how learning how to do something (e.g., kayaking, rope climbing, and so on) results in higher self-regard and confidence.

## REFERENCES

Baumeister, R. (1996). "Relation of Threatened Egotism to Violence and Aggression." *Psychological Review* 103(1): 5–33.

Callaghan, A. (1997). "Desperate to Learn English." *New York Times*, August 15, p. A15.

Caplan, N., M. Choy, and J. Whitmore. (1992). "Indochinese Refugee Families and Academic Achievement." *Scientific American* 266(2) (February): 37–42.

Farkas, S., and J. Johnson. (1998). *Time to Move On: African-American and White Parents Set an Agenda for Public Schools*. New York: Public Agenda Foundation.

Maeroff, G. I. (1998). "Altered destinies: Making life better for schoolchildren in need." *Phi Delta Kappan* 79: 424–432.

Rothman, S. (1989). *The Myth of Black Low Self-Esteem*. Northampton, MA: Smith College Center for the Study of Social and Political Change.

Stevenson, H. (1992). *The Learning Gap*. New York: Summit Books.

## READING FOR INFORMATION

1. In your own words, explain why students want higher standards and more demanding teachers.
2. Summarize the authors' argument against bilingual education.
3. On the topic of self-esteem and academic achievement, how do the views of African Americans differ from those of whites?
4. In your own words, describe the difference between Asian and American students and parents.

## READING FOR FORM, ORGANIZATION, AND EXPOSITORY FEATURES

1. Frase and Streshly divide the selection into four parts. How does each part contribute to their argument?
2. Underline the sentences that best express Frase and Streshly's position.
3. Explain the function of the six examples in paragraph 2. Would the impact of Frase and Streshly's argument change if they had omitted the examples?
4. Give examples of the various types of evidence—facts, statistics, and references to authorities—that Frase and Streshly use to support their position.

## READING FOR RHETORICAL CONCERNS

1. Describe Frase and Streshly's rhetorical goal. Do you think they achieve it?
2. Describe the organizational features that make the argument easy to follow.
3. Do you think Frase and Streshly are addressing their argument to a wide general audience or to specialized scholarly readers? How did you arrive at your conclusion?

## WRITING ASSIGNMENTS

1. Do as Frase and Streshly suggest in paragraph 14 and "name the two events that occurred to you in high school that you felt best about." Then write a brief essay describing the events and read it to the class. After everyone has shared, evaluate the experiences. Did most students describe an achievement or accomplishment, as Frase and Streshly predict? Did any report a "touchy-feely activity"?
2. Summarize Frase and Streshly's argument for an audience of students who have not read the selection.

3. Write an argumentative essay in which you support or reject Frase and Streshly's claim that "American parents and students . . . lack faith in the efficacy of hard work in school" (paragraph 11).

4. Write an essay in which you compare and contrast the views expressed by Frase and Streshly and those held by Bempechat in "Challenging Our Assumptions."

# Manufacturing a Crisis in Education

## David C. Berliner and Bruce J. Biddle

*David C. Berliner, professor in the College of Education at Arizona State University, writes extensively about education. His books include* Educational Psychology, *6th edition, coauthored with N. L. Gage;* The Handbook of Educational Psychology, *edited with R. L. Calfee; and* The Manufactured Crisis: Myths, Fraud, and the Attack on America's Public Schools, *from which this selection is taken.*

*Bruce J. Biddle, Professor Emeritus of Psychology and Sociology at the University of Missouri, is founding editor of the journal* Social Psychology of Education *and author of numerous articles and books, including* The Study of Teaching, *coauthored with M. J. Dunkin;* Role Theory, Identities, and Behaviors; Social Class, Poverty, and Education; Research Knowledge Use in Education: Principal Effects, *coauthored with L. J. Saha; and* The Manufactured Crisis: Myths, Fraud, and the Attack on America's Public Schools, *from which this selection is taken.*

### PREREADING

Could it be that the claims of the authors you have read in this chapter are false or exaggerated? Could it be that calls for school reform are unnecessary because education in the United states is actually in good shape? Respond in your journal.

Seldom in the course of policymaking in the U.S. have so many firm convictions held by so many been based on so little convincing proof.

—*Clark Kerr, President Emeritus of the University of California (1991)*

Why have so many Americans come to believe that *American*   1
education is so deficient and that we should look to the Japanese to find out how to run our schools? The answer is that for more than a dozen years this groundless and damaging message has been proclaimed by major leaders of our government and industry and has been repeated endlessly by a compliant press. Good-hearted Americans have come to believe that the public schools of their nation are in a crisis state because they have so often been given this false message by supposedly credible sources.

To illustrate, in 1983, amid much fanfare, the White House re-   2
leased an incendiary document highly critical of American education. Entitled *A Nation at Risk*[1] this work was prepared by a prestigious committee under the direction of then Secretary of Education Terrel Bell and was endorsed in a speech by President Ronald Reagan. It made many claims about the "failures" of American education, how those "failures" were confirmed by "evidence," and how this would inevitably damage the nation. (Unfortunately, none of the supposedly supportive "evidence" actually appeared in *A Nation at Risk*, nor did this work provide citations to tell Americans where that "evidence" might be found.)

But leaders of this disinformation campaign were not content   3
merely to attack American schools. *A Nation at Risk* charged that American students never excelled in international comparisons of student achievement and that this failure reflected systematic weaknesses in our school programs and lack of talent and motivation among American educators. Thus, it came as little surprise when the White House soon sent a team of Americans to Japan to discover and report on why Japanese education was so "successful." Following this visit, the then Assistant Secretary of Education, Chester Finn, a leader of the team, said of the Japanese,

> They've demonstrated that you can have a coherent curriculum, high standards, good discipline, parental support, a professional teaching force and a well-run school. They have shown that the average student can learn a whole lot more.[2]

This enthusiasm was echoed by others on the team. According to   4
team member Herbert Walberg, an educational researcher, features of the Japanese system could be adopted in America and would help to solve the many "problems" of American education. Walberg suggested, "I think it's portable. Gumption and willpower, that's the key."[3]

This was far from the end of White House criticisms of American  5
education. Indeed, the next decade witnessed a veritable explosion of
documents and pronouncements from government leaders—two American presidents, Ronald Reagan and George Bush, secretaries of education, assistant secretaries, and chiefs and staff members in federal
agencies—telling Americans about the many "problems" of their public
schools. As in *A Nation at Risk*, most of these claims were said to reflect
"evidence," although the "evidence" in question either was not presented or appeared in the form of simplistic, misleading generalizations.

During the same years many leaders in industry claimed in docu-  6
ments and public statements that American education was in deep
trouble, that as a result our country was falling behind foreign competitors, and that these various charges were all confirmed by "evidence"
(which somehow was rarely presented or appeared in simple misleading
formats). And these many charges, documents, and pronouncements
from leaders of government and industry, often seconded by prominent
members of the educational community, were dutifully reported and
endlessly elaborated upon by an unquestioning press.

So it is small wonder that many Americans have come to believe  7
that education in our country is now in a deplorable state. Indeed, how
could they have concluded anything else, given such an energetic and
widely reported campaign of criticism, from such prestigious sources,
attacking America's public schools? To the best of our knowledge, no
campaign of this sort had ever before appeared in American history.
Never before had an American government been so critical of the public schools, and never had so many false claims been made about education in the name of "evidence." We shall refer to this campaign of
criticism as the Manufactured Crisis.

The Manufactured Crisis was not an accidental event. Rather, it  8
appeared within a specific historical context and was led by identifiable
critics whose political goals could be furthered by scapegoating educators. It was also supported from its inception by an assortment of questionable techniques—including misleading methods for analyzing data,
distorting reports of findings, and suppressing contradictory evidence.
Moreover, it was tied to misguided schemes for "reforming" education—
schemes that would, if adopted, seriously damage American schools.

Unfortunately, the Manufactured Crisis has had a good deal of in-  9
fluence—thus, too many well-meaning, bright, and knowledgeable
Americans have come to believe some of its major myths, and this has
generated serious mischief. Damaging programs for educational reform

have been adopted, a great deal of money has been wasted, effective school programs have been harmed, and morale has declined among educators.

But myths need not remain unchallenged; in fact, they become [10] shaky when they are exposed to the light of reason and evidence. When one actually *looks* at the evidence, one discovers that most of the claims of the Manufactured Crisis are, indeed, myths, half-truths, and sometimes outright lies.

One of the worst effects of the Manufactured Crisis has been to [11] divert attention away from the *real* problems faced by American education—problems that are serious and that are escalating in today's world. To illustrate, although many Americans do not realize it, family incomes and financial support for schools are *much* more poorly distributed in our country than in other industrialized nations. This means that in the United States, very privileged students attend some of the world's best private and public schools, but it also means that large numbers of students who are truly disadvantaged attend public schools whose support is far below that permitted in other Western democracies. Thus, opportunities are *not* equal in America's schools. As a result, the achievements of students in schools that cater to the rich and the poor in our country are also far from equal.

In addition, America's school system has expanded enormously [12] since World War II and now serves the needs of a huge range of students. This increased diversity has created many opportunities—but also many dilemmas—and debates now rage over how to distribute resources and design curricula to meet the needs of students from diverse backgrounds, with many different skills and interests. Problems such as these *must* be addressed if Americans are to design a school system that truly provides high standards and equal opportunities for all students.

Our second major task, then, is to direct attention away from the [13] fictions of the Manufactured Crisis and toward the real problems of American schools.

## NOTES

1. National Commission on Excellence in Education. (1983). *A Nation at Risk: The Imperative for Educational Reform*. Washington, DC: The Commission on Excellence in Education.
2. Richburg, Keith B. (1985). "Japanese Education: Admired but not Easily Imported." *Washington Post* (October 19), pp. A1, A4.
3. *Ibid.*  ✿

## READING FOR INFORMATION

1. Why do Berliner and Biddle find fault with the criticisms of American education that were published in the 1980s and 1990s?

2. In your own words, explain what Berliner and Biddle mean by a "manufactured crisis."

3. According to Berliner and Biddle, what are "the real problems" in American education? Can you think of others?

## READING FOR FORM, ORGANIZATION, AND EXPOSITORY FEATURES

1. Comment on the epitaph. Why is it an effective opener for this selection?

2. What effect do Berliner and Biddle achieve by referring to Americans as "good-hearted" (paragraph 1) and "well-meaning, bright, and knowledgeable" (paragraph 9)?

3. How does paragraph 7 affect the reader? What would be lost if it was omitted?

## READING FOR RHETORICAL CONCERNS

1. Describe Berliner and Biddle's rhetorical goal. Do you think they achieve their objective?

2. What assumptions do the authors make about their readers? Do you think those assumptions are correct?

3. How would you describe the authors' voice—complacent, matter-of-fact, worried, enraged? What led you to this conclusion?

## WRITING ASSIGNMENTS

1. Write an essay in which you agree or disagree that certain criticisms of education direct our attention away from the real problems in American schools.

2. Drawing upon the selections in Chapter 10, write an essay in which you argue that income and wealth inequality pose serious problems for American education.

3. Conduct research on Berliner and Biddle's claim that "opportunities are not equal in America's schools" (paragraph 11). You might investigate financial inequalities on district and state levels as well as resource inequalities resulting from factors such as tracking, assignment of teachers, and physical space. Formulate your own appraisal of the educational equality and write a research paper supporting your view.

## SYNTHESIS WRITING ASSIGNMENTS

1. In "The Revolt of the Black Bourgeoisie," Leonce Gaiter argues,

   Blacks must now see to it that our children face no such burden. We must see to it that the white majority, along with vocal minorities within the black community (generally those with a self-serving political agenda), does not perpetuate the notion that African-Americans are invariably doomed to the underclass (paragraph 16).

   Write an essay in which you compare and contrast Gaiter's views with those of Shelby Steele.

2. According to Herbert Gans, "Although a great deal of publicity is given to school dropouts, not enough has been said about the peer pressure in poor and working-class neighborhoods that discourages doing well in school" (paragraph 25). Gans would argue the behavior is poverty-related, whereas Steele would claim that it is partially due to black Americans' lack of agency. What is your position? Write an argument essay, using the selections by Gans, Steele, and, if you wish, other authors in this chapter.

3. Drawing on selections by McQuillan, Steele, and Bempechat, write an essay in which you argue that schools and families have very low expectations for students and offer them little challenge.

4. Drawing on selections by Gross, Bempechat, and Frase and Streshly, write an Op Ed piece for your local newspaper in which you argue the need for a more demanding homework policy in your neighborhood schools.

5. Write an essay in which you compare and contrast the views of Frase and Streshly and those of Steele on the relationship between self-esteem and learning.

6. Drawing on the selections in this chapter, write an essay arguing for or against the claim that U.S. students need to be held more accountable for their own learning.

7. In "Manufacturing a Crisis in Education," Berliner and Biddle refer to criticisms of American schools that appeared in the 1980s and 1990s. What about the current call for educational reform? Do you think that it, too, is "manufactured"? Drawing on the selections in Chapter 11 and other sources you acquire through library research, write an essay in which you state and defend your position.

8. The authors in this chapter offer different reasons for the problems in schooling epitomized by McQuillan in his description of Rafael Jackson's "day." Compare the various arguments and then formulate your appraisal of the quality of U.S. schools.

# Humanities

## SUBJECTS OF STUDY IN THE HUMANITIES

The subjects that humanists study have theoretical, historical, and critical orientations. The theoretical subjects are philosophy, linguistics, and semiotics. Humanists approach them from a broad perspective and at close range by examining thought, language, structures of meaning and expression, and other significant evidence of human rationality. The historical subjects are history; various area studies, such as ancient classical civilization, Latin American studies, and Asian studies; and historical studies of particular disciplines, such as the history of science, the history of art, and historical linguistics. Humanists approach them by studying the causes, effects, development, and interaction of peoples, nations, institutions, ideas, fashions, styles, and the like. The critical subjects are literature, drama, music, the visual arts, and other expressive arts. Humanists approach them by analyzing, interpreting, and evaluating "texts," understood in the broadest sense of the term as novels, poems, plays, films, paintings, sculpture, dance, musical scores, musical performances, and so forth.

## METHODS OF STUDY IN THE HUMANITIES

The theoretical, historical, and critical orientations of the humanities also describe the methods that humanists use. The study of history, for example, requires a critical reading of documents from the past as well as a theoretical probing of their importance. The study of literature and the arts usually emphasizes critical interpretation, but it also calls for some historical study of how styles, forms, and themes developed, and for a theoretical study of how we understand them. When you are reading in the humanities, therefore, you need to recognize how the various theoretical, historical, and critical approaches work in the various disciplines. The chapters on the humanities in this anthology provide examples.

## WRITING IN THE HUMANITIES

Assignments for writing in the humanities require you to exercise your theoretical, historical, and critical judgment. In this anthology, for example, writing assignments in the humanities run the gamut from critical summary to theoretical speculation. Shorter assignments may call for various types of writing: a summary or précis of an article, a chapter, or a whole book; a critical report on an article, a chapter, or a whole book; or a review of research in several publications. All of these assignments require you to select important points to write about in logical order or in order of importance. Longer assignments may require a close analysis of several texts. Here's an example from Chapter 12 of this anthology:

> Benazir Bhutto, Elly Bulkin, and Mary Daly are respectively Muslim, Jewish, and Catholic women who seek to strengthen women's active roles in the public arena. Write an essay in which you discuss and evaluate the goals they set forth for women's participation in political leadership, their struggle against racism and sexism, and their efforts to advance the women's movement. Base your discussion on the essays that they have written in this anthology.

Note that this assignment implicitly requires you to summarize and paraphrase portions of Bhutto's, Bulkin's, and Daly's articles, indicating the goals that they set forth. It also implicitly requires you to speculate on how feasible these goals might be. For this purpose you will need to analyze their arguments and project their logical extensions.

Most writing assignments in the humanities will call upon you to use these critical skills in one way or another, but some higher-level writing assignments may also require you to use historical and theoretical skills as well. You may be asked to examine a certain problem in its historical context or to discuss the theoretical implications of another problem on a broad scale.

## ORGANIZATIONAL PATTERNS OF WRITING
## IN THE HUMANITIES

The organizational patterns for writing in the humanities follow the patterns for writing in the natural and social sciences. In the most common one, the writer takes each proposition, event, or detail in its order of occurrence and explains it as he or she sees it. The good writer, however, will vary this basic pattern in many subtle ways. Sometimes he or she may take a number of points from the same source and classify them under general headings—for example, all the negative arguments against a certain moral or ethical position; or all the long-term and short-term implications of an argument based on analyzing current political conditions. Or the writer may endorse and appropriate some conclusions from a given source but contest and refute others from the same source. In Chapter 12 Garry Wills acknowledges institutional flaws that his sources document in his church, but he also argues that these flaws should prompt the faithful to support and improve their church:

> It was said of Acton (and I have heard it too) that if he did not like the papacy, he should go join a church without the papacy. But how would that solve the problem? Where is a church not deeply flawed?…If one wants a pure or perfect church, one must go off to search for it on some other globe. (p. 570)

Still other organizational patterns may contrast statement with response or question with answer, each time penetrating deeper into the problem being investigated. Isaac Kramnick and R. Laurence Moore's "Is America a Christian Nation?" in Chapter 12 exemplifies this pattern. The authors evaluate Pat Robertson's argument in "America, a Christian Nation" by quoting its thesis, critiquing its claims, and offering a strong counterclaim based on historical study:

> Pat Robertson may think, as he claimed in 1993, that the wall of separation between church and state is "a lie of the left" and that "there is no such thing in the Constitution." History and victories won through the course of our American past tell us that he is wrong. (p. 583)

Further, some organizational patterns may establish cause-and-effect relationships in their critical assessment of diverse sources. In Chapter 13 Ronald Takaki reviews several sources and finds that "by 1900, 60 percent of Japan's industrial laborers were women" (p. 612).

He therefore speculates that "while it is not known how many of the women who emigrated had been wage-earners, this proletarianization of women already well underway in Japan paved the way for such laborers to consider working in America" (p. 612).

## STYLES OF WRITING IN THE HUMANITIES

Some styles of writing in the humanities suggest—within limits—the tone of the author's personal and idiosyncratic voice. This quality distinguishes it radically from impersonal styles of writing in the natural and social sciences. The major evidence for critical assessments of texts in the humanities is direct observation of details in the texts themselves, close reference to them, and pointed quotation from them. How the author of an article projects an attitude toward those texts often counts as much as what he or she directly says about them. Benazir Bhutto, for example, clearly projects a personal involvement in issues about the status of women in Islamic societies:

> All these considerations are there, and yet women are backward, and they are backward not because Islam has made them backward, but because the societies that they live in are societies which have upheld the privileged class and which have subsisted on a policy of discrimination against a wide segment of the population. (p. 549)

In Chapter 13, Primo Levi, an Italian Jew, conveys the horror of his imprisonment in a Nazi concentration camp when he recounts the sudden disappearance of his loved ones:

> Thus, in an instant, our women, our parents, our children disappeared. We saw them for a short while as an obscure mass at the other end of the platform; then we saw nothing more. (p. 601)

## PERSONAL VOICE

Writing in the humanities not only tolerates the development of a personal voice but also encourages it. Listen to Mary Daly's voice as she wittily compares herself to a pirate when as a budding feminist she embarks upon the male-dominated study of formal theology:

> Women who are Pirates in a phallocentric society are involved in a complex operation. First, it is necessary to Plunder—that is, righteously rip off—gems of knowledge that the patriarchs have stolen from us. Second, we must Smuggle back to other women our Plundered treasures. (p. 566)

Because the humanities propose to exercise and develop critical think-ing, the issue of "what you think and why" becomes crucial. The "what" and "why" seldom generate straightforward, unequivocal answers. To the casual observer, some answers may seem curious, whimsical, arbi-trary, entirely subjective. To others more deeply acquainted with the humanistic disciplines, open-endedness confers its own rewards. Among them is the light it casts upon our processes of thought, our un-derstanding of complex issues, and the wide-ranging and often contra-dictory interpretations of them. About the Christian Coalition's goals Pat Robertson tells us

> The coalition's clear mandate is to affirm and support America's historic and traditional political institutions, which happen to be founded upon ethical systems derived from (and strengthened by) Judeo-Christian values. (p. 574)

In contrast, Isaac Kramnick and R. Laurence Moore argue

> The creation of a godless constitution was not an act of irreverence. Far from it. It was an act of confidence in religion. It intended to let religion do what it did best, to preserve the civil morality necessary to democracy, without laying upon it the burdens of being tied to the fortunes of this or that political faction. (p. 583)

A writer in the humanities measures the success of an argument by how it accommodates divergent explanations and shows their rela-tionships. Significantly, most writers in the humanities do not agree on the universal applicability of any single formula, method, or approach for solving problems. The best solutions usually entail a combination of formulas, methods, and approaches.

Reading in the humanities, therefore, requires a tolerance for ambiguity and contradiction. Oddly enough, however, most writers in the humanities defend their assertions with a strong and aggressive rhetoric. At best, this rhetoric scrupulously avoids bloat, pomposity, and roundabout ways of saying things. Instead of "It was decided that they would utilize the sharp instrument for perforating and unsealing alu-minum receptacles," it prefers "They decided to use the can opener." It uses technical vocabulary when necessary, but it usually prefers clear, precise, intelligible diction to stilted, awkward jargon. It uses figurative language and analogy, but not for their own sake; it uses them to ex-press meanings and relationships that literal language sometimes obscures. In Chapter 13, Ronald Takaki concludes his study of Japanese immigration with a poem that expresses the emotions of young women leaving their place of birth for the uncertainties of a marriage in America. As their ships sailed from the harbor, many women gazed at the diminishing shore:

> With tears in my eyes
> I turn back to my homeland
> Taking one last look. (p. 614)

Writing in the humanities strives for a richness of texture and implication, but at the same time, it highlights important threads in that texture and designates them as central to the unraveling. Readers, however, should not allow its assertiveness to fool them. Few examples of good writing in the humanities are completely intolerant of opposing views. There's always room for another perspective.

# *twelve*

# Religion and Identity

Religion, as we all know, is a highly personal matter, and most people find it difficult to account for their religious beliefs without sounding solemn, apologetic, or occasionally arrogant. The respect given to science as an academic discourse often puts religion on the defensive. There seems to be no empirical way to verify the truth of one's religious commitment or the depth of one's religious experience. Arguments about religion require the serious writer to defuse the skepticism of the equally serious reader. Religion, because it isn't science, needs to be discussed with the same sort of rational precision and intellectual rigor that those who respect science demand.

Disciplines in the humanities approach religion from various perspectives: social, cultural, historical, political, literary, and artistic. Humanists might study religion in its social context to articulate features that contribute to the formation of personal or group identities. They might study it in its cultural context to articulate features that stem from ethnic or linguistic or other communal practices. Historians might focus on changes that have affected the development of particular religions over the course of time, including relationships between churches and forms of government supportive of or antithetical to each other. Literary scholars and historians of art or music might analyze, interpret, and evaluate the impact of religious thought or emotion on poetry, fiction, drama, visual forms, and musical composition.

The selections in this chapter explore connections between religion and personal or group identities associated with the Muslim, Jewish, Protestant, and Roman Catholic faiths. In "Excellent Things in Women" Sara Suleri recounts her experiences in a Muslim household during her youth in Pakistan, while in "Politics and the Muslim Woman" Benazir Bhutto, a political leader in Pakistan, argues that Islamic law does not regard women as inferior to men or incapable of leadership. The next two articles examine a wide range of identities in relation to the Jewish religion. In "I Still Hear the Cry," by Alina Bacall-Zwirn and Jared Stark, a Holocaust survivor recounts how the birth of her baby in the Auschwitz death camp challenged her identity as a Jew and as a mother, and in "Threads," by Elly Bulkin, the author links her Jewish identity to her other identities as an antiracist lesbian feminist.

Similar issues inform the following articles about questions of Christian theology. In "Sin Big" Mary Daly, a feminist theologian, describes the radical impact of her training in Roman Catholic theology. In "The Pope's Loyal Opposition" the historian Garry Wills argues that despite his criticism of past misconduct in the Roman Papacy, he still considers himself supportive of Catholicism. Finally, two articles examine the ambivalent relationship between church and state in American politics. In "America, a Christian Nation" Pat Robertson, a religious leader and one-time presidential candidate, claims that America is a Christian nation and that its Christianity explains its greatness, while in "Is America a Christian Nation?" the political scientist Isaac Kramnick and the historian R. Laurence Moore argue that the American Constitution explicitly dissociates religion from political institutions and topical political controversy.

# Excellent Things in Women

## *Sara Suleri*

*Sara Suleri Goodyear was born and raised in Lahore, Pakistan, an Islamic nation in south-central Asia. She emigrated to the United States and received her Ph.D. from Indiana University in 1983. She is currently Professor of English at Yale University.*

*The Islamic religion is central to Pakistan's national identity. That country was created in 1947 following religious strife between Hindus and Muslims in India when the latter gained its independence from Britain. Massive migrations brought Muslims to the eastern and western states of Pakistan that were partitioned from northern India. Ethnic discrimination, political corruption, and economic impoverishment soon led these states to a bitter civil war. In 1971 West Pakistan and East Pakistan were divided into two separate countries, the current Islamic Republic of Pakistan and Bangladesh, its former eastern wing.*

### PREREADING

Read the first paragraph of Sara Suleri's memoir below and underline all the names, dates, and terms that are not familiar to you. Either in the library or online, consult an atlas, almanac, encyclopedia, or historical digest to gather information about what you have underlined. Examples of your underlining might include "Meerut," the name of a city near Delhi in northwest India; "Urdu" and "Punjab," the dominant languages of northern India and western Pakistan that are largely identified with Muslim populations; "Inglestan," the Urdu name for "England"; "the fourteenth of August," the date in 1947 when India became independent from Britain and was subdivided into the separate states of India (chiefly Hindu) and Pakistan (chiefly Muslim); and "Quran" or "Koran," the book of Islamic scripture. As you continue to read through the memoir, underline other unfamiliar names, dates, or terms, and question whether the context might adequately explain their meaning.

Dadi, my father's mother, was born in Meerut toward the end  1
of the last century. She was married at sixteen and widowed in
her thirties, and by her latter decades could never exactly recall how

many children she had borne. When India was partitioned, in August of 1947, she moved her thin pure Urdu into the Punjab of Pakistan and waited for the return of her eldest son, my father. He had gone careening off to a place called Inglestan, or England, fired by one of the several enthusiasms made available by the proliferating talk of independence. Dadi was peeved. She had long since dispensed with any loyalties larger than the pitiless give-and-take of people who are forced to live together in the same place, and she resented independence for the distances it made. She was not among those who, on the fourteenth of August, unfurled flags and festivities against the backdrop of people running and cities burning. About that era she would only say, looking up sour and cryptic over the edge of her Quran, "And I was also burned." She was, but that came years later.

By the time I knew her, Dadi with her flair for drama had allowed  2 life to sit so heavily upon her back that her spine wilted and froze into a perfect curve, and so it was in the posture of a shrimp that she went scuttling through the day. She either scuttled or did not: It all depended on the nature of her fight with the Devil. There were days when she so hated him that all she could do was stretch herself out straight and tiny on her bed, uttering most awful imprecation. Sometimes, to my mother's great distress, Dadi could berate Satan in full eloquence only after she had clambered on top of the dining-room table and lain there like a little molding centerpiece. Satan was to blame: He had after all made her older son linger long enough in Inglestan to give up his rightful wife, a cousin, and take up instead with a white-legged woman. Satan had stolen away her only daughter Ayesha when Ayesha lay in childbirth. And he'd sent her youngest son to Swaziland, or Switzerland; her thin hand waved away such sophistries of name.

God she loved, and she understood him better than anyone. Her  3 favorite days were those when she could circumnavigate both the gardener and my father, all in the solemn service of her God. With a pilfered knife, she'd wheedle her way to the nearest sapling in the garden, some sprightly poplar or a newly planted eucalyptus. She'd squat, she'd hack it down, and then she'd peel its bark away until she had a walking stick, all white and virgin and her own. It drove my father into tears of rage. He must have bought her a dozen walking sticks, one for each of our trips to the mountains, but it was like assembling a row of briar pipes for one who will not smoke: Dadi had different aims. Armed with implements of her own creation, she would creep down the driveway unperceived to stop cars and people on the street and give them all the gossip that she had on God.

Food, too, could move her to intensities. Her eyesight always took a sharp turn for the worse over meals—she could point hazily at a perfectly ordinary potato and murmur with Adamic reverence "What *is* it, what *is* it called?" With some shortness of manner one of us would describe and catalog the items on the table. "*Alu ka bhartha*," Dadi repeated with wonderment and joy; "Yes, Saira Begum, you can put some here." "Not too much," she'd add pleadingly. For ritual had it that the more she demurred, the more she expected her plate to be piled with an amplitude her own politeness would never allow. The ritual happened three times a day.

We pondered it but never quite determined whether food or God constituted her most profound delight. Obvious problems, however, occurred whenever the two converged. One such occasion was the Muslim festival called Eid—not the one that ends the month of fasting, but the second Eid, which celebrates the seductions of the Abraham story in a remarkably literal way. In Pakistan, at least, people buy sheep or goats beforehand and fatten them up for weeks with delectables. Then, on the appointed day, the animals are chopped, in place of sons, and neighbors graciously exchange silver trays heaped with raw and quivering meat. Following Eid prayers the men come home, and the animal is killed, and shortly thereafter rush out of the kitchen steaming plates of grilled lung and liver, of a freshness quite superlative.

It was a freshness to which my Welsh mother did not immediately take. She observed the custom but discerned in it a conundrum that allowed no ready solution. Liberal to an extravagant degree on thoughts abstract, she found herself to be remarkably squeamish about particular things. Chopping up animals for God was one. She could not locate the metaphor and was uneasy when obeisance played such a truant to the metaphoric realm. My father the writer quite agreed: He was so civilized in those days.

Dadi didn't agree. She pined for choppable things. Once she made the mistake of buying a baby goat and bringing him home months in advance of Eid. She wanted to guarantee the texture of his festive flesh by a daily feeding of tender peas and clarified butter. Ifat, Shahid, and I greeted a goat into the family with boisterous rapture, and soon after he ravished us completely when we found him at the washingline nonchalantly eating Shahid's pajamas. Of course there was no argument: The little goat was our delight, and even Dadi knew there was no killing him. He became my brother's and my sister's and my first pet, and he grew huge, a big and grinning thing.

Years after, Dadi had her will. We were old enough, she must have thought, to set the house sprawling, abstracted, into a multitude of secrets. This was true, but still we all noticed one another's secretive ways. When, the day before Eid, our Dadi disappeared, my brothers and sisters and I just shook our heads. We hid the fact from my father, who at this time of life had begun to equate petulance with extreme vociferation. So we went about our jobs and tried to be Islamic for a day. We waited to sight moons on the wrong occasion, and watched the food come into lavishment. Dried dates change shape when they are soaked in milk, and carrots rich and strange turn magically sweet when deftly covered with green nutty shavings and smatterings of silver. Dusk was sweet as we sat out, the day's work done, in an evening garden. Lahore spread like peace around us. My father spoke, and when Papa talked, it was of Pakistan. But we were glad, then, at being audience to that familiar conversation, till his voice looked up, and failed. There was Dadi making her return, and she was prodigal. Like a question mark interested only in its own conclusions, her body crawled through the gates. Our guests were spellbound, then they looked away. Dadi, moving in her eerie crab formations, ignored the hangman's rope she firmly held as behind her in the gloaming minced, hugely affable, a goat.

That goat was still smiling the following day when Dadi's victory brought the butcher, who came and went just as he should on Eid. The goat was killed and cooked: a scrawny beast that required much cooking and never melted into succulence, he winked and glistened on our plates as we sat eating him on Eid. Dadi ate, that is: Papa had taken his mortification to some distant corner of the house; Ifat refused to chew on hemp; Tillat and Irfan gulped their baby sobs over such a slaughter. "Honestly," said Mamma, "honestly." For Dadi had successfully cut through tissues of festivity just as the butcher slit the goat, but there was something else that she was eating with that meat. I saw it in her concentration; I know that she was making God talk to her as to Abraham and was showing him what she could do—for him—to sons. God didn't dare, and she ate on alone.

Of those middle years it is hard to say whether Dadi was literally left alone or whether her bodily presence always emanated a quality of being apart and absorbed. In the winter I see her alone, painstakingly dragging her straw mat out to the courtyard at the back of the house and following the rich course of the afternoon sun. With her would go her Quran, a metal basin in which she could wash her hands, and her ridiculously heavy spouted waterpot, that was made of brass. None of us, according to Dadi, were quite pure enough to transport these particular items, but the rest of her paraphernalia we were allowed to carry out. These were baskets of her writing and sewing materials and her bottle of pungent and Dadi-like bitter oils, with which she'd coat the papery skin that held her brittle bones. And in the summer, when the night created an illusion of possible coolness and everyone held their breath while waiting for a thin and intermittent breeze, Dadi would be on the roof, alone. Her summer bed was a wooden frame latticed with a sweet-smelling rope, much aerated at its foot. She'd lie there all night until the wild monsoons would wake the lightest and the soundest sleeper into a rapturous welcome of rain.

In Pakistan, of course, there is no spring but only a rapid elision 11 from winter into summer, which is analogous to the absence of a recognizable loneliness from the behavior of that climate. In a similar fashion it was hard to distinguish between Dadi with people and Dadi alone: she was merely impossibly unable to remain unnoticed. In the winter, when she was not writing or reading, she would sew for her delight tiny and magical reticules out of old silks and fragments she had saved, palm-sized cloth bags that would unravel into the precision of secret and more secret pockets. But none such pockets did she ever need to hide, since something of Dadi always remained intact, however much we sought to open her. Her discourse, for example, was impervious to penetration, so that when one or two of us remonstrated with her in a single hour, she never bothered to distinguish her replies. Instead she would pronounce generically and prophetically, "The world takes on a single face." "Must you, Dadi...," I'd begin, to be halted then by her great complaint: "The world takes on a single face."

It did. And often it was a countenance of some delight, for Dadi 12 also loved the accidental jostle with things belligerent. As she went perambulating through the house, suddenly she'd hear Shahid, her first grandson, telling me or one of my sisters we were vile, we were disgusting women. And Dadi, who never addressed any one of us girls without first conferring the title of lady—so we were "Teellat Begum," "Nuzhat Begum," "Iffatt Begum," "Saira Begum"—would halt in reprimand and tell her grandson never to call her granddaughters women. "What else shall I call them, men?" Shahid yelled. "Men!" said Dadi, "Men! There is more goodness in a woman's little finger than in the benighted mind of man." "Hear, hear, Dadi! *Hanh, hanh*, Dadi!" my sisters cried. "For men," said Dadi, shaking the name off her fingertips like some unwanted water, "live as though they were unsuckled things." "And heaven," she grimly added, "is the thing Muhammad says (peace be upon him) lies beneath the feet of women!" "But he was a man," Shahid still would rage, if he weren't laughing, as all of us were laughing, while Dadi sat among us as a belle or a May queen.

Toward the end of the middle years my father stopped speaking to 13 his mother, and the atmosphere at home appreciably improved. They secretly hit upon a novel histrionics that took the place of their daily battle. They chose the curious way of silent things: Twice a day Dadi would leave her room and walk the long length of the corridor to my father's room. There she merely peered round the door, as though to see if he were real. Each time she peered, my father would interrupt whatever adult thing he might be doing in order to enact a silent paroxysm, an elaborate facial pantomime of revulsion and affront. At teatime in particular, when Papa would want the world to congregate in his room, Dadi came to peer her ghostly peer. Shortly thereafter conversation was bound to fracture, for we could not drown the fact that Dadi, invigorated by an outcast's strength, was sitting alone in the dining room, chanting an appeal: "God give me tea, God give me tea."

At about this time Dadi stopped smelling old and smelled instead 14 of something equivalent to death. It would have been easy to notice if she had been dying, but instead she conducted the change as a refinement, a subtle gradation, just as her annoying little stove could shift its hanging odors away from smoke and into ash. During the middle years there had been something more defined about her being, which sat in the world as solely its own context. But Pakistan increasingly complicated the question of context, as though history, like a pestilence, forbid any definition outside relations to its fevered sleep. So it was simple for my father to ignore the letters that Dadi had begun to write to him every other day in her fine wavering script, letters of advice about the house or the children or the servants. Or she transcribed her complaint: "Oh my son, Zia. Do you think your son, Shahid, upon whom God bestow a thousand blessings, should be permitted to lift up his grandmother's chair and carry it into the courtyard when his grandmother is seated in it?" She had cackled in a combination of delight and virgin joy when Shahid had so transported her, but that little crackling sound she omitted from her letter. She ended it, and all her notes, with her single endearment. It was a phrase to halt and arrest when Dadi actually uttered it: Her solitary piece of tenderness was an injunction, really, to her world—"Keep on living," she would say.  ❀

## READING FOR INFORMATION

1. How does Suleri characterize her parents in paragraph 6? Where was her mother born and raised? What is her father's profession? Do subsequent paragraphs clarify this information? Underline the evidence.

2. Explain in your own words how the ceremony of killing and cooking the goat in paragraph 9 might represent a threat "to sons." Does the reference to Abraham (and Isaac) in the last sentence explain the religious significance of this sacrifice?

3. How many women are members of Suleri's immediate household in this memoir? Underline their names as they occur in the text and jot in the margins their specific relationships to the author.

## READING FOR FORM, ORGANIZATION, AND EXPOSITORY FEATURES

1. What effect does the author achieve by including Urdu words in her text, as in paragraph 12 where "*Alu ka bhartha*" implicitly refers to "a perfectly ordinary potato" mentioned two sentences earlier?

2. How would you describe the overall organizational structure of this memoir? Does Suleri narrate a series of events in unvarying chronological sequence, or does she instead move back and forth between different moments in the past so as to relate them in striking patterns of association? Describe some of these patterns.

3. What are the "middle years" that the author refers to in paragraphs 13 and 14? If they recall political events in the history of Pakistan, might they evoke the period between the founding of that nation 1947 and the civil war that erupted in 1971?

## READING FOR RHETORICAL CONCERNS

1. Which members of her family do you think the author identifies with most strongly? Why? Do you think the author sees some aspects of herself in each member, or do you think that she expresses definite preferences for some rather than others?

2. Describe the author's tone. Does she relate generational rivalries among family members with detachment or with affection? How does she relate gendered rivalries among them?

3. What is the effect of Dadi's disparaging remarks about men in paragraph 12? Does Dadi justify these remarks by appealing to her religion? Does the author necessarily agree or disagree with her? What is her sentiment about Dadi's attitude?

## WRITING ASSIGNMENTS

1. Write a brief character analysis of Dadi as the author represents her in this memoir. Describe her faith in the teachings of Islam at a time when social and political conflict in her country must have tested it severely. Describe how she responds to individual members of the family at moments of particular crisis.

2. Write a brief character analysis of the author as she expresses her response to Dadi's behavior. What does the author say or imply about her own religious attitudes and beliefs, her own identification with her family's values and commitments, her own development as a young woman nurturing her personal identity?

# Politics and the Muslim Woman

### *Benazir Bhutto*

*Benazir Bhutto was born in Pakistan in 1953 and has served twice as Prime Minister of her country (1988–90 and 1993–96). She is the first woman freely elected to that office in the Muslim world.*

*As explained in the headnote to Sara Suleri's memoir, Pakistan was created as an Islamic republic when India received its independence from Britain in 1947. Political instability has long threatened that nation's fragile democracy with military rule and martial law. Benazir Bhutto's father served as its president after its division from Bangladesh, but he was overthrown and executed in 1977. Bhutto adopted his party's leadership in opposition to the military regime that displaced it. For her political activism, she has spent years in jail, under house arrest, and in foreign exile, as she recounts in her autobiography,* Daughter of Destiny *(1989). As a dynamic leader in an Islamic country, she refutes the charge that its religion prohibits women from holding public office.*

### PREREADING

Using the information about Pakistan recounted above as well as information offered in the Prereading exercise for Sara Suleri's "Excellent Things in Women," speculate about some of the problems that Benazir Bhutto might have confronted during her political career in Pakistan. What impact might Islamic religious teaching have had on her public service?

Benazir Bhutto, "Politics and the Muslim Woman." Unpublished audio recording, Rama Mehta lecture, April 11, 1985 at Radcliffe College. Radcliffe Archives, Radcliffe Institute, Harvard University.

I think one of the first things that we must appreciate about the 1
religion of Islam is that there is no one interpretation to it.
Islam has certain religious aspects and has some aspects which relate to
relations between man and man in society. . . .

I would describe Islam in two main categories: reactionary Islam 2
and progressive Islam. We can have a reactionary interpretation of
Islam which tries to uphold the status quo, or we can have a progressive
interpretation of Islam which tries to move with a changing world,
which believes in human dignity, which believes in consensus, and
which believes in giving women their due right.

I know that some authors have speculated that women in Islamic 3
countries can never achieve self-actualization or a degree of assertiveness unless they look at this from a non-Islamic point of view. I don't
agree with that at all. I believe that Islam within it provides justice and
equality for women, and I think that those aspects of Islam which have
been highlighted by the *mullas* [religious scholars] do not do a service
to our religion. When I use the term *mullas*, please don't try to think of
them in the same terms as the clergy. Christianity has a clergy. Islam
does not have a clergy. The relationship between a Muslim and God is
direct. There is no need for somebody to intervene. The *mullas* try to
intervene. The *mullas* give their own interpretation. But I think there
are growing movements, as more and more people in Muslim countries, both men and women, achieve education and begin to examine
the Qur'an in the light of their education, they are beginning not to
agree with the *mullas* on their orthodox or reactionary version of Islam.

Let us start with the story of the Fall. Unlike Christianity, it is not 4
Eve who tempts Adam into tasting the apple and being responsible for
original sin. According to Islam—and I mention this because I believe
that Islam is an egalitarian religion—both Adam and Eve are tempted,
both are warned, both do not heed the warning, and therefore the Fall
occurs.

As far as opportunity is concerned, in Islam there is equal oppor- 5
tunity for both men and women. I refer to the Sura *Ya Sin* [Sura 36,
Verses 34–35], which says: "We produce orchids and date gardens and
vines, and we cause springs to gush forth, that they may enjoy the fruits
of it." God does not give fruits, orchids, or the fruit of the soil just for
men to enjoy or men to plow; he gives it for both men and women.
What, in terms of income and opportunity, is available, is available to
both man and woman. Sura *an-Nisa* [Sura 4, Verse 32]: "To men is allot-
ted what they earn, and to women what they earn."

As regards the law of inheritance, some scholars make a great de-   6
gree of the fact that inheritance law gives twice the amount to a son,
and half the amount to a daughter [Sura 4, Verse 11]. Well, maybe if
you look at it in isolation, but not if you look at it in the whole aspect,
because it is made abundantly clear that the woman's share is for the
use of the woman alone. A man gets two-thirds. One-third—the equivalent of the woman's—is for his own use. The additional one-third that a
man gets is to provide provision for his wife and children. This is the
obligation on the man. He gets that extra share so that he can provide
for the family, the wife, and the children. The wife is not responsible for
the welfare of the husband, nor is she responsible for the welfare of the
children. The wife is not even responsible for suckling her own child. If
she chooses not to suckle her child, she does not have to. If she chooses
to suckle her child, it is for the husband to provide her with the
provisions. . . .

As far as forgiveness and reward are concerned, similar conditions   7
are set down for both men and for women. I refer to Sura "The Clan"
[Sura 33, Verse 35]: "Men who surrender unto God, and women who
surrender, and men who believe, and women who believe, and men
who speak the truth, and women who speak the truth, and men who
persevere in righteousness, and women who persevere, and men who
are humble, and women who are humble, and men who give alms, and
women who give alms, and men who fast, and women who fast, and
men who guard their modesty, and women who guard their modesty,
and men who remember God much, and women who remember, God
has prepared for them forgiveness and a vast reward." There are no
special considerations set out for the male sex to show that in the eyes
of God they are deserving of special considerations.

In Sura "Repentance" [Sura 9, Verse 71], again emphasis is laid on   8
equal advice to men and women: "The believing man and the believing
woman, all loyalty to one another, they enjoin noble deeds and forbid
dishonor. They perform prayer and say the alms, and obey God and His
Messenger. On them will God have mercy." If it is a matter of entering
paradise, again Sura Luqman [Sura 31, Verse 8] says: "If any do righteousness"—be they male or female—"and have faith, they will enter
paradise." As regards theft, if you look at the Sura "Tablespread" [Sura 5,
Verse 38]: "As for the thief, both male and female, cut off their hand."

Now this doesn't have to do with Muslim women, but I would like   9
to add at this juncture that within Islam there are two kinds of interpretations: One is the rigid interpretation, and one is a conceptual interpre-

tation. Thus, in the rigid or *mulla*-istic sense, "Cut off their hand" would mean "Cut off their hand" even today. But in the conceptual analysis of Islam, "Cut off their hand" would mean "Adopt those means which will prevent thievery occurring again." And again, these means may change with the advance of society. It may involve psychiatric help, it may involve having them kept in a separate home, but the main idea is whether you look at it rigidly, "Cut off their hand," or whether you look at it conceptually, "Do not provide the means for them to do that theft again."

When it is adultery, again: "The adulterer and adulteress, give 10 them a hundred stripes." [Sura 24, Verse 2] That is Sura "Light." Again I would say that there is the rigid interpretation and the conceptual interpretation, and I think that most progressive Muslims believe in the conceptual interpretation because they believe Islam is a dynamic religion for all times and ages.

Now there are certain interpretations within the Qur'an Sharif [the Holy 11 Qur'an] which are extremely ambiguous. Some people interpret them in favor of the conservatives; some people interpret them in favor of the reactionaries. One of these occurs in Sura "The Romans" [Sura 30, Verse 21]: "He created from you help-mates from your self that you might find rest in them." This is an interpretation that progressives will give: Because it says, "He created from you," it does not say, "He created from men." "He created from you" means He created from mankind, or the human race, help-mates. But then other interpretations are given which claim what it said is, God created out of you, out of man, mates that you might find rest in them. And the conservatives use this to say that women were created for men to find rest. Or rather, that they were created to be in the service of man rather than being equal to man.

Arabic is a very complex language. It is a language that many Mus- 12 lims don't even understand, because Islam is not only in the Arab countries, but has spread far and beyond. These scholars and these *mullas* usually argue on these points. One *mulla* will say that God created women for rest and therefore women are to be used by men. Another one will say no, He created them from amongst yourself. So it depends very much on the matter of interpretation. But which way should interpretation go? Should it go against the basic grain of the entire message of the religion, or should it be in consonance with the basic message of that religion? When the basic message of Islam was for justice and for equality, when it came as a religion to liberate mankind from superstition and ignorance, to provide education and improvements, then I think it is quite clear for modern Islamic thinkers that it is a religion which did not provide for discrimination and ought to be interpreted in the light of its main thematic message, rather than to make ambiguous statements go against the basic theme of the message....

Another example concerns the right of divorce and polygamy. It is 13 often said that Islam provides for four wives for a man. But in my interpretation of this, and in the interpretation of many other Muslims, that is simply not true.

What the Qur'an does say, and I quote: "Marry as many women as 14 you wish, wives two or three or four. If you fear not to treat them equally, marry only one. [...] I doubt you will be able to be just between your wives, even if you try." [Sura 4, Verses 3 and 129] So if God Himself and His message says that He doubts that you can be equal, I don't know how any man can turn around and say that "God has given me this right to get married more than once."

... The Prophet Muhammad, throughout the life of his first wife, 15 Khadija, never married again. The Prophet's son-in-law, and who was more or less like an adopted son, *Hazrat* 'Ali [circa 596–661], during the lifetime of his first wife, *Bibi* [Madame] Fatima [circa 605–633], never married more than once. The marriages that took place later were more out of necessity of warfare, widows, or even of tribal connections. Thus to say that a man could be allowed to marry four times, at will, is not something that you can find a strong argument for in the Qur'an.

And if you look at Muslim society, it is not often that the vast Mus- 16 lim population goes on marrying two, three, four [wives]. It is something that is related just to the privileged class. They can afford to do that. And they didn't, as the caliphate ruled and the Muslim empire ruled, they didn't just marry two, three, or four women, they went on to keep harems with hundreds of concubines. None of that had anything to do with Islam, either.

A woman in Islam, when she marries, does not take her husband's 17 name. That is again something that has come about more as a matter of exposure to other customs or traditions. A woman in Islam is an identity in her own right. She is not an extension first of her father and then an extension of her husband. She asserts herself from the moment she is born; she is a person with the characteristics she develops, and she keeps her own name. The ideal of identity is just being appreciated in the West, where many people are beginning to keep their own name.

Aside from these provisions from the Qur'an Sharif, which I have 18 been drawing your attention to, I would like to say that within Islamic history there are very strong roles for women. For instance, the Prophet's wife, Bibi Khadija, was a woman of independent means. She had her own business, she traded, she dealt with society at large, she employed the Prophet Muhammad, peace be upon him, when he was a young boy, and subsequently, Bibi Khadija herself sent a proposal [of marriage] to the Prophet. So she is the very image of somebody who is independent, assertive, and does not conform to the passive description of women in Muslim societies that we have grown accustomed to hearing about. Bibi Khadija was fifteen years older than the Prophet, and she was also known, not only as the wife of the Prophet, but as the Mother of all believers....

I have tried to show you Islam as being a very liberal religion 19 toward women, as giving women their own identity, giving women the right to choose their husbands: If they are not happy with their spouse they don't have to keep him. When the divorce law [the nuptial agreement between a man and woman] is written, it is a contract of how you live together; you can write in that contract that "I want the right to divorce you"; you can write in that contract that "in the event of divorce I want to be maintained according to the style that I am accustomed to."

All these considerations are there, and yet women are backward, 20 and they are backward not because Islam has made them backward, but because the societies that they live in are societies which have upheld the privileged class and which have subsisted on a policy of discrimination against a wide segment of the population....

Before I conclude on this aspect of the powerful role within Islam 21 of women, I would like to quote from the Qur'an, the Sura "The Ant" [Sura 27, Verse 23]: "I found a woman ruling over them, and she has been given abundance of all things, and hers is a mighty throne." It is not Islam which is averse to women rulers, I think—it is men.  ❈

## READING FOR INFORMATION

1. Paraphrase and in your own words explain the difference between reactionary Islam and progressive Islam in paragraph 2.
2. Paraphrase and in your own words explain the difference between the two kinds of scriptural interpretation in paragraph 9.
3. Paraphrase and in your own words explain the principle of spiritual interpretation that aims for consonance with the religion's dominant beliefs in paragraph 12.

## READING FOR FORM, ORGANIZATION, AND EXPOSITORY FEATURES

1. Underline the focus of Bhutto's understanding of the Koran's teaching in paragraphs 4 to 8 about the Fall; about equal opportunity for women and men; about the law of inheritance; about forgiveness and reward; and about repentance.

2. Why does Bhutto devote particular attention to the Koran's teaching about theft and adultery in paragraphs 9 and 10? In your own words recount Bhutto's interpretation of this teaching.

3. Why does Bhutto explore the Koran's teaching about divorce and polygamy at great length in paragraphs 13 to 18? In your own words explain why this particular topic might have special relevance to the question of women's political rights and responsibilities.

## READING FOR RHETORICAL CONCERNS

1. This essay originated in oral form as a talk that the author delivered at Radcliffe College. What features of style suggest this format? In your own words speculate upon the author's rhetorical purpose in addressing this talk to students and faculty at Radcliffe College.

2. What assumptions does Bhutto make about her audience? Do you think that she addresses listeners deeply familiar with the Islamic religion, or do you think she addresses readers who know relatively little about Islamic practices?

3. Underline passages in paragraphs 3, 4, 6, 10, 12, 13, and 19 where Bhutto forthrightly states her own beliefs about Islamic teaching even when she assumes that her audience might have a different preconception of this teaching.

## WRITING ASSIGNMENTS

1. Write a summary of Bhutto's argument for students and faculty at your college who have not heard her speak or read her published work. Address your summary to those who profess to know very little about the Islamic religion.

2. Write a critical analysis of Bhutto's argument about the difference between reactionary Islam and progressive Islam with particular attention to her interpretation of Islamic teaching about women's equality with men and their mutual capacity for public action and political leadership. Address your essay to students who might have a different assessment of Islamic teaching.

3. How do you think Sara Suleri might react to Bhutto's argument? Compose an imagined conversation between Suleri and Bhutto. Have the

former react to four or five points in the essay and imagine the latter's response.

# I Still Hear the Cry

## *Alina Bacall-Zwirn and Jared Stark*

*Alina Bacall-Zwirn was born in the Jewish ghetto of Warsaw, Poland, in 1922. During World War II at the age of nineteen she married Leon Bacall, another resident of the ghetto. Upon Hitler's plan for eliminating the Jewish population, the couple was separated and sent to Nazi death camps in 1943, she to the women's camp at Birkenau in Auschwitz and he to the men's camp in nearby Buna-Monowitz. At the time she did not know that she was pregnant. A few months after arriving at Auschwitz she gave birth to a baby boy. A midwife took the child from her, explaining that he was sick and would probably die. When Alina asked to stay with her child in the infirmary, the midwife warned that Nazi officers would likely send her to the gas chamber because their policy was to hasten the deaths of those in the infirmary. Alina had then to choose between acting upon her identity as the mother of her child and protecting her identity as a vulnerable Jew.*

*After Germany's defeat in 1945 Alina was liberated and reunited with her husband. In 1949 the couple moved to the United States.*

*The testimony here unfolds in several stages. In April 1993 Alina presented her story orally in an interview videotaped for the Fortunoff Holocaust Archive at Yale University. A few months earlier (in January 1993) Jared Stark, a Yale graduate student appointed to transcribe her oral account into written form, visited her at her home in Tamarac, Florida, to prepare her for the interview. Nearly a year after the taping (in March 1994) he visited her again at her home to review details in her testimony. In the following excerpt Jared Stark, now a college professor, has labeled his transcriptions according to the date and place of their delivery. Note that he rearranges them to clarify Alina's story. Note also that he preserves the oral texture of Alina's broken English, a language that she learned only after emigrating to the United States.*

### PREREADING

In your journal explain your understanding of the term "holocaust." List some of the experiences that survivors such as Alina Bacall-Zwirn might have undergone. Read Jared Stark's first two questions (paragraph 1) and respond to her reply: "What was I feeling? Pain."

Reprinted from *No Common Place: The Holocaust Testimony of Alina Bacall-Zwirn* by Alina Bacall-Zwirn and Jared Stark by permission of the University of Nebraska Press. Copyright © 1999 by the University of Nebraska Press.

*March 16, 1994*    ₁

*Tamarac*

*JARED:* Do you remember what you were thinking?

*ALINA:* What?

*JARED:* Do you remember what you were thinking? What you were feeling?

*ALINA:* What I was feeling? Pain. And I just was thinking about my husband. My husband was sick. I didn't know if he was having typhus. In the same time I find out. And my sister-in-law die, from pneumonia, I think. And I'm giving birth to my child, and I have to go with the child to crematorium. Because that's what . . . I didn't think about to live.

And I think, I couldn't save the baby. And I'm giving the baby . . . I give birth to the baby to be killed. And I didn't have time to be too much in pain, because the baby was born in one second. And normal. I didn't rip anything inside because it was normal birth.

*JARED:* And the midwife assisted you?

*ALINA:* Yes. She pick up the baby, and I only ask her, what is it?

She said, it's a boy.

And I went to the bed and I said, I wish my husband were with me. And then I thought she going to clean up the baby and give me to my bed, to feed the baby. I hear the baby crying and crying and crying. And one day, and second day . . .

And I said to her, give me my baby. I want to feed him, feed the baby.

And she came to my bed and she start to talk to me and she said . . .

I said, where is the baby?

She said, it's in the, in the . . . you know, the sick people, some go there, too. Sick people.

*JARED:* Yes.

*ALINA:* And she put the baby into the sick person *Revier* and wait until the baby die. Because she was religious person, very religious, too. And she will not kill the baby. She will not do anything wrong.

And I hear the baby crying. And I said, give me the baby. I'm going to . . .

And she said, if I give you the baby, you're going with the baby. You know what I mean?

I said, that's what I want. I want to go. I'm tired already. And I want to go with the baby to the crematorium. I want to die with my baby.

And she said to me, you're young. You going to see your husband. I remember the words what she said. You're young, you going to have more children. You know?

And I said, I want my baby, and I cry. And I scream, give me my baby, give me my baby. And I cry.

Maybe a week the baby was alive, because I hear the crying. Maybe five days, maybe six days, the baby was crying.

And I want the baby, and I still hear the cry.

*April 21, 1993*
*New Haven*
*Fortunoff Video Archive at Yale*

*ALINA:* She said, you have a boy. And she took away the boy, and until today I don't know where is the boy.

I beg her, I hear crying, and I ask her to give me the baby. I'm very . . . I said, I don't want to live. I want to die with my baby, give me my baby. I don't have any, you know, how do you say it? I lost my strength and everything. I can't fight anymore. I want to die.

*March 16, 1994*
*Tamarac*

*JARED:* When did you first realize the baby wasn't there anymore?

*ALINA:* When I didn't hear the cry. I didn't have any more tears, you know? I think I didn't care, I want to die. You know, when comes a minute when you just want to die, you don't want to live anymore, like everything is closing.

You're tired, you're tired, you're sleepy, tired to go on with your life. It's nothing any more.

*JARED:* Did you see them take the baby away?

*ALINA:* No, no.

*JARED:* Were you asleep, or . . .

*ALINA:* No, I wasn't asleep. She said go on to the bed, I have to walk to the bed. And I was waiting for the baby, and I ask, and then she gave me this speech. She saved my life, she really saved my life.

*Evening of January 9, 1993*                                                    4
*Tamarac*

> *I myself wonder why I couldn't cry. When I wanted to, I couldn't cry, my tears never came out of my eyes. And all of a sudden I can't stop.*

*January 9, 1993*                                                               5
*Tamarac*

ALINA: I remember I want to die with my baby together. You get so, you know, fed up with everything. You didn't want to live. You don't care even, you know. You get some moment, you know, fed up with everything. What I have to fight for? They going to kill me anyway. So better to, you know, to shorten my misery. How you say it, misery?

JARED: Misery.

ALINA: Misery. And I didn't . . . until I got a letter from my husband, you know, when I told you they were looking, the two brothers, my husband and his brother. They didn't know which wife is dead, and I received a letter from him.

> That's what keep me a little, you know, give me more strength to go through. Knowing that he's alive, that he's going to make it probably.

*April 21, 1993*                                                               6
*New Haven*
*Fortunoff Video Archive at Yale*

ALINA: She looked at me, she sat down, she begged me to quiet down and she said, you are so beautiful, you're going to find your husband, you're going to have children, still children.

> I still remember the words what she told me. I said, I can't live anymore, I want to die.
>
> Until now I don't know where is my baby.

*March 18, 1994*                                                               7
*Tamarac*

ALINA: Because I didn't see when the baby start to cry . . . stopped to cry. Every day I asked to give me my baby, give me my baby. And then they told me, baby is dead.

JARED: And you always believed that?

*ALINA:* I didn't think much about it.

*JARED:* Until when?

*ALINA:* One and a half years. But that was before. I didn't speak out, you know. After the war, I talked to my husband. I said, who knows, I'm not sure if my sister is dead, because I wasn't witness to these deaths. So you're never sure, if he's dead or in some other place.

　　With my mother and father, I have witnesses to it. Because my husband was with my father in the camp and he saw how he's going to the place to die. My mother, it's my cousin, first cousin, came, they let her go to the camp, and she told me about my mother, that my mother went to crematorium.

　　But the rest, my sister, I don't know, and the baby too, I don't know either.

　　But then I'm thinking, it was such a hard time in concentration camp. Who would like to raise a baby in such circumstances, right? I am thinking about it. Nobody probably.

　　But a lot of times I think about the baby crying.

*JARED:* Was there ever a moment when you thought about trying to find out?

*ALINA:* You cannot find out, it's not that easy to find out. You don't have a name. The people around me, they're dead. Some of them dead, some of them went back to Russia. And the Yugoslavia girl, who knows where she is, I don't even know her name. Everything was secret, you don't know anything, the number only.

　　But I don't remember numbers.

8

*March 16, 1994*
*Tamarac*

*ALINA:* But now I realize she did a good thing for me.

*JARED:* This was the Czech woman?

*ALINA:* Yes. I have the family. I have children. That's the way she brought me. She said, you young. You going to find your husband, and you going to have many children. If I give you the baby, you go with the baby. But I was young, and I didn't understand how I could give the baby without me, you know.

It's like they taking my sense and everything, my body, everything.

✿  ✿  ✿

*ALINA:* And that's what happened. So I was already blaming my-    9
self that I brought something to the world. But, you see, you
never know if you die or not. You shouldn't decide anything.

It was a beautiful feeling, you know. I'm a mother. I have a baby.
And it's like a . . . fruit . . . love . . . you know? I can't explain. But it
was a big love, and the fruit from love.

How you say it? Right? I'm saying good? You going to call it different. I don't know.

And it was so beautiful. It was so . . . I have, you know . . . I don't
think . . .

So I was thinking about it. The whole nine months what I was
pregnant, about the time what I had with my husband. The good
time, I mean.

You know who suffer? I'm a mother, and they taking away my
love from me. Killing.

*March 18, 1994*    10
*Tamarac*

*JARED:* So how did you feel on Wednesday, after we talked?

*ALINA:* I was really sick. Going over things in my mind, and I start
to think how the baby looked . . .

*JARED:* Do you know how the baby looked?

*ALINA:* Beautiful. A lot of black hair. My husband was blonde, but
the baby had my hair. Healthy, compared with the circumstances,
with me pregnant in such terrible circumstances, not enough
food, and hungry, and everything, yet the baby was healthy.    ✿

## READING FOR INFORMATION

1. In your own words explain what Alina Bacall-Zwirn means when she recounts the midwife's warning, "If I give you the baby, you're going with
the baby" (paragraph 1).

2. In your own words explain what Alina Bacall-Zwirn means when she recounts the midwife's consolation, "You're young, you going to have more
children" (paragraph 1).

3. How do you react to Alina Bacall-Zwirn's statement, "I myself wonder
why I couldn't cry" (paragraph 4)?

## READING FOR FORM, ORGANIZATION, AND EXPOSITORY FEATURES

1. Like Benazir Bhutto's essay, this selection originated as an oral account. Unlike the former, however, it is transcribed so as to preserve the spontaneity, informality, and even disorganization of the occasion. Underline words, phrases, expressions, and ungrammatical features of style that convey the oral manner of presentation. Do they add to or detract from the importance of the testimony?

2. Underline Jared Stark's questions to Alina Bacall-Zwirn in paragraph 3. Does the respondent fully and clearly answer the questions asked? What further questions would you ask of her?

3. Underline Jared Stark's questions to Alina Bacall-Zwirn in paragraph 7. Does she answer them fully and clearly? What further questions would you ask of her?

## READING FOR RHETORICAL CONCERNS

1. Underline passages where the interviewer or the interviewed returns to an earlier statement and repeats or modifies it. How do these repetitions or modifications call attention to inevitable gaps between memory and testimony? How do they deepen the important truths of the testimony?

2. Many scholars of the Nazi Holocaust warn against trying to draw a heroic or redemptive message from survivor testimony. They argue that to focus on the survivors' resourcefulness or ingenuity diminishes the horror of what happened to those who did not survive, as though to imply that the latter had somehow failed to escape. How does Alina Bacall-Zwirn's testimony avert this result by focusing on ordinary details, unknowable motivations, and incomplete memories of the events?

3. Do you think that Jared Stark anticipates the reader's (or video viewer's) questions about Alina Bacall-Zwirn's testimony? Give specific examples of how his questions and comments might guide the reader through the testimony.

## WRITING ASSIGNMENTS

1. Write a brief account of what you have learned from Alina Bacall-Zwirn's testimony, how you pieced together information about her experience from the repetitions and out-of-sequence fragments that she recounts, and how you might summarize her story if you retold it in chronological order. Address your account to classmates who have not read this selection.

2. Write an essay in response to Alina Bacall-Zwirn's understanding of her identity as a victim of the Holocaust and as a mother in her concluding statement, "I'm a mother, and they taking away my love from me. Killing" (paragraph 9). Analyze the series of complex choices that she had to make at each stage of her experience.

3. Write an essay describing the impact of Alina Bacall-Zwirn's testimony on you. Explain how this testimony made you think about experiences you might never have imagined and about the way you would now read or listen to other people's accounts of such experience.

# Threads

## *Elly Bulkin*

*Elly Bulkin (born 1944) is a founding editor of* Conditions, *a feminist magazine with an emphasis on writing by lesbians, and is active in the local and national work of New Jewish Agenda.*

### PREREADING

Many people assume that the practice of organized religion is incompatible with the exercise of homosexual gender preferences. Is this assumption necessarily true? How, for example, do some religions accommodate their teachings and practice to homosexual individuals or communities? Jot down a few particular examples that you might be aware of concerning same-sex partnering, gay parenting, homosexual clergy, civil rights for homosexuals, and so forth.

A traditional view of Jewish identity divides the world into "We" and "They." Seeing this as a lesson passed on from mother to child "in all cultures, classes, and societies," Holocaust historian Lucy Dawidowicz describes how "the Jewish mother enlarges the We to embrace all Jews, those living now and those of the past, those living here, there, and everywhere."[1] Certainly I was taught this by parents whose first question about a new friend was, "Is she Jewish?" I

Reprinted from *Yours in Struggle* by permission of Elly Bulkin. Published 1984.

relearn it again in hard times: In July, 1982, on our way back from a New Jewish Agenda vigil against the Israeli invasion of Lebanon, another Jewish lesbian mentioned that she had simply stopped *talking* to non-Jewish friends about the Middle East; while she shares their objections to Israeli policies on the West Bank, Gaza Strip, and Lebanon, as well as their opposition to anti-Arab racism, she cannot cope with the anti-Jewish attitudes which her friends also express.

Although I value greatly the "We" assumed in such conversations, I balk at a framework that sets everything in a context of "We" and "They." As a woman, a lesbian, a Jew, I know that the division expresses both the joy and strength of who "We" are *and* the justified fear and mistrust of a dominant society which views us with hostility, a society which places us outside the boundaries of what it values, even when we are temporarily safe from its violence. At the same time, while I see sharply my link with the "We" in Dawidowicz' discussion, I also see other "We's" with whom I identify. In each instance, I feel bound by our shared identity and oppression, but also find that, where political views and actions diverge significantly, I experience little sense of commonality. I have learned a tremendous amount from Dawidowicz, for instance, and certainly identify with the "We" in her descriptions of Jew-hating. But I lose that feeling of connection when, in a discussion of the book *Adolescent Prejudice*, she writes, "anti-Semitism and racial prejudice were more prevalent among the poor and *the stupid* (the study characterized them euphemistically as 'the economically and academically disadvantaged') than among *'the privileged'* "[2] (my emphasis), because in this statement her analysis of oppression does not extend beyond the lives of "We" Jews. . . .

The problem as I—and, I think, a great many other Jewish feminists—see it is to embrace the "We" of our Jewish identities without seeing "They" as totally Other. We strive to acknowledge Jewish identity and Jewish oppression as fundamental components of our lives and histories, individually and collectively, and, at the same time, to use what we know of being Jewish—as of our other identities and oppressions—to understand generations of experience that have some parallels, yet are different from our own. This process is complicated, and the history between non-Jewish people of color and white Jews has not made it less so.

When I tell a friend, an Ashkenazi Jew, of my plan to write about some similarities between experiences of oppression and about their common roots in theories of "racial" inferiority, she tells me, "Be careful." She knows, as I do, how often such parallels have been used—and continue to be used—by some white Jewish people to discount the oppression of people of color or to imply that "we all have the same understanding, the same daily intimate experience of oppression," thereby suggesting that each oppression does not have its unique aspects. She knows too the frustration of pointing out Jewish oppression to some non-Jewish women of color who, in barely acknowledging its existence and in refusing to confront it, reflect society's prevalent anti-Semitism....

Considering both the complexity and the sensitivity of such inter-  5
actions, I move along rather gingerly. But I remain unwilling to ignore the connections that I do see. I think, for example, of how, since coming to the Americas, to Africa, to Asia, to Australia, to all of the continents where people of color had lived free of whites for thousands of years, white Europeans have attempted—often with success—to exterminate these indigenous peoples. I see similarities going way back to the earliest recorded attempts to enslave Jews, to ghettoize us, to destroy us.

Developed during centuries of Christian political domination,  6
Jew-hating myths provided a basis for "racial" theories propounding Germanic and Anglo-Saxon supremacy which emerged in the mid-1800s and contributed to the Jewish history of the following hundred years. In Germany, virulent political anti-Semitism during the last century continued on into the Nazi era. In the United States, 1920s immigration laws lumped Arabs and Asians and Blacks and Jews and Latinos together as "undesirable races."[3] Anti-alien laws in the United States remained despite a 1939 attempt to admit 20,000 children from Germany, two-thirds of them Jewish; the American Legion, one of the groups opposed to the Child Refugee Bill, maintained that "it was traditional American policy that home life should be preserved and that the American Legion therefore strongly opposed the breaking up of families."[4] The politics of the Ku Klux Klan of the 1920s with its 3.5 to 5 million members continue to be reflected in those of today's Klan, American Neo-Nazis, the Liberty Lobby, and other groups whose platforms violently oppose "mongrelizing" the white Christian "race." These groups clearly deny the rights—even the right to exist—of people of color, Jews, lesbians, and gay men. The connections are brought into bold relief by the Invisible Empire of the Knights of the Ku Klux Klan, whose membership application requires one to "swear that I am a White Person of Non-Jewish ancestry."[5] It is only class which divides these groups from the "respectable" men in business suits who commit

the far greater atrocities: the "scientific" advocates of Anglo-Saxon superiority in the 1920s, the Reagan administration in the 1980s.

If we are uncertain about who our enemies are, they have no [7] doubt as to their prey. For them, hatred of Jews and hatred of people of color dovetail nicely. In writing about "the Boers' extermination of Hottentot tribes, the wild murdering by Carl Peters in German Southeast Africa, the decimation of the peaceful Congo population—from 20 to 40 million reduced to 8 million people" which occurred between 1890 and 1911, Hannah Arendt makes explicit such connections:

> African colonial possessions became the most fertile soil for the flowering of what later was to become the Nazi elite. Here they had seen with their own eyes how people could be converted into race and how, simply by taking the initiative in this process, one might push one's own people into the position of the master race.[6]

I think we can recognize the similarities without blurring the dis- [8] tinctions. The Middle Passage during which rows and rows of enslaved Africans lay chained in their excrement on their way to the "New World"; the cattle cars that crammed Jews standing up, befouled, on their way to Nazi death camps. The U.S. government decision to drop atomic bombs on the "non-white" enemies of the allies, while people of Japanese—but not German or Italian—ancestry in this country and Canada were "relocated," their property confiscated, as they were forcibly interned.[7] More recently, the Haitian refugees imprisoned for over a year, despite objections, despite multiracial demonstrations led by Black people, despite the signs of members of Brooklyn New Jewish Agenda: "Our ancestors were held in camps too. Let these people go."

A Native American woman makes these connections from her [9] own perspective. In a letter, she describes reading Helen Epstein's *Children of the Holocaust*, a book about children of survivors, and then passing it on to her mother and sister.[8] Like her, she writes, they have also survived a Holocaust and wonder at their luck, cope with their guilt. Among the 1.3 million surviving Native Americans in a land that once contained ten to twelve million of their people, they find a means to further understand and interpret their own history through a book about some of those who survived a genocide which killed a third of the world's 18 million Jews.

The issue is not only one of physical survival, but of survival as a [10] group of people with a specific culture, language, history, tradition.

Here too I can see parts of my own experiences and those of some other Jewish women mirrored in certain experiences of some non-Jewish women of color. One example: I am sitting in a coffee shop with Carmen, a Puerto Rican used to speaking Spanish daily, and Sylvia, a Chicana who is relearning the Spanish of her parents. Carmen, who works closely with a group of Salvadoran refugee women who have no knowledge of English, describes her frustration at a Chicana colleague who makes little personal contact with them. Her colleague, Carmen tells us, is "not a real Chicana." I start at the word "real," and sense Sylvia stiffen. Carmen explains that, by being unwilling to speak Spanish to the refugees, her co-worker has left them alone, acted inhospitably to other Latinas. Sylvia responds by talking about her own experience as a Chicana who has, to a certain extent, been assimilated, been severed from her roots because she was not raised to speak Spanish fluently.

Days later, I told Sylvia my response to the coffee shop inter- 11 change. It reminded me of some Ashkenazi women I know: our ambivalent relationship to Yiddish; the discussion in my Jewish lesbian group three years before about going to a Yom Kippur service—measuring our childhood experiences of religious rituals, our recollections of Hebrew prayers and songs, against the concept of being "a real Jew." It reminded me too of hearing about a Sephardic Jew who "as a child . . . had wanted to learn Yiddish to be part of what she then thought were the 'real Jews'," the Ashkenazim.[9] Sylvia and I do not understand all of the nuances of each other's reactions. But I find some comfort, as I work out the implications of my Jewish identity, in sharing some common ground with a woman of color who is not Jewish and who is also working out her relationship to her own culture and history.

Though our specific experiences differ, depending on class, age, 12 region, and other variables, as well as on racial/ethnic identity, I know that I share with some women of color, non-Jewish and Jewish, as well as with other white Jewish women, a history of assimilation and reclamation. I think, for example, of the history of different Asian-American peoples, sorting out the meaning of both aspects of their self-description—Japanese-American, Korean-American, Chinese-American; the parts of their parents', their grandparents' languages and traditions they have held onto and those they have let go. And I think too of the decisions to celebrate one's identity: for those Native American women, Latinas, and Black women who could "pass" as white; for the Jewish woman whose father changed his name in the 1930s so he could "make it," and raised her, ignorant of her identity, as a Christian; for the Arab-American woman, who, after internalizing her racial oppression, came only in the last few years to identify as a woman of color; for the Jewish-Latina, the Arab-Jewish woman, for any Jewish woman of color who is too often, as one Jamaican-Jewish woman has said, "a token to everybody"; for any woman of color of mixed heritage—Chinese-Korean, Native American-Black, Asian-Black, Chicana; for the Arab-American dyke who is shunned because she is a lesbian by the only other Arab woman in town, the Jewish lesbian whose family sits *shivah** for her, the "bulldagger" whose Black community rejects her. All of the women who, told to choose between or among identities, insist on selecting all.

## NOTES

1. Lucy S. Dawidowicz, "Jewish Identity: A Matter of Fate, a Matter of Choice," *The Jewish Presence: Essays in Identity and History* (New York: Harcourt Brace Jovanovich, 1978), p. 5.
2. Dawidowicz, "Can Anti-Semitism Be Measured?" *The Jewish Presence*, p. 196.
3. See John Higham, *Strangers in the Land: Patterns of American Nativism, 1860–1925* (New York: Atheneum, 1966) and Thomas F. Gossett, *Race: The History of an Idea in America* (New York: Schocken Books, 1965). Between 1890 and 1920, over 250,000 Arab immigrants came to the United States. In response to attempts during the century's first decade to keep all but Anglo-Saxons from entering the country and to an Alabama congressional representative's 1907 comment, "I regard the Syrian and peoples from other parts of Asia Minor as the most undesirable" of immigrants, Dr. H.A. El-Kourie "wrote a short essay entitled 'Facts Establishing That the Semitic is the Equal of Any Race and Superior to Many.' The writings detail the positive attributes of the Syrian immigrants and the positive role the Semitic race and its descendants— 'the Syrians, Hebrews, German Jews, Russian Jews, Bedouins, and Sedentary Arabs'— had played in history" (Alan Dehmer, "The Politics of Survival: Birmingham, Alabama," *Taking Root/Bearing Fruit: The Arab-American Experience*, American Arab Anti-Discrimination Committee (Washington, DC: ADC, 1984), p. 37.
4. Arthur D. Morse, *While Six Million Died: A Chronicle of American Apathy* (New York: Hart Publishing Company, 1967), p. 263.
5. Connecticut Education Association, Council on Interracial Books for Children, and National Education Association, *The Ku Klux Klan and the Struggle for Equality: An Informational and Instructional Kit* (New York: CIBC, 1981), p. 7.
6. Hannah Arendt, *The Origins of Totalitarianism* (New York and London: Harcourt Brace Jovanovich, 1951), pp. 185, 206.
7. See Michi Weglyn, *Years of Infamy: The Untold Story of America's Concentration Camps* (New York: Morrow, 1976) and Ken Adachi, *The Enemy That Never Was: A History of the Japanese Canadians* (Toronto: McClelland & Stewart, 1976).
8. Helen Epstein, *Children of the Holocaust: Conversations with Sons and Daughters of Survivors* (New York: G.P. Putnam's Sons, 1979).
9. Quoted in Rita Arditti, "Sephardic Jewry," *Sojourner* (July 1983), p. 3.

*Shivah*—seven-day mourning period after burial observed by the deceased's family.

## READING FOR INFORMATION

1. Paraphrase Bulkin's statement of agreement with but also dissent from the Holocaust historian whom she mentions in paragraph 2.
2. Paraphrase Bulkin's statement of agreement with and dissent from her Jewish friend whose warning she recounts in paragraphs 4 and 5.
3. List the similarities and distinctions among oppressed groups of African-Americans, Jews, Japanese, Haitians, and Native Americans whom Bulkin evokes in paragraphs 8 and 9.

## READING FOR FORM, ORGANIZATION, AND EXPOSITORY FEATURES

1. What is the effect of the author's many references to conversations with her friends, both in agreement and in disagreement, recounted in paragraphs 1, 4, 10, and 11?
2. Underline passages in paragraphs 1, 2, 7, and 9 where the author quotes from books either in agreement or in disagreement. Does the effect of these quotations differ from the effect of her quotations from conversations with friends? Explain the difference.
3. Mark the passages in paragraphs 1, 2, 5, 8, 11, and 12 that are organized according to patterns of comparison and contrast, and explain what elements are being compared and contrasted.

## READING FOR RHETORICAL CONCERNS

1. Identify for this article a "rhetorical context" as described on pp. 26–27. What is the author trying to emphasize in paragraphs 2, 3, 5, 8, and 12?
2. Describe the author's tone. Is the author respectful of the differences between herself and the writers or friends with whom she disagrees in paragraphs 2, 4, 5, 10, and 11?
3. What assumptions does the author make about similarities and differences in various forms of ethnic, racial, religious, and gender discrimination? Does she effectively argue that as a lesbian Jew she is in a good position to defend all women and people of color who have been victims of prejudice?

## WRITING ASSIGNMENTS

1. Write a critical essay in response to Bulkin's claim that among persons with various ethnic, racial, religious, and gender identifications "we can recognize the similarities without blurring the distinctions" (paragraph 8). Do different forms of identification (for example, racial or gender

identifications as opposed to ethnic or religious ones) generate different sorts of prejudice and discrimination, or are all types inherently the same? Address your essay to members of an ethnic, racial, religious, or gender group with which you identify.

2. Which of the tensions that Bulkin describes among different forms of identity have you experienced the most? Respond in an essay of two or three pages addressed to members of an ethnic, racial, religious, or gender group different from your own.

3. As a Prereading question we asked you to consider whether organized religion is incompatible with the exercise of some ethnic, racial, or homosexual gender identities. Rewrite your response in the light of Bulkin's argument that "I balk at a framework that sets everything in a context of 'We' and 'They' " (paragraph 2).

# Sin Big

## *Mary Daly*

*Mary Daly is associate professor of Theology at Boston College. Raised as a Roman Catholic, she has published several books in feminist theology, including* Beyond God the Father *(1973),* Gyn/Ecology *(1978),* Quintessence: Recalling the Outrageous, Contagious Courage of Women *(1996), and* Webster's First Intergalactic Wickedary of the English Language *(1987), a dictionary for wicked women conjured in cahoots with Jane Caputi.*

### PREREADING

Many people assume that the study of theology and religion should be solemn, serious, pious, and grave. Is it possible for you to imagine that such a study may instead be pert, witty, cheerful, and ironic without compromising its honesty or reverence? Read the first paragraph of Mary Daly's account of her training in formal theology. How do you respond to her sense of humor about religion?

Ever since childhood, I have been honing my skills for living    1
the life of a Radical Feminist Pirate and cultivating the Courage to Sin. The word "sin" is derived from the Indo-European root

By Mary Daly, as appeared in *The New Yorker*, vol. 72 (Feb. 26 & March 4, 1996): 76–80.

"es-," meaning "to be." When I discovered this etymology, I intuitively understood that for a woman trapped in patriarchy, which is the religion of the entire planet, "to be" in the fullest sense is "to sin."

Women who are Pirates in a phallocratic society are involved in a complex operation. First, it is necessary to Plunder—that is, righteously rip off—gems of knowledge that the patriarchs have stolen from us. Second, we must Smuggle back to other women our Plundered treasures. In order to invent strategies that will be big and bold enough for the next millennium, it is crucial that women share our experiences: the chances we have taken and the choices that have kept us alive. They are my Pirate's battle cry and wake-up call for women who want to hear.... 2

After I graduated from college, my lust for learning and adventure led me to graduate school. First, I went to the Catholic University of America, in Washington, D.C., which had offered me a full-tuition scholarship while I studied for an M.A. in English. One night, after tedious hours of translating Middle English, I fell into a deep sleep and dreamed of green: Elemental, Be-dazzling Green. When I woke up, I had a revelation: "Study philosophy!" However, there was no scholarship money available there for a woman to study philosophy. 3

One day, when I was sitting in class, I suddenly had a vision of myself standing at a blackboard teaching *theology*. This was mystifying, since I had no ambition to pursue that subject. Moreover, such a thing was unheard of in 1952, when Catholic women were still not allowed to teach or study theology. 4

Shortly after this unusual event, I "just happened" to see an ad for a School of Sacred Theology for women at St. Mary's College in Notre Dame, Indiana. I learned that this program had been initiated by the president of the college, Sister Madeleva. That fiery nun was exasperated that no university in this country would admit women to study catholic theology at the doctoral level. When I wrote to her, she immediately offered me a scholarship and a part-time teaching job to support my studies. Having armed myself with the M.A., I jumped at the chance. On the train headed for St. Mary's, I felt that I was riding a Great Wind. 5

At St. Mary's, I acquired the habit of thinking philosophically in a rigorously logical manner. Medieval theology, especially that of Aquinas, who became my teacher, was philosophy carried into an Other dimension. After earning my Ph.D. in religion at the ripe old age of twenty-five, I decided to keep on Searching. I applied to the University 6 of Notre Dame, but I was refused admission to the doctoral program in philosophy solely on the basis of my sex. Moreover, I was unable to find a suitable teaching position, and found myself marooned for five years at a mediocre college in Brookline, Massachusetts. So, in 1959, I crossed the Atlantic to study at the University of Fribourg in Switzerland, where there was scholarship money available and where no obstacle was placed in the path of women who wanted to study for degrees in theology. My purpose was to obtain the highest of higher degrees in theology and philosophy, and between 1959 and 1965 I accumulated four degrees in Fribourg. I was getting ready to Sin Big.

The question may well arise: *Why did you go on and on pursuing*   7 *doctorates—especially in theology?* Was I a learned lunatic? Well, sure. But what else could I do that would prepare me so adequately for my work in the women's movement that was soon to come?

Theology—especially medieval catholic theology—is a treasure   8 chest containing archaic gems. By studying arduously, I equipped myself to reverse the reversals inherent in Christian dogma and decode its doctrines with precision. Subsequently, I would take these myths, symbols, and "mysteries" out of their phallocentric framework and make them Visible in a woman-centered context. In my books *Beyond God the Father* (1973) and *Gyn/Ecology* (1978), the doctrines of the male-god and of the trinity are revealed as distorted reflections of ancient female images of divinity. So, also, the idea of the "virgin birth" of Jesus is exposed as both a pale derivative and a reversal of pre-patriarchal myths of parthenogenesis (which produces divine daughters, not sons).

During those years in Fribourg, I followed my own interior com-   9 pass. In fact, I Plundered with a vengeance—flying to university classes on my Velosolex motor bicycle, teaching in three junior-year-abroad programs, and exploring Europe on a very skimpy shoestring. In 1964, I published an article in *Commonweal* magazine on women and the church, which led to a letter from a British publisher inviting me to write a book on the subject. My Smuggling career was about to begin.   ✿

### READING FOR INFORMATION

1. List the colleges and universities that Mary Daly attended, with the degrees and academic majors that she pursued, as indicated in paragraphs 3, 5, and 6 of this essay.

2. Paraphrase Daly's explanation of her decision to study theology as she presents it in paragraphs 4 and 7.

3. Summarize the goal that Daly sets for herself in the first three sentences of paragraph 8.

## READING FOR FORM, ORGANIZATION, AND EXPOSITORY FEATURES

1. Explain in your own words the metaphor of Piracy that Daly develops in paragraph 2. What does she mean by "Plunder" and "Smuggle"?
2. Describe the organizational features that make this text easy to follow. In addition to the chronological order that narrates the author's education and publications, does the author use other patterns to organize this essay?
3. What is the purpose of the author's sketch of Sister Madeleva in paragraph 5? How does it serve to anchor the seriousness with which Daly approaches her own academic career?

## READING FOR RHETORICAL CONCERNS

1. Underline the words in italics and quotation marks that Daly uses to describe her experiences in paragraphs 3, 4, 5, and 7. What is her attitude toward the ideas that they evoke?
2. Describe the author's tone. Who and what are the objects of her irony in paragraph 6?
3. What assumptions does Daly make about her readers? Does she seem confident that they will share her criticism of the male hierarchy that dominates the academic study of theology?

## WRITING ASSIGNMENTS

1. Like Elly Bulkin, Mary Daly identifies herself as a feminist who views her religion differently but no less seriously than her counterparts do. How do you think Bulkin would react to Daly's account of her training and objectives? Compose a conversation in which Bulkin and Daly compare their experiences.
2. Like Sara Suleri, Mary Daly identifies herself as a university professor with feminist interests. How do you think Suleri would react to Daly's account of her training and objectives? Compose a conversation in which Suleri and Daly compare their experiences.
3. Which of the tensions in her academic training that Daly describes can you identify with the most? Respond in an essay that tries to assess them with a sense of humor.

# The Pope's Loyal Opposition

## *Garry Wills*

*Garry Wills (born 1934) is a historian and cultural critic who teaches at North-western University. He has written many award-winning books, including Reagan's America (1988), the Pulitzer Prize-winning Lincoln at Gettysburg (1992), Saint Augustine (1999), Papal Sin (2000), and James Madison (2002).*

### PREREADING

Read paragraph 1 and the first italicized sentences in paragraphs 2, 6, 8, 10, and 11. Do you expect that this essay will attack religion rather than celebrate it? Respond to the paradox by speculating how the author might transform each of his criticisms of the papacy into support for it and for the Roman Catholic Church as a religious institution.

Support of the papacy is possible for the conscientious only if 1 certain things are recognized. I believe there are a number of such conditions to be met. One must recognize, for a start, that

1. *The papacy is a deeply flawed institution.* Saying such a thing is 2 considered by some Catholics to be disloyal. Apparently they believe that the only real Catholic is one able and willing to deny a long history of abuses and corruption. That assertion is usually prefaced with an "of course." *Of course* there have been individual popes who were bad, certain persons' peccadilloes or individual sins, usually committed long ago—Boniface VIII's political vendettas, Alexander VI's bastards, Julius II's war crimes, and so on. Sure, Dante and others in the Middle Ages put this or that pope in hell. But these were blemishes on an essentially noble and holy record, extraneous faults not connected with the core of papal teaching.

This is an evasion, an attempt to deny that the institution itself has 3 been at fault over long stretches of time. The record shows centuries of principled and authoritatively ordered repression, centuries in which the papacy or its agents tortured and executed people for thought crimes, persecuted Jews and other non-Christians, persecuted (for that matter) Christians who differed with Rome's doctrines, suborned or excused political assassinations, sang a papal Te Deum for the Saint Bartholomew's Day Massacre, opposed political freedoms and democracy, burned books, burned witches—and called all these actions holy, blessed by God, even commanded by God.

Admittedly, the popes have been around so long that they have   4
lived through stupid and criminal times, and have been infected by their surroundings. And power of itself tends to corrupt, especially when a combination of maximum spiritual and temporal power tempts men to a combination of apparent opposites, fanaticism and cynicism. Although early popes were automatically canonized, and an unworthy one was canonized as recently as 1954 (Pius X), few of the popes were saints, even by the standards of powerful men. In terms of basic decency, the average president of the United States has been a better human being than the average pope.

Are we to make it a test of faith that one denies or minimizes so   5
soiled, so incriminating a record? Are only two stands possible—defending the essential righteousness of the papacy, the only *Catholic* opinion; and admitting a dark legacy, an entirely *non-Catholic* option? Where, then, does an honest historian like Lord Acton stand? He took neither of those positions. He thought the government of the church, like all governments, was corrupted by the very nature of power's exercise; yet he remained a believer in the church *and the papacy.* There should be nothing surprising about this attitude when we consider the larger truth of which it is only one aspect, namely that:

2. *The church itself is a deeply flawed institution.* It was said of   6
Acton (and I have heard it too) that if he did not like the papacy, he should go join a church without the papacy. But how would that solve the problem? Where is a church not deeply flawed? Such a thing has never existed. Some Protestants like to imagine a "primitive church" that preceded the corruptions of Rome. Some Catholics (like Leo XIII) like to imagine a golden age of benign papal supremacy in the Middle Ages, one centered on the thirteenth century. Others talk as if only the apostolic time was true to the pure gospel. None of these views is even remotely accurate.

The thirteenth century saw the vicious crusades against the   7
Cathars and others and the rise of the Inquisition. The "primitive

church" was riven with disagreement and the clash of egos—between "Hellenist" and Jewish Christians, between Gnostics and the orthodox, between Pauline and Petrine factions. Paul's own churches rang with bitter feuds and jealousies. Ignatius was thrown out of his church of Antioch. Clement of Rome had to tell the Corinthians that brother-hurting-brother was an old story in the church—even Peter and Paul were turned over to Nero by their fellow Christians. For that matter, the apostles were driven by ambition, blindness, and rivalry during Christ's life. If one wants a pure or perfect church, one must go off to search for it on some other globe.

A further point must be made when it is said that a Catholic must 8 agree with the papacy. *Which* papacy? The truth is that

3. *There have been many papacies.*... The papacy that persecuted 9 Jews is not the papacy of John Paul II, who went to Yad Vashem to honor victims of the Holocaust. The papacy that opposed democracy is not the same as the one that endorsed the Vatican II document on religious liberty. The papacy of Pius X saying that doctrine can never change is not the papacy of Paul VI, who endorsed the Vatican Council's assertion that it can change.

There have been popes elected by the people, deposed by coun- 10 cils, subjected to the control of corrupt families. Indeed, there was a whole millennium when the papacy had nothing like the primacy later claimed for it. Popes were chosen or deposed by secular rulers; they themselves chose or deposed secular rulers; they let secular rulers choose bishops. None of those things would seem acceptable in the modern papacy. The papacy has at one time or another backed almost any political arrangement available in the West, and has eventually opposed the same kinds of regimes it endorsed. It has itself been collegiate, subordinate, autocratic. Since papacies have differed so widely, we must recognize that:

4. *One is obliged to differ from the papacy.* If that were not true, 11 we would all have to honor papacies that persecuted, lapsed into heresy, or supported despotism. We would have to believe in the many frauds used in canon law to define the papacy—the Symmachan forgeries, the false Isadore, the Donation of Constantine. We would still be believing that Jews are cursed and non-Catholics damned. It is not an honest "out" to say that we must agree only with the papacy of our time, not the straying ones of the past, since the claim of papalists is precisely that the institution defies time and change, that it spans the centuries

with a single truth. We can thank God that this is not true. We must differ from some forms of the papacy because:

5. *The papacy, like the church, changes.* Newman said, "In a   12
higher world it is otherwise, but here below to live is to change, and to
be perfect is to have changed often."[1] Since he thought that the church
is "here below," he obviously was asserting that the church must
change—and if the church (the *whole*), then how not the papacy (a *part*
of the church)? . . . Christ promised a Spirit-guided church, not a
changeless one. The Spirit is perfectly able to steer the church through
changes. If she were not able to, the church would never have survived
so many divagations, so many dangers, so many disasters.   ❀

## READING FOR INFORMATION

1. List the four claims about flaws in the papacy and the church that Wills
   makes in paragraphs 6, 8, 10, and 11. How does Wills implicitly distinguish between the papacy and the church, between its leadership and its
   congregation?

2. What specific flaws in the papacy and the church does Wills cite in paragraphs 2, 3, and 11? How does he explain that these institutions may be
   flawed but still useful?

3. What specific information about historical change does Wills recount
   in paragraphs 9 through 11? What conclusions does he draw about
   the inevitability of historical change and its potential for institutional
   improvement?

## READING FOR FORM, ORGANIZATION, AND EXPOSITORY FEATURES

1. What transitions does the author provide at the ends of paragraphs 1, 5,
   7, 9, and 10? How effective are these transitions in linking the separate
   claims of his argument?

2. How would you describe the organizational structure of this essay? Comment on how Wills takes pains to heighten the logic and rigor of his argument by calling attention to the connections and relationships among his
   various ideas.

3. Do you think the author does a good job of acknowledging the strengths
   as well as weaknesses of the institution that he defends? Do you think
   that his emphasis on its negative qualities might defeat his argument in
   support of it? Explain your reasoning.

## READING FOR RHETORICAL CONCERNS

1. Underline the questions that Wills asks in paragraphs 5, 6, and 8. Does Wills use these questions to put his church on the defensive, or does he use them ultimately to bolster his support for it?

2. Do you think that the author anticipates his readers' criticisms and objections to his claims? What evidence of planning to meet these criticisms and objections does Wills provide?

3. Describe the author's tone. Which words apply to it, and why: scholarly, earnest, alert, rueful, dispassionate, skeptical, circumspect, calm, agitated, accusatory? Is the tone appropriate for his rhetorical purpose?

## WRITING ASSIGNMENTS

1. Do you agree or disagree with Wills's premise that "if one wants a pure or perfect church, one must go off to search for it on some other globe" (paragraph 7)? Write an argumentative essay attacking or defending this premise with respect to a believer's (yours or someone else's) commitment to the church of his or her choice.

2. Like Wills, Mary Daly identifies herself as a serious student of Catholic theology and church history. While both criticize institutional flaws in their church, he professes implicit loyalty to it and she works for explicit change. Compose a conversation in which they exchange their views and discuss whether and how change might occur.

3. Using the strategies presented in Chapter 4, write a critical analysis of the logic of Wills's argument. Address your essay to classmates who might offer a different critical assessment of the argument.

# America, a Christian Nation

## *Pat Robertson*

*Pat Robertson (b. 1930) is a televangelist and founder of the Christian Coalition, a faith-oriented citizen action group that aims to influence public policy on local, state, and national levels. In 1988 he ran as a candidate for president in the Republican Party primary elections; since then he has emerged as an important figure in that party's politics. He has written several books, including Amer-ica's Date with Destiny (1986), New World Order (1991), and The Turning Tide (1993), from which this selection is taken.*

### PREREADING

Review your knowledge of colonial and early American history and jot down the names of religious groups and denominations that have figured prominently in this history. Examples might include Puritans, Quakers, Anglicans, and so forth. Which of these religions continue to figure in current history? Consult a local or campus telephone direc-tory to see which churches or church services are available in your community. Do the results concur with your sense of religious diver-sity in present-day America?

Contrary to the calumnies of its opponents, no one in the    1 Christian Coalition believes the goal of political action is to take over in matters of religious faith. Nor do they have any interest in co-opting any other group's personal or moral beliefs. The coalition's clear mandate is to affirm and support America's historic and traditional political institutions, which happen to be founded upon ethical systems derived from (and strengthened by) Judeo-Christian values. The dem-ocracy conceived by George Washington, John Adams, and Thomas Jefferson was a system of principled administration of the public affairs of a nation of free men and women, with respect for the individual lib-erty of each citizen and tolerance for individual differences. That is the vision of democracy we all support....

What Americans really hope for is a return to common-sense lead- 2
ership, where things are what they seem to be, and where men, women,
and children can live together in peace and in harmony, free of the
plague of experts that has flooded this country for more than half a century. This is one of the main reasons that we are beginning to hear new
voices from middle America telling us that there is hope, that there is a
right and wrong, and that the values this nation has always cherished
are just and right and worth fighting for....

With all of the negative changes impacting our society, it is in- 3
creasingly important for Christians to be involved in all the things that
affect our communities. They need to be involved not only in the
church, but in government, education, civic activities, and every other
area of life. Unfortunately, secular involvement has not been something
that Christians have been very good at or very eager to do until now.
Many are well educated and successful, but they have kept silent up
to now....

One of the foundational principles of coalition building is that we must 4
cooperate with those groups with whom we agree on cardinal issues in
order to achieve our mutual political goals. We agree not to attempt to
coerce or unduly influence others to subscribe to our beliefs that do not
directly impinge upon the issues at stake. In other words, Protestants,
Catholics, Mormons, Seventh-Day Adventists, and Orthodox Jews, for
example, may disagree on some important theological issues. Yet on
certain important political issues they see eye-to-eye; therefore, where
they agree they must unite so that together they can achieve their mutual goals with greater unanimity, force, and effectiveness.

One of my dear friends, Orrin Hatch, is an outstanding senator 5
from the state of Utah. He is a Mormon, and while we disagree on
many issues of doctrine and biblical understanding, we are very much
in unison in our dedication to family values, on creating a healthy moral
climate in America, and on protecting and preserving our rights as believers to practice our faith without restriction. When he was appointed
chairman of the Senate Labor Committee, I wrote him a letter and
said, "Thank God you're there!" I really meant it.

I think people have to hear this. We may differ on some important 6
spiritual issues, and we do, but that does not in any way keep me from
making an alliance with Senator Hatch on the major political issues
confronting our nation. A political party is not a church. It does not
need to maintain a rigid orthodoxy and a statement of faith. Christians

who are novices in politics have been concerned about party platforms as statements of faith because that's the way they operate as Christians. But in politics, legislative action flows from holding office, and those who hold office are able to make decisions concerning the lives of the people. It is ridiculous to spend a lot of time arguing over the arcane points of a platform only to see positions of great power won by the proponents of the philosophy we are opposing.

Professional politicians say, Give on principle, but hold on offices.    7
They understand that the principles are at the heart of everything, but the specific wording of any resolution is not legislation; legislation has to be hammered out through debate and compromise. There has to be give-and-take in legislation. The Christian or anybody else who gets into politics has to understand that the name of the game is to win offices, and from that position it is possible to pass laws and appoint others to positions of authority. Only after these victories is there any chance that basic philosophies can be transformed into legislative and administrative action.    ❀

## READING FOR INFORMATION

1. Paraphrase in paragraph 1 Robertson's statement of goal for the Christian Coalition to support a democracy based on Judeo-Christian values.

2. Paraphrase in paragraph 4 Robertson's statement of toleration for differences in religious belief among Christians and Orthodox Jews.

3. Underline the specific religious denominations that Robertson mentions throughout the essay. List as many religions or denominations as you can that he does not mention.

## READING FOR FORM, ORGANIZATION, AND EXPOSITORY FEATURES

1. What is the function of paragraph 2? What does Robertson mean by the general term "American"?

2. Do you think the author does a good job of acknowledging the scope of religious diversity in contemporary America? How, for example, does he represent his own relationships with people of other faiths in paragraphs 5 and 6?

3. What is the impact of the last two sentences in paragraph 7? Does the author convey a positive impression of his goal to secure the election of candidates favorable to his cause?

## READING FOR RHETORICAL CONCERNS

1. Underline passages where the author presents alternatives to his own convictions. How much tolerance does he display for opposing points of view?

2. Identify for this article a "rhetorical context" as described on pp. 26–27. What is the author trying to accomplish in paragraphs 3 and 7?

3. What assumptions does Robertson make about his readers? Is he addressing an audience of general readers, political campaigners, or academic historians? Is he addressing an audience of like-minded persons?

## WRITING ASSIGNMENTS

1. Briefly summarize Robertson's argument for classmates who might belong to religious groups that the author does not mention in his writing. Try to accommodate his argument to their religious convictions.

2. Do you agree or disagree with Robertson's "vision of democracy" that he offers in paragraph 1? Write a critical essay that explains your agreement or disagreement by refining the general position set forth in Robertson's argument.

3. Write a brief essay in response to Robertson's final paragraph. Do you think that religious groups should try to sway voters to elect particular candidates?

# Is America a Christian Nation?

## *Isaac Kramnick and R. Laurence Moore*

*Isaac Kramnick is the R. J. Schwartz Professor of Government at Cornell University; his books include* The Rage of Edmund Burke *(1977);* Age of Ideology: Political Thought from 1750 to the Present *(1979); and* Republicanism and Bourgeois Radicalism *(1990). R. Laurence Moore is the H. A. Newman Professor of American Studies at Cornell University; his books include* European Socialists and the Promised Land *(1970);* Religious Outsiders and the Making of America *(1986); and* Selling God: American Religion in the Marketplace of Culture *(1995).*

### PREREADING

As you did for the preceding selection, review your knowledge of American history and read the names that you jotted down for religious groups and denominations that have figured prominently in it. Once again ask yourself which of these groups continue to figure in it. If you have not already done so, consult a local or campus telephone directory to see which churches or church services are available in your community. Do you find there any groups or denominations that you did not imagine available in your community?

Americans seem to fight about many silly things: whether a   1
copy of the Ten Commandments can be posted in a city courthouse; whether a holiday display that puts an image of the baby Jesus next to one of Frosty the Snowman violates the Constitution; whether fidgeting grade-schoolers may stand for a minute in silent "spiritual" meditation before classes begin. Common sense might suggest that these are harmless practices whose actual damage is to trivialize religion. Otherwise they threaten no one. Not children, who ignore them as the incomprehensible designs of absurd grown-ups. Not atheists, who may find them hypocritical and vulgar but hardly intimidating. Not Buddhists and Muslims, who in these small areas of daily practice can

demand equal access to the public landscape. So why do they raise ideological storms?

The answer lies in what history has done to us. Some Americans  2 have inherited extravagant hopes about what religion, specifically Christianity, may accomplish in solving social problems through moral instruction. Others look to a different legacy, one that suggests how easily partisan religion in the hands of a purported majority can become a dangerous form of intellectual and political tyranny. Both groups have become masters of hyperbolic language. However, their quarrels are not about nothing. If Americans have learned to make constitutional mountains out of religious molehills, it is because crucial principles may become endangered. The crèche or the menorah on public property becomes the nose of the camel sneaking into the tent where Americans have carefully enshrined the constitutional separation of church and state.

Should we be worried? Our answer is yes, at least with respect to  3 one area of ongoing controversy. We are concerned about current pronouncements made by politically charged religious activists, what is called in journalistic parlance the religious right. Their crusade is an old one. Now a prime target is abortion clinics. Before it was mail delivery on Sundays, or Catholic immigrants, or Darwinian biology in school curriculums. Whenever religion of any kind casts itself as the one true faith and starts trying to arrange public policy accordingly, people who believe that they have a stake in free institutions, whatever else might divide them politically, had better look out.

What follows, then, is a polemic. Since before the founding of the  4 United States, European colonists in North America were arguing about the role of religion in public and political life. Broadly speaking, two distinct traditions exist. We intend to lay out the case for one of them—what we call the party of the godless Constitution and of godless politics. In brief, this position recognizes that the nation's founders, both in writing the Constitution and in defending it in the ratification debates, sought to separate the operations of government from any claim that human beings can know and follow divine direction in reaching policy decisions. They did this despite their enormous respect for religion, their faith in divinely endowed human rights, and their belief that democracy benefited from a moral citizenry who believed in God. The party we defend is based on a crucial intellectual connection, derived historically from both religious and secular thinkers, between a godless Constitution and a God-fearing people.

We will call the other side in this debate that runs through Ameri- 5 can history the party of religious correctness. It maintains that the United States was established as a Christian nation by Christian people, with the Christian religion assigned a central place in guiding the nation's destiny. For those who adhered to this party in the past, it followed that politicians and laws had to pass the test of furthering someone's definition of a Christian public order. Recently some who belong to this party have suggested that the stress upon "Christian" be downplayed in their political pronouncements. By referring more ecumenically to the United States as a religious nation, they invite other religious traditions to join a family-values crusade launched originally by a particular form of Christian faith. However, . . . a shift in rhetorical strategy to widen political appeal does not affect the substantive issues at stake. . . .

We believe, we believe passionately, that the party of religious cor- 6 rectness represents an approach to public policy that is damaging— damaging to the American Constitution, damaging to political debate, and damaging to American children whose social and educational needs are seriously misstated by the programs of religious correctness. We argue with some confidence because over the long years of American history the party of religious correctness has lost most of the major wars. It lost because it was wrong, not because Americans despise religion. . . .

So let us be as clear as we can be at the outset. We are aware of 7 the crucial role that religion played in America's revolutionary struggle, of the importance that many Constitution makers attached to it, and of the energy it gave to many American crusades for social justice. We both in fact have written about these points. . . . Suffice it to say that our intention is not to marginalize religion. If anything, it is to warn against the ways that some aggressive proponents of religious correctness are doing exactly that in their political battles, even as they try to lay the blame elsewhere.

Americans are a people who like to argue about their origins. We 8 think that if we could just get straight what the founding fathers really thought, we might do everything right. This is an illusion. However, there are far worse intellectual exercises than arguing about the founding fathers. They were uncommonly bright people. One problem, however, is that Washington, Jefferson, and Madison said a variety of things. A handy quotation plucked from this or that letter can serve a lot of partisan causes. It is not the purpose of this project to prove that all the founding fathers would agree with everything we say. Nonetheless, a little attention to a few hard facts can clear away phony arguments on both sides....

Some of the founding fathers fretted that Americans weren't  9 much interested in religion and most definitely weren't securely Christian. They had reason to be concerned. Although some versions of our national myths tell us that the English colonists to North America were more religious than the people who stayed behind in England, that they carried Christian crosses ashore, fell on their knees, and dedicated themselves to the Christian God, the fact is that most English Protestants acted in these matters with less fervor than Spanish and French Catholics who had preceded them into many parts of the New World. In the middle of the seventeenth century many more zealous Puritans lived in London than in New England. And run-of-the-mill Anglicans, who always outnumbered Puritans in the American colonies during the seventeenth and eighteenth centuries, tended to be lazy church organizers, especially indifferent in the Carolinas, Virginia, and Georgia to the problems of staffing outlying parishes with competent clerics....

The figure of church affiliation has gone up dramatically since the  10 early years of the Republic. To be sure, if we are to judge from the biblical literacy of Americans (in a recent poll fewer than half could name one of the four Gospels), the doctrinal investment of most Americans in organized religion is light. Yet that is scarcely the result of a secularist-led conspiracy. Christian churches, in fact, have no cause to complain about their public visibility. In numerical terms they are doing as well as or better than anything else that engages Americans' interest and energy. Professional sports is possibly a close competitor among men. Politics for either sex is not. These days dire warnings about the marginalization of religion come usually from the religious right. How seriously can we take such warnings if the religious right can claim anywhere near the constituency that its literature boasts, about a quarter of the American voting population—24 million Protestant evangelicals and a large proportion of America's 58 million Catholics? Most groups would relish marginalization of that sort.

The truly curious thing about some of the complaints from the  11 Christian Coalition, the most vocal group of religious activists on the scene today, is that the last two Democratic presidents in this country, Jimmy Carter and Bill Clinton, have been Bible-quoting Southern Baptists. Rather than welcoming them as spiritual allies, the Christian Coalition has turned to far more dubious men of faith: Ronald Reagan, whose odd California blend of Armageddon prophecy, astrology, and un-family values was largely indifferent to church institutions; and George Bush, who manipulated his old-line Episcopalian faith so weirdly to serve political opportunism that even the Christian Coalition blushed.

Pat Robertson, one prominent spokesman for the Christian right, 12 insists that America was founded as a Christian polity, which persisted until subverted by a cabal of twentieth-century liberals and freethinkers who replaced it with an un-American secular state. The rhetoric of the Christian right repeatedly calls for a return to America's lost Christianhood, as shaped by its founders. Ralph Reed proclaimed, before political realities modified his tone, that "what Christians have got to do is to take back this country" and "make it a country once again governed by Christians." Pat Robertson uses the same imagery of return. "If Christian people work together," he urges, "they can succeed during this decade in winning back control of the institutions that have been taken from them over the past 70 years." . . .

One of the Christian right's most visible spokesmen, the evangelist- 13 psychologist James Dobson, distributes through his organization Focus on the Family a set of history lessons that seeks to show that . . . "The Constitution was designed to perpetuate a Christian order." Many of America's disorders, Dobson argues, stem from abandoning this unity of state and church. "This really was a Christian nation," he claims, "and, as far as its founders were concerned, to try separating Christianity from government is virtually impossible and would result in unthinkable damage to the nation and its people. Much of the damage we see around us must be attributed to this separation."

This reading of the mind of the men who wrote the godless Con- 14 stitution is wrong. The principal framers of the American political system wanted no religious parties in national politics. They crafted a constitutional order that intended to make a person's religious convictions, or his lack of religious convictions, irrelevant in judging the value of his political opinion or in assessing his qualifications to hold political office. . . . Yet, so successful were the drafters of the Constitution in defining government in secular terms that one of the most powerful criticisms of the Constitution when ratified and for succeeding decades was that it was indifferent to Christianity and God. It was denounced by many as a godless document, which is precisely what it is.

Those who crafted American national government as a secular in- 15 stitution called upon two traditions. They used the strong vision of separate spiritual and worldly realms found in the American religious thought of Roger Williams and the Baptists of the founding era. They also enlisted the English liberal tradition, which put at the center of its political philosophy individuals free of government, enjoying property and thinking and praying as they wished. From these two sources came America's Constitution in 1787, today still our fundamental law. Pat Robertson may think, as he claimed in 1993, that the wall of separation between church and state is "a lie of the left" and that "there is no such thing in the Constitution." History and victories won through the course of our American past tell us that he is wrong.

The paradox we confront in telling our story is the one we mentioned in the beginning. The creation of a godless constitution was not an act of irreverence. Far from it. It was an act of confidence in religion. It intended to let religion do what it did best, to preserve the civil morality necessary to democracy, without laying upon it the burdens of being tied to the fortunes of this or that political faction. The godless Constitution must be understood as part of the American system of voluntary church support that has proved itself a much greater boon to the fortunes of organized religion than the prior systems of church establishment ever were. &#10070;    16

## READING FOR INFORMATION

1. Summarize the two sides of the debate about whether or not it is proper for religion to play a role in American political life as the authors represent it in paragraphs 4 to 7.

2. Underline the facts about American history that the authors present in paragraphs 8 to 10. Is this information sufficient to support their argument, or does it need further elaboration? If it needs elaboration, do you think additional information would generally confirm or confute the authors' claims?

3. Explain why the authors are critical of "religious correctness" in paragraphs 14 and 15. Summarize their argument in your own words.

## READING FOR FORM, ORGANIZATION, AND EXPOSITORY FEATURES

1. What worries about "religious correctness" do the authors express in paragraphs 1 to 3? Are their concerns serious enough to warrant their subsequent defense of a "godless Constitution" in paragraph 4?

2. What is the effect of the authors' conclusion that "The creation of a godless constitution . . . was an act of confidence in religion" (paragraph 16)?

Do they sustain an argument in paragraphs 4 to 15 that successfully leads to this conclusion?

3. Construct for this article a graphic overview of the dominant argument. Does it correspond to the sample graphic overview given on pp. 24–25? What elements have you included that do not appear in the sample? What elements have you excluded that appear there?

## READING FOR RHETORICAL CONCERNS

1. Underline passages where the authors present alternatives to their own convictions. How much tolerance do they display for opposing points of view?

2. Is the argument one-sided, or do the authors concede alternative viewpoints? Do they fairly represent the position of "religious correctness" as they discuss it in paragraphs 12 and 13?

3. What assumptions do Kramnick and Moore make about their readers? Are they addressing an audience of general readers or of like-minded academic historians?

## WRITING ASSIGNMENTS

1. Write a critical essay in response to Kramnick and Moore's final paragraph and in particular to their claim that a separation of church and state proves to benefit organized religion because it guarantees that the state will not interfere with religion.

2. How do you think that Pat Robertson would react to Kramnick and Moore's argument and to their representation of his position? Compose a conversation among them. Have Robertson object to three or four points in the article, and supply Kramnick and Moore's response.

3. Like Garry Wills who argues that the institutional flaws in his church provide reason for its followers to support that church, Kramnick and Moore pose an apparent paradox when they argue that a godless constitution offers the best possible support for organized religion. Using the strategies presented in Chapter 4, write a critical analysis of the latters' argument. Address your essay to classmates who might hold a different opinion from yours about the separation of church and state.

## SYNTHESIS WRITING ASSIGNMENTS

1. Benazir Bhutto, Elly Bulkin, and Mary Daly are respectively Muslim, Jewish, and Catholic women who seek to strengthen women's active roles in the public arena. Write an essay in which you discuss and evaluate the goals they set forth for women's participation in political leadership, their

struggle against racism and sexism, and their efforts to advance the women's movement. Base your discussion on the essays that they have written in this anthology.

2. Sara Suleri, Alina Bacall-Zwirn, and Mary Daly recount complex personal perspectives on their respective experiences as a Pakistani Muslim, a Polish Jew, and a North American Catholic. In each case their gendered identities as women play important roles in shaping their experiences. Write an essay in which you explain how gender puts a particular mark on one's religious identity by setting standards for behavior, posing choices, and summoning role models. Illustrate your argument with examples from their writing and address it to classmates who have not read their essays.

3. Benazir Bhutto, Elly Bulkin, Garry Wills, and Isaac Kramnick and R. Laurence Moore write complex arguments in which they acknowledge opposing views, competing claims, and alternative hypotheses. After reading their work, what do you think of other arguments whose authors try to defend their beliefs by ignoring criticisms or objections and concentrating only on the positive attributes of their position? Write a brief essay expressing your views of how you might go about defending an unusual choice or unpopular commitment with respect to some aspect of your (or someone else's) personal identity.

4. Each selection in this chapter explores overlapping relationships between one's religious identity as a Muslim, Jew, or Christian and other sorts of personal identity in public, private, political, and professional settings. Some of these selections further explore relationships between religion and gender and racial identities. How might their questions relate to issues that recur in this book's section on natural sciences and technology? How, for example, does John J. Conley's "Narcissus Cloned" in Chapter 6 or Steve Mann's "Cyborg Seeks Community" in Chapter 7 deal with matters of personal identity at stake in this current chapter? Write an essay that discusses such concerns as topics in science and technology intersect with those in the humanities.

5. Each selection in this chapter explores overlapping relationships between religious identity and other sorts of personal identity. Some of the selections focus especially on relationships between religious identity and gender and racial identities. How might the questions they raise relate to issues that recur in this book's section on the social sciences? How, for example, does Barbara Ehrenreich's "Serving in Florida" in Chapter 10 or Shelby Steele's "Educating Black Students" in Chapter 11 deal with matters of gender and racial identity at stake in this current chapter? Write an essay that discusses such concerns as topics in the social sciences intersect with those in the humanities.

C H A P T E R
# *thirteen*

# Literatures of Diaspora:
# Fiction and Nonfiction

Within the humanities, the various disciplines of literary criticism, theater arts, history of art, and musicology attempt to assess the cultural products of human civilization. Courses in literature, drama, art, and music train students to analyze, interpret, and evaluate meaningful "texts." We use the word "text" in a broad sense to refer to any composition, whether of words, as in poetry, drama, and prose fiction or nonfiction; of color, line, and texture, as in painting, sculpture, and architecture; or of sound and movement, as in music and dance, film, and television. The questions one might ask about one sort of text resemble those one might ask about other sorts. They concern the selection and arrangement of appropriate materials; the tone, attitude, and point of view that govern their selection and arrangement; similarities to and comparisons and contrasts with other texts; and further questions about relationships between texts and the sociocultural contexts of their production and reception.

One aim of literary criticism, art history, and music theory is to make the meaning of such "texts" more accessible to us. This aim is especially visible when the text displays a social, historical, or cultural otherness whose assumptions differ from ours. Shakespeare's plays, for example, profit from a critical and historical analysis that illuminates differences between early modern attitudes and our own. Sometimes the technical jargon of an analysis may have the opposite effect: It may make the object of study appear more impenetrable than ever. A musicological study of flats and sharps, harmonies and counterpoints, arpeggios and staccatos in one of Mozart's string quarters may distance us entirely from the sound of the music. If we reflect upon its purpose, however, we may find that it evokes complexity only because the process of understanding any worthwhile text is correspondingly complex. It does not seek to replace an experience of the work of art. It seeks, rather, to explore the ramifications of that experience as they connect with social, historical, moral, political, philosophical, ideological, psychological, aesthetic, and other experiences. The outcome of good criticism shows us that what we take for granted in a text may be not so simple after all.

If academic approaches to expressive forms demonstrate the otherness, difference, and complexity of those forms, many of the texts that they study deal with otherness, difference, and complexity in a primary way. Fiction, nonfiction, poetry, drama, painting, sculpture, photography, film, television, song, dance, and instrumental music all provide us with glimpses into other worlds. They can represent customs, conventions, ways of life, and human experiences that different audiences might not otherwise have. Or, if they represent a world accessible to their audience, they do so best when they afford a new perspective on that world.

The selections in this chapter deal with otherness, difference, and accessibility by focusing on a range of fictional and nonfictional texts from a heterogeneous world culture. The word *diaspora* refers to the scattering and dispersion of people with a common ethnic origin. The first selection is a short story by the South American writer Isabel Allende, now a resident of the United States, and it concerns the dubious rise to prosperity and prestige of an oddly matched couple—she is Scotch, he is Spanish—amid varied immigrant and indigenous groups in Latin America. The second selection is a stark account of deportation from Italy to a Nazi death camp in Poland by a Jewish chemist, Primo Levi, who uses literary techniques of dramatic dialogue, story-telling, and interlocking structure to report his real-life experience. In the third selection, Ronald Takaki, a professional historian, uses similar techniques to describe patterns of Japanese immigration to America in the nineteenth century. The last two selections are works of fiction. Bharati Mukherjee's short story narrates the assimilation of an illegal immigrant from the West Indies into the academic community of Ann Arbor, Michigan. Alice Walker's short story depicts the bonds that relate three generations of African American women to their ancestors despite the scattering of their origins and dispersion of their roots.

# The Proper Respect

## *Isabel Allende*

*Isabel Allende, niece of the assassinated Marxist president of Chile, Salvador Allende, has worked as a journalist in Chile, Venezuela, and the United States. Currently residing in California, she has written best-selling novels, including* The House of the Spirits *(1982),* Love and Shadows *(1985),* Eva Luna *(1987),* Infinite Plan *(1991), and* Paula *(1994); nonfiction such as* Paths of Resistance: The Art and Craft of the Political Novel *(1989); and many short stories.*

### PREREADING

To an even greater extent than the mixed peoples of North America, the population of South America represents a multicultural patchwork of ethnic and national origins. Though significantly influenced by Spain and the Spanish language, its racial composition includes Native Americans, Asians, Africans, Middle Easterners, and Europeans, with sometimes profound cultural differences among them. Consult an atlas, an almanac, and a world encyclopedia to learn more about these differences.

They were a pair of scoundrels. He had the face of a pirate, 1 and he dyed his hair and mustache jet black; with time, he changed his style and left the gray, which softened his expression and lent him a more circumspect air. She was fleshy, with the milky skin of reddish blondes, the kind of skin that in youth reflects light with opalescent brush strokes, but with age becomes crinkled paper. The years she had spent in the oil workers' camps and tiny towns on the frontier had not drained her vigor, the heritage of her Scots ancestors. Neither mosquitoes nor heat nor abuse had spoiled her body or diminished her desire for dominance. At fourteen she had run away from her father, a Protestant pastor who preached the Bible deep in the jungle; his was a totally futile labor, since no one understood his English palaver and, furthermore, in those latitudes words, even the word of God, were lost in the jabbering of the birds. At fourteen the girl had reached her full growth and was in absolute command of her person. She was not sentimental. She rejected one after another of the men who, attracted by the incandescent flame of her hair, so rare in the tropics, had offered her their protection. She had never heard love spoken of, and it was not in her nature to invent it; on the other hand, she knew how to make the most of the only commodity she possessed, and by the time she was twenty-five she had a handful of diamonds sewed into the hem of her petticoat. She handed them over without hesitation to Domingo Toro, the bull of a man who had managed to tame her, an adventurer who trekked through the region hunting alligators and trafficked in arms and bootleg whiskey. He was an unscrupulous rogue, the perfect companion for Abigail McGovern.

In their first years together, the couple had fabricated bizarre schemes for accumulating capital. With her diamonds, his alligator hides, funds he had obtained dealing contraband, and chicanery at the gaming tables, Domingo had purchased chips at the casino he knew were identical to those used on the other side of the border where the value of the currency was much stronger. He filled a suitcase with chips, made a brief trip, and traded them for good hard cash. He was able to repeat the operation twice more before the authorities became suspicious, and even when they did they could not accuse him of anything illegal. In the meantime, Abigail had been selling clay pots and bowls she bought from the Goajiros and sold as archeological treasures to the gringos who worked with National Petroleum—with such success that soon she branched out into fake Colonial paintings produced by a student in his cubbyhole behind the cathedral and preternaturally aged with sea water, soot, and cat urine. By then Abigail, who had outgrown her roughneck manners and speech, had cut her hair and now dressed in expensive clothes. Although her taste was a little extreme and her effort to appear elegant a little too obvious, she could pass as a lady, which facilitated social relationships and contributed to the success of her business affairs. She entertained clients in the drawing rooms of the Hotel Inglés and, as she served them tea with the measured gestures she had learned by imitation, she would natter on about big-game hunting and tennis tournaments in hypothetical places with British-sounding names that no one could locate on a map. After the third cup she would broach in a confidential tone the subject of the meeting. She would show her guests photographs of the purported antiquities, making it clear that her proposal was to save those treasures from local neglect. The government did not have the resources to preserve these extraordinary objects, she would say, and to slip them out of the country, even though it was against the law, constituted an act of archeological conscience.

Once the Toros had laid the foundations for a small fortune, Abigail's next plan was to found a dynasty, and she tried to convince Domingo of the need to have a good name.     3

"What's wrong with ours?"     4

"No one is called Toro, that's a barroom name," Abigail argued.

"It was my father's name, and I don't intend to change it."

"In that case, we will have to convince the world that we are wealthy."

She suggested that they buy land and plant bananas or coffee, as     5
social snobs had done before them; but he did not like the idea of moving to the interior, a wild land fraught with the danger of bands of thieves, the army, guerrillas, snakes, and all the diseases known to man. To him it seemed insane to head off into the jungle in search of a future when a fortune was theirs for the taking right in the capital; it would be less risky to dedicate themselves to commerce, like the thousands of Syrians and Jews who had debarked with nothing but misery in the packs slung over their backs, but who within a few years were living in the lap of luxury.

"No small-time stuff!" objected Abigail. "What I want is a re-     6
spectable family; I want them to call us *don* and *doña* and not dare speak to us without removing their hats."

But Domingo was adamant, and finally she accepted his decision.     7
She nearly always did, because anytime she opposed her husband, he punished her by withdrawing communication and sexual favors. He would disappear from the house for days at a time, return hollow-eyed from his clandestine mischief, change his clothes, and go out again, leaving Abigail at first furious and then terrified at the idea of losing him. She was a practical person totally devoid of romantic notions, and if once there had been a seed of tenderness in her, the years she had spent on her back had destroyed it. Domingo, nevertheless, was the only man she could bear to live with, and she was not about to let him get away. The minute Abigail gave in, Domingo would come home and sleep in his own bed. There were no noisy reconciliations; they merely resumed the rhythm of their routines and returned to the complicity of

their questionable dealings. Domingo Toro set up a chain of shops in poor neighborhoods, where he sold goods at low prices but in huge quantities. The stores served as a screen for other, less legal, activities. Money continued to pile up, and they could afford the extravagances of the very wealthy, but Abigail was not satisfied: she had learned that it is one thing to have all the comforts but something very different to be accepted in society.

"If you had paid attention to me, they wouldn't be thinking of us  8 as Arab shopkeepers. Why did you have to act like a ragpicker?" she protested to her husband.

"I don't know why you're complaining; we have everything."

"Go ahead and sell that trash, if that's what you want, but I'm going to buy racehorses."

"Horses? What do you know about horses, woman?"

"I know that they're classy. Everyone who is anyone has horses."

"You'll be the ruin of us."

For once Abigail had her way, and in a very short time had proved  9 that her idea was not a bad one. Their stallions gave them an excuse to mingle with the old horse-breeding families and, in addition, were extremely profitable, but although the Toros appeared frequently in the racing section, their names were never in the society pages. Disheartened, Abigail compensated with even more vulgar ostentation. She bought a china service with her hand-painted portrait on every piece, cut-glass goblets, and furniture with raging gargoyles carved on the feet. Her prize, however, was a threadbare armchair she passed off as a Colonial relic, telling everyone it had belonged to El Libertador, which was why she had tied a red cord across the arms, so no one would place his unworthy buttocks where the Father of the Nation had sat. She hired a German governess for her children, and a Dutch vagabond who affected an admiral's uniform as custodian of the family yacht. The only vestiges of their past life were Domingo's buccaneer's tattoos and an old injury to Abigail's back, a consequence of spread-legged contortions during her oil-field days; but long sleeves covered his tattoos, and she had a silk-padded iron corset made to prevent pain from infringing upon her dignity. By then she was obese, laden with jewels, the spit and image of Nero. Greed had wrought the physical havoc her jungle adventures had not imposed upon her.

For the purpose of attracting the most select members of society,  10 every year the Toros hosted a masked ball at Carnival time: the Court of Baghdad with the elephant and camels from the zoo and an army of

waiters dressed as Bedouins; a Bal de Versailles at which guests in bro-
cade gowns and powdered wigs danced the minuet amid beveled mirrors; and other scandalous revels that became a part of local legend and
gave rise to violent diatribes in leftist newspapers. The Toros had to
post guards before the house to prevent students—outraged by such
extravagance—from painting slogans on the columns and throwing excrement through the windows, alleging that the newly rich filled their
bathtubs with champagne, while to eat, the newly poor hunted cats on
the rooftops. Such lavish displays had afforded the Toros a degree of re-
spectability, because by then the line that divided the social classes was
vanishing; people were flocking into the country from every corner of
the globe, drawn by the miasma of petroleum. Growth in the capital
was uncontrolled, fortunes were made and lost in the blink of an eye,
and it was no longer possible to ascertain the ancestry of every individual. Even so, the old families kept their distance from the Toros, despite the fact they themselves had descended from other immigrants
whose only merit was to have reached these shores a half-century
sooner. They attended Domingo and Abigail's banquets and sometimes
sailed around the Caribbean in the yacht piloted by the firm hand of
the Dutch captain, but they did not return the invitations. Abigail might
have been forced to resign herself to second-class status had an unforeseen event not changed their luck.

On a late August afternoon Abigail had awakened unrefreshed 11
from her siesta; it was unbearably hot and the air was heavy with
presages of a coming storm. She had slipped a silk dress over her corset
and ordered her chauffeur to drive her to the beauty salon. They drove
through the heavy traffic with the windows closed, to forestall any mal-
content who might spit at the *señora* through an open window—something that happened more and more frequently. They stopped before
the salon at exactly five o'clock, which Abigail entered after instructing
the chauffeur to come for her one hour later. When he returned to pick
her up, Abigail was not there. The hairdresser said that about five minutes after she had arrived, the *señora* had said she had a brief errand to
run, and had not returned. Meanwhile, in his office Domingo Toro had
received a call from the Red Pumas, an extremist group no one had
heard of until then, announcing that they had kidnapped his wife.

That was the beginning of the scandal that was to assure the Toros' 12
reputation. The police had taken the chauffeur and the hairdressers
into custody, searched entire barrios, and cordoned off the Toros' man-
sion, to the subsequent annoyance of their neighbors. During the day a

television van blocked the street, and a throng of newspaper reporters, detectives, and curiosity seekers trampled the lawns. Domingo Toro appeared on television, seated in a leather chair in his library between a globe of the world and a stuffed mare, imploring the kidnappers to release the mother of his children. The cheapgoods magnate, as the press had labeled him, was offering a million in local currency in exchange for his wife—an inflated amount considering that a different guerrilla group had obtained only half that much for a Middle East ambassador. The Red Pumas, however, had not considered the sum sufficient, and had doubled the ransom. After seeing Abigail's photograph in the newspaper, many believed that Domingo Toro's best move would be to pay the ransom—not for the return of his wife, but to reward the kidnappers for keeping her. Incredulity swept the nation when the husband, after consultations with bankers and lawyers, accepted the deal despite warnings by police. Hours before delivering the stipulated sum, he had received a lock of red hair through the mail, with a note indicating that the price had gone up another quarter of a million. By then, the Toro children had also appeared on television, sending desperate filial messages to their mother. The macabre auction was daily rising in pitch, and given full coverage by the media.

The suspense ended five days later, just as public curiosity was beginning to be diverted by other events. Abigail was found, bound and gagged, in a car parked in the city center, a little nervous and bedraggled but without visible signs of harm and, if anything, slightly more plump. The afternoon that she returned home, a small crowd gathered in the street to applaud the husband who had given such strong proof of his love. In the face of harassment from reporters and demands from the police, Domingo Toro had assumed an attitude of discreet gallantry, refusing to reveal how much he had paid, with the comment that his wife was beyond price. People wildly exaggerated the figure, crediting to him a payment much greater than any man would have given for a wife, least of all his. But all this speculation had established the Toros as the ultimate symbol of opulence; it was said they were as rich as the President, who for years had profited from the proceeds of the nation's oil and whose fortune was calculated to be one of the five largest in the world. Domingo and Abigail were raised to the peak of high society, the inner sanctum from which they had previously been excluded. Nothing clouded their triumph, not even public protests by students, who hung banners at the University accusing Abigail of arranging her own kidnapping, the magnate of withdrawing millions from one pocket and putting them into another without penalty of taxes, and the police of swallowing the story of the Red Pumas in order to frighten the populace and justify purges against opposition parties. But no evil tongue could destroy the glorious result of the kidnapping, and a decade later the Toro-McGoverns were known as one of the nation's most respectable families.    ✿

## READING FOR INFORMATION

1. Explain the differences between settling on a plantation and living in the capital as Domingo Toro perceives them in paragraph 5. What businesses does he conduct in paragraph 7?

2. Summarize the events that precede Abigail's disappearance in paragraph 11. Does she appear to shape the event?

3. List the major details that suggest a time frame for the story. When do you think it takes place?

## READING FOR FORM, ORGANIZATION, AND EXPOSITORY FEATURES

1. Summarize from paragraph 2 the process and intention of Abigail's first efforts to pass as a lady.

2. Explain in your own words what the "vestiges of their past life" signify in paragraph 9.

3. List the details in paragraphs 12 and 13 that suggest the couple has staged Abigail's kidnapping.

## READING FOR RHETORICAL CONCERNS

1. Explain in your own words what the narrator means by characterizing Abigail in paragraph 7 as "a practical person totally devoid of romantic notions." What does her practicality suggest about her motivations for seeking respect?

2. Describe the narrator's tone in paragraph 12. What is the significance of identifying Domingo as a "cheapgoods magnate" and of emphasizing his inflated ransom?

3. Describe the narrator's tone in paragraph 13.

## WRITING ASSIGNMENTS

1. Write an analytical profile of the narrator. Does he or she admire the Toros? trust them? sympathize with their efforts? How does the narrator encourage the reader to adopt a skeptical attitude?

2. Write an analytical critique of how the story represents mass culture and popular opinion. What implications does the multicultural diversity of the setting have for the Toros's success? How do the Toros manipulate media and appearances, and what does their manipulation imply about those taken in by it? Though the story is set in Latin America, could its outcome happen elsewhere?

# The Journey

## Primo Levi

*Primo Levi (1919–87) was a Jewish Italian citizen who worked as a chemist in Turin. In 1943 he was arrested by Italian Fascists and was deported to the Polish death camp at Auschwitz. The following excerpt is taken from his book,* Survival in Auschwitz *(1958), a testimony of cruelty and endurance in which he recounts his ten months in the camp.*

### PREREADING

Review Alina Bacall-Zwirn's Holocaust testimony about her experience in Auschwitz, "I Still Hear the Cry," in the preceding chapter. That testimony was a written transcription of an oral account. Levi's testimony originated entirely as an act of writing. How might you expect it to differ in style and tone from the earlier account? Jot your impressions in freewritten form.

As a Jew, I was sent to Fossoli, near Modena, where a vast   1
detention camp, originally meant for English and American prisoners-of-war, collected all the numerous categories of people not approved of by the new-born Fascist Republic.

At the moment of my arrival, that is, at the end of January 1944,   2
there were about one hundred and fifty Italian Jews in the camp, but within a few weeks their number rose to over six hundred. For the most part they consisted of entire families captured by the Fascists or Nazis through their imprudence or following secret accusations. A few had given themselves up spontaneously, reduced to desperation by the

vagabond life, or because they lacked the means to survive, or to avoid separation from a captured relation, or even—absurdly—"to be in conformity with the law." There were also about a hundred Jugoslavian military internees and a few other foreigners who were politically suspect.

The arrival of a squad of German SS men should have made even the optimists doubtful; but we still managed to interpret the novelty in various ways without drawing the most obvious conclusions. Thus, despite everything, the announcement of the deportation caught us all unawares.

On 20 February, the Germans had inspected the camp with care and had publicly and loudly upbraided the Italian commissar for the defective organization of the kitchen service and for the scarce amount of wood distribution for heating; they even said that an infirmary would soon be opened. But on the morning of the 21st we learned that on the following day the Jews would be leaving. All the Jews, without exception. Even the children, even the old, even the ill. Our destination? Nobody knew. We should be prepared for a fortnight of travel. For every person missing at the roll-call, ten would be shot.

Only a minority of ingenuous and deluded souls continued to hope; we others had often spoken with the Polish and Croat refugees and we knew what departure meant.

For people condemned to death, tradition prescribes an austere ceremony, calculated to emphasize that all passions and anger have died down, and that the act of justice represents only a sad duty towards society which moves even the executioner to pity for the victim. Thus the condemned man is shielded from all external cares, he is granted solitude and, should he want it, spiritual comfort; in short, care is taken that he should feel around him neither hatred nor arbitrariness, only necessity and justice, and by means of punishment, pardon.

But to us this was not granted, for we were many and time was short. And in any case, what had we to repent, for what crime did we need pardon? The Italian commissar accordingly decreed that all services should continue to function until the final notice: the kitchens remained open, the corvées for cleaning worked as usual, and even the teachers of the little school gave lessons until the evening, as on other days. But that evening the children were given no homework.

And night came, and it was such a night that one knew that human eyes would not witness it and survive. Everyone felt this: not one of the guards, neither Italian nor German, had the courage to come and see what men do when they know they have to die.

All took leave from life in the manner which most suited them. 9
Some praying, some deliberately drunk, others lustfully intoxicated for
the last time. But the mothers stayed up to prepare the food for the
journey with tender care, and washed their children and packed the
luggage; and at dawn the barbed wire was full of children's washing
hung out in the wind to dry. Nor did they forget the diapers, the toys,
the cushions and the hundred other small things which mothers remember and which children always need. Would you not do the same?
If you and your child were going to be killed tomorrow, would you not
give him to eat today?

In hut 6A old Gattegno lived with his wife and numerous children 10
and grandchildren and his sons- and daughters-in-law. All the men were
carpenters; they had come from Tripoli after many long journeys, and
had always carried with them the tools of their trade, their kitchen
utensils and their accordions and violins to play and dance to after the
day's work. They were happy and pious folk. Their women were the
first to silently and rapidly finish the preparations for the journey in
order to have time for mourning. When all was ready, the food cooked,
the bundles tied together, they unloosened their hair, took off their
shoes, placed the Yahrzeit candles on the ground and lit them according
to the customs of their fathers, and sat on the bare soil in a circle for the
lamentations, praying and weeping all the night. We collected in a
group in front of their door, and we experienced within ourselves a grief
that was new for us, the ancient grief of the people that has no land, the
grief without hope of the exodus which is renewed every century.

Dawn came on us like a betrayer; it seemed as though the new sun 11
rose as an ally of our enemies to assist in our destruction. The different
emotions that overcame us, of resignation, of futile rebellion, of religious abandon, of fear, of despair, now joined together after a sleepless
night in a collective, uncontrolled panic. The time for meditation, the
time for decision was over, and all reason dissolved into a tumult, across
which flashed the happy memories of our homes, still so near in time
and space, as painful as the thrusts of a sword.

Many things were then said and done among us; but of these it is 12
better that there remain no memory.

With the absurd precision to which we later had to accustom our- 13
selves, the Germans held the roll-call. At the end the officer asked
"*Wieviel Stück?*" The corporal saluted smartly and replied that there

were six hundred and fifty "pieces" and that all was in order. They then loaded us on to the buses and took us to the station of Carpi. Here the train was waiting for us, with our escort for the journey. Here we received the first blows: and it was so new and senseless that we felt no pain, neither in body nor in spirit. Only a profound amazement: How can one hit a man without anger?

There were twelve goods wagons for six hundred and fifty men; in mine we were only forty-five, but it was a small wagon. Here then, before our very eyes, under our very feet, was one of those notorious transport trains, those which never return, and of which, shuddering and always a little incredulous, we had so often heard speak. Exactly like this, detail for detail: goods wagons closed from the outside, with men, women and children pressed together without pity, like cheap merchandise, for a journey towards nothingness, a journey down there, towards the bottom. This time it is us who are inside. 14

Sooner or later in life everyone discovers that perfect happiness is unrealizable, but there are few who pause to consider the antithesis: that perfect unhappiness is equally unattainable. The obstacles preventing the realization of both these extreme states are of the same nature: they derive from our human condition which is opposed to everything infinite. Our ever-insufficient knowledge of the future opposes it: and this is called, in the one instance, hope, and in the other, uncertainty of the following day. The certainty of death opposes it: for it places a limit on every joy, but also on every grief. The inevitable material cares oppose it: for as they poison every lasting happiness, they equally assiduously distract us from our misfortunes and make our consciousness of them intermittent and hence supportable. 15

It was the very discomfort, the blows, the cold, the thirst that kept us aloft in the void of bottomless despair, both during the journey and after. It was not the will to live, nor a conscious resignation: for few are the men capable of such resolution, and we were but a common sample of humanity. 16

The doors had been closed at once, but the train did not move until evening. We had learnt of our destination with relief. Auschwitz: a name without significance for us at that time, but it at least implied some place on this earth. 17

The train travelled slowly, with long, unnerving halts. Through the slit we saw the tall pale cliffs of the Adige Valley and the names of the last Italian cities disappear behind us. We passed the Brenner at 18 midday of the second day and everyone stood up, but no one said a word. The thought of the return journey stuck in my heart, and I cruelly pictured to myself the inhuman joy of that other journey, with doors open, no one wanting to flee, and the first Italian names...and I looked around and wondered how many, among that poor human dust, would be struck by fate. Among the forty-five people in my wagon only four saw their homes again; and it was by far the most fortunate wagon.

We suffered from thirst and cold; at every stop we clamoured for 19 water, or even a handful of snow, but we were rarely heard; the soldiers of the escort drove off anybody who tried to approach the convoy. Two young mothers, nursing their children, groaned night and day, begging for water. Our state of nervous tension made the hunger, exhaustion and lack of sleep seem less of a torment. But the hours of darkness were nightmares without end.

There are few men who know how to go to their deaths with dignity, 20 and often they are not those whom one would expect. Few know how to remain silent and respect the silence of others. Our restless sleep was often interrupted by noisy and futile disputes, by curses, by kicks and blows blindly delivered to ward off some encroaching and inevitable contact. Then someone would light a candle, and its mournful flicker would reveal an obscure agitation, a human mass, extended across the floor, confused and continuous, sluggish and aching, rising here and there in sudden convulsions and immediately collapsing again in exhaustion.

Through the slit, known and unknown names of Austrian cities, 21 Salzburg, Vienna, then Czech, finally Polish names. On the evening of the fourth day the cold became intense: the train ran through interminable black pine forests, climbing perceptibly. The snow was high. It must have been a branch line as the stations were small and almost deserted. During the halts, no one tried any more to communicate with the outside world: we felt ourselves by now "on the other side." There was a long halt in open country. The train started up with extreme slowness, and the convoy stopped for the last time, in the dead of night, in the middle of a dark silent plain.

On both sides of the track rows of red and white lights appeared 22 as far as the eye could see; but there was none of that confusion of sounds which betrays inhabited places even from a distance. By the wretched light of the last candle, with the rhythm of the wheels, with every human sound now silenced, we awaited what was to happen.

Next to me, crushed against me for the whole journey, there had 23 been a woman. We had known each other for many years, and the misfortune had struck us together, but we knew little of each other. Now, in the hour of decision, we said to each other things that are never said among the living. We said farewell and it was short; everybody said farewell to life through his neighbour. We had no more fear.

The climax came suddenly. The door opened with a crash, and the dark echoed with outlandish orders in that curt, barbaric barking of Germans in command which seems to give vent to a millennial anger. A vast platform appeared before us, lit up by reflectors. A little beyond it, a row of lorries. Then everything was silent again. Someone translated: we had to climb down with our luggage and deposit it alongside the train. In a moment the platform was swarming with shadows. But we were afraid to break that silence: everyone busied himself with his luggage, searched for someone else, called to somebody, but timidly, in a whisper. 24

A dozen SS men stood around, legs akimbo, with an indifferent air. At a certain moment they moved among us, and in a subdued tone of voice, with faces of stone, began to interrogate us rapidly, one by one, in bad Italian. They did not interrogate everybody, only a few: "How old? Healthy or ill?" And on the basis of the reply they pointed in two different directions. 25

Everything was as silent as an aquarium, or as in certain dream sequences. We had expected something more apocalyptic: they seemed simple police agents. It was disconcerting and disarming. Someone dared to ask for his luggage: they replied, "luggage afterwards." Someone else did not want to leave his wife: they said, "together again afterwards." Many mothers did not want to be separated from their children: they said "good, good, stay with child." They behaved with the calm assurance of people doing their normal duty of every day. But Renzo stayed an instant too long to say good-bye to Francesca, his fiancée, and with a single blow they knocked him to the ground. It was their everyday duty. 26

In less than ten minutes all the fit men had been collected together in a group. What happened to the others, to the women, to the children, to the old men, we could establish neither then nor later: the night swallowed them up, purely and simply. Today, however, we know that in that rapid and summary choice each one of us had been judged capable or not of working usefully for the Reich; we know that of our convoy no more than ninety-six men and twenty-nine women entered the respective camps of Monowitz-Buna and Birkenau, and that of all 27 the others, more than five hundred in number, not one was living two days later. We also know that not even this tenuous principle of discrimination between fit and unfit was always followed, and that later the simpler method was often adopted of merely opening both the doors of the wagon without warning or instructions to the new arrivals. Those who by chance climbed down on one side of the convoy entered the camp; the others went to the gas chamber.

This is the reason why three-year-old Emilia died: the historical 28 necessity of killing the children of Jews was self-demonstrative to the Germans. Emilia, daughter of Aldo Levi of Milan, was a curious, ambitious, cheerful, intelligent child; her parents had succeeded in washing her during the journey in the packed car in a tub with tepid water which the degenerate German engineer had allowed them to draw from the engine that was dragging us all to death.

Thus, in an instant, our women, our parents, our children disap- 29 peared. We saw them for a short while as an obscure mass at the other end of the platform; then we saw nothing more.

Instead, two groups of strange individuals emerged into the light 30 of the lamps. They walked in squads, in rows of three, with an odd, embarrassed step, head dangling in front, arms rigid. On their heads they wore comic berets and were all dressed in long striped overcoats, which even by night and from a distance looked filthy and in rags. They walked in a large circle around us, never drawing near, and in silence began to busy themselves with our luggage and to climb in and out of the empty wagons.

We looked at each other without a word. It was all incomprehen- 31 sible and mad, but one thing we had understood. This was the metamorphosis that awaited us. Tomorrow we would be like them.

Without knowing how, I found myself loaded on to a lorry with 32 thirty others; the lorry sped into the night at full speed. It was covered and we could not see outside, but by the shaking we could tell that the road had many curves and bumps. Are we unguarded? Throw ourselves down? It is too late, too late, we are all "down." In any case we are soon aware that we are not without guard. He is a strange guard, a German soldier bristling with arms. We do not see him because of the thick darkness, but we feel the hard contact every time that a lurch of the lorry throws us all in a heap. At a certain point he switches on a pocket torch and instead of shouting threats of damnation at us, he asks us courteously, one by one, in German and in pidgin language, if we have any money or watches to give him, seeing that they will not be useful to us any more. This is no order, no regulation: it is obvious that it is a small private initiative of our Charon. The matter stirs us to anger and laughter and brings relief.  ✤

## READING FOR INFORMATION

1. List the author's emotions as he names them in paragraph 11. Annotate passages in the rest of the essay where these emotions dominate the account.

2. Underline the place names mentioned in paragraphs 18 and 21. Using an atlas or map of Europe, locate these places and trace Levi's journey from Turin, Italy, to Auschwitz, Poland.

3. Summarize the narrative in paragraphs 24 to 32. What specific events does Levi recount in these paragraphs?

## READING FOR FORM, ORGANIZATION, AND EXPOSITORY FEATURES

1. Underline the beginning of passages where Levi refers to the actions of specific individuals such as the Italian commissar in paragraph 7 and old Gattegno in paragraph 10. How many vivid accounts of human behavior occur in the essay?

2. Underline particular words and phrases that refer to meanings or concepts unfamiliar to you. For example, in paragraph 13 *Wieviel Stück?* means "How many pieces?" in German, and the phrase evokes the cynicism of the Nazi officers who regard human beings as "pieces [of flesh]." In your college library ask a reference librarian how you might find information to identify the unfamiliar words or phrases that you encounter.

3. How would you describe the organizational plan of this essay? Although it follows a chronological sequence in a time-order plan, it also pauses for meditation and reflection as in paragraphs 6, 15, and 20. What is the effect of these pauses?

## READING FOR RHETORICAL CONCERNS

1. Why does the author say "it is better that there remain no memory" (paragraph 12) in the middle of an essay in which he works hard to recount his memory of traumatic events? In your own words explain his purpose for doing this.

2. What is the effect of the author's announcement in paragraph 24 that "the climax came suddenly"? Why does the author then write another

eight paragraphs before ending the essay? How do paragraphs 1 to 23 prepare for the climax?

3. What is the effect of the author's statement, "This is the reason why three-year-old Emilia died" (paragraph 28)? How does the author prepare for this sudden statement? How explicitly does he narrate the child's death?

## WRITING ASSIGNMENTS

1. In paragraph 12 Levi states that "it is better that there remain no memory," and yet he continues to write about his traumatic experience in the Auschwitz death camp. The selection here represents only a single chapter in a full-length book of testimony that he completed and published fourteen years after the events. Write an analytic essay of four pages based on the essay above in which you examine specific details in Levi's account. How might the techniques of dramatic narrative enhance the importance of the account?

2. For students who might not have read this essay, write a summary of Levi's narrative and describe its emotional effect. What philosophical attitudes does Levi evoke in his account, and how do they modify the emotion?

3. Review Alina Bacall-Zwirn's testimony of her experience in the same Auschwitz death camp, testimony that she offered thirty-five years after Levi published his. Whereas his account follows a chronological order punctuated by philosophical reflection, hers moves back and forth in its time order and keeps returning to the memory of a particular event. Write an analytical essay in which you compare and contrast the different approaches of these Holocaust victims to recounting their traumatic experience.

# A Different Mirror

## *Ronald Takaki*

*Ronald Takaki is a professor and Chair of the Department of Ethnic Studies at the University of California, Berkeley. He is the author of* Iron Cages: Race and Culture in Nineteenth-Century America *(1979),* Strangers from a Different Shore: A History of Asian Americans *(1989),* A Different Mirror *(1993),* From Different Shores: Perspectives on Race and Ethnicity in America, *and other historical studies.*

## PREREADING

In paragraph 5 of the following essay, Takaki cites an article in *Time* magazine that reports that "white Americans will become a minority group" within the next century. How might our knowledge of past history illuminate this future? What kinds of attention should historians pay to accounts about the multicultural foundation, growth, and development of the United States? How might personal narratives contribute to this history? Freewrite some responses to these questions.

## A DIFFERENT MIRROR

I had flown from San Francisco to Norfolk and was riding in a taxi to     1
my hotel to attend a conference on multiculturalism. Hundreds of educators from across the country were meeting to discuss the need for greater cultural diversity in the curriculum. My driver and I chatted about the weather and the tourists. The sky was cloudy, and Virginia Beach was twenty minutes away. The rearview mirror reflected a white man in his forties. "How long have you been in this country?" he asked. "All my life," I replied, wincing. "I was born in the United States." With a strong southern drawl, he remarked: "I was wondering because your English is excellent!" Then, as I had many times before, I explained: "My grandfather came here from Japan in the 1880s. My family has

been here, in America, for over a hundred years." He glanced at me in the mirror. Somehow I did not look "American" to him; my eyes and complexion looked foreign.

Suddenly, we both became uncomfortably conscious of a racial di-  2
vide separating us. An awkward silence turned my gaze from the mirror to the passing landscape, the shore where the English and the Powhatan Indians first encountered each other. Our highway was on land that Sir Walter Raleigh had renamed "Virginia" in honor of Eliza-beth I, the Virgin Queen. In the English cultural appropriation of America, the indigenous peoples themselves would become outsiders in their native land. Here, at the eastern edge of the continent, I mused, was the site of the beginning of multicultural America. Jamestown, the English settlement founded in 1607, was nearby: the first twenty Africans were brought here a year before the Pilgrims ar-rived at Plymouth Rock. Several hundred miles offshore was Bermuda, the "Bermoothes" where William Shakespeare's Prospero had landed and met the native Caliban in *The Tempest*. Earlier, another voyager had made an Atlantic crossing and unexpectedly bumped into some is-lands to the south. Thinking he had reached Asia, Christopher Colum-bus mistakenly identified one of the islands as "Cipango" (Japan). In the wake of the admiral, many peoples would come to America from differ-ent shores, not only from Europe but also Africa and Asia. One of them would be my grandfather. My mental wandering across terrain and time ended abruptly as we arrived at my destination. I said goodbye to my driver and went into the hotel, carrying a vivid reminder of why I was attending this conference.

Questions like the one my taxi driver asked me are always jarring,  3
but I can understand why he could not see me as American. He had a narrow but widely shared sense of the past—a history that has viewed American as European in ancestry. "Race," Toni Morrison explained, has functioned as a "metaphor" necessary to the "construction of Amer-icanness": in the creation of our national identity, "American" has been defined as "white."[1]

But America has been racially diverse since our very beginning on  4
the Virginia shore, and this reality is increasingly becoming visible and ubiquitous. Currently, one-third of the American people do not trace their origins to Europe; in California, minorities are fast becoming a majority. They already predominate in major cities across the country— New York, Chicago, Atlanta, Detroit, Philadelphia, San Francisco, and Los Angeles.

This emerging demographic diversity has raised fundamental questions about America's identity and culture. In 1990, *Time* published a cover story on "America's Changing Colors." "Someday soon," the magazine announced, "white Americans will become a minority group." How soon? By 2056, most Americans will trace their descent to "Africa, Asia, the Hispanic world, the Pacific Islands, Arabia—almost anywhere but white Europe." This dramatic change in our nation's ethnic composition is altering the way we think about ourselves. "The deeper significance of America's becoming a majority nonwhite society is what it means to the national psyche, to individuals' sense of themselves and their nation—their idea of what it is to be American."[2]

...Our diversity was tied to America's most serious crisis: the Civil War was fought over a racial issue—slavery. In his "First Inaugural Address," presented on March 4, 1861, President Abraham Lincoln declared: "One section of our country believes slavery is *right* and ought to be extended, while the other believes it is *wrong* and ought not to be extended." Southern secession, he argued, would be anarchy. Lincoln sternly warned the South that he had a solemn oath to defend and preserve the Union. Americans were one people, he explained, bound together by "the mystic chords of memory, stretching from every battlefield and patriot grave to every living heart and hearthstone all over this broad land." The struggle and sacrifices of the War for Independence had enabled Americans to create a new nation out of thirteen separate colonies. But Lincoln's appeal for unity fell on deaf ears in the South. And the war came. Two and a half years later, at Gettysburg, President Lincoln declared that "brave men" had fought and "consecrated" the ground of this battlefield in order to preserve the Union. Among the brave were black men. Shortly after this bloody battle, Lincoln acknowledged the military contributions of blacks. "There will be some black men," he wrote in a letter to an old friend, James C. Conkling, "who can remember that with silent tongue, and clenched teeth, and steady eye, and well-poised bayonet, they have helped mankind on to this great consummation. . . ." Indeed, 186,000 blacks served in the Union Army, and one-third of them were listed as missing or dead. Black men in blue, Frederick Douglass pointed out, were "on the battlefield mingling their blood with that of white men in one common effort to save the country." Now the mystic chords of memory stretched across the new battlefields of the Civil War, and black soldiers were buried in "patriot graves." They, too, had given their lives to ensure that the "government of the people, by the people, for the people shall not perish from the earth."[3]

Like these black soldiers, the people in our study have been actors   7
in history, not merely victims of discrimination and exploitation. They
are entitled to be viewed as subjects—as men and women with minds,
wills, and voices.

In the telling and retelling
    of their stories,
They create communities
    of memory.

They also re-vision history. "It is very natural that the history written by the victim," said a Mexican in 1874, "does not altogether chime
with the story of the victor." Sometimes they are hesitant to speak,
thinking they are only "little people." "I don't know why anybody wants
to hear my history," an Irish maid said apologetically in 1900. "Nothing
ever happened to me worth the tellin'."[4]

But their stories are worthy. Through their stories, the people who   8
have lived America's history can help all of us, including my taxi driver,
understand that Americans originated from many shores, and that all of
us are entitled to dignity. "I hope this survey do a lot of good for Chinese people," an immigrant told an interviewer from Stanford University in the 1920s. "Make American people realize that Chinese people
are humans. I think very few American people really know anything
about Chinese." But the remembering is also for the sake of the children. "This story is dedicated to the descendants of Lazar and Goldie
Glauberman," Jewish immigrant Minnie Miller wrote in her autobiography. "My history is bound up in their history and the generations that
follow should know where they came from to know better who they
are." Similarly, Tomo Shoji, an elderly Nisei woman, urged Asian Americans to learn more about their roots: "We got such good, fantastic stories to tell. All our stories are different." Seeking to know how they fit
into America, many young people have become listeners; they are eager
to learn about the hardships and humiliations experienced by their parents and grandparents. They want to hear their stories, unwilling to remain ignorant or ashamed of their identity and past.[5]

The telling of stories liberates. By writing about the people on   9
Mango Street, Sandra Cisneros explained, "the ghost does not ache so
much." The place no longer holds her with "both arms. She sets me
free." Indeed, stories may not be as innocent or simple as they seem to
be. Native-American novelist Leslie Marmon Silko cautioned:

> I will tell you something about stories...
> They aren't just entertainment.
>  Don't be fooled.

Indeed, the accounts given by the people in this study vibrantly recreate moments, capturing the complexities of human emotions and thoughts. They also provide the authenticity of experience. After she escaped from slavery, Harriet Jacobs wrote in her autobiography: "[My purpose] is not to tell you what I have heard but what I have seen—and what I have suffered." In their sharing of memory, the people in this study offer us an opportunity to see ourselves reflected in a mirror called history.[6]

In his recent study of Spain and the New World, *The Buried Mirror*, Carlos Fuentes points out that mirrors have been found in the tombs of ancient Mexico, placed there to guide the dead through the underworld. He also tells us about the legend of Quetzalcoatl, the Plumed Serpent: when this god was given a mirror by the Toltec deity Tezcatlipoca, he saw a man's face in the mirror and realized his own humanity. For us, the "mirror" of history can guide the living and also help us recognize who we have been and hence are. In *A Distant Mirror*, Barbara W. Tuchman finds "phenomenal parallels" between the "calamitous 14th century" of European society and our own era. We can, she observes, have "greater fellow-feeling for a distraught age" as we painfully recognize the "similar disarray," "collapsing assumptions," and "unusual discomfort."[7]

But what is needed in our own perplexing times is not so much a "distant" mirror, as one that is "different." While the study of the past can provide collective self-knowledge, it often reflects the scholar's particular perspective or view of the world. What happens when historians leave out many of America's peoples? What happens, to borrow the words of Adrienne Rich, "when someone with the authority of a teacher" describes our society, and "you are not in it"? Such an experience can be disorienting—"a moment of psychic disequilibrium, as if you looked into a mirror and saw nothing."[8]

Through their narratives about their lives and circumstances, the people of America's diverse groups are able to see themselves and each other in our common past. They celebrate what Ishmael Reed has described as a society "unique" in the world because "the world is here"—a place "where the cultures of the world crisscross." Much of America's past, they point out, has been riddled with racism. At the same time, these people offer hope, affirming the struggle for equality as a central theme in our country's history. At its conception, our nation was dedicated to the proposition of equality. What has given concreteness to this powerful national principle has been our coming together in the creation of a new society. "Stuck here" together, workers of different backgrounds have attempted to get along with each other

> People harvesting
> Work together unaware
> Of racial problems,

wrote a Japanese immigrant describing a lesson learned by Mexican and Asian farm laborers in California.[9]

Finally, how do we see our prospects for "working out" America's racial crisis? Do we see it as through a glass darkly? Do the televised images of racial hatred and violence that riveted us in 1992 during the days of rage in Los Angeles frame a future of divisive race relations— what Arthur Schlesinger, Jr., has fearfully denounced as the "disuniting of America"? Or will Americans of diverse races and ethnicities be able to connect themselves to a larger narrative? Whatever happens, we can be certain that much of our society's future will be influenced by which "mirror" we choose to see ourselves. America does not belong to one race or one group, the people in this study remind us, and Americans have been constantly redefining their national identity from the moment of first contact on the Virginia shore. By sharing their stories, they invite us to see ourselves in a different mirror.[10]

## PACIFIC CROSSINGS: SEEKING THE LAND OF MONEY TREES

During the 1890s, American society witnessed not only the Wounded Knee massacre and the end of the frontier, but also the arrival of a new group of immigrants. Unlike the Irish, the Japanese went east to America. But they, too, were pushed here by external influences. During the nineteenth century, America's expansionist thrust reached all the way across the Pacific Ocean. In 1853, Commodore Matthew C. Perry had sailed his armed naval ships into Tokyo Bay and forcefully opened Japan's doors to the West. As Japanese leaders watched Western powers colonizing China, they worried that their country would be the next victim. Thus, in 1868, they restored the Meiji emperor and established a strong centralized government. To defend Japan, they pursued a twin strategy of industrialization and militarization and levied heavy taxes to finance their program.

Bearing the burden of this taxation, farmers suffered severe eco- 15 nomic hardships during the 1880s. "The distress among the agricultural class has reached a point never before attained," the *Japan Weekly Mail* reported. "Most of the farmers have been unable to pay their taxes, and hundreds of families in one village alone have been compelled to sell their property in order to liquidate their debts." Thousands of farmers lost their lands, and hunger stalked many parts of the country. "What strikes me most is the hardships paupers are having in surviving," reported a journalist. "Their regular fare consists of rice husk or buckwheat chaff ground into powder and the dregs of bean curd mixed with leaves and grass."[11]

Searching for a way out of this terrible plight, impoverished farm- 16 ers were seized by an emigration *netsu*, or "fever." Fabulous stories of high wages stirred their imaginations. A plantation laborer in the Kingdom of Hawaii could earn six times more than in Japan; in three years, a worker might save four hundred yen—an amount equal to ten years of earnings in Japan. When the Japanese government first announced it would be filling six hundred emigrant slots for the first shipment of laborers to Hawaii, it received 28,000 applications. Stories about wages in the United States seemed even more fantastic—about a dollar a day, or more than two yen. This meant that in one year a worker could save about eight hundred yen—an amount almost equal to the income of a governor in Japan. No wonder a young man begged his parents: "By all means let me go to America." Between 1885 and 1924, 200,000 left for Hawaii and 180,000 for the United States mainland. In haiku, one Japanese migrant captured the feeling of expectation and excitement:

> Huge dreams of fortune
> Go with me to foreign lands,
> Across the ocean.

To prospective Japanese migrants, "money grew on trees" in America.[12]

## PICTURE BRIDES IN AMERICA

Initially, most of the migrants from Japan were men, but what became 17 striking about the Japanese immigration was its eventual inclusion of a significant number of women. By 1920, women represented 46 percent of the Japanese population in Hawaii and 35 percent in California. Clearly, in terms of gender, the Japanese resembled the Irish and Jews rather than the Chinese. This difference had consequences for the two Asian groups in terms of the formation of families. In 1900, fifty years after the beginning of Chinese immigration, only 5 percent were women. In this community composed mostly of "bachelors," only 4 percent were American-born. "The greatest impression I have of my childhood in those days was that there were very few families in Chinatown," a resident recalled. "Babies were looked on with a kind of wonder." On the other hand, in 1930, 52 percent of the Japanese population had been born in America. But why did proportionately more women emigrate from Japan than China?[13]

Unlike China, Japan was ruled by a strong central government that was able to regulate emigration. Prospective immigrants were required to apply to the government for permission to leave for the United States and were screened by review boards to certify that they were healthy and literate and would creditably "maintain Japan's national honor." Japan had received reports about the Chinese in America and was determined to monitor the quality of its emigrants. Seeking to avoid the problems of prostitution, gambling, and drunkenness that reportedly plagued the predominantly male Chinese community in the United States, the Japanese government promoted female emigration. The 1882 Chinese Exclusion Act prohibited the entry of "laborers," both men and women, but militarily strong Japan was able to negotiate the 1908 Gentlemen's Agreement. While this treaty prohibited the entry of Japanese "laborers," it allowed Japanese women to emigrate to the United States as family members.[14]

Through this opening in immigration policy came over sixty thousand women, many as "picture brides." The picture bride system was based on the established custom of arranged marriage. In Japanese society, marriage was not an individual matter but rather a family concern, and parents consulted go-betweens to help them select partners for their sons and daughters. In situations involving families located far away, the prospective bride and groom would exchange photographs before the initial meeting. This traditional practice lent itself readily to the needs of Japanese migrants. "When I told my parents about my desire to go to a foreign land, the story spread throughout the town," picture bride Ai Miyasaki later recalled. "From here and there requests for marriage came pouring in just like rain!" Similarly, Riyo Orite had a "picture marriage." Her marriage to a Japanese man in America had

been arranged through a relative. "All agreed to our marriage, but I
didn't get married immediately," she recalled. "I was engaged at the age
of sixteen and didn't meet Orite until I was almost eighteen. I had seen
him only in a picture at first. . . . Being young, I was unromantic. I just
believed that girls should get married. I felt he was a little old, about
thirty, but the people around me praised the match. His brother in
Tokyo sent me a lot of beautiful pictures [taken in the United States]. . . .
My name was entered in the Orites' *koseki* [family register]. Thus we
were married."[15]

The emigration of Japanese women occurred within the context of 20
internal economic developments. While women in China were re-
stricted to farm and home, Japanese women were increasingly entering
the wage-earning work force. Thousands of them were employed in
construction work as well as in the coal mines where they carried heavy
loads on their backs out of the tunnels. Young women were leaving
their family farms for employment in textile mills where they worked
sixteen-hour shifts and lived in dormitories. By 1900, 60 percent of
Japan's industrial laborers were women. While it is not known how
many of the women who emigrated had been wage-earners, this proletarianization of women already well under way in Japan paved the way
for such laborers to consider working in America.[16]

Japanese women were also more receptive to the idea of traveling 21
overseas than Chinese women. The Meiji government required the education of female children, stipulating that "girls should be educated . . .
alongside boys." Emperor Meiji himself promoted female education.
Japanese boys as well as girls, he declared, should learn about foreign
countries and become enlightened about the world. Female education
included reading and writing skills as well as general knowledge. Japanese women, unlike their Chinese counterparts, were more likely to be
literate. "We studied English and Japanese, mathematics, literature,
writing, and religion," recalled Michiko Tanaka. Under the reorganiza-
tion of the school system in 1876, English was adopted as a major subject in middle school. This education exposed Japanese women to the
outside world. They also heard stories describing America as "heav-
enly," and some of the picture brides were more eager to see the new
land than to meet their husbands. "I wanted to see foreign countries
and besides I had consented to marriage with Papa because I had the
dream of seeing America," Michiko Tanaka revealed to her daughter
years later. "I wanted to see America and Papa was a way to get there."
"I was bubbling over with great expectations," said another picture

bride. "My young heart, 19 years and 8 months old, burned, not so much with the prospects of reuniting with my new husband, but with the thought of the New World."[17]

The emigration of women was also influenced by Japanese views [22] on gender. A folk saying popular among farmers recommended that a family should have three children: "One to sell, one to follow, and one in reserve." The "one to sell" was the daughter. Of course, this was meant only figuratively: she was expected to marry and enter her husband's family. "Once you become someone's wife you belong to his family," explained Tsuru Yamauchi. "My parents said once I went over to be married, I should treat his parents as my own and be good to them." One day, Yamauchi was told that she would be going to Hawaii to join her future husband: "I learned about the marriage proposal when we had to exchange pictures." Emigration for her was not a choice but an obligation to her husband.[18]

Whether a Japanese woman went to America depended on which [23] son she married—the son "to follow" or the son "in reserve." Unlike the Chinese, Japanese farmers had an inheritance system based on impartible inheritance and primogeniture. Only one of the sons in the family, usually the eldest, inherited the family's holdings: he was the son who was expected "to follow" his father. In the mountainous island nation of Japan, arable land was limited, and most of the farm holdings were small, less than two and a half acres. Division of a tiny family holding would mean disaster for the family. As the possessor of the family farm, the eldest son had the responsibility of caring for his aged parents and hence had to stay home. The second or noninheriting son—the one held "in reserve" in case something happened to the first son—had to leave the family farm and find employment in town. This practice of relocating within Japan could easily be applied to movement abroad. Thus, although the migrants included first sons, they tended to be the younger sons. Unlike Chinese sons who had to share responsibility for their parents, these Japanese men were not as tightly bound to their parents and were allowed to take their wives and children with them to distant lands.[19]

But whether or not women migrated was also influenced by the [24] needs in the receiving countries. In Hawaii, the government initially stipulated that 40 percent of the Japanese contract labor emigrants—laborers under contract to work for three years—were to be women. During the government-sponsored contract labor period from 1885 to 1894, women constituted 20 percent of the emigrants. During the period from 1894 to 1908, thousands of additional women sailed to Hawaii as private contract laborers. Planters viewed Japanese women as workers and assigned 72 percent of them to field labor. Furthermore, they promoted the Japanese family as a mechanism of labor control. In 1886, Hawaii's inspector-general of immigration reported that Japanese men were better workers on plantations where they had their wives: "Several of the planters are desirous that each man should have his wife." After 1900, when Hawaii became a territory of the United States, planters became even more anxious to bring Japanese women to Hawaii. Since the American law prohibiting contract labor now applied to the islands, planters had to find ways to stabilize their labor force. Realizing that men with families were more likely to stay on the plantations, managers asked their business agents in Honolulu to send "men with families."[20]

Meanwhile, Japanese women were pulled to the United States 25 mainland where they were needed as workers by their husbands. Shopkeepers and farmers sent for their wives, thinking they could assist as unpaid family labor. Wives were particularly useful on farms where production was labor intensive. "Nearly all of these tenant farmers are married and have their families with them," a researcher noted in 1915. "The wives do much work in the fields."[21]

As they prepared to leave their villages for Hawaii and America, 26 many of these women felt separation anxieties. One woman remembered her husband's brother saying farewell: "Don't stay in the [United] States too long. Come back in five years and farm with us." But her father quickly remarked: "Are you kidding? They can't learn anything in five years. They'll even have a baby over there. . . . Be patient for twenty years." Her father's words shocked her so much that she could not control her tears: suddenly she realized how long the separation could be. Another woman recalled the painful moment she experienced when her parents came to see her off: "They did not join the crowd, but quietly stood in front of the wall. They didn't say 'good luck,' or 'take care,' or anything. . . . They couldn't say anything because they knew, as I did, that I would never return." As their ships sailed from the harbor many women gazed at the diminishing shore:

> With tears in my eyes
> I turn back to my homeland,
> Taking one last look.[22]

## NOTES

1. Toni Morrison, *Playing in the Dark: Whiteness in the Literary Imagination* (Cambridge, Mass., 1992), p. 47.
2. William A. Henry III, "Beyond the Melting Pot," in "America's Changing Colors," *Time*, vol. 135, no. 15 (April 9, 1990), pp. 28–31.
3. Abraham Lincoln, "First Inaugural Address," in *The Annals of America*, vol. 9, *1863–1865; The Crisis of the Union* (Chicago, 1968), p. 255; Lincoln, "The Gettysburg Address," pp. 462–463; Abraham Lincoln, letter to James C. Conkling, August 26, 1863, in *Annals of America*, p. 439; Frederick Douglass, in Herbert Aptheker (ed.), *A Documentary History of the Negro People in the United States* (New York, 1951), vol. 1, p. 496.
4. Weber (ed.), *Foreigners in Their Native Land*, p. vi; Hamilton Holt (ed.), *The Life Stories of Undistinguished Americans as Told by Themselves* (New York, 1906), p. 143.
5. "Social Document of Pany Lowe, interviewed by C. H. Burnett, Seattle, July 5, 1924," p. 6, Survey of Race Relations, Stanford University, Hoover Institution Archives; Minnie Miller, "Autobiography," private manuscript, copy from Richard Balkin; Tomo Shoji, presentation, Ohana Cultural Center, Oakland, California, March 4, 1988.
6. Sandra Cisneros, *The House on Mango Street* (New York, 1991), pp. 109–110; Leslie Marmon Silko, *Ceremony* (New York, 1978), p. 2; Harriet A. Jacobs, *Incidents in the Life of a Slave Girl, written by herself* (Cambridge, Mass., 1987; originally published in 1857), p. xiii.
7. Carlos Fuentes, *The Buried Mirror: Reflections on Spain and the New World* (Boston, 1992), pp. 10, 11, 109; Barbara W. Tuchman, *A Distant Mirror: The Calamitous 14th Century* (New York, 1978), p. xiii, xiv.
8. Adrienne Rich, *Blood, Bread, and Poetry: Selected Prose, 1979–1985* (New York, 1986), p. 199.
9. Ishmael Reed, "America: The Multinational Society," in Rick Simonson and Scott Walker (Eds.), *Multi-cultural Literacy* (St. Paul, 1988), p. 160; Ito, *Issei*, p. 497.
10. Arthur M. Schlesinger, Jr., *The Disuniting of America: Reflections on a Multicultural Society* (Knoxville, Tenn., 1991); Carlos Bulosan, *America Is in the Heart: A Personal History* (Seattle, 1981), pp. 188–189.
11. *Japan Weekly Mail*, December 20, 1884, reprinted in Nippu Jiji, *Golden Jubilee of the Japanese in Hawaii, 1885–1935* (Honolulu, 1935), n.p.; Yuji Ichioka, *The Issei: The World of the First Generation Japanese Immigrants, 1885–1924* (New York, 1988), p. 45. Ichioka's is the best book on the subject.
12. Kazuo Ito, *Issei: A History of the Japanese Immigrants in North America* (Seattle, 1973), pp. 27, 38, 29. Ito's study is a massive and wonderful compilation of stories, oral histories, and poems. It is indispensable.
13. Victor and Brett de Bary Nee, *Longtime Californ': A Documentary Study of an American Chinatown* (New York, 1972), p. 148.
14. Robert Wilson and Bill Hosokawa, *East to America: A History of the Japanese in the United States* (New York, 1980), pp. 47, 113–114.
15. Eileen Sunada Sarasohn (ed.), *The Issei: Portrait of a Pioneer, An Oral History* (Palo Alto, Calif., 1983), pp. 44, 31–32.
16. Thomas C. Smith, *Nakahara: Family Farming and Population in a Japanese Village, 1717–1830* (Stanford, Calif., 1977), pp. 134, 152, 153; Sheila Matsumoto, "Women in Factories," in Joyce Lebra *et al.* (eds.), *Women in Changing Japan* (Boulder, Colo., 1976), pp. 51–53; Sharon L. Sievers, *Flowers in Salt: The Beginnings of Feminist Consciousness in Modern Japan* (Stanford, Calif., 1983), pp. 55, 62, 66, 84; Yukiko Hanawa, "The Several Worlds of Issei Women," unpublished M.A. thesis, California State University, Long Beach, 1982, pp. 31–34; Yasuo Wakatsuki, "Japanese

Emigration to the United States, 1866–1924," *Perspectives in American History*, vol. 12 (1979), pp. 401, 404; Wilson and Hosokawa, *East to America*, p. 42.

17. Hanawa, "Several Worlds," pp. 13–16; Susan McCoin Kataoka, "Issei Women: A Study in Subordinate Status," unpublished Ph.D. thesis, University of California, Los Angeles, 1977, p. 6; Akemi Kikumura, *Through Harsh Winters: The Life of a Japanese Immigrant Woman* (Novato, Calif., 1981), pp. 18, 25; Emma Gee, "Issei: The First Women," in Emma Gee (ed.), *Asian Women* (Berkeley, Calif., 1971), p. 11.

18. Tsuru Yamauchi is quoted in Ethnic Studies Oral History Project (ed.), *Uchinanchu: A History of Okinawans in Hawaii* (Honolulu, 1981), pp. 490, 491; the folk saying can be found in Tadashi Fukutake, *Japanese Rural Society* (Ithaca, N.Y., 1967), p. 47.

19. Fukutake, *Japanese Rural Society*, pp. 6, 7, 39, 40, 42; Victor Nee and Herbert Y. Wong, "Asian American Socioeconomic Achievement: The Strength of the Family Bond," *Sociological Perspectives*, vol. 28, no. 3 (July 1985), p. 292.

20. Katherine Coman, *The History of Contract Labor in the Hawaiian Islands* (New York, 1903), p. 42; Allan Moriyama, "Causes of Emigration: The Background of Japanese Emigration to Hawaii, 1885–1894," in Edna Bonacich and Lucie Cheng (eds.), *Labor Immigration under Capitalism: Asian Workers in the United States before World War II* (Berkeley, Calif., 1984), p. 273; Republic of Hawaii, Bureau of Immigration, *Report* (Honolulu, 1886), p. 256; manager of the Hutchinson Sugar Company to W. G. Irwin and Company, February 5, 1902, and January 25, 1905, Hutchinson Plantation Records; for terms of the Gentlemen's Agreement, see Frank Chuman, *The Bamboo People: The Law and Japanese-Americans* (Del Mar, Calif., 1976), pp. 35–36.

21. H. A. Millis, *The Japanese Problem in the United States* (New York, 1915), p. 86.

22. Sarasohn (ed.), *Issei*, p. 34; Yuriko Sato, "Emigration of Issei Women" (Berkeley, 1982), in the Asian American Studies Library, University of California, Berkeley; Ito, *Issei*, p. 34.  ✿

## READING FOR INFORMATION

1. In paragraph 6, Takaki refers to the American Civil War as a struggle "to defend and preserve the Union." Summarize the ideas about "union" that motivate his discussion. What use does Takaki make of Lincoln's phrase "the mystic chords of memory"?

2. List features of Japanese history in paragraphs 14 and 15 that Takaki regards as important for understanding patterns of Japanese emigration to America.

3. Summarize Japanese views on gender that Takaki discusses in paragraphs 22 and 23 as they bear upon the history of Japanese emigration. How do Takaki's stories about "picture brides" relate to those views?

## READING FOR FORM, ORGANIZATION, AND EXPOSITORY FEATURES

1. List the immigrant groups that Takaki mentions in paragraphs 6 to 8. Could you add other groups to this list? Why does Takaki propose that their stories are worth telling?

2. Describe the use that Takaki makes of statistics in paragraph 17. How does he interpret them to fashion an account of distinctive features about Japanese immigration?

3. Summarize the contrasts between Chinese and Japanese patterns of immigration that Takaki develops in paragraphs 18 and 20. Describe the major features of this contrast.

## READING FOR RHETORICAL CONCERNS

1. Explain why Takaki begins his essay in paragraphs 1 and 2 with a personal account of his conversation with a taxicab driver. How does that account color his scholarly presentation of historical materials in the rest of the essay?

2. In paragraphs 10 and 11, Takaki cites two recent books with *Mirror* in their titles and suggests that his use of the world will differ from theirs. Explain how it differs. What role does he attribute to the idea of "mirroring" in the study of history?

3. Paraphrase Takaki's discussion of the family as a "mechanism of labor control" in paragraph 24. Describe Takaki's attitude toward that development.

## WRITING ASSIGNMENTS

1. Write an argumentative essay about how American history should record patterns of racial diversity since the beginning. Reflect upon your own racial roots and comment upon how they are represented in American history.

2. Write a comparison and contrast essay drawing points of similarity and difference between Takaki's case history of Japanese picture brides and the case history of women in some other immigrant group who arrived in America with expectations of marrying and raising a family.

# Jasmine

### *Bharati Mukherjee*

*Bharati Mukherjee was born in Calcutta and currently teaches English at the University of California, Berkeley. She has published many short stories, four novels, including* The Tiger's Daughter *(1972),* Darkness *(1985),* Jasmine *(1989), and* The Holder of the World *(1993); and two works of nonfiction written with her husband, Clark Blaise,* Days and Nights in Calcutta *(1977) and* The Sorrow and Terror *(1987).*

## PREREADING

Inquire at the reference desk of your college library to obtain a copy of the Immigration Reform and Control Act of 1986. Designed to restrict the flow of illegal immigrants into the United States, it imposes harsh penalties on employers who knowingly hire undocumented aliens. Read its provisions, and freewrite on some of the likely consequences of this act, including subtle and sometimes blatant racism, economic hardships, and class tensions.

Jasmine came to Detroit from Port-of-Spain, Trinidad, by way   1
of Canada. She crossed the border at Windsor in the back of a gray van loaded with mattresses and box springs. The plan was for her to hide in an empty mattress box if she heard the driver say, "All bad weather seems to come down from Canada, doesn't it?" to the customs man. But she didn't have to crawl into a box and hold her breath. The customs man didn't ask to look in.

The driver let her off at a scary intersection on Woodward Avenue   2
and gave her instructions on how to get to the Plantations Motel in Southfield. The trick was to keep changing vehicles, he said. That threw off the immigration guys real quick.

Jasmine took money for cab fare out of the pocket of the great big   3
raincoat that the van driver had given her. The raincoat looked like something that nuns in Port-of-Spain sold in church bazaars. Jasmine

was glad to have a coat with wool lining, though; and anyway, who would know in Detroit that she was Dr. Vassanji's daughter?

All the bills in her hand looked the same. She would have to be  4 careful when she paid the cabdriver. Money in Detroit wasn't pretty the way it was back home, or even in Canada, but she liked this money better. Why should money be pretty, like a picture? Pretty money is only good for putting on your walls maybe. The dollar bills felt businesslike, serious. Back home at work, she used to count out thousands of Trinidad dollars every day and not even think of them as real. Real money was worn and green, American dollars. Holding the bills in her fist on a street corner meant she had made it in okay. She'd outsmarted the guys at the border. Now it was up to her to use her wits to do something with her life. As her Daddy kept saying, "Girl, is opportunity come only once." The girls she'd worked with at the bank in Port-of-Spain had gone green as bananas when she'd walked in with her ticket on Air Canada. Trinidad was too tiny. That was the trouble. Trinidad was an island stuck in the middle of nowhere. What kind of place was that for a girl with ambition?

The Plantations Motel was run by a family of Trinidad Indians  5 who had come from the tuppenny-ha'penny country town, Chaguanas. The Daboos were nobodies back home. They were lucky, that's all. They'd gotten here before the rush and bought up a motel and an ice cream parlor. Jasmine felt very superior when she saw Mr. Daboo in the motel's reception area. He was a pumpkin-shaped man with very black skin and Elvis Presley sideburns turning white. They looked like earmuffs. Mrs. Daboo was a bumpkin, too; short, fat, flapping around in house slippers. The Daboo daughters seemed very American, though. They didn't seem to know that they were nobodies, and kept looking at her and giggling.

She knew she would be short of cash for a great long while. Be-  6 sides, she wasn't sure she wanted to wear bright leather boots and leotards like Viola and Loretta. The smartest move she could make would be to put a down payment on a husband. Her Daddy had told her to talk to the Daboos first chance. The Daboos ran a service fixing up illegals with islanders who had made it in legally. Daddy had paid three thousand back in Trinidad, with the Daboos and the mattress man getting part of it. They should throw in a good-earning husband for that kind of money.

The Daboos asked her to keep books for them and to clean the  7 rooms in the new wing, and she could stay in 16B as long as she liked.

They showed her 16B. They said she could cook her own roti; Mr. Daboo would bring in a stove, two gas rings that you could fold up in a metal box. The room was quite grand, Jasmine thought. It had a double bed, a TV, a pink sink and matching bathtub. Mrs. Daboo said Jasmine wasn't the big-city Port-of-Spain type she'd expected. Mr. Daboo said that he wanted her to stay because it was nice to have a neat, cheerful person around. It wasn't a bad deal, better than stories she'd heard about Trinidad girls in the States.

All day every day except Sundays Jasmine worked. There wasn't  8 just the bookkeeping and the cleaning up. Mr. Daboo had her working on the match-up marriage service. Jasmine's job was to check up on social security cards, call clients' bosses for references, and make sure credit information wasn't false. Dermatologists and engineers living in Bloomfield Hills, store owners on Canfield and Woodward: she treated them all as potential liars. One of the first things she learned was that Ann Arbor was a magic word. A boy goes to Ann Arbor and gets an education, and all the barriers come crashing down. So Ann Arbor was the place to be.

She didn't mind the work. She was learning about Detroit, every  9 side of it. Sunday mornings she helped unload packing crates of Caribbean spices in a shop on the next block. For the first time in her life, she was working for a black man, an African. So what if the boss was black? This was a new life, and she wanted to learn everything. Her Sunday boss, Mr. Anthony, was a courtly, Christian, church-going man, and paid her the only wages she had in her pocket. Viola and Loretta, for all their fancy American ways, wouldn't go out with blacks.

One Friday afternoon she was writing up the credit info on a  10 Guyanese Muslim who worked in an assembly plant when Loretta said that enough was enough and that there was no need for Jasmine to be her father's drudge.

"Is time to have fun," Viola said. "We're going to Ann Arbor."

Jasmine filed the sheet on the Guyanese man who probably now  11 would never get a wife and got her raincoat. Loretta's boyfriend had a Cadillac parked out front. It was the longest car Jasmine had ever been in and louder than a country bus. Viola's boyfriend got out of the front seat. "Oh, oh, sweet things," he said to Jasmine. "Get in front." He was a talker. She'd learned that much from working on the matrimonial match-ups. She didn't believe him for a second when he said that there were dudes out there dying to ask her out.

Loretta's boyfriend said, "You have eyes I could leap into, girl."    12

Jasmine knew he was just talking. They sounded like Port-of-Spain 13
boys of three years ago. It didn't surprise her that these Trinidad country boys in Detroit were still behind the times, even of Port-of-Spain.
She sat very stiff between the two men, hands on her purse. The Daboo
girls laughed in the back seat.

On the highway the girls told her about the reggae night in Ann 14
Arbor. Kevin and the Krazee Islanders. Malcolm's Lovers. All the big
reggae groups in the Midwest were converging for the West Indian Students Association fall bash. The ticket didn't come cheap but Jasmine
wouldn't let the fellows pay. She wasn't that kind of girl.

The reggae and steel drums brought out the old Jasmine. The rum 15
punch, the dancing, the dreadlocks, the whole combination. She hadn't
heard real music since she got to Detroit, where music was supposed to
be so famous. The Daboos girls kept turning on rock stuff in the motel
lobby whenever their father left the area. She hadn't danced, really
*danced*, since she'd left home. It felt so good to dance. She felt hot and
sweaty and sexy. The boys at the dance were more than sweet talkers;
they moved with assurance and spoke of their futures in America. The
bartender gave her two free drinks and said, "Is ready when you are,
girl." She ignored him but she felt all hot and good deep inside. She
knew Ann Arbor was a special place.

When it was time to pile back into Loretta's boyfriend's Cadillac, 16
she just couldn't face going back to the Plantations Motel and to the
Daboos with their accounting books and messy files.

"I don't know what happen, girl," she said to Loretta. "I feel all
crazy inside. Maybe is time for me to pursue higher studies in this
town."

"This Ann Arbor, girl, they don't just take you off the street. It *cost*
like hell."

She spent the night on a bashed-up sofa in the Student Union. 17
She was a well-dressed, respectable girl, and she didn't expect anyone
to question her right to sleep on the furniture. Many others were doing
the same thing. In the morning, a boy in an army parka showed her the
way to the Placement Office. He was a big, blond, clumsy boy, not bad-
looking except for the blond eyelashes. He didn't scare her, as did most
Americans. She let him buy her a Coke and a hotdog. That evening she
had a job with the Moffits.

Bill Moffitt taught molecular biology and Lara Hatch-Moffitt, his 18
wife, was a performance artist. A performance artist, said Lara, was very
different from being an actress, though Jasmine still didn't understand

what the difference might be. The Moffitts had a little girl, Muffin, whom Jasmine was to look after, though for the first few months she might have to help out with the housework and the cooking because Lara said she was deep into performance rehearsals. That was all right with her, Jasmine said, maybe a little too quickly. She explained she came from a big family and was used to heavy-duty cooking and cleaning. This wasn't the time to say anything about Ram, the family servant. Americans like the Moffitts wouldn't understand about keeping servants. Ram and she weren't in similar situations. Here mother's helpers, which is what Lara called her—Americans were good with words to cover their shame—seemed to be as good as anyone.

Lara showed her the room she would have all to herself in the fin- 19 ished basement. There was a big, old TV, not in color like the motel's, and a portable typewriter on a desk which Lara said she would find handy when it came time to turn in her term papers. Jasmine didn't say anything about not being a student. She was a student of life, wasn't she? There was a scary moment after they'd discussed what she would expect as salary, which was three times more than anything Mr. Daboo was supposed to pay her but hadn't. She thought Bill Moffitt was going to ask her about her visa or her green card number and social security. But all Bill did was smile and smile at her—he had a wide, pink, baby face—and play with a button on his corduroy jacket. The button would need sewing back on, firmly.

Lara said, "I think I'm going to like you, Jasmine. You have a 20 something about you. A something real special. I'll just bet you've acted, haven't you?" The idea amused her, but she merely smiled and accepted Lara's hug. The interview was over.

Then Bill opened a bottle of Soave and told stories about camping 21 in northern Michigan. He'd been raised there. Jasmine didn't see the point in sleeping in tents; the woods sounded cold and wild and creepy. But she said, "Is exactly what I want to try out come summer, man. Campin and huntin."

Lara asked about Port-of-Spain. There was nothing to tell about 22 her hometown that wouldn't shame her in front of nice white American folk like the Moffitts. The place was shabby, the people were grasping and cheating and lying and life was full of despair and drink and wanting. But by the time she finished, the island sounded romantic. Lara said, "It wouldn't surprise me one bit if you were a writer, Jasmine."

Ann Arbor was a huge small town. She couldn't imagine any kind 23 of school the size of the University of Michigan. She meant to sign up for courses in the spring. Bill brought home a catalogue bigger than the phonebook for all of Trinidad. The university had courses in everything. It would be hard to choose; she'd have to get help from Bill. He wasn't like a professor, not the ones back home where even high school teachers called themselves professors and acted like little potentates. He wore blue jeans and thick sweaters with holes in the elbows and used phrases like "in vitro" as he watched her curry up fish. Dr. Parveen back home—he called himself "doctor" when everybody knew he didn't have even a Master's degree—was never seen without his cotton jacket which had gotten really ratty at the cuffs and lapel edges. She hadn't learned anything in the two years she'd put into college. She'd learned more from working in the bank for two months than she had at college. It was the assistant manager, Personal Loans Department, Mr. Singh, who had turned her on to the Daboos and to smooth, bargain-priced emigration.

Jasmine liked Lara. Lara was easygoing. She didn't spend the time 24 she had between rehearsals telling Jasmine how to cook and clean American-style. Mrs. Daboo did that in 16B. Mrs. Daboo would barge in with a plate of stale samosas and snoop around giving free advice on how mainstream Americans did things. As if she were dumb or something! As if she couldn't keep her own eyes open and make her mind up for herself. Sunday mornings she had to share the butcher-block workspace in the kitchen with Bill. He made the Sunday brunch from new recipes in *Gourmet* and *Cuisine*. Jasmine hadn't seen a man cook who didn't have to or wasn't getting paid to do it. Things were topsy-turvy in the Moffitt house. Lara went on two- and three-day road trips and Bill stayed home. But even her Daddy, who'd never poured himself a cup of tea, wouldn't put Bill down as a woman. The mornings Bill tried out something complicated, a Cajun shrimp, sausage, and beans dish, for instance, Jasmine skipped church services. The Moffitts didn't go to church, though they seemed to be good Christians. They just didn't talk church talk, which suited her fine.

Two months passed. Jasmine knew she was lucky to have found a 25 small, clean, friendly family like the Moffitts to build her new life around. "Man!" she'd exclaim as she vacuumed the wide-plank wood floors or ironed (Lara wore pure silk or pure cotton). "In this country Jesus givin out good luck only!" By this time they knew she wasn't a student, but they didn't care and said they wouldn't report her. They never asked if she was illegal on top of it.

To savor her new sense of being a happy, lucky person, she would 26 put herself through a series of "what ifs": what if Mr. Singh in Port-of-

Spain hadn't turned her on to the Daboos and loaned her two thousand! What if she'd been ugly like the Mintoo girl and the manager hadn't even offered! What if the customs man had unlocked the door of the van! Her Daddy liked to say, "You is a helluva girl, Jasmine."

"Thank you, Jesus," Jasmine said, as she carried on.

Christmas Day the Moffitts treated her just like family. They gave 27 her a red cashmere sweater with a V neck so deep it made her blush. If Lara had worn it, her bosom wouldn't hang out like melons. For the holiday weekend Bill drove her to the Daboos in Detroit. "You work too hard," Bill said to her. "Learn to be more selfish. Come on, throw your weight around." She'd rather not have spent time with the Daboos, but that first afternoon of the interview she'd told Bill and Lara that Mr. Daboo was her mother's first cousin. She had thought it shameful in those days to have no papers, no family, no roots. Now Loretta and Viola in tight, bright pants seemed trashy like girls at Two-Johnny Bissoondath's Bar back home. She was stuck with the story of the Daboos being family. Village bumpkins, ha! She would break out. Soon.

Jasmine had Bill drop her off at the RenCen. The Plantations 28 Motel, in fact, the whole Riverfront area, was too seamy. She'd managed to cut herself off mentally from anything too islandy. She loved her Daddy and Mummy, but she didn't think of them that often anymore. Mummy had expected her to be homesick and come flying right back home. "Is blowin sweat-of-brow money is what you doing, Pa," Mummy had scolded. She loved them, but she'd become her own person. That was something that Lara said: "I am my own person."

The Daboos acted thrilled to see her back. "What you drinkin, Jas- 29 mine girl?" Mr. Daboo kept asking. "You drinkin sherry or what?" Pouring her little glasses of sherry instead of rum was a sure sign he thought she had become whitefolk-fancy. The Daboo sisters were very friendly, but Jasmine considered them too wild. Both Loretta and Viola had changed boyfriends. Both were seeing black men they'd danced with in Ann Arbor. Each night at bedtime, Mr. Daboo cried. "In Trinidad we stayin we side, they stayin they side. Here, everything mixed up. Is helluva confusion, no?"

On New Year's Eve the Daboo girls and their black friends went to 30 a dance. Mr. and Mrs. Daboo and Jasmine watched TV for a while. Then Mr. Daboo got out a brooch from his pocket and pinned it on Jasmine's red sweater. It was a Christmasy brooch, a miniature sleigh loaded down with snowed-on mistletoe. Before she could pull away, he kissed her on the lips. "Good luck for the New Year!" he said. She lifted her head and saw tears. "Is year for dreams comin true."

Jasmine started to cry, too. There was nothing wrong, but Mr. 31
Daboo, Mrs. Daboo, she, everybody was crying.

What for? This is where she wanted to be. She'd spent some 32
damned uncomfortable times with the assistant manager to get approval for her loan. She thought of Daddy. He would be playing poker
and fanning himself with a magazine. Her married sisters would be
rolling out the dough for stacks and stacks of roti, and Mummy would
be steamed purple from stirring the big pot of goat curry on the stove.
She missed them. But. It felt strange to think of anyone celebrating
New Year's Eve in summery clothes.

In March Lara and her performing group went on the road. Jas- 33
mine knew that the group didn't work from scripts. The group didn't
use a stage, either; instead, it took over supermarkets, senior citizens'
centers, and school halls, without notice. Jasmine didn't understand the
performance world. But she was glad that Lara said, "I'm not going to
lay a guilt trip on myself. Muffie's in super hands," before she left.

Muffie didn't need much looking after. She played Trivial Pursuit 34
all day, usually pretending to be two persons, sometimes Jasmine, whose
accent she could imitate. Since Jasmine didn't know any of the answers,
she couldn't help. Muffie was a quiet, precocious child with see-through
blue eyes like her dad's, and red braids. In the early evenings Jasmine
cooked supper, something special she hadn't forgotten from her island
days. After supper she and Muffie watched some TV, and Bill read.
When Muffie went to bed, Bill and she sat together for a bit with their
glasses of Soave. Bill, Muffie, and she were a family, almost.

Down in her basement room that late, dark winter, she had trou- 35
ble sleeping. She wanted to stay awake and think of Bill. Even when she
fell asleep it didn't feel like sleep because Bill came barging into her
dreams in his funny, loose-jointed, clumsy way. It was mad to think of
him all the time, and stupid and sinful; but she couldn't help it. Whenever she put back a book he'd taken off the shelf to read or whenever
she put his clothes through the washer and dryer, she felt sick in a
giddy, wonderful way. When Lara came back things would get back to
normal. Meantime she wanted the performance group miles away.

Lara called in at least twice a week. She said things like, "We've fi- 36
nally obliterated the margin between realspace and performancespace."
Jasmine filled her in on Muffie's doings and the mail. Bill always closed
with, "I love you. We miss you, hon."

One night after Lara had called—she was in Lincoln, Nebraska— 37
Bill said to Jasmine, "Let's dance."

She hadn't danced since the reggae night she'd had too many rum 38
punches. Her toes began to throb and clench. She untied her apron and
the fraying, knotted-up laces of her running shoes.

Bill went around the downstairs rooms turning down lights. "We 39
need atmosphere," he said. He got a small, tidy fire going in the living
room grate and pulled the Turkish scatter rug closer to it. Lara didn't
like anybody walking on the Turkish rug, but Bill meant to have his way.
The hissing logs, the plants in the dimmed light, the thick patterned rug:
everything was changed. This wasn't the room she cleaned every day.

He stood close to her. She smoothed her skirt down with both 40
hands.

"I want you to choose the record," he said.

"I don't know your music."

She brought her hand high to his face. His skin was baby smooth.

"I want *you* to pick," he said. "You are your own person now."

"You got island music?"

He laughed, "What do you think?" The stereo was in a cabinet 41
with albums packed tight alphabetically into the bottom three shelves.
"Calypso has not been a force in my life."

She couldn't help laughing. "Calypso? Oh, man." She pulled dust 42
jackets out at random. Lara's records. The Flying Lizards. The Violent
Fems. There was so much still to pick up on!

"This one," she said finally.

He took the record out of her hand. "God!" he laughed. "Lara 43
must have found this in a garage sale!" He laid the old record on the
turntable. It was "Music for Lovers," something the nuns had taught
her to fox-trot to way back in Port-of-Spain.

They danced so close that she could feel his heart heaving and 44
crashing against her head. She liked it, she liked it very much. She
didn't care what happened.

"Come on," Bill whispered. "If it feels right, do it." He began to
take her clothes off.

"Don't Bill," she pleaded.

"Come on, baby," he whispered again. "You're a blossom, a
flower."

He took off his fisherman's knit pullover, the corduroy pants, the 45
blue shorts. She kept pace. She'd never had such an effect on a man. He
nearly flung his socks and Adidas into the fire. "You feel so good," he
said. "You smell so good. You're really something, flower of Trinidad."

"Flower of Ann Arbor," she said, "not Trinidad."

She felt so good she was dizzy. She'd never felt this good on the is-  46
land where men did this all the time, and girls went along with it always
for favors. You couldn't feel really good in a nothing place. She was
thinking this as they made love on the Turkish carpet in front of the
fire: she was a bright, pretty girl with no visa, no papers, and no birth
certificate. No nothing other than what she wanted to invent and tell.
She was a girl rushing wildly into the future.

His hand moved up her throat and forced her lips apart and it felt  47
so good, so right; that she forgot all the dreariness of her new life and
gave herself up to it.   ✿

## READING FOR INFORMATION

1. List the business and commercial enterprises of the Daboo family in
   paragraphs 5, 6, and 8. What attitude does the narrator project toward
   those activities?

2. List the various racial and ethnic groups with which Jasmine has contact
   in paragraphs 5, 9, 10, 17, and 18.

3. Paraphrase and compare the story's representations of Christmastime
   with the Hatch-Moffits, the Daboos, and Jasmine's parents in paragraphs
   27, 30, and 32.

## READING FOR FORM, ORGANIZATION, AND EXPOSITORY FEATURES

1. Summarize the features of Lara's first meeting with Jasmine in paragraphs 18, 19, 20, and 22. Why does Lara assume that Jasmine is a student actress and writer?

2. Explain why in paragraph 24 Jasmine thinks that the Hatch-Moffit
   household is "topsy-turvy."

3. Explain the significance of Bill's "Learn to be more selfish" in paragraph
   27, of Jasmine's "But" in paragraph 32, and of Lara's "guilt trip" in paragraph 33.

## READING FOR RHETORICAL CONCERNS

1. Describe Jasmine's attitude toward the Daboo family in paragraph 5.
   Why does she feel superior to them?

2. Summarize the account of Jasmine's upbringing in Jamaica as related in
   paragraphs 3, 4, 6, and 18.

3. Explain the significance of Bill's "If it feels right, do it" in paragraph 44.

## WRITING ASSIGNMENTS

1. Write a critical analysis of the story's action from the points of view of the Daboos, the Hatch-Moffits, and Jasmine. Comment upon the narrator's implied attitude toward each of these points of view.

2. Write a critical evaluation of Jasmine's character. Is she an outright opportunist? Or does she acquiesce to her crises, accepting the provisional good that comes to her? To what extent does she control what's happening to her? In the final scene, who seduces whom?

# Everyday Use

## *Alice Walker*

*Alice Walker (b. 1944) was born in Eatonton, Georgia, the daughter of a sharecropper and a maid. After graduating from Sarah Lawrence College, she began publishing novels, poems, short stories, and essays. Her novels include* The Third Life of Grange Copeland *(1970),* Meridian *(1976), and* The Color Purple *(1982, winner of the Pulitzer Prize). She has also served as contributing editor for* Ms. *magazine and has taught and lectured at several colleges and universities.*

### PREREADING

Do you or your family cherish any artifacts that through time have acquired value as works of art in your own or others' eyes? They may include everyday objects of clothing, furniture, or tools or special ones such as fancy pottery, jewelry, or ornaments. Try to describe them in a way that will communicate to others the qualities that make them valuable to you. Freewrite your response as though you were composing a letter to a friend.

 *for your grandmama*

I will wait for her in the yard that Maggie and I made so clean     1
and wavy yesterday afternoon. A yard like this is more comfortable than

most people know. It is not just a yard. It is like an extended living room. When the hard clay is swept clean as a floor and the fine sand around the edges lined with tiny, irregular grooves, anyone can come and sit and look up into the elm tree and wait for the breezes that never come inside the house.

Maggie will be nervous until after her sister goes: she will stand  2 hopelessly in corners, homely and ashamed of the burn scars down her arms and legs, eying her sister with a mixture of envy and awe. She thinks her sister has held life always in the palm of one hand, that "no" is a word the world never learned to say to her.

You've no doubt seen those TV shows where the child who has  3 "made it" is confronted, as a surprise, by her own mother and father, tottering in weakly from backstage. (A pleasant surprise, of course: What would they do if parent and child came on the show only to curse out and insult each other?) On TV mother and child embrace and smile into each other's faces. Sometimes the mother and father weep, the child wraps them in her arms and leans across the table to tell how she would not have made it without their help. I have seen these programs.

Sometimes I dream a dream in which Dee and I are suddenly  4 brought together on a TV program of this sort. Out of a dark and soft-seated limousine I am ushered into to a bright room filled with many people. There I meet a smiling, gray, sporty man like Johnny Carson who shakes my hand and tells me what a fine girl I have. Then we are on the stage and Dee is embracing me with tears in her eyes. She pins on my dress a large orchid, even though she has told me once that she thinks orchids are tacky flowers.

In real life I am a large, big-boned woman with rough, man-  5 working hands. In the winter I wear flannel nightgowns to bed and overalls during the day. I can kill and clean a hog as mercilessly as a man. My fat keeps me hot in zero weather. I can work outside all day, breaking ice to get water for washing; I can eat pork liver cooked over the open fire minutes after it comes steaming from the hog. One winter I knocked a bull calf straight in the brain between the eyes with a sledge hammer and had the meat hung up to chill before nightfall. But of course all this does not show on television. I am the way my daughter would want me to be: a hundred pounds lighter, my skin like an un-cooked barley pancake. My hair glistens in the hot bright lights. Johnny Carson has much to do to keep up with my quick and witty tongue.

But that is a mistake. I know even before I wake up. Who ever    6
knew a Johnson with a quick tongue? Who can even imagine me looking a strange white man in the eye? It seems to me I have talked to
them always with one foot raised in flight, with my head turned in
whichever way is farthest from them. Dee, though. She would always
look anyone in the eye. Hesitation was no part of her nature.

"How do I look, Mama?" Maggie says, showing just enough of her    7
thin body enveloped in pink skirt and red blouse for me to know she's
there, almost hidden by the door.
"Come out into the yard," I say.

Have you ever seen a lame animal, perhaps a dog run over by    8
some careless person rich enough to own a car, sidle up to someone
who is ignorant enough to be kind to him? That is the way my Maggie walks. She has been like this, chin on chest, eyes on ground, feet
in shuffle, ever since the fire that burned the other house to the
ground.

Dee is lighter than Maggie, with nicer hair and a fuller figure.    9
She's a woman now, though sometimes I forget. How long ago was it
that the other house burned? Ten, twelve years? Sometimes I can still
hear the flames and feel Maggie's arms sticking to me, her hair smoking
and her dress falling off her in little black papery flakes. Her eyes
seemed stretched open, blazed open by the flames reflected in them.
And Dee. I see her standing off under the sweet gum tree she used to
dig gum out of; a look of concentration on her face as she watched the
last dingy gray board of the house fall in toward the red-hot brick chim-
ney. Why don't you do a dance around the ashes? I'd wanted to ask her.
She had hated the house that much.

I used to think she hated Maggie, too. But that was before we    10
raised the money, the church and me, to send her to Augusta to school.
She used to read to us without pity; forcing words, lies, other folks'
habits, whole lives upon us two, sitting trapped and ignorant underneath her voice. She washed us in a river of make-believe, burned us
with a lot of knowledge we didn't necessarily need to know. Pressed us
to her with the serious way she read, to shove us away at just the moment, like dimwits, we seemed about to understand.

Dee wanted nice things. A yellow organdy dress to wear to her    11
graduation from high school; black pumps to match a green suit she'd
made from an old suit somebody gave me. She was determined to stare
down any disaster in her efforts. Her eyelids would not flicker for

minutes at a time. Often I fought off the temptation to shake her. At six-teen she had a style of her own: and knew what style was.

I never had an education myself. After second grade the school 12 was closed down. Don't ask *me* why: in 1927 colored asked fewer ques-tions than they do now. Sometimes Maggie reads to me. She stumbles along good-naturedly but can't see well. She knows she is not bright. Like good looks and money, quickness passed her by. She will marry John Thomas (who has mossy teeth in an earnest face) and then I'll be free to sit here and I guess just sing church songs to myself. Although I never was a good singer. Never could carry a tune. I was always better at a man's job. I used to love to milk till I was hooked in the side in '49. Cows are soothing and slow and don't bother you, unless you try to milk them the wrong way.

I have deliberately turned my back on the house. It is three 13 rooms, just like the one that burned, except the roof is tin; they don't make shingle roofs any more. There are no real windows, just some holes cut in the sides, like the portholes in a ship, but not round and not square, with rawhide holding the shutters up on the outside. This house is in a pasture, too, like the other one. No doubt when Dee sees it she will want to tear it down. She wrote me once that no matter where we "choose" to live, she will manage to come see us. But she will never bring her friends. Maggie and I thought about this and Maggie asked me, "Mama, when did Dee ever *have* any friends?"

She had a few. Furtive boys in pink shirts hanging about on wash- 14 day after school. Nervous girls who never laughed. Impressed with her they worshiped the well-turned phrase, the cute shape, the scalding humor that erupted like bubbles in lye. She read to them.

When she was courting Jimmy T she didn't have much time to pay 15 to us, but turned all her faultfinding power on him. He *flew* to marry a cheap city girl from a family of ignorant flashy people. She hardly had time to recompose herself.

When she comes I will meet—but there they are! 16

Maggie attempts to make a dash for the house, in her shuffling way, but I stay her with my hand. "Come back here," I say. And she stops and tries to dig a well in the sand with her toe.

It is hard to see them clearly through the strong sun. But even the 17 first glimpse of leg out of the car tells me it is Dee. Her feet were al-ways neat-looking, as if God himself had shaped them with a certain style. From the other side of the car comes a short, stocky man. Hair is all over his head a foot long and hanging from his chin like a kinky mule tail. I hear Maggie suck in her breath. "Uhnnnh," is what it sounds like. Like when you see the wriggling end of a snake just in front of your foot on the road. "Uhnnnh."

Dee next. A dress down to the ground, in this hot weather. A dress  18 so loud it hurts my eyes. There are yellows and oranges enough to throw back the light of the sun. I feel my whole face warming from the heat waves it throws out. Earrings gold, too, and hanging down to her shoulders. Bracelets dangling and making noises when she moves her arm up to shake the folds of the dress out of her armpits. The dress is loose and flows, and as she walks closer, I like it. I hear Maggie go "Uhnnnh" again. It is her sister's hair. It stands straight up like the wool on a sheep. It is black as night and around the edges are two long pig-tails that rope about like small lizards disappearing behind her ears.

"Wa-su-zo-Tean-o!" she says, coming on in that gliding way the  19 dress makes her move. The short stocky fellow with the hair to his navel is all grinning and he follows up with "Asalamalakim, my mother and sister!" He moves to hug Maggie but she falls back, right up against the back of my chair. I feel her trembling there and when I look up I see the perspiration falling off her chin.

"Don't get up," says Dee. Since I am stout it takes something of a  20 push. You can see me trying to move a second or two before I make it. She turns, showing white heels through her sandals, and goes back to the car. Out she peeks next with a Polaroid. She stoops down quickly and lines up picture after picture of me sitting there in front of the house with Maggie cowering behind me. She never takes a shot without making sure the house is included. When a cow comes nibbling around the edge of the yard she snaps it and me and Maggie *and* the house. Then she puts the Polaroid in the back seat of the car, and comes up and kisses me on the forehead.

Meanwhile Asalamalakim is going through motions with Maggie's  21 hand. Maggie's hand is as limp as a fish, and probably as cold, de-spite the sweat, and she keeps trying to pull it back. It looks like Asalamalakim wants to shake hands but wants to do it fancy. Or maybe he don't know how people shake hands. Anyhow, he soon gives up on Maggie.

"Well," I say. "Dee."                                                22

"No, Mama," she says. "Not 'Dee,' Wangero Leewanika Kemanjo!"

"What happened to 'Dee'?" I wanted to know.

"She's dead," Wangero said. "I couldn't bear it any longer, being named after the people who oppress me."

"You know as well as me you was named after your aunt Dicie," I said. Dicie is my sister. She named Dee. We called her "Big Dee" after Dee was born.

"But who was *she* named after?" asked Wangero.

"I guess after Grandma Dee," I said.

"And who was she named after?" asked Wangero.

"Her mother," I said, and saw Wangero was getting tired. "That's about as far back as I can trace it," I said. Though, in fact, I probably could have carried it back beyond the Civil War through the branches.

"Well," said Asalamalakim, "there you are."

"Uhnnnh," I heard Maggie say.

"There I was not," I said, "before 'Dicie' cropped up in our family, so why should I try to trace it that far back?"

He just stood there grinning, looking down on me like somebody 23 inspecting a Model A car. Every once in a while he and Wangero sent eye signals over my head.

"How do you pronounce this name?" I asked.

"You don't have to call me by it if you don't want to," said Wangero.

"Why shouldn't I?" I asked. "If that's what you want us to call you, we'll call you."

"I know it might sound awkward at first," said Wangero.

"I'll get used to it," I said. "Ream it out again."

Well, soon we got the name out of the way. Asalamalakim had a 24 name twice as long and three times as hard. After I tripped over it two or three times he told me to just call him Hakim-a-barber. I wanted to ask him was he a barber, but I didn't really think he was, so I didn't ask.

"You must belong to those beef-cattle peoples down the road," I 25 said. They said "Asalamalakim" when they met you, too, but they didn't shake hands. Always too busy: feeding the cattle, fixing the fences, putting up salt-lick shelters, throwing down hay. When the white folks poisoned some of the herd the men stayed up all night with rifles in their hands. I walked a mile and a half just to see the sight.

Hakim-a-barber said, "I accept some of their doctrines, but farm- 26 ing and raising cattle is not my style." (They didn't tell me, and I didn't ask, whether Wangero (Dee) had really gone and married him.)

We sat down to eat and right away he said he didn't eat collards 27 and pork was unclean. Wangero, though, went on through the chitlins and corn bread, the greens and everything else. She talked a blue streak over the sweet potatoes. Everything delighted her. Even the fact that we still used the benches her daddy made for the table when we couldn't afford to buy chairs.

"Oh, Mama!" she cried. Then turned to Hakim-a-barber. "I never 28 knew how lovely these benches are. You can feel the rump prints," she said, running her hands underneath her and along the bench. Then she gave a sigh and her hand closed over Grandma Dee's butter dish. "That's it!" she said. "I knew there was something I wanted to ask you if I could have." She jumped up from the table and went over in the corner where the churn stood, the milk in it clabber by now. She looked at the churn and looked at it.

"This churn top is what I need," she said. "Didn't Uncle Buddy 29 whittle it out of a tree you all used to have?"

"Yes," I said.

"Uh huh," she said happily. "And I want the dasher, too."

"Uncle Buddy whittle that, too?" asked the barber.

Dee (Wangero) looked up at me.

"Aunt Dee's first husband whittled the dash," said Maggie so low you almost couldn't hear her. "His name was Henry, but they called him Stash."

"Maggie's brain is like an elephant's," Wangero said, laughing. "I 30 can use the churn top as a centerpiece for the alcove table," she said, sliding a plate over the churn, "and I'll think of something artistic to do with the dasher."

When she finished wrapping the dasher, the handle stuck out. I 31 took it for a moment in my hands. You didn't even have to look close to see where hands pushing the dasher up and down to make butter had left a kind of sink in the wood. In fact, there were a lot of small sinks; you could see where thumbs and fingers had sunk into the wood. It was beautiful light yellow wood, from a tree that grew in the yard where Big Dee and Stash had lived.

After dinner Dee (Wangero) went to the trunk at the foot of my 32 bed and started rifling through it. Maggie hung back in the kitchen over the dishpan. Out came Wangero with two quilts. They had been pieced by Grandma Dee and then Big Dee and me had hung them on the quilt frames on the front porch and quilted them. One was in the Lone Star pattern. The other was Walk Around the Mountain. In both of them were scraps of dresses Grandma Dee had worn fifty and more years ago. Bits and pieces of Granpa Jarrell's Paisley shirts. And one teeny faded blue piece, about the size of a penny matchbox, that was from Great Grandpa' Ezra's uniform that he wore in the Civil War.

"Mama," Wangero said sweet as a bird. "Can I have these old 33 quilts?"

I heard something fall in the kitchen, and a minute later the 34 kitchen door slammed.

"Why don't you take one or two of the others?" I asked. "These old things was just done by me and Big Dee from some tops your grandma pieced before she died."

"No," said Wangero. "I don't want those. They are stitched around the borders by machine."

"That'll make them last better," I said.

"That's not the point," said Wangero. "These are all pieces of dresses Grandma used to wear. She did all this stitching by hand. Imagine!" She held the quilts securely in her arms, stroking them.

"Some of the pieces, like those lavender ones, come from old clothes her mother handed down to her," I said, moving up to touch the quilts. Dee (Wangero) moved back just enough so that I couldn't reach the quilts. They already belonged to her.

"Imagine!" she breathed again, clutching them closely to her bosom.

"The truth is," I said. "I promised to give them quilts to Maggie, for when she marries John Thomas."

She gasped like a bee had stung her.

"Maggie can't appreciate these quilts!" she said. "She'd probably 35 be backward enough to put them to everyday use."

"I reckon she would," I said. "God knows I been saving 'em for long enough with nobody using 'em. I hope she will!" I didn't want to bring up how I had offered Dee (Wangero) a quilt when she went away to college. Then she had told me they were old-fashioned, out of style.

"But they're *priceless!*" she was saying now, furiously; for she has a temper. "Maggie would put them on the bed and in five years they'd be in rags. Less than that!"

"She can always make some more," I said. "Maggie knows how to quilt."

Dee (Wangero) looked at me with hatred. "You just will not un- 36 derstand. The point is these quilts, *these* quilts!"

"Well," I said, stumped. "What would *you* do with them?"

"Hang them," she said. As if that was the only thing you *could* do with quilts.

Maggie by now was standing in the door. I could almost hear the 37 sound her feet made as they scraped over each other.

"She can have them, Mama," she said, like somebody used to never winning anything, or having anything reserved for her. "I can 'member Grandma Dee without the quilts."

I looked at her hard. She had filled her bottom lip with checker- 38 berry snuff and it gave her face a kind of dopey, hangdog look. It was Grandma Dee and big Dee who taught her how to quilt herself. She stood there with her scarred hands hidden in the folds of her skirt. She looked at her sister with something like fear but she wasn't mad at her. This was Maggie's portion. This was the way she knew God to work.

When I looked at her like that something hit me in the top of my 39 head and ran down to the soles of my feet. Just like when I'm in church and the spirit of God touches me and I get happy and shout. I did something I never had done before: hugged Maggie to me, then dragged her on into the room, snatched the quilts out of Miss Wangero's hands and dumped them into Maggie's lap. Maggie just sat there on my bed with her mouth open.

"Take one or two of the others," I said to Dee.

But she turned without a word and went out to Hakim-a-barber.    40

"You just don't understand," she said, as Maggie and I came out to the car.

"What don't I understand?" I wanted to know.

"Your heritage," she said. And then she turned to Maggie, kissed her, and said, "You ought to try to make something of yourself, too, Maggie. It's really a new day for us. But from the way you and Mama still live you'd never know it."

She put on some sunglasses that hid everything above the tip of 41 her nose and her chin.

Maggie smiled; maybe at the sunglasses. But a real smile, not 42 scared. After we watched the car dust settle I asked Maggie to bring me a dip of snuff. And then the two of us sat there just enjoying, until it was time to go in the house and go to bed.   ✿

## READING FOR INFORMATION

1. List examples of Dee's superior attitude toward others, and describe instances where she flaunts her newly acquired tastes and refinement.

2. List corresponding examples of Maggie's sense of inferiority and low self-esteem. Is there any evidence that Maggie still has a nucleus of self-confidence that may help her to survive and triumph?

3. Explain in your own words any family resemblances that link Mama and her two daughters, and recount any sharp differences that distinguish them. Note important differences in the characters' responses to the burning of the old house in paragraph 9.

## READING FOR FORM, ORGANIZATION, AND EXPOSITORY FEATURES

1. Circle usages of the word "style" in paragraphs 11 and 35. Explain how each context modifies the meaning of the word. Underline references to reading and education in paragraphs 10, 12, 35, and 40. Explain how each context modifies the significance of those activities.
2. Explain why the word "choose" appears in quotation marks in paragraph 13. Explain what Maggie's "uhnnnh" means in paragraphs 17, 18, and 22. Does this word change its meaning in different contexts?
3. Paraphrase Dee's argument about the value of the quilts in paragraphs 34, 35, and 36. What attitude does she project about her own taste and refinement? Rewrite the dialogue in these paragraphs as a statement that clarifies the differences in attitudes.

## READING FOR RHETORICAL CONCERNS

1. Recount Mama's description of her own appearance and physique in paragraphs 5, 12, and 20.
2. Compare and contrast Mama's self-descriptions with her descriptions of each daughter's appearance in paragraphs 2, 7, 8, 9, 11, 12, 18, and 38.
3. Describe how ironically the narrator treats the names of her daughter and Hakim-a-barber in paragraphs 22, 24, 26, 29, 32, 34, and 35.

## WRITING ASSIGNMENTS

1. On one level, this story depicts a mother's progress from a world of fantasy where she idolizes one daughter at the other's expense into a world of reality where she becomes critical of that daughter and appreciative of the other. Write an analytical essay about her progress and the experiences that influence it.
2. On another level, the story encourages us to make positive value judgments about culture and possessions, history, and human relationships. It also encourages us to recognize mistaken value judgments about them. The artistic worth of the quilts focuses all of these meanings. Write an analytical essay about the characters' various assumptions concerning the quilts and about how their judgments of their value define their own individuality.

## SYNTHESIS WRITING ASSIGNMENTS

1. Drawing on selections by Takaki and Mukherjee, write a five- to six-page essay in which you synthesize their representational views about the immigrant experience in America. Address your essay to an audience of classmates from high school with whom you have not been in contact since starting college.

2. Drawing on selections by Allende and Takaki, write a five- to six-page essay in which you compare and contrast the experiences of different ethnic groups as they interact with one another in North and South America. What conditions drive members of these groups to different forms of economic survival? Address your essay to an audience of students who have not read these texts.

3. Drawing on selections by Mukherjee and Walker, write a five- to six-page essay in which you respond to the characters' various efforts, both successful and unsuccessful, to preserve their ethnic identities. Address your essay to members of the academic community at large as a critical review in your college newspaper.

4. Drawing on selections by Levi and Takaki, write a five- to six-page essay in which you analyze the writers' appropriation of fictional techniques (narrative, dialogue, vivid description) to represent nonfictional experience. Address your essay to an audience of students who have read these texts.

5. Drawing on selections by Allende and Mukherjee, write a five- to six-page essay in which you evaluate their narrative representations of outsiders' efforts to succeed as insiders in multicultural societies. Address your essay to members of the academic community at large as a critical review in your college newspaper.

# Appendix:
# Documenting Sources

## MLA DOCUMENTATION STYLE

Chapters 2 to 4 contain sample essays written according to the MLA (Modern Language Association) rules for page format (margins, page numbering, titles, and so forth) and source documentation. In addition to providing many sample pages that illustrate MLA style, we describe how to type papers in MLA format (pp. 73–75); follow MLA guidelines for using parenthetical documentation to cite sources that you summarize (pp. 23–29), paraphrase (pp. 16–21), or quote (pp. 30–35); and construct a works cited list (pp. 57–58). Most of our examples, however, are based on the articles and book excerpts that are reprinted in the anthology section of this book. As a college student, you may need to document materials that differ from our earlier examples. You may need, for instance, to document an Internet source, a television newscast, or a personal interview. The first section of the appendix is an MLA "quick guide" that includes examples of how to document the types of sources that students use most often in academic papers. The next section explains the principles and rules for MLA documentation. The third section is a list of MLA documentation examples that covers a wider range of situations than does the quick guide. For an exhaustive discussion of MLA documentation style, see the *MLA Handbook for Writers of Research Papers*, 6th edition.

## MLA QUICK GUIDE

The following examples illustrate how to document in MLA style the types of sources that most often appear in college students' essays. They are arranged beginning with the most commonly cited source types. If you are unable to find in this quick guide a model that works for the source you are citing, look through the more extensive list of examples on pages 646–57.

*Magazine or journal article obtained through a library-based online subscription service*

> Simpson, Michael D. "Supreme Court to Hear Student
>     Drug Testing." <u>NEA Today</u> Mar. 2002: 20. <u>Expanded</u>
>     <u>Academic ASAP</u>. Ithaca College Library, Ithaca, NY.
>     2 July 2002 <http://infotrac.galegroup.com>.

*Article, essay, poem, or short story that is reprinted in a textbook anthology*

> Vogel, Steven. "Grades and Money." <u>Dissent</u> Fall 1997:
>     102-4. Rpt. in <u>Reading and Writing in the Academic</u>
>     <u>Community</u>. 2nd ed. Eds. Mary Lynch Kennedy and
>     Hadley M. Smith. Upper Saddle River, NJ: Prentice
>     Hall, 2001. 337-40.

*Document on a World Wide Web site*

> <u>American Civil Liberties Union Freedom Network</u>.
>     "Security and Freedom." 19 Feb. 2002. American
>     Civil Liberties Union. 26 Aug. 2002
>     <http://aclu.org/students/>.

*Article, essay, poem, or short story in a magazine*

> Dickinson, Amy. "Video Playgrounds: New Studies Link
>     Violent Video Games to Violent Behavior. So Check
>     Out These Cool Alternatives." <u>Time</u> 8 May 2000: 100.

*Article in a newspaper*

> Becker, Elizabeth. "A New Villain in Free Trade: The
>     Farmer on the Dole." <u>New York Times</u> 25 Aug. 2002,
>     sec. 4: 10.

*Article, essay, poem, or short story in an academic*
*or professional journal*

> Mirskin, Jerald. "Writing as a Process of Valuing."
>      <u>College Composition and Communication</u> 46 (1995):
>      387-410.

*Book*

> Hower, Edward. <u>Shadows and Elephants</u>. Wellfleet, MA:
>      Leapfrog, 2002.

*Article, essay, poem, or short story that appears in print*
*for the first time in an anthology*

> McPherson, Diane. "Adrienne Rich." <u>Contemporary Lesbian</u>
>      <u>Writers of the United States: A Bio-Bibliographical</u>
>      <u>Critical Sourcebook</u>. Eds. Sandra Pollack and Denise
>      D. Knight. Westport, CT: Greenwood, 1993. 433-45.

*Section, chapter, article, essay, poem, short story, or play*
*in a book with one author*

> Brown, Cory. "Drought." <u>A Warm Trend</u>. Wesley Chapel,
>      FL: Swallow's Tale Press, 1989. 29.

## PRINCIPLES AND RULES FOR MLA DOCUMENTATION

### Books

When documenting books, arrange the documentary information in the
following order:

1. Author's name
2. Title of the part of the book (if you are referring to a section or
   chapter)
3. Title of the book
4. Name of the editor or translator
5. Edition
6. Number of volumes
7. Name of the series if the book is part of a series
8. City of publication
9. Abbreviated name of the publisher

10.  Date of publication
11.  Page numbers (if you are referring to a section or chapter)

## Books Without Complete Publication Information or Pagination

Supply as much of the missing information as you can, enclosing the information you supply in square brackets to show your reader that the source did not contain this information—for example, Metropolis: U of Bigcity P, [1971]. Enclosing the date in brackets shows your reader that you found the date elsewhere: another source that quotes your source, the card catalog, your professor's lecture, and so on. If you are not certain of the date, add a question mark—for example, [1971?]. If you only know an approximate date, put the date after a "c." (for *circa*, meaning "around"). However, when you cannot find the necessary information, use one of the following abbreviation models to show this to your reader: n.d. (no date); N. pag. (no pagination); N.p. (no place of publication); n.p. (no publisher). For example, the following works cited entry would be used if you knew only the title of the book that served as your source:

> Photographic View Album of Cambridge. [England]: N.p.,
>     n.d. N. pag.

## Book Cross-References

If you cite two or more articles from the same anthology, list the anthology itself with complete publication information, then cross-reference the individual articles. In the cross-reference, the anthology editor's last name and the page numbers follow the article author's name and the title of the article. In the example below, the first and third entries are for articles reprinted in the second entry, the anthology edited by Kennedy, Kennedy, and Smith.

> Frude, Neil. "The Intimate Machine." Kennedy, Kennedy,
>     and Smith 268-73.
> Kennedy, Mary Lynch, William J. Kennedy, and Hadley M.
>     Smith, eds. Writing in the Disciplines. 4th ed.
>     Upper Saddle River, NJ: Prentice Hall, 2000.
> Rifkin, Jeremy. "The Age of Simulation." Kennedy,
>     Kennedy, and Smith 284-93.

## Periodicals

When documenting articles in a periodical, arrange the documentary information in the following order:

1. Author's name
2. Title of the article
3. Name of the periodical
4. Series number or name
5. Volume number (followed by a period and the issue number, if needed)
6. Date of publication
7. Page numbers

## Online Sources That Are Also Available in Print

The World Wide Web offers electronic versions of many publications that are available in print, ranging from newspaper articles to full-length books. Entries for sources that have electronic addresses (URLs) should include as many of the following items as are available:

1. Author
2. Title of the source (book, article, poem, or other source type)
3. Editor, compiler, or translator (if relevant)
4. Complete publication information for the print version
5. Title of the Web site (if no title is given, provide a label such as "Home page") or name of the database.
6. Name of the Web site editor or compiler (if available)
7. Version, volume, or issue number of the source (if relevant)
8. Date of electronic publication (latest update)
9. For articles accessed through a subscription service (InfoTrac, Pro-Quest, and so forth), the name of the service and, if a library is the subscriber, the name of the library and the city (state, if necessary) in which it is located.
10. Number of total pages, paragraphs, or sections (if available)
11. Organization or institution associated with the Web site
12. Date when the researcher collected the information from the Web site
13. Electronic address, or URL, of the source (enclosed in angle brackets)

Each element listed above should follow the format specifications on pages 646–55. For example, article titles should be placed in quotation marks, while book titles should be underlined.

## Sources That Are Available Only Online

Certain electronic sources are available only online (on the World Wide Web, at Gopher sites, etc.). A myriad of organizations and individuals maintain Web sites that provide information that is not published in print form. For sources that do not appear in print, MLA works-cited entries should include as many of the following items as possible:

1. Author
2. Title of the source (essay, article, poem, short story, or other source type); or title of a posting to an online discussion, followed by the label "Online posting"
3. Editor, compiler, or translator (if relevant)
4. Title of the Web site (if no title is given, provide a label such as "Home page")
5. Name of the Web site editor or compiler (if available)
6. Version, volume, or issue number of the source (if relevant)
7. Date of electronic publication (latest update) or of posting
8. Name of discussion list or forum (for a posting only)
9. Number of total pages, paragraphs, or sections (if available)
10. Organization or institution associated with the Web site
11. Date when the researcher collected the information from the Web site
12. Electronic address, or URL, of the source (enclosed in angle brackets)

All elements within entries should follow the format guidelines presented on pages 646–55. For example, article titles should be placed in quotation marks, while book titles should be underlined.

Some electronic sources are "portable," as is a CD-ROM, for example, and may or may not have print versions. Other electronic sources do not have URLs. In each case, use the style that applies, listing the publication medium (CD-ROM, for example), publisher, and the computer network or service for an online source (for example, a computer database such as PsychINFO reached through CompuServe). Give the electronic publication information after the author, title, editor or compiler, and print publication information.

## Content Endnotes

In addition to a works-cited list, MLA style provides for a list of comments, explanations, or facts that relate to the ideas discussed in the essay but do not fit into the actual text. You may occasionally need these content endnotes to provide information that is useful but must, for some reason, be separated from the rest of the essay. The most common uses of endnotes are listed below.

1. Providing additional references that go beyond the scope of the essay but could help the reader understand issues in more depth
2. Discussing a source of information in more detail than is possible in a works-cited list
3. Acknowledging help in preparing an essay
4. Giving an opinion that does not fit into the text smoothly
5. Explaining ideas more fully than is possible in the text
6. Mentioning concerns not directly related to the content of the essay
7. Providing additional necessary details that would clutter the text
8. Mentioning contradictory information that goes against the general point of view presented in the essay
9. Evaluating ideas explained in the essay

In MLA style, endnotes are listed on separate pages just before the works-cited list. The first page of the endnote list is titled *Notes.* Notes are numbered sequentially (1, 2, 3, ...), and a corresponding number is included in the text of the essay, typed halfway between the lines (in superscript), to show the material to which the endnote refers. Notice in the example below that the reference numeral (that is, the endnote number) is placed in the text of the essay immediately after the material to which it refers. Usually, the reference numeral will appear at the end of a sentence. No space is left between the reference numeral and the word or punctuation mark that it follows. However, in the notes list, one space is left between the numeral and the first letter of the note. Notes are numbered according to the order in which they occur in the essay.

Any source that you mention in an endnote must be fully documented in the works-cited list. Do not include this complete documentation in the endnote itself. Never use endnotes as a substitute for the works-cited list, and do not overuse endnotes. If possible, include all information in the text of your essay. For most essays you write, no endnotes will be necessary.

The following excerpts from the text of an essay and its list of endnotes illustrate MLA endnote format. For example, in your text you would type

For hundreds of years, scientists thought that the sun's energy came from the combustion of a solid fuel such as coal.[1] However, work in the early twentieth century convinced researchers that the sun sustains a continuous nuclear fusion reaction.[2] The sun's nuclear furnace maintains a temperature . . . .

The notes on the notes page would be formatted with the first line of each note indented five spaces.

[1] Detailed accounts of pre-twentieth-century views of solar energy can be found in Banks and Rosen (141-55) and Burger (15-21).

[2] In very recent years, some scientists have questioned whether or not the sun sustains a fusion reaction at all times. Experiments described by Salen (68-93) have failed to detect the neutrinos that should be the by-products of the sun's fusion. This raises the possibility that the sun's fusion reaction turns off and on periodically.

## MLA DOCUMENTATION MODELS

### Books

*Book with one author*

Kennedy, William J. Rhetorical Norms in Renaissance Literature. New Haven: Yale UP, 1978.

*Two or more books by the same author (alphabetize by title)*

Kennedy, William J. Jacopo Sannazaro and the Uses of the Pastoral. Hanover, NH: UP of New England, 1983.
---. Rhetorical Norms in Renaissance Literature. New Haven: Yale UP, 1978.

*Book with two authors*

Kramnick, Isaac, and R. Laurence Moore. The Godless Constitution: The Case against Religious Correctness. New York: Norton, 1996.

*Book with three authors*

Bulkin, Elly, Minnie Bruce Pratt, and Barbara Smith. <u>Yours in Struggle: Three Feminist Perspectives on Anti-Semitism and Racism</u>. Ithaca, NY: Firebrand, 1988.

*Book with more than three authors*

Glock, Marvin D., et al. <u>Probe: College Developmental Reading</u>. 2nd ed. Columbus, OH: Merrill, 1980.

*Book with a corporate author*

Boston Women's Health Collective Staff. <u>Our Bodies, Ourselves</u>. Magnolia, MA: Peter Smith, 1998.

*Book with an anonymous author*

<u>Writers' and Artists' Yearbook, 1980</u>. London: Adam and Charles Black, 1980.

*Book with an editor instead of an author*

DiRenzo, Anthony, ed. <u>If I Were Boss: The Early Business Stories of Sinclair Lewis</u>. Carbondale, IL: Southern Illinois UP, 1997.

*Book with two or three editors*

Anderson, Charles M., and Marian M. MacCurdy, eds. <u>Writing and Healing: Toward an Informed Practice</u>. Urbana, IL: National Council of Teacher of English, 1999.

*Book with more than three editors*

Kermode, Frank, et al., eds. <u>The Oxford Anthology of English Literature</u>. 2 vols. New York: Oxford UP, 1973.

*Book with a translator*

> Allende, Isabel. <u>The Stories of Eva Luna</u>. Trans. Margaret Sayers Peden. New York: Macmillan, 1991.

*Book with more than one edition*

> Kennedy, Mary Lynch, William J. Kennedy, and Hadley M. Smith. <u>Writing in the Disciplines</u>. 4th ed. Upper Saddle River, NJ: Prentice Hall, 2000.

*Book that has been republished*

> Conroy, Frank. <u>Stop-time</u>. 1967. New York: Penguin, 1977.

## Parts of Books

*Section, chapter, article, essay, poem, short story, or play in a book with one author*

> Chomsky, Noam. "Psychology and Ideology." <u>For Reasons of State</u>. New York: Vintage, 1973. 318-69.
> Walker, Alice. "Everyday Use." <u>In Love and Trouble: Stories of Black Women</u>. San Diego: Harcourt, 1973. 47-59.

*Introduction, preface, or foreword written by someone other than the book's author*

> Piccone, Paul. General Introduction. <u>The Essential Frankfurt Reader</u>. Eds. Andrew Arato and Eike Gebhardt. New York: Urizen, 1978. xi-xxiii.

*Article or essay reprinted in an anthology*

> Au, Kathryn H. "Literacy for All Students: Ten Steps Toward Making a Difference." <u>The Reading Teacher</u> 51.3 (1997): 186-94. Rpt. in <u>Perspectives: Literacy</u>. Ed. C. Denise Johnson. Madison, WI: Coursewise, 1999. 3-9.

*Article, essay, poem, or short story that appears in print*
*for the first time in an anthology*

> Horn, Wade F. "Promoting Marriage as a Means for Pro-
> moting Fatherhood." <u>Revitalizing the Institution of</u>
> <u>Marriage for the Twenty-First Century: An Agenda</u>
> <u>for Strengthening Marriage</u>. Eds. Alan J. Hawkins,
> Lynn D. Wardle, and David Orgon Coolidge. Westport,
> CT: Praeger, 2002. 101-109.

*Novel or play in an anthology*

> Gay, John. <u>The Beggar's Opera</u>. <u>Twelve Famous Plays of</u>
> <u>the Restoration and Eighteenth Century</u>. Ed. Cecil
> A. Moore. New York: Random, 1960. 573-650.

*Signed article in a reference work*

> Tilling, Robert I. "Vocanology." <u>McGraw Hill</u>
> <u>Encyclopedia of Science and Technology</u>. 8th ed.
> 1997.

*Unsigned article in a reference work*

> "Tenancy by the Entirety." <u>West's Encyclopedia of</u>
> <u>American Law</u>. 1998.

## Periodicals

*Article in a scholarly/professional journal; each issue numbers*
*its pages separately*

> McCarty, Roxanne. "Reading Therapy Project." <u>Research</u>
> <u>and Teaching in Developmental Education</u> 18.2
> (2002): 51-56.

*Article in a scholarly/professional journal; the entire volume*
*has continuous page numbering*

> Trainor, Jennifer Seibel, and Amanda Godley. "After
> Wyoming: Labor Practices in Two University Writing
> Programs." <u>College Composition and Communication</u> 50
> (1998): 153-81.

*Signed article in a weekly or monthly magazine*

> Jenkins, Henry. "Cyberspace and Race." <u>Technology
> Review</u> April 2002: 89.

*Unsigned article in a weekly or monthly magazine*

> "Dip into the Future, Far as Cyborg Eye Can See: And
> Wince." <u>The Economist</u> 3 Jan. 1998: 81-83.

*Poem or short story in a magazine*

> Flanagan, David. "Pilgrimage." <u>Creations Magazine</u>
> June/July 2001: 8.

*Signed article in a newspaper (in an edition
with lettered sections)*

> Miller, Marjorie. "Britain Urged to Legalize Cloning of
> Human Tissue." <u>Los Angeles Times</u> 9 Dec 1998: A1.

*Unsigned article in a newspaper (in a daily
without labeled sections)*

> "Justice Proposes Immigration Laws." <u>Ithaca Journal</u>
> [Ithaca, NY] 28 Aug. 2002: 2.

*Editorial or special feature (in an identified edition
with numbered sections)*

> "The Limits of Technology." Editorial. <u>New York Times</u> 3
> Jan. 1999, early ed., sec. 4: 8.

*Published letter to the editor of a newspaper*

> Plotnick, Mermine. Letter. <u>New York Times</u> 25 Aug. 2002,
> sec. 4: 8.

*Review*

> Hoberman, J. "The Informer: Elia Kazan Spills His
> Guts." Rev. of <u>Elia Kazan: A Life</u>, by Elia Kazan.
> <u>Village Voice</u> 17 May 1988: 58-60.

*Article whose title contains a quotation*

> Nitzsche, Jane Chance. "'As swete as is the roote of
> lycorys, or any cetewale': Herbal Imagery in
> Chaucer's Miller's Tale." Chaucerian Newsletter 2.1
> (1980): 6-8.

*Article from Dissertation Abstracts International (DAI)*

> Webb, John Bryan. "Utopian Fantasy and Social Change,
> 1600-1660." Diss. SUNY Buffalo, 1982. DAI 43
> (1982): 8214250A.

## Other Written Sources

*Government publication*

> U. S. Dept. of Energy. Winter Survival: A Consumer's
> Guide to Winter Preparedness. Washington: GPO,
> 1980.

*Congressional Record*

> Cong. Rec. 13 Apr. 1967: S505457.

*Pamphlet*

> Bias-Related Incidents. Ithaca, NY: Ithaca College
> Bias-Related Incidents Committee, 2001.

*Dissertation*

> Boredin, Henry Morton. "The Ripple Effect in Classroom
> Management." Diss. U of Michigan, 1970.

*Personal letter*

> Siegele, Nancy. Letter to the author. 13 Jan. 2002.

*Public document*

> U. S. Depart. of Agriculture. "Shipments and Unloads of
> Certain Fruits and Vegetables. 1918-1923."
> Statistical Bulletin 7 Apr. 1925: 10-13.

*Information service*

> Edmonds, Edward L., ed. <u>The Adult Student: University Challenge</u>. Charlottetown: Prince Edward Island U, 1980. ERIC ED 190 008.

*CD-ROM*

> Stucky, Nathan. "Performing Oral History: Storytelling and Pedagogy." <u>Communication Education</u> 44.1 (1995): 1-14. <u>CommSearch</u> 2nd ed. CD-ROM. Electronic Book Technologies. 1995.

## Online Sources That Are Also Available in Print

*Book originally available in print that was located online*

> Shaw, Bernard. <u>Pygmalion</u>. 1912. <u>Bartleby Archive</u>. 6 Mar. 1998 <http://www.columbia.edu/acis/bartleby/shaw/>.

*Poem originally available in print that was located online*

> Carroll, Lewis. "Jabberwocky." 1872. 6 Mar. 1998 <http://www.jabberwocky.com/carroll/jabber/jabberwocky.html>.

*Journal article originally available in print that was located online*

> Rehberger, Dean. "The Censoring of Project #17: Hypertext Bodies and Censorship." <u>Kairos</u> 2.2 (Fall 1997): 14 sec. 6 Mar. 1998 <http:english.ttu.edu/kairos/2.2/index_f.html>.

*Magazine article originally available in print that was located online*

> Viagas, Robert, and David Lefkowitz. "Capeman Closing Mar. 28." <u>Playbill</u> 5 Mar. 1998. 6 Mar. 1998 <http:www1.playbill.com/cgi-bin/plb/news?cmd=show&code=30763>.

*Journal article originally available in print that was located through a library-based subscription service*

> Davidson, Margaret. "Do You Know Where Your Children Are?" <u>Reason</u> 31.6 (Nov. 1999): 39. <u>Expanded Academic ASAP</u>. Ithaca College Library, Ithaca, NY. 8 Feb. 2000 <http://infotrac.galegroup.com>.

## Sources That Are Only Available Online

*Posting to an online discussion list*

> Grumman, Bob. "Shakespeare's Literacy." Online posting. 6 Mar. 1998. Deja News. 13 Aug. 1998 <humanities. lit.author.>.

*Scholarly project available online*

> Voice of the Shuttle: Web Page for Humanities Research. Ed. Alan Liu. 3 March 1998. U. California, Santa Barbara. 8 Mar. 1998 <http://humanitas.ucsb.edu/>.

*Professional Web site*

> The Nobel Foundation Official Website. The Nobel Foundation. Dec. 1998. 28 Feb. 1999 <http:// www.nobel.se/>.

*Personal Web site*

> Thiroux, Emily. Home page. 7 Mar. 1998. 12 Jan. 1999 <http://academic.csubak.edu/home/acadpro/ departments/english/engthrx.htmlx>.

*Synchronous communication (such as MOO, MUD, and IRC)*

> "Ghostly Presence." Group discussion. Telenet 16 Mar. 1997 <moo.du.org:8000/80anon/anonview/1 4036#focus>.

*Gopher site*

> Banks, Vickie, and Joe Byers. "EDTECH." 18 Mar. 1997 <gopher://ericyr.syr.edu:70/00/Listervi/EDTECH/ README>.

*FTP (File Transfer Protocol) site*

> U.S. Supreme Court directory. 6 Mar. 1998
>     <ftp://<ftp.cwru.edu/U.S.Supreme.Court/>.

## Nonprint Sources

*Film*

> Rebel without a Cause. Dir. Nichols Ray. Perf. James
>     Dean, Sal Mineo, and Natalie Wood. Warner Brothers,
>     1955.

*Television or radio program*

> Comet Halley. Prod. John L. Wilhelm. PBS. WNET, New
>     York. 26 Nov. 1986.

*Personal (face-to-face) interview*

> Hall, Donald. Personal interview. 19 Apr. 2001.

*Telephone interview*

> Grahn, Judy. Telephone interview. 23 Mar. 2000.

*Performance of music, dance, or drama*

> Corea, Chick, dir. Chick Corea Electrik Band. Cornell
>     U., Ithaca, New York. 15 Oct. 1985.

*Lecture*

> Gebhard, Ann O. "New Developments in Young Adult Liter-
>     ature." New York State English Council. Buffalo,
>     NY. 15 Nov. 1984.

*Recording: CD*

> Cohen, Leonard. Ten New Songs. Sony, 2001.

## Recording: Cassette

> Tchaikovsky, Piotr Ilich. Violin Concerto in D, op. 35. Itzhak Perlman, violinist. Audiocassette. RCA, 1975.

## Recording: LP

> Taylor, James. "You've Got a Friend." <u>Mud Slide Slim and the Blue Horizon</u>. LP. Warner, 1971.

## Videotape

> <u>The Nuclear Dilemma</u>. BBC-TV. Videocassette. Time-Life Multimedia, 1974.

## Computer program

> <u>Corel WordPerfect</u> 7. Academic Ed. CD-ROM. Ottawa: Corel Corp., 1996.

## Work of art

> da Vinci, Leonardo. <u>The Virgin, the Child and Saint Anne</u>. Louvre, Paris.

## Map or chart

> <u>Ireland</u>. Map. Chicago: Rand, 1984.
> <u>Adolescents and AIDS</u>. Chart. New York: Earth Science Graphics, 1988.

## Cartoon

> Addams, Charles. Cartoon. <u>New Yorker</u> 16 May 1988: 41.

## APA DOCUMENTATION STYLE

While MLA documentation style is an important standard in the humanities, APA (American Psychological Association) style is used widely in the social sciences. APA style differs from MLA style in many details, but both share the basic principles of including source names and page numbers (APA also adds the publication date) in parentheses within the text of the paper and of listing complete publication information for each source in an alphabetized list. Below is a point-by-point comparison of APA and MLA styles. For a complete explanation of APA style, consult the *Publication Manual of the American Psychological Association,* 5th edition. Pages 176–89 of this book contain a sample student paper written in APA style.

## APA QUICK GUIDE

The following examples illustrate how to document in APA style the types of sources that most often appear in college students' essays. They are arranged beginning with the most commonly cited source types. It may be helpful to contrast them with the MLA quick guide on pages 640–41, since the same examples are used in both quick guides.

*Magazine or journal article obtained through a library-based online subscription service*

> Simpson, M. D. (2002, March). Supreme court to hear student drug testing. *NEA Today, 20,* 20. Retrieved July 2, 2002 from Expanded Academic ASAP database.

*Article, essay, poem, or short story that is reprinted in a textbook anthology*

> Vogel, S. (2001). Grades and money. In M. L. Kennedy & H. M. Smith (Eds.), *Reading and writing in the academic community* (pp. 337-340). Upper Saddle River, NJ: Prentice Hall. (Reprinted from [1997, Fall] *Dissent, 44.4,* 102-104)

*Unsigned document on a World Wide Web site*

> American Civil Liberties Union. (2002, February 19). Security and freedom. Retrieved August 26, 2002 from American Civil Liberties Union Web site: http://aclu.org/students/

*Article, essay, poem, or short story in a magazine*

> Dickinson, A. (2000, May 8). Video playgrounds: New studies link violent video games to violent behavior. So check out these cool alternatives. *Time, 155,* 100.

*Signed article in a newspaper*

> Becker, E. (2002, August 25). A new villain in free
>     trade: The farmer on the dole. *New York Times*,
>     p. 4.10.

*Article, essay, poem, or short story in an academic*
*or professional journal*

> Mirskin, J. (1995). Writing as a process of valuing.
>     *College Composition and Communication, 46,* 387-410.

*Book*

> Hower, E. (2002). *Shadows and elephants*. Wellfleet, MA:
>     Leapfrog.

*Article, essay, poem, or short story that appears in print*
*for the first time in an anthology*

> McPherson, D. (1993). Adrienne Rich. In S. Pollack &
>     D. D. Knight (Eds.), *Contemporary lesbian writers*
>     *of the United States: A bio-bibliographical*
>     *critical sourcebook* (pp. 433-445). Westport, CT:
>     Greenwood.

*Section, chapter, article, essay, poem, short story, or play*
*in a book with one author*

> Brown, C. (1989). Drought. *A warm trend*. (p. 39) Wesley
>     Chapel, FL: Swallow's Tale Press.

## COMPARISON OF MLA AND APA
## DOCUMENTATION STYLES

### Parenthetical Documentation

*MLA*

Give the last name of the author and the page number if you are quoting a specific part of the source.

> The question has been answered before (O'Connor
> 140-43).

> O'Connor has already answered the question (140-43).

*APA*

Give the last name of the author, the publication date, and the page number if you are quoting a specific part of the source.

```
The question has been answered before (O'Connor, 2002,
pp. 140-143).

O'Connor (2002) has already answered the question (pp.
140-143).
```

---

*MLA*

Omit the abbreviation for page. Drop redundant hundreds digit in final page number.

```
Walsh discusses this "game theory" (212-47).
```

*APA*

Use the abbreviation "p." for page or "pp." for pages to show page citation. Retain redundant hundreds digit in final page number.

```
Walsh (1979) discusses this "game theory" (pp.
212-247).
```

---

*MLA*

Omit commas in parenthetical references.

```
The question has been answered before (O'Connor
140-43).
```

*APA*

Use commas within parentheses.

```
The question has been answered before (O'Connor, 2002,
pp. 140-143).
```

---

*MLA*

Use a shortened form of the title to distinguish between different works by the same author.

```
Jones originally supported the single-factor explana-
tion (Investigations) but later realized that the
phenomenon was more complex (Theory).
```

*APA*

Use publication date to distinguish between different works by the same author.

> Jones originally supported the single-factor explana-
> tion (1996) but later realized that the phenomenon was
> more complex (2001).

## List of Sources

*MLA*

The title of the page listing the sources is Works Cited.

*APA*

The title of the page listing the sources is References.

*MLA*

Use the author's full name.

> O'Connor, Mary Beth.

*APA*

Use the author's last name, but only the initials of the author's first and middle names.

> O'Connor, M. B.

*MLA*

When there are two or more authors, invert the first author's name, insert a comma and the word "and," and give the second author's first name and surname in the common order.

> Kennedy, Mary Lynch, and Hadley M. Smith.

*APA*

When there are two or more authors, invert all the names. After the first author's name, insert a comma and an ampersand (&).

> Kennedy, M. L., & Smith, H. M.

*MLA*

Capitalize major words in the titles of books and periodicals and underline all words in those titles.

```
Silicon Snake Oil: Second Thoughts about the Information
Highway.
```

```
Reading Research Quarterly.
```

*APA*

Capitalize only the first word and all proper nouns of the titles (and subtitles) of books. Capitalize all major words in the titles of periodicals. Do not underline book and periodical titles but rather use italics.

```
Silicon snake oil: Second thoughts about the
information highway.
```

```
Reading Research Quarterly.
```

---

*MLA*

List book data in the following sequence: author, title of book, city of publication, shortened form of the publisher's name, date of publication.

```
Ozeki, Ruth L. My Year of Meats. New York: Penguin,
    1998.
```

*APA*

List book data in the following sequence: author, date of publication, title of the book, place of publication, publisher.

```
Ozeki, R. L. (1998). My year of meats. New York:
    Penguin.
```

---

*MLA*

List journal article data in the following sequence: author, title of the article, title of the journal, volume number, date of publication, inclusive pages.

```
Yagelski, Robert P. "The Ambivalence of Reflection."
    College Composition and Communication 51 (1999):
    32-50.
```

*APA*

List journal article data in the following sequence: author, date of publication, title of the article, title of the journal, volume number, inclusive pages.

> Yagelski, R. P. (1999). The ambivalence of reflection. *College Composition and Communication, 51,* 32-50.

---

*MLA*

List the data for an article in an edited book in the following sequence: author of the article, title of the article, title of the book, editor of the book, place of publication, publisher, date of publication, inclusive pages.

> Donaldson, E. Talbot. "Briseis, Briseida, Criseyde, Cresseid, Cressid: Progress of a Heroine." <u>Chaucerian Problems and Perspectives: Essays Presented to Paul E. Beichner, C.S.C.</u> Eds. Edward Vasta and Zacharias P. Thundy. Notre Dame: Notre Dame UP, 1979. 3-12.

*APA*

List the data for an article in an edited book in the following sequence: author of the article, date, title of the article, name of the editor, title of the book, inclusive pages, place of publication, and publisher.

> Donaldson, E. T. (1979). Briseis, Briseida, Criseyde, Cresseid, Cressid: Progress of a heroine. In E. Vasta & Z. P. Thundy (Eds.), *Chaucerian problems and perspectives: Essays presented to Paul E. Beichner, C.S.C.* (pp. 3-12). Notre Dame: Notre Dame University Press.

Note: The proper names in the article title are capitalized, as is the word following the colon.

---

## Content Endnotes

*MLA*

Title the list of endnotes: Notes.

*APA*

Title the list of endnotes: Footnotes.

*MLA*

Place the endnote list immediately before the works-cited page.

*APA*

Place the endnote list immediately after the references page.

*MLA*

Skip one space between the reference numeral and the endnote.

> [1] For more information, see Jones and Brown.

*APA*

Do not skip any space between the reference numeral and the endnote.

> [1]For more information, see Jones (1983) and Brown (1981).

# R H E T O R I C A L
## *index*

## Antecedent-Consequent Plan

John J. Conley, "Narcissus Cloned" (p. 211)

Charles Krauthammer, "Crossing Lines: A Secular Argument Against Research Cloning" (p. 217)

Malcolm Tait, "Bessie and the Gaur" (p. 232)

Sherry Turkle, "Love by Any Other Name" (p. 252)

Raymond Kurzweil, "Live Forever" (p. 260)

Clifford Stoll, "Isolated by the Internet" (p. 269)

Jeff Barbian, "The Gist Generation" (p. 278)

Thomas D. Colbridge, "Kyllo v. United States: Technology v. Individual Privacy" (p. 298)

Wendy Kaminer, "Trading Liberty for Illusions" (p. 318)

Joshua Quittner, "Invasion of Privacy" (p. 321)

Robert L. Barret and Bryan E. Robinson, "Children of Gay Fathers" (p. 340)

Wade F. Horn, "Promoting Marriage as a Means for Promoting Fatherhood" (p. 378)

Judith Stacey, "Toward Revels or a Requiem for Family Diversity?" (p. 389)

Leon Botstein, "High School, an Institution Whose Time Has Passed" (p. 472)

Janine Bempechat, "Challenging Our Assumptions" (p. 500)

Martin L. Gross, "Homework" (p. 510)

Larry E. Frase and William Streshly, "Myth 5: Self-esteem Must Come First—Then Learning" (p. 514)

David C. Berliner and Bruce J. Biddle, "Manufacturing a Crisis in Education" (p. 522)

Garry Wills, "The Pope's Loyal Opposition" (p. 569)

## Comparison Plan

Lee M. Silver, "Jennifer and Rachel" (p. 198)

Charles Krauthammer, "Crossing Lines: A Secular Argument Against Research Cloning" (p. 217)

Rodney A. Brooks, "We Are Not Special" (p. 240)

James Q. Wilson, "Cohabitation Instead of Marriage" (p. 373)

Charmion Browne, "When Shelter Feels Like a Prison" (p. 442)

Shelby Steele, "Educating Black Students" (p. 490)

Benazir Bhutto, "Politics and the Muslim Woman" (p. 544)

Elly Bulkin, "Threads" (p. 558)

Ronald Takaki, "A Different Mirror" (p. 604)

## Description Plan

Lee M. Silver, "Jennifer and Rachel" (p. 198)
Charles Krauthammer, "Crossing Lines: A Secular Argument Against Research Cloning" (p. 217)
Karen Wright, "Species on Ice" (p. 228)
Steve Mann, "Cyborg Seeks Community" (p. 245)
Sherry Turkle, "Love by Any Other Name" (p. 252)
David Brooks, "Time to Do Everything but Think" (p. 281)
Francis X. Clines, "Computer Project Seeks to Avert Youth Violence" (p. 286)
Thomas D. Colbridge, "Kyllo v. United States: Technology v. Individual Privacy" (p. 298)
Christian Parenti, "DC's Virtual Panopticon" (p. 311)
Joshua Quittner, "Invasion of Privacy" (p. 321)
Pauline Irit Erera, "What Is A Family?" (p. 350)
Jeremy Seabrook, "What Are 'Class' and 'Inequality'?" (p. 399)
Dirk Johnson, "White Standard for Poverty" (p. 445)
Pat Robertson, "America, a Christian Nation" (p. 574)

## Time-Order Plan

Steve Mann, "Cyborg Seeks Community" (p. 245)
Raymond Kurzweil, "Live Forever" (p. 260)
Wendy Kaminer, "Trading Liberty for Illusions" (p. 318)
Kimberly Mistysyn, "Brave New Family" (p. 337)
Patricia Clark Smith, "Grandma Went to Smith, All Right, But She Went from Nine to Five: A Memoir" (p. 412)
Barbara Ehrenreich, "Serving in Florida" (p. 449)
Patrick James McQuillan, "A Day in the Life of Rafael Jackson" (p. 475)
Sara Suleri, "Excellent Things in Women" (p. 537)
Alina Bacall-Zwirn and Jared Stark, "I Still Hear the Cry" (p. 551)
Mary Daly, "Sin Big" (p. 565)
Isabel Allende, "The Proper Respect" (p. 588)
Primo Levi, "The Journey" (p. 595)
Bharati Mukherjee, "Jasmine" (p. 618)
Alice Walker, "Everyday Use" (p. 628)

## Response Plan

Lee M. Silver, "Jennifer and Rachel" (p. 198)
Jonathan Colvin, "Me, My Clone, and I (Or In Defense of Human Cloning)" (p. 208)
John J. Conley, "Narcissus Cloned" (p. 211)
Charles Krauthammer, "Crossing Lines: A Secular Argument Against Research Cloning" (p. 217)
Malcolm Tait, "Bessie and the Gaur" (p. 232)
David Brooks, "Time to Do Everything but Think" (p. 281)
Kelly Patricia O'Meara, "Rooting Out the Bad Seeds?" (p. 291)
Christian Parenti, "DC's Virtual Panopticon" (p. 311)
Joshua Quittner, "Invasion of Privacy" (p. 321)
David Popenoe, "Seven Tenets for Establishing New Marital Norms" (p. 368)
Leonce Gaiter, "The Revolt of the Black Bourgeoisie" (p. 427)
Herbert Gans, "The War Against the Poor Instead of Programs to End Poverty" (p. 432)
Isaac Kramnick and R. Laurence Moore, "Is America a Christian Nation?" (p. 578)

# *index*

abstract, 23, 55
abstracts in indexes, 163
accessing periodicals, 160–163
active reading, 3–36, 40–44, 145
adjacency operator, 151
Allende, Isabel, 587, 588–95, 638
analogy, 9, 13, 26, 47
analysis, 13, 122–141
analysis-classification, 13
analysis and evaluation, 13, 123–41
analytical essays, 123–41
analyzing assignments, 41–43, 123–24
annotations, 3, 5, 9–11, 16, 24, 37, 43, 46, 126
antecedent-consequent, 13, 26, 47
APA documentation style, 655–62
argument, 13, 40, 103–22, 132–33, 138–40
argument essay, 103–23
argumentative voice, 8
assignments, clarifying, 41–43, 123–24
audience, 110, 123–24
author's persona, 129

Bacall-Zwirn, Alina, 535, 551–58, 585
Barbian, Jeff, 239, 278–81
Barret, Robert L., 332, 336, 340–50, 397
Bempechat, Janine, 333, 334, 471, 500–10, 533
Berliner, David C., 471, 522–27, 533
biographical information, 6
Bhutto, Benazir, 532, 535, 544–51, 585
Biddle, Bruce J., 471, 522–27, 533
block organizational pattern, 47–48, 84, 86–87
body of paper, 4, 6, 38, 48, 51, 84, 113–14, 131–34
book documentation
    in APA style, 656–62
    in MLA style, 646–49
book reviews, 122
Boolean searching, 152–53
Botstein, Leon, 333, 471, 472–75, 533
brainstorming, 5, 7–8, 46, 111, 146–47
Branwyn, Gareth, 30–31, 35
Brontë, Emily, 54
Brooks, David, 239, 281–83
Brooks, Rodney A., 239, 240–45
Browne, Charmion, 398, 442–45
Bulkin, Elly, 535, 558–65

catalogs, library, 157–60, 168
case study in social science writing, 332, 340–50, 375–90
cause-effect, 28, 96, 131
characterization, 126, 129–30, 137
classifying items, 44, 47
Clines, Francis X., 285, 286–91
close reading, 3, 8–15, 37
Colbridge, Thomas D., 285, 298–311
collaborative exercise, xviii–xix, 15, 22, 29, 35, 39, 45, 70, 76–77, 94, 102, 111–12, 121–22, 141, 147, 156–57, 164, 189
Colvin, Jonathan, 197, 208–11
combining sentences, 18, 20, 26
community of readers, 15
comparing and contrasting sources, 78–94, 131–32
comparison/contrast, 8, 13, 41, 47, 78–94, 127, 131–32
computer online catalogs, 157–60
conclusions, 4, 6, 38, 48, 52, 57, 84, 93, 113, 114, 121, 140, 175
Conley, John J., 197, 211–17, 238
content endnotes, 644–46, 661–62
content notes, 10–11, 23
Corbett, Edward P. J., 112, 141
critical reading strategies, 122
cross-references, in documentation, 642

Daly, Mary, 532, 535, 565–69
definition, 13, 26, 47
description, 13, 26, 47
Dewey decimal classification, 158–59
diagrams, 6
diaspora, definition, 587
Dickens, Charles, 31, 35
directives for assignments, 41–42
documentation, 13, 18, 21, 23, 27, 28, 32–33, 34, 42, 52, 54, 70, 72, 87, 93, 97, 121, 138, 176
documentation styles, 646–62
drafting, 4, 38, 51–59, 86–92, 134–38, 174

editing, 4, 37, 69–75, 93, 122, 140, 175
Ehrenreich, Barbara, 333, 398, 449–69, 638
elaborations, 9–10, 23, 37, 40, 43–45, 79, 92
Elbow, Peter, 108, 141
electronic retrieval systems, 148–56

ellipsis, 31–32
endnotes, 644–46, 661–62
enumeration, 6
Erera, Pauline Irit, 331, 332, 334, 336, 350–68
evaluating sources, 168–69
evaluation and analysis, 13, 124–41
evaluative essays, 124–41
evidence, 105–12, 126
examples, 9, 13, 26, 110
excerpting information from sources, 169–170
*Expanded Academic Index*, 160–62
expository features, 3, 5, 12–14, 35, 128

fictional sources, 126, 129–30, 135–37
Flower, Linda, 14, 35, 64, 77
footnotes, 6
formal outline, 49–50, 172
formulating a thesis, 46–47, 170–72
Frase, Larry E., 471, 514–22
freewriting, 3, 7–8, 37, 38, 42, 125, 143–44, 170–71
Freud, Sigmund, 144, 146, 167–68

Gaiter, Leonce, 333, 334, 398, 427–32, 470
Gans, Herbert J., 80–83, 85–86, 91–92, 94, 398,
    432–42, 470
general subject indexes, 160
genre, 12
graphic overview, 24–25, 48–49
Gross, Martin C., 471, 510–14

Haas, Christina, 14, 35
headings, 6, 11
Heim, Michael, 17, 31, 35
Herman, Judith Lewis, 158–59
highlighters, 10
Horn, Wade F., 332, 336, 378–89, 397

indexes and abstracts, computerized, 160–63
indexes and abstracts, printed, 160–63
ineffective expressions, 64, 68
information, 3, 12, 15, 19, 37, 95–96, 110, 121,
    142–70
InfoTrac, 160–62
instructor conferences, 92
interviews, conducting and using, 166–67
introduction, reading of, 6, 11
introduction, writing, 4, 38, 48, 51–52, 53–57, 84–86,
    113–14, 131–133
introductory paragraphs, 55–57

Johnson, Dirk, 398, 445–49

Kaminer, Wendy, 285, 318–21
Keats, John, 54
keyword searching (computer), 151
Kramnick, Isaac, 531, 533, 535, 578–84, 585
Krauthammer, Charles, 217–28
Kurzweil, Raymond, 260–69

*Lancet, The,* 17–18, 31–32, 35
Lanham, Richard, 66–67, 77
lengthening, 4, 38
Levi, Primo, 532, 587, 595–603, 638
library catalog, 157–60
library collection, 156–60
library orientation, 156–57
Library of Congress classifications, 158–59
library staff, 154–56
lists of references, 58
literary analysis, 126, 129–30, 134–37
literature review, 13
literature, writing about, 587

Mann, Steve, 245–52
manuscript checklist, 72
manuscript form, 4, 38, 72, 139, 175–76
marginal notes, 9–10
McQuillan, Patrick James, 331, 332, 471, 475–90
mechanics of style, 4, 38, 59, 70, 94, 175
method of study in social science writing, 331–35
methods of study in the humanities, 529–34
methods of study in the natural sciences, 193–96
microforms, 157
misplaced modifiers, 71
Mistysyn, Kimberly, 336, 337–40
MLA documentation style, 70, 646–55
MLA manuscript style, 73
model or theory in social science writing, 332, 398
Moore, R. Laurence, 531, 533, 535, 578–84, 585
Mukherjee, Bharati, 587, 618–28, 638

narration, 13, 26
nonprint sources in documentation, 654–55
note taking, 11, 16, 23, 24, 81–82, 106, 125, 169–70

O'Meara, Kelly Patricia, 285, 291–98
opening strategies, 55–56, 91, 140
organization of text, 3, 12–13, 23–26, 37
organizational plans for writing in the humanities,
    529–34
organizational plans for writing in the natural sci-
    ences, 195–96
organizational plans for writing in the social sciences,
    332
organizational signals, 6
organizing, 4, 38, 47–51, 63, 84–86, 112–14, 131–34,
    172–74
organizing a comparison/contrast essay, 84–86
organizing a response essay, 47–51
organizing an analysis or synthesis essay, 131–34
organizing an argument, 112–14
organizaing a research paper, 172–74
outlines, 10, 11, 48–51, 85–86, 131–34, 172–74

parallelism, 13, 26, 72
paraphrasing, 3, 4, 5, 10, 16–22, 37, 38, 39, 54, 87,
    122, 131, 134, 139, 169–70